Understanding Health Insurance

A Guide to Professional Billing

7TH EDITION

JoAnn C. Rowell

Founder and Former Chairperson,
Medical Assisting Department
Anne Arundel Community College,
Arnold, MD
Adjunct Faculty
Community College of Baltimore County—
Catonsville Campus
Catonsville, MD

Michelle A. Green, MPS, RHIA

Professor,
Department of Physical & Life Sciences
Alfred State College
Alfred, NY

THOMSON

DELMAR LEARNING™   Australia Canada Mexico Singapore Spain United Kingdom United States

THOMSON

DELMAR LEARNING

Understanding Health Insurance, A Guide to Professional Billing, 7th Edition
by JoAnn C. Rowell and Michelle A. Green

Vice President, Health Care
William Brottmiller

Editorial Director:
Cathy L. Esperti

Acquisitions Editor:
Rhonda Dearborn

Developmental Editor:
Marjorie A. Bruce

Marketing Director:
Jennifer McAvey

Marketing Coordinator:
Mona Caron

Editorial Assistant:
Natalie Wager

Technology Project Manager:
Laurie Davis

Production Director:
Karen Leet

Art/Design Coordinator:
Connie Lundberg-Watkins

Project Editor:
Mary Ellen Cox

Production Coordinator:
Catherine Ciardullo

Library of Congress Cataloging-in-Publication Data

Rowell, Jo Ann C., 1934–
    Understanding health insurance : a guide to professional billing. – 7th ed. / JoAnn C. Rowell, Michelle A. Green.
        p. cm.
    Includes bibliographical references and index.
    ISBN 1-4018-3791-3 (alk. paper)
    1. Health insurance claims—United States. 2. Insurance, Health—United States. I. Green, Michelle A. II. Title

HG9396.R68 2003
368.38'2'00973—dc21   2003051669

International Divisions List

Asia (Including India):
Thomson Learning
60 Albert Street, #15-01
Albert Complex
Singapore 189969
Tel 65 336-6411
Fax 65 336-7411

Australia/New Zealand:
Nelson
102 Dodds Street
South Melbourne
Victoria 3205
Australia
Tel 61 (0)3 9685-4111
Fax 61 (0)3 9685-4199

Latin America:
Thomson Learning
Seneca 53
Colonia Polanco
11560 Mexico, D.F. Mexico
Tel (525) 281-2906
Fax (525) 281-2656

Canada:
Nelson
1120 Birchmount Road
Toronto, Ontario
Canada M1K 5G4
Tel (416) 752-9100
Fax (416) 752-8102

UK/Europe/Middle East/Africa:
Thomson Learning
Berkshire House
1680-173 High Holborn
London WC1V 7AA
United Kingdom
Tel 44 (0)20 497-1422
Fax 44 (0)20 497-1426

Spain (includes Portugal):
Paraninfo
Calle Magallanes 25
28015 Madrid
España
Tel 34 (0)91 446-3350
Fax 34 (0)91 445-6218

Notice to the Reader

Contents

Chapter 9

CMS Reimbursement Issues 271

Chapter 10

Coding for Medical Necessity 287

Chapter 11

Essential CMS-1500 Claim Instructions 317

Chapter 12

Filing Commercial Claims 339

Chapter 17

Appendices

List of Tables

Preface

INTRODUCTION

Accurately processing health insurance claims has become more exacting at the same time health insurance plan options have rapidly expanded. These changes, combined with modifications in state and federal regulations affecting the health insurance industry, are a constant challenge to health care personnel. Those responsible for processing health insurance claims require thorough instruction in all aspects of medical insurance, including plan options, carrier requirements, state and federal regulations, selecting relevant information from source documents, accurately completing claims, and coding diagnoses and procedures. *Understanding Health Insurance*, 7th edition provides the required information in a clear and comprehensive manner.

OBJECTIVES

The objectives of the seventh edition of this text are to:

1. Introduce information about major insurance programs and federal health care legislation.
2. Provide a basic knowledge of national diagnosis and procedure coding systems.
3. Simplify the process of completing claims.

This text is designed to be used by college and vocational school programs to train medical assistants, medical insurance specialists, and health information technicians. It can also be used as an in-service training tool for new medical office personnel and independent billing services, or individually by claims processors in the health care field who want to develop those skills.

FEATURES OF THE TEXT

Major features of this text have been updated and expanded.

- Key terms and learning objectives at the beginning of each chapter help to organize the material. They can be used as a self-test for checking comprehension and mastery of the chapter. Key terms are bold-faced throughout each chapter to help students master the technical vocabulary associated with claims processing.

- Coding exercises are located within the respective coding chapters: ICD-9-CM Coding, CPT Coding, HCPCS Coding System, and Coding for Medical Necessity. Answers to diagnosis and procedure coding exercises are located in Appendix IV at the back of the text for quick feedback.

- Exercises in other chapters are located after major topics. These exercises provide an opportunity to apply concepts and skills immediately. In Chapters 11 through 17, exercises help develop skills in accurately completing claims.

- Numerous examples are provided in each chapter to illustrate the correct application of rules and guidelines.

- Coding tips provide practical suggestions for mastering the use of the CPT and ICD-9-CM coding manuals.

- End-of-chapter reviews and challenge exercises reinforce learning and identify topics requiring further study.

- A practice disk (CD-ROM) is provided on the inside back cover. The case studies on the disk are contained in Appendix I and Appendix II and include billing data and patient encounter forms with case histories. Appendix V (Using the Student Practice CD-ROM) provides a brief introduction to setting up and running the CD-ROM. The complete *Disk Procedure Manual* is easily accessed on the CD-ROM and provides complete instructions for working with the software.

THE SEVENTH EDITION

- Internet links throughout the text have been updated so that the latest information about insurance claims processing can be researched.

- End-of-chapter bulleted summaries are included to provide a concise review of key topics and concepts.

- A Study Checklist at the end of each chapter integrates the various components of this teaching/learning package and directs students to the various methods of review, reinforcement, and testing.

- The *Legal and Regulatory Considerations* (Chapter 5) emphasizes:
  - confidentiality of patient information.
  - retention of patient information and health insurance records.
  - Federal False Claims Act.
  - Health Insurance Portability and Accountability Act of 1996.

- Chapter 6, *ICD-9-CM Coding,* contains CMS's ICD-9-CM Coding Guidelines. The ICD-9-CM coding rules include examples. The coding conventions for the Index to Diseases and the Tabular List are located in tables within the chapter, and examples of coding book entries are included. The chapter review includes coding exercises, which are organized according to the chapters in the ICD-9-CM Tabular List

- Chapter 7, *CPT Coding,* contains examples from the coding book as chapter figures. The CPT Evaluation and Management Section contains additional information to assist in the assignment of E/M codes, and an explanation of each category also includes additional examples. The table that includes CPT 2003 modifiers in a quick view format is revised, and a new table was created to more clearly define and explain modifiers. The chapter review includes coding exercises, organized by CPT section.

- Chapter 9 is renamed *CMS Reimbursement Issues,* and new reimbursement systems are included.

- Chapter 10 is renamed *Coding for Medical Necessity.* Exercises are revised throughout, and tables allow students to organize answers to exercises. A chapter review contains evaluation and management coding practice exercises.

- Chapter 11 is renamed *Essential CMS-1500 Claim Instructions* to better reflect its content. Updated information about CMS's national provider identifier (NPI) is included.
- The step-by-step claims completion instructions located in Chapters 12–17 are revised according to changes implemented by third-party payers.
- Chapter 14, *Medicare*, contains updated information.
- Chapter 15, *Medicaid*, contains an example and a case study for completing mother/baby claims.
- Chapter 16, *TRICARE*, is rewritten to include the historical perspective of CHAMPUS and TRICARE development and an explanation of how TRICARE programs are administered and developed (including demonstration projects). In addition, CHAMPVA is differentiated from CHAMPUS, and instructions for primary TRICARE with supplemental policy claims completion is included.
- Chapter 17, *Workers' Compensation*, includes a legislative history, expanded information about managed care, and instructions for completing the First Report of Injury form.
- Appendix I, *Case Studies: Set One,* is revised using a newly created encounter form, which makes it easier to review for claims processing. Additional case studies are added, along with a table that organizes case studies according to type of payer.
- Appendix II, *Case Studies: Set Two*, contains revised encounter forms, new tables, and new case studies.
- Appendix III, *Forms*, includes a list of forms, and the E/M CodeBuilder form has been revised.
- Appendix IV, *Answers to Coding Exercises*, facilitates feedback to learners during completion of coding exercises in Chapters 6–8 and 10.
- Appendix V, *Using the Student Practice CD-ROM*, contains instructions for installing the software. The CD-ROM procedure manual and tutorials are located only on the CD-ROM and can be accessed by opening the software and clicking on Help. The manual and tutorials can be printed from the CD-ROM.
- Appendix VI includes UB-92 (Uniform Bill) claims processing instructions for institutional services (including hospitals and skilled nursing facilities).
- An updated bibliography and glossary follow the Appendices.

Additional resources can be found online at:
    http://www.delmarlearning.com
    http://www.MedicalBillingandCoding.com

- Abbreviations related to Medical Billing and Coding
- Medical Terminology: Common Prefixes, Suffixes, and Combining Forms
- Web sites related to Medical Billing and Coding
- Dental claims processing instructions

SUPPLEMENTS

The following supplements accompany the seventh edition of this text.

Instructor's Manual

The Instructor's Manual consists of two parts, one for the text and one for the workbook. Both have been updated, and continue to serve as a guide for a course of study in health insurance claims processing. Case studies not provided in the text can be used as a final examination. Answers to coding exercises not included in Appendix IV of the text and completed claims for all case studies in the text and workbook are also included.

Student Workbook

The workbook developed for the text follows the text's chapter organization with questions grouped under main topic headings also found in the text. The exercises provide additional practice to reinforce learning and improve skills in basic coding and completion of claim forms. In Chapters 11 through 17, new case studies allow more practice in completing the CMS-1500 claim.

Electronic Classroom Manager

The electronic classroom manager on CD-ROM contains a computerized test bank, PowerPoint® slides, and an electronic version of the Instructor's Manual.

The computerized test bank provides test creation, delivery, and reporting capability. Instructors have the option of adding questions to further individualize the tests created. Organized by chapter, the test bank contains approximately 1,000 questions.

A PowerPoint® presentation covers key topics and clarifies difficult concepts. Organized by chapter, the slides provide another way to enhance learning.

An electronic version of the Instructor's Manual is included for the instructor's convenience. The electronic version contains all the content in the printed manual.

WEBTUTOR

WebTutor is an Internet-based course management and delivery system designed to accompany the text. Its content is available for use in either WebCT or Blackboard. Available to supplement on-campus course delivery or as the course management platform for an on-line course, WebTutor contains:

- On-line quizzes for each chapter.
- Discussion topics and learning links.
- On-line glossary, organized by chapter.
- Answers to textbook challenge exercises.
- Communication tools including a course calendar, chat, email, and threaded discussions.

To learn more, visit http://e.thomsonlearning.com

REVIEWERS

A special thank you is extended to the reviewers who have provided recommendations and suggestions for improvement throughout the development of the seventh edition. Their experience and knowledge has been a valuable resource for the authors.

Robin Berenson, M.S., JCTC
    Faculty Instructor
    Spartanburg Technical College
    Spartanburg, SC
Karen M. Bogdan
    Director of Operations
    North American Health Plans
    Amherst, NY

Susan A. Brisky, BPS
    Adjunct Faculty
    Alfred State College
    Alfred, NY
Ron Deamer
    Instructor
    Concorde Career Institute
    Portland, OR

Sebelle Deese, MS
  Director of Medical Assisting Program
  Mount Washington Community College
  Gardner, MA

Cheryl Hutchinson, CMA, CPC
  Coordinator/Instructor in Medical
    Assistant Program
  Southwestern Illinois College
  Belleville, IL

Mary E. McGillivray Walker, M.Ed., RHIA, CMT
  Instructor
  Minnesota West Community and
    Technical College, Jackson Campus
  Jackson, MN

Dr. Karen Minchella
  Consulting Management Associates, LLC
  Fraser, MI

Peggy Oakes, RN BSN, CPC
  Special Claims Investigator
  Claims Administration Corp.
  Rockville, MD

Julie Orloff, CPC, RMA, CMA, CPT
  Program Coordinator for Medical
    Assisting and Medical Coding
  National School of Technology
  North Miami Beach, FL

Vicki Slevinski, CMA, RN
  Instructor of Medical Assisting
  Career and Technical Education Center
    at Ellicottville
  Ellicottville, NY

ACKNOWLEDGMENTS

To my husband and son, Michael and Eric, who understand and support my passion for teaching and writing.

To my students, throughout the world, who motivate me to want to learn everything so I can teach them everything. You are my inspiration.

To my coauthor, JoAnn Rowell, who provided me with this wonderful opportunity.

To Ruth Burke, thank you for your attention to detail!

To my Developmental Editor, Marge Bruce, who has infinite patience for my perfectionism.

To my Acquisitions Editor, Rhonda Dearborn, who listens to my ideas and makes them happen.

To my sixth and ninth grade English teacher, Mrs. Hourihan, who made me believe I could write, and to Mr. Odum, my tenth grade English teacher, who just expected that I would write.

To Alice, who told an undecided 16-year-old girl, "Pick a career and go to college." So I did, and then during my career as a health information manager, she said, "You could fill out insurance claims for people who don't know how to." So, I did—sort of—in the form of this textbook. Thanks, Mom.

Special appreciation is expressed to Ingenix Publishing Group for granting permission to reprint selected tables and pages from:

- *HCPCS Level II Expert, 2003 (Spiral).*
- *ICD-9-CM Professional for Physicians, Vol. 1 & 2, 2003 (Softbound).*
- *Medicare Part B Correct Coding and Fee Guide*

KEY TERMS

Alliance of Claims Assistance
    Professionals (ACAP)
American Academy of
    Professional Coders (AAPC)
American Health Information
    Management Association
    (AHIMA)
Centers for Medicare and
    Medicaid Services (CMS,
    formerly HCFA)
coding
Current Procedural Terminology
    (CPT)
electronic claims processing
electronic data interchange
    (EDI)

ethics
explanation of benefits
    (EOB)
health care provider
Healthcare Common Procedure
    Coding System (HCPCS)
health insurance claim
hold harmless clause
*International Classification of
    Diseases, 9th Revision,
    Clinical Modification*
    (ICD-9-CM)
local codes (level III codes)
medical necessity
national codes (level II codes)
preauthorization

Chapter 1

Health Insurance Specialist— Roles and Responsibilities

OBJECTIVES

Upon successful completion of this chapter, you should be able to:

1. Define key terms.

2. Explain the reasons for increasing employment opportunities for health insurance specialists.

3. Prepare a list of career opportunities for health insurance specialists.

4. List and discuss the basic skill requirements for aspiring health insurance specialists.

5. Describe the responsibilities of health insurance specialists.

6. Name three professional organizations dedicated to working with health insurance specialists, and identify professional credentials for each.

INTRODUCTION

The career of a health insurance specialist is a challenging one with new opportunities arising continuously. Job security is high for an individual who understands claims processing and billing regulations, possesses accurate coding skills, and successfully appeals underpaid or denied insurance claims. A review of medical office personnel help wanted advertisements indicates the need for individuals with these skills.

● **NOTE:** Health information specialist is another title for health insurance specialist. ●

1

HEALTH INSURANCE OVERVIEW

Most health care practices in the United States accept responsibility for filing health insurance claims and some payers (e.g., Medicare) require providers to file claims. A **health insurance claim** is the documentation submitted to an insurance plan requesting reimbursement for health care services provided. In the past few years, many practices have increased the number of employees assigned to some aspect of the claims filing process. This increase is a result of more patients having some form of health insurance, many of whom require **preauthorization** (prior approval) for treatment by specialists and post-treatment reports. If preauthorization requirements are not met, payment of the claim is denied. If the insurance plan has a **hold harmless clause** (patient is not responsible for paying what the insurance plan denies) in the contract, the health care provider cannot collect the fees from the patient. In addition, patients referred to nonparticipating providers (e.g., physician who does not participate in a particular health care plan) have significantly higher out-of-pocket costs than anticipated. Competitive insurance companies are fine tuning procedures to reduce administrative costs and overall expenditures. This cost-reduction campaign forces closer scrutiny of the entire claims process, which in turn increases the time and effort medical practices must devote to billing and filing claims according to the insurance policy filing requirements. Poor attention to claims requirements will result in lower reimbursement rates to the practices and increased expenses.

A number of managed care contracts are signed by health care providers. A **health care provider** is a physician or other health care practitioner (e.g., physician's assistant). Each new provider-managed care contract increases the practice's patient base, the number of claims requirements and reimbursement regulations, the time the office staff must devote to fulfilling contract requirements, and the complexity of referring patients for specialty care. Each insurance plan has its own authorization requirements, billing deadlines, claims requirements, and a list of participating providers or networks. If a health care provider has signed ten participating contracts, there are ten different sets of requirements to follow and ten different panels of participating health care providers from which referrals can be made.

Rules associated with health insurance processing (especially government programs) change frequently, and to remain up-to-date, insurance specialists should be sure they are on mailing lists to receive newsletters from insurance payers. It is also important to remain current regarding news released from the **Centers for Medicare and Medicaid Services** (CMS, formerly HCFA or the Health Care Financing Administration), the administrative agency within the federal Department of Health and Human Services (DHHS). The Secretary of the DHHS is often reported by the news media as having announced the implementation of new regulations.

INTERNET LINK

Go to http://cms.hhs.gov for the latest information on federal regulations, payment systems, and more.

NOTE: Internet links will appear throughout the text, and a comprehensive listing can be found online for Medical Billing and Coding sites.

Another reason for the increased hiring of insurance specialists is a direct result of employers attempting to reduce the cost of providing employee health insurance coverage. Employers renegotiate benefits with existing plans or change insurance carriers altogether. The employees often receive retroactive notice of these contract changes and, in some cases, once notified may have to wait several weeks before new health benefit books and new insurance identification cards are issued. These changes in employer-sponsored plans have made it necessary for the health care provider's staff to check on patients' current eligibility and benefit status at the time of each office visit.

Career Opportunities

According to the *Occupational Outlook Handbook* published by the U.S. Department of Labor—Bureau of Labor Statistics, health care facilities and insurance companies will hire claims examiners (insurance specialists) to process routine medical claims at an increased rate of 10 to 20% through the year 2010. As the use of software for processing insurance claims is implemented, insurance specialist positions will become more automated, requiring a background in word processing and other computer applications as well as anatomy and physiology, medical terminology, and health insurance processing. Providers who implement **electronic claims processing** send data in a standardized machine-readable format to an insurance company via disk, telephone, or cable. The insurance company receives the data, reviews it, and sends an acknowledgment to the provider. This mutual exchange of data between the provider and insurance company is called **electronic data interchange (EDI)**, often used by claims clearinghouses. (EDI must be in compliance with HIPAA regulations, discussed in Chapter 5.)

In addition to the increase of insurance specialist positions available in health care practices, opportunities are increasing in other settings for experienced health insurance specialists as:

- claims benefit advisors in health, malpractice, and liability insurance companies.
- coding or insurance specialists in state, local, and federal government agencies, legal offices, private insurance billing offices, and medical societies.
- educators in schools and companies specializing in medical office staff training.
- writers and editors of health insurance textbooks, newsletters, and other publications.
- self-employed consultants who provide assistance to medical practices with billing practices and claims appeal procedures.
- consumer claims assistance professionals, who file claims and appeal low reimbursement for private individuals. In the latter case, individuals may be dissatisfied with the handling of their claims by the health care provider's insurance staff.
- practices with poorly trained health insurance staff who are unwilling or unable to file a proper claims appeal.
- private billing practices dedicated to claims filing for elderly or disabled patients.

Coding is the process of reporting diagnoses, procedures, and services as numeric and alphanumeric characters on the insurance claim form. Two systems used are ICD-9-CM and HCPCS. The *International Classification of Diseases, 9th Revision, Clinical Modification* (**ICD-9-CM**, often abbreviated as ICD) is the coding system used to report diagnoses (e.g., diseases, signs, and symptoms) and reasons for encounters (e.g., annual physical examination, and surgical follow-up care) on physician office claims. Codes are reported either numerically or alphanumerically and include a decimal (e.g., 401.9 is the code for hypertension; V20.2 is the code for a well-child office visit). The **Healthcare Common Procedure Coding System** (HCPCS, pronounced "hick picks") consists of three levels: (1) *Current Procedural Terminology* **(CPT)**, which is published by the American Medical Association and includes five-digit numeric codes and descriptors for procedures and services performed by providers (e.g., 99203 identifies a detailed office visit for a new patient); (2) **national codes**, commonly referred to as HCPCS level II codes, which are published by CMS and include five-digit alphanumeric codes for procedures, services, and supplies that are not classified in CPT (e.g., J-codes are used to assign drugs administered); and (3) **local codes** that are developed by local insurance companies and include five-digit alphanumeric codes for procedures, services, and supplies that are also not classified in CPT.

NOTE: CMS will phase out local codes by December 31, 2003.

BASIC SKILL REQUIREMENTS

Anyone who aspires to become a health insurance specialist needs to possess the following:

- Strong foundation in medical terminology
- Basic knowledge of anatomy and physiology
- Knowledge of diagnosis and procedure coding conventions and rules
- Critical reading and comprehension skills
- Sufficient math skills to maintain patient financial records
- Excellent oral and written communication skills
- Ability to enter financial and demographic data into a patient database
- Ability to access information through the Internet
- Strong sense of ethics
- Attention to detail
- Knowledge of health insurance contractual language

The Importance of Medical Terminology

Health insurance specialists must be fluent in the language of medicine and have access to a comprehensive medical dictionary as a reference. A background in medical terminology is also important, and individuals can enroll in formal coursework or obtain a medical terminology textbook and complete it as self-paced instruction (e.g., *Medical Terminology for Health Professions,* 4th Edition, by Ann Ehrlich and Carol Schroeder). Health insurance specialists are required to take diagnoses, symptoms, and treatments or services reported in the patient's chart and translate them into numerical or alphanumerical codes (e.g., ICD) required by state and federal health care agencies and the commercial health insurance industry. These three-, four-, or five-digit codes are reported on all health insurance claim forms and insurance payment documents without narrative descriptions of the diagnoses, symptoms, or procedures performed. Frequently, descriptions in the patient record/chart do not match the precise wording found in the coding systems. Therefore, health insurance specialists must draw on their knowledge of medical terminology to assign codes to the written narratives documented by health care providers.

Practice

As a review, or to become familiar with common medical terms, refer to the online listing of Medical Terminology: Common Prefixes, Suffixes, and Combining Forms.

Basic Knowledge of Anatomy and Physiology

A basic understanding of anatomy and physiology is crucial in recognizing abnormal body conditions. Insurance companies determine the medical necessity for procedure(s) or service(s) performed before payment is issued. **Medical necessity** involves *linking every procedure or service code reported on the CMS-1500 claim to a condition code that justifies the necessity for performing that procedure or service.*

EXAMPLE 1

Procedure: Knee X-ray (CPT code)

Documented diagnosis: Shoulder pain (ICD code)

In this example, the procedure is not covered because the X-ray is not medically justified.

EXAMPLE 2

Procedure: Knee X-ray (CPT code)

Documented diagnosis: Fractured patella (knee bone) (ICD code)

In this example, the procedure is covered because it is medically justified.

Knowledge of Diagnosis and Procedure Coding Conventions/Rules

Computerization of the medical practice and insurance claims processing function requires the translation of diagnoses, procedures, and services into logical and systematic coding systems. Working with coded information requires an understanding of the rules, conventions, and applications of these coding systems to ensure proper selection of individual codes.

EXAMPLE

Chief Complaint: Patient is seen for facial laceration.

Procedure: Suture of 3 cm facial laceration, simple.

When referring to the CPT coding manual, there is no listing for "Suture, facial laceration." There is, however, an instructional notation just below the entry for

"Suture" that refers the coder to "Repair." When "Repair" is referenced in the Index, the coder must then locate subterm "Skin," and then "Wound" and "Simple." The code range for "Repair, Skin, Wound, Simple" is 12020–12021. The final step is to verify the code selection in the tabular section of the coding manual and to enter it on the insurance claim. Because skin is integumentary, you will find the code in the Integumentary section of CPT. ●

Critical Reading

Reading and comprehension skills are critical to differentiating the technical description of two different but similar procedures or diagnoses. For example, a professional coder or biller should be able to readily identify the differences in the following examples:

● EXAMPLE 1

Ureteral endoscopy through a ureter*otomy* versus ureteral endoscopy through a ureter*ostomy*

Answer: When a ureteral endoscopy is performed via ureterotomy, the physician is examining the kidney and ureteral structures using an endoscope after an incision is made through the skin and the ureter. After the examination, the scope is removed and the surgical wound is sutured.

For a ureteral endoscopy via ureterostomy, the endoscope is passed into the ureter through an ureterostomy tube that has been in place since a previous surgery. After the examination is completed, the scope is removed and the ureterostomy is either left in place or it is removed and the passageway allowed to seal on its own.

● EXAMPLE 2

Spond*ylosis* versus spondyl*olysis*

Answer: Spondylosis is defined as any condition of the spine. Spondylolysis is a defect (breakdown) of the articulating portion of the vertebra. ●

Misreading or misinterpreting any word or diagnosis may result in assignment of incorrect code numbers and the possibility of a delay in payment or total rejection of a claim. For example, consider "facial" versus "fascial" from the example on page 5. The patient has a wound of the face, not the layer of tissue that covers muscle (called fascia). Including, excluding, or substituting one letter in a word can result in misinterpretation (e.g., "golf" versus "gulf"—while friends await your arrival at the golf course, you are expecting to meet them at the beach).

Excellent Communication Skills

All health insurance specialists must possess excellent oral and written communication skills. They must be comfortable discussing insurance concepts and regulations on several levels. Patients often need assistance in translating complex insurance concepts and regulations into basic terms they can understand. The ability to communicate intelligently with health care providers regarding documentation of services and/or procedures can reduce coding and billing errors. At the same time, the health insurance specialist must communicate effectively with insurance company personnel using the language of the health care industry.

Written communication is necessary when appealing underpaid claims. Some appeals are straightforward and only take a short note to correct the error. Many claims, however, will require long, detailed, written appeals. A poorly written appeal of a complex claim may not get the reconsideration the case deserves. An incorrect diagnosis or procedure code on the original claim may result in a denial. The appeal for reconsideration of the case requires notification that a coding error occurred along with the submission of a corrected claim. Other appeals may be generated because the insurance company recoded a complex case. If the recoding is not justified, an appeal for reconsideration must contain a detailed defense of the original claim's coding and the rationale that supports the original codes submitted.

Data Entry Ability

Because federal legislation (e.g., HIPAA) requires all claims to be electronically submitted, insurance specialists must have good keyboarding skills and the ability to enter basic financial and insurance data into the practice's accounting system. Accurate and precise data entry of the patient's demographic (identification) and account information ensures that required data is electronically placed in proper fields on claim forms generated by the computer. In some computer programs, insurance information screens with different titles otherwise appear identical. For example, primary and secondary insurance screens require the entry of similar information. Electronic claim forms will be rejected by the insurance company for missing or misplaced critical data on the form. Improper payment or charge data entered on the patient account will also result in incorrect data displayed on the claim form.

Internet Access

The ability to access the Internet is a necessary function of insurance claims processing. Online information sources provide access to a large volume of medical reference materials, insurance carrier manuals, and procedure guidelines that are not accessible in printed form or are too costly for the majority of practices to purchase. In addition, most insurance companies and government agencies use Web sites to release reimbursement and billing changes prior to adoption. By prereleasing major changes, insurers and government agencies receive feedback from medical practices on how changes will affect operations in the field. When a designated comment period ends, the issue is either re-evaluated or the final rule is adopted and reported. By checking Web sites, practices can anticipate changes and plan for a smooth transition to implementing new rules before the announced effective date of these changes. Access to this resource may allow for several weeks' advanced notification of the new rule before it is available to practices in newsletters and bulletins. Insurance company Web sites also provide quick access to provider information departments without the long delays caused by the limited number of telephone lines.

The Internet offers numerous opportunities to network with other health insurance specialists across the country. Access to solutions and insight into billing and coding problems through specialized chat rooms or forums sponsored by the various medical coding and nongovernment insurance information organizations are invaluable.

Strong Sense of Ethics

The *American Heritage® Concise Dictionary* defines **ethics** as the principle of right or good conduct, and rules that govern the conduct of members of a profession. The insurance specialist, upon joining a professional association, is responsible for upholding the code of ethics (see Internet Links—Code of Ethics for Professional Associations). Related to ethics is the importance of maintaining confidentiality of privileged patient information (discussed in Chapter 5).

INTERNET LINKS

CODE OF ETHICS FOR PROFESSIONAL ASSOCIATIONS

American Association of Medical Assistants	http://www.aama-ntl.org
American Health Information Management Association	http://www.ahima.org

Attention to Detail

Processing insurance claims requires careful consideration and thorough follow-up. Tasks are completed one at a time, including those that may appear to be unimportant. This attention to detail is an essential characteristic of an insurance specialist.

HEALTH INSURANCE SPECIALIST RESPONSIBILITIES

This section provides an overview of major responsibilities delegated to health insurance specialists. In practices with just one or two persons working with insurance billing, each individual must be capable of performing all the listed responsibilities. In large multispecialty practices with many insurance department positions, each insurance specialist usually processes claims for a limited number of insurance payers (e.g., an insurance specialist may be assigned to process only Medicare claims). In some practices, there is a clear division of labor with specific individuals accepting responsibility for only a few assigned tasks. Typical tasks are listed in the following job description.

Health Insurance Specialist Job Description

1. Review patient record documentation to accurately code all diagnoses, procedures, and services using ICD-9-CM for diagnoses, and CPT and HCPCS level II for procedures and services.

The accurate coding of diagnoses, procedures, and services rendered to the patient allows a medical practice to:

- communicate diagnostic and treatment data to a patient's insurance plan to assist the patient in obtaining maximum benefits.
- facilitate analysis of the practice's patient base to improve patient care delivery and efficiency of practice operations to contain costs.

2. Research and apply knowledge of all insurance rules and regulations for major insurance programs in the local or regional area.

3. Accurately post charges, payments, and adjustments to patient accounts and office accounts receivable records.

4. Prepare or review claims generated by the practice to ensure that all required data are accurately reported, and to ensure prompt reimbursement for services provided (contributing to the practice's cash flow).

5. Review all insurance payments and transmittal notices to ensure proper processing and payment of each claim. The patient receives an **explanation of benefits (EOB)**, which is a report that details the results of processing a claim (e.g., payer reimburses provider $80 on a submitted charge of $100).

6. Correct all data errors and resubmit all unprocessed or returned claims.

7. Research and prepare appeals for all underpaid, unjustly recoded, or denied claims.

8. Rebill all claims not paid within 30 to 45 days, depending on individual practice policy and the payers' policies.

9. Inform health care providers and the staff of changes in fraud and abuse laws, coding changes, documentation guidelines, and insurance carrier requirements that may affect the billing and claims submission procedures.

10. Assist with the timely updating of the practice's internal documents, patient registration forms, and billing forms as required by changes in coding or insurance billing requirements.

11. Maintain an internal audit system to ensure that required pretreatment authorizations have been received and entered into the billing and treatment records. Audits comparing provider documentation with codes assigned should also be performed.

12. Explain insurance benefits, policy requirements, and filing rules to patients.

PROFESSIONAL CREDENTIALS

The health insurance specialist who becomes affiliated with one or more professional associations receives useful information available in several formats including professional journals and newsletters, access to members-only Web sites, notification of professional development, and so on. A key feature of membership is an awareness of the importance of professional certification. Once certified, the professional is responsible for maintaining that credential by fulfilling continuing education requirements established by the sponsoring association.

The **American Health Information Management Association (AHIMA)** sponsors three certification exams for coding specialists. AHIMA represents more than 40,000 health information management professionals who work throughout the health care industry. Health information management professionals manage, analyze, and utilize patient care data, making it accessible to health care providers when needed. AHIMA's *Certified Coding Associate* (CCA) fulfills the need for an entry-level coding credential. The *Certified Coding Specialist* (CCS) demonstrates competence in ICD-9-CM and CPT Surgery coding as well as in patient documentation and data integrity/quality issues, anatomy, physiology, and pharmacology. The *Certified Coding Specialist—Physician-Based* (CCS-P) demonstrates expertise in multispecialty CPT, ICD-9-CM, and HCPCS national (level II) coding. For information on membership and certification, call AHIMA at (312) 233-1100, or e-mail inquiries to **info@ahima.org**. Their mailing address is 233 N. Michigan Avenue, Chicago, IL 60611-5519.

The **American Academy of Professional Coders (AAPC)** offers four certification exams. The AAPC was established to provide a national certification and credentialing process, to support the national and local membership by providing educational products and opportunities to network, and to increase and promote national recognition and awareness of professional coding. The *Certified Professional Coder Apprentice* (CPC-A) and *Certified Professional Coder—Hospital Apprentice* (CPC-HA) is available to applicants who have not yet met the required medical field experience for certification as a CPC or CPC-H. The *Certified Professional Coder* (CPC) is available for physician practice and clinic coders, and the *Certified Professional Coder—Hospital* (CPC-H) examination is written for outpatient facility coders. Contact the AAPC at (800) 626-8699, or e-mail them at **aapc@aapcnatl.org**. Their mailing address is 309 West 700 South, Salt Lake City, UT 84101.

The **Alliance of Claims Assistance Professionals (ACAP)** endorses the Healthcare Reimbursement Specialist (HRS) credential, offered by the National Electronic Billers Alliance (NEBA). The ACAP represents professionals dedicated to the effective management of health insurance claims, and its membership includes professional electronic billers who work for providers as well as professional claims assistance professionals who work for patients. For information on services, contact ACAP at **askus@claims.org**. Their mailing address is 873 Brentwood Drive, W. Chicago, IL 60185-3743.

INTERNET LINKS

American Health Information Management Association (AHIMA)	http://www.ahima.org
American Academy of Professional Coders (AAPC)	http://www.aapcnatl.org
Alliance of Claims Assistance Professionals (ACAP)	http://www.claims.org
National Electronic Billers Alliance (NEBA)	http://www.nebazone.com

SUMMARY

- The submission of health insurance claims is the responsibility of health care providers. The number of patients subscribing to health insurance plans has resulted in increased employment opportunities for health insurance specialists.

- Basic skill requirements of the health insurance specialist include training in medical terminology, anatomy and physiology, diagnosis and procedure coding, reading and comprehension, math, oral and written communication, data entry, Internet access, and ethics, along with an attention to detail.

- The duties performed by the health insurance specialist include reviewing patient records and other source documents to code diagnoses, procedures, and services. In addition, the specialist is expected to understand insurance rules and regulations, operate office bookkeeping systems, post charges and payments, prepare and review claims for accuracy, review insurance payments and explanation of benefits forms, appeal claims when necessary, update staff about new regulations, and assist patients with understanding how their insurance affects the services they receive.

- Becoming credentialed through one of several professional associations (e.g., AAPC, ACAP, AHIMA) demonstrates competence and knowledge in the field of health insurance processing as well as coding and reimbursement.

STUDY CHECKLIST

- ☐ Read textbook chapter, and highlight key concepts. (Use colored highlighter sparingly throughout chapter.)
- ☐ Create an index card for each key term. (Write key term on one side of the index card and the concept on the other. Learn the definition of each key term, and match the term to the concept.)
- ☐ Access chapter Internet links to learn more about concepts.

- ☐ Answer the chapter review questions, verifying answers with your instructor.
- ☐ Complete Web Tutor assignments and take online quizzes.
- ☐ Complete Workbook chapter, verifying answers with your instructor.
- ☐ Form a study group with classmates to discuss chapter concepts in preparation for an exam.

REVIEW

MATCHING

Match the credential with the sponsoring professional association.

_____ 1. CAP
_____ 2. CCS
_____ 3. CPC
_____ 4. ECP
_____ 5. CCA

a. AAPC
b. ACAP
c. AHIMA

MULTIPLE CHOICE

Select the most appropriate response.

6. The document submitted to the payer requesting reimbursement is called a(n):
   a. explanation of benefits.
   b. health insurance claim.
   c. hold harmless document.
   d. preauthorization form.

7. The Centers for Medicare and Medicaid Services was previously called the:
   a. Department of Health and Human Services.
   b. Health, Education and Welfare Agency.
   c. Health Care Financing Administration.
   d. Office of the Inspector General.

8. A health care practitioner is also called a:
   a. dealer.
   b. provider.
   c. purveyor.
   d. supplier.

9. The mutual exchange of data between provider and payer is called electronic:
   a. claims processing.
   b. data interchange.
   c. information analysis.
   d. statistical investigation.

10. The process of assigning diagnoses, procedures, and services using numeric and alphanumeric characters is called:
    a. coding.
    b. data processing.
    c. programming.
    d. reimbursement.

SHORT ANSWER

Briefly respond to each of the following.

11. Describe the basic skills needed to become a health insurance specialist.

12. List career opportunities available to health insurance specialists.

13. Identify the organizations that credential health insurance specialists.

14. Describe how the health insurance specialist maintains credentials.

15. Explain the relationship between ethics and confidentiality of patient information.

KEY TERMS

Ambulatory Payment Classification (APC)

Association of Medical Care Plans

Balanced Budget Act of 1997 (BBA)

base period

Blue Cross Association (BCA)

BlueCross BlueShield Association (BCBSA)

CHAMPUS Reform Initiative (CRI)

Civilian Health and Medical Program of the Department of Veterans Affairs (CHAMPVA)

Civilian Health and Medical Program–Uniformed Services (CHAMPUS)

Clinical Laboratory Improvement Act (CLIA)

CMS-1500

Consolidated Omnibus Budget Reconciliation Act of 1986 (COBRA)

consumer-driven health plan

copayment (copay)

Correct Coding Initiative (CCI)

deductible

Dependents' Medical Care Act of 1956

diagnosis-related group (DRG)

disability insurance

Employment Retirement Income Security Act of 1974 (ERISA)

end-stage renal disease (ESRD)

Evaluation and Management (E/M)

Federal Employees' Compensation Act (FECA)

fee schedule

group health insurance

group medical practices

HCFA-1500

health care

health insurance

Health Insurance Portability and Accountability Act of 1996 (HIPAA)

health maintenance organization (HMO)

Health Maintenance Organization Assistance Act of 1973

Health Plan Employer Data and Information Set (HEDIS)

Hill-Burton Act

Home Health Prospective Payment System (HH PPS)

inpatient

Inpatient Rehabilitation Facilities Prospective Payment System (IRF PPS)

insurance

International Classification of Diseases (ICD)

liability insurance

lifetime maximum amount

major medical insurance

managed care

Medicaid

medical care

Medicare

Minimum Data Set (MDS)

National Association of Blue Shield Plans

Occupational Safety and Health Administration Act of 1970 (OSHA)

Omnibus Budget Reconciliation Act of 1981 (OBRA)

Outcomes and Assessment Information Set (OASIS)

Outpatient Prospective Payment System (OPPS)

Peer Review Organization (PRO)

per diem

prepaid health plan

preventive services

Professional Standards Review Organization (PSRO)

prospective payment system (PPS)

quality improvement organization (QIO)

Resource Utilization Groups (RUGs)

Resource-Based Relative Value Scale system (RBRVS)

Skilled Nursing Facility Prospective Payment System (SNF PPS)

subrogation

Tax Equity and Fiscal Responsibility Act of 1982 (TEFRA)

third-party administrator (TPA)

usual and reasonable payments

workers' compensation

World Health Organization (WHO)

Chapter 2

Introduction to Health Insurance

OBJECTIVES

Upon successful completion of this chapter, you should be able to:

1. Define key terms.
2. State the difference between medical care and health care.
3. Differentiate between disability and liability insurance.
4. Discuss the history of health care reimbursement from 1860 to the present.
5. Identify and explain the impact of significant events in the history of health care reimbursement.
6. Interpret health insurance coverage statistics.

INTRODUCTION

According to the *American Heritage® Concise Dictionary*, **insurance** is a contract that protects the insured from loss. An insurance company guarantees payment to the insured for an unforeseen event (e.g., death, accident, and illness) in return for the payment of premiums. The types of insurance include disability, liability, malpractice, property, life, and health, which is covered in this text. This chapter includes explanations of terms and concepts as an introduction to health insurance processing. These terms and concepts are covered in greater detail in later chapters of this text.

WHAT IS HEALTH INSURANCE?

To understand the meaning of the term "health insurance" as it is used in this text, differentiation between medical care and health care must be made. **Medical care** includes the identification of disease and the provision of care and treatment as that provided by members of the health care team to persons who are sick, injured, or concerned about their health status. **Health care** expands the definition of medical care to include **preventive services**, which are designed to help individuals avoid health and injury problems. Preventive or proactive examinations may bring about early detection of problems resulting in treatment options that are less drastic and less expensive.

Health care insurance or **health insurance** is a contract between a policy holder and a third-party payer or government program to reimburse the policy holder for all or a portion of the cost of medically necessary treatment or preventive care provided by health care professionals. Because both the government and the general public speak of "health insurance," this text will use that term exclusively. Health insurance is available to individuals who participate in group (e.g., employer sponsored), individual (or personal insurance), or prepaid health plans (e.g., managed care).

NOTE: Some group plans can be converted to individual plans when the employee leaves the organization. •

DISABILITY AND LIABILITY INSURANCE

Disability Insurance

Disability insurance, for the purpose of this text, is defined as reimbursement for income lost as a result of a temporary or permanent illness or injury. When patients are treated for disability diagnoses and other medical problems, separate patient records must be maintained. It is also a good idea to organize the financial records separately for these patients. Offices that generate one patient record both for the treatment of disability diagnoses and other medical problems often confuse the submission of diagnostic and procedural data for insurance processing. This can result in payment delays and claims denials. Other insurance coverage (e.g., workers' compensation) is usually primary to basic medical coverage.

NOTE: Disability insurance generally does not pay for health care services, but provides the disabled person with financial assistance. •

Disability benefits are usually paid if an individual:

- has been unable to do regular or customary work for a certain number of days (number of days depends on the policy).
- was employed when disabled (e.g., individuals must have lost wages because of a disability).
- has disability insurance coverage.
- was under the care and treatment of a licensed provider during initial disability, and to continue receiving benefits, remains under care and treatment.

- completes and mails a claim form within a certain number of days after the date individual was disabled (number of days depends on the policy).
- has the licensed provider complete the disability medical certification document(s).

Individuals may be found ineligible for disability benefits if they:
- are claiming or receiving unemployment insurance benefits.
- became disabled while committing a crime that resulted in a felony conviction.
- are receiving workers' compensation benefits at a weekly rate equal to or greater than the disability rate.
- are in jail, prison, or recovery home (e.g., half way house) because of being convicted of a crime.
- fail to have an independent medical examination when requested to do so.

A disability claim begins on the date of disability, and the disability payer calculates an individual's weekly benefit amount using a base period. The **base period** usually covers 12 months and is divided into four consecutive quarters. It includes taxed wages paid approximately 6 to 18 months before the disability claim begins. The base period does not include wages being paid at the time the disability began.

A final payment notice is sent when records show an individual has been paid through the doctor's estimated date of recovery. If the individual is still disabled, the doctor needs to submit appropriate documentation so that the case is reviewed. When an individual has recovered or returned to work and becomes disabled again, a new claim form should be submitted along with a reporting of the dates worked.

INTERNET LINK

For more information and sample claim forms, click on the Disability Insurance link at the California Employment Development Department's Web site at http://www.edd.ca.gov

Liability Insurance

Although liability insurance is not covered in this text, it is important to understand how it influences the processing of health insurance claims. **Liability insurance** is a policy that covers losses to a third party caused by the insured, by an object owned by the insured, or on premises owned by the insured. Liability insurance claims are made to cover the cost of medical care for traumatic injuries, lost wages, and in many cases, remuneration for the "pain and suffering" of the injured party. Most health insurance contracts state that health insurance benefits are secondary to liability insurance. In this situation, the patient is *not* the insured. This means that the insured (e.g., employer) is responsible for payment, and the patient's health insurance plan is billed as secondary (and reimburses only the remaining costs of health care *not* covered by the insured). When negligence by another party is suspected in an injury claim, the health insurance carrier will not reimburse the patient for medical treatment of the injury until one of two factors is established: (1) it is determined there was no third-party negligence, or (2) in cases where third-party negligence did occur, the liability carrier determines the incident is not covered by the negligent party's liability contract.

● **EXAMPLE**

Dr. Small treated Jim Keene in the office for scalp lacerations (cuts) that resulted from a work-related injury. Mr. Keene is covered by an employer-sponsored group health plan called HealthCareUSA, and his employer provides workers' compensation insurance coverage for on-the-job injuries.

The insurance claim for treatment of Mr. Keene's lacerations should be submitted to the employer's workers' compensation insurance carrier (company).

If the claim was submitted to HealthCareUSA, it would be subject to review because the diagnosis code submitted would indicate trauma (injury), which activates the review of patient records by an insurance company. Upon reviewing requested copies of patient records, HealthCareUSA would determine that another insurance plan should have been billed for this treatment. HealthCareUSA would deny payment of the claim, and Dr. Small's office would then submit the claim to the workers' compensation carrier. With this scenario, a delay in payment for treatment has resulted. ●

To file a claim with a liability carrier, a regular patient billing statement addressed to the liability carrier is often used rather than an insurance claim form. Be sure to include the name of the policy holder and the liability policy identification numbers. If the liability insurer denies payment, a claim is then filed with the patient's health insurance plan. *A photocopy of the written denial of responsibility must accompany the health insurance claim form.*

● **NOTE:** Third-party payers pursue the recovery of payments from those legally responsible for injuries and/or illnesses (e.g., malpractice cases, public property injuries, automobile accidents). When health care expenses are the liability of another party, the third-party payer has the right to recover payment from that party, a process called **subrogation**. It is important that health insurance specialists submit proper information on claims (e.g., when, where, and how an injury occurred) so as to avoid payment delays that occur when third-party payers rule out liability insurance coverage before issuing reimbursement for health care services. ●

MAJOR DEVELOPMENTS IN HEALTH INSURANCE

From the early 1900s when solo practices prevailed to the new millennium, which has seen an increase in managed care and group practices, health care services (like other aspects of society in this country) have undergone tremendous changes (Table 2-1).

TABLE 2-1 History of health care reimbursement

YEAR	EVENT	DESCRIPTION
1860	First health insurance policy	The Franklin Health Assurance Company of Massachusetts was the first commercial insurance company in the United States to provide private health care coverage for injuries that did not result in death.
1880	Expansion of private health insurance	Sixty additional insurance companies offer health insurance policies. Such policies covered loss of income and a limited number of illnesses (e.g., typhoid, scarlet fever, and smallpox).
1900	Self-pay prevails	Most Americans continued to pay their own health care expenses, which usually meant either charity care or no care.
1908	Workers' compensation	President Theodore Roosevelt signed legislation to provide workers' compensation for certain federal employees in unusually hazardous jobs. **Workers' compensation** is a program mandated by federal and state governments, which requires employers to cover medical expenses and loss of wages for workers who are injured on the job or who have developed job-related disorders.
1915	Campaign for health insurance begins	The American Association of Labor Legislation (AALL) drafted model health insurance legislation, which limited coverage to the working class and others who earned less than $1,200 a year, including their dependents. The American Medical Association (AMA) supported this legislation, but it was never passed into law.
1916	FECA	The **Federal Employees' Compensation Act (FECA)** replaced the 1908 workers' compensation legislation, and civilian employees of the federal government were provided medical care, survivors' benefits, and compensation for lost wages. The Office of Workers' Compensation Programs (OWCP) administers FECA as well as the Longshore and Harbor Workers' Compensation Act of 1927 and the Black Lung Benefits Reform Act of 1977.
1920	Introduction of prepaid health plans	The first contracts between employers and local hospitals and physicians were developed. Participating hospitals and physicians performed specified medical services for a predetermined fee that was paid on either a monthly or yearly basis. These **prepaid health plans** were the forerunner of today's managed care plans.
1921	Indian Health Service	The Snyder Act of 1921 and the Indian Health Care Improvement Act (IHCIA) of 1976 provided legislative authority for Congress to appropriate funds specifically for the care of Indian people, creating and supporting the Indian Health Service (IHS).
1929	First Blue Cross policy	Justin Ford Kimball, an official at Baylor University in Dallas, introduced a plan to guarantee schoolteachers 21 days of hospital care for $6 a year. Other groups of employees in Dallas joined, and the idea attracted nationwide attention. This is generally considered the first Blue Cross plan.
1930	Health care reform is initiated	The Committee on the Cost of Medical Care (CCMC) was funded by charitable organizations to address concerns about the cost and distribution of medical care. It recommended the allocation of national resources for health care and that voluntary health insurance be provided to cover medical costs. This initiative failed.
1939	Wagner National Health Act of 1939	The Tactical Committee on Medical Care drafted the Wagner National Health Act, which proposed that a federally funded national health program be administered by states and localities. The proposal called for compulsory national health insurance and a payroll tax. Extensive national debate occurred, but Congress did not pass it into law.

(continues)

TABLE 2-1 *(continued)*

YEAR	EVENT	DESCRIPTION
1939 *(cont.)*	Blue Cross symbol is officially adopted	The Blue Cross symbol was officially adopted by a commission of the American Hospital Association (AHA) as the national emblem for plans that met certain guidelines.
	Blue Shield	The first Blue Shield plan was founded in California. The Blue Shield concept grew out of the lumber and mining camps of the Pacific Northwest at the turn of the century. Employers wanted to provide medical care for their workers, so they paid monthly fees to *medical service bureaus*, which were composed of groups of physicians.
1940s	Group health insurance	To attract wartime labor during World War II, group health insurance was offered to full-time employees. The insurance was not subject to income or Social Security taxes, making it an attractive part of an employee benefit package. **Group health insurance** is health care coverage available through employers and other organizations (e.g., labor unions, rural and consumer health cooperatives); employers usually pay part, or all, of premium costs. It was during this time that more **group medical practices** were formed, which consisted of three or more health care providers who shared equipment, supplies, and personnel, and who divided income by a prearranged formula.
1945	Universal comprehensive national health insurance	Harry Truman was one of the first American presidents to support a plan for universal comprehensive national health insurance, including private insurance for those who could afford it and public welfare services for the poor. This legislation was not passed into law.
1946	Hill-Burton Act	The **Hill-Burton Act** provided federal grants for modernizing hospitals that had become obsolete because of a lack of capital investment during the Great Depression and WWII (1929 to 1945). In return for federal funds, facilities were required to provide services free or at reduced rates to patients unable to pay for care.
	Blue Shield	The **Association of Medical Care Plans**, with the Blue Shield as an emblem, was created as a national coordinating agency for physician sponsored health insurance plans.
1947	Taft-Hartley Act	The Taft-Hartley Act of 1947 amended the National Labor Relations Act of 1932, restoring a more balanced relationship between labor and management. An indirect result of Taft-Hartley was the creation of **third-party administrators (TPAs)**, which administer health care plans and process claims, serving as a system of "checks and balances" for labor-management.
1948	ICD	The **World Health Organization (WHO)** developed the **International Classification of Diseases (ICD)**, which is a classification system used to collect data for statistical purposes. Codes were later reported for hospital inpatient and physician office reimbursement purposes. **Inpatients** are admitted to a hospital for treatment with the expectation that the patient will remain in the hospital for a period of 24 hours or more.
	Blue Shield symbol is informally adopted	The Blue Shield symbol was informally adopted in 1948 by a group of nine Plans known as the Associated Medical Care Plans, which eventually became the **National Association of Blue Shield Plans**.

(continues)

TABLE 2-1 *(continued)*

YEAR	EVENT	DESCRIPTION
1950	Major medical insurance is offered	Insurance companies began offering major medical insurance, which provided coverage for catastrophic or prolonged illnesses and injuries. Most of these programs incorporate large deductibles and lifetime maximum amounts. A deductible is the amount for which the patient is financially responsible before an insurance policy provides coverage. A lifetime maximum amount is the maximum benefits payable to a health plan participant.
1956	Dependents' Medical Care Act of 1956	The Dependents' Medical Care Act was signed into law, and provided health care to dependents of active military personnel.
1960	Blue Cross Association	In 1960 the commission of the American Hospital Association (AHA) was replaced with the Blue Cross Association (BCA), with formal ties to the AHA ending in 1972.
1966	Social Security Amendments of 1965 were implemented	Medicare (Title XVIII of the SSA of 1965) provides health care services to Americans over the age of sixty-five. (It was originally administered by the Social Security Administration.)
		Medicaid (Title XIX of the SSA of 1965) is a cost-sharing program between the federal and state governments to provide health care services to low-income Americans. (It was originally administered by the Social and Rehabilitation Service [SRS].)
	Amendments to the Dependents' Medical Care Act of 1956	Amendments to the Dependents' Medical Care Act of 1956 created the Civilian Health and Medical Program—Uniformed Services (CHAMPUS), which was designed as a benefit for dependents of personnel serving in the armed forces and uniformed branches of the Public Health Service and the National Oceanic and Atmospheric Administration. The program is now called TRICARE.
	CPT is developed	Current Procedural Terminology (CPT) was developed by the American Medical Association in 1966. Each year, an annual publication is prepared, which includes changes that correspond to significant updates in medical technology and practice.
1970	Employer-based self-insurance plans	Many large employers determined they would be able to save money by self-insuring their employee health plans rather than purchasing coverage from private insurers.
	OSHA	The Occupational Safety and Health Administration Act of 1970 (OSHA) was legislation designed to protect all employees against injuries from occupational hazards in the workplace.
1972	PSROs	Created as part of Title XI of the Social Security Amendments Act of 1972, Professional Standards Review Organizations (PSROs) were physician-controlled nonprofit organizations that contracted with HCFA (now called CMS) to provide for the review of hospital inpatient resource utilization, quality of care, and medical necessity. (PSROs were replaced with Peer Review Organizations [PROs], as a result of the Tax Equity and Fiscal Responsibility Act of 1982, or TEFRA.)
1973	Medicare benefits expanded	Medicare coverage became available to those also entitled to receive Social Security or Railroad Retirement disability cash benefits after twenty-four months of disability based on SSA criteria, most persons with end-stage renal disease (ESRD), and certain individuals over sixty-five who were not eligible for paid coverage but elected to pay for Medicare benefits. End-stage renal disease (ESRD) is a chronic

(continues)

TABLE 2-1 *(continued)*

YEAR	EVENT	DESCRIPTION
1973 *(cont.)*		kidney disorder that requires long-term hemodialysis or kidney transplantation because the patient's filtration system in the kidneys has been destroyed.
	CHAMPVA	The Veterans Healthcare Expansion Act of 1973 authorized Veterans Affairs (VA) to establish the **Civilian Health and Medical Program of the Department of Veterans Affairs (CHAMPVA)** program to provide health care benefits for dependents of veterans rated as 100% permanently and totally disabled as a result of service-connected conditions, veterans who died as a result of service-connected conditions, and veterans who died on duty with less than 30 days of active service.
	HMO Act of 1973	The **Health Maintenance Organization Assistance Act of 1973** authorized federal grants and loans to private organizations that wished to develop **health maintenance organizations (HMOs)**, which are responsible for providing health care services to subscribers in a given geographic area for a fixed fee.
1974	ERISA	The **Employment Retirement Income Security Act of 1974 (ERISA)** mandated reporting and disclosure requirements for group life and health plans (including managed care plans), permitted large employers to self-insure employee health care benefits, and exempted large employers from taxes on health insurance premiums. **Managed care** allows patients to receive care from a group of participating providers to whom a copayment is paid for each service. A **copayment (copay)** is a provision in an insurance policy that requires the policyholder or patient to pay a specified dollar amount to a health care provider for each visit or medical service received.
1977	HCFA	To combine health care financing and quality assurance programs into a single agency, the Health Care Financing Administration (HCFA) was formed within the Department of Health and Human Services (HHS). The Medicare and Medicaid programs were also transferred to the newly created agency. (HCFA is now called the Centers for Medicare & Medicaid Services, or CMS.)
1980	HHS	With the departure of the Office of Education, The Department of Health, Education and Welfare (HEW) became the Department of Health and Human Services (HHS).
1981	OBRA	The **Omnibus Budget Reconciliation Act of 1981 (OBRA)** was federal legislation that expanded Medicare and Medicaid programs.
1982	BCBS Association	The Blue Cross Association and the National Association of Blue Shield Plans merged to create the **BlueCross BlueShield Association (BCBSA)**, which is an association of independent Blue Cross and Blue Shield Plans.
1983	TEFRA of 1982	The **Tax Equity and Fiscal Responsibility Act of 1982 (TEFRA)** created Medicare risk programs, which allowed federally qualified HMOs and competitive medical plans that met specified Medicare requirements to provide Medicare-covered services under a risk contract. TEFRA also enacted a **prospective payment system (PPS)**, which issues a predetermined payment for services. Previously, reimbursement was generated on a **per diem** basis, which issued payment based on daily rates. The PPS implemented in 1983 is called **diagnosis-related groups (DRGs)**, which reimburses hospitals for inpatient stays. **Peer review organizations (PROs)** were also created as part of TEFRA, replacing PSROs. PROs review medical necessity issues, determine appropriateness of care provided through retrospective analysis of medical records, assess specific aspects of care (e.g., cesarean

(continues)

TABLE 2-1 *(continued)*

YEAR	EVENT	DESCRIPTION
1983 *(cont.)*		sections) to determine whether variations in practice patterns exist, conduct physician office site reviews, and review reimbursement appeals to evaluate medical necessity and appropriateness of services denied by third-party payers.
1984	Standardization of information submitted on Medicare claims	HCFA (now called CMS) required providers to use the **HCFA-1500** (now called the **CMS-1500**) to submit Medicare claims. The HCFA Common Procedure Coding System (HCPCS) (now called Healthcare Procedure Coding System) was created. CPT was adopted as level I in the three-level system. HCFA created national (level II) codes. Local carriers created regional (level III) codes. Commercial payers also adopted HCPCS coding and use of the HCFA-1500 claim form.
1985	COBRA	The **Consolidated Omnibus Budget Reconciliation Act of 1985 (COBRA)** allows employees to continue health care coverage beyond the benefit termination date.
1988	TRICARE	The **CHAMPUS Reform Initiative (CRI)** of 1988 resulted in a new program, TRICARE, which includes three options: TRICARE Prime, TRICARE Extra, and TRICARE Standard.
	ICD-9-CM reporting on physician office claims	Medicare began requiring physician offices to submit ICD-9-CM codes on HCFA-1500 (now called CMS-1500) claims.
	CLIA	The **Clinical Laboratory Improvement Act (CLIA)** established quality standards for all laboratory testing to ensure the accuracy, reliability, and timeliness of patient test results regardless of where the test was performed.
1989	Medicare requires claims on all Medicare patients	HCFA (now called CMS) requires all physicians to submit claims on behalf of Medicare patients regardless of the physician's participation status in the Medicare program.
	HEDIS	The National Committee for Quality Assurance (NCQA) developed the **Health Plan Employer Data and Information Set (HEDIS),** which created standards to assess managed care systems using data elements that are collected, evaluated, and published to compare the performance of managed health care plans.
1991	E/M codes created	The American Medical Association (AMA) and HCFA (now called CMS) implemented major revisions of CPT, creating a new section called **Evaluation and Management (E/M),** which describes patient encounters with health care professionals for the purpose of evaluation and management of general health status.
	HCFA-1500 (1-90) new version released	HCFA (now called CMS) also released a new version of the HCFA-1500 (now called CMS-1500) claim and required its use for all government claims.
1992	RBRVS is implemented	A new fee schedule for Medicare services was implemented as part of the Omnibus Reconciliation Acts (OBRA) of 1989 and 1990, which replaced the regional usual and reasonable payment basis with a fixed fee schedule calculated according to the Resource Based Relative Value Scale system (RBRVS). The **Resource-Based Relative Value Scale (RBRVS) system** is a payment system that reimburses physicians' practice expenses based on relative values for three components of each physician's service: physician work, practice expense, and malpractice insurance expense. **Usual and reasonable payments** were based on

(continues)

TABLE 2-1 *(continued)*

YEAR	EVENT	DESCRIPTION
1992 *(cont.)*		fees typically charged by providers by specialty within a particular region of the country. A **fee schedule** is a list of predetermined payments for health care services provided to patients (e.g., a fee is assigned to each CPT code).
1996	CCI	HCFA (now called CMS) developed the National **Correct Coding Initiative (CCI)** to promote national correct coding methodologies and to eliminate improper coding. CCI edits are developed based on coding conventions defined in the American Medical Association's Current Procedural Terminology (CPT) Manual, current standards of medical and surgical coding practice, input from specialty societies, and analysis of current coding practice.
	HIPAA	The **Health Insurance Portability and Accountability Act of 1996 (HIPAA)** mandates regulations that govern privacy, security, and electronic transactions standards for health care information. The primary intent of HIPAA is to provide better access to health insurance, limit fraud and abuse, and reduce administrative costs.
1997	BBA of 1997	The **Balanced Budget Act of 1997 (BBA)** addresses health care fraud and abuse issues, and the Department of HHS Office of the Inspector General (OIG) provides investigative and audit services in health care fraud cases.
1998	SNF PPS	The **Skilled Nursing Facility Prospective Payment System (SNF PPS)** is implemented (as a result of the BBA of 1997) to cover all costs (routine, ancillary and capital) related to services furnished to Medicare Part A beneficiaries. The SNF PPS generates per diem payments for each admission that are case-mix adjusted using a resident classification system called **Resource Utilization Groups (RUGs)**, which is based on data collected from resident assessments (using data elements called the **Minimum Data Set**, or **MDS**) and relative weights developed from staff time data.
1999	HH PPS	The Omnibus Consolidated and Emergency Supplemental Appropriations Act (OCE-SAA) of 1999 amended the BBA of 1997 to require the development and implementation of a **Home Health Prospective Payment System (HH PPS)**, which reimburses home health agencies at a predetermined rate for health care services provided to patients. The HH PPS was implemented October 1, 2000, and uses the **Outcomes and Assessment Information Set (OASIS)**, a group of data elements that represent core items of a comprehensive assessment for an adult home care patient and form the basis for measuring patient outcomes for purposes of outcome-based quality improvement.
2000	OPPS	The **Outpatient Prospective Payment System (OPPS)**, which uses **Ambulatory Payment Classifications (APCs)** to calculate reimbursement, is implemented for billing of hospital-based Medicare outpatient claims.
	Consumer-driven health plans	**Consumer-driven health plans** are introduced as a way to encourage individuals to locate best health care at the lowest possible price with the goal of holding down health care costs. These plans are organized into three categories: 1. *Employer-paid high-deductible insurance plans* with special health spending accounts to be used by employees to cover deductibles and other medical costs when covered amounts are exceeded. 2. *Defined contribution plans,* which provide a selection of insurance options, and employees pay the difference between what the employer pays and the actual cost of the plan they select.

(continues)

TABLE 2-1 *(continued)*

YEAR	EVENT	DESCRIPTION
2000 *(cont.)*		3. *After-tax savings accounts,* which combine a traditional health insurance plan for major medical expenses with a savings account that the employee uses to pay for routine care.
2001	CMS	On June 14, 2001, HCFA changed its name to the Centers for Medicare and Medicaid Services (CMS).
2002	IRF PPS	The Inpatient Rehabilitation Facilities Prospective Payment System (IRF PPS) is implemented (as a result of the BBA of 1997), which utilizes information from a patient assessment instrument to classify patients into distinct groups based on clinical characteristics and expected resource needs. Separate payments are calculated for each group, including the application of case and facility level adjustments.
	Quality Improvement Organizations (QIOs)	CMS announced that peer review organizations (PROs) will be known as quality improvement organizations (QIOs), and they will continue to perform utilization and quality control review of health care furnished, or to be furnished, to Medicare beneficiaries.

HEALTH INSURANCE COVERAGE STATISTICS

U.S. Census Bureau data from 2002 estimates that 85% of people in the United States are covered by some form of health insurance; and of that percentage:

- 63% are covered by employment-based plans
- 25% are covered by government plans (e.g., Medicare, Medicaid, TRICARE)
- 8% are covered by privately sponsored plans

The reason the insurance coverage breakdown does not total 85% is because approximately 10% of people in the United States are covered by more than one insurance plan (e.g., employment-based plan plus Medicare).

SUMMARY

- Health insurance is a contract between a policyholder and an insurance carrier or government program for the purpose of providing reimbursement of all or a portion of medical and heath care costs.
- Disability insurance provides an individual with reimbursement for lost wages, while liability insurance covers losses to a third party caused by the insured or on premises owned by the insured.
- The history of health care reimbursement can be traced back to 1860 when the Franklin Health Assurance Company of Massachusetts wrote the first health insurance policy.
- Subsequent years, through the present, have seen great changes and advances in health care insurance and reimbursement, from the development of the first Blue Cross and Blue Shield plans to legislation that resulted in government health care programs (e.g., to cover individuals age 65 and older), payment systems to control health care costs (e.g., diagnosis-related groups), and regulations to govern privacy, security, and electronic transaction standards for health care information.

STUDY CHECKLIST

☐ Read the textbook chapter, and highlight key concepts.

☐ Create an index card for each key term.

☐ Access the chapter Internet links to learn more about concepts.

☐ Answer the chapter review questions, verifying answers with your instructor.

☐ Complete Web Tutor assignments and take online quizzes.

☐ Complete Workbook chapter, verifying answers with your instructor.

☐ Form a study group with classmates to discuss chapter concepts in preparation for an exam.

REVIEW

MATCHING

Match the definition with the appropriate term.

_____ 1. Identification of disease and provision of care/treatment to the sick and injured

_____ 2. Includes preventive services, designed to help individuals avoid health problems

_____ 3. Contract between policyholder and payer that reimburses medically necessary treatment

_____ 4. Reimbursement for lost income as the result of temporary or permanent illness or injury

_____ 5. Policy that covers losses to a third party caused by the insured

a. disability insurance
b. health care
c. health insurance
d. liability insurance
e. medical care

MULTIPLE CHOICE

Select the most appropriate response.

6. Which was the first commercial insurance company in the United States to provide private health care coverage for injuries that did not result in death?

a. Baylor University Health Plan

b. Blue Cross and Blue Shield Association

c. Franklin Health Assurance Company

d. Office of Workers' Compensation Program

7. By 1880, how many insurance companies offered health insurance policies?

a. 60

b. 500

c. 1000

d. 10,000

8. In the early 1900s, most Americans continued to pay for their own health care, which meant:

a. their employers reimbursed them for reasonable medical expenses.

b. they either received charitable health care services or no care at all.

c. the federal government provided them with health care coverage.

d. physician medical group practices pooled resources to provide care.

9. Which U.S. President signed legislation to provide workers' compensation for certain federal employees in unusually hazardous jobs?

    a. Hill-Burton   c. Roosevelt

    b. Kimball   d. Truman

10. Workers' compensation is an insurance program that requires employers to cover medical expenses and:

    a. create medical service bureaus.

    b. implement prepaid health plan services.

    c. limit lifetime maximum amounts of coverage.

    d. provide lost wages for injured workers.

11. Which organization drafted model health insurance legislation in 1915 to limit coverage to the working class who earned less than $1,200 per year?

    a. AALL   c. AMA

    b. AHA   d. FECA

12. In what year were prepaid health plans introduced?

    a. 1915   c. 1920

    b. 1916   d. 1929

13. Which of the following replaced the 1908 workers' compensation legislation and provided civilian employees of the federal government with medical care, survivors' benefits, and compensation for lost wages?

    a. Black Lung Benefits Reform Act

    b. Federal Employees' Compensation Act

    c. Longshore and Harbor Workers' Compensation Act

    d. Office of Workers' Compensation Programs

14. The first Blue Cross policy was introduced by:

    a. Baylor University in Dallas, Texas.

    b. Harvard University in Cambridge, Massachusetts.

    c. Kaiser Permanente in Los Angeles, California.

    d. American Medical Association representatives.

15. Health care reform was initiated in 1930 when the _____ was funded by charitable organizations to address concerns about the cost and distribution of medical care.

    a. Committee on the Cost of Medical Care

    b. Hill-Burton Act

    c. Tactical Committee on Medical Care

    d. Wagner National Health Care Act

16. In 1939, the AHA adopted the _____ symbol as the national emblem for plans that met certain guidelines.

    a. Blue Cross

    b. Blue Shield

17. Which concept was developed from lumber and mining camps of the Pacific Northwest, in which employers provided medical care for workers through medical service bureaus.

    a. Blue Cross

    b. Blue Shield

18. In the 1940s, group health insurance was offered as part of a full-time employee benefit package to attract wartime labor. This insurance was:

    a. not subject to income and Social Security taxes.

    b. subject to income and Social Security taxes.

19. Which term describes three or more health care providers who share equipment, supplies, and personnel, and who divide income according to a prearranged formula?

    a. Corporation

    b. Group medical practice

    c. Health maintenance organization

    d. Sole proprietorship

20. Which organization was created in 1946 as a coordinating agency for physician-sponsored health plans?

    a. Association of Medical Care Plans

    b. Blue Cross and Blue Shield Association

    c. Blue Cross Association

    d. National Association of Blue Shield Plans

TRUE/FALSE

Indicate whether each statement is true or false.

21. ☐ T ☐ F PROs were replaced with PSROs in 1982, as a result of TEFRA.

22. ☐ T ☐ F The reimbursement system that issues payments based on daily rates is called PPS.

23. ☐ T ☐ F HCFA was formed in 1977 within the Department of Health and Human Services.

24. ☐ T ☐ F The ICD was developed by the National Center for Healthcare Statistics.

25. ☐ T ☐ F The BBA of 1997 addresses health care fraud and abuse issues.

MATCHING

Match the reimbursement system with its description.

____ 26. Inpatient hospitalizations

____ 27. Physician practice expenses

____ 28. Skilled nursing facility services

____ 29. Home health agency services

____ 30. Hospital-based outpatient claims

a. APCs

b. DRGs

c. OASIS

d. RBRVS

e. RUGs

MATCHING

Match the program with its description.

____ 31. Provides health care services to those over the age of 65

____ 32. Provides health care services to low-income Americans

____ 33. Created as a benefit for dependents of personnel serving in the armed forces

____ 34. Provides health care benefits to dependents of veterans

____ 35. Cover medical expenses and loss of wages for employees who are injured or become ill on the job

a. CHAMPUS

b. CHAMPVA

c. Medicaid

d. Medicare

e. Workers' compensation

MATCHING

Match the legislation with its description.

____ 36. Provided federal grants for modernizing hospitals that had become obsolete

____ 37. Designed to protect all employees against injuries from occupational hazards in the workplace

____ 38. Authorized federal grants and loans to private organizations that wished to develop HMOs

____ 39. Legislation that provided health care to dependents of active military personnel

____ 40. Mandated reporting and disclosure requirements for group life and health plans

____ 41. Federal legislation that expanded the Medicare and Medicaid programs

____ 42. Created Medicare risk programs and enacted DRGs

____ 43. Allows employees to continue health care coverage beyond the benefit termination date

____ 44. Established quality standards for all laboratory testing

____ 45. Mandated regulations that govern privacy, security, and electronic transactions for health care information

a. CLIA of 1988
b. COBRA of 1985
c. Dependents Medical Care Act
d. ERISA of 1974
e. Hill-Burton Act
f. HIPAA of 1996
g. HMO Act of 1973
h. OBRA of 1981
i. OSHA of 1970
j. TEFRA of 1983

MATCHING

Match the term with its description.

____ 46. Provides coverage for catastrophic illnesses

____ 47. Maximum benefits payable to a health plan participant

____ 48. Amount for which the patient is financially responsible before an insurance policy provides coverage

____ 49. Amount the patient pays for each visit or medical service covered

____ 50. List of predetermined payments for services provided to patients

a. Copayment
b. Deductible
c. Fee schedule
d. Lifetime maximum
e. Major medical

KEY TERMS

accreditation
adverse selection
Amendment to the HMO Act of 1973
cafeteria plan
capitation
case management
case manager
closed-panel HMO
CMS Office of Managed Care
competitive medical plan (CMP)
concurrent review
covered lives
direct contract model HMO
discharge planning
enrollees
exclusive provider organization (EPO)
external quality review organization
    (EQRO)
federally qualified HMO
fee-for-service
gag clauses
gatekeeper
group model HMO
group practice without walls (GPWW)
independent practice association (IPA)
    HMO
individual practice association (IPA)
    HMO
integrated delivery system (IDS)
integrated provider organization (IPO)
Joint Commission on Accreditation of
    Healthcare Organizations (JCAHO)
legislation
managed care organization (MCO)
managed health care (managed care)
management service organization (MSO)
mandates

medical foundation
medical savings account (MSA)
Medicare+Choice (M+C or Medicare
    Part C)
Medicare Risk Programs
National Committee for Quality
    Assurance (NCQA)
network model HMO
network provider
open-panel HMO
physician incentive plan
physician incentives
physician-hospital organization (PHO
point-of-service plan (POS)
preadmission certification (PAC)
preadmission review
Preferred Provider Health Care Act o
    1985
preferred provider organization (PPO
primary care provider (PCP)
quality assessment and performance
    improvement (QAPI)
quality assurance program
Quality Improvement System for
    Managed Care (QISMC)
report card
retrospectively
risk contract
risk pool
second surgical opinion (SSO)
self-referral
staff model HMO
standards
survey
triple option plan
utilization management (utilization
    review)
utilization review organization (URO)

Managed Health Care

OBJECTIVES

Upon successful completion of this chapter, you should be able to:

1. Define key terms.

2. Compare managed care with traditional health care insurance.

3. Discuss the history of managed care in the United States.

4. List managed health care federal legislation according to year, and provide legislative summaries of each.

5. Delineate the role of a managed care organization.

6. Apply the concept of capitation as it is associated with managed care.

7. Interpret a managed care profile map that details HMO penetration rates.

8. Explain the role of a gatekeeper in managed care.

9. Identify and explain activities conducted by managed care organizations or their representative organizations (e.g., third-party administrators).

10. Describe six managed care models, and provide details about each.

11. Differentiate between the two organizations that accredit managed care organizations.

12. Implement administrative procedures so that the physician's practice appropriately responds to managed care organization program activities.

INTRODUCTION

Managed health care (or managed care) combines health care delivery with the financing of services provided. The intent was to replace conventional fee-for-service plans with more affordable quality care to health care consumers and providers who agreed to certain restrictions (e.g., patients would receive care only from providers who are members of a managed care organization.)

HISTORY OF MANAGED HEALTH CARE

Managed health care (or managed care) (Tables 3-1 and 3-2) was developed as a way to provide affordable, comprehensive, prepaid health care services to **enrollees** (employees and dependents who join a managed care plan; known as beneficiaries in private insurance plans).

TABLE 3-1 History of managed care

YEAR	MANAGED CARE ACTIVITY
1910	• For 50 cents/month, the Western Clinic in Tacoma, Washington, offered medical services to lumber mill owners and their employees.
1929	• Baylor Hospital (Texas) provided prepaid hospital coverage to approximately 1,500 teachers, representing the origins of Blue Cross. • Rural Farmers Cooperative in Elk City (Oklahoma) was established by Dr. Michael Shadid and area farmers, and sold $50 shares to fund a hospital (known today as the Great Plains Regional Medical Center). In exchange for shares, discounted medical care was provided. • Ross-Loos medical group provided prepaid health care services to Los Angeles Department of Water and Power employees and their families.
1933	• Dr. Sidney Garfield and several associates provided prepaid health care services to 5,000 Southern California aqueduct construction workers.
1937	• Kaiser Foundation Health Plans were created to finance medical care for its employees and their families. • The Group Health Association (GHA) nonprofit cooperative was created in Washington, DC for employees of the Federal Home Loan Bank.
1938	• Dr. Sidney Garfield and Henry Kaiser created a group practice prepayment plan for Grand Coulee Dam construction workers and their families. • Dr. Garfield established group practice prepayment plans for Kaiser shipyard (California) and steel mill (Washington) employees and their families, eventually serving 200,000 members.
1930s	• The American Medical Association (AMA) opposed prepaid cooperative plans and attempted to suppress their growth by expelling participating physicians from local medical societies, preventing them from obtaining consultations and referrals, and persuading hospitals to deny them admitting privileges.
1947	• The AMA was indicted and convicted of violating the Sherman Antitrust Act, which was upheld in 1947 by the Supreme Court. However, state laws were established to limit the establishment of prepaid health care plans, and the AMA implemented "watchful coexistence" instead of sponsoring reprisals against prepaid group practices. • The Health Insurance Plan (HIP) of Greater New York was created to provide health care coverage to City of New York employees. • The Group Health Cooperative of Puget Sound (Seattle, Washington) was created as the result of 400 families contributing $100 each.
1954	• San Joaquin Medical Foundation (California) formed in response to competition from Kaiser. This plan is considered the earliest example of an independent practice association (IPA).
1955	• The nationally recognized health maintenance organization (HMO), Kaiser-Permanente, was created.
1960s	• Implementation of Medicare and Medicaid resulted in dramatically increased health care costs, and politicians and interest groups proposed reform of the health care system. • Key issues related to reform included: consumer rights, cost containment, coverage for the uninsured, efficient health care delivery systems, and health care access for the poor and minorities.
1970s	• States restricted development and/or operation of HMOs. • Employers and labor unions supported the concept of managed care. • President Nixon's State of the Union address called for "new programs to encourage preventive medicine by attacking the cause of disease and injury, and by providing incentives for doctors to keep people well, rather than just treat them when they are sick." (Table 3-2 details federal legislation implemented in response to health care industry needs and changes.)

TABLE 3-2 Timeline for managed health care federal legislation

YEAR	LEGISLATIVE TITLE	LEGISLATIVE SUMMARY
1973	Health Maintenance Organization Assistance Act of 1973 (HMO Act of 1973)	• authorized grants and loans to develop HMOs under private sponsorship • defined a **federally qualified HMO** (certified to provide health care services to Medicare and Medicaid enrollees) as one that has applied for and met federal standards established in the HMO Act of 1973 • required most employers with more than 25 employees to offer HMO coverage if local plans were available
1974	Employee Retirement Income Security Act of 1974 (ERISA)	• mandated reporting and disclosure requirements for group life and health plans (including managed care plans) • permitted large employers to self-insure employee health care benefits • exempted large employers from taxes on health insurance premiums
1981	Omnibus Budget Reconciliation Act of 1981 (OBRA)	• provided states with flexibility to establish HMOs for Medicare and Medicaid programs • increased managed care enrollment resulted
1982	Tax Equity and Fiscal Responsibility Act of 1982 (TEFRA)	• modified the HMO Act of 1973 • created **Medicare Risk Programs**, which allowed federally qualified HMOs and competitive medical plans (CMPs) that met specified Medicare requirements to provide Medicare covered services under a risk contract • defined **risk contract** as an arrangement among providers to provide capitated (fixed, prepaid basis) health care services to Medicare beneficiaries • defined **competitive medical plan (CMP)** as an HMO that meets federal eligibility requirements for a Medicare risk contract, but is not licensed as a federally qualified plan.
1985	**Preferred Provider Health Care Act of 1985**	• eased restrictions on preferred provider organizations (PPOs) • allowed subscribers to seek health care from providers outside of the PPO
	Consolidated Omnibus Budget Reconciliation Act of 1985 (COBRA)	• established an employee's right to continue health care coverage beyond scheduled benefit termination date (including HMO coverage)
1988	**Amendment to the HMO Act of 1973**	• allowed federally qualified HMOs to permit members to occasionally use non-HMO physicians and be partially reimbursed
1989	Health Plan Employer Data and Information Set (HEDIS) is developed by National Committee for Quality Assurance (NCQA)	• created standards to assess managed care systems in the terms of membership, utilization of services, quality, access, health plan management and activities, and financial indicators
1994	**HCFA's Office of Managed Care** is established	• facilitated innovation and competition among Medicare HMOs

(continues)

TABLE 3-2 *(continued)*

YEAR	LEGISLATIVE TITLE	LEGISLATIVE SUMMARY
1996	Health Insurance Portability and Accountability Act of 1996 (HIPAA)	• created federal standards for insurers, HMOs, and employer plans, including those who self-insure
1997	Medical Savings Accounts (MSA) pilot program created as part of IRS legislation	A **medical savings account (MSA)** allows individuals to withdraw tax-free funds for health care expenses, which are not covered by a qualifying high-deductible health plan. Health care expenses that may be reimbursed from the MSA include: • dental expenses, including uncovered orthodontia • eye exams, contact lenses and eyeglasses • hearing care expenses • health plan deductibles and copayments • prescription drugs NOTE: 2002 IRS legislation expanded MSA provisions, increasing individual eligibility, lowering deductibles, and allowing employers and employees to contribute to accounts.
1997	Balanced Budget Act of 1997 (BBA)	• encouraged formation of provider service networks (PSNs) and provider service organizations (PSOs) • mandated risk-based managed care organizations to submit encounter data related to inpatient hospital stays of members • established the **Medicare+Choice** (**M+C** or **Medicare Part C**) program, which expanded Medicare coverage options by creating managed care plans, to include HMOs, PPOs, and MSAs • required M+C organizations to implement a **quality assessment and performance improvement (QAPI)** program, so that quality assurance activities are performed to improve the functioning of M+C organizations

INTERNET LINK

For more information about Kaiser Permanente, visit http://www.kaiserpermanente.org.

Go to http://www.gprmc-ok.com/about.htm to learn more about Dr. Shadid and the history of the Great Plains Regional Medical Center.

MANAGED CARE ORGANIZATIONS

A **managed care organization (MCO)** is responsible for the health of a group of enrollees, and can be a health plan, hospital, physician group, or health system. Unlike traditional **fee-for-service** plans, which reimburse providers for individual health care services rendered, managed care is financed according to a method called **capitation**, where providers accept pre-established payments for providing health care services to enrollees over a period of time (usually one year). If the physician provides services that cost less than the capitation amount, there is a profit (which the physician keeps). If services provided to subscribers cost more than the capitation amount, the physician loses money.

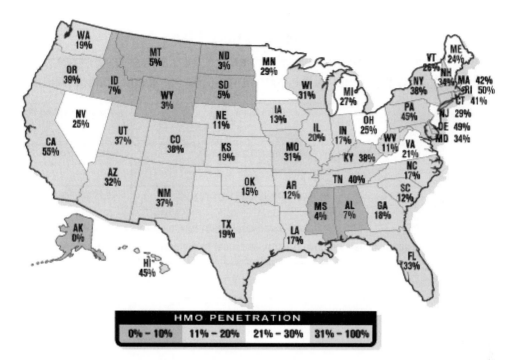

FIGURE 3-1 Managed Care Profile Map—HMO Penetration Rates (Reprinted with permission from Medical Data International, Inc. Copyright 2000, Medical Data International, Inc., http://www.medicaldata.com.)

The concentration of MCOs varies widely across the country (Figure 3-1), with the heaviest in California and Rhode Island.

NOTE: Some managed care organizations have discontinued capitation and have adopted fee-for-service payment plans. ●

EXAMPLE

In June, Hillcrest Medical Group received a capitated payment of $15,000 for the 150 members (enrollees) of the ABC Managed Care Health Plan. The Group spent $12,500 of the capitated payment on preventive, chronic, and acute health care services provided to member patients. The services were provided at the Group's office and local hospital, which included inpatient, outpatient, and emergency department care. (The Group is responsible for paying the enrollees' hospital bills.) In this scenario, health care services provided to enrollees cost less than the capitated payment received. The Hillcrest Medical Group, therefore, made a profit of $2,500. If health care services had cost more than the capitated amount of $15,000, the Group would have experienced a loss. ●

Primary Care Providers

Managed care plan enrollees receive care from a primary care provider that is selected from a list of participating providers. The **primary care provider (PCP)** is responsible for supervising and coordinating health care services for enrollees and preauthorizing referrals to specialists and inpatient hospital admissions (except in emergencies) (Figure 3-2). The PCP serves as a **gatekeeper** by providing essential health care services at the lowest possible cost, avoiding nonessential care, and referring patients to specialists.

Managed Care Plan

PRIMARY CARE PROVIDER PREAUTHORIZATION FORM FOR CONSULTATION

Patient Name	Preauthorization Number	Name of Consulting Physician
Member Identification Number	Member Name (Last, First, MI)	Member Birthdate
Primary Care Physician Identification Number	Name of Primary Care Physician (PCP)	PCP Phone Number

This referral authorizes the services listed below. All services must be rendered by provider stated below.

Diagnosis

Medical History

Reason for Referral

Consultant may provide services listed below. All authorized visits must occur within 90 days of date authorized by PCP. If surgical procedure is listed below, Consultant Treatment Plan is not required. For initial consultation, specialist must submit Consultant Treatment Report of findings and treatment recommendations.

Diagnostic tests indicated:

Procedure(s) to be performed:

Primary Care Physician Signature	Date

Consultant billing procedures for services authorized by Primary Care Physician:

1. Enter Preauthorization Number listed above in Block 23 of the CMS-1500 form.
2. For first submission, submit CMS-1500 with original PCP Preauthorization Form for consultation.
3. For subsequent submissions, no attachments are required.
4. Consultant must complete Consultant Treatment Plan to obtain authorization for any surgical procedure not specified on the Preauthorization Form PCP Referral.

Improperly completed forms will be returned.

FIGURE 3-2 Sample primary care provider preauthorization referral form

Quality Assurance

Managed care plans that are "federally qualified" and those that must comply with state quality review **mandates** (laws) are required to establish quality assurance programs. A **quality assurance program** includes activities that assess the quality of care provided in a health care setting. Many states have enacted **legislation** (laws) requiring an **external quality review organization (EQRO)** (e.g., QIO) to review health care provided by managed care organizations. The types of quality reviews performed include government oversight, patient satisfaction surveys, data collected from grievance procedures, and reviews conducted by independent organizations. Independent organizations that perform reviews include accreditation agencies such as the National Committee for Quality Assurance and Joint Commission on Accreditation of Healthcare Organizations.

Medicare established the **Quality Improvement System for Managed Care (QISMC)** to assure the accountability of managed care plans in terms of objective, measurable **standards** (requirements). Plans are required to meet minimum performance levels and to show demonstrable and measurable improvement in specified broad clinical areas (e.g., preventive services, acute ambulatory care, chronic care, and hospital care) based on performance improvement projects that each plan identifies. The Health Plan Employer Data and Information Set (HEDIS), sponsored by the National Committee for Quality Assurance, consists of performance measures used to evaluate managed care plans (e.g., rate of Pap smears performed among women of a certain age). The National Committee for Quality Assurance (NCQA) reviews managed care plans and develops report cards to allow health care consumers to make informed decisions when selecting a plan. The **report card** contains data regarding a managed care plan's quality, utilization, customer satisfaction, administrative effectiveness, financial stability, and cost control.

INTERNET LINK

The NCQA's Web site at http://hprc.ncqa.org allows health care consumers to create a customized report card or to view report cards for all managed care plans.

Utilization Management

Utilization management (or **utilization review**) is a method of controlling health care costs and quality of care by reviewing the appropriateness and necessity of care provided to patients prior to the administration of care (or **retrospectively**, which is conducted after care has been administered). Utilization management activities are performed by managed care plans and include:

- *preadmission certification* (**PAC**, or **preadmission review**) which is a review for medical necessity of inpatient care prior to the patient's admission.
- *preauthorization*, which is a review that grants prior approval for reimbursement of a health care service (e.g., elective surgery).
- *concurrent review*, which is a review for medical necessity of tests and procedures ordered during an inpatient hospitalization.
- *discharge planning*, which involves arranging appropriate health care services for the discharged patient (e.g., home health care).

Some managed care plans contract out utilization management services to a **utilization review organization (URO)**, which is an entity that establishes a utilization management program and performs external utilization review services. Other plans contract with a *third-party administrator (TPA),* which is an organization that provides health benefits claims administration and other outsourcing services for self-insured companies.

Case Management

Case management involves the development of patient care plans for the coordination and provision of care for complicated cases in a cost-effective manner. For example, instead of admitting a patient to the hospital, a managed care plan might authorize 24-hour home health care services when appropriate. The case manager submits written confirmation, authorizing treatment, to the provider (Figure 3-3).

Managed Care Plan

DATE:

RE:
DATE OF BIRTH:
IDENTIFICATION NUMBER:
START TREATMENT DATE:

NAME OF CONSULTANT:
MAILING ADDRESS:

Dear Dr. _____

_____ was referred to you by the Managed Care Insurance Company on _____. I am authorizing the following medically necessary treatment. This is subject to patient eligibility and contract limitations at the time treatment is performed.

Procedure	Units	From	To	Authorization Number

When filing for reimbursement, please send the CMS-1500 claim form to me in care of the Managed Care Insurance Company at the above address. In order to expedite payment, please be certain to include in Block 23 all appropriate authorization number(s) as indicated above.

Please note that any services provided beyond those listed in this letter require additional authorization. If you anticipate that the patient will require additional services, you must complete an outpatient treatment report two weeks prior to rendering any additional treatment. If the patient fails to keep appointments, please inform us by telephone. If treatment is discontinued, submit a written discharge summary within two weeks of termination.

Although eligibility and benefit information has been corroborated to the best of our ability, certification for medically necessary care does not guarantee financial reimbursement related to these matters. If you need further information, or if there are any significant changes in the patient's medical status, please contact me at the Managed Care Plan at (800) 555-1212, extension 1234.
Thank you for your cooperation.

Sincerely,

Case Manager
Original:
cc:

FIGURE 3-3 Sample case manager written confirmation order

Second Surgical Opinions

Prior to scheduling elective surgery, managed care plans sometimes require a **second surgical opinion (SSO)** in which a second physician is asked to evaluate the necessity of surgery and recommend the most economic, appropriate facility in which to perform the surgery (e.g., outpatient clinic or doctor's office versus inpatient hospitalization).

NOTE: Managed care programs have been successful in containing costs and limiting unnecessary services, resulting in the current trend for health care plans to offer the SSO as a benefit, not a requirement. ●

Gag Clauses

Medicare and many states prohibit managed care contracts from containing **gag clauses**, which prevent providers from discussing all treatment options with patients, whether or not the plan would provide reimbursement for services. Medicare beneficiaries are entitled to advice from their physicians on medically necessary treatment options that may be appropriate for their condition or disease. Because a gag clause would have the practical effect of prohibiting a physician from giving a patient the full range of advice and counsel that is clinically appropriate, it would result in the managed care plan not providing all covered Medicare services to its enrollees, in violation of the managed care plan's responsibilities.

Physician Incentives

Physician incentives include payments made directly or indirectly to health care providers to serve as encouragement to reduce or limit services (e.g., discharge an inpatient from the hospital more quickly) so as to save money for the managed care plan. The federal **physician incentive plan** requires managed care plans that contract with Medicare or Medicaid to disclose information about physician incentive plans to CMS or State Medicaid agencies before a new or renewed contract receives final approval.

SIX MANAGED CARE MODELS

Managed care originally focused on cost reductions by restricting health care access through utilization management and availability of limited benefits. Managed care organizations (MCOs) were created to manage benefits and to develop participating provider networks. Managed care can now be categorized according to six models:

1. Exclusive Provider Organization (EPO)

2. Integrated Delivery System (IDS)

3. Health Maintenance Organization (HMO)
   a. direct contract model
   b. group model
   c. individual practice association (IPA)
   d. network model
   e. staff model

4. Point-of-Service Plan (POS)

5. Preferred Provider Organization (PPO)

6. Triple Option Plan

Exclusive Provider Organization (EPO)

An **exclusive provider organization (EPO)** is a managed care plan that provides benefits to subscribers if they receive services from network providers. A **network provider** is a physician or health care facility under contract to the managed care plan. Usually, network providers sign exclusive contracts with the EPO, which means they cannot contract with other managed care plans. Subscribers are generally required to coordinate health care services through their primary care physician (PCP). EPOs are regulated by state insurance departments (unlike HMOs that are regulated by either the state commerce or department of corporations, depending on state requirements).

Integrated Delivery System (IDS)

An **integrated delivery system (IDS)** is an organization of affiliated providers sites (e.g., hospitals, ambulatory surgical centers, or physician groups) that offer joint health care services to subscribers. Models include physician-hospital organizations, management service organizations, group practices without walls, integrated provider organizations, and medical foundations. A **physician-hospital organization (PHO)** is owned by hospital(s) and physician groups that obtain managed care plan contracts; physicians maintain their own practices and provide health care services to plan members. A **management service organization (MSO)** is usually owned by physicians or a hospital and provides practice management (administrative and support) services to individual physician practices. A **group practice without walls (GPWW)** establishes a contract that allows physicians to maintain their own offices and share services (e.g., appointment scheduling and billing). An **integrated provider organization (IPO)** manages the delivery of health care services offered by hospitals, physicians (who are employees of the IPO), and other health care organizations (e.g., an ambulatory surgery clinic and a nursing facility). A **medical foundation** is a nonprofit organization that contracts with and acquires the clinical and business assets of physician practices; the foundation is assigned a provider number and manages the practice's business. An *integrated delivery system* may also be referred to by any of the following names: integrated service network (ISN), delivery system, vertically integrated plan (VIP), vertically integrated system, horizontally integrated system, health delivery network, or accountable health plan.

INTERNET LINK

Go to http://www.healtheast.org to view information about HealthEast, an integrated care delivery system located in St. Paul, Minnesota, that provides acute care, chronic care, senior services, community-based services, ambulatory/outpatient services, physician clinics, and preventive services.

Health Maintenance Organization (HMO)

A **health maintenance organization (HMO)** is an alternative to traditional group health insurance coverage and provides comprehensive health care services to voluntarily enrolled members on a prepaid basis. In contrast, **traditional health insurance coverage** is usually provided on a fee-for-service basis in which reimbursement increases if the health care service fees increase, if multiple units of service are provided, or if more expensive services are provided instead of less expensive services (e.g., brand-name vs. generic prescription medication).

HMOs provide preventive care services to promote "wellness" or good health, thus reducing the overall cost of medical care. Annual physical examinations are encouraged for the early detection of health problems. Health risk assessment instruments (surveys) and resources are also available to subscribers. A primary care provider (PCP) assigned to each subscriber is responsible for coordinating health care services and referring subscribers to other health care providers.

HMOs often require patients to pay a *copayment* (or *copay*), which is a fee paid by the patient to the provider at the time health care services are rendered. Copayments range from $1 to $35 per visit, and some services are exempt because coinsurance payments are required instead. Coinsurance is usually associated with traditional health insurance plans, and can apply to managed care plans when out-of-network (nonparticipating) providers render health care services to plan subscribers. Generally, the coinsurance amount is a fixed percent (e.g., 50% of mental health care services of an out-of-network provider) for which the subscriber is financially responsible, usually after a deductible has been met. The *deductible* (another term usually associated with traditional health insurance plans) is the amount of money the subscriber must pay before plan benefits are reimbursable.

HMOs must meet the requirements of the HMO Act of 1973 as well as rules and regulations of individual states. There are five HMO models (Table 3-3): direct contract model, group model, individual practice association, network model, and staff model.

Point-of-Service Plan (POS)

To create flexibility in managed care plans, some HMOs and PPOs (preferred provider organizations) have implemented a **point-of-service plan (POS),** where patients have freedom to use the HMO panel of providers or to self-refer to non-HMO providers. If the enrollee chooses to receive all medical care from the HMO network of health care providers or obtains an authorization from the POS primary care physician for specialty care outside the HMO network, the enrollee pays only the regular copayment or a small charge for the visit. Also no deductible or coinsurance responsibility applies. If the enrollee sees a non-HMO panel specialist without a referral from the primary care physician, this is known as a **self-referral**. The enrollee will have greater out-of-pocket expenses as the enrollee must pay both a large deductible (usually $200 to $250) and the 20% to 25% coinsurance charges similar to those paid by persons with fee-for-service plans.

Preferred Provider Organization

A **preferred provider organization (PPO)** is a network of physicians and hospitals that have joined together to contract with insurance companies, employers or other organizations to provide health care to subscribers for a discounted fee. PPOs do not routinely establish contracts for laboratory or pharmacy services, but they do offer reduced-rate contracts with specific hospitals. Most PPOs are open-ended plans that allow patients to use non-PPO providers in exchange for larger out-of-pocket expenses. Premiums, deductibles, and copayments are usually higher than those paid for HMOs, but lower than regular fee-for-service plans.

TABLE 3-3 Closed-Panel and Open-Panel Health Maintenance Organization (HMO) models

CLOSED-PANEL HMO	Health care is provided in an HMO-owned center or satellite clinic or by physicians who belong to a specially formed medical group that serves the HMO.
CLOSED-PANEL MODELS	**DESCRIPTION**
Group Model HMO	Contracted health care services are delivered to subscribers by *participating physicians who are members of an independent multispecialty group practice.* The HMO reimburses the physician group, which is then responsible for reimbursing physician members and contracted health care facilities (e.g., hospitals). The physician group can be owned or managed by the HMO, or it can simply contract with the HMO.
Staff Model HMO	Health care services are provided to subscribers by *physicians employed by the HMO.* Premiums and other revenue are paid to the HMO. Usually, all ambulatory services are provided within HMO corporate buildings.
OPEN-PANEL HMO	Health care is provided by individuals who are *not* employees of the HMO or who do not belong to a specially formed medical group that serves the HMO.
OPEN-PANEL MODELS	**DESCRIPTION**
Direct Contract Model HMO	Contracted health care services are delivered to subscribers by *individual physicians in the community.*
Individual Practice Association (IPA) HMO	Also called **Independent Practice Association (IPA)**, contracted health services are delivered to subscribers by *physicians who remain in their independent office settings.* The IPA is an intermediary (e.g., physician association) that negotiates the HMO contract and receives and manages the capitation payment from the HMO so physicians are paid on either a fee-for-service or capitation basis.
Network Model HMO	Contracted health care services are provided to subscribers by *two or more physician multispecialty group practices.*

Triple Option Plan

A **triple option plan** is usually offered by either a single insurance plan or as a joint venture among two or more insurance carriers, and provides subscribers or employees with a choice of HMO, PPO, or traditional health insurance plans. It is also called a **cafeteria plan** because of different benefit plans and extra coverage options provided through the insurer or third party administrator. Triple option plans are intended to prevent the problem of covering members who are sicker than the general population (called **adverse selection**). A **risk pool** is created when a number of people are grouped for insurance purposes (e.g., employees of an organization); the cost of health care coverage is determined by employees' health status, age, sex, and occupation.

NOTE: State and federal governments have embraced some form of managed care in an effort to control health care costs. Because each program has developed a unique approach to managed care, details are discussed within individual chapters for these programs (Chapters 14–17).

ACCREDITATION OF MANAGED CARE ORGANIZATIONS

Two groups evaluate managed care organizations—the National Committee for Quality Assurance (NCQA) and the Joint Commission on Accreditation of Healthcare Organizations (JCAHO, pronounced jāy cō). **Accreditation** is a voluntary process that a health care facility or organization (e.g., hospital or managed care plan) undergoes to demonstrate that it has met standards beyond those required by law. Accreditation organizations develop **standards** (requirements) that are reviewed during a **survey** (evaluation) process that is conducted both off-site (e.g., managed care plan submits an initial document for review) and on-site (at the managed care plan's facilities).

INTERNET LINKS

Visit the NCQA at http://www.ncqa.org

Visit the JCAHO at http://www.jcaho.org

National Committee for Quality Assurance (NCQA)

The **National Committee for Quality Assurance (NCQA)**, of Washington D.C., is a private, not-for-profit organization that assesses the quality of managed care plans in the United States and releases the data to the public for consideration when selecting a managed care plan. The NCQA began accrediting managed care programs in 1991 when a need for consistent, independent information about the quality of care provided to patients was originally identified.

Joint Commission on Accreditation of Healthcare Organizations (JCAHO)

The **Joint Commission on Accreditation of Healthcare Organizations (JCAHO)**, located in Oakbrook Terrace, Illinois, provides voluntary accreditation of a variety of health care organizations (e.g., hospitals, long-term care and ambulatory care facilities). In 1989, the accreditation program for managed care was implemented as part of the 1990 Ambulatory Care Accreditation Program. In 1997, accreditation for PPOs was created under the Network Accreditation Program. In that same year, the accreditation program for managed behavioral health care organizations was implemented under the Behavioral Health Care Accreditation Program.

EFFECTS OF MANAGED CARE ON A PHYSICIAN'S PRACTICE

Managed care programs have tremendous impact on a practice's administrative procedures. A sampling of some procedures that must be in place include:

- separate bookkeeping systems for each capitated plan to ensure financial viability of the contract.
- a tracking system for preauthorization of specialty care and documented requests for receipt of the specialist's treatment plan or consultation report.

- preauthorization and/or precertification for all hospitalizations and continued certification if the patient's condition requires extension of the number of authorized days.
- up-to-date lists for referrals to participating health care providers, hospitals, and diagnostic test facilities used by the practice.
- up-to-date list of special administrative procedures required by each MCO contract.
- maintenance of up-to-date lists of patient copayments and fees for each plan the providers use.
- special patient interviews to ensure preauthorization and explain out-of-network requirements if patient is self-referring.
- additional paperwork for specialists to complete and file treatment and discharge plans.
- some **case managers** who are employed by the MCO to monitor services provided to enrollees require notification if a patient fails to keep a preauthorized appointment.
- some MCOs require the attachment of preauthorization documentation to all health insurance claims.

NOTE: It is important to realize that managed care is one of many systems in place to reimburse health care. The other major systems are covered in Chapers 12–17.

SUMMARY

- The financing of America's health care system has changed the way health care services are organized and delivered, as evident by a movement from traditional fee-for-service systems to managed care networks. These range from structured staff model HMOs to less structured preferred provider organizations (PPOs).
- Currently, more than 60 million Americans are enrolled in some type of managed care program in response to regulatory initiatives affecting health care cost and quality.
- Legislation resulting in regulations included:
  - HMO Act (1973)
  - ERISA (1974)
  - OBRA (1981)
  - TEFRA (1982)
  - Preferred Provider Health Care Act (1985)
  - COBRA (1985)
  - Amendment to the HMO Act of 1973 (1989)
  - HEDIS (1989)
  - HCFA Office of Managed Care (1994)
  - HIPAA (1996)
  - BBA (1997)

- A managed care organization (MCO) is responsible for the health of its enrollees, which can be administered by the MCO that serves as a health plan, or contracts with a hospital, physician group, or health system.
- Most managed care financing is achieved through a method called capitation, and enrollees are assigned or select a primary care provider, who serves as the patient's gatekeeper.
- Federal legislation mandated that MCOs participate in quality assurance programs, and other activities, including utilization management, case management, requirements for second surgical opinions, prohibition from including gag clauses in MCO contracts, and disclosure of any physician incentives.
- Managed care is categorized according to six models:
  - Exclusive provider organizations
  - Integrated delivery systems
  - Health maintenance organizations
  - Point-of-service plans
  - Preferred provider organizations
  - Triple option plans.
- Accreditation organizations, including the NCQA and JCAHO, evaluate MCOs according to pre-established standards.

STUDY CHECKLIST

☐ Read the textbook chapter, and highlight key concepts.

☐ Create an index card for each key term.

☐ Access the chapter Internet links to learn more about concepts.

☐ Answer the chapter review questions, verifying answers with your instructor.

☐ Complete Web Tutor assignments and take online quizzes.

☐ Complete Workbook chapter, verifying answers with your instructor.

☐ Form a study group with classmates to discuss chapter concepts in preparation for an exam.

REVIEW

MULTIPLE CHOICE

Select the most appropriate response.

1. The intent of managed health care was to:
   a. dramatically improve the health care delivery system in the United States.
   b. have employees of a managed care organization provide patient care.
   c. replace fee-for-service plans with affordable quality care to consumers.
   d. retrospectively reimburse patients for health care services provided.

2. Which term best describes those who receive managed health care plan services?
   a. employees
   b. enrollees
   c. payers
   d. providers

3. When was the first managed care program created?
   a. 1929
   b. 1933
   c. 1938
   d. 1940

4. Which was the first nationally recognized health maintenance organization?
   a. Harvard Plan
   b. Kaiser Permanente
   c. Preferred Care
   d. TRICARE

5. During the 1960s, debates on how to improve the health care delivery system ensued because:
   a. health care costs had dramatically increased.
   b. labor unions supported the concept of managed care.
   c. new programs were developed to encourage preventive care.
   d. states restricted the development and operation of HMOs.

6. Which allows federally qualified HMOs to provide covered services under a risk contract?
   a. Competitive medical plans
   b. HEDIS (of the NCQA)
   c. Medicare Risk Programs
   d. Office of Managed Care control

7. The Medical Center received a $100,000 capitation payment in January to cover the health care costs of 150 managed care enrollees. By the following January, $80,000 had been expended to cover services provided. The remaining $20,000 is:
   a. distributed equally among the 150 enrollees.
   b. retained by the Medical Center as profit.
   c. submitted to the managed care organization.
   d. turned over to the federal government.

8. Refer to Figure 3-1, Managed Care Profile Map, and identify the state with the lowest HMO penetration rate.

a. Alaska

b. California

c. Florida

d. Texas

9. Which is responsible for supervising and coordinating health care services for enrollees?

a. case manager

b. gatekeeper

c. third-party administrator

d. utilization review organization

10. Which term describes requirements created by accreditation organizations?

a. laws

b. mandates

c. regulations

d. standards

MATCHING

Match the legislative title with its summary.

_____ 11. Authorized grants and loans to develop HMOs under private sponsorship

_____ 12. Provided states with flexibility to establish HMOs for Medicare and Medicaid programs

_____ 13. Established an employee's right to continue health care coverage (including HMO coverage)

_____ 14. Mandated reporting and disclosure requirements for group and health plans (including managed care plans)

_____ 15. Created Medicare risk programs

a. COBRA

b. ERISA

c. HMO Act

d. OBRA

e. TEFRA

MATCHING

Match the legislative title with its summary.

_____ 16. Created standards to assess managed care systems

_____ 17. Created federal standards for insurers (HMOs) and employer plans

_____ 18. Defined a federally qualified HMO

_____ 19. Defined competitive medical plans

_____ 20. Encouraged formation of PSNs and PSOs

a. BBA

b. HEDIS

c. HIPAA

d. HMO Act

e. TEFRA

MATCHING

Match the type of utilization management activity with its definition.

_____ **21.** Review for medical necessity of
inpatient care prior to admission

_____ **22.** Review that grants prior approval
for reimbursement of a service

_____ **23.** Review for medical necessity of tests during
hospitalization

_____ **24.** Arranging appropriate health care services for
released patients

a. Concurrent review
b. Discharge planning
c. Preadmission certification
d. Preadmission review

MATCHING

Match the managed care model with its description.

_____ **25.** Organization of affiliated provider
sites that offer joint health care
to subscribers

_____ **26.** Offered by a single insurance
company or as a joint venture to
provide subscribers with a choice of
HMOs, PPO, or traditional insurance

_____ **27.** An alternative to traditional health insurance
coverage, which provides comprehensive services
to voluntarily enrolled members on a prepaid basis

_____ **28.** Managed care plan that provides benefits to
subscribers if they receive services from network
providers

_____ **29.** Network of physicians and hospitals that join
together to contract with insurance companies,
employers, and other organizations to provide
care to subscribers for a discounted fee

_____ **30.** Patients have the freedom to use an HMO panel
of providers or to self-refer to non-HMO providers

a. Exclusive provider organization
b. Integrated delivery system
c. Health maintenance organizations
d. Point-of-service plan
e. Preferred provider organization
f. Triple option plan

MATCHING

Match the status of the HMO with its panel type.

_____ **31.** Direct contract model HMO
_____ **32.** Group model HMO
_____ **33.** Individual practice association HMO
_____ **34.** Network model HMO
_____ **35.** Staff model HMO

a. Closed-panel
b. Open-panel

TRUE/FALSE

Indicate whether each statement is true or false.

36. ☐ T   ☐ F   Accreditation organizations, such as the JCAHO, perform routine surveys to determine whether an organization or facility has met standards required by the accrediting body.

37. ☐ T   ☐ F   A utilization management program measures the cost of care provided in a health care setting.

38. ☐ T   ☐ F   An example of an External Qualify Review Organization (EQRO) would be a QIO, which contracts its services from CMS.

39. ☐ T   ☐ F   The JCAHO started its accreditation program for managed care in 1989 as part of the 1990 Ambulatory Care Accreditation Program.

40. ☐ T   ☐ F   Gag clauses prevent physicians from discussing all treatment options with patients.

41. ☐ T   ☐ F   The National Committee for Quality Assurance (NCQA) is located in Chicago, IL.

42. ☐ T   ☐ F   Regulation is the voluntary process that a health care organization or facility undergoes to demonstrate that it has met standards beyond those required by law.

43. ☐ T   ☐ F   A surgical inpatient admission is denied, and the patient is approved for outpatient surgery instead. This is an example of case management.

44. ☐ T   ☐ F   Health care consumers can create a customized report card for managed care plans at the NCQA Web site.

45. ☐ T   ☐ F   Managed care organizations require second surgical opinions on all cases.

KEY TERMS

accept assignment

accounts receivable aging report

allowed charge

appeal

assignment of benefits

batched EOB

beneficiary

birthday rule

chargemaster

clean claim

closed assigned claims

coinsurance

coinsurance payment

common data file

day sheet

delinquent claim

delinquent claim cycle

downcoding

encounter form

established patient

explanation of benefits (EOB)

Fair Debt Collection Practices Act
(FDCPA)

guarantor

litigation

manual daily accounts receivable
journal

medically unnecessary

new patient

noncovered procedure

nonparticipating provider
(nonPAR)

open assigned claims

outsource

participating provider (PAR)

patient account record

patient ledger

policyholder

pre-existing condition

primary insurance

primary policyholder

source document

subscriber

superbill

suspense

transmittal notice

two-party check

unassigned claim

unauthorized procedures and
services

unbundling

uncovered benefit

uncovered procedure

Life Cycle of an Insurance Claim

Upon successful completion of this chapter, you should be able to:

1. Define key terms.

2. Conduct a new patient interview.

3. Discuss the life cycle of an insurance claim.

4. Determine insurance coverage when a patient has more than one policy or a child covered by both parents.

5. Explain how to process an established patient return visit insurance claim.

6. Perform postclinical checkout procedures.

7. Differentiate between manual and electronic claims processing procedures.

8. Detail the processing of a claim by an insurance company.

9. Interpret information on an explanation of benefits form.

10. Maintain a medical practice's insurance claim files

11. Identify problems that result in delinquent claims, and resolve those problems.

INTRODUCTION

This chapter provides an overview of the development of a health insurance claim in the health care provider's office and the major steps taken to process that claim by the insurance company.

● NOTE: Figures 4-5 (page 60) and 4-8 (page 64) through 4-13 (page 72) are illustrations of sample documents generated during the life cycle of an insurance claim for a single encounter with the same patient. ●

DEVELOPMENT OF THE CLAIM

The development of an insurance claim begins when the patient contacts a health care provider's office and schedules an appointment. At this time, it is important to determine whether the patient is requesting an initial appointment or is returning to the practice for additional services.

NOTE: The interview and check-in of a new hospital patient is more extensive than that for an established patient. •

A **new patient** is defined as a person who has not received any professional services from the health care provider or another provider of the same specialty in the same group practice within the last 36 months. An **established patient** is a person who has been seen within the last 36 months by the health care provider or another provider of the same specialty in the same group practice.

The development of a claim consists of three parts:

- Patient interview and check-in
- Clinical assessment and treatment
- Patient check-out

NOTE: Procedures discussed in this chapter are for practices that are not computerized. The icon ☑ identifies steps completed for computerized practices. •

NEW PATIENT INTERVIEW AND CHECK-IN PROCEDURE

The purpose of the new patient interview and check-in procedure is to obtain information, schedule the patient for an appointment, and generate a patient record. Basic office policies and procedures (e.g., copayments must be paid at the time of visit) should also be explained to each new patient.

NOTE: To increase office efficiency, mail new patients an information form to be completed and brought to the office 15 minutes prior to the scheduled appointment. •

S T E P 1 Preregister the new patient who calls to schedule an appointment. After determining that the patient has contacted the appropriate office, obtain the following information:

- Patient's name (last, first, and middle initial)

    NOTE: For a minor child, obtain the name and address of the parent or guardian. •

- Home address and telephone number
- Employer, address, and telephone number
- Date of birth
- **Guarantor** (person responsible for paying the charges)
- Social security number
- Spouse's name, occupation, and place of employment
- Referring provider's name

- Emergency contact (e.g., relative), including address and telephone number
- Health insurance information (so the claim can be processed)
  * Name and phone number of health insurance company
  * Name of **policyholder** (or **subscriber** or **beneficiary**), who is the person in whose name the insurance policy is issued
  * Health insurance identification number, which is sometimes the policyholder's social security number (SSN)

    NOTE: Some payers require reporting of the SSN, while others do not. •

  * Health insurance group number
  * Whether health care treatment must be preauthorized

NOTE: Be sure to instruct the patient to bring the health insurance card (Figure 4-1) to the appointment because the office will need to make a copy of its front and back. The card contains the subscriber's insurance and group number, as well as payer telephone numbers and provider network information. •

Managed Care Plan	**HMO Any State**
Subscriber Doe, John	Plan Codes: 301 / 293
Participant's Name Jane	Group No. A5423

Identification No.
    ABC123456789
	Copays: Office Visit: $20
	                    Emergency: $25

Medical Group Number & Name
    1234 SMGH /
	Medical Group Telephone:
	    (101) 555-1234

Benefit Plan: COLLEGE	Effective Date: 01-01-90

IN CASE OF EMERGENCY - CALL YOUR MEDICAL GROUP / PRIMARY CARE PHYSICIAN

FIGURE 4-1 Health insurance card

Be sure to explain office policies regarding appointment cancellations, billing and collections (e.g., copayments are to be paid at the time of office visit), and health insurance filing. Patients may ask whether the provider participates in their health insurance plan. A **participating provider (PAR)** contracts with a health insurance plan and accepts whatever the plan pays for procedures or services performed. PARs are not allowed to bill patients for the difference between the contracted rate and their normal fee.

NOTE: The patient is responsible for copayments and/or deductibles, but does not pay more than the allowed negotiated charge. •

A **nonparticipating provider (nonPAR)** does not contract with the insurance plan, and patients who elect to receive care from nonPARs will incur higher out-of-pocket expenses. The patient is expected to pay the difference between the insurance payment and the provider's fee, up to the usual and customary fee.

EXAMPLE 1

Dr. Smith is a participating provider for the ABC Health Insurance Plan. Kathe Bartron is treated by Dr. Smith in the office, for which a $50 fee is charged.

Provider fee	$50
Provider contracted rate (or allowable charge)	$40
Patient copayment	- $10
Insurance payment	$30
Provider write-off amount	$10

EXAMPLE 2

Dr. Jones is a nonparticipating provider. Lee Noffsker is treated by Dr. Jones in the office, for which a $50 fee is charged.

Provider fee	$50
Usual and customary (U&C) rate	$45
Patient coinsurance	- $ 9
Insurance payment	$36
Provider may bill patient over U&C rate	$ 5

! MANAGED CARE ALERT: Prior to scheduling an appointment with a specialist, a managed care patient must obtain preauthorization from the primary care provider (Figure 4-2) or case manager (i.e., preauthorization number is required). In addition, depending on the managed care plan, certain procedures and services must be preauthorized prior to the patient's undergoing treatment.

STEP 2 Upon arrival for the office appointment, have the patient complete a patient registration form (Figure 4-3).

The patient registration form is used to create the patient's financial and medical records. Be sure to carefully review the completed form for identification, financial, and medical history information. Sometimes patients don't know how to answer a question or they feel that the requested information does not apply to their situation. If information is missing, be sure to interview the patient appropriately to complete the form.

NOTE: It is fraudulent for patients to withhold information about secondary health insurance coverage, and penalties may apply.

STEP 3 Photocopy the front and back of the patient's insurance identification card(s), and file in the patient's financial record.

NOTE: Consider generating a financial record and a medical record for each patient to separately maintain each type of information.

Consultation Referral Form

Date of Referral:

Patient Information:

Name (Last, First, MI)

Date of Birth (MM/DD/YYYY)   Phone:
(   )

Member #:

Site #:

Carrier Information:

Name:

Address:

Phone Number: (   )

Facsimile / Data #: (   )

Primary or Requesting Provider:

Name: (Last, First, MI)   Specialty:

Institution / Group Name: Provider ID #:   1   Provider ID #:   2 (If Required)

Address: (Street #, City, State, Zip)

Phone Number: (   )   Facsimile / Data Number: (   )

Consultant / Facility / Provider:

Name: (Last, First, MI)   Specialty:

Institution / Group Name: Provider ID #:   1   Provider ID #:   2 (if Required)

Address: (Street #, City, State, Zip)

Phone Number: (   )   Facsimile / Data Number: (   )

Referral Information:

Reason for Referral:

Brief History, Diagnosis and Test Results: _____

Services Desired: Provide Care as indicated:
☐ Initial Consultation Only
☐ Diagnostic Test: (specify) _____
☐ Consultation with Specific Procedures: (specify) _____
_____
☐ Specific Treatment: _____
☐ Global OB Care & Delivery
☐ Other: (explain) _____

Place of Service:
☐ Office
☐ Outpatient Medical/Surgical Center*
☐ Radiology   ☐ Laboratory
☐ Inpatient Hospital*
☐ Extended Care Facility*
☐ Other: (explain)
*(Specific Facility Must be Named)

Number of visits:
(If blank, 1 visit
is assumed)   Authorization #: (If Required)

Referral is Valid Until: (Date)
(See Carrier Instructions)

Signature: (Individual Completing This Form)   Authorizing Signature (If Required)

Referral certification is not a guarantee of payment. Payment of benefits is subject to a member's eligibility on the date that the service is rendered and to any other contractual provisions of the plan / carrier.

White: Carrier • Yellow: Primary or Requesting Provider • Pink: Consultant / Facility / Provider • Goldenrod: Patient

See Carrier/ Plan Manual For Specific Instructions.

FIGURE 4-2 Sample consultation referral form

STEP 4 Confirm the patient's insurance information by contacting the plan (or payer) based on information on the insurance ID card.

NOTE: Due to HIPAA privacy standards, when contacting the payer to verify insurance eligibility and benefit status, be prepared to provide the following information:
- Beneficiary last name and first initial
- Beneficiary date of birth
- Beneficiary Health Insurance Claim (HIC) number
- Beneficiary gender

DOCTORS GROUP • MAIN STREET • ALFRED, NY 12345   PATIENT REGISTRATION FORM

PATIENT INFORMATION

Last Name	First Name	Middle Name

Street	City	State/Zip Code

Patient's Date of Birth	Social Security Number	Home Phone Number

Student Status
❏ Full-time   ❏ Part-time

Employment Status
❏ Full-time   ❏ Part-time   ❏ Unemployed

Marital Status
❏ Single   ❏ Married   ❏ Separated
❏ Divorced   ❏ Widowed

Sex   ❏ Male   ❏ Female | Name/Address of Employer | Occupation

Employer Phone Number	Referred by

Emergency Contact	Address	Telephone Number

Visit is related to on-the-job injury
❏ No   ❏ Yes   Date: _____

Prior treatment received for injury
❏ No   ❏ Yes   Doctor: _____   WC Number: _____

Visit is related to automobile accident   ❏ No   ❏ Yes   Date: _____ | Name & Address of Insurance Company/Policy Number

GUARANTOR'S BILLING INFORMATION

Last Name	First Name	Middle Name

Street	City	State/Zip Code

Relationship to Patient	Social Security Number	Home Phone Number

Employer	Employer Address	Employer Phone Number

INSURANCE INFORMATION

PRIMARY INSURED INFORMATION		SECONDARY INSURED INFORMATION	
Last Name	First Name/Middle Initial	Last Name	First Name/Middle Initial
Address	City/State/Zip Code	Address	City/State/Zip Code
Relationship to Insured ❏ Self ❏ Spouse ❏ Child ❏ Other		Relationship to Insured ❏ Self ❏ Spouse ❏ Child ❏ Other	
Sex ❏ Male ❏ Female		Sex ❏ Male ❏ Female	
Insured's Date of Birth	Home Phone Number	Insured's Date of Birth	Home Phone Number
Name and Address of Insurance Company		Name and Address of Insurance Company	
Insured Identification Number Group Number Effective Date		Insured Identification Number Group Number Effective Date	
Name of Employer Sponsoring Plan		Name of Employer Sponsoring Plan	

CONSENT TO PAYMENT

I have listed all health insurance plans from which I may receive benefits. I hereby authorize payment of medical benefits billed to my insurance to the Doctors Group. I hereby accept responsibility for payment for any service(s) provided to me that is not covered by my insurance. I also accept responsibility for fees that exceed the payment made by my insurance, if the Doctors Group does not participate with my insurance. I agree to pay all copayments, coinsurance, and deductibles at the time services are rendered. I, (Patient's Name), hereby authorize the Doctors Group to use and/or disclose my health information which specifically identifies me or which can reasonably be used to identify me to carry out my treatment, payment, and health care operations.

I understand that while this consent is voluntary, if I refuse to sign this consent, the Doctors Group can refuse to treat me.

I have been informed that the Doctors Group has prepared a notice ("Notice") that more fully describes the uses and disclosures that can be made of my individually identifiable health information for treatment, payment and health care operations. I understand that I have the right to review such Notice prior to signing this consent. I understand that I may revoke this consent at any time by notifying the Doctors Group, in writing, but if I revoke my consent, such revocation will not affect any actions that the Doctors Group took before receiving my revocation.

I understand that the Doctors Group has reserved the right to change his/her privacy practices and that I can obtain such changed notice upon request. I understand that I have the right to request that the Doctors Group restrict how my individually identifiable health information is used and/or disclosed to carry out treatment, payment or health operations. I understand that the Doctors Group does not have to agree to such restrictions, but that once such restrictions are agreed to, the Doctors Group must adhere to such restrictions.

_____   _____
Signature of Patient or Patient's Representative   Date

Printed Name of Patient: _____   Relationship of representative to patient: _____

FIGURE 4-3 Sample patient registration form

S T E P 5   ☑ Enter all information using computer data entry software. Verify information with the patient or subscriber, and make appropriate changes.

When the patient reports more than one insurance company, check to be sure the patient has correctly determined which policy is primary, secondary, and so on. The determination of primary or secondary status for patients with two or more commercial policies is different for adults than for children.

- *Adult patient named as primary policyholder:* The patient is the policyholder or subscriber.

- *Adult patient named as secondary policyholder:* The patient is listed as a dependent on a primary insurance policy.

    EXAMPLE: Mary Jones works for Alfred State College and is enrolled in the group health insurance's family plan. She is named as the primary policyholder on this plan. Her husband, Bill, is a full-time college student and is named as the secondary policyholder on Mary's health insurance plan. Bill does not subscribe to any other health insurance policy. ●

- *Primary versus secondary insurance:* There is a difference between the terms *primary policyholder* and *primary insurance*. The **primary policyholder** is the person to whom the policy is issued. **Primary insurance** is the insurance plan responsible for paying health care insurance claims first. Once the primary insurance is billed and pays the contracted amount (e.g., 80% of billed amount), the secondary plan is billed for the remainder, and so on. *Health insurance reimbursement cannot exceed the total cost of services rendered.*

    NOTE: Certain insurance plans are always considered primary to other plans (e.g., workers' compensation insurance is primary to an employee's group health care plan if the employee is injured on-the-job). These situations are discussed in Chapters 12 through 17. ●

    EXAMPLE: Cindy Thomas has two health insurance policies, a group insurance plan through her full-time employer and another group insurance plan through her husband's employer. Cindy's plan through her own employer is primary, while the plan through her husband's employer is secondary. When Cindy receives health care services at her doctor's office, the office first submits the insurance claim to Cindy's employer's health plan; once that health plan has paid, the insurance claim can be submitted to Cindy's secondary insurance (her husband's group insurance plan). ●

    NOTE: Total reimbursement cannot exceed the total charges for health care services rendered by Cindy's doctor. ●

- *Child of divorced parents:* The custodial parent's plan is primary. If the parents are remarried, the custodial parent's plan is primary, the custodial step-parent's plan is secondary, and the noncustodial parent's plan is tertiary (third). An exception is made if a court order specifies that a particular parent must cover the child's medical expenses.

- *Child living with both parents:* If each parent subscribes to a different health insurance plan, the primary and secondary policies are determined by applying the birthday rule. Physician office staff must obtain the birth date of each policyholder because the **birthday rule** states that the policyholder whose birth month and day occurs earlier in the calendar year holds the primary policy for dependent children. The year of birth is not considered when applying the birthday rule determination. If the policyholders have identical birthdays, the policy in effect the longest is considered primary.

EXAMPLE 1

A child is listed as a dependent on each of his father's and mother's group policy. Which policy is primary?

    Mother—birthdate 03/06/59—works for IBM

    Father—birthdate 03/20/57—works for General Motors

Answer: Mother's policy is primary; her birthday is earlier in the calendar year.

EXAMPLE 2

A child has the same coverage as in Example 1; however, in this case the mother was born on 03/04/45 and the father was born on 01/01/56. Which policy is primary?

Answer: Father's policy is primary.

EXAMPLE 3

A dependent child is covered by both parent's group policies. The parents were born on the same day. Which policy is primary?

    Father's policy took effect 03/06/86

    Mother's policy took effect 09/06/92

Answer: Father's policy is primary because it has been in effect six years longer.

- *Gender rule:* Some self-funded health care plans use the *gender rule*, which states that the father's plan is always primary when a child is covered by both parents. This provision can cause problems if one parent's coverage uses the *birthday rule* and the other uses the *gender rule*. Be sure to contact the health plan administrators to determine which rule to follow.

NOTE: Determination of primary and secondary coverage involving one or more government-sponsored programs is discussed in detail in the respective Medicare, Medicaid, and TRICARE (formerly CHAMPUS) chapters.

 All patients with insurance must sign a Consent to Payment form. (Figure 4-4).

 Create a new patient's medical record.

STEP 8 Generate the patient's encounter form (Figure 4-5).

I consent to the disclosure of my protected health information (PHI) for the purpose of treatment, payment or health care operations. My PHI refers to health and demographic information collected from me and created or received by my provider, another health care provider, a health plan, my employer, a health care clearinghouse, or a third-party administrator. This PHI relates to my past, present and/or future physical or mental health and identifies me.

I hereby authorize ____*[Name of Health Care Provider]*____ to release my health care information to __*[Name of Third-Party Payer]*__ for the purpose of obtaining reimbursement for health care provided.

I understand that I have the right to review the _*[Name of Health Care Provider's]*_ Privacy Notice for a more complete description of uses and disclosures and that I have the right to review the notice prior to signing this consent.

I understand that I have the right to request that ___*[Name of Health Care Provider]*___ restrict how my protected health information is used or disclosed to carry out treatment and payment of health care operations.

I further understand that ___*[Name of Health Care Provider]*___ is not required to agree to requested restrictions, but if ___*[Name of Health Care Provider]*___ agrees to a requested restriction, the restriction is binding on ___*[Name of Health Care Provider]*___.

I understand that I have the right to revoke this consent in writing except to the extent that the ___*[Name of Health Care Provider]*___ has already taken action in reliance on this consent.

I understand that ___*[Name of Health Care Provider]*___ reserves the right to change the privacy practices described in their Privacy Notice and that I may obtain a revised notice by accessing the ___*[Name of Health Care Provider]*___ Web site, calling the office and requesting a revised notice be sent in the mail, or requesting one at my next appointment.

_____
Signature of Patient or Personal Representative

_____
Name of Patient or Personal Representative/Relationship to Patient

_____
Date

FIGURE 4-4 Sample consent to payment (HIPAA compliant)

The **encounter form** is the financial record source document used by health care providers and other personnel to record treated diagnoses and services rendered to the patient during the current encounter. In the physician's office, it is also called a **superbill**; in the hospital it is called a **chargemaster**. The minimum information entered on the form at this time is the date of service, patient's name, and balance due on the account.

Attach the encounter form to the front of the patient's medical record so that it is available for clinical staff when the patient is escorted to the treatment area.

Tom Smith, M.D.
OTOLARYNGOLOGY

Yorktown Medical Group

Name:	MR#:	DOB:
Address:	Ins. #:	Copay:
Phone #:	Referring MD:	Balance Due:
Date of Service:		

FEE | *** P R O C E D U R E S *** | *FEE*

Evaluation and Management

		FEE
[ ] 99203	office/outpatient visit, new	....
[ ] 99212	office/outpatient visit, est., limited	....
[ ] 99213	office/outpatient visit, est., intermediate	....
[ ] 99214	office/outpatient visit, est., extended	....
[ ] 99261	follow-up inpatient consult	....
[ ] 99271	confirmatory consultation	....
[ ] 99284	emergency dept visit	....
[ ] 99341	home visit, new patient	....
[ ] ____	Other	

Medicine

[ ] 92552	pure tone audiometry, air	....
[ ] 92553	audiometry, air & bone	....
[ ] 92553	audiometry, air & bone	....
[ ] 92557	comprehensive hearing test	....
[ ] 92567	tympanometry	....
[ ] 92568	acoustic reflex testing	....
[ ] 92569	acoustic reflex decay test	....
[ ] 99050	medical services after hrs	....
[ ] 99052	medical services at night	....
[ ] 99054	medical servcs, unusual hrs	....
[ ] ____	Other	

Surgery

[ ] 21315	treatment of nose fracture, w/o stabiliza	....
[ ] 21320	treatment of nose fracture, with stabiliza	....

* P R O C E D U R E S *

		FEE
[ ] 30100	intranasal biopsy	....
[ ] 30110	removal of nose polyp(s)	....
[ ] 30200	injection treatment of nose	....
[ ] 30300	remove nasal foreign body	....
[ ] 30560	release of nasal adhesions	....
[ ] 30901	control of nosebleed, simple	....
[ ] 30903	control of nosebleed, complex	....
[ ] 30905	control of nosebleed, posterior	....
[ ] 30906	repeat control of nosebleed	....
[ ] 31000	irrigation, maxillary sinus	....
[ ] 31254	revision of ethmoid sinus	....
[ ] 31287	nasal/sinus endoscopy, surg	....
[ ] 31511	remove foreign body, larynx	....
[ ] 31575	diagnostic laryngoscopy	....
[ ] 38505	needle biopsy, lymph nodes	....
[ ] 40490	biopsy of lip	....
[ ] 42100	biopsy roof of mouth	....
[ ] 42330	removal of salivary stone	....
[ ] 42400	biopsy of salivary gland	....
[ ] 42650	dilation of salivary duct	....
[ ] 42700	drainage of tonsil abscess	....
[ ] 42720	drainage of throat abscess	....
[ ] 42804	biopsy of upper nose/throat	....
[ ] 60100	biopsy of thyroid	....
[ ] 69210	remove impacted ear wax	....

* D I A G N O S I S *

Digestive System

- [ ] 527.2 sialoadenitis
- [ ] 527.6 salivary gland mucocele
- [ ] 528.2 oral aphthae
- [ ] 528.9 oral soft tissue dis nec
- [ ] ____ Other

Injury and Poisoning

- [ ] 802.0 nasal bone fx-closed
- [ ] 873.43 marginal wound of lip
- [ ] 873.64 opn wnd tongue/mouth flr
- [ ] 910.0 abrasion head
- [ ] 931 foreign body in ear
- [ ] 932 foreign body in nose
- [ ] ____ Other

Musculoskeletal System

- [ ] 738.0 acq nose deformity
- [ ] 738.7 cauliflower ear
- [ ] ____ Other

Neoplasms

- [ ] 210.4 benign neo mouth nec/nos
- [ ] 225.1 benign neo cranial nerve
- [ ] ____ Other

Nervous System and Sense Organs

- [ ] 380.11 acute infection of pinna
- [ ] 380.14 malignant otitis externa
- [ ] 380.15 chr mycot otitis externa
- [ ] 380.22 acute otitis externa nec
- [ ] 380.23 chr otitis externa nec
- [ ] 380.31 hematoma auricle/pinna

- [ ] 380.4 impacted cerumen
- [ ] 380.81 exostosis ext ear canal
- [ ] 381.01 ac serous otitis media
- [ ] 381.10 chr serous om simp/nos
- [ ] 381.81 dysfunct eustachian tube
- [ ] 382.00 ac supp otitis media nos
- [ ] 382.01 ac supp om w drum rupt
- [ ] 384.21 cent perf tympanic memb
- [ ] 384.23 marginal perf tymp nec
- [ ] 384.25 total perf tympanic memb
- [ ] 385.33 cholestma mid ear/mstoid
- [ ] 386.01 meniere dis cochlvestib
- [ ] 386.04 inactive meniere's dis
- [ ] 386.10 peripheral vertigo nos
- [ ] 386.11 benign paxy smal vertigo
- [ ] 386.35 viral labyrinthitis
- [ ] 387.0 otoscler-oval wnd nonobl
- [ ] 388.2 sudden hearing loss nos
- [ ] 388.31 subjective tinnitus
- [ ] 388.72 referred pain of ear
- [ ] 389.01 conduc hear loss ext ear
- [ ] 389.02 conduct hear loss tympan
- [ ] 389.03 conduc hear loss mid ear
- [ ] 389.10 sensomeur hear loss nos
- [ ] 389.2 mixed hearing loss
- [ ] ____ Other

Respiratory System

- [ ] 461.0 ac maxillary sirusitis
- [ ] 461.1 ac frontal sinusitis

- [ ] 461.2 ac ethmoidal sinusitis
- [ ] 461.3 ac sphenoidal sinusitis
- [ ] 461.8 other acute sinusitis
- [ ] 463 acute tonsillitis
- [ ] 465.9 acute uri nos
- [ ] 470 deviated nasal septum
- [ ] 471.0 polyp of nasal cavity
- [ ] 471.8 nasal sinus polyp nec
- [ ] 471.8 nasal sinus polyp nec
- [ ] 472.0 chronic rhinitis
- [ ] 472.2 chronic nasopharyngitis
- [ ] 473.0 chr maxillary sinusitis
- [ ] 473.1 chr frontal sinusitis
- [ ] 473.2 chr ethmoidal sinusitis
- [ ] 473.3 chr sphenoidal sinusitis
- [ ] 473.8 chronic sinusitis nec
- [ ] 474.00 chronic tonsillitis
- [ ] 477.9 allergic rhinitis nos
- [ ] 478.0 hypertrph nasal turbinat
- [ ] 478.1 nasal & sinus dis nec

- [ ] ____ Other

Symptoms, Signs, and Ill-Defined Conditions

- [ ] 784.7 epistaxis
- [ ] ____ Other

Skin and Subcutaneous Tissue

- [ ] 680.0 carbuncle of face
- [ ] 701.4 keloid scar
- [ ] ____ Other

2001 Country Road, Yorktown Heights, NY 15555   License#: 123456789

FIGURE 4-5 Sample encounter form generated from Encounter Form Maker software

If all patient scheduling is performed on the computer, generate encounter forms for all patients scheduled on a given day by selecting the "print encounter forms" function from the computer program.

NOTE: At this point, clinical assessment and/or treatment of the patient is performed, after which the provider documents all current and pertinent diagnoses, services rendered, and special follow-up instructions on the encounter form. The medical record and encounter form are then returned to the staff member responsible for checking out patients. •

ESTABLISHED PATIENT RETURN VISIT

S T E P 1 Depending on the provider's plan of treatment, either schedule a return appointment when checking out the patient or when the patient contacts the office.

EXAMPLE S: Patient states her stomach hurts, and she has been vomiting.

O: Abdominal exam reveals mild tenderness. Her throat is red.

A: Flu.

P: Bed rest. Return to office if symptoms worsen.

(SOAP notes are typically used in a provider's office to document patient visits. S = subjective, O = objective, A = assessment, and P = plan. SOAP notes are discussed in Chapter 10.) •

MANAGED CARE ALERT: Approximately one week prior to an appointment with a specialist for nonemergency services, the status of preauthorization for care must be verified. If the preauthorization has expired, the patient's nonemergency appointment may have to be postponed until the required treatment reports have been filed with the primary care provider or case manager and a new preauthorization for additional treatment has been obtained.

S T E P 2 Verify the patient's registration information when the patient checks in at the front desk.

As the cost of health care increases and competition for subscribers escalates among insurers, many employers who pay a portion of health care costs for their employees purchase health insurance contracts that cover only a 3- or 6-month period. Therefore, it is important to ask all returning patients if there have been any changes in their name, address, phone number, employer, and insurance program. If the answer is yes, a new registration form should be completed and necessary changes made in the computerized patient database.

S T E P 3 Generate an encounter form for the patient's current visit.

Attach the encounter form to the front of the patient's medical record so it is available for clinical staff when the patient is escorted to the treatment area.

NOTE: Once the clinical assessment and/or treatment has been completed, the patient enters the postclinical phase of the visit. The services and diagnosis(es) are added to the encounter form, and the patient's medical record and encounter form are given to the staff member responsible for checking out patients. •

POSTCLINICAL CHECK-OUT PROCEDURES

The following procedures are the same for new and established patients.

STEP 1   Assign CPT and level II (national) codes to procedures and services, and assign ICD-9-CM codes to diagnoses documented on the encounter form.

CODING TIP: Make sure that diagnoses, procedures, and services listed on the encounter form are documented in the patient's medical record before reporting codes on the insurance claim.

STEP 2   Enter charges for procedures and/or services performed, and total the charges on the encounter form.

STEP 3   Post all charges to the patient's ledger/account record and the daily accounts receivable journal either manually or on the pertinent computer screens.

The **patient ledger** (Figure 4-6), known as the **patient account record** (Figure 4-7) in a computerized system, is a permanent record of all financial transactions between the patient and the practice. The charges along with personal or third-party payments are all posted on the patient's account.

```
BC/BS R2345678                    STATEMENT                 PATIENT, IMA

                         IMA PATIENT
                         900 RANDELL RD
                         ANYWHERE MD 20000
```

DATE	CODE	DESCRIPTION	CHARGE	CREDITS PAYMENTS	CREDITS ADJ	CURRENT BALANCE
			BALANCE FORWARD →			30 -
5/23/YYYY		ROA per ck		30 -		0
6/25/YYYY	99213	OV ROA per ck	38 -	38 -		0
		Ins billed				

PLEASE PAY LAST AMOUNT IN THIS COLUMN ▲

OV — Office Visit	**HOSP** — Hospital Visit	**ROA** — Received on Account
OS — Office Surgery	**HS** — Hospital Surgery	**NC** — No Charge
TC — Telephone Consultation	**SA** — Surgical Assistant	**INS** — Insurance
FA — Failed Appointment	**SC** — Surgical Consultation	
RP — Report	**ER** — Emergency Room	

THIS IS A COPY OF YOUR ACCOUNT AS IT APPEARS ON YOUR LEDGER CARD

FIGURE 4-6
Sample patient ledger card

M.I.S.C. (Management Information System for Clinics)

File   Edit   Patient   Billing   Service Codes   Clinic   Daily   Reports   Utilities   Window   Help

Ledger Card

Name	Jim L. Henderson		Bill Type	5	Account	00003	Doctor	1
Curr	0.00	+60.	0.00	+120.	149.00	Surplus	0.00	Ins.	119.20
+30.	0.00	+90	0.00	Total	149.00	End Bal	149.00	Pat.	29.80

Eff Date	#	Doc	CPT	Description	Bill	%	Ins. Bal.	Pat. Bal.	Amount	Total
09/05/1999	1	1	73020-	Shoulder - Limit	1		25.60	6.40	32.00	32.00
09/05/1999	2	1	73070-	Elbow - Limited	1		28.00	7.00	35.00	67.00
09/05/1999	3	1	73100-	Wrist - Limited	1		24.80	6.20	31.00	98.00
09/05/1999	4	1	73120-	Hand - Limited	1		24.80	6.20	31.00	129.00
09/06/1999	1	1	97014-	ELECTRIC STIMULA	1		16.00	4.00	20.00	149.00
	***			End of Ledger for Patient			***			149.00

Done   Pay/Adj   Σ Sum Service   Recalculate   Ledger Notes / Patient Notes   Rebill

FIGURE 4-7 Sample patient account record generated from practice management software (Permission to reprint granted by DataCom Software Business Products)

Each procedure performed must be individually described and priced on the patient's ledger/account record.

The **manual daily accounts receivable journal**, also known as the **day sheet**, is a chronologic summary of all transactions posted to individual patient ledgers/accounts on a specific day (Figure 4-8).

S T E P 4   Collect payment from the patient.

Most health care policies require the patient to pay a portion of the fee at the time services are rendered. The policy may stipulate a copayment and/or coinsurance payment. The *copayment*, commonly called a *copay*, is the amount the patient pays each time a specific service is rendered. Health care providers often require the copayment to be paid at the time of registration because it eliminates costly patient billing for these amounts. A **coinsurance payment**, commonly called **coinsurance**, is the percentage the patient pays for covered services after the deductible has been met and the copayment has been paid. For example, with an 80/20 plan, the insurance company pays 80% and the patient pays 20%.

HINT: To save the expense of mailing invoices, ask patients to pay their portion of the bill as they depart the office. ●

PT. NAME	DESCRIPTION	OLD BAL.	CHARGE	PAYMENT	NEW BAL.
1. Patient, Ima	OV-99213 per ck	0	38 —	38 —	0

DATE 6/25/YYYY

DAY SHEET

PROOF
Old Bal. _____
+ Charges _____
- Payments _____
= New Bal. _____

TOTALS

FIGURE 4-8 Sample day sheet

S T E P 5   Post payment to the patient's account.

The source of each payment should be identified, either as cash, money order, credit card, insurance, or personal check (see the 5/23/YYYY entry on Figure 4-6).

S T E P 6   Complete the insurance claim.

The insurance claim used to report professional and technical services is known as the **CMS-1500 claim** (formerly HCFA-1500) (Figure 4-9). The provider's claim for payment is generated from information located on the patient's encounter form, ledger/account record, and source document (e.g., patient record or chart). Information located on these documents is transferred to the CMS-1500 claim. Such information includes patient and insurance policy identification, codes and charges for procedures and/or services, and codes for diagnoses treated and/or managed during the encounter. The selection of codes for procedures, services, and diagnoses is discussed in later chapters.

The CMS-1500 claim requires responses to standard questions pertaining to whether the patient's condition is related to employment, auto accident, and/or any other accident; additional insurance coverage; use of an outside lab; and whether or not the provider

PLEASE DO NOT STAPLE IN THIS AREA

APPROVED OMB-0938-0008

CARRIER

[ ] [ ] PICA

HEALTH INSURANCE CLAIM FORM

PICA [ ] [ ]

1. MEDICARE (Medicare #) MEDICAID (Medicaid #) CHAMPUS (Sponsor's SSN) CHAMPVA (VA File #) GROUP HEALTH PLAN (SSN or ID) FECA BLK LUNG (Medicaid #) [X] OTHER (ID)

1a. INSURED'S I.D. NUMBER (FOR PROGRAM IN ITEM 1)
R0001001

2. PATIENT'S NAME (Last Name, First Name, Middle Initial)
PATIENT IMA

3. PATIENT'S BIRTH DATE MM DD YY 03 08 1934 SEX M [ ] F [X]

4. INSURED'S NAME (Last Name, First Name, Middle Initial)
PATIENT H E

5. PATIENT'S ADDRESS (No. Street)
1 FEELBETTER STREET

6. PATIENT RELATIONSHIP TO INSURED
Self [ ] Spouse [X] Child [ ] Other [ ]

7. INSURED'S ADDRESS (No. Street)
SAME

CITY
ANYWHERE USA
STATE

8. PATIENT STATUS
Single [ ] Married [X] Other [ ]

CITY
STATE

ZIP CODE
00001
TELEPHONE (Include Area Code)
(001) 001 3456

Employed [ ] Full-Time Student [ ] Part-Time Student [ ]

ZIP CODE
TELEPHONE (INCLUDE AREA CODE)
( )

9. OTHER INSURED'S NAME (Last Name, First Name, Middle Initial)

10. IS PATIENT'S CONDITION RELATED TO:

11. INSURED'S POLICY GROUP OR FECA NUMBER

a. OTHER INSURED'S POLICY OR GROUP NUMBER

a. EMPLOYMENT? (CURRENT OR PREVIOUS)
[ ] YES [X] NO

a. INSURED'S DATE OF BIRTH MM DD YY 12 30 YYYY SEX M [X] F [ ]

b. OTHER INSURED'S DATE OF BIRTH MM DD YY SEX M [ ] F [ ]

b. AUTO ACCIDENT?
[ ] YES [X] NO PLACE (State)

b. EMPLOYER'S NAME OR SCHOOL NAME
ANY COMPANY

c. EMPLOYER'S NAME OR SCHOOL NAME

c. OTHER ACCIDENT?
[ ] YES [X] NO

c. INSURANCE PLAN NAME OR PROGRAM NAME
BC/BS

d. INSURANCE PLAN NAME OR PROGRAM NAME

10d. RESERVED FOR LOCAL USE

d. IS THERE ANOTHER HEALTH BENEFIT PLAN?
[ ] YES [X] NO If yes, return to and complete item 9 a – d.

READ BACK OF FORM BEFORE COMPLETING & SIGNING THIS FORM.
12. PATIENT'S OR AUTHORIZED PERSON'S SIGNATURE I authorize the release of any medical or other information necessary to process this claim. I also request payment of government benefits either to mysel or to the party who accepts assignment below.
SIGNED *Ima Patient* DATE 6/25/YYYY

13. INSURED'S OR AUTHORIZED PERSON'S SIGNATURE I authorize payment of medical benefits to the undersigned physician or supplier for services described below.
SIGNED *Ima Patient*

14. DATE OF CURRENT: MM DD YY 06 25 YYYY ILLNESS (First symptom) OR INJURY (Accident) OR PREGNANCY (LMP)

15. IF PATIENT HAS HAD SAME OR SIMILAR ILLNESS, GIVE FIRST DATE MM DD YY

16. DATES PATIENT UNABLE TO WORK IN CURRENT OCCUPATION MM DD YY MM DD YY FROM TO

17. NAME OF REFERRING PHYSICIAN OR OTHER SOURCE

17a. I.D. NUMBER OF REFERRING PHYSICIAN

18. HOSPITALIZATION DATES RELATED TO CURRENT SERVICES MM DD YY MM DD YY FROM TO

19. RESERVED FOR LOCAL USE

20. OUTSIDE LAB? [ ] YES [X] NO $ CHARGES

21. DIAGNOSIS OR NATURE OF ILLNESS OR INJURY. (RELATE ITEMS 1, 2, 3, OR 4 TO ITEM 24E BY LINE)
1. 401 .9
2. 272 .0
3.
4.

22. MEDICAID RESUBMISSION CODE ORIGINAL REF. NO.

23. PRIOR AUTHORIZATION NUMBER

24. A DATE(S) OF SERVICE From MM DD YY	To MM DD YY	B Place of Service	C Type of Service	D PROCEDURES, SERVICES, OR SUPPLIES (Explain Unusual Circumstances) CPT/HCPCS MODIFIER	E DIAGNOSIS CODE	F $ CHARGES	G DAYS OR UNITS	H EPSDT Family Plan	I EMG	J COB	K RESERVED FOR LOCAL USE
1 0625YYYY	0625YYYY	11		99213	1	38 00	001				
2											
3											
4											
5											
6											

25. FEDERAL TAX I.D. NUMBER
52-1581586 SSN [ ] EIN [X]

26. PATIENT'S ACCOUNT NO.
9804

27. ACCEPT ASSIGNMENT? (For govt. claims, see back)
[X] YES [ ] NO

28. TOTAL CHARGE
$ 38 00

29. AMOUNT PAID
$

30. BALANCE DUE
$ 38 00

31. SIGNATURE OF PHYSICIAN OR SUPPLIER INCLUDING DEGREES OR CREDENTIALS (I certify that the statements on the reverse apply to this bill and are made a part thereof.)
HEEZA FRIEND MD 0626YYYY
SIGNED DATE

32. NAME AND ADDRESS OF FACILITY WHERE SERVICES WERE RENDERED (If other than home or office)

33. PHYSICIAN'S SUPPLIER'S BILLING NAME, ADDRESS, ZIP CODE & PHONE #
(001) 001 0101
HEEZA FRIEND MD
1 INTERNAL STREET
ANYWHERE, USA
PIN# HE0010 GRP#

(APPROVED BY AMA COUNCIL ON MEDICAL SERVICE 8/88)

PLEASE PRINT OR TYPE

FORM CMS-1500 (12-90) FORM RRB-1500 FORM OWCP-1500

PATIENT AND INSURED INFORMATION

PHYSICIAN OR SUPPLIER INFORMATION

FIGURE 4-9 Completed CMS-1500 claim

accepts assignment. To **accept assignment** means the provider has made the choice to accept as payment in full what is paid by the insurance company on the claim (except for any copayment and/or coinsurance amounts).

NOTE: To *accept assignment* is sometimes confused with **assignment of benefits**, which is taken by the patient and/or insured advising the payer to reimburse the provider directly.

The health insurance specialist will also complete portions of the form that identify the type of insurance, patient's sex, patient's relationship to insured, and provider's federal tax ID number. The CMS-1500 claim includes several areas that require the signature of the patient and the provider. When submitting claims, *SIGNATURE ON FILE* can be substituted for the patient's signature (as long as the patient's signature is actually on file in the office).

The completed claim is then proofread and double-checked for accuracy (e.g., verification that signature statement is on file, and so on). Any necessary attachments are copied from the patient's chart (e.g., operative report) or developed (e.g., letter delineating unlisted service provided, referred to in the CPT coding manual as a "special report").

The computer generates the claims when the "print claim" function is selected. Most computer programs can generate a specific patient's claim as well as claims for a number of patients (e.g., patients treated on a particular day). It is essential that office staff responsible for entering patient registration information understand data entry requirements so that the claims are formatted properly.

STEP 7 Staple any required attachments to the claim, such as copies of operative reports, pathology reports, and written authorization. ☑ For electronic claims, check with the insurance carrier to determine how to submit the attachments (e.g., fax or postal mail).

STEP 8 Obtain the provider's signature on the claim, if manually processed. Special arrangements may be made with some insurance plans to allow the provider's name to be typed or a signature stamp to be used. No signature is possible on electronic claims.

NOTE: In July 2000, federal electronic signature legislation was enacted. Physicians who contract with government and/or managed care plans are considered to have valid signatures on file.

STEP 9 File a copy of the claim and copies of the attachment(s) in the practice's insurance files. ☑ Electronic claims are stored in the computer.

STEP 10 Log completed claims in an insurance registry if the practice's procedure manual requires this step (Figure 4-10). Be sure to include the date the claim was filed with the insurance carrier. ☑ For computerized claims processing, medical office management software should generate a claims log.

STEP 11 Mail or electronically send the claims to the insurance carrier. Paper claims must be generated when attachments are to accompany the claims. ☑ Most practices electronically transmit claims, and federal HIPAA legislation was enacted requiring that government claims be electronically processed (implemented October, 16, 2002). They receive a transmittal notice listing the patient names for claims success-

INSURANCE CLAIMS REGISTRY

Date Filed	Patient Name	Insurance Company	Unusual Procedure Reported	Amount Due	Amount Paid
6/13/YYYY	Patient, Ima	BC/BS FEP	n/a	$ 38.00	

FIGURE 4-10 Insurance claims registry

fully transmitted. The transmittal notice also contains names of patients whose claims have preliminary processing errors. When the transmittal notice is received, compare it to the list of claims transmitted. If a disruption in service occurred, claims may not have transmitted successfully. Claims reported as not processed must be investigated and data errors corrected. Missing and corrected claims are then transmitted a second time and checked against a second transmittal notice.

INSURANCE COMPANY PROCESSING OF A CLAIM

The processing of paper claims starts in the mailroom, where the envelopes are opened and attachments are unstapled and clipped to the claim. Claims are then optically scanned into a computer.

The processing of electronic claims begins when a file of transmitted claims is opened in the claims processing computer.

S T E P 1 The computer analyzes each claim for patient and policy identification for comparison with the computerized database.

Claims are automatically rejected if the patient and subscriber names do not match exactly with names in the computerized database. Use of nicknames or typographical errors on claims will cause rejection and return, or delay in reimbursement to the provider because the claim cannot be matched.

S T E P 2 Procedure and service codes on the claim are matched with the policy's master benefit list.

MANAGED CARE ALERT: In the case of a managed care claim, both the procedures and the dates of service are checked to ensure that services performed were preauthorized and performed within the preauthorized timeframe.

Any procedure or service determined to be a noncovered benefit is marked either as an **uncovered procedure, noncovered procedure, uncovered benefit** or **medically unnecessary,** and rejected for payment. Procedures and services that are provided to a patient without proper authorization from a payer or that are not covered by a current authorization are marked as **unauthorized procedures and services.** Patients may be billed for uncovered or noncovered procedures, but not for unauthorized services.

S T E P 3   Procedure and service codes are cross-matched with diagnosis codes reported on the CMS-1500 claim to ensure the medical necessity of all procedures/services provided.

Any service that is considered medically unnecessary may be disallowed, which means the procedure or service does not match up with an appropriate diagnosis.

S T E P 4   The claim is checked against the common data file.

The information presented on each claim is checked against the insurer's **common data file**, an abstract of all recent claims filed on each patient. This step determines whether the patient is receiving concurrent care for the same condition by more than one provider. This function further identifies services that are related to recent surgeries, hospitalizations, or liability coverages.

S T E P 5   A determination is made of "allowed charges."

If no irregularity or inconsistency is found on the claim, the allowed charge for each covered procedure is determined. The **allowed charge** is the maximum amount the insurance company will allow for each procedure or service, according to the patient's policy. The exact amount allowed varies according to the contract and is less than or equal to the fee charged by the provider. Payment is never greater than the fee submitted by the provider (see the shaded total benefit column in Figure 4-11.

S T E P 6   Determination of the patient's annual deductible is made.

The **deductible** is the total amount of covered out-of-pocket medical expenses a policyholder must incur each year before the insurance company is obligated to pay any benefits.

S T E P 7   The copayment and/or coinsurance requirement is determined.

S T E P 8   The explanation of benefits and transmittal notice forms (or computer-generated transmittal notice) are generated.

The **explanation of benefits (EOB)** form (called the Medicare Summary Notice, or MSN, by CMS) is a statement telling the patient how the insurance company determined its share of the reimbursement (Figure 4-11). The payer sends the provider a **transmittal notice** with similar information (Figure 4-12). The EOB report includes the following:

- patient and provider identification
- list of all procedures, dates of service, and charges submitted on the claim form
- list of any procedures submitted but not considered a benefit of the policy
- list of allowed charges for each covered procedure
- amount of the patient deductible, if any, subtracted from the total allowed charges
- patient's financial cost-sharing responsibility (copayment and/or coinsurance) for this claim
- total amount payable by the insurance company on this claim

XYZ Insurance Company

P.O. Box 1234
Anywhere USA 00000-0000
(800) 555-1234
(800) 555-1235 TTY

PATIENT: Dee Post
1 Main St
Alfred NY 14802

EXPLANATION OF BENEFITS

Insured:	Dee Post
Member ID #:	123456789
Group ID #:	1001

10-15-YYYY

For Services From To	Type of Service	CPT Code	Total Charges	Disallowed Charges	Deductible (-)	Remaining Covered Charges	Co-Pay	Total Benefit	Patient Responsibility	Comments
PATIENT: Dee Post		CLAIM: 89562462-00			PROVIDER: Joy Small, MD				PAYEE: Joy Small, MD	
0730 0730YY	Xray	73510	65.00	31.65	.00	0.00	0.00	33.35	0.00	P1
0730 0730YY	E&M	99203	90.00	.00	.00	0.00	15.00	75.00	15.00	P3
	TOTALS		155.00	31.65	.00	0.00	15.00	108.35	15.00	P2

COMMENTS:

P1   PREFERRED PROVIDER ORGANIZATION DISCOUNT OF $31.65 PROVIDED, PATIENT NOT RESPONSIBLE.
P2   PAYMENT IN THE AMOUNT $108.35 WAS MADE TO JOY SMALL MD ON 10/15/YY.
P3   PATIENT IS RESPONSIBLE FOR PAYMENT OF $15.00 TO PROVIDER.

DEE POST   HAS MET $200.00 OF THE $200.00 PATIENT DEDUCTIBLE FOR THE 2000 BENEFIT YEAR.
HAS MET $ 0.00 OF THE OUT-OF-POCKET MAXIMUM FOR THE 2000 BENEFIT YEAR.

THIS IS NOT A BILL. PLEASE SAVE THIS COPY FOR YOUR RECORDS.

FIGURE 4-11 Sample explanation of benefits form sent to patients

Transmittal Notice

XYZ INSURANCE COMPANY   10-15-YYYY

Provider ID	Provider Name	Date of Service	Patient Name	Member ID	CPT Code	Total Charge	CoPay Amount	Amount Paid	Total
001	Small, Joy	07/30/YY	Dael, Tim	125627	29888	2,400.00	0.00	0.00	0.00
001	Small, Joy	07/30/YY	Post, Dee	236594	73510	65.00	0.00	0.00	0.00
001	Small, Joy	07/30/YY	Post, Dee	236594	99203	90.00	15.00	75.00	90.00
					Practice Total	2555.00	15.00	75.00	90.00

FIGURE 4-12 Sample transmittal notice (or batched EOB) sent to providers

STEP 9   EOB, transmittal notice, and benefit check, if payment is approved, are mailed (or transmitted electronically) by payer.

NOTE: If the claim is denied, a transmittal notice and an EOB are sent to the provider and patient, respectively. •

The transmittal notice and check are mailed (or electronically transmitted) to the provider, and a copy of the EOB (or Medicare Summary Notice) is mailed to the patient if one of the following occurred:

1. The patient signed an authorization of benefits statement for the provider, and Block 13 on the CMS-1500 claim contains the statement, SIGNATURE ON FILE.

2. The insurance specialist entered an X in the YES box in Block 27 of the CMS-1500 claim.

3. The provider has signed an agreement with the payer for direct payment of all claims. •

If the check is mailed to the patient, the policyholder and provider receive an EOB and transmittal notice, respectively. It is then the office's responsibility to obtain payment from the patient.

NOTE: The Privacy Act of 1974 prohibits payers from notifying providers about payments on or rejections of *unassigned claims*. Therefore, *providers who do not accept assignment of Medicare benefits do not receive a copy of the Medicare Summary Notice (MSN)* sent to the Medicare beneficiary (patient). Information released to providers is limited to whether the claim was received, processed, and approved or denied. To assist in an appeal, the patient must furnish the nonparticipating provider with a copy of the MSN, and a letter signed by the patient must accompany the request for review. If the beneficiary writes the appeal, the provider must supply supporting documentation (e.g., copy of medical record). •

MAINTAINING INSURANCE CLAIM FILES

The federal Omnibus Budget Reconciliation Act of 1987 (OBRA 1987) requires providers to retain copies of any government insurance claims and copies of all attachments filed by the provider for a period of six years.

NOTE: Do not confuse retention of claims with retention of medical records. Medicare Conditions of Participation require providers to maintain medical records for at least five years, and state retention laws are sometimes more strict (e.g., New York state requires medical records to be maintained at least six years). •

CMS stipulated in March 1992 that providers and billing services filing claims electronically can comply with this federal regulation by retaining the financial **source document** (routing slip, charge slip, encounter form, or superbill) from which the insurance claim was generated. In addition, the provider should keep the e-mailed report of the summary of electronic claims received from the insurance company.

It is recommended that electronic and manual claim files be set up as follows:

1. *Open assigned claims* are organized by month and insurance company. **Open assigned claims** have been submitted to the carrier, but processing is not complete.

2. *Closed assigned claims* are filed according to year and insurance company. **Closed assigned claims** include those for which all processing, including appeals, has been completed.

3. *Transmittal notices* are organized according to date of service. A transmittal notice (or **batched EOB**) is an efficient way for payers to report the results of insurance claims processed on different patients for the same date of service and provider.

> **NOTE:** If a patient requests a copy of the transmittal notice received by the provider, all patient identification except that of the requesting patient must be removed. ●

> **EXAMPLE:** Samantha Bartlett contacts the office to request a copy of the transmittal notice for her last date of service, explaining that she did not receive her copy. Because the information is on a batched EOB, the insurance specialist makes a copy of the page on which Samantha's information is found. Using the copy, the insurance specialist removes patients' information other than Samantha's, and mails the redacted (edited) copy to Samantha. The rest of the copy, which contains other patients' information, is shredded. ●

4. *Unassigned claims* are organized by year. An **unassigned claim** is generated for providers who do not accept assignment; the file includes all unassigned claims for which the provider is not obligated to perform any follow-up work.

> **NOTE:** For offices that submit electronic claims, create folders on your computer to store the above types of claims and files. Offices that submit manual claims should label folders according to the above guidelines, and file them in a secure filing cabinet. ●

Transmittal Notice Reconciliation

When the transmittal notice and payment are received, retrieve the claim(s), and review and post payments to the patient accounts. Be sure to post the date payment was received, amount of payment, processing date, and any applicable transmittal notice number. Claims that do not contain errors are moved to the *closed assigned claims* file. (Single-payment notices are attached to paper claims before filing in the *closed assigned claims* file. Batched EOBs are placed in the *batched EOB* file.)

Handling an Error in Claims Processing

If a transmittal notice is received without corresponding payment, review it to determine whether an error in processing occurred or payment is denied for another reason. If an error in claims processing is found, complete the following steps:

S T E P 1 Review the denial to determine the issue (e.g., coding error, inaccurate reporting of medical necessity).

S T E P 2 Appeal the denial for reconsideration of payment. An **appeal** is documented as a letter (Figure 4-13) signed by the provider explaining why the claim should be reconsidered for payment. If appropriate, include copies of medical record documentation. Be sure the patient has signed a release of information authorization.

Doctors Group
Main Street
Alfred NY 00000
March 15, 2004

Medicare B Review Department
P.O. Box 1001
Anywhere, US 12345

NAME OF PATIENT: _____
MEDICARE HICN*: _____
I do not agree with the determination you made on HICN* _____ .

The reason I disagree with this determination is/are: (Check all that apply.)
❑ Service/Claim underpaid/reduced   ❑ Service/Claim overpaid   ❑ Service(s) overutilized
❑ Services not medically necessary   ❑ Duplicate Claim submitted   ❑ Other: _____

Services in question are delineated as follows:

Date(s) of Service:	Quantity Billed:	Modifier:	Procedure Code(s):
_____	_____	_____	_____
_____	_____	_____	_____
_____	_____	_____	_____

Additional information to consider, including specific diagnosis, illness and/or condition:
_____
_____

Attachments to consider: (Check all that apply)
❑ Medical Records   ❑ Ambulance Run Sheet   ❑ Copy of Claim   ❑ Certificate of Medical Necessity
❑ Other: _____

_____   _____
Signature of Claimant or Representative   Telephone Number

* HICN = Health Insurance Claim Number

FIGURE 4-13 Sample Medicare appeal letter

S T E P 3 Make a copy of the claim (found in the *open assigned claims* file) and the transmittal notice, and attach it to the letter of appeal.

● **NOTE:** If the denial was reported on a batched EOB, circle the case. ●

S T E P 4 Enter the amount of any payment received (including check number) on the claim and on the patient's ledger card. If the office electronically processes claims, post this information in the *patient account record* of the office's computerized medical office management software.

S T E P   5   Refile the claim in the appropriate *open assigned claims* file.

S T E P   6   Mail, fax, or electronically transmit the appeal and attachments to the payer.

Handling Denials of Payment

A transmittal notice may indicate that payment was denied for a reason other than a processing error. The reasons for denials may include (1) procedure or service not medically necessary, (2) pre-existing condition not covered, (3) noncovered benefit, (4) termination of coverage, (5) failure to obtain preauthorization, (6) out-of-network provider used, or (7) lower level of care could have been provided. The following steps should be taken for each type of denial.

1. *Procedure or service not medically necessary:* The payer has determined that the procedure performed or service rendered was not medically necessary based on information submitted on the claim. To respond, first review the original source document (e.g., patient record) for the claim to determine whether significant diagnosis codes or other important information has been clearly documented or may have been overlooked. Next, write an appeal letter to the payer providing the reasons the treatment is medically necessary.

    NOTE: If the medical record does not support medical necessity, discuss the case with the office manager and provider. ●

2. *Pre-existing condition:* The payer has denied this claim based on language of the pre-existing condition clause in the patient's insurance policy. A **pre-existing condition** is any medical condition that was diagnosed and/or treated within a specified period of time immediately preceding the enrollee's effective date of coverage. The wording associated with these clauses varies from policy to policy (e.g., length of time pre-existing condition clause applies). It is possible for an insurance company to cancel a policy (or at least deny payment on a claim) if the patient failed to disclose pre-existing conditions. Respond to this type of denial by determining that the condition associated with treatment for which the claim was submitted was indeed pre-existing. If it is determined that an incorrect diagnosis code was submitted on the original claim, for example, correct the claim and resubmit it for reconsideration of payment.

    NOTE: A payer can cancel a patient's policy or deny payment on a claim if the patient failed to disclose a pre-existing condition. It is also likely a payer would simply refuse to process the claim. ●

    NOTE: Office staff must be familiar with federal regulations regarding insurance coverage of pre-existing conditions when a patient changes jobs and/or an employer switches insurance plans. ●

3. *Noncovered benefit:* The claim was denied based on a list developed by the insurance company that includes a description of items covered by the policy as well as those excluded. Excluded items may include procedures such as cosmetic surgery. Respond to this type of denial by determining that the treatment submitted on the claim for payment is indeed excluded

from coverage. If it is determined that an incorrect procedure code was submitted, for example, correct the claim and resubmit it for reconsideration of payment along with a copy of medical record documentation to support the code charge.

4. *Termination of coverage:* The payer has denied this claim because the patient is no longer covered by the insurance policy. Respond to this type of denial by contacting the patient to determine appropriate coverage, and submit the claim accordingly. For example, a patient may have changed jobs and no longer be covered by his former employer's health insurance plan. The office needs to obtain correct insurance carrier information and submit a claim accordingly. This type of denial reinforces the need to interview patients about current address, telephone number, employment, and insurance coverage each time they come to the office for treatment.

   NOTE: Denial types 5 and 6 are *not* restricted to managed care plans. ●

5. *Failure to obtain preauthorization:* Many health plans require patients to call a toll-free number located on their insurance card to obtain prior authorization for particular treatments. Problems can arise during an emergency situation when there is a lack of communication between provider and health plan (payer) because treatment cannot be delayed while awaiting preauthorization. While the claim is usually paid, payment might be less and/or penalties may apply because preauthorization was not obtained. If failure to obtain preauthorization was due to a medical emergency, it is possible to have penalties waived. Respond to this situation by requesting a retrospective review of a claim, and be sure to submit information explaining special circumstances that might not be evident by reviewing the patient's chart.

   EXAMPLE: The patient was admitted to the labor and delivery unit, which resulted in an emergency cesarean section. The patient's EOB contained a $250 penalty notice (patient's responsibility) and a reduced payment to the provider (surgeon). The EOB legend stated that preauthorization for the surgical procedure (cesarean section) was not obtained. The provider appealed the claim explaining the circumstances of the emergency surgery, and the payer waived the $250 penalty and reimbursed the provider the regular rate. ●

6. *Out-of-network provider used:* The payer has denied payment because treatment was provided outside the provider network. Respond to this denial by writing a letter of appeal explaining why the patient sought treatment from outside the provider network (e.g., medical emergency when patient was out of town). Payment received could be reduced and penalties could also apply.

7. *Lower level of care could have been provided:* This type of denial applies when (a) care rendered on an inpatient basis is normally provided as an outpatient, (b) outpatient surgery could have been performed in a provider's office, or (c) skilled nursing care could have been performed by a home health agency. Respond to this type of denial by writing a letter of appeal explaining why the higher level of care was required. Be prepared to forward copies of the patient's chart for review by the insurance carrier.

DELINQUENT CLAIMS

A **delinquent claim** is usually more than 120 days past due, but some practices establish time frames that are less than and more than 120 days past due. The **delinquent claim cycle** advances through various aging periods (30 days, 60 days, 90 days, and so on), with practices typically focusing internal recovery efforts on older delinquent accounts (e.g., 120 days or more). As a result, many accounts in the earlier stages of the delinquency cycle (e.g., 30- to 60-day accounts) are overlooked as they begin to age. In turn, if the practice focuses on the early delinquent accounts, the older accounts often get overlooked.

NOTE: Payers establish time frames after which they will not process a claim. For example, HMOs typically establish a 180-day limit from the date of service for claims processing. Once the claims filing date has passed, it is extremely difficult to obtain reimbursement from the payer, and *the provider is prohibited from billing the patient for payment.*

The best way to deal with delinquent claims is to prevent them by:

- verifying health plan identification cards on all patients.

- determining patient's health care coverage (e.g., to ensure that a pre-existing condition was not submitted for reimbursement on the claim).

- electronically submitting a **clean claim**, which is a correctly completed standardized claim (e.g., CMS-1500).

- contacting the payer to determine that the claim was received.

- reviewing records to determine whether the claim was paid, denied, or is in **suspense** (pending) (e.g., subject to recovery of benefits paid in error on another patient's claim).

- submitting documentation requested by the payer to support the claim.

Collecting on Delinquent Claims

To determine whether a claim is delinquent, generate an **accounts receivable aging report**, which shows the status (by date) of outstanding claims from each payer as well as payments due from patients. At this point, many practices **outsource** (contract out) delinquent payments from patients to a full-service collections agency that utilizes collection tactics, including written contacts and multiple calls from professional collectors. Such agencies are regulated by the **Fair Debt Collection Practices Act (FDCPA)**, which specifies what a collection source may or may not do when pursuing payment of past due accounts. Agencies that collect past due charges directly from patients add a fee to the delinquent account balance, only if the practice originally notified the patient that a fee would be added if the account was sent to an outside collection source for resolution.

NOTE: Litigation, which uses legal action to recover a debt, is usually a last resort for a medical practice.

NOTE: *Delinquent claims awaiting payer reimbursement are never outsourced. They are resolved with the payer.*

Resolving Problems with Payers

While the status of most claims is indicated on the explanation of benefits submitted by the payer, other problems must be resolved by submitting an inquiry to the payer to determine the status of the claim. For each problem listed in Table 4-1, the practice must review the claims submitted and make appropriate corrections so the claim is paid.

TABLE 4-1 Claims submission problems, descriptions, and resolutions

PROBLEM	DESCRIPTION
Coding errors	• Downcoding (assigning lower level codes than documented in the record) • Incorrect code reported (e.g., incomplete code) • Incorrect coding system used (e.g., CPT code reported when level II national code should have been reported) • Medical necessity does not correspond with procedure and service codes • Unbundling (submitting multiple CPT codes when one code should be submitted) • Unspecified diagnosis codes are reported
Delinquent	• Payment is overdue, based on practice policy
Denied	• Medical coverage cancelled • Medical coverage lapsed beyond renewal date • Medical coverage policy issues prevent payment (e.g., pre-existing condition, noncovered benefit) • No-fault, personal injury protection (PIP), automobile insurance applies • Patient did not first pay coinsurance, copayment, and/or deductible • Payer determines services were not medically necessary • Procedure performed was experimental and, therefore, not reimbursable • Services should have been submitted to workers' compensation carrier • Services were not preauthorized, as required under the health plan • Services were provided before medical coverage was in effect
Lost	• Claim was not received by payer
Overpayment	• Payer may apply offsets to future provider payments to recuperate funds • Payer overpays provider's fee or managed care contract rate • Provider receives payment intended for patient • Provider receives duplicate payments from multiple payers • Payment is received on a claim not submitted by the provider
Payment errors	• Patient is paid directly by the payer when the provider should have been paid • Patient cashes a two-party check in error (check made out to both patient and provider)
Pending (suspense)	• Claim contains an error • Need for additional information • Review required by payer (e.g., high reimbursement, utilization management, complex procedures)
Rejected	• Also called *soft denials* • Claim contains a technical error (e.g., transposition of numbers, missing or incorrect data, duplicate charges or dates of service) • Payer instructions when submitting the claim were not followed • Resubmitted claim is returned (consider submitting a review request to payer)

State Insurance Regulators

Insurance is regulated by the individual states, not the federal government. State regulatory functions include registering insurance companies, overseeing compliance and penalty provisions of the state insurance code, supervising insurance company formation within the state, and monitoring the reinsurance market. State regulators ascertain that all authorized insurance companies meet and maintain financial, legal, and other requirements for doing business in the state. Regulators also license a number of insurance-related professionals, including agents, brokers and adjusters.

If the practice has a complaint about an insurance claim, contact the state insurance regulatory agency (e.g., state insurance commission) for resolution. While the commissioner will usually review a health care policy to determine whether the claims denial was based on legal provisions, the commissioner does not have legal authority to require a payer to reimburse a specific claim.

INTERNET LINK

Go to http://www.ambest.com/directory/govdir.html to view the list of government regulators by state.

SUMMARY

- The development of an insurance claim begins when the new or established patient contacts the medical practice to schedule an appointment for health care.

- New patients should be preregistered so that identification and health insurance information can be obtained prior to the scheduled office visit.

- Established patients are usually rescheduled at check out of a current appointment.

- Postclinical checkout procedures include coding diagnoses, procedures, and services; entering and posting charges; collecting and posting patient payments; completing insurance claims; attaching reports to claims; logging claims in an insurance registry; and submitting claims to payers.

- Insurance company claims processing includes optically scanning claims or opening electronic files that contain submitted claims; analyzing claims for patient/policy identification information; matching procedure and service codes with the payer's list of allowed codes; ensuring medical necessity of procedures and services; generating transmittal notices; and reimbursing providers.

- Insurance claim files are to be retained for a period of six years, according to the Omnibus Budget Reconciliation Act of 1987 (OBRA). For electronic claims, providers are to retain the financial source document.

- Transmittal notice reconciliation is an essential medical practice function that allows providers to determine the status of outstanding claims.

- Insurance claims processing problems are generated as a result of a variety of issues, including coding errors, delinquent claims, denied claims, lost claims, overpayment, payment errors, pending (suspense) claims, and rejected claims.

- The Fair Debt Collection Practices Act (FDCPA) specifies what a collection source may or may not do when pursuing payment of past due accounts.

- Insurance is regulated by the individual states, usually by a state insurance commission.

STUDY CHECKLIST

☐ Read the textbook chapter, and highlight key concepts.

☐ Create an index card for each key term.

☐ Access the chapter Internet links to learn more about concepts.

☐ Answer the chapter review questions, verifying answers with your instructor.

☐ Complete Web Tutor assignments and take online quizzes.

☐ Complete Workbook chapter, verifying answers with your instructor.

☐ Form a study group with classmates to discuss chapter concepts in preparation for an exam.

REVIEW

ORDERING

1. Sequence the new patient initial interview and check-in steps listed below by placing the correct step number to the left of the statement.

_____ Create the patient's encounter form.

_____ Patient completes registration form.

_____ Preregister the patient.

_____ Enter information into computer database.

_____ Make photocopy of patient insurance cards.

_____ Verify patient's insurance.

_____ Patient signs the authorization for release of medical information.

_____ Create patient's chart.

2. Sequence the postclinical check-out steps listed below by placing the correct step number to the left of the statement.

_____ Collect payment from the patient.

_____ Log claim in the insurance registry.

_____ Post all payments to the patient's account.

_____ Provider signs the claim.

_____ Mail claim to insurance company.

_____ Post all charges on the day sheet.

_____ Generate the claim.

_____ File office copy of the claim.

_____ Affix any required attachments to the claim.

_____ Code all procedures/services and diagnoses.

_____ Enter and total charges for all procedures performed.

3. Sequence the insurance company processing of a claim steps below by placing the correct step number to the left of the statement.

_____ The transmittal notice is generated.

_____ Deductible requirements are determined.

_____ Code numbers are matched with the master benefits list.

_____ Transmittal notice and benefit check are mailed.

_____ Determination is made of "allowed charges."

_____ Copayment requirement is determined.

_____ Procedure codes are cross-matched with diagnosis codes.

_____ Claim is scanned for patient and policy identification numbers.

_____ Claim is checked against common data file.

SHORT ANSWER

Briefly respond to each of the following.

4. Explain how the managed care authorization for specialty care for a new patient is obtained.

5. Discuss how to determine primary and secondary coverage for an adult patient covered by two full benefit policies.

6. Determine the primary, secondary, and tertiary policyholder for a child in the following scenarios:

   a. Parent A was born on March 13, 1956; Parent B was born on April 13, 1954.

   b. Parent A was born on January 1, 1956, and has had the insurance policy for three years; Parent B was born on January 1, 1960, and has had the policy for six years.

   c. The parents of the patient are divorced and both have remarried. The child is covered under three policies: the father, the stepmother, and the mother, who has custody of the child. The court has not made any stipulation about medical insurance.

   d. Child is covered exactly as described above; however, the court has stipulated the father is responsible for the medical expenses.

KEY TERMS

abuse

ANSI ASC X12N 837

authorization

black box edit

breach of confidentiality

business associate

carrier

case law

check digit

civil law

clearinghouse

Clinical Data Abstraction Centers
(CDACs)

code pairs (edit pairs)

common law

confidentiality

consent

contract

criminal law

Current Dental Terminology (CDT)

deposition

direct treatment provider

electronic transaction standards

encrypted

Federal Claims Collection Act of 1966

Federal False Claims Act

Federal Register

first party

fiscal intermediary (FI)

flat file

fraud

guardian(s)

interrogatory

listserv

Medicare Bulletin

minimum data

modifier

National Drug Code (NDC)

National Health PlanID (PlanID)

National Individual Identifier

National Provider Identifier (NPI)

National Standard Employer Identifier
Number (EIN)

National Standard Format (NSF)

overpayment

Payment Error Prevention Program
(PEPP)

payment error rate

precedent

privacy

Privacy Act of 1974

Privacy Rule

qui tam

regulation

second party

security

Stark II regulations

statute

statutory law

subpoena

subpoena duces tecum

third party

UB-92

upcoding

verbal contract

Chapter 5 Legal and Regulatory Considerations

OBJECTIVES

Upon successful completion of this chapter, you should be able to:

1. Define key terms.
2. Provide examples of a statute, regulation, and case law.
3. Explain the use of the *Federal Register*.
4. Discuss ways the insurance specialist can obtain information about new laws and regulations.
5. Give examples of breaches of confidentiality.
6. State the importance of obtaining the patient's signature for the "Authorization for Release of Information" statement on the CMS-1500 claim.
7. Identify two classifications of patients who are not required to sign the "Authorization for Release of Information" statement on the CMS-1500 claim.
8. Explain how the patient authorization for release of information is obtained for electronic claims.
9. Verify a legitimate telephone request for patient information.
10. Process facsimile (fax) requests for patient information.
11. Prepare a confidentiality notice to serve as the first page of faxed patient information.
12. Establish a patient record retention policy for the physician's office.
13. Summarize the *CMS Internet Security Policy* and the *Stark II regulations*.
14. List the components of the Health Insurance Portability and Accountability Act of 1996 (HIPAA), and explain the health care impact of each.
15. Outline the elements of the *Compliance Program Guidance for Physician Practices* and the *Payment Error Prevention Program*.
16. Implement *CMS's National Correct Coding Initiative* (CCI).
17. Provide an example of *unbundling*.
18. Differentiate among the NPI, PlanID, EIN, and patient identifier.
19. List the scheduled implementation dates for CMS's *electronic health care standards* and *privacy standards*.
20. Explain how overpayments are recovered.

INTRODUCTION

The health insurance specialist must be knowledgeable about laws and regulations for maintaining patient records and processing health insurance claims. This chapter defines legal and regulatory terminology and summarizes laws and regulations that affect health insurance processing. Internet links are also included as a resource for remaining up-to-date and obtaining clarification of legal and regulatory considerations.

INTRODUCTION TO LEGAL AND REGULATORY CONSIDERATIONS

Federal and state **statutes** (or **statutory law**) are laws passed by legislative bodies (e.g., federal congress and state legislatures). These laws are then implemented as **regulations**, which are guidelines written by administrative agencies (e.g., CMS). **Case law** (or **common law**) is based on court decisions that establish a **precedent** (or standard).

Federal regulations govern programs such as Medicare, Medicaid, TRICARE, and the Federal Employees Health Benefit Plans (FEHBP). State laws regulate insurance companies, patient record keeping practices, and provider licensing. State insurance departments determine coverage issues for insurance policies (contracts) and state workers' compensation plans.

Civil law deals with all areas of the law that are not classified as criminal. **Criminal law** is public law governed by statute or ordinance that deals with crimes and their prosecution. A **subpoena** is an order of the court that requires a witness to appear at a particular time and place to testify. A **subpoena duces tecum** requires documents (e.g., patient record) be produced. A subpoena is used to obtain witness testimony at trial and at **deposition**, which is testimony under oath taken outside of court (e.g., at the provider's office). In civil cases (e.g., malpractice), the provider might be required to complete an **interrogatory**, which is a document containing a list of questions that must be answered in writing.

Qui tam is an abbreviation for the Latin phrase *qui tam pro domino rege quam pro sic ipso in hoc parte sequitur* meaning "who as well for the king as for himself sues in this matter." It is a provision of the Federal Civil False Claims Act, which allows a private citizen to file a lawsuit in the name of the U.S. Government charging fraud by government contractors and other entities that receive or use government funds, and share in any money recovered. A common defendant in *qui tam* actions involving Medicare/Medicaid fraud includes physicians, hospitals, HMOs, and clinics.

To accurately process health insurance claims, especially for government programs like Medicare and Medicaid, you should become familiar with the *Code of Federal Regulations* (Figure 5-1). Providers and health insurance specialists can locate legal and regulatory issues found in such publications as the *Federal Register* and *Medicare Bulletin*. The **Federal Register** (Figure 5-2) is a legal newspaper published every business day by the National Archives and Records Administration (NARA). It is available in paper form, on microfiche, and online.

Title 42--Public Health

CHAPTER IV--CENTERS FOR MEDICARE & MEDICAID SERVICES, DEPARTMENT OF HEALTH AND HUMAN SERVICES

PART 405--FEDERAL HEALTH INSURANCE FOR THE AGED AND DISABLED

405.201	Scope of subpart and definitions.
405.203	FDA categorization of investigational devices.
405.205	Coverage of a non-experimental/investigational (Category B) device.
405.207	Services related to a noncovered device.
405.209	Payment for a non-experimental/investigational (Category B) device.
405.211	Procedures for Medicare contractors in making coverage decisions for a non-experimental/investigational (Category B) device.
405.213	Re-evaluation of a device categorization.
405.215	Confidential commercial and trade secret information.
405.301	Scope of subpart.
405.350	Individual's liability for payments made to providers and other persons for items and services furnished the individual.
405.351	Incorrect payments for which the individual is not liable.

FIGURE 5-1 Portion of table of contents from Code of Federal Regulations, Title 42, Public Health, Chapter IV, Centers for Medicare & Medicaid Services (Reprinted according to National Archives and Records Administration Permissions Notice)

The *Medicare Bulletin* (Figure 5-3) is published by CMS as a legal notice to providers (e.g., physicians, suppliers, and so on) about requirements imposed by Medicare laws, regulations, and guidelines. It is mailed to providers by their Medicare **carrier**, which is the organization (e.g., insurance company) that contracts with CMS to process Medicare Part B claims. (Hospitals receive the *Medicare Bulletin* from their **fiscal intermediary (FI)**, which is the organization that contracts with CMS to process Medicare Part A claims.)

● **NOTE:** Health care organizations should appoint one individual to review CMS transmittals (e.g., *Medicare Bulletin*), update the Medicare carriers manual, and educate staff about changes. ●

● **EXAMPLE 1:** FEDERAL STATUTE, IMPLEMENTED AS STATE PROGRAM

Congress passed Title XXI of the Social Security Act as part of the Balanced Budget Act of 1997, which called for implementation of the State Children's Health Insurance Program. In response, New York implemented Child Health Plus, which expanded insurance eligibility to children under age 19 who are not eligible for Medicaid and have limited or no health insurance. Even if family income is high, children can be eligible to enroll in Child Health Plus; an insurance premium in the form of a monthly family contribution may be required (e.g., a family of two with an income ranging from $24,977–$25,920 pays $15.00 per month per child).

41244   **Federal Register** / Vol. 67, No. 116 / Monday, June 17, 2002 / Notices

Exposure Cohort Petitioning Process

Procedures, NIOSH-IREP concerns and model transparency, dose reconstruction workgroup discussion and issues, and Board discussion.

Agenda items are subject to change as priorities dictate.

For Further Information Contact: Larry Elliott, Executive Secretary, ABRWH, NIOSH, CDC, 4676 Columbia Parkway, Cincinnati, Ohio 45226, telephone (513) 841–4498, fax (513) 458–7125.

The Director, Management Analysis and Services Office, has been delegated the authority to sign **Federal Register** notices pertaining to announcements of meetings and other committee management activities for both the Centers for Disease Control and Prevention and the Agency for Toxic Substances and Disease Registry.

Dated: June 12, 2002.

John C. Burckhardt,

Acting Director, Management Analysis and Services Office, Centers for Disease Control and Prevention.

[FR Doc. 02–15273 Filed 6–14–02; 8:45 am]

BILLING CODE 4163–19–P

DEPARTMENT OF HEALTH AND HUMAN SERVICES

Centers for Medicare & Medicaid Services
Privacy Act of 1974; Report of Modified or Altered System

AGENCY: Centers for Medicare & Medicaid Services (CMS), (formerly the Health Care Financing Administration), Department of Health and Human Services (HHS).

ACTION: Notice of proposal to modify or alter a System of Records (SOR).

SUMMARY: In accordance with the requirements of the Privacy Act of 1974, we are proposing to modify or alter an SOR, "End Stage Renal Disease (ESRD) Program Management and Medical Information System (PMMIS)," System

No. 09–70–0520. We propose to broaden the scope of this system to include the collection and maintenance of ESRD Core Indicators or Clinical Performance Measures (CPM). Data contained in CPM Data Set are being added to meet statutory requirements and to augment the usefulness of the information for research, quality improvement projects, and policy formulation. We are deleting routine use number 2 authorizing disclosures to organizations deemed qualified to carry out quality assessments; number 5, authorizing disclosures to a contractor; number 6, authorizing disclosures to an agency of a state government; and an unnumbered routine use which authorizes the release of information to the Social Security Administration (SSA).

Routine use number 2 is being deleted because it is not clear what "organizations" are being identified and who should receive information referred to in this routine use. We will add a new routine use to accomplish release of information in this system to ESRD Network Organizations and Quality Improvement Organizations (QIO) to carry out quality assessments, medical audits, quality improvement projects, and/or utilization reviews. Disclosures allowed by routine use number 6 and to SSA will be covered by a new routine use to permit

release of information to "another Federal and/or state agency, agency of a state government, an agency established by state law, or its fiscal agent." Disclosures previously allowed by routine use number 5 will now be covered by proposed routine use number 1.

The security classification previously reported as "None" will be modified to reflect that the data in this system is considered to be "Level Three Privacy Act Sensitive." We are modifying the language in the remaining routine uses to provide clarity to CMS' intention to disclose individual-specific information contained in this system. The proposed routine uses will be prioritized and reordered according to their proposed usage. We will also update any sections of the system that were affected by the recent reorganization and update language in the administrative sections to correspond with language used in other CMS SORs.

The primary purpose of the system of records is to maintain information on Medicare ESRD beneficiaries, non-Medicare ESRD patients, Medicare approved ESRD hospitals and dialysis facilities, and Department of Veterans Affairs (DVA) patients. The ESRD/ PMMIS is used by CMS and the renal community to perform their duties and responsibilities in monitoring the Medicare status, transplant activities, dialysis activities, and Medicare utilization (inpatient and physician/supplier bills) of ESRD patients and their Medicare providers, as well as in calculating the Medicare covered periods of ESRD. Information retrieved from this system of records will also be disclosed to:

FIGURE 5-2 Sample page from the *Federal Register* (Reprinted according to National Archives and Records Administration Permissions Notice)

PROGRAM MEMORANDUM

Department of Health and Human Services

INSURANCE COMMISSIONERS
INSURANCE ISSUERS

Centers for Medicare & Medicaid Services

Transmittal No. 02-01

Date March 2002

Title: Medigap Insurance Standards Bulletin Series — INFORMATION

Subject: Processing Applications for Medigap Guaranteed Issue Policies and Policies Sold during Open Enrollment Periods

Market: Medigap

I. PURPOSE

The purpose of this bulletin is to clarify the interpretation of certain statutory requirements of sections 1882(s)(2) and (3) of the Social Security Act (the Act). These sections govern a Medicare beneficiary's right to purchase a Medicare supplemental policy (commonly referred to as a Medigap policy) during the six-month Medigap open enrollment period, or on a guaranteed issue basis when certain circumstances apply.

Specifically, this bulletin will focus on the actions an issuer is required to take when an applicant has federally-mandated open enrollment or guaranteed issue rights. This bulletin does not address issues that have arisen about how to determine **whether** an individual has open enrollment or guaranteed issue rights. Rather, it specifies the issuer's obligations with respect to beneficiaries who clearly have those rights.

II. BACKGROUND

Section 1882(s)(2) of the Act requires an issuer to make available any Medigap policy it sells in a state to any Medicare beneficiary during the first six months the individual is both age 65 or older and is enrolled in Part B of Medicare. During the Medigap open enrollment period, an issuer may not deny or condition the issuance or effectiveness of a Medigap policy, or discriminate in the pricing of the policy because of health status, claims experience, receipt of health care, or medical condition.

FIGURE 5-3 Sample *Medicare Bulletin* (Reprinted in accordance with CMS Content Reuse policy)

 EXAMPLE 2: FEDERAL STATUTE, IMPLEMENTED AS A FEDERAL REGULATION, AND PUBLISHED IN THE *FEDERAL REGISTER*

Congress passed the Balanced Budget Refinement Act of 1999 (Public Law 106-113), which called for a number of revisions to Medicare, Medicaid, and the State Children's Health Insurance Program. On May 5, 2000, the Department of Health and Human Services published a proposed rule in the *Federal Register* to revise the Medicare hospital inpatient prospective payment system for operating costs. This proposed rule was entitled "Medicare Program; Changes to the Hospital Inpatient Prospective Payment Systems and Fiscal Year 2001 Rates; Proposed Rule." The purpose of publishing the proposed rule is to allow for comments from health care providers. Once the comment period has ended, the final rule is published in the *Federal Register*.

EXAMPLE 3: CASE LAW

When originally passed, New York State Public Health Law (PHL) sections 17 and 18 allowed a *reasonable charge* to be imposed for copies of patient records.

Health care facilities, therefore, charged fees for locating the patient's record and making copies. These fees were later challenged in court, and reasonable charge language in the PHL was interpreted in *Hernandez v. Lutheran Medical Center* (1984), *Ventura v. Long Island Jewish Hillside Medical Center* (1985), and *Cohen v. South Nassau Communities Hospital* (1987). The interpretation permitted charges of $1.00 to $1.50 per page, plus a search and retrieval fee of $15. ●

● **NOTE:** Sections 17 and 18 of the PHL were amended in 1991 when the phrase, "the reasonable fee for paper copies shall not exceed seventy-five cents per page" was added to the law. ●

INTERNET LINKS

The *Federal Register* can be accessed online at http://www.archives.gov

CMS press releases can be viewed at http://www.cms.gov

Medicare bulletins can be viewed at a carrier's or fiscal intermediary's official Web site. The Trailblazer Health Enterprises, LLC™ Medicare site can be viewed at http://www.trailblazerhealth.com

Consider subscribing to an online service, such as CodeCorrect.com located at http://www.codecorrect.com, that posts up-to-date billing and coding news. Most online services provide a free trial membership to try out their products before actually purchasing them.

State departments of health Web sites can be accessed at http://www.cdc.gov by clicking on the Other Sites link.

Membership in professional associations can also prove helpful in accessing up-to-date information about the health insurance industry (refer to Chapter 1 for information on joining professional associations). Newsletters and journals published by professional associations routinely include articles that clarify implementation of new legal and regulatory issues. They also provide resources for obtaining the most up-to-date information about such issues. Another way to remain current is to subscribe to a **listserv**, which is a subscriber-based question-and-answer forum that is available through e-mail.

INTERNET LINKS

CMS offers free subscriptions to electronic mailing listservs at http://cms.hhs.gov/medlearn/listserv.asp. Notices are sent to your e-mail address.

Join Medicare Part-B listserv at http://lyris.ucg.com/cgi-bin/listserv/listserv.pl/ partb-l. This listserv is very active (50+ postings per day), and you may want to join the digest version to receive one daily e-mail that contains all postings for that day.

CONFIDENTIALITY OF PATIENT INFORMATION

Confidentiality of patient information includes the related concepts of privacy and security. **Privacy** is the right of individuals to keep their information from being disclosed to others. Once information is disclosed (e.g., for the purpose of obtaining health care), it is essential that confidentiality of the information be maintained. **Confidentiality** involves restricting patient information access to those with proper authorization and maintaining the security of patient information. **Security** involves the safekeeping of patient information by:

- controlling access to hard copy and computerized records (e.g., implementing password protection for computer-based patient records).
- protecting patient information from alteration, destruction, tampering, or loss (e.g., establishing office policies).
- providing employee training in confidentiality of patient information (e.g., conducting annual in-service education programs).
- requiring employees to sign a confidentiality statement that details the consequences of not maintaining patient confidentiality (e.g., employee termination).

Because patient information is readily available through computerized databases and other means, it is essential to take steps to maintain confidentiality. **Breach of confidentiality**, often unintentional, involves the unauthorized release of patient information to a third party. Examples include:

- discussing patient information in public places (e.g., elevators).
- leaving patient information unattended (e.g., computer screen display).
- communicating patient information to family members without the patient's consent.
- publicly announcing patient information in a waiting room or registration area.
- accessing patient information without a job-related reason.

To understand the legality of this issue, it is first necessary to define contract and third party. A **contract** is an agreement between two or more parties to perform specific services or duties. A **third party** is one who is not involved in the patient/provider relationship. (The **first party** is the person designated in the contract to receive a contracted service. The **second party** is the person or organization providing the service.)

A **verbal contract** is established between the patient and the health care provider when the patient asks a provider to perform medical services. In exchange for services, the patient agrees to promptly pay the provider's customary fee for those services. The parties to this contract are the patient, the health care provider, and the office staff. If the patient is a minor or a legally incompetent adult, parents or stated **guardian(s)** (the person(s) legally designated to be in charge of the patient's affairs) contract for the services of the health care provider on behalf of the patient. The parents or guardians, therefore, become a party to the *patient-health care provider contract.*

For patients to receive proper treatment they must be willing to be examined and touched by medical professionals. Patients must also reveal the reason they sought medical advice and how this problem has affected them. At times, this requires the patient to reveal intimate thoughts and feelings, as well as their bodies. If the patient is to feel comfortable in confiding to a health care provider, the patient must be assured that the office will protect and control the confidential information given to the health care provider. Breach of confidentiality cannot be charged against a health care provider if written permission to release necessary medical information to an insurance company or other third party has been obtained from the patient, the parent, or the guardian. A good maxim to follow is:

"When in doubt, have them write it out."

Authorized Release of Information to Payers

To prevent breach of patient confidentiality, all health care professionals involved with processing insurance claims of the CMS-1500 should check to be sure the patient has signed an "Authorization for Release of Medical Information" statement before completing the claim. The release can be obtained in one of two ways:

- Ask the patient to sign block 12, Patient's or Authorized Person's Signature, on the CMS-1500 claim (Figure 5-4) or
- Ask the patient to sign a special release form that is customized by each practice and specifically names the patient's insurance company (Figure 5-5).

NOTE: Computerized practices must obtain the patient's signature on the special release form and provide a copy to the patient's insurance company upon request. With this method, the CMS-1500 claim generated will contain SIGNATURE ON FILE in Block 12 (Figure 5-6).

NOTE: A dated, signed special release form is generally considered valid for one year. Be sure to obtain the patient's signature on the special release form each year. Undated signed forms are assumed to be valid until revoked by the patient or guardian. CMS regulations permit government programs to accept both dated and undated authorizations.

Established medical practices must update patient information and obtain the necessary authorization forms. Patients who regularly seek care must sign a new authorization each year.

Authorization Exceptions

The federal government allows three exceptions to the required authorization for release of medical information to insurance companies:

1. Patients covered by Medicaid
2. Patients covered by Workers' Compensation
3. Patients seen by a provider in a hospital, but who do not receive follow-up care in the provider's office

READ BACK OF FORM BEFORE COMPLETING & SIGNING THIS FORM.
12. PATIENT'S OR AUTHORIZED PERSON'S SIGNATURE I authorize the release of any medical or other information necessary to process this claim. I also request payment of government benefits either to myself or to the party who accepts assignment below.

SIGNED _____*Mary Sue Patient*_____ DATE _____

FIGURE 5-4 Patient signature in Block 12

(Insert Letterhead)

Authorization for Release of Medical Information to the Payer and Assignment of Benefits to Physician

COMMERCIAL INSURANCE

I hereby authorize releaase of medical information necessary to file a claim with my insurance company and ASSIGN BENEFITS OTHERWISE PAYABLE TO ME TO _____ *(fill in provider's name)* _____

I understand that I am financially responsible for any balance not covered by my insurance carrier. A copy of this signature is as valid as the original.

Signature of patient or guardian_____ Date _____

MEDICARE

BENEFICIARY _____   Medicare Number _____

I request that payment of authorized medicare benefits be made on my behalf to ____ *(fill in provider's name)* for any service furnished to me by that provider. I authorize any custodian of medical information about me to release to the Centers for Medicare & Medicaid Services and its agents any information needed to determine these benefits or the benefits payable for related services.

Beneficiary Signature _____   Date _____

MEDICARE SUPPLEMENTAL INSURANCE

BENEFICIARY _____   Medicare Number _____

Medigap ID Number _____

I hereby give ____ *(Name of Physician or Practice)* ____ permission to bill for Medicare Supplemental Insurance payments for my medical care.

I understand that ____ *(Name of Medicare Supplemental Insurance Carrier)* ____ needs information about me and my medical condition to make a decision about these payments. I give permission for that information to go to ____ *(Name of Medicare Supplemental Insurance Company)* ____ .

I request that payment of authorized Medicare Supplemental benefits be made either to me or on my behalf to (Name of Physician or Practice) for any services furnished me by that physician. I authorize any holder of medical information about me to release to (Name of Medicare Supplemental Insurance Company) any information required to determine and pay these benefits.

Beneficiary Signature _____   Date _____

FIGURE 5-5 Sample authorization form for release of medical information and assignment of benefits

READ BACK OF FORM BEFORE COMPLETING & SIGNING THIS FORM.

12. PATIENT'S OR AUTHORIZED PERSON'S SIGNATURE I authorize the release of any medical or other information necessary to process this claim. I also request payment of government benefits either to myself or to the party who accepts assignment below.

SIGNED ____ **SIGNATURE ON FILE** ____   DATE ____

13. INSURED'S OR AUTHORIZED PERSON'S SIGNATURE I authorize payment of medical benefits to the undersigned physician or supplier for services described below.

SIGNED ____

FIGURE 5-6 Release of medical information (Blocks 12 and 13 on a CMS-1500 claim)

For the first two exceptions, the federal government mandated that when a patient enrolls in Medicaid or requests benefits under the Workers' Compensation program, the patient becomes a third-party beneficiary in a contract between the health care provider and the government agency that sponsors the specific program. When health care providers agree to treat either a Medicaid or a Workers' Compensation case, they agree to accept the program's payment as payment in full for covered procedures rendered to these patients. The patient may be billed only if services rendered are not covered by the payer, or if the payer determines the patient was ineligible for benefits on the date(s) of service.

For the third exception, patients are required to sign an authorization for treatment and an authorization for release of medical information at the hospital before being treated by the hospital or seen by the provider. If the hospital's medical information release form includes both the authorization for release of information from the hospital and the treating physician's services, claims may be submitted by the physician's office without obtaining a separate medical information release from the patient. The words SIGNATURE ON FILE are entered in Block 12 of the CMS-1500 claim filed by the provider (Figure 5-6). If, at a later date, proof of the signature authorizing the release of information is requested, a copy of the signed authorization may be obtained from the hospital's files.

Release of HIV/AIDS Status

Patients who undergo screening for the human immunodeficiency virus (HIV) or AIDS infection should sign an additional authorization statement for release of information regarding their HIV/AIDS status (Figure 5-7). Several states require very specific wording on this form. Be sure to determine if your state requires a special form.

(Insert letterhead)

Authorization to Release HIV-Related Information

Patient Name _____   Date of Service _____

Address _____   Date of Birth _____

I authorize _____*(name of practice)*_____ to release HIV-related information to the following organization for the purpose of processing payment for services rendered. I understand that this is a required consent and I voluntarily and knowingly sign this authorization for release of information to:

Name of Requestor _____

Address _____

I understand this consent can be cancelled at any time, but that information already disclosed is exempt. I release _____*(name of practice)*_____ from any liability arising from the release of information to the individual or agency stated above.

Patient signature: _____   Date: _____

Patient representative signature: _____   Date: _____

Reason patient is unable to sign: _____

Witness signature: _____   Date: _____

Information released shall include a statement prohibiting the requestor from redisclosing patient information without the prior consent of the patient. Unless otherwise specified, *this authorization will expire one year from date signed.*

FIGURE 5-7 Sample authorization to release HIV-related information

Release of Information to Other Third Parties

The patient's signature on the release of medical information form restricts the release of information to the party specified. Release of the same information or copies of the patient medical record to any other third party is not authorized. To release medical information to an individual other than the payer, be sure to have the patient complete an authorization to release medical information (Figure 5-8).

Most states have special laws covering release of mental health services records. There also are federal laws covering confidentiality when the patient is enrolled in a federally assisted alcohol and drug abuse program. If you work with a substance abuse facility or have a patient receiving mental health services, acquaint yourself with federal and state laws.

Need To Know Rule

Confidentiality is breached when a health care professional in the practice releases confidential information to a person who has no demonstrable legal need to receive this information. Persons in this category may include spouses, friends, relatives, other patients, or colleagues working in a practice where the patient has had no previous contact.

NOTE: There is a demonstrable need to provide limited patient information to office personnel when making a referral of a patient to that office. ●

(Insert letterhead)

Authorization to Release Medical Information

Patient Name _____   Date of Service _____

Address _____   Date of Birth _____

I authorize _____ *(name of practice)* _____ to release information contained in my medical record concerning treatment provided from _____ to _____ . I understand that this is a required consent and I voluntarily and knowingly sign this authorization for release of information to:

Name of Requestor _____

Address _____

I release _____ *(name of practice)* _____ from any liability arising from the release of information to the individual or agency stated above.

Patient signature: _____   Date: _____

Patient representative signature: _____   Date: _____

Reason patient is unable to sign: _____

Witness signature: _____   Date: _____

Information released shall include a statement prohibiting the requestor from redisclosing patient information without the prior consent of the patient.

FIGURE 5-8 Sample authorization to release general medical information

This does not preclude the sharing of case studies or specific insurance billing problems with colleagues or acquaintances. In these discussions, however, great care must be taken to ensure that a third party (a person or entity not involved in the patient-provider relationship) cannot identify the patient or family involved.

EXAMPLE: Mary Sue Patient is seen in Dr. Day's office with the complaint of abdominal pain. After examining the patient and evaluating test results, Dr. Day refers Mary Sue to Dr. Shaw, a gastroenterologist. Dr. Day's medical assistant schedules the patient's appointment with Dr. Shaw. According to individual state law, only **minimum data** may be shared with Dr. Shaw's office, which means enough information to schedule the appointment (e.g., reason for the referral and office visit). •

NOTE: Each state defines what is meant by *minimum data.* The HIPAA Privacy Rule also specifies that the minimum amount of information necessary for the purpose of the use or disclosure is to be disclosed. •

CLAIMS INFORMATION TELEPHONE INQUIRIES

Another area of concern regarding breach of confidentiality involves the clarification of insurance data by telephone. A signed release statement from the patient may be on file, but the office has no assurance of the identity or credentials of the inquirer. It is very simple for a curious individual to place a call to a physician's office and claim to be an insurance company benefits clerk. The rule to follow here is:

Never give information over the phone or in person until you have verified that the party making the request is entitled to the information.

To verify insurance company telephone inquiries for clarification of claims data, place the caller on hold until you have the file copy of the patient's insurance claim in hand. Ask the caller to read the line on the claim that needs clarification. When sufficient information from the caller's copy is obtained to ensure validity of the inquiry, clarifying statements or data may be released by phone. Be sure to follow up this action by writing a memo detailing the conversation, and file it with the practice's file copy of the claim. Computerized practices should access the patient account and/or demographic screens to confirm the data. If an error is detected, it should be corrected and a notation made to explain the change in the message section of the patient's computer file.

If there are multiple questions or if a detailed clarification is needed, it is best to ask for a written request for information. The written request and a copy of the response then become an official addendum to the practice's file copy of the claim.

Another way to verify a caller's identity is to use a "Caller ID" service. You should also ask how you can return the call. Then, place the call through the caller's switchboard to verify that the caller was a valid insurance company employee. If verification cannot be made, the caller must submit a request in writing on company stationery.

Phone Requests from Lawyers

Great care should be taken when attorneys request information over the telephone. Lawyers are well aware that offices must have the patient's signed release of information in the practice's files before answering questions. Never assume that the attorney has a signed release from the patient, and do not submit to pressure from the attorney to breach confidentiality.

Law offices are required to send any patient's authorized release of information statement the lawyers have obtained to the provider. After comparing and matching the signature on the release form sent by the lawyer with the patient's or guardian's signature and handwriting on the registration form, you should respond to the lawyer's request in writing.

FACSIMILE TRANSMISSION

Great care must be taken to ensure that sensitive information sent by fax reaches the intended receiver and is handled properly. It is recommended that health information be faxed only when there is:

1. an urgent need for the health record and mailing the record will cause unnecessary delays in treatment, or

2. immediate authorization for treatment is required from a primary care physician or other third-party case manager.

In such cases, information transmitted should be limited only to the information required to satisfy the immediate needs of the requesting party. Each transmission of sensitive material should have a cover sheet including the following information:

- Name of the facility to receive the facsimile
- Name and phone number of the person authorized to receive the transmission
- Name and phone number of the sender
- Number of pages being transmitted
- A confidentiality notice or disclaimer (Figure 5-9)
- Instructions to authorized recipient to send verification of receipt of transmittal to the sender.

The practice should keep a dated log of the transmission of all medically sensitive facsimiles and copies of all "receipt of transmittal" verifications signed and returned by the authorized recipient. Special care must be taken to ensure that proper facsimile destination numbers are keyed into the fax machine prior to transmission.

If you have received this transmittal in error, please notify the sender immediately.

The material in this transmission contains confidential information that is legally privileged. This information is intended only for the use of the individual or entity named above.

If you are not the intended recipient, you are hereby notified that any disclosure, copying, distribution, or action taken based on the contents of this transmission is strictly prohibited.

FIGURE 5-9 Sample fax confidentiality notice

CONFIDENTIALITY AND THE INTERNET

At present there is no guarantee of confidentiality when patient records are transmitted via the Internet. If time constraints prevent sending sensitive information through a more secure delivery system, special arrangements may be made with the requesting party to transmit the document after deleting specific patient identification information. It is best to call the party requesting the documents to arrange for an identifier code to be added to the document so that the receiving party is assured that the information received is that which was requested. This transmission should be followed by an official unedited copy of the record sent by overnight delivery including specific patient material that was deleted in the previous transmission.

On November 24, 1998, the *HCFA Internet Security Policy* issued guidelines for the security and appropriate use of the Internet for accessing and transmitting sensitive information (e.g., Medicare beneficiary information). The information must be **encrypted** so that information is converted to a secure language format for transmission, and authentication or identification procedures must be implemented to assure that the sender and receiver of data are known to each other and are authorized to send and/or receive such information.

RETENTION OF PATIENT INFORMATION AND HEALTH INSURANCE RECORDS

OBRA of 1987 requires patient information and health insurance records to be maintained for six years, unless state law specifies a longer period. The records must be available as references for use by CMS, fiscal intermediaries, DHHS audit, or as designated for billing review and other references. It is acceptable to microfilm patient information and insurance records (including attachments submitted to insurance companies), if the microfilm accurately reproduces all original documents. All other categories of health insurance records are to be maintained in their original form.

EMPLOYEE RETIREMENT INCOME SECURITY ACT (ERISA)

The *Employee Retirement Income Security Act (ERISA)* was enacted in 1974 to ensure that pension and other benefits were provided to employees as promised by their employers. ERISA rules cover pensions, profit-sharing stock bonuses, health care, life insurance, prepaid legal services, and disability insurance (both long- and short-term). The Consolidated Omnibus Budget Reconciliation Act of 1985 (COBRA) amended ERISA to include provisions for continuation of health care, which apply to group health plans of employers with 20 or more employees. Participants and beneficiaries have the right to maintain, at their own expense, health care plan coverage that would be lost due to a triggering event (e.g., termination of employment). The cost of this coverage is to be comparable to what it would be if they were still members of the employer's group. Individuals are required to receive an initial general notice informing them of their rights under COBRA. The Health Insurance Portability and Accountability Act of 1996 (HIPAA) further amended ERISA to improve the portability and continuity of health insurance coverage in connection with employment. Provisions include rules relating to pre-existing conditions, exclusions, special enrollment rights, and prohibition of discrimination against individuals based on health status-related factors.

MEDICAL NECESSITY

Today's concept of medical necessity determines the extent to which individuals with health conditions receive health care services. (The concept was introduced in the 1970s when health insurance contracts intended to exclude care, such as voluntary hospitalizations prescribed primarily for the convenience of the provider or patient.) *Medical necessity* is the measure of whether a health care procedure or service will be reimbursed by a payer, and this decision-making process is based on the payer's contractual language and the treating provider's documentation. Generally the following criteria are used to determine medical necessity:

- *Purpose:* the procedure or service is performed to treat a medical condition
- *Scope:* the most appropriate level of service is provided, taking into consideration potential benefit and harm to the patient
- *Evidence:* the treatment is known to be effective in improving health outcomes
- *Value:* the treatment is cost-effective for this condition when compared to alternative treatments, including no treatment.

NOTE: Cost-effective does not necessarily mean least expensive. •

FEDERAL FALSE CLAIMS ACT

The federal government passed the **Federal False Claims Act** during the Civil War to regulate fraud associated with military contractors selling supplies and equipment to the Union Army. Since then, this Act has been used by federal agencies to regulate the conduct of any contractor submitting claims for payment to the federal government for any program, including Medicare. Control of fraud and abuse has been a key regulatory interest ever since the hospital prospective payment system legislation (called Diagnosis Related Groups, or DRGs) was passed as part of the Tax Equity & Fiscal Responsibility Act (TEFRA) of 1982. Prior to TEFRA, the cost-based reimbursement system for Medicare claims made fraud almost unnecessary because the system rewarded high utilization of services. The implementation of DRGs resulted in the first serious "gaming" of the system to find ways to maximize revenues for hospitals. Because the diagnosis and procedure codes reported impact the DRG selected (and resultant payment), some hospitals engaged in a practice called **upcoding**, which is the assignment of an ICD-9-CM diagnosis code that does not match patient record documentation for the purpose of illegally increasing reimbursement (e.g., assigning the ICD-9-CM code for heart attack code when angina was actually documented in the record). As a result, upcoding became a serious fraud concern under DRGs.

Stark II Regulations

In the 1980's, the issue of self-referral was presented as a serious legislative item in Congress. **Self-referral** involves providers ordering services to be performed for patients by organizations in which they have a financial interest (e.g., laboratories, or durable medical equipment). Commercial laboratories were targeted first, followed by most methods of physician or provider investment in health care delivery entities. Representative Stark led legislative efforts to treat any types of referral practices by physicians to entities in which they had a material financial interest as fraud. Examples of material financial interest include ownership interest and kickbacks to induce referrals (e.g., free or less than fair market value terms for office space, consulting services, and practice management). In 1998, **Stark II regulations** were released for implementation to regulate physician referral for Medicare services from which the doctor profits. Studies revealed that when a doctor has an investment interest in a lab, for example, the doctor orders more tests and more expensive services.

Hospitals are also required to comply with the Stark II self-referral law because of relationships they establish with physicians. They must make sure that the financial arrangements they make with physicians who refer patients to them (e.g., inpatient admissions, and outpatient services) conform to exceptions to the Stark II law (e.g., personal service exception, space lease exception, and equipment lease exception). In addition, hospitals should make sure that contracts are negotiated for hospital-physician relationships.

HEALTH INSURANCE PORTABILITY AND ACCOUNTABILITY ACT OF 1996

In 1996, Congress passed the Health Insurance Portability and Accountability Act (HIPAA) due to additional concerns about fraud (e.g., coding irregularities, medical necessity issues, and waiving of copays and deductibles). While the Federal False Claims Act provided HCFA with regulatory authority to enforce fraud and abuse statutes for the Medicare program, HIPAA extends that authority to all federal and state health care programs.

The **Health Insurance Portability and Accountability Act of 1996 (HIPAA)**, Public Law 104-191, amended the Internal Revenue Code of 1986, to:

- improve the portability and continuity of health insurance coverage in the group and individual markets.

- combat waste, fraud, and abuse in health insurance and health care delivery.

- promote the use of medical savings accounts.

- improve access to long-term care services and coverage.

- simplify the administration of health insurance by creating unique identifiers for providers, health plans, employers, and individuals.

- create standards for electronic health information transactions.

- create privacy standards for health information.

A discussion on each HIPAA component follows, and although HIPAA standards are still being finalized, health care organizations should develop and implement a response to each component.

INTERNET LINKS

CMS business activities with regard to HIPAA can be found at http://.cms.gov/hipaa

Educate your staff about HIPAA and Medicare issues. Download free interactive computer-based training courses and learn about satellite programs designed to teach Medicare billing guidelines at http://.cms.hhs.gov/medlearn.

Portability and Continuity of Health Insurance Coverage

HIPAA provisions were designed to improve the portability and continuity of health coverage by:

- limiting exclusions for pre-existing medical conditions.
- providing credit for prior health coverage and a process for transmitting certificates and other information concerning prior coverage to a new group health plan or issuer.
- providing new rights that allow individuals to enroll for health coverage when they lose other health coverage, change from group to individual coverage, or have a new dependent.
- prohibiting discrimination in enrollment and premiums against employees and their dependents based on health status.
- guaranteeing availability of health insurance coverage for small employers and renewability of health insurance coverage in both the small and large group markets.
- preserving, through narrow preemption provisions, the states' traditional role in regulating health insurance, including state flexibility to provide greater protections.

Fraud and Abuse

HIPAA defines **fraud** as "an intentional deception or misrepresentation that someone makes, knowing it is false, that could result in an unauthorized payment." The attempt itself is considered fraud, regardless of whether it is successful. **Abuse** "involves actions that are inconsistent with accepted, sound medical, business, or fiscal practices. Abuse directly or indirectly results in unnecessary costs to the program through improper payments." The difference between fraud and abuse is the individual's intent; however, both have the same impact in that they steal valuable resources from the health care industry. The most common forms of Medicare fraud include:

- billing for services not furnished.
- misrepresenting the diagnosis to justify payment.
- soliciting, offering, or receiving a kickback.
- unbundling codes (reporting multiple CPT codes to increase reimbursement, when a single combination code should be reported).
- falsifying certificates of medical necessity, plans of treatment, and medical records to justify payment.
- billing for a service that was not furnished.

Examples of abuse include:

- excessive charges for services, equipment, or supplies.
- submitting claims for items or services that are not medically necessary to treat the patient's stated condition.
- improper billing practices that result in a payment by a government program when the claim is the legal responsibility of another third-party payer.
- violations of participating provider agreements with insurance companies.

When a Medicare provider commits fraud, an investigation is conducted by the Department of Health and Human Services (DHHS) Office of the Inspector General (OIG). The OIG Office of Investigations prepares the case for referral to the Department of Justice for criminal and/or civil prosecution. A person found guilty of Medicare fraud faces criminal, civil, and/or administrative sanction penalties including:

- civil penalties of $5,000 to $10,000 per false claim plus triple damages under the False Claims Act. (The provider pays an amount equal to three times the claim submitted in addition to the civil penalties fine.)
- criminal fines and/or imprisonment of up to ten years if convicted of the crime of health care fraud as outlined in HIPAA or, for violations of the Medicare/Medicaid Anti-Kickback Statute, imprisonment of up to five years and/or a criminal fine of up to $25,000.
- administrative sanctions including up to a $10,000 civil monetary penalty per line item on a false claim, assessments of up to triple the amount falsely claimed, and/or exclusion from participation in Medicare and state health care programs.

In addition to the penalties outlined above, those who commit health care fraud can also be tried for Mail and Wire Fraud.

EXAMPLE: Medical review of claims submitted to Medicare by a physician group practice that contains mental health providers identified a pattern of psychiatric services billed on behalf of nursing facility patients with a medical history of dementia. Review of patient record documentation revealed no mental health care physician orders or plans of treatment. This is an example of billing for services not furnished.

The DHHS Office of Inspector General (OIG) published the final *Compliance Program Guidance for Individual and Small Group Physician Practices* in the October 5, 2000 *Federal Register.* The intent of the guidance is to help physicians in individual and small group practices design voluntary compliance programs that best fit the needs of individual practices. By law, physicians are not subject to civil, administrative or criminal penalties for innocent errors, or even negligence. The civil False Claims Act covers only offenses that are committed with *actual knowledge* of the falsity of the claim, *reckless disregard* or *deliberate ignorance* of the truth or falsity of a claim. (The False Claims Act does not cover mistakes, errors or negligence.) The OIG has stated that it is mindful of the difference between innocent errors (e.g., erroneous claims) and reckless or intentional conduct (e.g., fraudulent claims).

A voluntary compliance program can help physicians identify erroneous and fraudulent claims by ensuring that submitted claims are true and accurate, expediting and optimizing proper payment of claims, minimizing billing mistakes, and avoiding conflicts with self-referral and antikickback statutes. Unlike other guidance previously issued by the OIG (e.g., *Third-Party Medical Billing Company Compliance Program Guidance*), the final physician guidance does not require that physician practices implement all seven standard components of a full scale compliance program. (While the seven components provide a solid basis upon which a physician practice can create a compliance program, the OIG acknowledges that full implementation of all components may not be feasible for smaller physician practices.) Instead, the guidance emphasizes a step-by-step approach for those practices to follow in developing and implementing a voluntary compliance program.

As a first step, physician practices can begin by identifying risk areas which, based on a practice's specific history with billing problems and other compliance issues, might benefit from closer scrutiny and corrective/educational measures. The step-by-step approach is as follows:

1. Perform periodic audits to internally monitor billing practices.

2. Develop written practice standards and procedures.

3. Designate a compliance officer to monitor compliance efforts and enforce practice standards.

4. Conduct appropriate training and education about practice standards and procedures.

5. Respond appropriately to detected violations by investigating allegations and disclosing incidents to appropriate government entities.

6. Develop open lines of communication (e.g., discussions at staff meetings regarding erroneous or fraudulent conduct issues) to keep practice employees updated regarding compliance activities.

7. Enforce disciplinary standards through well-publicized guidelines.

The final guidance further identifies four specific compliance risk areas for physicians: (1) proper coding and billing; (2) ensuring that services are reasonable and necessary; (3) proper documentation; and (4) avoiding improper inducements, kickbacks and self-referrals. These risk areas reflect areas in which the OIG has focused its investigations and audits related to physician practices. The final guidance also provides direction to larger practices in developing compliance programs by recommending that they use both the physician guidance and previously issued guidance, such as the *Third-Party Medical Billing Company Compliance Program Guidance* or the *Clinical Laboratory Compliance Program Guidance*, to create a compliance program that meets the needs of the larger practice.

INTERNET LINK

The OIG Fraud Prevention and Detection program is available at http://oig.hhs.gov

Payment Error Prevention Program (PEPP)

In 1997, the Office of Inspector General (OIG) of Health and Human Services (HHS) reported that approximately $4 billion in improper Medicare payments were made for inpatient services under the diagnosis related group (DRG) prospective payment system (PPS). The **Payment Error Prevention Program (PEPP)** was initiated, and requires facilities to identify and reduce improper Medicare payments and, specifically, the Medicare payment error rate. (CMS defines the **payment error rate** as the number of dollars found to be paid in error out of the total of all dollars paid for inpatient PPS services.) CMS determines the inpatient payment error rate for each state, and facility performance is evaluated in part on the basis of reductions in this payment error rate. **Clinical Data Abstraction Centers (CDACs)** were established and became responsible for initially requesting and screening medical records for the PEPP surveillance sample for medical review, DRG validation, and medical necessity. Medical review criteria applied by the CDACs to screen medical records were developed by Peer Review Organizations (PROs), now called Quality Improvement Organizations (QIOs).

Overpayment Recovery

Overpayments are funds a provider or beneficiary has received in excess of amounts due and payable under Medicare and Medicaid statutes and regulations. Once a determination of overpayment has been made, the amount so determined is a debt owed to the United States Government. The **Federal Claims Collection Act of 1966** requires carriers and fiscal intermediaries (as agents of the federal government) to attempt the collection of overpayments. Examples of overpayments include:

- payment based on a charge that exceeds the reasonable charge.
- duplicate processing of charges/claims.
- payment to a physician on a nonassigned claim or to a beneficiary on an assigned claim. (Payment made to wrong payee.)
- payment for noncovered items and services, including medically unnecessary services.
- incorrect application of the deductible or coinsurance.
- payment for items or services rendered during a period of nonentitlement.
- primary payment for items or services for which another entity is the primary payer.
- payment for items or services rendered after the beneficiary's date of death. (Post-payment reviews are conducted to identify and recover payments with a billed date of service that is after the beneficiary's date of death.)

When a carrier or fiscal intermediary determines that an overpayment was made, it proceeds with recovery by issuing an overpayment demand letter (Figure 5-10) to the provider. The letter contains information about the review and statistical sampling methodology used as well as corrective actions to be taken. (An explanation of the sampling methodology that was followed is included.) Corrective actions include payment suspension, imposition of civil money penalties, institution of pre- or post-payment review, additional edits, and so on.

Providers and beneficiaries can receive a waiver of recovery of overpayments if one or more of the following provisions apply:

- Overpayment was discovered subsequent to the third calendar year after the year of payment.
- If an overpaid physician is found to be without fault or is deemed without fault, overpayment shifts to the beneficiary (e.g., medically unnecessary services).
- When both provider and beneficiary are without fault with respect to an overpayment on an assigned claim for medically unnecessary services, liability is waived for the overpayment (e.g., no action taken to recover the overpayment).
- If a beneficiary is liable for an incorrect payment, CMS or SSA may waive recovery if the beneficiary was without fault with respect to the overpayment and recovery would cause financial hardship or would be against equity and good conscience.

Carriers and fiscal intermediaries are prohibited from seeking overpayment recovery when the following two time limitations apply:

- Overpayment is not reopened within four years (48 months) after the date of payment, unless the case involves fraud or similar fault.

(Insert Medicare carrier letterhead here)

May 15, YYYY

Doug M. Smith, M.D.
393 Main St
Anywhere US 12345

RE: EMPLOYEE: **Nathan A. Sanders**   CLAIM #:   **939395SLD0005**
      SSN: **123-45-6789**   GROUP #:   **02365**
      PATIENT: **Nathan A. Sanders**   DIV DESC: **PRODUCTION MAIL**
      EMPLOYER: **Global Center**   LOC DESC: **NY**

Dear Provider:

Please be advised that an overpayment of benefits has been made for the above named patient. In order to resolve this matter we are asking you to make reimbursement. Please make your check payable to:

GLOBAL CARE MEDICAL CENTER

in the amount of

$675.00

and forward it to:

EMPIRE STATE HEALTH PLAN
P.O. BOX 93902
ANYWHERE US 12345

We are requesting this refund due to the following reason:

CLAIM WAS PROCESSED UNDER THE WRONG PATIENT FOR DATES OF SERVICE 4/15 & 4/20/YYYY.

If you have any questions, please feel free to contact us.

Sincerely,

Mary Louise Smith
Claims Analyst (39-392)

FIGURE 5-10 Sample overpayment letter

- Overpayment is discovered later than three full calendar years after the year of payment unless there is evidence that the provider or beneficiary was at fault with respect to the overpayment.

Provider Liability for Overpayments

Providers are liable for refunding an overpayment in the following situations:

- Overpayment resulted from incorrect reasonable charge determination (because providers are responsible for knowing Medicare reasonable charges for services).

   Exception: If the provider's reasonable charge screen was increased and the physician had no reason to question the amount of the increase, the physician is not liable and the case is referred to CMS for review.

● **NOTE:** If the provider has reason to believe the increase was excessive, the provider is liable unless the question was brought promptly to the attention of the carrier or fiscal intermediary who assured the physician that the increase was correct. ●

● Provider received duplicate payments from the carrier or fiscal intermediary (because the claim was processed more than once, or the provider submitted duplicate claims).

● **NOTE:** The provider does not have a reasonable basis for assuming that the total payment received was correct and thus should have questioned it. The provider is, therefore, at fault and liable for the overpayment. ●

● Provider received payment on the basis of **assignment** (the provider agreed to accept as payment whatever the payer deemed a reasonable charge), and a beneficiary received payment on an itemized bill and submitted that payment to the provider.

● **NOTE:** The provider is liable for the portion of the total amount paid in excess of the reasonable charge (including any copayment paid by the beneficiary). The beneficiary is liable for the balance of the overpayment. If the provider protests recovery of the overpayment on the grounds that all or part of the check received from the beneficiary was applied to amounts the beneficiary owed for other services, the beneficiary, rather than the physician, is liable for refunding such amounts. ●

● **EXAMPLE:** Mary Sue Patient underwent office surgery on May 15 performed by Dr. Smith. Medicare determined the reasonable charge for the office surgery to be $375. In July, Dr. Smith and Mary Sue Patient each received a check from Medicare in the amount of $300. Mary Sue Patient then signed her $300 over to Dr. Smith. Thus, Dr. Smith received a total of $600 for services provided on May 15, an overpayment of $225 (the amount received in excess of the reasonable charge). Mary Sue Patient is liable for the remaining $75 of the duplicate payment. (If Mary Sue Patient had also previously paid Dr. Smith the $75 as coinsurance, Dr. Smith would be liable for the entire $300 overpayment.) *Dr. Smith is responsible for contacting the Medicare carrier to report the overpayment and make arrangements to provide a refund to the carrier.* ●

● Provider received duplicate payments from Medicare and another payer directly or through the beneficiary, which happens to be the primary payer (e.g., automobile medical or no-fault insurer, liability insurer, or workers' compensation).

● **NOTE:** The provider is liable for the portion of the Medicare payment in excess of the amount Medicare is obligated to pay as a secondary payer. However, if the provider signs the other insurance payment over to the beneficiary, the beneficiary is liable. ●

● Provider was paid but does not accept assignment.

● **NOTE:** The provider is liable whether or not the beneficiary had also been paid. ●

- Provider furnished erroneous information, or provider failed to disclose facts known or that should have been known and that were material to payment of benefit.

  EXAMPLE 1: A beneficiary is referred to a provider by an employer for a fracture that occurred during a fall at work. The physician billed Medicare and neglected to indicate on the claim that the injury was work-related (although that information had been provided by the patient). If Medicare benefits are paid to the provider for services and the injury would have been covered by workers' compensation, the provider is liable for an overpayment because of failure to disclose that the injury was work-related.

  EXAMPLE 2: A provider submitted an assigned claim showing total charges of $1,000. The provider did not indicate on the claim that any portion of the bill had been paid by the patient. The carrier determined the reasonable charge to be $600 and paid the physician $480 (80% of $600) on the assumption that no other payment had been received. The carrier later learned that the beneficiary had paid the physician $200 before the provider submitted his claim. Thus, the payment should have been split between provider and beneficiary with $400 paid to the provider and $80 to the beneficiary. The provider is liable for causing the $80 overpayment as the amount received from the beneficiary was not reported on the claim. ●

- Provider submitted a claim for services other than medically unnecessary services, but should have known they would not be covered (e.g., conversation with a relative of a beneficiary).

  NOTE: Generally, allegations by a provider as not liable for payments received for noncovered services because provider was unaware of coverage provisions is not a basis for finding the provider without fault.

- Provider submitted a claim for medically unnecessary services.

  NOTE: In these matters, criteria for determining whether the provider knew or should have known that services were not covered are followed by carriers and fiscal intermediaries. ●

- Items or services were furnished by provider or supplier not qualified for Medicare reimbursement.

  EXAMPLE 1: A lab test is performed by a nonqualified independent laboratory.

  EXAMPLE 2: Services are rendered by a naturopath. ●

- Overpayment was due to a mathematical or clerical error.

  NOTE: The failure to properly assess the deductible is not considered a mathematical error. ●

- Provider does not submit documentation to substantiate services billed or where there is question as to whether services were actually performed (e.g., fraud is suspected).

- Overpayment was for rental of durable medical equipment, and supplier billed under the one-time authorization procedure.

NOTE: Suppliers of durable medical equipment who have accepted assignment may be reimbursed for rental items on the basis of a one-time authorization by the beneficiary (e.g., without the need to obtain beneficiary's signature each month). A supplier using the procedure must have filed with the carrier a statement that it assumes unconditional responsibility for rental overpayments for periods after the beneficiary's death or while beneficiary was institutionalized or no longer needed or used the equipment. ●

Absence of Provider Liability for Overpayments

A provider is liable for overpayments received unless found to be *without fault* as determined by the carrier or fiscal intermediary. A provider can be considered without fault if reasonable care was exercised in billing for and accepting payment, and the provider had a reasonable basis for assuming that payment was correct. In addition, if the provider had reason to question the payment and promptly brought the question to the attention of the carrier or fiscal intermediary, he may be found without liability.

NOTE: The provider must make full disclosure to the carrier or fiscal intermediary of all material facts and the basis on which information was made available, including, but not limited to, Medicare regulations. ●

The above criteria are always met in the case of overpayments due to an error with respect to the beneficiary's entitlement to Medicare benefits and the carrier's or fiscal intermediary's failure to properly apply the deductible. Normally, it is clear from the circumstances of the overpayment whether the provider was without fault in causing the overpayment. When this is not clear from the record, the carrier or fiscal intermediary must review the issue (as long as the review occurs within three calendar years after the year in which the overpayment was made).

Correct Coding Initiative

The Centers for Medicare and Medicaid Services (CMS) developed the National *Correct Coding Initiative (CCI)* in 1996 to reduce Medicare program expenditures by detecting inappropriate codes submitted on claims and denying payment for them, promoting national correct coding methodologies, and eliminating improper coding practices. (Table 5-1 contains a list of CCI terms, definitions and examples.) There are over 140,000 CCI **code pairs** (or **edit pairs**) that cannot be reported on the same claim, and they are based on coding conventions defined in CPT, current standards of medical and surgical coding practice, input from specialty societies, and analysis of current coding practices. CMS contracts with AdminaStar Federal, Inc., an Indiana Medicare carrier, to develop and maintain coding edits, which are published by the National Technical Information Service (NTIS).

INTERNET LINKS

CCI Edits Manual from NTIS	http://www.ntis.gov
AdminaStar Federal, Inc.	http://www.adminastar.com
Medicare's National CCI Edits	http://www.cms.hhs.gov/medlearn/ncci.asp

TABLE 5-1 Medicare's National CCI terms and definitions

TERM	DEFINITION	EXAMPLE
CCI Edits	Pairs of CPT and/or HCPCS level II codes, which are not separately payable except under certain circumstances (e.g., reporting appropriate modifier). The edits are applied to services billed by the same provider for the same beneficiary on the same date of service.	The surgeons intends to perform laparoscopic cholecystectomy; upon visualization of the gallbladder, it is determined than an open cholecystectomy is required. If the surgeon reports CPT codes for removal of an organ through an open incision as well as with laparoscopy, the CCI edit results in claims denial. NOTE: If a laparoscopic procedure becomes an open procedure, report only the open procedure code. ●
Comprehensive Code	The major procedure or service when reported with another code. The *comprehensive code* represents greater work, effort, and time as compared to the other code reported. (Also called "column 1 codes.") Higher payments are associated with comprehensive codes.	The patient undergoes deep biopsy as well as superficial biopsy of the same site. If the surgeon reports CPT codes for the deep and superficial biopsy, the CCI edit results in claims denial. NOTE: Report only the deep biopsy when both deep and superficial biopsies are performed at the same location. ● If the surgeon determines that the superficial biopsy code should be reported in addition to the deep biopsy code, supporting documentation in the patient's record must be evident. NOTE: A modifier must be added to the code.
Component Code	The lesser procedure or service when reported with another code. The *component code* is part of a major procedure or service, and is often represented by a lower work relative value unit (RVU) under the Medicare Physician Fee Schedule as compared to the other code reported. (Also called *column 2 codes*.) Lower payments are associated with component codes.	A **modifier** is a two-digit code added to the main code to indicate a procedure/service has been altered (e.g., bilateral procedure). ●
Comprehensive/ Component Edit Table (Figure 5-11	Code combinations (or edit pairs), where one of the codes is a component of the more comprehensive code and only the comprehensive code is paid. (If clinical circumstances justify appending a CCI associated modifier to either code of a code pair edit, payment of both codes may be allowed.)	Figure 5-11 contains a partial listing of comprehensive/component codes. Refer to Column 1 code 10140. If code 10140 is reported on a CMS-1500 claim, none of the codes from Column 2 can be reported on the same claim (unless a modifier is attached and supporting documentation is found in the patient's record).

(continues)

TABLE 5-1   *(continued)*

TERM	DEFINITION	EXAMPLE
Mutually Exclusive Codes	Procedures or services that could not reasonably be performed at the same session by the same provider on the same beneficiary.	A claim that contains codes for cystourethros-scopy, with internal urethrotomy of a female (CPT code 52270) with that of a male (CPT code 52275) will result in denial as a result of this CCI edit.
Mutually Exclusive Edit Table (Figure 5-12)	Code combinations (or edit pairs), where one of the procedures/services would not reasonably be performed with the other. (If clinical circumstances justify adding a CCI modifier to either code of a code pair edit, payment of both codes may be allowed.)	Figure 5-12 contains a partial listing of mutually exclusive codes. Refer to Column 1 code 10060. If code 10060 is reported on a CMS-1500 claim, none of the codes from Column 2 can be reported on the same claim (unless a modifier is attached and supporting documentation is found in the patient's record).

CORRECT CODING EDITS FOR COMPREHENSIVE CODES 10000-19999   CPT codes only © Copyright AMA

Comprehensive	Component	Comprehensive	Component
10021	19290	10140	11055, 11056, 11057, 11719,
10022	10021, 19290		11720, 11721, 69990, G0127
10040	69990	10160	11055, 11056, 11057, 11719,
10060	11055, 11056, 11057, 11719,		11720, 11721, 69990, G0127

FIGURE 5-11 Partial listing of Correct Coding Edits for Comprehensive/Component Code Edits (This figure is for illustrative purposes only and may not represent current version published in NTIS manual.)

CORRECT CODING EDITS FOR MUTUALLY EXCLUSIVE CODES 10000-19999   CPT codes only © Copyright AMA

Column 1	Column 2	Column 1	Column 2
10060	11401, 11402, 11403, 11404,	10160	10061, 10140
	11406, 11421, 11422, 11423,	11000	11010, 11011, 11012, 11056,
	11424, 11426, 11441, 11442,		11057, 15000, 97601
	11443, 11444, 11446, 11450,	11010	20150, 20561, 20662, 20663

FIGURE 5-12 Partial Listing of Mutually Exclusive Correct Coding Edits (This figure is for illustrative purposes only and may not represent current version published in NTIS manual.)

CCI edits are also available as part of vendor encoder software, including the CodeCorrect.com online product at http://www.codecorrect.com, which is updated as new versions of CCI edits become available.

EncoderPro software from Ingenix includes CCI unbundling edits. Go to http://www.ingenixonline.com and click on Software for more information.

NOTE: Under a previous CMS contract, a private company refused to publish code edits they developed because they considered them proprietary; these nonpublished code edits were called **black box edits**. Use of these edits was discontinued when CMS did not renew its contract with the company, and future CMS contracts do not allow for such restrictions. ●

Medical Savings Accounts

HIPAA permits eligible individuals to establish a *medical savings account (MSA)*, a tax-exempt trust or custodial account established for the purpose of paying medical expenses in conjunction with a high-deductible health plan. Individuals eligible to establish an MSA include:

- an employee (or spouse of an employee) of a "small employer" that maintains an individual or family "high-deductible health plan" covering that individual (employee or spouse), or
- a self-employed person (or spouse of self-employed person) that maintains an individual or family "high-deductible health plan" covering that individual (self-employed person or spouse).

Access to Long-Term Care Services

HIPAA contains tax clarification provisions for long-term care insurance to assure that the tax treatment for private long-term care insurance is the same as for major medical coverage. Insurance companies must also follow certain administrative and marketing practices or face significant fines.

EXAMPLE 1: Consumers must be provided with a description of the policy's benefits and limitations before making a commitment to allow consumers to compare policies from different companies.

EXAMPLE 2: Companies must report annually the number of claims denied, information on policy replacement sales, and policy terminations data. ●

No policy can be sold as a long-term care insurance policy if it limits or excludes coverage by type of treatment, medical condition, or accident. An exception to this rule, however, includes policies that may limit or exclude coverage for pre-existing conditions or diseases, mental or nervous disorders (but not Alzheimer's), or alcoholism or drug addiction. The law also prohibits a company from canceling a policy except for nonpayment of premiums.

Administrative Simplification

HIPAA was part of a Congressional attempt at incremental health care reform, with the *Administrative Simplification* aspect requiring DHHS to develop standards for maintenance and transmission of health information required to identify individual patients. These standards are designed to:

- improve efficiency and effectiveness of the health care system by standardizing the interchange of electronic data for specified administrative and financial transactions.
- protect the security and confidentiality of electronic health information.

The requirements outlined by law and the regulations implemented by DHHS require compliance by *all* health care organizations that maintain or transmit electronic health information (e.g., health plans; health care clearinghouses; and health care providers, from large integrated delivery networks to individual physician offices).

The law also provides for significant financial penalties for violations.

General penalty for failure to comply:

- each violation: $100
- maximum penalty for all violations of an identical requirement: may not exceed $25,000

Wrongful disclosure of individually identifiable health information:

- wrongful disclosure offense: $50,000; imprisonment of not more than one year; or both
- offense under false pretenses: $100,000; imprisonment of not more than 5 years; or both
- offense with intent to sell information: $250,000; imprisonment of not more than 10 years; or both.

Unique Identifiers

The administrative simplification (AS) provision of HIPAA requires establishment of standard identifiers for third-party payers (e.g., insurance companies, Medicare, and Medicaid), providers, and employers, as follows:

- **National Health PlanID (PlanID)** (formerly called PAYERID) will be assigned to third-party payers; it is expected to have ten numeric positions, including a check digit as the tenth position. (A **check digit** is a one-digit character, alphabetic or numeric, which is used to verify the validity of a unique identifier.)
- **National Individual Identifier** (patient identifier) has been put on hold. Several bills in Congress would eliminate the requirement to establish a National Individual Identifier.

  NOTE: California implemented a regulation that prohibits the use of social security numbers on health plan ID cards and health-related correspondence.

- **National Provider Identifier (NPI)** will be assigned to health care providers as an 8- or possibly 10-character alphanumeric identifier, including a check digit in the last position.

- **National Standard Employer Identifier Number (EIN)** is assigned to employers who, as sponsors of health insurance for their employees, need to be identified in health care transactions. It is the federal employer identification number (EIN) assigned by the Internal Revenue Service (IRS) and has nine digits with a hyphen (00-0000000). EIN assignment by the IRS began in January 1998.

Electronic Health Care Transactions

HIPAA requires payers to implement **electronic transaction standards** (or transactions rule), which is a uniform language for electronic data interchange. **Electronic data interchange (EDI)** is the process of sending data from one party to another using computer linkages. The CMS Standard EDI Enrollment Form must be completed prior to submitting electronic media claims (EMC) to Medicare. The agreement must be executed by each provider of health care services, physician, or supplier that intends to submit EMC.

EXAMPLE: Health care providers submit electronic claims data to payers on computer tape, diskette, or by computer modem or fax. The payer receives the claim, processes the data, and sends the provider the results of processing electronic claims (an electronic transmittal notice). ●

NOTE: Computer-generated paper claims are not categorized as EDI. ●

The final rule on transactions and code sets was effective October 16, 2002 for large plans and October 16, 2003 for small plans. It requires the following to be used by health plans, health care **clearinghouses** (which perform centralized claims processing for providers and health plans), and health care providers who participate in electronic data interchanges:

- Three electronic formats are supported for health care claim transactions, including the UB-92 flat-file format, the National Standard Format (NSF), and the ANSI ASC X12 837 (American National Standards Institute (ANSI), Accredited Standards Committee (ASC), Insurance Subcommittee (X12N), Claims validation tables (837).

    NOTE: A **flat file** consists of a series of fixed-length records (e.g., 25 spaces for patient's name). The **UB-92** flat file is used to bill institutional services, such as services performed in hospitals. The **National Standard Format (NSF)** flat file format is used to bill physician and noninstitutional services, such as services reported by a general practitioner on a CMS-1500 claim. The **ANSI ASC X12 837** variable-length file format is used to bill institutional, professional, dental, and drug claims. ●

- Dental services are using *Current Dental Terminology* (CDT) codes. **Current Dental Terminology (CDT)** is a medical code set that is maintained and copyrighted by the American Dental Association.

- Diagnoses and inpatient hospital services are reported using *International Classification of Diseases, 9th Revision, Clinical Modification* (ICD-9-CM) codes.

    NOTE: This will change to ICD-10-CM when adopted for implementation (possibly 2005). ●

- Physician services are reported using *Current Procedural Terminology* (CPT) codes.

- Procedures are reported using: ICD-9-CM (Index to Procedures and Tabular List of Procedures) and the *Healthcare Common Procedure Coding System* (HCPCS), *Level I* (CPT) and *Level II (national)* codes.

- Institutional and professional pharmacy transactions are reported using HCPCS, *Level II (national)* codes.

- Retail pharmacy transactions are reported using the *National Drug Code* (NDC) manual.

The **National Drug Code** (NDC) is maintained by the Food and Drug Administration (FDA) and identifies prescription drugs and some over the counter products. Each drug product is assigned a unique 11-digit, 3-segment number, which identifies the vendor, product, and trade package size.

INTERNET LINKS

ANSI ASC X12N 837 implementation guides are available at http://www.wpc-edi.com

Retail pharmacy standards implementation guide is available at http://www.ncpdp.org

Go to http://cms.hhs.gov and click the Medicare link, and then the Electronic Data Interchange (EDI) link to download the CMS Standard EDI Enrollment Form.

Privacy Standards

HHS published the final Privacy Rule on December 28, 2000, and the final rule took effect on April 14, 2001. The **Privacy Rule** creates national standards to protect individuals' medical records and other personal health information. This rule also gives patients greater access to their own medical records and more control over how their personal health information is used. The rule addresses the obligations of health care providers and health plans to protect health information. By law, covered entities (health plans, health care clearinghouses, and health care providers who conduct certain financial and administrative transactions electronically) have until April 14, 2003, to comply. (Small health plans have until April 14, 2004, to comply.) The HHS Office for Civil Rights (OCR) has implementation and enforcement responsibility for the Privacy Rule.

NOTE: Covered entities are bound by the Privacy Rule even if they contract with business associates to perform some of their essential functions. A **business associate** is a person or entity that provides certain functions, activities, or services for or to a covered entity, involving the use and/or disclosure of protected health information (PHI).

On July 6, 2001, OCR issued the first in a series of guidance materials that answer some of the questions about the new protections for consumers and requirements for doctors, hospitals, other providers, health plans and health insurers, and health care clearinghouses. It also clarifies some of the confusion regarding the meaning of key provisions of the rule. Final modifications to the Privacy Rule were published in the August 14, 2002 *Federal Register*, and a new subpart was added—*Subpart E: Privacy of Individually Identifiable Health Information*. The Privacy Rule requires the implementation of activities, such as:

- providing information to patients about their privacy rights and how their information can be used.
- adopting clear privacy procedures for its practice, hospital, or plan.
- training employees so they understand the privacy procedures.
- designating an individual to be responsible for seeing that the privacy procedures are adopted and followed.
- securing patient records containing individually identifiable health information so that they are not readily available to those who do not need them.

To ease the burden of complying with the new requirements, the Privacy Rule incorporates flexibility for providers and plans to create their own privacy procedures, tailored to fit their size and needs. For example:

- The privacy official at a small physician practice may be the office manager, who will have other nonprivacy related duties; the privacy official at a large health plan may be a full-time position, and may have the regular support and advice of a privacy staff or board.
- The training requirement may be satisfied by a small physician practice's providing each new member of the workforce with a copy of its privacy policies and documenting that new members have reviewed the policies, whereas a large health plan may provide training through live instruction, video presentations, or interactive software programs.
- The policies and procedures of small providers may be more limited under the rule than those of a large hospital or health plan, based on the volume of health information maintained and the number of interactions with those within and outside of the health care system.

INTERNET LINKS

Guidance materials can be found at http://aspe.hhs.gov by clicking on the *Administrative Simplification in the Health Care Industry (HIPAA)* link

The HHS Office for Civil Rights provides information on the new regulation at http://www.hhs.gov/ocr/hipaa

Sample business associate contract provisions can be found at http://www.hhs.gov/ocr/hipaa/contractprov.html

> **NOTE:** Patient access to personal information in CMS's records is also governed by the *Privacy Act of 1974,* which protects Federal records that can be retrieved by a personal identifier. ●

> **NOTE:** The Privacy Rule does not preempt state laws that are more restrictive than federal regulations. ●

HHS recognizes that the privacy standards are restrictive, and the following revisions are under consideration:

- *Phoned-in Prescriptions:* Pharmacists will be permitted to continue filling prescriptions phoned in by a patient's doctor before obtaining the patient's written consent.

- *Referral Appointments:* Direct treatment providers receiving a first time patient referral will be permitted to schedule appointments, surgery, or other procedures before obtaining the patient's signed consent. A **direct treatment provider** is one who treats a patient directly, rather than based on the orders of another provider, and/or provides health care services or test results directly to patients.

- *Allowable Communications:* Covered entities will be free to engage in whatever communications are required for quick, effective, high quality health care, including routine oral communications with family members, treatment discussions with staff involved in coordination of patient care, and using patient names to locate them in waiting areas.

- *Minimum Necessary Scope:* Certain common practices, such as the use of sign-up sheets and X-ray lightboards, and maintenance of patient medical charts at the bedside are allowed under the rule.

- *Parents and Minors:* Parents will continue to have appropriate access to information about the health and well-being of their children.

The Privacy Rule establishes a federal requirement that doctors, hospitals, or other health care providers obtain a patient's written consent and an authorization before using or disclosing the patient's protected health information (PHI) to carry out *treatment, payment, or health care operations (TPO)*. A **consent** is a general document that gives health care providers, who have a direct treatment relationship with a patient, permission to use and disclose all PHI for TPO. It gives permission only to that provider, not to any other person, and one consent covers all uses and disclosures for TPO by that provider indefinitely.) The Privacy Rule establishes a uniform standard for certain health care providers to obtain their patients' consent for uses and disclosures of health information about the patient to carry out TPO. An **authorization** is a customized document that gives covered entities permission to use specified PHI for specified purposes, which are generally other than TPO, or to disclose PHI to a third party specified by the individual. It covers only the uses and disclosures and only the PHI stipulated in the authorization; it has an expiration date; and, in some cases, it also states the purpose for which the information may be used or disclosed. The Privacy Rule also requires that "reasonable steps" be taken to ensure that patient records are secured at all times (e.g., storing records in locked cabinets to prevent unauthorized access).

NOTE: Privacy violations are subject to no more than $100 per person per violation not to exceed $25,000 per person per year per violation of a single standard. More serious violations are subject to more severe penalties, including:

- $50,000 and/or up to one year in prison for persons who knowingly obtain and disclose protected health information.

- $100,000 and/or up to five years in prison for persons who under "false pretense" obtain and disclose protected health information.

- $250,000 and up to 10 years in prison for persons with intent to sell, transfer, or use for malicious reasons or personal gain, protected health information.

SUMMARY

- Federal and state statutes are laws passed by legislative bodies, which are implemented as regulations (guidelines written by administrative agencies).

- Case law (or common law) is based on court decisions that establish a precedent (or standard).

- The *Federal Register* is a legal newspaper published every business day by the federal government.

- The *Medicare Bulletin* serves as a legal notice to providers about Medicare laws, regulations, and guidelines.

- A Medicare carrier contracts with CMS to process Medicare Part B claims, and a fiscal intermediary processes Medicare Part A claims.

- A listserv is a subscriber-based question-and-answer forum that is available through e-mail.

- Patient health care information must be maintained in a confidential and secure manner. Confidentiality restricts access to patient information (a patient authorization is required to release information). Privacy is the right of individuals to keep information from being disclosed to others. Security involves the safekeeping of patient information. Breach of confidentiality is the unauthorized release of information to a third party.

- A contract is an agreement between two or more parties to perform specific services or duties. A verbal contract is established between patient and provider when the patients seeks medical services.

- Patients must sign the "Authorization for Release of Medical Information" located in Block 12 of the CMS-1500 claim or sign a special release form that is maintained by the practice. (Enter SIGNATURE ON FILE in Block 12 of the CMS-1500 claim.)

- Special rules apply to the release of HIV/AIDS, drug/alcohol, and mental health information.

- Do not release information over the telephone unless you have verified that the person making the request is entitled to the information.

- Limit the submission of faxed information to that required to satisfy the immediate needs of the requesting party or to assist emergency health care situations.

- Sensitive information submitted via the Internet must be encrypted (converted to a secure language for transmission).

- Patient information and health insurance records must be maintained for a minimum of six years unless state law specifies a longer period.

- The Federal False Claims Act regulates fraudulent practices, such as upcoding (assigning an ICD-9-CM diagnosis code that does not match documentation to increase inpatient reimbursement).

- Stark II regulations legislate self-referrals by providers who order services to be performed for patients at a facility in which they have a financial interest.

- ERISA ensures that pension and other benefits are provided to employees as promised by their employers, and COBRA includes provisions for continuation of health care coverage if employment is discontinued due to a triggering event (e.g., layoff).

- Medical necessity is the measure of whether a health care procedure or service will be reimbursed by a payer. It is usually based on the recommendations of the provider and the payer's representative.

- HIPAA is the acronym for the Health Insurance Portability and Accountability Act of 1996, which includes many provisions: health insurance reform, administrative simplification, fraud and abuse guidelines, use of medical savings accounts, improved access to long-term care services and coverage, electronic health information transaction standards, and privacy and security standards for health information.

- The Payment Error Prevention Program (PEPP) identifies and reduces improper Medicare payments and the payment error rate. Overpayment recovery involves the collection of overpayments made to health care provided by Medicare, Medicaid, and other payers.

- The Correct Coding Initiative (CCI) was implemented to reduce Medicare program expenditures by detecting inappropriate coding on claims and denying payment for them.

STUDY CHECKLIST

- ☐ Read the textbook chapter and highlight key concepts.
- ☐ Create an index card for each key term.
- ☐ Access the chapter Internet links to learn more about concepts.
- ☐ Answer the chapter review questions, verifying answers with your instructor.

- ☐ Complete Web Tutor assignments and take online quizzes.
- ☐ Complete Workbook chapter, verifying answers with your instructor.
- ☐ Form a study group with classmates to discuss chapter concepts in preparation for an exam.

REVIEW

TRUE/FALSE

Indicate whether each statement is true or false.

1. ☐ T ☐ F Breach of confidentiality is the release of confidential patient information to a third party.

2. ☐ T ☐ F Fraud is the deception or misrepresentation made by an individual, knowing it to be false, which could result in some unauthorized benefit.

3. ☐ T ☐ F A contract is an agreement between two or more parties to perform specific services or duties.

4. ☐ T ☐ F A patient/provider contract for medical services is negotiated so that the payer will agree to promptly pay the physician's usual fee for services performed.

5. ☐ T ☐ F A guardian is a person who has legal responsibility for a minor child or incompetent adult.

SHORT ANSWER

Briefly respond to each of the following.

6. Identify the problem in each case scenario that results in a breach of confidentiality.

   a. An insurance company sends a letter on company letterhead requesting a copy of a patient's records in order to process payment. No other documents accompany the letter.

   b. An attorney calls the office and requests that a copy of his client's medical record be immediately faxed to the attorney's office.

   c. An insurance company calls the office to request information about a claim. Dates of service are confirmed as well as the patient's HIV status.

   d. Diagnostic and treatment data about a competent adult is requested by the patient's spouse.

   e. Case studies about patients are discussed in the classroom.

7. Explain how a health insurance specialist could unwittingly be involved in committing fraud by interacting with the following individuals:

   a. health care provider

   b. patient

   c. widow/widower of a deceased patient

8. List the monetary and/or prison term penalties for committing Medicare fraud.

9. Identify the overpayment amount for the following cases along with the liable party.

   a. Patient received services on April 5, totaling $1,000. The provider accepted assignment, and the payer established the reasonable charge as $450. On July 1, the provider received $360 from the insurance company, representing an 80% payment of the reasonable charge. The patient had paid a $90 coinsurance at the time of the visit. On August 1, the patient received a check from the insurance company in the amount of $450.

   b. Patient underwent office surgery on October 10, and Medicare determined the reasonable charge to be $650. The provider and patient each received a check for $500, and the patient signed the check over to the provider. The patient had not paid a coinsurance at the time of the office surgery.

   c. Patient was treated in the Emergency Department for a fractured arm. The chief complaint was "I was moving a file cabinet for my boss when it tipped over and fell on my arm." The facility billed the patient's employer group insurance policy and received reimbursement of $550.

   d. The provider submitted an assigned claim for which the payer determined the reasonable charge was $500. The payer reimbursed the provider $400 (80% of the reasonable charge). It was later determined that the patient had paid $200 at the time of the visit.

10. Identify the monetary and/or prison term penalties established by HIPAA for breaching a patient's protected health information.

KEY TERMS

Upon successful completion of this chapter, you should be able to:

1. Define key terms.
2. Discuss the difference between "primary diagnosis" and "principal diagnosis."
3. Explain the purpose of reporting diagnosis codes on insurance claims.
4. List and apply CMS guidelines in coding diagnoses.
5. Identify and properly use ICD-9-CM's special terms, marks, abbreviations, and symbols.
6. Accurately code all diagnoses according to ICD-9-CM.

INTRODUCTION

There are two related classifications of diseases with similar titles. The *International Classification of Diseases (ICD)* is published by the World Health Organization (WHO) and is used to code and classify **mortality** (death) data from death certificates. The *International Classification of Diseases, Clinical Modification* (ICD-9-CM) is developed in the United States and is used to code and classify **morbidity** (disease) data from inpatient and outpatient records, physician office records, and most statistical surveys. The health insurance specialist assigns ICD-9-CM codes to diagnoses, signs, and symptoms documented by the health care provider. Entering ICD-9-CM codes on the CMS-1500 claim results in uniform reporting of medical reasons for health services provided.

INTERNET LINK

If the ICD-9-CM coding system is being introduced to you for the first time, consider completing a workbook such as *Understanding Medical Coding: A Comprehensive Guide*, by Sandra J. Johnson, available for purchase from Delmar Learning at http://www.delmarhealthcare.com

INTRODUCTION TO ICD-9-CM

ICD-9-CM was sponsored in 1979 as the official system for assigning codes to diagnoses (inpatient and outpatient care, including physician offices) and procedures (inpatient care). The ICD-9-CM is organized into three volumes:

- Volume 1 (Tabular List)
- Volume 2 (Index to Diseases)
- Volume 3 (Index to Procedures and Tabular List)

The **National Center for Health Statistics (NCHS)** and CMS are U.S. Department of Health and Human Services agencies responsible for overseeing all changes and modifications to the ICD-9-CM. The NCHS works with the World Health Organization (WHO) to coordinate official disease classification activities for ICD-9-CM (Index to Diseases and Tabular List), which includes the use, interpretation, and periodic revision of the classification system. CMS is responsible for creating annual procedure classification updates for ICD-9-CM (Index to Procedures and Tabular List). Updates are available as downloads (DOS, Windows, and Macintosh versions) from the official ICD-9-CM Web site of the NCHS, and a CD-ROM version that contains official coding guidelines as well as the complete, official version of the ICD-9-CM is available for purchase online, by telephone, or by fax from the:

Superintendent of Documents
U.S. Government Printing Office
(888) 293-6498 or
(866) 512-1800
(202) 512-2250 (fax)
http://bookstore.gpo.gov

ICD-9-CM coding books are also available from commercial publishing companies and are helpful in manual coding because they contain color-coded entries that identify required additional digits, nonspecific and unacceptable principal diagnoses, and more.

INTERNET LINK

ICD-9-CM updates are available through a free download at http://www.cdc.gov/nchs/icd9.htm

You may purchase a CD-ROM that contains official coding guidelines and the complete official version of ICD-9-CM at http://bookstore.gpo.gov

Mandatory Reporting of ICD-9-CM Codes

The Medicare Catastrophic Coverage Act of 1988 mandated the reporting of ICD-9-CM diagnosis codes on Medicare claims. Private insurance carriers adopted similar diagnosis coding requirements for claims submission in subsequent years (reporting procedure codes is discussed in Chapters 7 and 8). Requiring codes to be reported on submitted claims ensures the medical necessity of procedures and services rendered to patients during an encounter (office visit, outpatient visit, or emergency department visit). *Medical necessity* is defined by Medicare as "the determination that a service or procedure rendered is reasonable and necessary for the diagnosis or treatment of an illness or injury." If it is possible that scheduled tests or services/procedures may be found "medically unnecessary" by Medicare, have the patient sign an **Advance Beneficiary Notice (ABN)**, which acknowledges patient responsibility for payment if Medicare denies the claim (the ABN is discussed in greater detail in Chapter 14).

NOTE: Be sure to clarify the definition of *medical necessity* by insurance companies (other than Medicare) because the definition can vary. ●

EXAMPLE: A patient with insulin-dependent diabetes is treated at the physician's office for treatment of a leg injury sustained from a fall. When the physician questions the patient about his general health status since the last visit, the patient admits to knowing that a person on insulin should perform a daily blood sugar level check; the patient also admits to usually skipping this check 1 or 2 times a week and not performing this check today. The physician orders an X-ray of the leg, which proves to be positive for a fracture, and a test of the patient's blood glucose level. If the only stated diagnosis on the claim is a fractured tibia, the blood glucose test would be rejected for payment by the insurance company as an unnecessary medical procedure. The diagnostic statement on the claim should include both the fractured tibia and insulin-dependent diabetes to permit reimbursement consideration for the X-ray and the blood glucose test. ●

ICD-9-CM Annual Updates

CMS and the NCHS annually update ICD-9-CM, so providers should order new code books no later than September of each year. New diagnosis codes officially go into effect on January 1 of each year, although some commercial carriers do not require or accept the new codes until March 1 because electronic systems must be updated to accept new codes.

ICD-10-CM and ICD-10-PCS

In 1992, the World Health Organization (WHO) completed work on the tenth revision, which has a new title: *The International Statistical Classification of Diseases and Related Health Problems* and a new alphanumeric coding system. It is expected that the change from ICD-9-CM to the NCHS-developed ICD-10-CM and the CMS-developed ICD-10-PCS (Procedure Coding System) will be mandated for 2005 or later. An overview of ICD-10-CM is included at the end of this chapter.

NOTE: There is not yet a scheduled implementation date for ICD-10-CM. There will be a two-year implementation window once the final notice to implement has been published in the *Federal Register.* ●

OUTPATIENT CODING GUIDELINES

The **Diagnostic Coding and Reporting Guidelines for Outpatient Services: Hospital-Based and Physician Office** were developed by the federal government for use in reporting diagnoses for claims submission. Four cooperating parties are involved in the continued development and approval of the guidelines:

1. American Hospital Association (AHA)
2. American Health Information Management Association (AHIMA)
3. Centers for Medicare & Medicaid Services (CMS, formerly HCFA)
4. National Center for Health Statistics (NCHS)

Although the guidelines were originally developed for use in submitting government claims, insurance companies have also adopted them (sometimes with variation).

● **NOTE:**

- Because variations may contradict the official guidelines, be sure to obtain each insurance company's official coding guidelines.
- When reviewing the guidelines, the terms *encounter* and *visit* are used interchangeably in describing outpatient and physician office services.
- Diagnoses often are not established at the time of the initial encounter/visit. It may take two or more visits before the diagnosis is confirmed. ●

CODING TIP:

The most critical rule involves beginning the search for the correct code assignment through the Alphabetic Index. Never begin searching for a code in the Tabular List because this will lead to coding errors.

A. ICD-9-CM Tabular List of Diseases

The appropriate code or codes from 001.0 through V82.9 must be used to identify diagnoses, symptoms, conditions, problems, complaints, or any other reason for the encounter/visit.

B. Accurate Reporting of ICD-9-CM Codes

For accurate reporting of ICD-9-CM diagnosis codes, the documentation should describe the patient's condition using terminology that includes specific diagnoses as well as symptoms, problems, or reasons for the encounter. There are ICD-9-CM codes to describe all of these.

C. Reason for Encounter

The selection of codes 001.0 through 999.9 will frequently be used to describe the reason for the encounter. These codes are from the section of ICD-9-CM for the classification of diseases and injuries (e.g. infectious and parasitic diseases; neoplasms; symptoms, signs, and ill-defined conditions).

D. Signs and Symptoms

Codes that describe signs and symptoms, as opposed to definitive diagnoses, are acceptable for reporting purposes when the physician has not documented a confirmed diagnosis. Chapter 16 of ICD-9-CM, "Symptoms, Signs, and Ill-defined Conditions" (codes 780.0–799.9), contains many, but not all, codes for symptoms. Some symptom codes are located in other ICD-9-CM chapters, which can be found by properly using the ICD-9-CM Index to Diseases.

E. Factors Influencing Health Status and Contact with Health Services (V Codes)

ICD-9-CM provides codes to deal with encounters for circumstances other than a disease or injury. The Supplementary Classification of Factors Influencing Health Status and Contact with Health Services (V01.0–V82.9) is provided to deal with occasions when circumstances other than a disease or injury are recorded as diagnosis or problems.

F. Category, Subcategory, and Subclassification Codes

ICD-9-CM is composed of codes that contain 3, 4, or 5 digits. Codes with 3 digits are included in ICD-9-CM as the heading of a category of codes that may be further subdivided by the use of fourth and/or fifth digits, which provide greater specificity.

A three-digit code is to be used only if it is not further subdivided. Where fourth-digit subcategories and/or fifth-digit subclassifications are provided, they must be assigned. A code is invalid if it has not been coded to the full number of digits required for that code.

G. Sequencing of the Primary and Secondary Diagnoses

List first the ICD-9-CM code for the diagnosis, condition, problem, or other reason for encounter/visit shown in the medical record to be chiefly responsible for the services provided. List additional codes that describe coexisting conditions that were treated or medically managed or influenced the treatment of the patient during the encounter.

H. Qualified Diagnoses

Do not code diagnoses documented as *probable, suspected, questionable, rule out,* or *working diagnosis* (these are considered *qualified diagnoses*). Instead, code condition(s) to the highest degree of certainty for that encounter/visit, such as symptoms, signs, abnormal test results, or other reasons for the visit.

NOTE: This is contrary to inpatient coding practices, where assigning codes to qualified diagnoses (e.g., probable) is permitted. ●

I. Chronic Conditions

Chronic diseases treated on an ongoing basis may be coded and reported as many times as the patient receives treatment and care for the condition(s).

J. Coexisting Conditions

Code all documented conditions that coexist at the time of the encounter/visit and require or affect patient care treatment or management. Do not code conditions that were previously treated and no longer exist. However, history codes (V10–V19) may be assigned as secondary codes if the historical condition or family history has an impact on current care or influences treatment.

NOTE: Payers review claims for "family history of" classification to determine reimbursement eligibility. Some plans reimburse for conditions that may not normally be eligible for payment when "family history of" a related condition is documented in the patient's record. ●

K. Encounter for Diagnostic Services

For patients receiving *diagnostic services only* during an encounter/ visit, sequence first the diagnosis, condition, problem, or other reason for the encounter/visit that is documented in the patient record as that which is chiefly responsible for the outpatient services provided during the encounter/visit (this is the *primary diagnosis*).

Assign code(s) to other diagnoses (e.g., chronic conditions) that are treated or medically managed or would affect the patient's receipt of diagnostic services during this encounter/visit.

L. Encounter for Therapeutic Services

For patients receiving *therapeutic services only* during an encounter/ visit, sequence first the diagnosis, condition, problem, or other reason for the encounter/visit shown in the medical record to be chiefly responsible for the outpatient services provided during the encounter/visit.

Assign code(s) to other diagnoses (e.g., chronic conditions) that are treated or medically managed or would affect the patient's receipt of therapeutic services during this encounter/visit.

M. Exceptions to Rules K and L

The only exception to rules K and L is the one for patients receiving chemotherapy, radiation therapy, or rehabilitation. In this instance, the appropriate V code for the service is sequenced first, and the diagnosis or problem for which the service is being performed is sequenced second.

N. Encounter for Preoperative Evaluation

For patients receiving *preoperative evaluation only*, assign the appropriate subclassification code located under subcategory V72.8, Other specified examinations, to describe the preoperative consultation.

Assign an additional code to the condition that describes the reason for the surgery. Also, assign additional code(s) to any findings discovered during the preoperative evaluation.

NOTE: Preadmission testing (PAT) is routinely completed prior to an inpatient admission or outpatient surgery to facilitate the patient's treatment and reduce the length of stay. Some payers provide higher reimbursement for PAT, making it important to properly assign codes (e.g., V72.6, Laboratory examination). ●

O. Ambulatory Surgery (or Outpatient Surgery)

For *ambulatory surgery* (or *outpatient surgery*), assign a code to the diagnosis for which the surgery was performed. If the postoperative diagnosis is different from the preoperative diagnosis when the diagnosis is confirmed, assign a code to the postoperative diagnosis instead (because it is more definitive).

PRIMARY AND PRINCIPAL DIAGNOSES

Before undertaking the study of diagnosis coding for provider practices, it is necessary to have an understanding of two issues:

1. The definition of *primary diagnosis* versus *principal diagnosis* and how claims submission is affected by each definition

2. How to deal with diagnostic statements that are qualified by terms and phrases such as: *probable, suspected, rule out,* and *ruled out*

Rules for coding diagnoses on medical insurance claims differ for outpatients and inpatients. An **outpatient** is a person treated in one of three settings:

● health care provider's office

- hospital clinic, emergency department, hospital same-day surgery unit, or ambulatory surgical center (ASC) where the patient is released within 23 hours

- hospital admission solely for observation where the patient is released after a short stay

An *inpatient* is a person admitted to the hospital for treatment with the expectation that the patient will remain in the hospital for a period of 24 hours or more. The inpatient admission status is stipulated by the admitting physician.

The primary diagnosis is reported on physician office claims (CMS-1500) and hospital outpatient and emergency department claims (UB-92). The principal diagnosis is reported on inpatient hospital claims (UB-92). The *CMS-1500 claim* is the standard claim used to report physician office services and procedures. It was originally approved by the American Medical Association in 1975 for group and individual claims processing and was called the *Universal Claim Form*. The CMS-1500 claim was revised in 1990 and printed with red ink for optical scanning purposes. In 1992, Medicare required the CMS-1500 (10/90) claim to be submitted by physicians and suppliers (except for ambulance services). (The *UB-92* [or *CMS-1450*] is the uniform bill [standard claim] used to report inpatient admissions and outpatient and emergency department services and procedures.)

INTERNET LINKS

Information about the CMS-1500 claim is available at http://www.nucc.org.

Information about the UB-92 claim is available at http://www.nubc.org.

Primary Diagnosis versus Principal Diagnosis

The **primary diagnosis** is the most significant condition for which services and/or procedures were provided, and it is entered first in Block 21 of the CMS-1500 claim. The **principal diagnosis** is defined as "the condition determined *after study* that resulted in the patient's admission to the hospital." It is listed in Form Locator 67 on the UB-92 (CMS-1450) claim.

In addition to reporting the primary diagnosis, up to three *secondary diagnosis* codes may be reported in Block 21 of the CMS-1500 claim and linked to services and/or procedures reported in Block 24. If more than four conditions are to be reported, it will be necessary to generate a second CMS-1500 claim. A **secondary diagnosis** is a *concurrent condition* or **comorbidity** that coexists with the primary condition, has the potential to affect treatment of the primary condition, and is an active condition for which the patient is treated or monitored. (The UB-92 claim also allows secondary diagnosis codes to be reported in Form Locators 68 through 75; these diagnoses include comorbidities [conditions that coexist with the principal diagnosis] and **complications** [conditions that develop subsequent to inpatient admission].)

EXAMPLE 1: A patient seeks care at the health care provider's office for an injury to the right leg that, upon X-ray in the office, is diagnosed as a fractured tibia. While in the office, the physician also reviews the current status and treatment of the patient's insulin-dependent diabetes.

Answer: The primary diagnosis is "fracture, shaft, right tibia"; the secondary diagnosis is "insulin-dependent diabetes mellitus." On the CMS-1500 claim, report the diagnoses codes in Block 21, and enter the diagnosis link in Block 24E for the corresponding service or procedure.

DIAGNOSIS	LINK TO SERVICE OR PROCEDURE
Fracture, shaft, right tibia	X-ray of leg
Insulin-dependent diabetes mellitus	Office visit

EXAMPLE 2: The patient has a history of arteriosclerotic heart disease and was admitted to the hospital because of severe shortness of breath. After study, a diagnosis of congestive heart failure is added. What is the principal diagnosis?

Answer: The principal diagnosis is congestive heart failure. (This diagnosis was determined after study to be the cause of the patient's admission to the hospital. Arteriosclerosis alone would not have caused the hospitalization. Shortness of breath is not coded because it is a symptom of the actual condition, congestive heart failure.)

EXAMPLE 3: A patient was admitted with hemoptysis. The following procedures were performed: upper GI series, barium enema, chest X-ray, bronchoscopy with biopsy of the left bronchus, and resection of the upper lobe of the left lung. The discharge diagnosis was bronchogenic carcinoma. What is the principal diagnosis?

Answer: The principal diagnosis is bronchogenic carcinoma, left lung. (The hemoptysis precipitated the need for hospitalization but is a symptom of the underlying problem, bronchogenic carcinoma. After admission to the hospital and after study, the diagnostic tests revealed the carcinoma.) ●

PRINCIPAL VERSUS SECONDARY PROCEDURES

Hospital coders are required to differentiate between principal and secondary procedures rendered using the criteria discussed below. These criteria do not affect coding for health care providers' offices but are discussed here to introduce the full scope of ICD-9-CM diagnosis and procedure coding.

Hospitals are required to rank all inpatient procedures according to specific criteria for selection of principal and secondary procedures and to code them using the ICD-9-CM procedure index and tabular list.

NOTE: Outpatient procedures and services, whether performed in the hospital or in the health care provider's office, are coded using the CPT and HCPCS level II national coding systems. ●

A **principal procedure** is a procedure performed for definitive treatment rather than diagnostic purposes, or one performed to treat a complication, or that which is most closely related to the principal diagnosis. There may be cases in which the only procedures performed are not directly related to the principal diagnosis but are related to secondary conditions. In such cases, the principal procedure is considered to be the major definitive treatment performed. **Secondary procedures** are additional procedures performed during the same encounter as the principal procedure.

EXAMPLE 1: A patient was admitted to the hospital because of a fractured left hip. During the hospital stay, the patient developed a pulmonary embolism. The following procedures were performed: X-rays of the right and left hips, a lung scan, and a surgical pinning of the hip. Which is the principal procedure?

Answer: Pinning of the hip, also known as open reduction with internal fixation (ORIF), is the principal procedure; it is the major definitive treatment for the principal diagnosis of fractured hip. The lung scan was a necessary diagnostic procedure for confirmation of a pulmonary embolism. This diagnosis is the most life-threatening problem for the patient, but it does not meet the principal diagnosis criterion, which is the major cause, determined after study, for the hospitalization.

EXAMPLE 2: A patient entered the hospital with symptoms of profuse sweating, tremors, and polyuria. The patient has an existing problem with control of insulin-dependent diabetes mellitus as well as carpal tunnel syndrome. The diabetes was controlled within 18 hours by adjusting the patient's insulin dosage. A surgical carpal tunnel release was performed. The final diagnoses were carpal tunnel syndrome and uncontrolled insulin-dependent diabetes mellitus. What is the principal procedure?

Answer: The principal procedure is the carpal tunnel release. The principal diagnosis is uncontrolled insulin-dependent diabetes mellitus (IDDM). (Carpal tunnel syndrome is not the principal diagnosis because it was not the problem that brought the patient to the hospital. Uncontrolled diabetes caused the admission in this case.)

CODING QUALIFIED DIAGNOSES

Another difference in coding inpatient hospitalizations versus outpatient and/or provider office encounters involves the assignment of codes for qualified diagnoses. A **qualified diagnosis** is a working diagnosis that is not yet proven or established. Terms and phrases associated with qualifying diagnoses include *suspected, rule out, possible, probable, questionable, suspicious for,* and *ruled out.* For office visits do *not* assign an ICD-9-CM code to qualified diagnoses; instead, code the sign(s) and/or symptom(s) documented in the patient's chart.

EXAMPLE:

For Qualified Diagnosis	Code the Sign or Symptom
Suspected pneumonia	Shortness of breath, wheezing, rales, rhonchi
Questionable Raynaud's	Numbness of hands
Rule out wrist fracture	Wrist pain and swelling
Ruled out pneumonia	Influenza (flu)

Qualified diagnoses are a necessary part of the hospital and office chart until a specific diagnosis can be determined. While qualified diagnoses are routinely coded for hospital inpatient admissions and reported on the UB-92 claim, CMS *specifically outlaws the reporting of such diagnoses on the CMS-1500 claim submitted by health care provider offices.* CMS regulations permit the reporting of patients' signs and/or symptoms instead of the qualified diagnoses.

An additional incentive for not coding qualified diagnoses resulted from the Missouri case of *Stafford v. Neurological Medicine Inc., 811 F. 2d 470 (8th Cir., 1987).* In this case, the diagnosis stated in the physician's office chart was "rule out brain tumor." The claim submitted by the office listed the diagnosis code for "brain tumor," although test results were available that proved a brain tumor did not exist. The physician assured the patient, before she left the hospital, that although she had lung cancer, there was no metastasis to the brain. Sometime after the insurance carrier received the provider's claim, it was inadvertently sent to the patient. Upon receipt of the claim, the patient, devastated by the diagnosis, committed suicide. The husband sued and was awarded $200,000 on the basis of "negligent paperwork" because the physician's office was responsible for reporting a "qualified diagnosis."

ICD-9-CM CODING SYSTEM

The official version of ICD-9-CM was originally published in three volumes:

- Volume 1 (Tabular List)
- Volume 2 (Index to Diseases)
- Volume 3 (Index to Procedures and Tabular List)

Provider offices and health care facilities use the Tabular List and Index to Diseases (Volumes 1 and 2 of ICD-9-CM) to code diagnoses. The Index to Procedures and Tabular List (Volume 3) is used by hospitals to code inpatient procedures. Many publishers offer their own version of ICD-9-CM, and as a result hospital (Volumes 1, 2 and 3) and outpatient (Volumes 1 and 2) editions of the coding manual are available. In addition, to make the coding procedure easier, publishers often place the Index to Diseases (Volume 2) in front of the Tabular List (Volume 1).

Diseases—Tabular List (Volume 1)

The **Tabular List (Volume 1)** contains 17 chapters that classify diseases and injuries, two supplemental classifications, and five appendices. The 17 chapters are organized as follows:

Chapter 1	Infectious and Parasitic Diseases (001–139)
Chapter 2	Neoplasms (140–239)
Chapter 3	Endocrine, Nutritional and Metabolic Diseases, and Immunity Disorders (240–279)
Chapter 4	Diseases of the Blood and Blood-forming Organs (280–289)
Chapter 5	Mental Disorders (290–319)
Chapter 6	Diseases of the Nervous System and Sense Organs (320–389)
Chapter 7	Diseases of the Circulatory System (390–459)
Chapter 8	Diseases of the Respiratory System (460–519)
Chapter 9	Diseases of the Digestive System (520–579)
Chapter 10	Diseases of the Genitourinary System (580–629)
Chapter 11	Complications of Pregnancy, Childbirth, and the Puerperium (630–679)
Chapter 12	Diseases of the Skin and Subcutaneous Tissue (680–709)
Chapter 13	Diseases of the Musculoskeletal System and Connective Tissue (710–739)

Chapter 14   Congenital Anomalies (740–759)

Chapter 15   Certain Conditions Originating in the Perinatal Period (760–779)

Chapter 16   Symptoms, Signs, and Ill-defined Conditions (780–799)

Chapter 17   Injury and Poisoning (800–999)

The two supplemental classifications include:

V codes   Supplemental Classification of Factors Influencing Health Status and Contact with Health Services (V01–V82)

E codes   Supplementary Classification of External Causes of Injury and Poisoning (E800–E999)

The five appendices include:

Appendix A   Morphology of Neoplasms (M Codes)

Appendix B   Glossary of Mental Disorders

Appendix C   Classification of Drugs by American Hospital Formulary Service List Number and Their ICD-9-CM Equivalents

Appendix D   Classification of Industrial Accidents According to Agency

Appendix E   Three-Digit Categories

Supplementary Classifications: V Codes and E Codes

V codes are located in the Tabular List and are assigned for patient encounters when a circumstance other than a disease or injury is present. (V codes are indexed in the *Alphabetic Index of Diseases and Injuries.*) Examples of V Code assignment include:

- Removal of a cast applied by another physician (V54.8)
- Exposure to tuberculosis (V01.1)
- Personal history of breast cancer (V10.3)
- Well baby check-up (V20.2)
- Annual physical examination (V70.0)

E codes are located in the Tabular List and describe external causes of injury, poisoning, or other adverse reactions affecting a patient's health. They are reported for environmental events, industrial accidents, injuries inflicted by criminal activity, and so on. While assignment of these codes does not directly affect reimbursement to the provider, reporting E codes can expedite insurance claims processing because the circumstances related to an injury are indicated. (E codes are indexed in the *Index to External Causes of Injury and Poisoning.*)

EXAMPLE 1: A patient who falls at home and breaks his leg would have code E849.0 (preceded by the appropriate fracture code) reported on the insurance claim (in addition to the fracture code). This code indicates that the patient's health insurance policy, and not a liability policy, should cover treatment.

EXAMPLE 2: A patient who falls at the grocery store and breaks his leg would have code E849.6 reported on the insurance claim (in addition to the fracture code). This code indicates that the store's liability insurance should be billed, not the patient's health insurance.

Appendices

ICD-9-CM appendices serve as a resource in coding neoplasms, mental disorders, adverse effects of drugs and chemicals, and external causes of disease and injury. In addition, the three-digit disease category codes are listed as an appendix. Some publishers (e.g., Medicode's *Hospital & Payor ICD-9-CM Volumes 1, 2, & 3)* include adjunct appendices such as Major Diagnostic Categories (MDCs) (associated with Diagnosis Related Groups), Diagnosis Related Groups (DRG) Categories, valid three-digit ICD-9-CM codes (those that do not require a fourth or fifth digit), and differences and similarities between inpatient and outpatient coding guidelines.

Morphology of Neoplasms (M codes) (found in Appendix A of ICD-9-CM) contains a reference to the World Health Organization publication entitled *International Classification of Diseases for Oncology* (ICD-O). The appendix also interprets the meaning of each digit of the morphology code number. **Morphology** indicates the tissue type of a neoplasm, and while M Codes are *not reported on provider office claims*, they are reported to state cancer registries. A basic knowledge of morphology coding can be helpful to a coder because the name of the neoplasm documented in the patient's chart does not always indicate whether the neoplasm is **benign** (not cancerous) or **malignant** (cancerous).

Referring to the morphology entry in the Index to Diseases helps determine which column in the Neoplasm Table should be referenced to select the correct code. In addition, coding should be delayed until the pathology report is available in the patient's chart for review.

EXAMPLE: The patient's chart documents carcinoma of the breast. The Index to Diseases entry for *Carcinoma* says "*see also* Neoplasm by site, malignant." This index entry directs the coder to the Neoplasm Table, and the code is selected from one of the first three columns (depending on whether the cancer is primary, secondary, or *in situ*— check the pathology report for documentation). ●

The **Glossary of Mental Disorders** (found in Appendix B of ICD-9-CM) corresponds to the psychiatric terms that appear in Chapter 5, "Mental Disorders," and consists of an alphabetic listing of terms and definitions based on those contained in ICD-9-CM and input from the *American Psychiatric Association's Task Force on Nomenclature and Statistics*. Some definitions are based on those in *A Psychiatric Glossary, Dorland's Illustrated Medical Dictionary*, and *Stedman's Medical Dictionary, Illustrated*.

EXAMPLE: The diagnosis *Chronic Alcoholism* (303.9x) requires the addition of a fifth-digit to completely code the condition. Often providers do not document the term necessary to assign the fifth-digit (e.g., chronic alcoholism that is continuous, episodic, or in remission); therefore, the coder must assign a fifth-digit for "unspecified" (0). The Glossary of Mental Disorders, located in Appendix B of ICD-9-CM, defines alcoholism according to *continuous, episodic,* and in *remission*—if the coder reviewed these definitions, it is likely that the appropriate fifth-digit could be assigned based on documentation in the patient's chart (even though the provider did not specify the term). ●

The **Classification of Drugs by AHFS List** (found in Appendix C of ICD-9-CM) contains the American Hospital Formulary Services List number and its ICD-9-CM equivalent code number, organized in numerical order according to AHFS List number. The List is published under the direction of the American Society of Hospital Pharmacists.

EXAMPLE: The patient's chart documents that the patient experienced a reaction to *substance 76:00*. By referring to the Classification of Drugs by AHFS List in Appendix C of ICD-9-CM, the coder can determine that *76:00* refers to *oxytocics*. The coder can then turn to the Table of Drugs and Chemicals in the Index to Diseases of ICD-9-CM and look up *Oxytocics* (found in alphabetical order) to locate the reportable codes. ●

NOTE: The AHFS List can also be referenced within the Table of Drugs and Chemicals by looking up the word *Drug*. Because providers infrequently document the List number, it *may be* easier for coders to remember to reference the appendix. ●

The **Classification of Industrial Accidents According to Agency** (found in Appendix D of ICD-9-CM) is based on employment injury statistics adopted by the Tenth International Conference of Labor Statisticians. Because it may be difficult to locate the E Code entry in the ICD-9-CM Index to External Causes, coders may find the Industrial Accidents According to Agency appendix more helpful in identifying the category of equipment, and so on. for an external cause of injury.

EXAMPLE: The patient sustained an injury as the result of a malfunctioning combine. While the E code for "accident, caused by, combine" can be easily located in the Index to External Causes, if the coder doesn't know what a combine is, the location of the accident cannot be properly coded. The Industrial Accidents According to Agency appendix can be referenced to determine that a combine is categorized as agricultural equipment. Thus, the coder can assign the location E code as "Accident, occurring (at), farm." ●

The **List of Three-Digit Categories** (found in Appendix E of ICD-9-CM) contains a breakdown of three-digit category codes organized beneath section headings.

EXAMPLE: Acute rheumatic fever (390–392)

390	Rheumatic fever without mention of heart involvement
391	Rheumatic fever with heart involvement
392	Rheumatic chorea ●

Index to Diseases (Volume 2)

The **Index to Diseases (Volume 2)** contains three sections:

- *Alphabetical Index of Diseases and Injuries.* This index includes two official tables that make it easier to code hypertension and neoplasms. Some publishers print special editions of ICD-9-CM manuals that contain additional tables to simplify the search for the correct code of other complex conditions.

- *Table of Drugs and Chemicals.* Adverse effects and poisonings associated with medicinal, chemical, and biological substances are coded by referring to this table.

- *Index to External Causes of Injury and Poisoning* (E codes). This separate index is often forgotten; it is helpful to mark it with a tab as a reminder of its usefulness.

Tabular List and Index to Procedures (Volume 3)

The **Tabular List and Index to Procedures (Volume 3)** is included in the hospital version of commercial ICD-9-CM books. It is a combined alphabetical index and numerical listing of inpatient procedures. Hospital outpatient departments and health care providers' offices use the *Current Procedural Terminology, Fourth Edition* (CPT) published by the American Medical Association (AMA), and/or additional codes created by CMS to augment CPT codes on Medicare claims. These special CMS codes are known as HCPCS level II and III codes. HCPCS stands for *Healthcare Financing Administration Common Procedure Coding System.* (CPT and HCPCS codes are further discussed in Chapters 7 and 8 of this text.)

NOTE: HCPCS level III local codes will be eliminated by December 31, 2003 because they may duplicate national codes, may identify brand names rather than product categories, and/or may vary in use from locality to locality. This decision was also based on the HIPAA requirement to adopt standards for coding systems used for reporting health care transactions. ●

ICD-9-CM INDEX TO DISEASES

The Index to Diseases is an alphabetical listing of main terms or conditions printed in boldface type that may be expressed as nouns, adjectives, or eponyms (Figure 6-1).

Main Terms

Main terms (conditions) are printed in boldface type and are followed by the code number. Main terms may or may not be followed by a listing of parenthetical terms that serve as nonessential modifiers of the main term (see the Main Term in Figure 6-1). **Nonessential modifiers** are qualifying words that do not have to be included in the diagnostic statement for the code number listed at the end of the parenthetical statements to apply.

Subterms

Subterms (or **essential modifiers**) qualify the main term by listing alternate sites, etiology, or clinical status. A list of subterms is indented 2 spaces under the main term. Secondary qualifying conditions are indented 2 spaces under a subterm. Great care must be taken when moving from the bottom of one column to the top of the next column or when turning the page. The main term will be repeated and followed by "*continued.*" Watch carefully to determine if the subterm has changed or new second or third qualifiers appear when moving from one column to another.

EXAMPLE: The ICD-9-CM Index to Diseases entries are organized according to main terms, subterms, 2nd qualifiers, and 3rd qualifiers. Refer to the index entry for Deformity of aortic arch, acquired (447.8) and note the indented subterm and qualifiers. Notice when the main term continues at the top of a column (or on the next page of the Index to Diseases), the term "*—continued*" appears after the main term, and subterms and qualifiers are indented below the main term. ●

Dextrocardia (corrected) (false) (isolated)
      (secondary) (true)   746.87
   with
      complete transposition of viscera   759.3
      situs invertus 759.3
Dextroversion, kidney (left)   753.3
Dhobie itch   110.3
Main Term ———————— Diabetes, diabetic (brittle) (congenital)
Nonessential Modifier ——————— (familial) (mellitus) (severe) (slight)
      (without complication)   250.0

> **Note: Use the following fifth-digit subclassification with category 250:**
>
> **0**   type II [non-insulin dependent type] [NIDDM type] [adult-onset type] or unspecified type, not stated as uncontrolled
>
> **1**   type I [insulin dependent type] [IDDM] [juvenile type], not stated as uncontrolled
>
> **2**   type II [non-insulin dependent type] [NIDDM type] [adult-onset type] or unspecified type, uncontrolled
>
> **3**   type I [insulin dependent type] [IDDM type] [juvenile type], uncontrolled

   with
Subterm ——————————— coma (with ketoacidosis) 250.3
Second Qualifier ——————————— hyperosmolar (nonketotic) 250.2
      complication NEC   250.9
         specified NEC   250.8
      gangrene   250.7 *[785.4]*
      ketosis, ketoacidosis   250.1
Bracketed code ———————— osetomyelitis 250.8 *[731.8]*
(requires second   specified manifestations NEC   250.8
code)   acetonemia   250.1

FIGURE 6-1 ICD-9-CM Index to Diseases (Courtesy of *St. Anthony's Illustrated ICD-9-CM,* 2004, (800) 632-0123)

START OF MAIN TERM IN INDEX TO DISEASES		CONTINUATION OF MAIN TERM AT TOP OF NEXT COLUMN	
Main Term:	Deformity 738.10	Main Term:	Deformity—continued
Subterm:	aortic	Subterm:	appendix 751.5
2nd Qualifier:	arch 747.21	Subterm:	arm (acquired) 736.89
3rd Qualifier:	acquired 447.8	3rd Qualifier:	congenital 755.50

CODING TIPS:

1. A subterm or "essential modifier" provides greater specificity when included in the diagnosis. Select the code number stated after the essential modifier, not the one stated after the main condition. For example, the code to investigate in the Tabular List for *acquired AC globulin deficiency* is 286.7.

2. Always consult the code description in the Tabular List before assigning a code because one or more instructional notes not included in the Index to Diseases may change the code selection.

BASIC STEPS FOR USING THE INDEX TO DISEASES

S T E P 1 Locate the main term in the Index to Diseases (Volume 2).

This is accomplished by first locating the condition's boldfaced main term and then reviewing the subterms listed below the main term to locate the proper disorder.

Underlined terms in the following examples are the conditions to locate in the Index to find possible codes.

> **EXAMPLE:** <u>Irritability</u> of the bladder
>
> <u>Impacted</u> feces
>
> Comminuted <u>fracture</u>, left radius
>
> Upper respiratory <u>infection</u> •

Table 6-1 is a list of special main terms that should be considered when the main condition is not obvious from the health care provider's diagnostic statement. Those marked with an asterisk are associated with V codes.

S T E P 2 If the phrase "—*see condition*" is found after the main term, a descriptive term (an adjective) or the anatomic site has been referenced instead of the disorder or the disease (the condition) documented in the diagnostic statement.

> **EXAMPLE:** The provider's diagnostic statement is *myocardial infarction.*
>
> In the ICD-9-CM Index to Diseases, look up the word *myocardial.*
>
> Notice that the phrase —*see condition* appears next to the word *myocardial.*
>
> The phrase is instructing you to refer to the condition instead. In this case, the condition is *infarction.* •

S T E P 3 When the condition listed is not found, locate main terms such as syndrome, disease, disorder, derangement of, or abnormal. See Table 6-1, which lists Special Main Terms for additional help.

> **NOTE:** Sometimes terms found in the ICD-9-CM Index to Diseases are not found in the Tabular List of Diseases when the code number is reviewed for verification. When this occurs, the coder should "trust the index" because to save space in the tabular list, more terms are listed in the index than in the tabular list. •

> **EXAMPLE:** For the condition, *gum attrition*, main term *attrition* and subterm *gum* are found in the ICD-9-CM Index to Diseases. When code 523.2 is verified in the tabular list, the term *attrition* is not found; however, code 523.2 is still the correct code. •

If unsuccessful in finding a code using the main terms suggested in Table 6-1, turn to Appendix E—Three-Digit Categories—in the back of the ICD-9-CM code book. Review the categories listed under the chapter heading to determine which best fits the site of the patient's problem.

If looking for a code that describes an External Cause of Injury, these conditions are found in the separate E Code Index located after the Table of Drugs and Chemicals at the back of the Index.

TABLE 6-1 Special main terms associated with V codes

Abnormal	Infection
Admission*	Injury
Aftercare*	Late Effects
Anomaly	Lesion
Attention to*	Newborn*
Complication	Observation*
Delivery	Outcome*
Disease	Pregnancy
Disorder	Problem With*
Examination*	Puerperal
Exposure to*	Status*
Foreign Body	Syndrome
History (family)*	Vaccination*
History (personal)*	

EXERCISE 6-1 Finding the Condition in the Index

Underline the condition in each of the following items, then, *using only the Index*, locate the main term and the code number. Write the code number on the blank line provided.

NOTE: Items 6 through 8 are rather uncommon disorders, but are listed in the Index.

1. Bronchiole spasm _____
2. Congenital candidiasis _____
3. Irritable bladder _____
4. Earthquake injury _____
5. Exposure to AIDS _____
6. Ground itch _____
7. Nun's knees _____
8. Mice in right knee joint _____

After completing this exercise, refer to Appendix IV to check your answers.

Coding Conventions

Coding conventions are rules that apply to the assignment of ICD-9-CM codes. They can be found in the Index to Diseases, Tabular List, and Index to Procedures and Tabular List (Table 6-2).

TABLE 6-2 Coding conventions for Index to Diseases. The coding convention is explained in column one, and the coding manual entry is highlighted in column two.

CODING CONVENTION & EXAMPLE	INDEX TO DISEASES ENTRY
CODES IN SLANTED BRACKETS are always listed as secondary codes because they are manifestations (results) of other conditions. **Example:** *diabetic cataract.*	**Diabetes, diabetic** (brittle) (congenital) (familial) (mellitus) (severe) (slight) (without complication) 250.0 cataract 250.5 *[366.41]*
EPONYMS are diseases (or procedures) named for an individual (e.g., physician who originally discovered the disease, first patient diagnosed with the disease). **Example:** *Barlow's Syndrome.*	**Syndrome** Barlow's (mitral valve prolapse) 424.0
ESSENTIAL MODIFIERS are subterms that are indented below the main term in alphabetical order (except for "with" and "without"). The essential modifier clarifies the main term and must be contained in the diagnostic statement for the code to be assigned. **Example:** *acute necrotizing encephalitis.*	**Encephalitis** (bacterial) (chronic) (hemorrhagic) (idiopathic) (nonepidemic) (spurious) (subacute) 323.9 acute—*see also* Encephalitis, viral disseminated (postinfectious) NEC 136.9 *[323.6]* postimmunization or postvaccination 323.5 inclusional 049.8 inclusion body 049.8 necrotizing 049.8
NEC (not elsewhere classifiable) identifies codes to be assigned when information needed to assign a more specific code cannot be located in the ICD-9-CM coding book. **Example:** *disseminated encephalitis.*	**Encephalitis** (bacterial) (chronic) (hemorrhagic) (idiopathic) (nonepidemic) (spurious) (subacute) 323.9 acute—*see also* Encephalitis, viral disseminated (postinfectious) NEC 136.9 *[323.6]*
NONESSENTIAL MODIFIERS are subterms that are enclosed in parentheses following the main term. They clarify the code selection, but they do not have to be present in the provider's diagnostic statement. **Example:** *cerebral pseudomeningocele.*	**Pseudomeningocele** (cerebral) (infective) (surgical) 349.2 spinal 349.2 NOTE: Cerebral pseudomeningocele is assigned code 349.2, and pseudomeningocele is also assigned code 349.2 ●

NOTES are contained in boxes to define terms, clarify index entries, and list choices for additional digits (e.g., fourth- and fifth-digits). **Example:** *spontaneous breech delivery.*	**Delivery**
	NOTE: Use the following fifth-digit subclassification with categories 640–648, 651–676
	  0 unspecified as to episode of care
	  1 delivered, with or without mention of antepartum condition
	  2 delivered, with mention of postpartum complication

(continues)

TABLE 6-2 *(continued)*

CODING CONVENTION & EXAMPLE	INDEX TO DISEASES ENTRY
NOTES (continued)	3 antepartum condition or complication 4 postpartum condition or complication breech (assisted) (spontaneous) 652.2

SEE directs the coder to a more specific term under which the code can be found. **Example:** *traumatic delirium, with spinal cord lesion.*	**Delirium, delirious** 780.09
	   traumatic—*see also* injury, intracranial
	     with
	      lesion, spinal cord—*see* injury, spinal, by site
	The coder is directed to the index entry below, and code 952.9 would be assigned.
	Injury
	   Spinal (cord) 952.9

SEE ALSO refers the coder to an index entry that may provide additional information to assign the code. **Example:** *mucus inhalation.*
The coder is directed to also check the index entry below; in this case, there is no added information that would change the code.
	Inhalation
	   mucus (*see also* Asphyxia, mucus) 933.1
	
	Asphyxia, asphyxiation (by) 799.0
	   mucus 933.1

SEE CATEGORY refers the coder directly to the Tabular List category (three-digit code) for code assignment. **Example:** *late effect of intracranial abscess.*	**Late**—*see also* condition
	   effect(s) (of)—*see also* condition
	     abscess
	      intracranial or intraspinal (conditions
	      classifiable to 324)—*see* category 326

EXERCISE 6-2 **Working with Coding Conventions (Index to Diseases)**

Underline the main term (condition) found in the Index to Diseases, and enter the ICD-9-CM code number and index convention on the blank lines.

Condition	ICD-9-CM Code	Index Convention Used
1. Acute purulent *sinusitis*	461.9	nonessential & essential modifiers
2. Fracture, mandible		
3. Actinomycotic meningitis		
4. Psychomotor akinetic epilepsy		
5. 3-cm laceration, right forearm		
6. Contusion, abdomen		
7. Pneumonia due to *H. influenzae*		

(continues)

8. Delayed healing, open wound, abdomen

9. Bile duct cicatrix

10. Uncontrolled non-insulin dependent diabetes mellitus with osteomyelitis

After completing this exercise, refer to Appendix IV to check your answers.

ICD-9-CM TABULAR LIST OF DISEASES

ICD-9-CM codes for Chapters 1 through 17 (codes 001–999.9) are organized according to three-digit category codes. Specificity is achieved by assigning a decimal point and one or two digits, known as fourth (subcategory codes) and fifth (subclassification codes) digits, to the main three-digit code number (Figure 6-2). Two supplemental classifications also classify health status (V codes) and external causes of injuries and diseases (E codes).

V codes (supplementary classification) are expressed as a three-character alphanumeric code (the letter V plus two digits) that can be subdivided into fourth and fifth digits to provide a more definitive description (Figure 6-3).

E codes (supplementary classification) are expressed as a four-character alphanumeric code (the letter E plus three digits). One additional decimal digit may be required to provide a more specific description of the external cause of the injury or poisoning (Figure 6-3). E codes are always secondary diagnostic codes. *They are never reported as the primary code on claims.*

Chapters

The **chapter heading** is printed in uppercase letters and is preceded by the chapter number. The instructional "Notes" that follow the chapter heading detail general guidelines for code selections within the entire chapter. If the note(s) include an italicized excludes statement, the reference applies to the entire chapter (Figure 6-2).

EXAMPLE: Refer to Figure 6-2 and the Chapter 3 heading, "Endocrine, Nutritional and Metabolic Diseases, and Immunity Disorders" (240–279). Notice that an *Excludes* note is located just below the chapter heading along with a regular note. Both references apply to all codes contained within the chapter. •

Major Topic Heading

ICD-9-CM chapters are subdivided into **major topic headings** printed in bold uppercase letters and followed by a range of codes enclosed in parentheses. Any note or italicized excludes note printed below a major topic heading applies only to the code numbers listed in parentheses after the major topic heading, not to the entire chapter.

EXAMPLE: **PSYCHOSES (290–299)**

 mental retardation (317–319) •

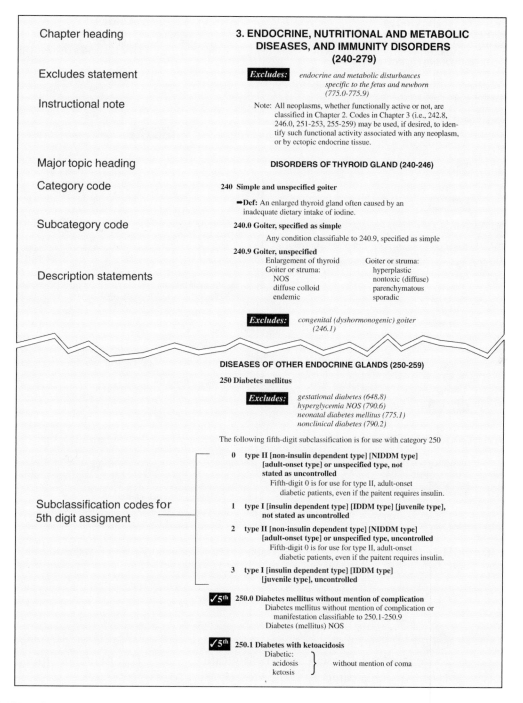

Chapter heading

3. ENDOCRINE, NUTRITIONAL AND METABOLIC DISEASES, AND IMMUNITY DISORDERS (240-279)

Excludes statement

Excludes: endocrine and metabolic disturbances specific to the fetus and newborn (775.0-775.9)

Instructional note

Note: All neoplasms, whether functionally active or not, are classified in Chapter 2. Codes in Chapter 3 (i.e., 242.8, 246.0, 251-253, 255-259) may be used, if desired, to identify such functional activity associated with any neoplasm, or by ectopic endocrine tissue.

Major topic heading

DISORDERS OF THYROID GLAND (240-246)

Category code

240 Simple and unspecified goiter

➡**Def:** An enlarged thyroid gland often caused by an inadequate dietary intake of iodine.

Subcategory code

240.0 Goiter, specified as simple

Any condition classifiable to 240.9, specified as simple

240.9 Goiter, unspecified
Enlargement of thyroid
Goiter or struma:
  NOS
  diffuse colloid
  endemic

Goiter or struma:
  hyperplastic
  nontoxic (diffuse)
  parenchymatous
  sporadic

Description statements

Excludes: congenital (dyshormonogenic) goiter (246.1)

DISEASES OF OTHER ENDOCRINE GLANDS (250-259)

250 Diabetes mellitus

Excludes: gestational diabetes (648.8)
hyperglycemia NOS (790.6)
neonatal diabetes mellitus (775.1)
nonclinical diabetes (790.2)

The following fifth-digit subclassification is for use with category 250

Subclassification codes for 5th digit assigment

0 **type II [non-insulin dependent type] [NIDDM type] [adult-onset type] or unspecified type, not stated as uncontrolled**
Fifth-digit 0 is for use for type II, adult-onset diabetic patients, even if the paitent requires insulin.

1 **type I [insulin dependent type] [IDDM type] [juvenile type], not stated as uncontrolled**

2 **type II [non-insulin dependent type] [NIDDM type] [adult-onset type] or unspecified type, uncontrolled**
Fifth-digit 0 is for use for type II, adult-onset diabetic patients, even if the paitent requires insulin.

3 **type I [insulin dependent type] [IDDM type] [juvenile type], uncontrolled**

✓5ᵗʰ **250.0 Diabetes mellitus without mention of complication**
Diabetes mellitus without mention of complication or manifestation classifiable to 250.1-250.9
Diabetes (mellitus) NOS

✓5ᵗʰ **250.1 Diabetes with ketoacidosis**
Diabetic:
  acidosis } without mention of coma
  ketosis

FIGURE 6-2 ICD-9-CM Diseases Tabular List (Courtesy of *St. Anthony's Illustrated ICD-9-CM*, 2004, (800) 632-0123)

Categories

Major topics are divided into three-digit categories. The **categories** are printed in bold upper- and lowercase type and are preceded by a three-digit code. Any italicized *Excludes* note that appears at this point applies to all three-, four-, or five-digit codes in the category.

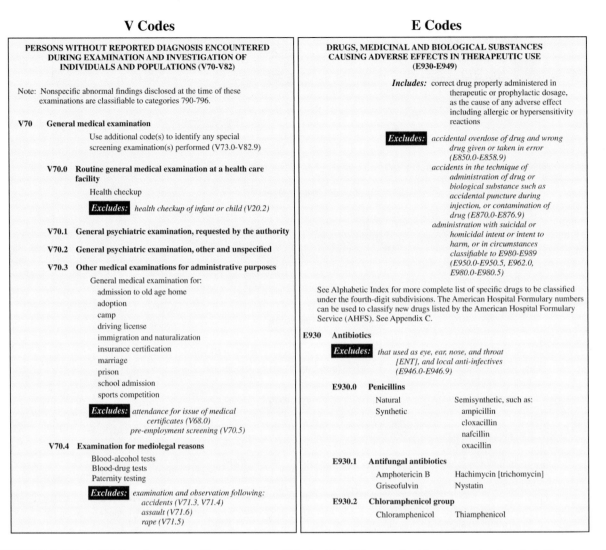

V Codes

PERSONS WITHOUT REPORTED DIAGNOSIS ENCOUNTERED DURING EXAMINATION AND INVESTIGATION OF INDIVIDUALS AND POPULATIONS (V70-V82)

Note: Nonspecific abnormal findings disclosed at the time of these examinations are classifiable to categories 790-796.

V70 General medical examination

Use additional code(s) to identify any special screening examination(s) performed (V73.0-V82.9)

V70.0 Routine general medical examination at a health care facility

Health checkup

Excludes: health checkup of infant or child (V20.2)

V70.1 General psychiatric examination, requested by the authority

V70.2 General psychiatric examination, other and unspecified

V70.3 Other medical examinations for administrative purposes

General medical examination for:
admission to old age home
adoption
camp
driving license
immigration and naturalization
insurance certification
marriage
prison
school admission
sports competition

Excludes: attendance for issue of medical certificates (V68.0)
pre-employment screening (V70.5)

V70.4 Examination for mediolegal reasons

Blood-alcohol tests
Blood-drug tests
Paternity testing

Excludes: examination and observation following:
accidents (V71.3, V71.4)
assault (V71.6)
rape (V71.5)

E Codes

DRUGS, MEDICINAL AND BIOLOGICAL SUBSTANCES CAUSING ADVERSE EFFECTS IN THERAPEUTIC USE (E930-E949)

Includes: correct drug properly administered in therapeutic or prophylactic dosage, as the cause of any adverse effect including allergic or hypersensitivity reactions

Excludes: accidental overdose of drug and wrong drug given or taken in error (E850.0-E858.9)
accidents in the technique of administration of drug or biological substance such as accidental puncture during injection, or contamination of drug (E870.0-E876.9)
administration with suicidal or homicidal intent or intent to harm, or in circumstances classifiable to E980-E989 (E950.0-E950.5, E962.0, E980.0-E980.5)

See Alphabetic Index for more complete list of specific drugs to be classified under the fourth-digit subdivisions. The American Hospital Formulary numbers can be used to classify new drugs listed by the American Hospital Formulary Service (AHFS). See Appendix C.

E930 Antibiotics

Excludes: that used as eye, ear, nose, and throat [ENT], and local anti-infectives (E946.0-E946.9)

E930.0 Penicillins

Natural   Semisynthetic, such as:
Synthetic   ampicillin
                         cloxacillin
                         nafcillin
                         oxacillin

E930.1 Antifungal antibiotics

Amphotericin B   Hachimycin [trichomycin]
Griseofulvin   Nystatin

E930.2 Chloramphenicol group

Chloramphenicol   Thiamphenicol

FIGURE 6-3 ICD-9-CM Supplementary Classifications, Tabular List (Diseases)—V and E codes (partial) (Courtesy of *St. Anthony's Illustrated ICD-9-CM,* 2004, (800) 632-0123)

EXAMPLE: Refer to Figure 6-2 and locate category code *250 Diabetes mellitus.* Notice the *Excludes* statement below category 250. This reference applies to all codes classified within category 250 codes.

Subcategories

Fourth-digit **subcategories** are indented and printed in the same fashion as the major category headings (see Figure 6-2). An italicized *Excludes* note found at this level applies only to the specific fourth-digit code.

EXAMPLE: Refer to Figure 6-2 and locate subcategory codes *240.0 Goiter, specified as simple* and *240.9 Goiter, unspecified.* As this condition contains codes at the subcategory (fourth-digit) level, it is incorrect to report the 3-digit code (240) on an insurance claim.

Subclassifications

Some fourth-digit subcategories are further subdivided into **subclassifications**, which require the assignment of a fifth digit. This requirement is indicated by the presence of a section mark (§), a red dot, or some other symbol, depending on the publisher of the code book. The placement and appearance of fifth digits are not standardized throughout ICD-9-CM. As you assign codes, you will notice varying fifth-digit placement.

Remember! Fifth digits are required when indicated in the code book.

Fifth-digit entries are associated with:

- chapters.
- major topic headings.
- categories.
- subcategories.

EXAMPLE 1: Fifth-Digit Entries Associated with Chapters

Refer to Chapter 13, "Diseases of the Musculoskeletal System and Connective Tissue" (710–739). The fifth-digit subclassification listed below the chapter heading is limited to certain categories (711–712, 715–716, 718–719, 730) in Chapter 13. The remaining categories in Chapter 13 either do not require the use of a fifth-digit subclassification (e.g., category 713) or the subclassification is listed within specific subcategories (e.g., 714.3, 717.4, 717.8, 720.81).

EXAMPLE 2: Fifth-Digit Entries Associated with Major Topic Headings

Refer to major topic heading, *Tuberculosis (010-018)*. The fifth-digit subclassification listed below the major topic heading is to be used with codes 010 through 018.

EXAMPLE 3: Fifth-Digit Entries Associated with Categories

Refer to category code *250 Diabetes mellitus*. The fifth-digit subclassification listed below the category code is to be used with all category 250 codes

EXAMPLE 4: Fifth-Digit Entries Associated with Subcategories

Refer to subcategory code 438.1. The fifth-digit subclassification listed is to be used only with subcategory 438.1. There is a different subclassification list for subcategory 438.2, 438.3, and so on. Notice that subcategory codes 438.0 and 438.9 do not contain a subclassification list. They are considered complete as four-digit codes. ●

NOTE: Major topic heading *Other Pregnancy with Abortive Outcome (634–639)* lists fourth-digit subcategory codes that are used with categories 634–638. Do not confuse this subcategory listing with similarly styled fifth-digit subclassifications that are often associated with major topic headings. The fifth-digit subclassification for category codes 634–637 is located below each three-digit category code. ●

NOTE: E-Codes—Supplementary Classification of External Causes of Injury and Poisoning (E800–E999) contains fourth-digit subcategories at the beginning of the following major section headings:

- Railway Accidents (E800–E807)
- Motor Vehicle Traffic Accidents (E810–E819)
- Motor Vehicle Accidents (E820–E825)
- Other Road Vehicle Accidents (E826–E829)
- Air and Space Transport Accidents (E840–E845)

Basic Steps for Using the Tabular List

STEP 1 Locate the first possible code number after reviewing main terms and subterms in the Index to Diseases.

STEP 2 Locate the code number in the Tabular List and review the code descriptions. Review any excludes notes to determine whether the condition being coded is excluded.

If the condition is excluded, locate the code number listed as an alternative in the excludes note to determine whether it is the condition to be coded.

STEP 3 Assign any required fifth digit.

STEP 4 Check to be sure the code number is appropriate for the age and sex of the patient.

STEP 5 Return to the Index to Diseases for other possible code selections if the code description in the Tabular List does not appear to fit the condition or reason for the visit.

STEP 6 Enter the final code selection.

EXERCISE 6-3 **Confirming Codes Found in the Index**

Using only the Tabular List, verify the following code numbers to determine whether the code matches the stated diagnosis or an excludes statement applies.

Place a "C" on the blank line if the code number is confirmed.

Place an "E" on the blank line if the condition is excluded.

Enter required fifth digits if applicable.

1. 515   Postinflammatory pulmonary fibrosis   _____
2. 250.1   Non-insulin dependent diabetes   _____
3. 727.67   Nontraumatic rupture of Achilles' tendon   _____
4. 422.0   Acute myocarditis due to Coxsackie virus   _____
5. 813.22   Malunion, closed right radial fracture   _____
6. 483.0   Mycoplasmic pneumonia   _____
7. 795.71   Positive HIV test, asymptomatic   _____
8. 796.2   Elevated blood pressure   _____
9. 718.06   Old tear of right knee meniscus   _____

After completing this exercise, refer to Appendix IV to check your answers.

Tabular List (Diseases) Coding Conventions

Tabular List (Diseases) coding conventions (Table 6-3) apply to disease and condition codes and to supplementary classification codes (e.g., factors influencing health status and contact with health services [V codes], and external causes of injury and poisoning [E codes]).

TABLE 6-3 Coding conventions for the Tabular List (Diseases). The coding convention is explained in column one, and the coding manual entry is located in column two.

CODING CONVENTION	TABULAR LIST ENTRY (DISEASES)	
AND: when two disorders are separated by the word "and," it is interpreted as "and/or" and indicates that either of the two disorders is associated with the category code.	**466**	**Acute bronchitis and bronchiolitis**
	466.0	**Acute bronchitis**
	466.1	**Acute bronchiolitis**
BOLD TYPE: all category and subcategory codes and descriptions are printed in bold type.	**421**	**Acute and subacute endocarditis**
	421.0	**Acute and subacute endocarditis**
	421.1	**Acute and subacute infective endocarditis in diseases classified elsewhere**
BRACES enclose a series of terms, each of which modifies the statement located to the right of the brace.	**478.5**	**Other diseases of vocal cords**
		Abscess ⎫
		Cellulitis ⎬ of vocal cords
		Granuloma ⎪
		Leukoplakia ⎭
BRACKETS enclose synonyms, alternate wording, or explanatory phrases.	**428.2**	**Pneumonia due to *Hemophilus influenzae* [*H. influenzae*]**
CODE FIRST UNDERLYING DISEASE appears when the code referenced is to be sequenced as a secondary code. The code, title, and instructions are italicized.	**366.42**	*Tetanic cataract*
		Code first underlying disease, as:
		calcinosis (275.4)
		hypoparathyroidism (252.1)
COLON: used after an incomplete term and is followed by one or more modifiers (additional terms)	**472.0**	**Chronic rhinitis**
		Ozena
		Rhinitis:
		NOS
		atrophic
		granulomatous
		hypertrophic
		obstructive
		purulent
		ulcerative
EXCLUDES: an excludes note directs the coder to another location in the codebook for proper assignment of the code	**250**	**Diabetes mellitus**
		EXCLUDES *gestational diabetes (648.8)*
		hyperglycemia NOS (790.6)
		neonatal diabetes mellitus (775.1)
		nonclinical diabetes (790.2)
FORMAT: all additional terms are indented below the term to which they are linked, and if a definition or disease requires more than one line, that text is printed on the next line and further indented.	**455.2**	**Internal Hemorrhoids with other complications**
		Internal hemorrhoids:
		bleeding
		prolapsed
		strangulated
		ulcerated

(continues)

TABLE 6-3 *(continued)*

CODING CONVENTION	TABULAR LIST ENTRY (DISEASES)
FOURTH & FIFTH DIGITS: the assignment of a fourth and/or fifth digit is indicated by an instructional note located below the category or subcategory description	**250** **Diabetes mellitus** EXCLUDES *gestational diabetes (648.8)* *hyperglycemia NOS (790.6)* *neonatal diabetes mellitus (775.1)* *nonclinical diabetes (790.2)* **The following fifth-digit subclassification is for use with category 250:** **0** **type II [non-insulin dependent type] [NIDDM type] [adult-onset type] or unspecified type, not stated as uncontrolled** **1** **type I [insulin dependent type] [IDDM] [juvenile type], not stated as uncontrolled** **2** **type II [non-insulin dependent type] [NIDDM type] [adult-onset type] or unspecified type, uncontrolled** **3** **type I [insulin dependent type] [IDDM] [juvenile type], uncontrolled**
INCLUDES: includes notes appear below a three-digit category code description to further define, clarify, or provide an example.	**244** **Acquired hypothyroidism** INCLUDES athyroidism (acquired) hypothyroidism (acquired) myxedema (adult) (juvenile) thyroid (gland) insufficiency (acquired)
NOS is the abbreviation for not otherwise specified and indicates that the code is unspecified. Coders should ask the provider for a more specific diagnosis before assigning the code.	**008.8** Other organism, not elsewhere classified Viral enteritis NOS gastroenteritis EXCLUDES influenza with involvement of gastrointestinal tract (487.8)
NOTES define terms, clarify information, and list choices for fourth- and fifth-digits.	**1. INFECTIONS AND PARASITIC DISEASES (001–139)** NOTE: Categories for "late effects" of infectious and parasitic diseases are found at 137–139.●
PARENTHESES enclose supplementary words that may be present or absent in the diagnostic statement, without affecting assignment of the code number.	**241.1** **Nontoxic multinodular goiter** Multinodular goiter (nontoxic)
USE ADDITIONAL CODE indicates a second code is to be reported to provide more information about the diagnosis.	**510** **Empyema** Use additional code to identify infectious organism (041.0–041.9)
WITH: when codes combine one disorder with another (e.g., code that combines primary condition with a complication), the provider's diagnostic statement must clearly indicate that both conditions are present and that a relationship exists between the conditions.	**487** **Influenza with bronchopneumonia** **487.0** **With pneumonia** **487.1** **With other respiratory manifestations** Influenza NOS Influenzal: laryngitis pharyngitis respiratory infection (upper) (acute)

EXERCISE 6-4   Working with Tabular List (Diseases) Coding Conventions

Underline the main term (condition) to be referenced in the Index to Diseases, and apply index coding conventions in locating the code. Verify the code selected in the Tabular List. Enter the ICD-9-CM code number(s) and Tabular List Coding Convention used on the blank lines provided. If more than one code number is assigned, be sure to list the primary condition code first.

Condition	ICD-9-CM Code(s)	Index Convention(s) Used
1. Pregnancy complicated by chronic gonorrhea; gonococcal endometritis	647.13, 098.3	fifth-digit required; use additional code
2. Benign neoplasm, ear cartilage		
3. Cervicitis, tuberculous		
4. Uncontrolled Type II diabetes with polyneuropathy		
5. Congenital hemangioma on face		
6. Hiss-Russell shigellosis		
7. Closed fracture, right leg		
8. Diabetic cataract		
9. Muscular atrophy, left leg		
10. Chronic smoker's bronchitis with acute bronchitis		

After completing this exercise, refer to Appendix IV to check your answers.

INDEX TO PROCEDURES AND TABULAR LIST OF PROCEDURES

As mentioned previously, the Tabular List and Index to Procedures (Volume 3) is included only in the hospital version of commercial ICD-9-CM books. It is a combined alphabetical index and numerical listing of inpatient procedures. Hospital outpatient departments and health care providers' offices report the *Current Procedural Terminology, Fourth Edition* (CPT) and HCPCS level II national codes created by CMS on Medicare claims.

Coding Conventions—Index to Procedures and Tabular List of Procedures

Although the purpose of this textbook is to cover physician office coding (for which ICD-9-CM Index to Diseases and Tabular List is used), Table 6-4 is included to provide comprehensive coverage of ICD-9-CM coding conventions.

TABLE 6-4 Coding conventions for the Index to Procedures and Tabular List. The coding convention is explained in column one and the coding manual entry is located in column two.

CODING CONVENTION	INDEX TO PROCEDURES ENTRY
OMIT CODE is a term that identifies procedures or services that may be components of other procedures. The *omit code* instruction means that the procedure or service is not coded.	**Laparotomy** NEC 54.19 As operative approach—*omit code*

CODING CONVENTION	TABULAR LIST (PROCEDURES) ENTRY
CODE ALSO ANY SYNCHRONOUS PROCEDURES refers to operative procedures that are to be coded to completely classify a procedure.	**08.2** **Excision or destruction of lesion or tissue of eyelid** Code also any synchronous reconstruction (08.61–08.74)

ICD-9-CM INDEX TO DISEASES TABLES

Three tables appear in the Index to Diseases: Hypertension, Neoplasm, and the Table of Drugs and Chemicals. The discussion that follows provides a basic understanding of how to use each table. Because the official tables consist of three to six columns, it will be helpful if you use a ruler or paper guide when working within a table to ensure that you stay on the same horizontal line as you work with a specific diagnosis.

Hypertension/Hypertensive Table

The Hypertension/Hypertensive table contains a complete listing of hypertension codes and other conditions associated with it. Column headings are shown in Figure 6-4.

- Malignant—A severe form of hypertension with vascular damage and a diastolic pressure reading of 130 mm Hg or greater. (Hypertension is out of control or there was a rapid change from a benign state for a prolonged period.)
- Benign—Mild and/or controlled hypertension, with no damage to the patient's vascular system or organs.
- Unspecified—No notation of benign or malignant status is found in the diagnosis or in the patient's chart.

CODING TIPS:

1. Always check the Tabular List before assigning a code for hypertension/hypertensive conditions.

2. The table uses all three levels of indentations when the word "with" is included in the diagnostic statement. Be sure you review the subterms carefully. You may need to assign two codes when "with" separates two conditions in the diagnostic statement.

3. Secondary hypertension is a unique and separate condition listed on the table. In this case hypertension was caused by another primary condition (e.g., cancer).

4. Use the fourth digit 9 sparingly.

Most insurance companies insist on conditions being coded to the highest degree of specificity known at the time of the encounter. They will not accept 401.9 Hypertension, unspecified except during the first few weeks of treatment for hypertension. After that point, the physician usually knows whether or not the patient has benign (controlled by medication) or malignant (out-of-control) hypertension. If "benign" or "malignant" is not specified in the diagnosis, ask the physician to document the type of hypertension.

	Malignant	Benign	Unspecified
Hypertension, hypertensive (arterial) (arteriolar) (crisis) (degeneration) (disease) (essential) (fluctuating) (idiopathic) (intermittent) (labile) (low renin) (orthostatic) (paroxysmal) (primary) (systemic) (uncontrolled) (vascular)......................	401.0	401.1	401.9
with			
heart involvement (conditions classifiable to 425.8, 428, 429.0–429.3, 429.8, 429.9 due to hypertension) (*see also* Hypertension, heart)	402.00	402.10	402.90
with kidney involvement — *see* Hypertension, cardiorenal			
renal involvement (*only* conditions classifiable to 585, 586, 587) (*excludes conditions classifiable to 584*) (*see also* Hypertension, kidney)	403.00	403.10	403.90
renal sclerosis or failure	403.00	403.10	403.90
with heart involvement—*see* Hypertension, cardiorenal			
failure (and sclerosis) (*see also* Hypertension, kidney)...........	403.01	403.11	403.91
sclerosis without failure (*see also* Hypertension, kidney).......	403.00	403.10	403.90
accelerated (*see also* Hypertension, by type, malignant)...........	401.0	—	—
antepartum—*see* Hypertension, complicating pregnancy, childbirth, or the puerperium			
cardiorenal (disease)..	404.00	404.10	404.90
with			
heart failure (congestive)	404.01	404.11	404.91
and renal failure..	404.03	404.13	404.93
renal failure	404.02	404.12	404.92
and heart failure (congestive)	404.03	404.13	404.93
cardiovascular disease (arteriosclerotic) (sclerotic)...................	402.00	402.10	402.90
with			
heart failure (congestive)	402.01	402.11	402.91
renal involvement (conditions classifiable to 403) (*see also* Hypertension, cardiorenal)	404.00	404.10	404.90

FIGURE 6-4 ICD-9-CM Hypertension table (partial) (Courtesy of *St. Anthony's Illustrated ICD-9-CM,* 2004, (800) 632-0123)

EXERCISE 6–5 | **Hypertension/Hypertensive Coding**

Code the following conditions.

1. Essential hypertension with cardiomegaly   _____
2. Transient hypertension due to pregnancy   _____
3. Malignant hypertensive crisis   _____
4. Renal and heart disease due to hypertension   _____

After completing this exercise, refer to Appendix IV to check your answers.

Neoplasm Table

Neoplasms are new growths, or tumors, in which cell reproduction is out of control. For coding purposes, the provider should specify whether the tumor is *benign* (non-cancerous, nonmalignant, noninvasive) or *malignant* (cancerous, invasive, capable of spreading to other parts of the body). It is highly advisable that neoplasms be coded directly from the pathology report (generated by a hospital's or stand-alone laboratory's pathology department and mailed to the provider's office); however, until the diagnostic statement specifies whether the neoplasm is benign or malignant, coders should code the patient's sign (e.g., breast lump) or report a subcategory code from the "unspecified nature" column of the documented site using the Disease Index Neoplasm table.

Another term associated with neoplasms is **lesion**, defined as any discontinuity of tissue (e.g., skin or organ) that may or may not be malignant. Disease index entries for "lesion" contain subterms according to anatomic site (e.g., organs or tissue), and that term should be referenced if the diagnostic statement does not confirm a malignancy. In addition, the following conditions are examples of benign lesions and are listed as separate Disease Index entries:

- Mass (unless the word "neoplasm" is included in the diagnostic statement)
- Cyst
- Dysplasia
- Polyp
- Adenosis

The Neoplasm Table (Figure 6-5) is indexed by anatomic site and contains four cellular classifications: malignant, benign, uncertain behavior, and unspecified nature. The malignant classification is subdivided into three divisions: primary, secondary, and carcinoma *in situ*. The six neoplasm classifications are defined as follows:

- **Primary malignancy**—The original tumor site. All malignant tumors are considered primary unless otherwise documented as metastatic or secondary.
- **Secondary malignancy**—The tumor has metastasized (spread) to a secondary site, either adjacent to the primary site or to a remote region of the body.
- **Carcinoma (Ca) *in situ***—A malignant tumor that is localized, circumscribed, encapsulated, and noninvasive (has not spread to deeper or adjacent tissues or organs).
- **Benign**—A noninvasive, nonspreading, nonmalignant tumor.
- **Uncertain behavior**—It is not possible to predict subsequent morphology or behavior from the submitted specimen. In order to assign a code from this column, the pathology report must specifically indicate the "uncertain behavior" of the neoplasm.

	Malignant				Uncertain	Unspecified
	Primary	Secondary	Ca in situ	Benign	Behavior	Nature
Neoplasm, neoplastic............................	199.1	199.1	234.9	229.9	238.9	239.9

Notes— 1. *The list below gives the code numbers for neoplasms by anatomic site. For each site there are six possible code numbers according to whether the neoplasm in question is malignant, benign, in situ, of uncertain behavior, or of unspecified nature. The description of the neoplasm will often indicate which of the six columns is appropriate (e.g., malignant melanoma of skin, benign fibroadenoma of breast, carcinoma in situ of cervix uteri).*

Where such descriptors are not present, the remainder of the Index should be consulted where guidance is given to the appropriate column for each morphologic (histologic) variety listed; e.g., Mesonephroma — see Neoplasm, malignant; Embryoma — see also Neoplasm, uncertain behavior; Disease, Bowen's — see neoplasm, skin, in situ. However, the guidance in the Index can be overwritten if one of the descriptors mentioned above is present; e.g., malignant adenoma of colon is coded to 153.9 and not to 211.3 as the adjective "malignant" overrides the Index entry "adenoma — see also Neoplasm, benign."

2. *Sites marked with the sign * (e.g., face NEC*) should be classified to malignant neoplasm of skin of these sites if the variety of neoplasm is a squamous cell carcinoma or an epidermal carcinoma and to benign neoplasm of skin of these sites if the variety of neoplasm is a papilloma (any type).*

	Primary	Secondary	Ca in situ	Benign	Uncertain Behavior	Unspecified Nature
abdomen, abdominal	195.2	198.89	234.8	229.8	238.8	239.8
cavity	195.2	198.89	234.8	229.8	238.8	239.8
organ..	195.2	198.89	234.8	229.8	238.8	239.8
viscera...	195.2	198.89	234.8	229.8	238.8	239.8
wall	173.5	198.2	232.5	216.5	238.2	239.2
connective tissue............................	171.5	198.89	—	215.5	238.1	239.2
abdominopelvic......................................	195.8	198.89	234.8	229.8	238.8	239.8
accessory sinus — *see* Neoplasm, sinus ...						
acoustic nerve	192.0	198.4	—	225.1	237.9	239.7
acromion (process)	170.4	198.5	—	213.4	238.0	239.2

FIGURE 6-5 ICD-9-CM Neoplasm table (partial) (Courtesy of *St. Anthony's Illustrated ICD-9-CM,* 2004, (800) 632-0123)

- **Unspecified nature**—A neoplasm is identified, but there is no further indication of the histology or nature of the tumor reflected in the documented diagnosis. Assign a code from this column when the neoplasm was destroyed or removed and a tissue biopsy was performed and results are pending.

To go directly to the Neoplasm Table, you must know the classification and the site of the neoplasm. Some diagnostic statements specifically document "neoplasm" classification; others will not provide a clue.

If the diagnostic statement classifies the neoplasm, the coder can refer directly to the Index to Diseases Neoplasm table to assign the proper code (verifying the code in the Tabular List, of course). Because sufficient information is documented in the diagnostic statements in Example 1, coders can refer directly to the Index to Diseases Neoplasm table.

 **EXAMPLE 1:**

Diagnostic Statement	Neoplasm Table Reference
Tracheal carcinoma *in situ*	trachea, Malignant, Ca *in situ* (231.1)
Benign breast tumor, male	breast, male, Benign (217)

(continues)

● **EXAMPLE 1** *(continued):*

Diagnostic Statement	Neoplasm Table Reference
Cowpers gland tumor, uncertain behavior	Cowper's gland, Uncertain Behavior (236.99)
Metastatic carcinoma	unknown site or unspecified, Malignant—Secondary (199.1)
Cancer of the breast, primary	breast, Malignant—Primary (174.9)

If the diagnostic statement *does not* classify the neoplasm, the coder must refer to the Index to Diseases entry for the condition documented (instead of the Neoplasm table). That entry will either contain a code number that can be verified in the Tabular List or the coder will be referred to the proper Neoplasm table entry under which to locate the code.

● **EXAMPLE 2:**

Diagnostic Statement	Index to Diseases Entry
non-Hodgkin's lymphoma	Lymphoma, non-Hodgkin's type NEC (M9591/3) 202.8
Adrenal adenolymphoma	Adenolymphoma (M8561/0) Specified site—*see* Neoplasm, by site, benign
	Neoplasm (table), adrenal (cortex) (gland) (medulla), benign (227.0)

For *non-Hodgkin's lymphoma*, assign code 202.8 (after verification in the Tabular List) by referring to "lymphoma" in the Index to Diseases. There is no need to go to the Neoplasm table. In fact, referencing the Neoplasm table in this case would have been improper, and the coder would most likely have assigned an incorrect code (e.g., perhaps the coder would have referenced "lymph, lymphatic" within the Neoplasm table and selected code 171.9 from the Malignant—Primary column, the wrong code).

For *Adrenal adenolymphoma*, refer to "adenolymphoma" in the Index to Diseases and because "adrenal" is the site specified in the diagnostic statement, the coder should follow the Index to Diseases instructions to "see Neoplasm, by site, benign." This instructional note refers the coder to the Neoplasm table and the anatomic site for adrenal (cortex) (gland) (medulla). The coder would next refer to the "Benign" column and assign code 227.0 (after verifying the code in the Tabular List). ●

CODING TIPS:

1. Assigning codes from the Neoplasm table is a two-step process. First, classify the neoplasm by its behavior (e.g., malignant, secondary) and then classify the neoplasm by its anatomic site (e.g., acoustic nerve).

2. To classify the neoplasm's behavior, review the provider's diagnostic statement (e.g., carcinoma of the throat), and look up the term "carcinoma" in the Index to Diseases. The entry will classify the behavior for you, directing you to the proper column in the Neoplasm table. (If malignant, you will still need to determine whether primary, secondary or *in situ* based on documentation in the patient's record.)

EXERCISE 6-6 | ## Neoplasm Coding I

Underline the main term found in the Index to Diseases, and enter the code number (after verifying it in the Tabular List) on the blank line.

1. Kaposi's sarcoma _____
2. Lipoma, skin, upper back _____
3. Carcinoma *in situ*, skin, left cheek _____
4. Scrotum mass _____
5. Neurofibroma _____
6. Cyst on left ovary _____
7. Ganglion right wrist _____
8. Yaws, frambeside _____
9. Breast, chronic cystic disease _____
10. Hurtle cell tumor _____
11. Bile duct cystadenocarcinoma _____
12. Mixed glioma _____

After completing this exercise, refer to Appendix IV to check your answers.

Primary Malignancies

A malignancy is coded as the primary site if the diagnostic statement documents:

- metastatic *from* a site
- spread *from* a site
- *primary neoplasm* of a site
- a malignancy for which no specific classification is documented
- a *recurrent* tumor

⬤ **EXAMPLE:**

Carcinoma of cervical lymph nodes, metastatic from the breast
        Primary—breast
        Secondary—cervical lymph nodes

Oat cell carcinoma of the lung with spread to the brain
        Primary—lung
        Secondary—brain ⬤

Secondary Malignancies

Secondary malignancies are **metastatic** and indicate that a primary cancer has spread (**metastasize**) to another part of the body. Sequencing of neoplasm codes is dependent on whether the primary or secondary cancer is being managed and/or treated.

⬤ **NOTE:** Examples in this section consistently sequence the primary first. In practice, the insurance specialist makes the determination as to sequencing of reported codes. ⬤ To properly code secondary malignancies, consider the following:

- Cancer described as *metastatic from* a site is *primary of* that site. Assign one code to the primary neoplasm and a second code to the secondary neoplasm of the specified site (if secondary site is known) or unspecified site (if secondary site is unknown).

    EXAMPLE 1: Metastatic carcinoma from breast to lung

    Assign two codes:
    > primary malignant neoplasm of breast (174.9)
    > secondary neoplasm of lung (197.0)

    EXAMPLE 2: Metastatic carcinoma from breast

    Assign two codes:
    > primary malignant neoplasm of breast (174.9)
    > secondary neoplasm of unspecified site (199.1)

- Cancer described as *metastatic to* a site is considered *secondary of* that site. Assign one code to the secondary site and a second code to the specified primary site (if primary site is known) or unspecified site (if primary site is unknown). In the example below, the metastatic site is listed first; in practice, the sequencing of codes depends on the reason for the encounter (e.g., is the primary or secondary cancer site being treated or medically managed).

    EXAMPLE 1: Metastatic carcinoma from liver to lung

    Assign two codes:
    > secondary neoplasm of lung (197.0)
    > primary malignant neoplasm of liver (155.0)

    EXAMPLE 2: Metastatic carcinoma to lung

    Assign two codes as follows:
    > secondary neoplasm of lung (197.0)
    > primary malignant neoplasm of unspecified site (199.1)

- When anatomic sites are documented as *metastatic*, assign *secondary* neoplasm code(s) to those sites, and assign an *unspecified site* code to the *primary* malignant neoplasm.

    EXAMPLE 1: Metastatic renal cell carcinoma of lung

    Assign two codes:
    > secondary neoplasm of lung (197.0)
    > primary renal cell carcinoma (189.0)

    EXAMPLE 2: Metastatic osteosarcoma of brain

    Assign two codes:
    > secondary neoplasm of brain (198.3)
    > primary malignant neoplasm of bone (170.9)

    EXAMPLE 3: Metastatic melanoma of lung and liver

    Assign three codes:
    > secondary neoplasm of lung (197.0)
    > secondary neoplasm of liver (197.7)
    > primary malignant melanoma of unspecified site (172.9)

EXAMPLE 4: Metastatic adenocarcinoma of prostate and vertebra

Assign three codes:

primary adenocarcinoma of unspecified site (199.1)

secondary neoplasm of prostate (198.82)

secondary neoplasm of vertebra (198.5)

If the diagnostic statement does not specify whether the neoplasm site is primary or secondary, code the site as *primary* unless the documented site is bone, brain, diaphragm, heart, liver, lymph nodes, mediastinum, meninges, peritoneum, pleura, retroperitoneum, spinal cord, or classifiable to 195. These sites are considered *secondary* sites unless the physician specifies that they are primary.

EXAMPLE 1: Lung cancer

Assign one code:

primary malignant neoplasm of lung (162.9)

NOTE: Lung is not included in the above list of secondary (metastatic sites); therefore, this cancer is coded as primary.

EXAMPLE 2: Brain cancer

Assign two codes:

secondary neoplasm of brain (198.3)

primary malignant neoplasm of unspecified site (199.1)

EXAMPLE 3: Metastatic cancer of hip

Assign two codes:

secondary neoplasm of hip (198.89)

primary malignant neoplasm of unspecified site (199.1)

Anatomic Site Is Not Documented

If the cancer diagnosis does not contain documentation of the anatomic site, but the term *metastatic* is documented, assign codes for "unspecified site" for both the primary and secondary sites.

EXAMPLE: Metastatic chromophobe adenocarcinoma

Assign two codes as follows:

secondary neoplasm of unspecified site (199.1)

primary chromophobe adenocarcinoma of unspecified site (194.3)

Primary Malignant Site Is No Longer Present

If the primary site of malignancy is no longer present, do not assign the code for primary of unspecified site. Instead, classify the previous primary site by assigning the appropriate code from category V10 "Personal history of malignant neoplasm."

EXAMPLE: Metastatic carcinoma to lung from breast (left radical mastectomy performed last year)

Assign two codes as follows:

secondary neoplasm of lung (197.0)

personal history of malignant neoplasm of breast (V10.3)

Contiguous or Overlapping Sites

Contiguous sites (or **overlapping sites**) occur when the origin of the tumor (primary site) involves two adjacent sites. Neoplasms with overlapping site boundaries are classified to the fourth-digit subcategory .8, "Other."

EXAMPLE: Cancer of the jejunum and ileum

Go to the Index to Disease entry for "intestine, small, contiguous sites" in the Neoplasm table. Locate code 152.8 in the Malignant—Primary column, and verify the code in the Tabular List, which appears as:

152   Malignant neoplasm of small intestine, including duodenum

 152.8   Other specified sites of small intestine

  Duodenojejunal junction

  Malignant neoplasm of contiguous or overlapping sites of small intestine whose point of origin cannot be determined ●

Re-excision of Tumors

A **re-excision** of a tumor occurs when the pathology report recommends that the surgeon perform a second excision to widen the margins of the original tumor site. The re-excision is performed to ensure that all tumor cells have been removed and a clear border (margin) of normal tissue surrounds the excised specimen. Use the diagnostic statement found in the report of the original excision to code the reason for the re-excision. The pathology report for the re-excision may not specify a malignancy at this time, but the patient is still under treatment for the original neoplasm.

CODING TIPS:

1. Read all notes in the table that apply to the condition you are coding.
2. Never assign a code directly from the table or Index to Diseases.
3. Be certain you are submitting codes that represent the *current status of the neoplasm.*
4. Assign a neoplasm code if the tumor has been excised and the patient is still undergoing radiation or chemotherapy treatment.
5. Assign a V code if the tumor is no longer present or if the patient is not receiving treatment, but is returning for follow-up care.

 EXAMPLE: V10–V15 Personal history of a malignancy

     V67.X Examination follow-up, no disease found ●

6. Classification stated on a pathology report overrides the morphology classification stated in the Disease Index.

EXERCISE 6–7 Neoplasm Coding II

STEP 1 Review the notes located at the beginning of the Neoplasm table and at the beginning of Chapter 2 in the Tabular List.

STEP 2 Code the following diagnostic statements.

1. Ca of the lung _____

2. Metastasis from the lung _____

3. Abdominal mass _____

4. Carcinoma of the breast (female) with
   metastasis to the axillary lymph nodes _____

5. Carcinoma of axillary lymph nodes and
   lungs, metastatic from the breast (female) _____

6. Astrocytoma _____

7. Skin lesion, left cheek _____

After completing this exercise, refer to Appendix IV to check your answers.

Table of Drugs and Chemicals

The Table of Drugs and Chemicals is used to identify drugs or chemicals that caused poisonings and adverse effects (Figure 6-6).

The official ICD-9-CM table contains a listing of the generic names of the drugs or chemicals, one column for poisonings, and five separate columns to indicate the external causes of adverse effects or poisonings. (Some publishers are now adding brand names to the list of drugs and chemicals.)

Substance	Poisoning	External Cause (E Code)				
		Accident	Therapeutic Use	Suicide Attempt	Assault	Undetermined
1-propanol	980.3	E860.4	—	E950.9	E962.1	E980.9
2-propanol	980.2	E860.3	—	E950.9	E962.1	E980.9
2, 4-D (dichlorophenoxyacetic acid)	989.4	E863.5	—	E950.6	E962.1	E980.7
2, 4-toluene diisocyanate	983.0	E864.0	—	E950.7	E962.1	E980.6
2, 4, 5-T (trichlorophenoxyacetic acid)	989.2	E863.5	—	E950.6	E962.1	E980.7
14-hydroxydihydromorphinone	965.09	E850.2	E935.2	E950.0	E962.0	E980.0
A						
ABOB	961.7	E857	E931.7	E950.4	E962.0	E980.4
Abrus (seed)	988.2	E865.3	—	E950.9	E962.1	E980.9
Absinthe	980.0	E860.0	—	E950.9	E962.1	E980.9
beverage	980.0	E860.0	E934.2	E950.4	E962.0	E980.4
Acenocoumarin, acenocoumarol	964.2	E858.2	E934.2	E950.4	E962.0	E980.3
Acepromazine	969.1	E853.0	E939.1	E950.3	E962.0	E980.3
Acetal	982.8	E862.4	—	E950.9	E962.1	E980.9
Acetaldehyde (vapor)	987.8	E869.8	—	E952.8	E962.2	E982.8
liquid	989.89	E866.8	—	E950.9	E962.1	E980.9
Acetaminophen	965.4	E850.4	E935.4	E950.0	E962.0	E980.0
Acetaminosalol	965.1	E850.3	E935.3	E950.0	E962.0	E980.0
Acetanilid(e)	965.4	E850.4	E935.4	E950.0	E962.0	E980.0
Acetarsol, acetarsone	961.1	E857	E931.1	E950.4	E962.0	E980.4
Acetazolamide	974.2	E858.5	E944.2	E950.4	E962.0	E980.4
Acetic						
acid	983.1	E864.1	—	E950.7	E962.1	E980.6
with sodium acetate (ointment)	976.3	E858.7	E946.3	E950.4	E962.0	E980.4
irrigating solution	974.5	E858.5	E944.5	E950.4	E962.0	E980.4
lotion	976.2	E858.7	E946.2	E950.4	E962.0	E980.4
anhydride	983.1	E864.1	—	E950.7	E962.1	E980.6
ether						

FIGURE 6-6 ICD-9-CM Table of Drugs and Chemicals (partial) (Courtesy of *St. Anthony's Illustrated ICD-9-CM,* 2004, (800) 632-0123)

An **adverse effect** or **adverse reaction** is the appearance of a pathologic condition caused by ingestion or exposure to a chemical substance properly administered or taken.

Code first the adverse effect(s) (or manifestations)(e.g., coma) by referring to the Index to Diseases.

The chemical substance is coded by referring to the Therapeutic Use column of the Table of Drugs and Chemicals.

CODING TIP: Never assign a code from the Poisoning column with a code from the Therapeutic Use column. Consider highlighting the Therapeutic Use column (Figure 6-6) in your coding manual as a reminder that these codes are *not* assigned with any of the others in the Table of Drugs and Chemicals.

EXAMPLE: Gastritis due to prescribed tetracycline

In this statement, gastritis (535.50) is the adverse effect (or manifestation) of the properly administered drug, tetracycline (E930.4).

Poisonings occur as the result of an overdose, wrong substance administered or taken, or intoxication (e.g., combining prescribed drugs with nonprescribed drugs or alcohol). The Table of Drugs and Chemicals categorizes poisonings according to accident, suicide attempt, assault, or undetermined.

Poisonings are coded by referring first to the Poisoning column of the Table of Drugs and Chemicals and then the External Cause (E code) columns within the table (with the exception of the Therapeutic Use column).

EXAMPLE: Accidental overdose of tetracycline

In this statement, the poisoning code is listed first (960.4) followed by the accidental overdose E code (E856).

Review the patient's record to determine the manifestations of the poisoning (e.g., headache, coma); refer to the Index to Diseases and sequence these codes after the codes for the poisoning and external cause.

- **Poisoning** (codes 960–989) is assigned according to classification of the drug or chemical.

- **Accident** (codes E850–E869) is used for accidental overdosing, wrong substance given or taken, drug inadvertently taken, or accidents in the use of drugs and chemical substances during medical or surgical procedures, and to show external causes of poisonings classifiable to 980–989.

- **Therapeutic use** (codes E930–E952) is used for the external effect caused by correct substance properly administered in therapeutic or prophylactic dosages.

- **Suicide attempt** (codes E950–E952) is a self-inflicted poisoning.

- **Assault** (codes E961–E962) is a poisoning inflicted by another person who intended to kill or injure the patient.

- **Undetermined** (codes E980–E982) is used if the record does not state whether the poisoning was intentional or accidental.

CODING TIPS:

The term *intoxication* often indicates that alcohol was involved (e.g., alcohol intoxication) or an accumulation effect of a medication in the patient's bloodstream occurred (e.g., Coumadin intoxication). When *alcohol intoxication* occurs, assign a code from the Poisoning column along with the appropriate E code. When an accumulation effect of a medication occurs, assign the manifestation code first (e.g., dizziness) and an E code from the Therapeutic Use column (e.g., Coumadin).

E codes are used to explain the cause of the poisoning or the adverse effect. They are not diagnoses but external causes or results of injury. Therefore, *E codes are always secondary, never primary, codes.*

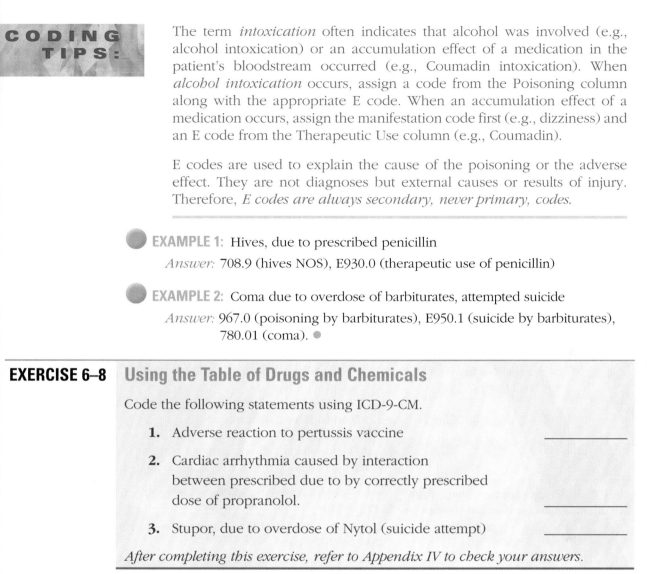 **EXAMPLE 1:** Hives, due to prescribed penicillin

Answer: 708.9 (hives NOS), E930.0 (therapeutic use of penicillin)

EXAMPLE 2: Coma due to overdose of barbiturates, attempted suicide

Answer: 967.0 (poisoning by barbiturates), E950.1 (suicide by barbiturates), 780.01 (coma). ●

EXERCISE 6–8 | Using the Table of Drugs and Chemicals

Code the following statements using ICD-9-CM.

1. Adverse reaction to pertussis vaccine _____

2. Cardiac arrhythmia caused by interaction between prescribed due to by correctly prescribed dose of propranolol. _____

3. Stupor, due to overdose of Nytol (suicide attempt) _____

After completing this exercise, refer to Appendix IV to check your answers.

SUPPLEMENTARY CLASSIFICATIONS

ICD-9-CM contains two supplementary classifications:

- V codes: factors influencing health status and contact with health services (V01–V82)
- E codes: external causes of injury and poisoning (E800–E999)

V Codes

V codes are contained in a supplementary classification of factors influencing the person's health status (Table 6-5A). These codes are used when a person seeks health care but does not have active complaints or symptoms, or when it is necessary to describe circumstances that could influence the patient's health care. These services fall into one of three categories:

1. Problems—issues that could affect the patient's health status

2. Services—Person is seen for treatment that is not caused by illness or injury

3. Factual reporting—used for statistical purposes (e.g., outcome of delivery or referral of patient without examination)

TABLE 6-5A ICD-9-CM V Code Sections, Descriptions, and Code Categories and Uses

SECTION	DESCRIPTION	CODE CATEGORY AND USE
V01–V06	Persons with potential health hazards related to communicable diseases	• V01—Patients who have been exposed to communicable diseases but have not been diagnosed • V02—Patients who have been identified as or are suspected of being infectious disease carriers • V03–V06—Patients who are seeking immunization against disease
V07–V09	Persons with need for isolation, other potential health hazards and prophylactic measures	• V07—Patients who are placed in an isolation area or who are receiving prophylactic measures (e.g., prophylactic fluoride administration by a dentist) • V08—Asymptomatic HIV infection status. NOTE: *Do not report code V08 if the patient is diagnosed with:* 　AIDS (042) 　Exposure to HIV (V01.7) 　Nonspecific serologic evidence of HIV (795.71) • V09—Patient's infection is drug-resistant; these are reported as a secondary code(s)
V10–V19	Persons with potential health hazards related to personal and family history	• V10–V15—Patient has personal history of malignant neoplasm, disease, allergy, hazard to health, or having undergone certain surgeries • V16–V19—Patient has family history of malignant neoplasm or other diseases/conditions CODING TIP: Be sure to verify history of codes in the Tabular List before reporting. Do not confuse *personal history of* with *family history of* codes.
V20–V29	Persons encountering health services in circumstances related to reproduction and development	• V20–V21—Patient is seen for a well baby or well child office visit CODING TIP: V20.x and V21.x may be reported with other ICD codes when documentation supports a well child visit as well as treatment of a condition. • V22–V23—Patient is supervised during pregnancy, whether normal or high-risk • V24—Patient is treated after having given birth • V25–V26—Patient is seen for contraceptive or procreative management • V27—Outcome of delivery is coded on the mother's insurance claim CODING TIP: V27.x is never reported as the first code on the insurance claim. Report from 650–659 first. • V28—Patient is screened during pregnancy • V29—Newborn is observed/evaluated, but no condition is diagnosed
V30–V39	Liveborn infants according to type of birth	• V30–V39—Type of birth is coded on the baby's insurance claim CODING TIP: V3x.xx is always reported as the first code on the insurance claim. If documented, also report congenital, perinatal, and other conditions.
V40–V49	Persons with a condition influencing their health status	• V40–V49—Patients who have not been diagnosed, but who have conditions that influence their health status EXAMPLE: Patient has colostomy as the result of colon cancer, which was successfully treated. Patient is seen for hay fever, and the provider documents that the patient is adjusting to having a colostomy. Code V44.3 is reported in addition to hay fever (477.9).

(continues)

TABLE 6-5A *(continued)*

SECTION	DESCRIPTION	CODE CATEGORY AND USE
V50–V59	Persons encountering health services for specific procedures and aftercare	• V50—Patient undergoes elective surgery (most payers will not provide reimbursement) • V51—Patient undergoes plastic surgery following injury EXAMPLE 1: Reconstructive surgery for healed third degree burns EXAMPLE 2: Breast implant following mastectomy • • V52–V54—Patient is fitted for prosthesis or implant or has device adjusted or removed • V55—Patient receives attention to artificial opening, such as colostomy cleansing • V56—Patient undergoes dialysis and dialysis catheter care CODING TIP: When reporting V56.xx, code also the associated condition (e.g., renal failure) • V57—Patient undergoes rehabilitation procedures CODING TIP: When reporting V57.xx, code also the associated condition (e.g., dysphasia) • V58—Patient receives other treatment or aftercare EXAMPLE: Patient is diagnosed with breast cancer, undergoes mastectomy, and is admitted for chemotherapy. Assign V58.1 as well as the appropriate breast cancer code. • • V59—Individual is donating an organ or tissue CODING TIP: Do not report V59.x on the recipient's insurance claim.
V60–V69	Persons encountering health services in other circumstances	• V60–V69—Individuals are seen for reasons other than resulting from illness or injury NOTE: Payers usually do not reimburse for these services. • EXAMPLE: Patient who pretends to be in pain so a narcotic will be prescribed, and the provider is alerted to the pretense by another provider (V65.2) •
V70–V83	Persons without reported diagnosis encountered during examination and investigation of individuals and populations	• V70—Patient seen for routine examination, such as annual physical CODING TIP: V70.x may be reported with other ICD codes when documentation supports the exam as well as treatment of a condition. • V71—Patient is observed and evaluated for a suspected condition, which is ruled out CODING TIP: Before reporting a V71 code, review the record to determine whether a sign or symptom can be coded instead. • V72–V82—Patient undergoes special investigations, examinations, or screenings EXAMPLE: Patient has extensive family history of ovarian cancer (e.g., mother, aunts, sisters) and elects to undergo screening as a preventive measure (V74.46). • • V83—Patient has generic carrier status

Refer to Table 6-5B for a list of main terms found in the ICD-9-CM Index to Diseases.

CODING TIP: Consult Appendix E (List of Three-Digit Categories) if you have trouble locating a V code category in the Disease Index.

EXERCISE 6–9 Exploring V Codes

Code the following statements using ICD-9-CM.

1. Family history of epilepsy with no evidence of seizures _____

2. Six-week postpartum checkup _____

3. Premarital physical _____

4. Consult with dietitian for patient with diabetes mellitus _____

5. Rubella screening _____

6. Exposure to TB _____

After completing this exercise, refer to Appendix IV to check your answers.

TABLE 6-5B Common V code indicators in the Index to Diseases

Admission to/for	History, personal
Aftercare follow-up	Maladjustment
Attention to	Newborn
Carrier of	Observation
Checkup for	Outcome
Closure of	Procedure (not performed because)
Contact with	Prophylactic
Contraception	Removal of
Dialysis	Replacement of
Encounter for	Routine examination
Exposure to	Screening (test) for
Examination of/for	Status
Fitting of	Test (for)
Follow-up (examination)	Vaccination
History, family	

CODING SPECIAL DISORDERS
HIV/AIDS

CAUTION: Before entering codes on a claim or any other official document that leaves the office, check to ensure that a signed Authorization for Release of HIV Status form was obtained from the patient. (See Figure 5-7 on page 90 for a sample authorization.) •

Code 042 is assigned when a documented diagnosis states the patient is HIV positive and exhibits manifestations associated with AIDS. Secondary codes are assigned to classify the manifestations such as Kaposi's sarcoma, candidiasis, coccidiosis, hemolytic anemia, and so on.

Assign code 079.53 in addition to 042 when HIV type 2 is identified by the provider.

Assign code 795.71 when screening for HIV was reported as nonspecific. For example, this code is used when a newborn tests positive upon HIV screening, but it cannot be determined whether the positive result reflects the true status of the baby or the seropositive status of the mother.

V01.7 is assigned for a patient who was exposed to the virus but not tested for infection.

V08 is assigned when the patient is HIV positive, asymptomatic, and does not exhibit manifestations of AIDS. Once the patient presents with symptoms, V08 can never again be reported.

Assign V65.44 when the reason for the encounter is counseling of a patient who has been tested for HIV. It does not matter whether the patient's HIV status is positive or negative.

Fracture Cases

CODING TIP: Study the fifth-digit classification note at the beginning of the Musculo-skeletal System chapter before coding fractures. This information is extremely helpful in selecting the correct code.

Distinction is required between closed and open fractures. If the diagnostic statement does not specify closed or open, select the appropriate closed fracture code. (It is important to realize that an open fracture does not always require an open reduction.) A list of common types of fractures appears in Table 6-6.

When a patient has suffered multiple injuries, list the injuries in descending order of severity on the claim.

EXERCISE 6–10 **Coding HIV/AIDS and Fracture Cases**

Code the following statements.

1. Patient is HIV positive with no symptoms _____

2. AIDS patient treated for candidiasis _____

3. Open fracture, maxilla _____

4. Greenstick fracture, 3rd digit right foot _____

5. Multiple fractures, right femur, distal end _____

After completing this exercise, refer to Appendix IV to check your answers.

TABLE 6-6 Common types of fractures

COMMON CLOSED FRACTURE TERMS	COMMON OPEN FRACTURE TERMS
Comminuted	Compound
Linear	Missile
Spiral	Puncture
Impacted	Fracture with a foreign body
Simple	Infected Fracture
Greenstick	
Compressed	

Late Effect

A **late effect** is a residual effect or sequela of a previous acute illness, injury, or surgery. The patient is currently dealing with long-term chronic effects of the disorder or trauma. The underlying acute condition no longer exists (Table 6-7).

In most cases, two codes will be required to classify diagnostic statements specifying residual conditions of an original illness or injury. The primary code is the residual (condition currently affecting the patient). The secondary code represents the original condition or etiology of the late effect. Locate the appropriate code by referencing the Index to Diseases under the main term, "Late." If the late effect is also due to an external cause, reference the External Causes Index under the word, "Late." Occasionally, one combination code is used to classify the diagnostic statement.

 EXAMPLE: Dysphasia due to CVA 6 months ago
Combination code is 438.12 ●

Occasionally, there will be a reversal of the primary and secondary positions. This occurs when the Index references the late effect first followed by a slanted bracketed residual code.

TABLE 6-7 Common late effects

ORIGINAL CONDITION/ETIOLOGY	LATE EFFECT/SEQUELA
Fracture	Malunion
CVA	Hemiplegia
Third-degree burn	Deep scarring
Polio	Contractures
Laceration	Keloid
Breast implant	Ruptured implant

EXAMPLE: Scoliosis due to childhood polio

Index reads: Scoliosis (acquired) (postural) 737.30

Due to or associated with

poliomyelitis 138 *[737.43]*

Primary code is 138

Secondary code is 737.43 (as dictated by the bracketed code in the index convention) •

Burns

Burns require two codes: one for the site and degree and a second for the percentage of body surface (not body part) affected.

The percentage of total body area or surface affected follows the "rule of nines":

• Head and neck	=	9%
• Back (trunk)	=	18%
• Chest (trunk)	=	18%
• Leg (each)	=	18%
		18%
• Arm (each)	=	9%
		9%
• Genitalia	=	1%

Total Body Surface (TBS)   100%

NOTE: To achieve the total percentage affected, health professionals add the affected extremities or regions together and state the combined total. •

EXERCISE 6–11 | **Coding Late Effect and Burns**

1. Malunion due to fracture, right ankle, 9 months ago _____
2. Brain damage due to subdural hematoma, 18 months previously _____
3. 2nd degree burn, anterior chest wall _____
4. Scalding with erythema, right forearm and hand _____
5. 3rd degree burn, back, 18% body surface _____

After completing this exercise, refer to Appendix IV to check your answers.

Congenital Versus Perinatal Conditions

Congenital anomalies (codes 740–759) are disorders diagnosed in infants at birth. (Adults can also be diagnosed with congenital anomalies because such disorders may have been previously undetected.)

● **EXAMPLE:** Congenital heart disease (746.x) describes heart defects that develop prior to birth and result from a failure of the heart or the blood vessels near the heart to develop normally. The causes are mostly unknown, but in some cases the disorder is due to alcohol consumption during pregnancy, heredity (genetics), or an infection during pregnancy. The disorder may be diagnosed before birth, or it may not be detected until birth (and even weeks or years after birth). ●

Perinatal conditions (codes 760–779) occur before birth, during birth, or within the **perinatal period**, or the first 28 days of life. Think of these conditions as something that happens to the patient.

● **NOTE:** Although CPT defines the *perinatal period* as the first 30 days of life, when assigning ICD-9-CM codes, you should use 28 days as the guideline. ●

● **EXAMPLE:** Drug withdrawal syndrome in a newborn (779.5) results when a mother is dependent on narcotics during the pregnancy. The narcotics taken by the mother pass from the mother's bloodstream through the placenta to the fetus, resulting in fetal addiction. At birth the baby's dependence continues but the narcotics are no longer available, and the baby's central nervous system becomes overstimulated causing withdrawal symptoms. The infant may also develop other related problems, such as low birth weight (765.x). ●

Use of E Codes

E codes consist of a four-character number (an E followed by three digits) and one digit after a decimal point. The Index to the External Cause of Injuries (E codes) is located separately in the Disease Index, after the Table of Drugs and Chemicals.

Although many states require the reporting of E codes, provider office insurance claims do not. However, reporting E codes on claims can expedite payment by health insurance carriers where no third-party liability for an accident exists. In such cases, it is necessary to report two E codes in addition to the appropriate injury codes *(E codes are never reported as primary codes).*

● **EXAMPLE:** Patient is seen for fractured pelvis sustained when he fell from a ladder while repairing his house. The fractured pelvis is coded and sequenced first on the claim followed by two E codes, one for the external cause and another for the place of occurrence: 808.8, E881.0, and E849.0.

Injury:	Fracture	
	pelvis	808.8
External Cause:	Fall (falling)	
	from, off	
	ladder	E881.0
Place of Occurrence:	Accident (to)	
	occurring (at) (in)	
	home (private) (residential)	E849.0

(Homeowners insurance covers injuries sustained by visitors, but not family members living in the home.) ●

CODING TIPS:

Review the note at the beginning of the E-Code Tabular List before coding External Causes of Injuries and Poisonings.

At the end of the Index to External Causes is a section entitled: "Fourth-Digit Subdivisions for the External Cause (E) Codes."

It may be necessary to consult the Appendix E List of Three-Digit Categories for assistance in locating possible main terms in the E-Code Index.

EXERCISE 6–12   **Coding External Cause of Injury**

Code the following statements.

1. Automobile accident, highway, passenger   _____
2. Worker injured by fall from ladder   _____
3. Accidental drowning, fell from power boat   _____
4. Soft tissue injury, right arm, due to snowmobile _____
    accident in patient's yard

After completing this exercise, refer to Appendix IV to check your answers.

CONSIDERATIONS TO ENSURE ACCURATE ICD-9-CM CODING

1. Preprinted diagnosis codes on encounter forms, routing slips, and coding lists should be reviewed to verify inclusion of fourth and fifth digits.

2. The latest edition code books should be purchased each year (new codes are effective each January) because they are annually updated (codes are added/deleted/revised).

3. Providers and insurance specialists should be kept informed of annual coding changes (e.g., newsletter subscription).

4. Diagnosis codes should be reviewed for accuracy when updates are installed in office management software.

5. A policy should be established to address assignment of codes when the office is awaiting the results of laboratory and pathology reports.

6. Reports of diagnostic tests performed at other facilities should be reviewed to ensure accurate coding.

7. The postoperative diagnosis should be coded (not the preoperative diagnosis).

8. Some computer programs automatically generate insurance claims for each encounter. Office staff should intercept these claims to verify diagnosis code(s) assigned (e.g., review for definitive diagnosis).

9. M codes (morphology codes) should not be reported on the CMS-1500 claim.

10. Diagnosis codes should be proofread to ensure proper entry in the permanent record (e.g., on-screen, paper, and electronic claim forms).

ICD-10-CM: DIAGNOSTIC CODING FOR THE FUTURE

The information presented in this section is excerpted and developed from the copyrighted Medicode publications, *Coders' Desk Reference* and *ICD-9-CM Volumes 1 & 2*. More comprehensive information on ICD-10-CM can be found in the Medicode/St. Anthony publication, *ICD-10 Made Easy*.

The tenth revision of the *International Classification of Diseases (ICD)*, and its clinical modification, is expected to replace the ICD-9-CM Index to Diseases and Tabular List by 2005. The World Health Organization (WHO) is responsible for revising ICD, and a clinical modification (CM) was developed by the Department of Health and Human Services (DHHS), National Center for Health Statistics (NCHS), for use in the United States.

ICD-10-CM includes more codes and applies to more users than ICD-9-CM because it is designed to collect data on every type of health care encounter (e.g., inpatient, outpatient, hospice, home health care, and long- term care). The ICD structure developed by WHO and clinically modified for use in the United States is also expected to improve the quality of data input into clinical databases and, thereby, provide more information about patients' health care encounters.

History of the ICD

The WHO's original intent for ICD was to serve as a statistical tool for the international collection and exchange of mortality (death) data. A subsequent revision was expanded to accommodate data collection for morbidity (disease) statistics. The seventh revision, published by WHO in 1955, was clinically modified for use in the United States after a joint study was conducted to evaluate the efficiency of **indexing** (cataloging diseases and procedures by code number) hospital diseases. The study participants included the American Hospital Association (AHA) and the American Association of Medical Record Librarians (AAMRL) (now called the American Health Information Management Association, or AHIMA). Results of that study led to the 1959 publication of the *International Classification of Diseases, Adapted for Indexing Hospital Records* (ICDA), by the federal Public Health Service. The ICDA uniformly modified ICD-7, and it gave the United States a way to classify patient operations and treatments.

An eighth edition of ICD, published by WHO in 1965, lacked the depth of clinical data required for America's emerging health care delivery system. In 1968, two widely accepted modifications were published in the United States: the *Eighth Revision of the International Classification of Diseases, Adapted for Use in the United States* (ICDA-8) and the *Hospital Adaptation of ICDA* (H-ICDA). Hospitals used either of these two systems until 1979 when ICD-9-CM was implemented. The ninth revision of the ICD by WHO, in 1975, once again prompted the development of a clinical modification. This time the incentive for creating a clinical modification of the ICD resulted from a process initiated in 1977 by the NCHS for hospital indexing and the retrieval of case data for clinical studies. After more than 30 years since its adoption in the United States, ICD has proven to be indispensable to anyone interested in payment schedules for the delivery of health care services to patients.

ICD-10

The WHO published ICD-10 in 1994 with a new name (*International Statistical Classification of Diseases and Related Health Problems*) and reorganized its three-digit categories (listed below). While the title was amended to clarify content and purpose and to reflect development of codes and descriptions beyond diseases and injuries, the familiar abbreviation "ICD" was kept. ICD-10 contains clinical detail, expands information about previously classified diseases, and classifies diseases discovered since the last revision.

ICD-10 also incorporates organizational changes and new features, but its format and conventions remain largely unchanged. Chapter titles, organization and *Includes* and *Excludes* notes are similar to ICD-9. The biggest difference is that the new codes are alphanumeric, and there is more detail in ICD-10-CM than in ICD-9-CM.

The ICD-10 coding system consists of 21 chapters:

Chapter 1	(A00–B99)	Certain Infectious and Parasitic Diseases
Chapter 2	(C00–D48)	Neoplasms
Chapter 3	(D50–D89)	Diseases of the Blood and Blood-forming Organs and Certain Disorders Involving the Immune Mechanism
Chapter 4	(E00–E90)	Endocrine, Nutritional, and Metabolic Diseases
Chapter 5	(F01–F99)	Mental and Behavioral Disorders
Chapter 6	(G00–G99)	Diseases of the Nervous System
Chapter 7	(H00–H59)	Diseases of the Eye and Adnexa
Chapter 8	(H60–H95)	Diseases of the Ear and Mastoid Process
Chapter 9	(I00–I97)	Diseases of the Circulatory System
Chapter 10	(J00–J99)	Diseases of the Respiratory System
Chapter 11	(K00–K93)	Diseases of the Digestive System
Chapter 12	(L00–L99)	Diseases of the Skin and Subcutaneous Tissue
Chapter 13	(M00–M99)	Diseases of the Musculoskeletal System and Connective Tissue
Chapter 14	(N00–N99)	Diseases of the Genitourinary System
Chapter 15	(O00–O99)	Pregnancy, Childbirth, and the Puerperium
Chapter 16	(P04–P94)	Certain Conditions Originating in the Perinatal Period
Chapter 17	(Q00–Q94)	Congenital Malformations, Deformations, and Chromosomal Abnormalities
Chapter 18	(R00–R99)	Symptoms, Signs, and Abnormal Clinical and Laboratory Findings, Not Elsewhere Classified
Chapter 19	(S00–T98)	Injury, Poisoning, and Certain Other Consequences of External Causes
Chapter 20	(V01–Y97)	External Causes of Morbidity
Chapter 21	(Z00–Z99)	Factors Influencing Health Status and Contact with Health Services

Two new chapters added to ICD-10 include "Diseases of the Eye and Adnexa" (Chapter 7) and "Disorders of the Ear and Mastoid Process" (Chapter 8). Supplementary classifications of the External Causes of Morbidity (called External Causes of Injury, or E codes, in ICD-9-CM) and Factors Influencing Health Status (or V codes) are incorporated into the core ICD-10 classification system. This means that these codes and descriptions are located throughout all chapters of ICD-10, and they are no longer designated as E codes and V codes.

Some chapter titles are revised for ICD-10. For example, ICD-9-CM Chapter 5 is titled "Mental Disorders" and the ICD-10 Chapter 5 title was changed to "Mental and Behavioral Disorders." The word "certain" was added to the title of Chapter 1, Infectious and Parasitic Diseases, to stress the fact that localized infections are classified to the pertinent body system (e.g., urinary tract infection would be classified to Chapter 14). The title of the ICD-9-CM chapter on congenital anomalies was expanded to include the terms, "deformations" and "chromosomal abnormalities."

ICD-10 chapters were rearranged to allow for expansion in the number of categories for disorders of the immune mechanism by including them in the chapter for diseases of the blood and blood-forming organs. In ICD-9-CM, these disorders are included with "Endocrine, Nutritional, and Metabolic Diseases." The chapters on "Diseases of the Genitourinary System, Pregnancy, Childbirth and the Puerperium," "Certain Conditions Originating in the Perinatal Period," and "Congenital Malformations, Deformations, and Chromosomal Abnormalities" are sequential in ICD-10.

Some conditions are reassigned to a different chapter because of new knowledge about the disorder. For example, in ICD-9-CM, gout is classified within the Endocrine, Nutritional, and Metabolic Diseases and Immunity Disorders chapter. In ICD-10, gout was moved to Chapter 13, "Diseases of the Musculoskeletal System and Connective Tissue."

ICD-10-CM

The NCHS emphasized problems identified in ICD-9-CM as it began to make clinical modifications to ICD-10 for the classification of mortality and morbidity data. In the United States, ICD-10 is being modified to:

- return to or exceed the level of specificity found in ICD-9-CM.
- expand the alphabetic index to diseases.
- provide code titles and language that complement accepted clinical practice.
- remove codes unique to mortality coding.

The modifications applied by the NCHS include:

- increasing ICD-10's five-character structure to six characters.
- incorporating common fourth-digit subcategories and fifth-digit subclassifications.
- creating codes that allow for laterality (e.g., unique code for right arm).
- adding trimesters to obstetric codes.
- creating combined diagnosis/symptoms codes.

Clinical modification does not affect the information reported to the WHO, but it expands that information for specificity purposes.

EXAMPLE 1: ICD-9 and ICD-9-CM Code Descriptions

ICD-9		ICD-9-CM	
140	Malignant neoplasm of the lip	140.0	Malignant neoplasm of the upper lip, vermilion border
374.1	Ectropion	374.13	Spastic ectropion

EXAMPLE 2: ICD-10 and ICD-10-CM Code Descriptions

ICD-10	**ICD-10-CM**
K57.3 Diverticular disease of large intestine without perforation or abscess	K57.31 Diverticular disease of large intestine without perforation or abscess with bleeding

ICD-10-CM codes begin with a letter and are followed by up to five numbers. All letters of the alphabet are used, and valid codes can contain three, four, five, or six characters.

EXAMPLE: ICD-10-CM Codes at Highest Level of Specificity

Z66   Do not resuscitate

Q90.1   Down syndrome, Trisomy 21, mosaicism (mitotic nondisjunction)

A69.21 Meningitis due to Lyme disease

J01.01 Acute recurrent maxillary sinusitis

ICD-10 Volumes

ICD-10 is published in three volumes, and publication dates were 1992 for Volume 1, 1993 for Volume 2, and 1994 for Volume 3.

ICD-10 Volume 1: Tabular List

Volume 1 contains a tabular list of alphanumeric disease codes. The same organizational structure in ICD-9 applies to ICD-10 so that all category codes with the same first three digits have common traits, and each digit beyond three adds specificity. In ICD-10, valid codes can contain anywhere from three to five digits; in the clinical modification, valid codes can contain up to six digits.

The ICD-9 organizational structure also applies to ICD-10 notes and instructions. When a note appears under a three-character category code, it applies to all codes within that category. Instructions located under a specific four- or five-character code apply only to that single code.

ICD-10 Volume 2: Instruction Manual

Volume 2 of ICD-10 contains rules and guidelines for mortality and morbidity coding. In ICD-10-CM, it is undecided whether a separate volume will be dedicated to rules, or if they will be organized under a different volume title. If Volume 2 of ICD-10-CM is titled "Instruction Manual," it will be important to remember that it does *not* refer to the Index to Diseases as in ICD-9-CM. CMS and the NCHS are modifying ICD-10 instructions for use in the United States, and these modifications may be available when the final draft of ICD-10-CM is published.

ICD-10 Volume 3: Alphabetic Index

Volume 3 of ICD-10 is an index to codes classified in the Tabular List. Like the ICD-9-CM Index to Diseases, terms in the ICD-10 index are organized alphabetically according to the name of the disease. The ICD-10-CM Alphabetic Index will consist of a similar arrangement of entities, diseases, and other conditions according to the axis of classification (organizing entities, diseases, and other conditions according to etiology, anatomy, or severity). In ICD-10-CM, anatomy is the primary axis of classification, which explains chapter titles like "Diseases of the Circulatory System" and "Diseases of the Genitourinary System."

Organizational Changes in ICD-10 and ICD-10-CM

ICD-10-CM will seem very familiar, but some classification changes include those related to iatrogenic illness, sequelae, and injury. **Iatrogenic illness** results from medical intervention (e.g., adverse reaction to contrast material injected prior to a scan). **Sequelae** (singular form is sequela) are late effects of injury or illness. In ICD-9-CM, these are classified within section 990–995, which is located at the end of the Injury and Poisoning chapter. In ICD-10, these codes appear at the end of each anatomic chapter, as appropriate.

EXAMPLE:

H59.2	Cystoid macular edema following cataract surgery (*Eye and Adnexa*)
K91.0	Vomiting following gastrointestinal surgery (*Digestive System*)
M96.2	Postradiation kyphosis (*Musculoskeletal System*)

An **injury** is a traumatic wound or some other damage to an organ. In ICD-9-CM, injuries are initially classified in the Injury and Poisoning chapter by type (e.g., all open wounds are classified in the same chapter). In ICD-10-CM, the axis of classification for injury is the anatomic site of injury. Thus, all injuries to the foot are classified together, as are all injuries to the head. Most of the multiple injury codes have been eliminated from ICD-10-CM, and injuries to the head are subdivided into the following three-digit categories:

Injuries to the head (S00–S09)

S00	Superficial injury of head
S01	Open wound of head
S02	Fracture of skull and facial bones
S03	Dislocation, sprain, and strain of joints and ligaments of head
S04	Injury of cranial nerves
S05	Injury of eye and orbit
S06	Intracranial injury
S07	Crushing injury of head
S08	Traumatic amputation of part of head
S09	Other and unspecified injuries of head

Other Issues of Importance When Comparing ICD-10-CM to ICD-9-CM

ICD-10-CM E codes classify diseases of the endocrine system, not external causes. External causes, currently classified in ICD-9-CM as E codes, will be V codes in ICD-10-CM. V codes, which are included in an ICD-9-CM supplemental classification to report factors influencing health status, have been changed to U Codes and Z Codes in ICD-10-CM.

EXAMPLE: ICD-10-CM External Cause and Health Status Codes

V01	Pedestrian injured in collision with pedal cycle
V79.3	Bus occupant (any) injured in unspecified nontraffic accident
W58	Bitten or struck by crocodile or alligator
X81	Confined or trapped in a low-oxygen environment
X39.41	Exposure to radon
X-5	Exposure to ignition or melting of nightwear
Y62.5	Failure of sterile precautions during heart catheterization
Y90.1	Blood alcohol level of 20–30 mg/100 ml
Z45.1	Encounter for adjustment and management of infusion pump
Z91.5	Personal history of self-harm

J Codes, included in the HCPCS Level II (National) coding system, are assigned to report drug administration. In ICD-10-CM, J Codes are used to report disorders of the respiratory system.

Implementing ICD-10-CM

Preparing all professionals—not just coders and insurance specialists—is key to the successful implementation of ICD-10-CM. Consider the following:

- *Create a task force.* Divide implementation of ICD-10-CM responsibilities into major working topics, and assign each member of the task force a job (e.g., coder training, physician training, and identification of software and application elements for information systems).

- *Be vigilant.* Assign one member of the task force to research, read, and summarize articles about ICD-10-CM implementation found in professional journals and newsletters, the Internet, and the *Federal Register*.

- *Alert the entire organization to the change to ICD-10-CM.* Don't wait until the implementation date to speak with information systems managers, vendors, business office, or physicians. The transition to ICD-10-CM affects all departments, so communication with everyone will avoid problems later. Open task force meetings to the entire organization, and invite representatives to become part of the working group.

- *Anticipate problems.* Plan for education and training of personnel, consider the costs associated with implementation of ICD-10-CM, and involve computer information systems personnel in the transition to ICD-10-CM (Table 6-8).

- *Train physicians.* The level of detail required in ICD-10-CM emphasizes physician participation. The patient's chart must specify terminology and provide complete documentation according to new standards. For example, in osteoporosis with pathologic fracture, the physician must identify the origin of osteoporosis as disuse, drug-induced, idiopathic, menopausal, postmenopausal, postsurgical, or postoophorectomy, along with the specific site.

- *Review patient charts.* Conduct a review of patient charts to identify documentation problems relevant to ICD-10-CM.

TABLE 6-8 Computer Information System (CIS) considerations for ICD-10-CM implementation

ICD-9-CM AND ICD-10-CM DIFFERENCES AND IMPLEMENTATION ISSUES FOR CIS			
CHARACTERISTIC	**ICD-9-CM**	**ICD-10-CM**	**IMPLEMENTATION ISSUE**
Number of characters	3–5	3–6	Fields that read ICD-10-CM codes must accommodate up to 6 characters.
Type of character	Numeric, except for V and E codes	Alphanumeric	Reprogramming may be necessary to distinguish between numbers (0,1) and alphabetic characters (O, I). EXAMPLE: Alphabetical characters may need to be capitalized to distinguish between the letter I and the number one (1); a slash may need to be used with the zero to distinguish between the number and the letter Ø, O). ● Use of the 10-key section of a keyboard is no longer appropriate for data entry.

Decimals	Decimals are used after the third character	Decimals are used after the third character	If your system currently accommodates decimals, make sure that up to three characters can be allowed after the decimal.
			 If your system does not accommodate decimals, there should be no implementation issues, other than the total number of characters required for each field.
			 NOTE: If your system accepts both ICD and HCPCS codes, the absence of a decimal may make it difficult for your system to distinguish between HCPCS codes and 5-character ICD-10-CM codes: both have five characters with an alpha character at the first position. ●
			 EXAMPLE:
			     E05.00 Thyrotoxicosis with diffuse goiter without thyrotoxic crisis or storm
			     E0500 Humidifier, durable for extensive supplemental humidification during IPPB treatments or oxygen delivery
			     Your system may need to be reprogrammed to use decimals with ICD-10-CM codes or to otherwise differentiate between those and HCPCS codes. ●

Hierarchy (organizational position of codes below three-digit categories)	Fourth- and fifth-digit codes have hierarchical relationships within three-digit categories.	Fourth-, fifth-, and sixth-character codes have hierarchical relationships within a three-character category	If your system recognizes ICD-9-CM's hierarchical relationship of fifth- to fourth-digit codes and fourth- to three-digit codes, reprogramming may be necessary to accommodate ICD-10-CM's additional hierarchical relationship—sixth- to fifth-character codes.

(continues)

TABLE 6-8 *(continued)*

ICD-9-CM AND ICD-10-CM DIFFERENCES AND IMPLEMENTATION ISSUES FOR CIS			
CHARACTERISTIC	**ICD-9-CM**	**ICD-10-CM**	**IMPLEMENTATION ISSUE**
Descriptions of codes	ICD-9-CM uses partial descriptions of codes in the Tabular List instead of restating category and subcategory code description.	Complete descriptions that stand alone.	Although the ICD-9-CM Tabular List uses partial descriptions for codes, data files are available that contain a complete description of each code. If your system uses such a data file, there should be no implementation issues. Some ICD-9-CM data files provide the code description in multiple fields: the three-digit category description, a four-digit subcategory description, and a five-digit subclassification description. If your system uses separate fields for category and subclassification descriptions, reprogramming may be necessary to accept the ICD-10-CM descriptions. Some ICD-9-CM data files contain abbreviate descriptions (e.g., 35-character, 48-character, or 150-character). If your code description field is limited by number of characters, be sure to use a vendor that can provide ICD-10-CM abbreviated descriptions in the length needed.
Coding Conventions	For example, excludes, includes, notes, essential modifiers, and nonessential modifiers.	For example, excludes, notes, essential modifiers, and nonessential modifiers.	ICD-10-CM incorporates coding conventions (e.g., includes, excludes, and notes) the same as ICD-9-CM. If your program contains this information, no changes should be necessary.
Quantity of codes	ICD-9-CM contains more than 15,000 Tabular List (Diseases) codes.	ICD-10-CM contains more than 25,000 codes.	ICD-10-CM contains more codes than ICD-9-CM. Reprogramming may be necessary to accommodate the increased number of codes and descriptions. Make sure your system has sufficient memory to handle the additional data. Remember that each ICD-10-CM code description is complete, which means more memory will be required.
Format and availability of data	Codes and descriptions are available both in print and electronic format.	Codes and descriptions are available in print. Access to electronic format has not yet been determined.	Most systems are set up to accept codes and descriptions electronically. Data files commonly provide codes and descriptions in specified formats (e.g., tab-delimited, fixed format, and comma-delimited). Because ICD-10-CM is not widely available, it may be difficult to acquire the codes and descriptions in the electronic format required by your system. Reprogramming may be required to accept a data file in a different format.

INTERNET LINKS

Accredited Standards Committee (ASC) (ASC X12)	http://www.x12.org
Department of Health and Human Services (DHHS)— HIPAA Administrative Simplification Provision	http://aspe.os.dhhs.gov/admnsimp
National Archives and Records Administration (NARA)—*Federal Register*	http://www.archives.gov
National Center for Health Statistics (NCHS)— ICD-9-CM and ICD-10-CM development	http://www.cdc.gov/nchs/icd9.htm
National Center for Vital and Health Statistics (NCVHS)—ICD-10-PCS development	http://cms.hhs.gov/paymentsystems/ icd9/icd10.asp
World Health Organization (WHO)—ICD-10 development (enter ICD-10 in Search and click OK)	http://www.who.int/whosis/icd10

Scheduling

ICD-10-CM is ready to be implemented in the United States, possibly in 2005, but a single procedural system has not been selected. In October 2000, the Department of Health and Human Services (HHS) selected Current Procedural Terminology (CPT) as the standard code set for reporting health care services in electronic transactions.

Planning for the Future

Procedures for updating subsequent editions in the United States will probably be similar to the process of updating ICD-9-CM. Revisions to ICD-9-CM are made once a year and are implemented January 1 of each year. Major changes in the time frame are published in the *Federal Register*. The ICD-9-CM Coordination and Maintenance Committee meets twice each year to discuss coding revisions proposed for the subsequent year.

INTERNET LINK

Ingenix will post updates about ICD-10-CM (and the inpatient procedural coding system, ICD-10-PCS) along with other coding issues at http://www.ingenixonline.com. Click Resources to view updates.

SUMMARY

- The *International Classification of Diseases* (ICD) was developed by the World Health Organization (WHO) to classify mortality (death) data from death certificates.

- The United States clinically modified ICD to facilitate the coding and classification and classify morbidity (disease) data from inpatient and outpatient records, physician office records, and statistical surveys. Currently in use is the *International Classification of Diseases, 9th Revision, Clinical Modification* (ICD-9-CM). ICD-10-CM and ICD-10-PCS are scheduled for possible implementation in 2005.

- The National Center for Health Statistics (NCHS) and the Centers for Medicare & Medicaid Services (CMS) oversee all changes and modifications to ICD-9-CM (and ICD-10-CM).

- The Medicare Catastrophic Coverage Act of 1988 mandated the reporting of ICD-9-CM diagnosis codes on Medicare claims. (Private insurers adopted similar requirements in subsequent years).

- Medical necessity is defined by the Medicare Program Integrity Manual as the determination that a service or procedure rendered is reasonable and necessary for the diagnosis or treatment of an illness or injury. If services/procedures might be found *medically unnecessary*, providers should have the patient sign an Advance Beneficiary Notice (ABN) that acknowledges patient responsibility for payment if Medicare denies the claim.

- NCHS and CMS annually update ICD-9-CM, and providers should order new coding manuals by September of each year. New codes usually go into effect on January 1 of each year, although some payers do not require/accept new codes until March 1.

- Diagnostic Coding and Reporting Guidelines for Outpatient Services: Hospital-Based and Physician Office were developed by the federal government for use in reporting diagnoses for claims submission. Four organizations develop and approve the guidelines, including AHA, AHIMA, CMS, and NCHS.

- Outpatient claims (CMS-1500) require the patient's primary diagnosis, secondary diagnoses, comorbidities, procedures, and services. Diagnoses are assigned ICD-9-CM codes, and procedures/services are assigned CPT and HCPCS national (level II) codes. Do *not* submit codes for qualified diagnoses on outpatient claims.

- Inpatient claims (UB-92) require the principal diagnosis, secondary diagnoses, comorbidities, principal procedure, and secondary procedures. All diagnoses and procedures are assigned ICD-9-CM codes. Submitting codes for qualified diagnoses *is* permitted on inpatient claims.

- When providers submit inpatient services and procedures for reimbursement, the CMS-1500 claim is used; diagnoses are assigned ICD-9-CM codes and procedures/services are assigned CPT/HCPCS National codes. (The hospital submits a claim for reimbursement of inpatient services on the UB-92 claim, and the provider submits a claim using the CMS-1500 claim. Each entity is entitled to reimbursement for the services/procedures provided to an inpatient.)

- ICD-9-CM consists of Volume 1 (Tabular List), Volume 2 (Index to Diseases), and Volume 3 (Index to Procedures and Tabular List). Volume 1 contains 17 chapters and five appendices, including two supplementary classifications (V codes and E codes). Volume 2 is often sequenced first for ease of use, and contains an alphabetical index of diseases and injuries, table of drugs and chemicals, and an index to external causes of injury and poisoning. Volume 3 contains an index to procedures (often sequenced first) and a tabular list of procedures.

- V codes classify factors influencing health status and contact with health services. E codes classify external causes of injury and poisoning.

- ICD-9-CM Index to Diseases is organized according to alphabetical main terms (boldfaced conditions), nonessential modifiers (in parentheses), and subterms (essential modifiers that are indented below main terms). It also includes several tables: Hypertensive/Hypertension Table, Neoplasms Table, and Table of Drugs and Chemicals.

● To properly assign an ICD-9-CM code locate the main term in the Index to Diseases, apply Index coding conventions (e.g., *See, See Also*), and verify the code in the Tabular List of Diseases (applying Tabular List coding conventions).

● Index to Diseases coding conventions include: codes in slanted brackets, eponyms, essential modifiers, NEC, nonessential modifiers, notes, *See, See Also*, and *See Category.* Tabular List coding conventions include: and, bold type, braces, brackets, code first underlying disease, colon, excludes, format, fourth and fifth digits, includes, NOS, notes, parentheses, use additional code, and with. Index to Procedures coding conventions include: *omit code.* Tabular List (Procedures) coding conventions include: *code also any synchronous procedures.*

STUDY CHECKLIST

☐ Read the textbook chapter, and highlight key concepts.

☐ Create an index card for each key term.

☐ Access the chapter Internet links to learn more about concepts.

☐ Complete the chapter review, verifying answers in Appendix IV.

☐ Complete Web Tutor assignments and take online quizzes.

☐ Complete workbook chapter, verifying answers with your instructor.

☐ Form a study group with classmates to discuss chapter concepts in preparation for an exam.

REVIEW

The ICD-9-CM Coding review is organized according to the ICD-9-CM chapters and supplemental classifications. To properly code, refer first to the Disease Index (to locate main term and subterm entries) and then to the Disease Tabular List (to review notes and verify the code selected).

● **NOTE:** Although the review is organized by chapter/supplemental classification, codes from outside a particular chapter/supplemental classification may be required to completely classify a case. ●

Underline the main term in each item; then use Index to Diseases and Tabular List coding rules and conventions to assign the code(s). Enter the code(s) on the line next to each diagnostic statement. Be sure to list the primary code first.

INFECTIOUS AND PARASITIC DISEASES (INCLUDING HIV)

1. Aseptic meningitis due to AIDS   _____

2. Asymptomatic HIV infection   _____

3. Septicemia due to streptococcus   _____

4. Dermatophytosis of the foot   _____

5. Measles; no complications noted   _____

6. Nodular pulmonary tuberculosis; confirmed histologically   _____

7. Acute cystitis due to *E. coli*   _____

8. Tuberculosis osteomyelitis of lower leg; confirmed by histology   _____

9. Gas gangrene   _____

NEOPLASMS

10. Malignant melanoma of skin of scalp   _____

11. Lipoma of face   _____

12. Glioma of the parietal lobe of the brain   _____

13. Adenocarcinoma of prostate   _____

14. Carcinoma *in situ* of vocal cord   _____

15. Hodgkin's granuloma of intra-abdominal lymph nodes and spleen   _____

16. Paget's disease with infiltrating duct carcinoma of breast,
    nipple and areola   _____

17. Liver cancer   _____

18. Metastatic adenocarcinoma from breast to brain
    (right mastectomy performed 5 years ago)   _____

19. Cancer of the pleura (primary site)   _____

ENDOCRINE, NUTRITIONAL AND METABOLIC DISEASES, AND IMMUNITY DISORDERS

20. Cushing's Syndrome   _____

21. Hypokalemia   _____

22. Non-insulin dependent diabetes mellitus, uncontrolled, with malnutrition   _____

23. Hypogammaglobulinemia   _____

24. Hypercholesterolemia   _____

25. Nephrosis due to type 2 diabetes   _____

26. Toxic diffuse goiter with thyrotoxic crisis   _____

27. Cystic fibrosis   _____

28. Panhypopituitarism   _____

29. Rickets   _____

DISEASES OF THE BLOOD AND BLOOD-FORMING ORGANS

30. Sickle cell disease with crisis

31. Iron deficiency anemia secondary to blood loss   _____

32. Von Willebrand's disease   _____

33. Chronic congestive splenomegaly   _____

34. Congenital nonspherocytic hemolytic anemia   _____

35. Essential thrombocytopenia   _____

36. Malignant neutropenia   _____

37. Fanconi's anemia   _____

38. Microangiopathic hemolytic anemia   _____

39. Aplastic anemia secondary to antineoplastic medication for breast cancer   _____

MENTAL DISORDERS

40. Acute exacerbation of chronic undifferentiated schizophrenia   _____
41. Reactive depressive psychosis due to the death of a child   _____
42. Hysterical neurosis   _____
43. Anxiety reaction manifested by fainting   _____
44. Alcoholic gastritis due to chronic alcoholism (episodic)   _____
45. Juvenile delinquency; patient was caught shoplifting   _____
46. Depression   _____
47. Hypochondria; patient also has continuous laxative habit   _____
48. Acute senile dementia with Alzheimer's disease   _____
49. Epileptic psychosis with generalized grand mal epilepsy   _____

DISEASES OF THE NERVOUS SYSTEM AND SENSE ORGANS

50. Neisseria meningitis   _____
51. Intracranial abscess   _____
52. Postvaricella encephalitis   _____
53. Hemiplegia due to old CVA   _____
54. Encephalitis   _____
55. Retinal detachment with retinal defect   _____
56. Congenital diplegic cerebral palsy   _____
57. Tonic-clonic epilepsy   _____
58. Infantile glaucoma   _____
59. Mature cataract   _____

DISEASES OF THE CIRCULATORY SYSTEM

60. Congestive rheumatic heart failure   _____
61. Mitral valve stenosis with aortic valve insufficiency   _____
62. Acute rheumatic heart disease   _____
63. Hypertensive cardiovascular disease, malignant   _____
64. Congestive heart failure; benign hypertension   _____
65. Secondary benign hypertension; stenosis of renal artery   _____
66. Malignant hypertensive nephropathy with uremia   _____
67. Acute renal failure; essential hypertension   _____
68. Acute myocardial infarction of inferolateral wall, initial episode of care   _____
69. Arteriosclerotic heart disease (native coronary artery) with angina pectoris   _____

DISEASES OF THE RESPIRATORY SYSTEM

70. Aspiration pneumonia due to regurgitated food   _____
71. Streptococcal Group B pneumonia   _____
72. Respiratory failure due to myasthenia gravis   _____

73. Intrinsic asthma in status asthmaticus _____

74. COPD with emphysema _____

DISEASES OF THE DIGESTIVE SYSTEM

75. Supernumerary tooth _____

76. Unilateral femoral hernia with gangrene _____

77. Cholesterolosis of gallbladder _____

78. Diarrhea _____

79. Acute perforated peptic ulcer _____

80. Acute hemorrhagic gastritis with acute blood loss anemia _____

81. Acute appendicitis with perforation and peritoneal abscess _____

82. Acute cholecystitis with cholelithiasis _____

83. Aphthous stomatitis _____

84. Diverticulosis and diverticulitis of colon _____

85. Esophageal reflux with esophagitis _____

DISEASES OF THE GENITOURINARY SYSTEM

86. Vesicoureteral reflux with bilateral reflux nephropathy _____

87. Acute glomerulonephritis with necrotizing glomerulolitis _____

88. Actinomycotic cystitis _____

89. Subserosal uterine leiomyoma, cervical polyp and endometriosis of uterus _____

90. Dysplasia of the cervix _____

DISEASES OF PREGNANCY, CHILDBIRTH, AND THE PUERPERIUM

91. Defibrination syndrome following termination of pregnancy procedure two weeks ago _____

92. Miscarriage at 19 weeks gestation _____

93. Incompetent cervix resulting in miscarriage _____

94. Postpartum varicose veins of legs _____

95. Spontaneous breech delivery _____

96. Triplet pregnancy, delivered spontaneously _____

97. Retained placental without hemorrhage, delivery this admission _____

98. Pyrexia of unknown origin during the puerperium (postpartum), delivery during previous admission _____

99. Late vomiting of pregnancy, undelivered _____

100. Pre-eclampsia complicating pregnancy, delivered this admission _____

DISEASES OF THE SKIN AND SUBCUTANEOUS TISSUE

101. Diaper rash _____

102. Acne vulgaris _____

103. Post-infectional skin cicatrix _____

104. Cellulitis of the foot; culture reveals staphylococcus _____

105. Infected ingrowing nail _____

DISEASES OF THE MUSCULOSKELETAL SYSTEM AND CONNECTIVE TISSUE

106. Displacement of thoracic intervertebral disc _____

107. Primary localized osteoarthrosis of the hip _____

108. Acute juvenile rheumatoid arthritis _____

109. Chondromalacia of the patella _____

110. Pathologic fracture of the vertebra due to metastatic carcinoma of the bone from the lung _____

CONGENITAL ANOMALIES

111. Congenital diaphragmatic hernia _____

112. Single liveborn male (born in the hospital) with polydactyly of fingers _____

113. Unilateral cleft lip and palate _____

114. Patent ductus arteriosus _____

115. Congenital talipes equinovalgus _____

CERTAIN CONDITIONS ORIGINATING IN THE PERINATAL PERIOD

116. Erythroblastosis fetalis _____

117. Hyperbilirubinemia of prematurity, prematurity (birthweight 2000 grams) _____

118. Erb's palsy _____

119. Hypoglycemia in infant with diabetic mother _____

120. Premature "crack" baby born in hospital to cocaine-dependent mother (birthweight 1,247 grams) _____

SYMPTOMS, SIGNS, AND ILL-DEFINED CONDITIONS

121. Abnormal cervical pap smear _____

122. Sudden infant death syndrome _____

123. Sleep apnea with insomnia _____

124. Fluid retention and edema _____

125. Elevated blood pressure reading _____

INJURY AND POISONING

Fractures, Dislocations and Sprains

126. Open frontal fracture with subarachnoid hemorrhage with brief loss of consciousness _____

127. Supracondylar fracture of right humerus and fracture of olecranon process of the right ulna _____

128. Anterior dislocation of the elbow

129. Dislocation of the 1st and 2nd cervical vertebra

130. Sprain of lateral collateral ligament of knee

Open Wounds and Other Trauma

131. Avulsion of eye

132. Traumatic below the knee amputation with delayed healing

133. Open wound of buttock

134. Open wound of wrist involving tendons

135. Laceration of external ear

136. Traumatic subdural hemorrhage with open intracranial wound;
loss of consciousness, 30 minutes

137. Concussion without loss of consciousness

138. Traumatic laceration of the liver, moderate

139. Traumatic hemothorax with open wound into thorax and
concussion with loss of consciousness

140. Traumatic duodenal injury

Burns

141. Third-degree burn of lower leg and second-degree burn of thigh

142. Deep third-degree burn of forearm

143. Third-degree burns of back involving 20% of body surface

144. Thirty percent body burns with 10%, third degree

145. First- and second-degree burns of palm

Foreign Bodies

146. Coin in the bronchus with bronchoscopy for removal of the coin

147. Foreign body in the eye

148. Marble in colon

149. Bean in nose

150. Q-Tip stuck in ear

Complications

151. Infected ventriculoperitoneal shunt

152. Displaced breast prosthesis

153. Leakage of mitral valve prosthesis

154. Postoperative superficial thrombophlebitis of the right leg

155. Dislocated hip prosthesis

V CODES

156. Exposure to tuberculosis _____

157. Family history of colon carcinoma _____

158. Status post unilateral kidney transplant, human donor _____

159. Encounter for removal of cast _____

160. Admitted to donate bone marrow _____

161. Encounter for chemotherapy for patient with Hodgkin's lymphoma _____

162. Reprogramming of cardiac pacemaker _____

163. Replacement of tracheostomy tube _____

164. Encounter for renal dialysis for patient in chronic renal failure _____

165. Encounter for speech therapy for patient with dysphasia secondary to an old CVA _____

166. Encounter for fitting of artificial leg _____

167. Encounter for observation of suspected malignant neoplasm of the cervix _____

168. Visit to radiology department for barium swallow; abdominal pain; findings are negative; barium swallow performed and the findings are negative _____

169. Follow-up examination of colon adenocarcinoma resected one year ago, no recurrence found _____

170. Routine general medical examination _____

171. Examination of eyes _____

172. Encounter for laboratory test; patient complains of fatigue _____

173. Encounter for physical therapy; status post below the knee amputation six months ago _____

174. Kidney donor _____

175. Encounter for chemotherapy; breast carcinoma _____

CODING LATE EFFECTS

Place an X on the line for each diagnostic statement that identifies a late effect of an injury/illness.

176. Hemiplegia due to previous cerebrovascular accident _____

177. Malunion of fracture, right femur _____

178. Scoliosis due to infantile paralysis _____

179. Keloid secondary to injury 9 months ago _____

180. Gangrene, left foot, following third-degree burn of foot 2 weeks ago _____

181. Cerebral thrombosis with hemiplegia _____

182. Mental retardation due to previous viral encephalitis _____

183. Laceration of tendon of finger 2 weeks ago. Admitted now for tendon repair _____

Code the following:

184. Residuals of poliomyelitis _____

185. Sequela of old crush injury to left foot _____

186. Cerebrovascular accident two years ago with late effects   _____

187. Effects of old gunshot wound, left thigh   _____

188. Disuse osteoporosis due to previous poliomyelitis   _____

189. Brain damage following cerebral abscess 7 months ago   _____

190. Hemiplegia due to old cerebrovascular accident   _____

ADVERSE REACTIONS AND POISONINGS

191. Ataxia due to interaction between prescribed Carbamazepine
and Erythromycin   _____

192. Vertigo as a result of dye administered for a scheduled IVP   _____

193. Accidental ingestion of mother's oral contraceptives
(no signs or symptoms resulted)   _____

194. Hemiplegia; patient had an adverse reaction to prescribed
Enovid one year ago   _____

195. Stricture of esophagus due to accidental lye ingestion three years ago   _____

196. Listlessness resulting from reaction between prescribed Valium and
ingestion of a six-pack of beer   _____

197. Lead poisoning (child had been discovered eating paint chips)   _____

198. Allergic reaction to unspecified drug   _____

199. Theophylline toxicity   _____

200. Carbon monoxide poisoning from car exhaust (suicide attempt)   _____

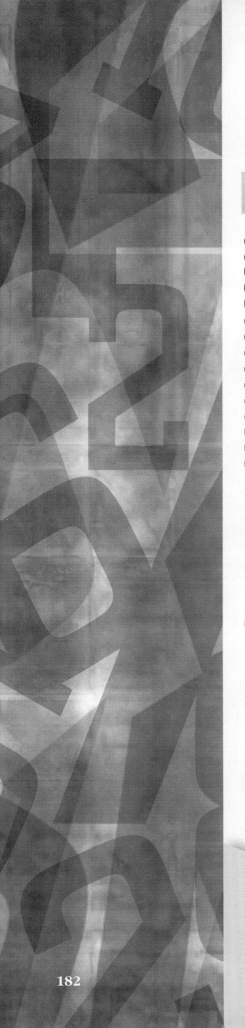

KEY TERMS

care plan oversight services
case management services
Category I codes
Category II codes
Category III codes
closed fracture treatment
comprehensive assessment
confirmatory consultation
consultation
contributory components
coordination of care
counseling
CPT-5
CPT-5 Project
CPT Coding Conventions
    boldface type
    cross-reference term *(See)*
    descriptive qualifier
    guidelines
    inferred words
    instructional notes
    italicized type
    separate procedure
    surgical package
CPT Extent of Examination
    problem focused
    expanded problem focused
    detailed
    comprehensive
CPT Extent of History
    problem focused
    expanded problem focused
    detailed
    comprehensive
CPT Symbols
    ●
    ▲
    ►◄
    ;
    *
    +
    ⊘
critical care services
cystourethroscopy
direct laryngoscopy
direct patient contact
disease oriented panel
domiciliary care

emergency department services
endoscopic guide-wire dilation
Evaluation and Management
    Documentation Guidelines
face-to-face time
global surgery
history
home services
hospital discharge services
indirect laryngoscopy
initial hospital care
key components
laboratory panel
major surgical procedure
manipulation of a fracture
medical decision making
minor surgical procedure
multiple surgical procedure
nature of the presenting problem
neonatal intensive care
newborn care
nursing facility services
observation services
open fracture treatment
organ panel
package concept
percutaneous skeletal fixation
physical examination
physician standby services
place of service
preoperative clearance
preventive medicine services
professional component
prolonged services
radiologic views
reduction of a fracture
referral
skin lesion
special report
subsequent hospital care
subsequent nursing facility care
surgical package
technical component
type of service
unit/floor time
unlisted procedure
unlisted service
without direct patient contact

Chapter 7 CPT Coding

OBJECTIVES

Upon successful completion of this chapter, you should be able to:

1. Define key terms.

2. Discuss the importance of carefully proofreading all code numbers reported on a claim.

3. Explain the format of CPT.

4. Compare ICD-9-CM to CPT.

5. Explain why modifiers were developed for CPT.

6. Determine the level of evaluation and management service.

7. Differentiate between a new and an established patient.

8. List requirements for assigning emergency department and critical care codes.

9. Explain the difference between a consultation and a confirmatory consultation.

10. Discuss qualifications for a "preventive medicine visit."

11. Define "global surgical period" as used in CPT and as applied by the insurance industry.

12. Explain the significance of the asterisk next to a CPT code (starred procedure).

INTRODUCTION

This chapter introduces the assignment of **Current Procedural Terminology (CPT)** service and procedure codes reported on the CMS-1500 claim. CPT is published by the American Medical Association and includes codes for procedures performed and services provided to patients. It is level one of the Healthcare Common Procedure Coding System (HCPCS), which also contains level two (national codes) and level three (local codes). Because of the introductory nature of this chapter, you are encouraged to obtain a comprehensive textbook that covers CPT principles and practice (e.g., Delmar's *Understanding Medical Coding: A Comprehensive Guide* by Sandra L. Johnson).

CPT CODING SYSTEM

Current Procedural Terminology (CPT) is a listing of descriptive terms and identifying codes for reporting medical services and procedures. It provides a uniform language that describes medical, surgical, and diagnostic services to facilitate communication among providers, patients, and insurers. The American Medical Association (AMA) first published CPT in 1966 and subsequent editions expanded its descriptive terms and codes for diagnostic and therapeutic procedures. Five-digit codes were introduced in 1970, replacing the four-digit classification. In 1983, CPT was adopted as part of the Healthcare Common Procedure Coding System (HCPCS) and its use was mandated for reporting Medicare Part B services. In 1986, HCPCS was required for reporting to Medicaid agencies, and in July 1987, as part of the Omnibus Budget Reconciliation Act (OBRA), CMS mandated that CPT codes be reported for outpatient hospital surgical procedures.

The AMA prepares an annual update of CPT that is available in late fall of each year preceding its implementation. Federal programs (e.g., Medicare and Medicaid) generally implement the new codes on January 1 of each year; other third-party payers may implement the new codes on the same date or later (e.g., March 1). Be sure to check with each payer to determine when to begin using the new codes. With each update, outdated procedures are deleted, new procedures are added, and narrative descriptions are revised. The ICD and CPT coding manuals are available from Delmar Learning as the exclusive distributor for Medicode and St. Anthony products. CPT may also be ordered from the AMA by calling (800) 621-8335.

INTERNET LINK

Order CPT coding books online at http://www.delmarhealthcare.com or http://www.ama-assn.org.

CPT codes are used to report services and procedures performed on patients:

- by providers in offices, clinics, and private homes.
- by providers in institutional settings such as hospitals, nursing facilities, and hospices.
- when the provider is employed by the health care facility (e.g., many of the physicians associated with Veterans Administration Medical Centers are employees of that organization).
- by a hospital outpatient department (e.g., ambulatory surgery, emergency department, and outpatient laboratory or radiographic procedures).

Procedures and services submitted on a claim must be linked to the ICD-9-CM code that justifies the need for the service or procedure. That ICD-9-CM code must demonstrate medical necessity for the service or procedure to receive reimbursement consideration by insurance payers.

The assignment of Current Procedural Terminology (CPT) codes simplifies reporting and assists in the accurate identification of procedures and services for third-party payer consideration. CPT codes and descriptions are based on consistency with contemporary medical practice as performed by clinical providers throughout the country.

NOTE: The inclusion or exclusion of procedures and services in the CPT manual does not automatically result in third-party payer reimbursement or health insurance coverage. Insurance specialists should verify coverage of procedures and services with payers and determine that claims submitted for reimbursement are coded accurately. ●

In response to the electronic data interchange requirements of the Health Insurance Portability and Accountability Act of 1996 (HIPAA), the American Medical Association initiated development of a fifth edition of CPT, entitled **CPT-5**. Among HIPAA's requirements is that code sets and classification systems be implemented in a cost-effective manner that includes the low cost, efficient distribution and application to all users. While CPT was identified as the procedure coding standard for the reporting of physician services in 2000, the May 7, 1998 *Federal Register* reported that "CPT is not always precise or unambiguous . . ." The CPT-5 project was the AMA's response.

Similarities Between CPT-4 and CPT-5

CPT codes will remain 5-digits in length, and code descriptions will continue to reflect health care services and procedures performed in modern medical practice. In addition, the process of periodically reviewing and updating codes and descriptions will continue.

Changes to CPT

CPT supports electronic data interchange (EDI), the computer-based patient record (CPR) or electronic medical record (EMR), and reference/research databases. CPT can also be used to track new technology and performance measures. Code descriptors were improved to eliminate ambiguous terms, and guidelines and notes underwent revision to make them more comprehensive, easier to interpret, and more specific. A CPT glossary was created to standardize definitions and differentiate the use of synonymous terms; and a searchable, electronic CPT index is under development along with a computerized database to delineate relationships among CPT code descriptions.

Improvements to CPT are underway to address the needs of hospitals, managed care organizations and long-term care facilities. In 2000, the AMA completed the **CPT-5 Project** (with changes phased in starting with CPT 2000 and concluding with CPT 2003), resulting in the establishment of three categories of CPT codes:

- **Category I codes:** procedures/services identified by a five-digit CPT code and descriptor nomenclature; these are codes traditionally associated with CPT and organized within six sections.

- **Category II codes:** contain "performance measurements" tracking codes that are assigned an alphanumeric identifier with a letter in the last field (e.g., 1234A); these codes will be located after the Medicine section, and *their use is optional.*

- **Category III codes:** contain "emergency technology" temporary codes assigned for data collection purposes that are assigned an alphanumeric identifier with a letter in the last field (e.g., 0001T); these codes are located after the Medicine section, and they will be archived after five years unless accepted for placement within Category I sections of CPT.

CPT Sections

CPT organizes Category I procedures and services within six sections:

- Evaluation and Management (E/M) (99201–99600)
- Anesthesia (00100–01999)
- Surgery (10040–69990)
- Radiology (70010–79999)
- Pathology and Laboratory (80048–89399)
- Medicine (90281–99199)

NOTE:

- The E/M section is located at the beginning of CPT because these codes are reported by all specialties.
- Codes (99100–99140) that classify *Qualifying Circumstances for Anesthesia Services* are located in the Medicine section (and explained in the Anesthesia section guidelines); they are to be reported with Anesthesia codes.

CPT Code Number Format

A five-digit code number and a narrative description identify each procedure and service listed in CPT. Most procedures and services contain stand-alone descriptions. To save space, some descriptions are not printed in their entirety next to a code number. Instead, the entry is indented and the coder must refer back to the common portion of the code description that is located before the semicolon.

EXAMPLE 1: Stand-alone code description

27870 Arthrodesis, ankle; any method

EXAMPLE 2: Indented code description

27780 Closed treatment of proximal fibula or shaft fracture; without manipulation

27781 with manipulation

The code description for 27781 is *closed treatment of proximal fibula or shaft fracture; with manipulation.*

CPT Appendices

CPT contains five appendices that are located between the Medicine section and the index. Insurance specialists should carefully review these appendices to become familiar with coding changes that affect the practice annually:

- *Appendix A:* detailed descriptions of each CPT modifier.

CODING TIP: Place a marker at the beginning of Appendix A because you will refer to this appendix often.

- *Appendix B:* annual CPT coding changes (added, deleted, and revised CPT codes).

Carefully review Appendix B of your current CPT manual because it will serve as the basis for updating interoffice documents and billing tools.

- *Appendix C:* clinical examples for codes found in Evaluation and Management.
- *Appendix D:* add-on codes.

Add-on codes are identified in CPT with a **+** symbol.

- *Appendix E:* codes exempt from modifier -51 reporting rules.

These codes are identified in CPT with a Ⓞ symbol.

CPT Symbols

Seven symbols are located throughout the CPT coding book:
- ● A bullet located to the left of a code number identifies new procedures and services added to CPT

   EXAMPLE: (CPT 2003)   CPT code 33215 was added.
   - ● **33215**   Repositioning of previously implanted transvenous pacemaker or pacing cardioverter-defibrillator (right atrial or right ventricular) electrode
- ▲ A triangle located to the left of a code number identifies a code description that has been revised.

   EXAMPLE: (CPT 2003)   CPT code 33216 was revised to delete the reference to "repositioning."
   - ▲ **33216**   Insertion or repositioning of a transvenous electrode (15 days or more after initial insertion); single chamber (one electrode) permanent pacemaker or single chamber pacing cardioverter-defibrillator
- ►◄ Horizontal triangles surround revised guidelines and notes. *This symbol is not used for revised code descriptions.*

   EXAMPLE: (CPT 2003)
   - ► **44238**   Unlisted laparoscopy procedure, intestine (except rectum) ◄

A complete list of code additions, deletions, and revisions is found in Appendix B of CPT. Revisions marked with horizontal triangles (►◄) are *not* included in Appendix B, and coders need to carefully review all CPT guidelines and notes in the new edition of CPT.

; To save space in CPT, some code descriptions are not printed in their entirety next to a code number. Instead, the entry is indented and the coder must refer back to the common portion of the code description that is located before the semicolon. The common portion begins with a capital letter, and the abbreviated (or subordinate) descriptions are indented and begin with lower-case letters.

> **EXAMPLE:** (CPT 2003)   The code description for 99316 is *Nursing facility discharge day management; more than 30 minutes*
>
> **99315**   Nursing facility discharge day management; 30 minutes or less
> **99316**   more than 30 minutes ●

CPT is printed using proportional spacing, and careful review of code descriptions to locate the semicolon may be necessary.

* The asterisk (or star) located next to minor procedure code numbers indicates variable preoperative and postoperative services. An asterisk (or star) indicates that the package concept *does not apply* to these procedures. Starred procedures are usually paid on a fee-for-service basis, which means that a charge for each service is generated.

The **package concept** (also called **global surgery** or **surgical package**) includes the procedure, local infiltration, metacarpal/digital block or topical anesthesia when used, and normal, uncomplicated follow-up care.

> **EXAMPLE:** (CPT 2003)
>
> **33010***   Pericardiocentesis; initial
> **33011***   subsequent ●

Include the asterisk next to applicable codes on preprinted documents (e.g., encounter form) as a reminder that individual services for these procedures are separately itemized and billed.

+ The plus symbol identifies add-on codes for procedures that are commonly, but not always, performed at the same time and by the same surgeon as the primary procedure. Parenthetical notes, located below add-on codes, often identify the primary procedure to which add-on codes apply.

> **EXAMPLE:** (CPT 2003)
>
> **22210**   Osteotomy of spine, posterior or posterolateral approach, one vertebral segment; cervical
> **+ 22216**   each additional vertebral segment (List separately in addition to primary procedure.) ●

Codes identified with **+** are never reported as stand-alone codes; they are reported with primary codes. Also, *do not* append add-on codes with modifier -51.

Ⓞ   This symbol identifies codes that are *not* to be used with modifier -51. These codes are reported in addition to other codes, but they are not classified as add-on codes.

> ⬤ **EXAMPLE:**   (CPT 2003)   The patient undergoes Hepatitis A vaccine.
>
> Ⓞ **90632**   Hepatitis A vaccine, adult dosage, for intramuscular use
>
> **90471**   Immunization administration (includes percutaneous, intradermal, subcutaneous, intramuscular and jet injections and/or intranasal or oral administration); one vaccine (single or combination vaccine/toxoid)

Both codes (90632 and 90471) are reported on the claim, but neither is assigned modifier -51. Because both are required to completely describe the administration of the Hepatitis A vaccine, payers automatically reduce reimbursement for the second code. If modifier -51 is reported with the second code, the payer further reduces reimbursement and the practice receives less money than entitled. ⬤

CPT CATEGORIES, SUBCATEGORIES, AND HEADINGS

CPT Category I codes are organized according to six sections that are subdivided into subsections, subcategories, and headings (Figure 7-1).

Guidelines

Guidelines are located at the beginning of each CPT section, and *they should be carefully reviewed before attempting to code.* **Guidelines** define terms and explain the assignment of codes for procedures and services located in a particular section (Figure 7-2). This means that guidelines in one section do not apply to another section in CPT.

Unlisted Procedures/Services

An **unlisted procedure** or **service** code is assigned when the provider performs a procedure or service for which there is no CPT code. When an unlisted procedure or service code is reported, a **special report** must accompany the claim to describe the nature, extent and need for the procedure or service.

> ⬤ **NOTE:**   Medicare and other third-party payers often require providers to report HCPCS level II (national) codes instead of unlisted procedure or service CPT codes. ⬤

Notes

Instructional notes appear throughout CPT sections to clarify the assignment of codes. They are typeset in two patterns (Figure 7-3, page 192):

1. A *blocked unindented note* is located below a category (or subsection) title and contains instructions that apply to all codes in the category.

2. An *indented parenthetical note* is located below a subsection title, code description, or code description that contains an example.

Parenthetical notes that contain the abbreviation "eg" are examples.

SYMBOL/CONVENTION	CPT ENTRY:
Section	**Surgery**
Category	**Integumentary System**
Subcategory	**Skin, Subcutaneous and Accessory Structures**
Heading	**Incision and Drainage**
Note	(For excision, see 11400, et seq)
Code number/description	**10040*** Acne surgery (eg, marsupialization, opening or removal of multiple milia, comedones, cysts, pustules)
Starred procedure	**10060*** Incision and drainage of abscess (eg, carbuncle, suppurative hidradenitis, cutaneous or subcutaneous abscess, cyst, furuncle, or paronychia); simple or single
Use of semicolon	**10061** complicated or multiple
	11000* Debridement of extensive eczematous or Infected skin; up to 10% of body surface
Use of plus symbol	**+11001** each additional 10% of the body surface (List separately in addition to code for primary procedure)
Use of -51 modifier exemption symbol	**⊘ 32000*** Thoracentesis, puncture of pleural cavity for aspiration, initial or subsequent
Use of revised instructional note symbol	(▶If imaging guidance is performed, ◀ see 76003, 76360, ▶ 76942 ◀)

FIGURE 7-1 Selection from CPT that illustrates symbols and conventions (CPT only © 2003 American Medical Association. All Rights Reserved.)

NOTE:

- Terminology in the example does not need to appear in the procedural statement documented by the provider.
- Parenthetical notes within a code series provide information about deleted codes.

Surgery Guidelines

Items used by all physicians in reporting their services are presented in the **Introduction**. Some of the commonalities are repeated here for the convenience of those physicians referring to this section on **Surgery**. Other definitions and items unique to Surgery are also listed.

Physicians' Services

Physicians' services rendered in the office, home, or hospital, consultations, and other medical services are listed in the section entitled **Evaluation and Management Services** (99200 series) found in the front of the book, beginning on page 9. "Special Services and Reports" (99000 series) is presented in the **Medicine** section.

Follow-Up Care for Therapeutic Surgical Procedures

Follow-up care for therapeutic surgical procedures includes only that care which is usually a part of the surgical service. complications, exacerbations, recurrence, or the presence of other diseases or injuries requiring additional services should be separately reported.

Materials Supplied by Physician

Supplies and materials provided by the physician (eg, sterile trays/drugs), over and above those usually included with the ▶procedure(s)◀ rendered ▶are reported◀ separately. List drugs, trays, supplies, and materials provided. Identify as 99070 ▶or specific supply code.◀

FIGURE 7-2 Portion of CPT Surgery Guidelines (CPT only © 2003 American Medical Association. All Rights Reserved.)

Descriptive Qualifiers

Descriptive qualifiers are terms that clarify the assignment of a CPT code. They can occur in the middle of a main clause or after the semicolon and may or may not be enclosed in parentheses. Be sure to read all code descriptions very carefully to properly assign CPT codes that require descriptive qualifiers.

EXAMPLE: **17000*** Destruction by any method (eg, laser surgery, electrosurgery, cryosurgery, surgical curettement), all benign or premalignant lesions (eg, actinic keratoses) <u>other than skin tags or cutaneous vascular proliferative lesions, first lesion</u>

+17003 second through 14 lesions, <u>each</u> (List separately in addition to code for first lesion)

The underlining in codes 17000 and 17003 identify descriptive qualifiers in each code description.

CODING TIP: Coders working in a provider's office should highlight descriptive qualifiers in CPT that pertain to the office's specialty. This will help ensure that qualifiers are not overlooked when assigning codes.

Cardiovascular System

Blocked unindented note

Selective vascular catheterizations should be coded to include introduction and all lesser order selective catheterizations used in the approach (eg, the description for a selective right middle cerebral artery catheterization includes the introduction and placement catheterization of the right common and internal carotid arteries).

Additional second and/or third order arterial catheterizations within the same family of arteries supplied by a single first order artery should be expressed by 36218 or 36248. Additional first order or higher catheterizations in vascular families supplied by a first order vessel different from a previously selected and coded family should be separately coded using the conventions described above.

Indented parenthetical note located below subsection title

(For monitoring, operation of pump and other Nonsurgical services, *see* 99190-99192, 99291, 99292, 99354-99360)

(For other medical or laboratory related services, *see* appropriate section)

(For radiological supervision and interpretation, *see* 75600-75978)

Heart and Pericardium

Pericardium

33010*   Pericardiocentesis; initial

Indented parenthetical note located below code description

(For radiological supervision and interpretation, use 76930)

Indented parenthetical note located below code description that contains an example

33250   Operative ablation of supraventricular arrhythmogenic focus pathway (eg, Wolff-Parkinson-White, atrioventricular node re-entry), tract(s) and/or focus (foci); without cardiopulmonary bypass

FIGURE 7-3 Selection from CPT that illustrates the two types of instructional notes (CPT only © 2003 American Medical Association. All Rights Reserved.)

EXERCISE 7- 1   Working with CPT Symbols and Conventions

If the statement is true, place a **T** in front of the number. If the statement is false, enter an **F** and correct the statement.

_____   **1.** The asterisk following a code number indicates a substantial change in the narrative of a code.

_____   **2.** The major sections of CPT are nuclear medicine, surgery, medicine, pathology, and radiology.

(continues)

(continued)

_____ **3.** The triangle is used to indicate a new procedure code number.

_____ **4.** The numerical format for a reported procedure should be expressed with a five-digit main number and a three-digit modifier.

_____ **5.** "Notes" should be applied to all codes located under a heading.

_____ **6.** The semicolon indicates a break between the main and subordinate clauses of procedure descriptions.

_____ **7.** All descriptive qualifiers for a particular code are found in an indented code description.

_____ **8.** When a parenthetical statement within a code description begins with "eg," one of the terms that follows must be included in the provider's description of the surgery for the code number to apply.

_____ **9.** Horizontal triangles (▶ ◀) are found in revised guidelines, notes, and procedure descriptions.

_____ **10.** The bullet (•) located to the left of a CPT code indicates a new code to that edition of CPT.

_____ **11.** Upon review of the CPT tabular listing below, code 50620 would be reported for a *ureterolithotomy performed on the upper or middle one-third of the ureter.*

50610	Ureterolithotomy; upper one-third of ureter
50620	middle one-third of ureter
50630	lower one-third of ureter

After completing this exercise, refer to Appendix IV to check your answers.

CPT INDEX

The CPT index (Figure 7-4) is organized by alphabetical main terms printed in bold-face. The main terms represent procedures or services, organs, anatomic sites, conditions, eponyms, or abbreviations. The main term may be followed by indented terms that modify the main term; these are called subterms.

Single Codes and Code Ranges

Index code numbers for specific procedures may be represented as a single code number, a range of codes separated by a dash, a series of codes separated by commas, or a combination of single codes and ranges of codes. All listed numbers should be investigated before assigning a code for the procedure or service.

EXAMPLE:

Liver

Repair

    Abscess...................................... 47300

    Cyst.. 47300

    Wound........................... 47350–47362 •

N

Cross-referenced term	**N. Meningitidis** *See* Neisseria Meningitidis
	Naffziger Operation *See* Decompression, Orbit; Section
	Nagel Test *See* Color Vision Examination

Main term
Subterm

Range of codes to investigate

Nails
Avulsion .11730-11732
Biopsy 11755
Debridement 11720-11721
Evacuation
    Hematoma, Subungual 11740
Excision 11750-11752
    Cyst
        Pilonidal 11770-11772
KOH Examination 87220
Removal 11730-11732, 11750-11752
Trimming 11719

FIGURE 7-4 Selection from CPT index (CPT only © 2003 American Medical Association. All Rights Reserved.)

Boldface Type

Main terms in the CPT index are printed in **boldface type**, along with CPT categories, subcategories, headings, and code numbers.

Cross-Reference Term

See is a **cross-reference** that directs coders to an index entry under which codes are listed. No codes are listed under the original entry.

> **EXAMPLE:** **AV Shunt**
>   *See* Arteriovenous Shunt

In this example, the coder is directed to the index entry for Arteriovenous Shunt because no codes are listed for AV Shunt. ●

Italicized Type

Italicized type is used for the cross-reference term, *See*, in the CPT Index.

Inferred Words

To save space in the CPT Index when referencing subterms, the practice of **inferred words** is used.

 EXAMPLE: **Abdomen**

Exploration (of) 49000, 49002

In this example, the word in parentheses (of) is inferred and does not appear in the CPT Index. ●

EXERCISE 7-2 **Working with the CPT Index**

1. Turn to code number 47300 and review all procedural descriptions through code 47362.

2. What does the term marsupialization mean? If you don't know the meaning, look it up in your medical dictionary.

   _____

   _____

3. How do codes 47350, 47360–47362 differ?

   47350 _____

   _____

   47360 _____

   _____

   47361 _____

   _____

   47362 _____

   _____

4. The cross-reference that directs coders to refer to a different index entry because no codes are found under the original entry is called *See*. TRUE or FALSE.

5. Main terms appear in *italics* in the CPT index. TRUE or FALSE.

6. Inferred words appear in the CPT index to assist coders in assigning appropriate codes. TRUE or FALSE.

After completing this exercise, refer to Appendix IV to check your answers.

 **CODING TIP:** The descriptions of *all* codes listed for a specific procedure must be carefully investigated before selecting a final code. As with ICD-9-CM, CPT coding must *never* be performed solely from the index.

CPT MODIFIERS

CPT modifiers clarify services and procedures performed by providers, and while the CPT code and description remains unchanged, modifiers indicate that the description of the service or procedure performed has been altered. CPT modifiers are reported as 2-digit numeric codes added to the 5-digit CPT code.

NOTE: Instructional notes about reporting 5-digit modifiers (e.g., 09977) were deleted starting with CPT 2003 because the CMS-1500 electronic claim format requires 2-digit modifiers.

EXAMPLE: 30630-77.

A patient undergoes repair of a deviated nasal septum (code 30630), which was unsuccessful. The patient undergoes repeat repair of the deviated nasal septum by a different surgeon (modifier -77). The same CPT code is assigned, and a modifier is added to indicate the repeat repair.

CPT modifiers have always been reported on claims submitted for provider office services and procedures. In April 2000, hospitals also began reporting CPT and HCPCS level II (national) modifiers for outpatient services.

CODING TIP: A list of all CPT modifiers with brief descriptions is located inside the front cover of the coding manual. CPT and HCPCS level II national modifiers approved for hospital outpatient reporting purposes are also identified.

NOTE: HCPCS Level II national modifiers are detailed in Chapter 8.

Not all CPT modifiers apply to each section of CPT. Table 7-1A summarizes modifiers in numeric order and identifies applicable CPT sections for each. The following example illustrates how and why modifiers are used.

EXAMPLE: Mrs. T has a history of gallbladder disease. After several hours of acute pain, she was referred to Dr. S for an evaluation of her condition. Dr. S performed a complete history and physical examination and decided to admit the patient to the hospital for an immediate work-up for cholecystitis. When the results of laboratory tests and sonogram were received, the patient was scheduled for an emergency laparoscopic cholecystectomy.

The surgeon was Dr. S and the assistant surgeon was Dr. A. The surgery was successful, and the patient was discharged the next day and told to return to the office in 7 days. Four days later, Mrs. T returned to Dr. S's office complaining of chest pains. Dr. S performed another examination and ordered the necessary tests. After reviewing the test results and confirming with the patient's primary care physician, it was determined that the patient was suffering from mild angina.

Dr. S submitted a claim (Figure 7-5) for the following services:

- Initial hospital visit, comprehensive, with medical decision making of high complexity (99223-57) (Modifier -57 indicates that the decision to perform surgery was made during the hospital evaluation)
- Laparoscopic cholecystectomy (47562)
- Office visit, established patient, expanded problem focused, with medical decision making of low complexity (99213-24) (Modifier -24 indicates that the re-examination of the patient revealed the problem to be unrelated to the nor-

TABLE 7-1A CPT modifiers in a quick view format

KEY

Shaded boxes that contain an "X" indicate modifiers restricted to a specific CPT Section.
Shaded boxes that contain "X-S" indicate modifiers restricted to CPT Surgery codes reported by ASC settings.
Unshaded boxes that contain an "X" indicate modifiers applicable to multiple CPT Sections.

ASC = Ambulatory Surgery Center, and this column is included to indicate CPT modifiers applicable to that setting. ASCs are located in hospital outpatient settings and as stand-alone surgical centers. HCPCS modifiers are located in Chapter 8.

MODIFIER	TITLE OF MODIFIER	E/M	ANESTHESIA	SURGERY	RADIOLOGY	PATHOLOGY & LABORATORY	MEDICINE	AMBULATORY SURGICAL CENTER (ASC)
-21	Prolonged Evaluation and Management Services	X						
-22	Unusual Procedural Services		X	X	X	X	X	
-23	Unusual Anesthesia		X					
-24	Unrelated Evaluation and Management Service by the Same Physician During a Postoperative Period	X						
-25	Significant, Separately Indentifiable Evaluation and Management Service by the Same Physician on the Same Day of the Procedure or Other Service	X						X
-26	Professional Component			X	X	X	X	
-27	Multiple Outpatient Hospital E/M Encounters on the Same Date	X						X
-32	Mandated Services	X	X	X	X	X	X	
-47	Anesthesia by Surgeon			X				
-50	Bilateral Procedure			X				X
-51	Multiple Procedures		X	X	X		X	
-52	Reduced Services	X		X	X	X	X	X
-53	Discontinued Procedure			X	X	X	X	
-54	Surgical Care Only			X				
-55	Postoperative Management Only			X			X	
-56	Preoperative Management Only	X		X			X	
-57	Decision for Surgery	X					X	
-58	Staged or Related Procedure or Service by the Same Physician During the Postoperative Period			X	X		X	X
-59	Distinct Procedural Service			X	X	X	X	X
-62	Two Surgeons			X	X			
-63	Procedure on Infants Less Than 4 kg	X	X	X	X	X	X	
-66	Surgical Team			X	X			
-73	Discontinued Outpatient Procedure Prior to Anesthesia Administration							X-S
-74	Discontinued Outpatient Procedure After Anesthesia Administration							X-S
-76	Repeat Procedure by Same Physician			X	X		X	X
-77	Repeat Procedure by Another Physician			X	X		X	X
-78	Return to the Operating Room for a Related Procedure During the Postoperative Period			X	X		X	
-79	Unrelated procedure or Service by the Same Physician During the Postoperative Period			X	X		X	
-80	Assistant Surgeon			X	X			
-81	Minimum Assistant Surgeon			X				
-82	Assistant Surgeon (when qualified resident surgeon not available)			X				
-90	Reference (Outside) Laboratory					X		
-91	Repeat Clinical Diagnostic Laboratory Test					X		X
-99	Multiple Modifiers			X	X		X	

24. A						B	C	D		E	F	G	H	I	J	K
DATE(S) OF SERVICE						Place	Type	PROCEDURES, SERVICES, OR SUPPLIES		DIAGNOSIS	$ CHARGES	DAYS	EPSDT	EMG	COB	RESERVED FOR LOCAL
From			To			of	of	(Explain Unusual Circumstances)		CODE		OR	Family			USE
MM	DD	YY	MM	DD	YY	Service	Service	CPT/HCPCS	MODIFIER			UNITS	Plan			
1								99223	57							
2								47562								
3								99213	24							

FIGURE 7-5 Completed block 24D on CMS-1500 claim

24. A						B	C	D		E	F	G	H	I	J	K
DATE(S) OF SERVICE						Place	Type	PROCEDURES, SERVICES, OR SUPPLIES		DIAGNOSIS	$ CHARGES	DAYS	EPSDT	EMG	COB	RESERVED FOR LOCAL
From			To			of	of	(Explain Unusual Circumstances)		CODE		OR	Family			USE
MM	DD	YY	MM	DD	YY	Service	Service	CPT/HCPCS	MODIFIER			UNITS	Plan			
1								47562	80							

FIGURE 7-6 Completed Block 24D on CMS-1500 claim

mal postoperative care provided to a cholecystectomy patient. The diagnosis linked to this visit is angina.)

Dr. A submits a claim (Figure 7-6) for the following service: Laparoscopic cholecystectomy 47562-80 (Modifier -80 indicates Dr. A is the assistant surgeon.) ●

The AMA and CMS develop new modifiers on a continuous basis, and next available numbers are assigned. This means there is no relationship among groups of modifier numbers. Reviewing modifiers in strict numerical order does not allow for comparison of those that are related to one other in terms of content; therefore, Table 7-1B organizes modifiers according to reporting similarity.

⬤ NOTE: In an attempt to simplify the explanation of modifiers, the wording does not correspond word-for-word with descriptions found in CPT. To determine which CPT section to apply a modifier, refer to Table 7-1A. ●

EXERCISE 7-3   Assigning CPT Modifiers

Assign the appropriate modifier(s) to each statement below.

1. Assistant surgeon reporting patient's cesarean section, delivery only.
2. Cholecystectomy reported during postoperative period for treatment of leg fracture.
3. Treatment for chronic conditions at same time preventive medicine is provided.
4. Inpatient visit performed by surgeon, with decision to perform surgery tomorrow.
5. Office consultation as preoperative clearance for surgery.
6. Postoperative management of vaginal hysterectomy.
7. Repeat gallbladder X-ray series, same physician.
8. Arthroscopy of right elbow and closed fracture reduction of left wrist.
9. Needle core biopsy of right and left breast.
10. Consultation required by payer.

After completing this exercise, refer to Appendix IV to check your answers.

TABLE 7-1B Organization of CPT modifiers according to reporting similarity

Special Evaluation and Management (E/M) Cases

MODIFIER	DESCRIPTION	INTERPRETATION
-21	Prolonged Evaluation and Management Services	Assign when services provided are prolonged and greater than the average highest reportable level of service required. Be sure to submit a copy of documentation with the claim to support assignment of this modifier.
	EXAMPLE: E/M of a patient seen in follow-up for continued treatment of anxiety with medication. The patient was very upset about family problems, and the provider spent 45 minutes counseling him. Report 992xx-21.	
-24	Unrelated Evaluation and Management Service by the Same Physician During a Postoperative Period	Assign to indicate that an E/M service was performed during the standard postoperative period for a condition unrelated to the surgery. The procedure to which the modifier is attached *must be* linked to a diagnosis that is *unrelated* to the surgical diagnosis previously submitted. Be sure to submit a copy of documentation with the claim to explain the circumstances.
	EXAMPLE: Five weeks after the surgical release of a frozen shoulder, a patient fell and severely sprained his ankle, which required strapping immobilization for support and comfort. Report 29540-24.	
-25	Significant, Separately Identifiable Evaluation and Management Service by the Same Physician on the Same Day of the Procedure or Other Service	Assign when a documented E/M service was performed on the same day as another procedure because the patient's condition required the assignment of significant, separately identifiable, additional E/M services normally not a part of the other procedure.
	EXAMPLE: During routine annual examination, it was discovered that the 65-year-old established patient had an enlarged liver expanding the scope of E/M services. Report 99397 and 992xx-25. (Be sure to submit supporting documentation to the payer.)	
-57	Decision for Surgery	Assign when the reported E/M service resulted in the initial decision to perform surgery within 24 to 48 hours of an examination. This modifier also permits payment of the required physical examination performed within 24 hours of the surgery.
	EXAMPLE: The patient was evaluated for chest pain in the emergency department, and a decision was made to insert a coronary arterial stent. Report 9928x-57.	

Greater, Reduced, or Discontinued Services

MODIFIER	DESCRIPTION	INTERPRETATION
-22	Unusual Procedural Services	Assign when a procedure requires greater than usual service(s). Documentation that would support using this modifier includes: difficult, complicated, extensive, unusual, or rare procedure. NOTE: This modifier has been overused. Be sure special circumstances are documented, and send a copy with the claim.
	EXAMPLE: Blood loss of 600 cc or greater. Prolonged operative time due to . . .	
-52	Reduced Services	Report when a service has been partially reduced at the physician's discretion and does not completely match the CPT code description. Attach documentation or an explanation to the claim.

(continues)

TABLE 7-1B *(continued)*

Greater, Reduced, or Discontinued Services *(continued)*

MODIFIER	DESCRIPTION	INTERPRETATION
	EXAMPLE: The provider began the 18-year-old new patient's first gynecologic exam, but discontinued it when it became apparent that the patient was experiencing extreme discomfort. Report 99285-52.	
-53	Discontinued Procedure	Report when provider has elected to terminate a procedure because of extenuating circumstances that threaten the well-being of the patient. **NOTE:** This modifier applies only to provider office settings *and only* if surgical prep has begun or induction of anesthesia has been initiated. Do *not* report for procedures electively canceled prior to induction of anesthesia and/or surgical prep.
	EXAMPLE: Procedure started and terminated due to equipment failure.	
-73	Discontinued Outpatient Procedure Prior to Anesthesia Administration	Report to describe discontinued procedures *prior to the administration of any anesthesia* because of extenuating circumstances threatening the well-being of the patient. Do not report for elective cancellations. **NOTE:** Report ICD-9-CM code V64.x to document reason procedure was halted.
	EXAMPLE: Patient developed heart arrhythmia prior to anesthesia administration.	
-74	Discontinued Outpatient Procedure After Anesthesia Administration	Report to describe discontinued procedures *after the administration of anesthesia* due to extenuating circumstances. **NOTE:** Report ICD-9-CM code V64.x to document reason procedure was halted.
	EXAMPLE: Patient prepped and draped, and general anesthesia administered. Anesthesiologist noted sudden increase in blood pressure, and procedure was terminated.	

Global Surgery

NOTE:
- These modifiers apply to the four areas related to the CPT *surgical package* (Figure 7-7), which includes the procedure, local infiltration, metacarpal/digital block or topical anesthesia when used, and normal, uncomplicated follow-up care.
- These modifiers do not apply to obstetric coding where the CPT description of specific codes clearly describes separate antepartum, postpartum and delivery services for both vaginal and cesarean deliveries.

MODIFIER	DESCRIPTION	INTERPRETATION
-54	Surgical Care Only	Report when surgeon performed only surgical portion of surgical package and personally administered required local anesthesia. **NOTE:** A different provider will have performed preoperative evaluation and/or provided postoperative care. The performing surgeon is usually responsible for the patient care until the patient is ready for hospital discharge.
	EXAMPLE: While on vacation, John Jones sustained tibial shaft fracture and underwent closed treatment by Dr. Charles. Upon return to his hometown, John received follow-up care from Dr. Smith, a local orthopedist. Dr. Charles should report 27750-54.	
-55	Postoperative Management Only	Report when a provider other than the surgeon is responsible for postoperative management only of a surgery performed by another physician.

(continues)

TABLE 7-1B *(continued)*

Global Surgery *(continued)*

MODIFIER	DESCRIPTION	INTERPRETATION
		Documentation in the patient's chart should detail the date of transfer of care to calculate the percentage of the fee to be billed for postoperative care. **NOTE:** • Be sure to complete CMS-1500 claim Blocks 14, 24A, and 24D, and attach surgeon's name/address. • Modifier -54 does not apply when a second provider occasionally covers for the surgeon and where no transfer of care has occurred.
	EXAMPLE: While on vacation, John Jones sustained tibial shaft fracture and underwent closed treatment by Dr. Charles. Upon return to his hometown, John received follow-up care from Dr. Smith, a local orthopedist. Dr. Smith should report 27750-55.	
-56	Preoperative Management Only	Report when a provider *other than* the operating surgeon performs preoperative clearance for surgery. **NOTE:** Report any problem found during examination *along with* reason for surgery. Report also ICD-9-CM code V72.8 for preoperative care.
	EXAMPLE: Dr. Berger preoperatively cleared a patient who underwent surgery by Dr. Charles. Dr. Berger reports 992xx-56.	

Special Surgical and Procedural Events

MODIFIER	DESCRIPTION	INTERPRETATION
-58	Staged or Related Procedure or Service by the Same Physician During the Postoperative Period	Report to indicate that additional related surgery was required during the postoperative period of a previously completed surgery and was performed by the same physician. Documentation should include one of the following: • Original plan for surgery included additional stages to be performed within postoperative period of first stage of procedure. • Underlying disease required a second related, but unplanned, procedure to be performed. • Additional related therapy is required after the performance of a diagnostic surgical procedure.
	EXAMPLE 1: A surgical wound is not healing properly because of the patient's underlying diabetes. Patient was told prior to the original surgery that if this happened, additional surgery would be required to debride or resuture the wound.	
	EXAMPLE 2: A biopsy of a breast lesion was performed. The pathology report documents carcinoma, and 4 days later a mastectomy will be performed.	
	EXAMPLE 3: A series of surgical steps was planned to correct a condition. An enteroscopy was performed, and a planned closure of the stoma is scheduled in 6 to 8 weeks.	

CODING TIP: Do not report modifier -58 if the CPT code description describes multiple sessions of an event. For example, code 67208 Destruction of localized lesion of retina (e.g., macular edema, tumors), one or more sessions; cryotherapy, diathermy. For example, code 17304 Chemosurgery (Mohs' micrographic technique)...; first stage, fresh tissue technique, up to 5 specimens... and code 17305... second stage, fixed or fresh tissue, up to 5 specimens.

(continues)

TABLE 7-1B *(continued)*

Special Surgical and Procedural Events *(continued)*

MODIFIER	DESCRIPTION	INTERPRETATION
-59	Distinct Procedural Service	Report when same physician performs one or more *distinctly independent procedures* on the same day as other procedures or services, according to the following criteria: ● Procedures are performed at different sessions or during different patient encounters. ● Procedures are performed on different sites or organs and require a different surgical prep. **NOTE:** modifier -51, multiple procedures, may also be reported. ● Procedures are performed for multiple or extensive injuries, using separate incisions/excisions, for separate lesions, or when not ordinarily encountered/ performed on the same day. **NOTE:** modifier -51, multiple procedures, may also be reported.
	EXAMPLE: Patient has two basal cell carcinomas removed, one from the forehead with a simple closure (11640) and the other from the nose requiring adjacent tissue transfer (14060). Report as: 14060, 11640-51, 11640-59.	
-63	Procedure Performed on Infants Less Than 4 kg	Report when infant weights less than 4 kilograms (kg) because procedures performed may require increased complexity and provider work.
	EXAMPLE: Baby Girl Markel's weight was 3.5 kg at the time she underwent radio frequency catheter ablation (RFCA). The provider reports modifier -63 with the procedure code.	
-78	Return to Operating Room for a Related Procedure During the Postoperative Period	Report for unplanned circumstances that require return to operating room for complications of initial operation.
	EXAMPLE: Surgical sutures did not hold, and the wound had to be resutured.	

CODING TIP: To ensure payment, medical necessity for the return to operating room must reflect the surgical complication.

MODIFIER	DESCRIPTION	INTERPRETATION
-79	Unrelated Procedure or Service by the Same Physician During the Postoperative Period	Report when a new procedure or service is performed by a surgeon during the normal postoperative period of a previously performed, but unrelated surgery.
	EXAMPLE: Six weeks following cataract surgery performed on the left eye, the patient undergoes a separate and unrelated surgery on the right eye.	

Bilateral and Multiple Procedures

MODIFIER	DESCRIPTION	INTERPRETATION
-50	Bilateral Procedure	Report when a procedure was performed bilaterally *during the same session and when the code description does not specify that the procedure is bilateral.*
	EXAMPLE: Patient underwent bilateral athrodesis, knee. Report 27580-50.	

(continues)

TABLE 7-1B *(continued)*

Bilateral and Multiple Procedures *(continued)*

MODIFIER	DESCRIPTION	INTERPRETATION
CODING TIP:		● Although CPT modifier -50 refers to *operative session*, both diagnostic and therapeutic procedures can be reported with the bilateral modifier *if the anatomic structures are found bilaterally and the identical procedure is performed on both sides.* ● Reporting HCPCS modifiers -LT (left side) and -RT (right side) with procedure codes is restricted to unilateral procedures. Documentation should accompany the submitted claim. *Do not report modifier -50 with HCPCS modifiers, -LT and -RT.*
-27	Multiple Procedures	Report for patients who receive multiple E/M services performed by *different providers.* **NOTE:** Do *not* report for multiple E/M services performed by the same provider on the same day.
	EXAMPLE: A patient is seen in the hospital's emergency department and then in its outpatient clinic on the same day. Report modifier -27 with each E/M code.	
-51	Multiple Procedures	Report when multiple procedures *other than E/M services*, are performed at the same session by the same provider. The procedures performed are characterized as: ● multiple, related surgical procedures performed at the same session. ● surgical procedures performed in combination, whether through the same or another incision, or involving the same or different anatomy. ● combination medical and surgical procedures performed at the same session. **NOTE:** This modifier is reported with the secondary or lesser procedure(s).
	EXAMPLE: Patient underwent right tibial shaft fracture repair and athrodesis of left knee. Report 27750 and 27580-51.	

CODING TIP: Do not report modifier -51 if:
- notes at the beginning of a category instruct the coder to *report additional codes in addition to....* (See note above code 22305 in CPT.)
- the code description states *List separately in addition to the code for primary procedure.* (See code 22116 in CPT.)
- the code description includes the words *each* or *each additional* segment, lesion. (See codes 22103, 17001, and 17003 in CPT.)
- the symbol **+** precedes a code, which designates an add-on code.
- codes are reported from the Laboratory and Pathology 80000 series.

Repeat Services

MODIFIER	DESCRIPTION	INTERPRETATION
-76	Repeat Procedure by Same Physician	Report when a procedure was repeated because of special circumstances involving the original service, and the same physician performed the repeat procedure.
	EXAMPLE: A repeat EKG is performed because of changes in the patient's condition or the need to assess the effect of therapeutic procedures.	

(continues)

TABLE 7-1B *(continued)*

Repeat Services *(continued)*

MODIFIER	DESCRIPTION	INTERPRETATION
-77	Repeat Procedure by Another Physician	Report when a physician *other than the original physician* performs a repeat procedure because of special circumstances involving the original study or procedure.
	EXAMPLE: Patient underwent sterilization procedure (e.g., tubal ligation), but became pregnant and after delivery underwent a second sterilization procedure.	

Multiple Surgeons

MODIFIER	DESCRIPTION	INTERPRETATION
-62	Two Surgeons	Report when two primary surgeons are required during an operative session, each performing distinct parts of a reportable procedure. Ideally, the surgeons represent different specialties.
	EXAMPLE: An orthopedist creates the surgical approach through a bone and a neurosurgeon repairs the nerve.	

CODING TIP: If either surgeon acts as the assistant surgeon for additional unrelated procedure(s) performed during the same operative session, report modifier -80 or -81 with the additional procedures code(s).

MODIFIER	DESCRIPTION	INTERPRETATION
-66	Surgical Team	Report when surgery performed is highly complex and requires the services of a skilled team of three or more physicians. The procedure reported on the claim for each participating physician must include this modifier. The operative report must document the complexity of the surgery and refer to the actions of each team member.
	EXAMPLE: Separation of conjoined twins.	
-80	Assistant Surgeon	Report when one physician assists another during an operative session. The assistant surgeon reports the same CPT code as the operating physician.
	EXAMPLE: Dr. Landry assisted Dr. Bartron during cardiovascular surgery. Dr. Landry reports the CPT code with modifier -80, and Dr. Bartron reports the CPT code with no modifier.	
-81	Minimum Assistant Surgeon	Report when primary operating physician planned to perform a surgical procedure alone, but operation circumstances arise that require the services of an assistant surgeon for a short time. The second surgeon reports the same CPT code as the operating physician.
	EXAMPLE: Dr. Kelly begins an elective surgical procedure on a patient, and finds it necessary to call in Dr. Pietro to assist for a short time.	
-82	Assistant Surgeon (when qualified resident surgeon not available)	Report when a qualified resident surgeon is unavailable to assist with a procedure. In teaching hospitals, the physician acting as the assistant surgeon is usually a qualified resident surgeon. If circumstances arise (e.g., rotational changes) and a qualified resident surgeon is not available, another surgeon may assist with a procedure. The nonresident-assistant surgeon reports the same CPT code as the operating physician.

(continues)

TABLE 7-1B *(continued)*

Multiple Surgeons *(continued)*

MODIFIER	DESCRIPTION	INTERPRETATION
		EXAMPLE: Resident surgeon Dr. Smith was to assist surgeon Dr. Manlin with a routine procedure. Dr. Smith was temporarily reassigned to the emergency department due to a staffing problem. Therefore, Dr. Manlin's partner, Dr. Lando, assisted with the procedure. Dr. Lando will attach modifier -82 to the procedure code.

CODING TIP: Do not report modifiers -80, -81, and -82 for nonphysician surgical assistant services (e.g., physician assistant, nurse practitioner) *unless the payer authorizes this reporting.*

Professional and Technical Components

MODIFIER	DESCRIPTION	INTERPRETATION
-26	Professional Component	Report when the physician either interprets test results or operates equipment for a procedure. *Do not report this modifier when a specific separately identifiable code describes the professional component of a procedure (e.g., 93010).*
		EXAMPLE: Independent radiologist Dr. Minion interprets an X-ray that was performed on Mary Sue Patient by another provider. Dr. Minion attaches modifier -26 to the X-ray code.

Mandated Services

MODIFIER	DESCRIPTION	INTERPRETATION
-32	Mandated Services	Report when services (e.g., second or third opinion on a surgical procedure) provided were mandated by a third-party (e.g., attorney, payer).
		EXAMPLE: Mary Sue Patient is seen by her primary care provider who recommends respiratory therapy. Before the payer will approve reimbursement for respiratory therapy, Mary Sue Patient is evaluated by respiratory specialist Dr. Powell. Dr. Powell attaches -32 to the E/M code submitted to the payer for reimbursement.

Unusual Anesthesia

MODIFIER	DESCRIPTION	INTERPRETATION
-23	Unusual Anesthesia	Report when circumstances (e.g., extent of service, patient's physical condition) require anesthesia for procedures that usually require either no anesthesia or local anesthesia.
		EXAMPLE: Patients who are mentally retarded, extremely apprehensive, or have a physical condition (e.g., tremors, spasticity) may require anesthesia for procedures that normally do not require anesthesia. The provider should attach modifier -23 to procedures performed under such circumstances.
-47	Anesthesia by Surgeon	Report when the surgeon provides the regional or general anesthesia for a surgical procedure he/she performs.
		EXAMPLE: Instead of calling in an anesthesiologist to assist with a surgical case, Dr. Borja administers the anesthesia and performs the procedure. Dr. Borja attaches modifier -47 to the procedure code to indicate these unusual circumstances.

(continues)

TABLE 7-1B *(continued)*

Unusual Anesthesia *(continued)*

MODIFIER	DESCRIPTION	INTERPRETATION
	CODING TIP: Modifier -47 is added to the CPT surgery code. It is not reported with Anesthesia codes 00100-01999.	

Laboratory Services

MODIFIER	DESCRIPTION	INTERPRETATION
-90	Reference (Outside) Laboratory	Report when a laboratory test is performed by an outside or reference laboratory.
	EXAMPLE: The provider orders a complete blood count (CBC) as part of a patient's annual physical exam. Because the office does not perform lab testing, arrangements are made with a laboratory to perform the CBC and bill the physician. The physician reports the CBC as code 85024-90. In addition, because office staff performed venipuncture, code 36415 is also reported.	
-91	Repeat Clinical Diagnostic Laboratory Test	Report when a clinical diagnostic laboratory test is repeated on the same day to obtain subsequent (multiple) test results. *This modifier is not reported when lab tests are repeated to confirm initial results* (e.g., due to equipment problems).
	EXAMPLE: The patient was in the emergency department for 18 hours for observation of chest pain. He underwent serial lab tests for cardiac enzyme testing every 6 hours. Modifier -91 is attached to the second and subsequent cardiac enzyme testing codes.	

Multiple Modifiers

MODIFIER	DESCRIPTION	INTERPRETATION
-99	Multiple Modifier	Report to alert third-party payers that more than one modifier is being reported with procedure/service codes.
	EXAMPLE: An assistant surgeon (-80) reports a bilateral (-50) surgical procedure as 43630 99 80 50.	

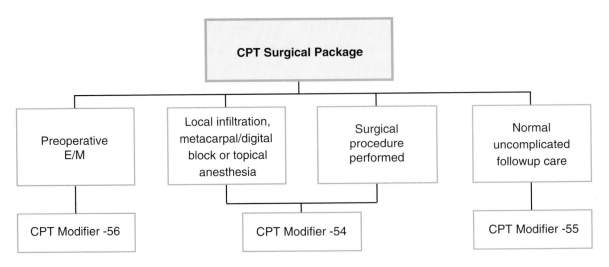

FIGURE 7-7 Modifiers that apply to components of the CPT Surgical Package

BASIC STEPS FOR CODING PROCEDURES AND SERVICES

STEP 1   Read the Introduction located in the CPT coding manual.

STEP 2   Review the guidelines located at the beginning of each CPT section.

STEP 3   Review the procedure or service listed on the office's source document (e.g, charge slip, progress note, operative report, laboratory report, or pathology report). Code only what is recorded on the office's source document; do not make assumptions about conditions, procedures, or services not stated. If necessary, obtain clarification from the provider.

STEP 4   Refer to the CPT Index, and locate the main term for the procedure or service documented. Main terms can be located by referring to the:

    a.   *Procedure or service* documented.

        EXAMPLE: Arthroscopy and consultation.

    b.   *Organ or anatomic site.*

        EXAMPLE: Arm, ankle, and backbone.

    c.   *Condition* documented in the record.

        EXAMPLE: Emboli, cyst, and chicken pox.

    d.   *Substance being tested.*

        EXAMPLE: Blood and urine are tested for cholesterol, chromium, and folic acid.

    e.   *Synonym* (terms with similar meanings).

        EXAMPLE: Intercarpal joint is a finger joint; both are listed in the index.

    f.   *Eponym* (procedures and diagnoses named for an individual).

        EXAMPLE: The Babcock Operation is the ligation of the saphenous vein; both are listed in the index.

    g.   *Abbreviation*

        EXAMPLE: CBC, HAAb, and MRI.

STEP 5   Locate necessary subterms, and follow cross references listed in the index.

STEP 6   Review the descriptions of service/procedure codes listed in the index. Note and compare all qualifiers in the descriptive statements.

HINT: If the last code description you read is located at the bottom of the page, turn the page and check to see if the description continues.

STEP 7   Assign the applicable primary code number and any add-on (+) or additional codes needed to accurately classify the statement being coded.

CODING TIP: You may have to refer to synonyms, translate medical terms to ordinary English, or substitute medical words for English terms documented in the provider's statement to find the main term in the index. Some examples are:

Procedure Statement	Word Substitution
Placement of a shunt	Insertion of shunt
Pacemaker implantation	Pacemaker insertion
Resection of tumor	Excision or removal of tumor
Radiograph of the chest	X-ray of chest
Suture laceration	Repair open wound
Placement of nerve block	Injection of nerve anesthesia

EXERCISE 7-4

Finding Procedures in the Index

Using only the index, find the code or range of codes to be investigated. Note the code or range of codes and any word substitution you made that lead to selected code numbers.

1. Closed treatment of wrist dislocation _____

2. Dilation of cervix _____

3. Placement of upper GI feeding tube _____

4. Radiograph and fluoroscopy of chest, 4 views _____

5. Magnetic resonance imaging, lower spine _____

6. Darrach procedure _____

7. Manual CBC _____

8. Electrosurgical removal, skin tags _____

After completing this exercise, refer to Appendix IV to check your answers.

SURGERY SECTION

The surgery section is organized by body system. Each system is subdivided first by the specific organ or anatomic site. Some subsections are further subdivided by procedure categories in the following order:

- Incision
- Destruction
- Excision
- Introduction
- Removal
- Repair
- Endoscopy
- Grafts
- Suture
- Other/miscellaneous procedures

To code surgeries properly, three questions must be asked:

1. What body system was involved?
2. What anatomic site was involved?
3. What type of procedure was performed?

Carefully read the procedure outlined in the operative report. Sometimes the discriminating factor between one code and another will be the surgical approach or type of procedure mentioned.

EXAMPLE 1: Surgical approach

57540   Excision of cervical stump, abdominal approach;

57545   with pelvic floor repair

57550   Excision of cervical stump, vaginal approach; ●

When reporting the code number for the excision of cervical stump, code 57540 would be reported for an abdominal approach, and code 57550 would be reported for a vaginal approach.

EXAMPLE 2: Type of procedure

11600   Excision, malignant lesion, trunk, arms, or legs; lesion
            diameter 0.5 cm or less

17260*   Destruction, malignant lesion (eg. laser surgery, electrosurgery,
            cryosurgery, chemosurgery, surgical currettement), trunk, arms or legs;
            lesion diameter 0.5 cm or less ●

When reporting the code for removal of a 0.5 cm malignant lesion of the arm, code 11600 would be reported for a surgical excision, and code 17260 would be reported for a destruction procedure (e.g., laser ablation).

Surgical Package

CPT divides surgical procedures into two groups: major surgery and minor surgery. A **major surgical procedure**, one with no asterisk (*****) after the code number, is considered by CPT to be a **surgical package** and includes the operation, any local anesthesia administered, and normal, uncomplicated follow-up care. (Figure 7-8). These are billed as one surgical fee for the services listed.

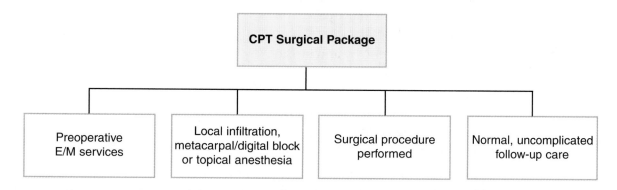

FIGURE 7-8 Components of the CPT Surgical Package

Minor surgical procedures (those with an asterisk (✱) following a code number) are considered by CPT to be a "relatively small surgical service too variable to be billed as an all-inclusive package." They are to be billed on a fee-for-service basis; all preoperative and postoperative services and supplies and materials provided over and above those usually included in an office visit are listed and billed separately.

Coders must be aware that **unbundling** is not allowed because it involves assigning multiple codes to procedures/services when just one comprehensive code *should be* reported. Be careful to differentiate reporting *minor surgical procedures* from *unbundling*. Examples of minor procedures that are bundled (included) with the surgical package code are:

- local infiltration of medication.
- closure of surgically created wounds.
- minor debridement.
- exploration of operative area.
- fulguration of bleeding points.
- application of dressings.
- application of splints with musculoskeletal procedures.

Read the descriptions of surgical procedures carefully, and remember that the main clause—the narrative to the left of the semicolon (;)—of an indented surgical description is stated only once in a series of related intraoperative procedures. The complexity of the related intraoperative procedures increases as you proceed through the listings of indented code descriptions. *Always report the comprehensive code rather than codes for individual components of a surgery.*

NOTE: Another indication that a code might not be reportable with another code is the presence of a parenthetical note (separate procedure) that indicates the procedure is part of a more comprehensive code. ●

EXAMPLE:

35001 Direct repair of aneurysm, pseudoaneurysm, or excision (partial or total) and graft insertion, with or without patch graft; for aneurysm and associated occlusive disease, carotid, subclavian artery, by neck incision

35002 for ruptured aneurysm, carotid, subclavian artery, by neck incision

35005 for aneurysm, pseudoaneurysm, and associated occlusive disease, vertebral artery

35011 for aneurysm and associated occlusive disease, axillary-brachial artery, by arm incision

35013 for ruptured aneurysm, axillary-brachial artery, by arm incision

Only one code from this series of five codes should be assigned *if the procedures performed and reported were rendered during the same operative session.* Note the increasing complexity of procedures as code numbers increase within a subsection. Thus, the higher the number the greater the complexity. ●

Exceptions to reporting one combination code occur when the code number is either marked by a ✚ symbol (add-on code) or a parenthetical note indicates that a code should be reported in addition to the primary code number. The following statements appear in CPT code descriptions or as parenthetical notes when it is appropriate to report additional codes:

- List separately in addition to code for primary procedure.
- Use . . . in conjunction with . . ..
- Each additional . . ..
- Each separate/additional . . ..

EXERCISE 7-5 **Working with the Surgical Package**

Code each statement.

1. Incision and drainage (I&D), finger abscess _____

2. Percutaneous I&D, abscess, appendix _____

3. Anesthetic agent injection, L-5 paravertebral nerve _____

4. Laparoscopic cholecystectomy with cholangiography _____

5. Flexible esophagoscopy with brushing, specimen collection, removal of foreign body, and radiologic supervision and interpretation _____

6. Anterior interbody approach, arthrodesis with minimal diskectomy, L-1 through L-3 vertebrae _____

After completing this exercise, refer to Appendix IV to check your answers.

Separate Procedure

The parenthetical note, **separate procedure**, follows a code description that identifies procedures that are an integral part of another procedure or service. In addition, a *separate procedure* code is reported if the procedure or service is performed independently of the comprehensive procedure or service or is unrelated to or distinct from another procedure or service performed at the same time. The *separate procedure* code is not reported if the procedure or service performed is included in the description of another reported code.

EXAMPLE:

The patient undergoes only a cystourethroscopy (passage of an endoscope through the urethra to visualize the urinary bladder). CPT codes for cystourethroscopy include:

52000 Cystourethroscopy (separate procedure)

52005 Cystourethroscopy, with ureteral catheterization, with or without irrigation, instillation, or ureteropyelography, exclusive of radiologic service;

52007 with brush biopsy of ureter and/or renal pelvis

52010 Cystourethroscopy, with ejaculatory duct catheterization, with or without irrigation, instillation, or duct radiography, exclusive of radiologic service

Report code 52000 because only the cystourethroscopy was performed. *A code from among 52005–52010 would be reported only if the operative report documented additional procedures that were included in the code description.* The placement of the phrase "separate procedure" is critical to correct coding. When it appears after the semicolon, it applies to that specific code.

● **EXAMPLE:**

> **57452*** Colposcopy (vaginoscopy); (separate procedure) ●

The phrase that appears to the left of the semicolon applies to all indented code descriptions.

● **EXAMPLE:**

> **32601** Thoracoscopy, diagnostic (separate procedure); lungs and pleural space, without biopsy
>
> **32602**   lungs and pleural space, with biopsy ●

EXERCISE 7-6 | **Coding Separate Procedures**

Code the following procedures.

1. Diagnostic arthroscopy, right wrist, with biopsy   _____
2. Simple vaginal mucosal biopsy   _____
3. Diagnostic nasal endoscopy, bilateral, and a facial chemical peel   _____
4. Diagnostic thoracoscopy, pleural space and biopsy right lung   _____

After completing this exercise, refer to Appendix IV to check your answers.

Multiple Surgical Procedures

Great care must be taken when billing **multiple surgical procedures** (two or more surgeries performed during the same operative session). The major surgical procedure (the procedure reimbursed at the highest level) should be listed first on the claim, and the lesser surgeries listed on the claim in descending order of expense. Modifier -51 is added to the CPT number for each lesser surgical procedure that does not have the symbol ⊘ or **+** in front of the code. (Appendix E in the CPT coding manual provides a complete list of modifier -51 exemptions.)

The ranking into major and minor procedures is done to accommodate the fact that most insurance companies will reduce the fee for the second surgery by 50 percent of the regular fee and the third, fourth, and so on, by 50 to 75% of the regular fee. If a lesser procedure is listed first, it may be paid at 100% and the major or most expensive surgery reduced by 50 to 75%, resulting in a lower payment for the combined surgeries. Insurance companies reason that when multiple surgical procedures are performed during the same operative session, they share the same pre- and postoperative session; therefore, the fee is reduced because the pre- and postoperative portion is covered in the full payment for the major procedure.

BILLING TIP: Computerized practices must be sure that *multiple surgeries performed during the same operative session are entered into the computer in the proper order* to ensure they are printed correctly on the computer-generated claim.

Do not confuse multiple procedures with bilateral procedures, which require a -50 modifier. Multiple procedures have different CPT code numbers. Bilateral procedures have the same CPT code number.

CODING SPECIAL SURGERY CASES
Skin Lesions

A **skin lesion** is defined as any alteration of the skin. When reporting the excision or destruction of lesions you must know the:

- site.
- size of the lesion measured before excision (reported in centimeters).
- number of lesions removed.
- benign or malignant status.
- method used for removal.

Read the provider's notes and reports carefully to determine the type of lesion and other qualifying information covered by specific codes. Carefully review the qualifiers for a code number before noting the number of units needed (number of lesions removed) for Item 24G on the CMS-1500 claim (Figure 7-9).

Excision of a lesion requires cutting through the dermal layer of the skin. Destruction (ablation) destroys a lesion, rather than cutting it out, and closure is not required (codes 17000–17286). The diagnosis code reported in Item 24E of the CMS-1500 claim must match the benign or malignant category used to describe the CPT code.

Simple (nonlayered) closure of skin and subcutaneous tissue is included in the excision of lesions code. If the report describes an excision deeper than the dermal layer (into the subcutaneous tissue), a **layered closure** or **plastic repair** of the excision may be coded. This refers to a separate closure made of deeper structures in addition to closure of the dermis. Layered closure requires two codes: one for the excision and one for an intermediate repair (codes 12031-12057.) Also, if other structures (e.g., nerves, veins, or tendons) are repaired these may be billed as well.

CPT codes for excisions, skin closures, and some destruction procedures are reported in centimeters; if the health care provider reports the size of the lesion in inches, you have to convert the inches to centimeters. One inch equals 2.54 cm.

24. A DATE(S) OF SERVICE			B Place of Service	C Type of Service	D PROCEDURES, SERVICES, OR SUPPLIES (Explain Unusual Circumstances) CPT/HCPCS MODIFIER	E DIAGNOSIS CODE	F $ CHARGES	G DAYS OR UNITS	H EPSDT Family Plan	I EMG	J COB	K RESERVED FOR LOCAL USE
From MM DD YY	To MM DD YY											

FIGURE 7-9 Block 24 on CMS-1500 claim

EXAMPLE:

Lesion size is 2 inches

2.54 multiplied by 2 equals 5.08 cm

A biopsy of the lesion is included in the procedure when it is performed after the removal of the lesion. A biopsy performed for the purpose of determining the morphology of the lesion is reported separately. To code a "radical excision" refer to "Excision" in the CPT Index and the specific body site.

Repair of Lacerations

Lacerations are also reported in centimeters. (See the conversion from inches to centimeters above.) The length and depth of lacerations must be documented in the record. *The length of multiple lacerations/wounds falling within the same coding classification (i.e., body region) are added together and reported as a single entry.* When multiple lacerations of different classifications are documented, list the code for the most complicated repair first.

EXERCISE 7-7 **Coding Lesions and Lacerations**

Code the following procedures.

1. Excision, 2.5 cm malignant lesion, left cheek   _____

2. Excision, 1-1/2 inch benign lesion, scalp   _____

3. Removal of 10 skin tags upper back, 3 right arm, 4 chest, 2 left thigh, 3 abdomen   _____

4. Suture of 1 inch simple laceration, left forearm,   _____

   and 2-1/2 inch simple laceration, right arm

5. Excision, 2.5 cm malignant lesion, forehead with intermediate closure   _____

After completing this exercise, refer to Appendix IV to check your answers.

Fractures and Dislocations

To code fractures and dislocations correctly, the coder must answer the following questions:

- What is the location of the fracture/dislocation?
- Was manipulation (reduction) documented?
- Was the fracture "open" or "closed," and was the treatment "open," "closed," or by percutaneous skeletal fixation?
- Was internal or external fixation required?
- Was skin or skeletal traction applied?
- Was closure of soft tissue required?

Closed fracture treatment means the fracture site was not surgically opened. **Open fracture treatment** means the fracture site was surgically opened, the bone ends visualized, aligned, and internal fixation may have been applied. **Percutaneous skeletal fixation** is considered open treatment. In this case the bone fragments are never directly visualized, but fixation (e.g., pins) is placed across the fracture site, usually under radiologic guidance.

Manipulation of a fracture or dislocation and **reduction of a fracture** or dislocation are the same thing—the application of manually applied forces to restore normal anatomic alignment. Before selecting a code that requires manipulation, be sure the documentation states that either manipulation or a reduction was performed.

The treatment of fractures should be documented in the patient's record as either open or closed. When it cannot be determined from the record whether the fracture was treated as opened or closed, it is assumed to be a closed fracture treatment; that is, no surgery was required to properly align the fracture.

Read the descriptions very carefully. When the description reads **open treatment of a closed fracture** or dislocation, an incision has been made over the fracture and some type of fixation device applied. Physicians often use the term **ORIF** as a shorthand for **open reduction with internal fixation**. Careful review is also necessary to pick out the terms "single" or "multiple" fractures.

Codes 20690 or 20692 may be reported in addition to the treatment of the fracture when the code description for the fracture procedure does not mention external fixation, but external fixation of a fracture is described in the procedure report.

The first casting, strapping, or traction is included in the fee for code numbers with no asterisk. All subsequent changes of casts or tractions are reported separately. Read the note located above code 29000.

Arthroscopy

Differentiation must be made between diagnostic and surgical arthroscopies. A diagnostic arthroscopy is always included in a surgical arthroscopy and should not be listed separately on the claim. You may bill for a diagnostic arthroscopy separately if the repair cannot be made through the scope. The arthrotomy is considered the primary procedure when it immediately follows an arthroscopy.

EXERCISE 7-8 | **Coding Fractures, Dislocation, and Arthroscopies**

Code the following statements.

1. Exploration of right wrist with removal of deep foreign body   _____

2. Manipulation of right thumb dislocation   _____

3. Reapplication of short leg walking cast   _____

4. Open reduction with screws, compound fracture, shaft, left tibia and fibula, and application of a long leg cast   _____

5. Diagnostic arthroscopy followed by removal of the medial meniscus by arthrotomy   _____

After completing this exercise, refer to Appendix IV to check your answers.

Endoscopy Procedures

Endoscopy codes in CPT are classified according to:

- anatomic site.
- extent of the examination.
- purpose of the endoscopy—diagnostic versus surgical.
- type of scope used.

Carefully review the procedure report, and CPT guidelines, notes, and code descriptions before selecting the final code. Endoscopies of the digestive system are always coded to the furthest site accessed by the scope. CPT codes for diagnostic endoscopies are included in a surgical endoscopy completed during the same operative session. CPT describes a colonoscopy as "examination of entire colon, from rectum to cecum and may include the examination of the terminal ileum." (See the long note above code 45300.)

EXAMPLE: The gastroscope was introduced with ease into the upper esophageal area under direct visualization and advanced to the second portion of the duodenum. No abnormalities were noted.

43235 Upper gastrointestinal endoscopy including esophagus, stomach and either the duodenum and/or jejunum as appropriate; diagnostic, with or without collection of specimen(s) by brushing or washing (separate procedure)

Endoscopic guide-wire dilation involves the passage of a guide-wire through an endoscope into the stomach. The endoscope is removed and dilators, each with a central lumen through which the guide-wire is placed, are used to widen a constricted esophagus. **Indirect laryngoscopy** means the larynx is visualized using a warm laryngeal mirror. **Direct laryngoscopy** is performed by passing a rigid or fiberoptic endoscope into the larynx.

CODING TIP: The surgical procedure is an "open procedure," one not performed through a scope, if the CPT code description is not listed under an anatomic site heading of Endoscopy, and the term "endoscopy" or the suffix "-scopy" does not appear in the description of the procedure.

EXERCISE 7-9 | **Coding Endoscopies**

Code the following statements.

1. Laparoscopic cholecystectomy with cholangiography _____

2. Anoscopy with removal of polyp by snare _____

3. Diagnostic flexible bronchoscopy _____

4. Fibroscopic full colonoscopy with removal
   of polyps by snare _____

5. Nasal endoscopy with partial ethmoidectomy _____

After completing this exercise, refer to Appendix IV to check your answers.

MEDICINE SECTION

The medicine section starts with code 90281. Noninvasive diagnostic procedures are found in all subsections.

 EXAMPLES:

92230 Fluorescein angioscopy with interpretation and report

93312 Echocardiography, transesophageal, real time with image documentation (2D) (with or without M-mode recording); including probe placement, image acquisition, interpretation and report

93501 Right heart catheterization

Cardiovascular System

Invasive procedures of the heart and pericardium are found in the surgery section of CPT; however, cardiac catheterizations, and so on, are located in the Medicine Section beginning with code 93501.

Some codes in this subsection include both the professional and technical components of the test in one code number. Other procedures have specific codes for the combined components and separate codes for the **professional component** (supervision of procedure, interpretation, and writing of the report) or **technical component** (use of equipment and supplies) only. When a physician performs only one component of a test, the CPT modifier -26 (professional component only) should be added to the global code to indicate that the full procedure was not performed.

Special Services and Reports

This is a miscellaneous section covering services billable as adjunct to basic services provided to the patient. Carefully read through this entire subsection to become familiar with aspects of coverage found here. The most commonly used codes are:

- 99000-99002   Procurement of specimens to be sent to an outside laboratory.

- 99050-99058   Special codes for E/M services that were performed at times other than the practice's normal hours or under unusual circumstances. These codes may be assigned to augment the regular visitation codes.

- 99080   Completion of special reports such as insurance forms, attorney and insurance reports, and so on.

Infusions and Injections

CPT contains codes to classify injections of antibiotic and intravenous therapy. Refer to codes 90780-90799; review their descriptions and the notes included below the Therapeutic or Diagnostic Infusions subsection.

Because of the variance in cost for therapeutic injections, over 400 HCPCS level II "J" series codes were developed by CMS to enable computer tracking of specific medications, including immunosuppressive drugs. Because of the potential for a higher level of reimbursement coupled with more accurate descriptions found in

HCPCS level II, "J" codes should be assigned instead of CPT codes. (A discussion of "J" codes appears in Chapter 8.)

Psychiatry (90801–90899)

The insurance industry usually refers to these services as "mental or behavioral health services." *Psychiatric codes are not reserved for use only by psychiatrists.* They may be used by any physician, clinical psychologist, licensed clinical social worker, mental health counselor, or psychiatric nurse specialist licensed to practice in their state.

Psychological and behavioral testing codes are found in the Central Nervous System Assessments/Tests (96100-96117) subsection of CPT. Psychiatric consultations are reported using E/M consultation codes that are limited to initial and follow-up evaluations and do not allow for psychiatric treatment of the patient. Inpatient or partial hospitalization services of psychiatric patients that are performed by the attending physicians may be reported using codes 99221–99233.

EXERCISE 7-10 | **Medicine Section Coding**

Code the following statements.

1. Cardiac catheterization, right side only, with conscious sedation, IV _____

2. Routine ECG, tracing only _____

3. Spirometry _____

4. CPR, in office _____

5. Diagnostic psychiatric examination _____

6. Influenza vaccine _____

7. Whirlpool and paraffin bath therapy _____

8. WAIS-R and MMPI psychological tests and report, 1 hour _____

9. Office services on emergency basis _____

After completing this exercise, refer to Appendix IV to check your answers.

RADIOLOGY SECTION

The radiology section includes subsections for diagnostic radiology, diagnostic ultrasound, radiation oncology, and nuclear medicine. These are further subdivided into anatomic categories. Read the category headings and code descriptions carefully.

The number of **radiologic views** (studies taken from different angles) described in the report or on the charge slip determines the code selection in many diagnostic radiologic procedures. The term "complete" in the discussion of views is a reference to the number of views required for a full study of a designated body part. Carefully review code descriptions to understand how many views constitute a "complete study" for a specific type of radiologic procedure.

EXAMPLE:

70120 Radiologic examination, mastoids; less than three views per side

70130   complete, minimum of three views per side

70134 Radiologic examination, internal auditory meati, complete

Complete Procedure

Do not confuse the use of the term "complete" found in the description with its use in a parenthetical note.

EXAMPLE:

70332 Temperomandibular joint arthrography, radiological supervision and interpretation

(70333 [complete procedure] has been deleted, see 21116, 70332)

The above example describes a diagnostic study that has two components: radiologic and surgical.

EXAMPLE:

21116 Injection procedure for temporomandibular joint arthrography

(For radiologic supervision and interpretation see 70332. Do not report 76003 in addition to 70332)

When both components (complete procedure) are performed by the same physician, two codes are reported. If two physicians are involved in performing the procedure, each physician will submit the code only for the portion performed.

Professional versus Technical Component

Another consideration in radiology coding involves determining which physician is responsible for the professional and technical components of an examination.

The professional component of a radiologic examination covers the supervision of the procedure and the interpretation and writing of a report describing the examination and its findings. The technical component of an examination covers the use of the equipment, supplies provided, and employment of the radiologic technicians. When the examination takes place in a clinic or private office that owns the equipment and its professional services are performed by a physician employed by the clinic or private office, both the professional and technical components are billed on the same claim. If, on the other hand, the equipment and supplies are owned by a hospital or other corporation and the radiologist performs only the professional component of the examination, two separate billings are generated: one by the physician for the professional component and one by the hospital for the technical component.

When two separate billings are required, the professional component is billed by adding the modifier -26 to the CPT code number. An exception to this rule is when the code description restricts the use of the code to "supervision and interpretation."

EXAMPLE:

75710 Angiography, extremity, unilateral, radiologic supervision and interpretation

Special care must be taken when coding interventional diagnostic procedures that involve injection of contrast media, local anesthesia, or needle localization of a mass. CPT assigns two separate codes to these interventional procedures: a 70000 series supervision and interpretation code, and a surgical code. This is done because these procedures may be performed by two physicians, each billing separately. If only one physician is involved, the claim should still include both codes.

CODING TIP: Report code 76140 when a physician consult is requested to review X-rays produced in another facility and the consultant generates a written report.

EXERCISE 7-11 **Radiology Coding**

Code the following statements.

1. GI series, with small bowel and air studies, without KUB _____

2. Chest X-ray, PA & left lateral _____

3. Cervical spine X-ray, complete, with flexion and extension _____

4. X-ray pelvis, AP _____

5. Abdomen, flat plate, AP _____

6. BE, colon, with air _____

7. Postoperative radiologic supervision and interpretation of cholangiography by radiologist _____

8. SPECT exam of the liver _____

9. Retrograde pyelography with KUB _____

After completing this exercise, refer to Appendix IV to check your answers.

PATHOLOGY/LABORATORY SECTION

This section is organized according to the type of pathology or laboratory procedure performed. The major subsections are titled organ or disease oriented panels, drug testing, therapeutic drug assays, evocative/suppression testing, consultations (clinical pathology), urinalysis, chemistry, hematology and coagulation, immunology, transfusion medicine, microbiology, anatomic pathology, cytopathology, cytogenic studies, surgical pathology, and other procedures. Procedures are listed alphabetically within each subsection.

Laboratory Panels

One code number is assigned to a specific **laboratory panel**, (also called **organ panel** or **disease oriented panel**). The panel consists of a series of blood chemistry studies routinely ordered by providers at the same time for the purpose of investigating a specific organ or disorder. The make-up of the panel is very specific; no substitutions are allowed.

 EXAMPLE:

> **80055** Obstetric panel
>> This panel must include the following:
>> Hemogram, automated, and manual differential WBC count (CBC) (85022) OR
>> Hemogram and platelet count, automated, and automated complete differential WBC count (CBC) (85025)
>> Hepatitis B surface antigen (HBsAg) (87340)
>> Antibody, rubella (86762)
>> Syphilis test, qualitative (eg, VDRL, RPR, ART) (86592)
>> Antibody screen, RBC, each serum technique (86850)
>> Blood typing, ABO (86900), AND
>> Blood typing, Rh (D) (86901) ●

The health care provider's laboratory request form may either state a specific panel or individually list all the specific tests.

When the request lists blood chemistry tests individually, check the Organ or Disease Oriented Panel (80048-80090) listing in the code book to determine whether any or all of the tests ordered fit into a specific panel description and, if so, use the panel code. If the request lists chemistry tests in addition to those that fit a specific panel description you will need to report a panel code and a code for each individual test that is not included in the panel.

 EXAMPLE:

Carbon dioxide, chloride, HDL cholesterol, alkaline phosphatase, potassium and sodium

This would be coded:

80051 Electrolyte panel

83718 Lipoprotein, direct measurement; high density cholesterol (HDL cholesterol)

84075 Phosphatase, alkaline; ●

CODING TIP: Refer to "Blood Tests, Panels" in the index for a codes list of panel options. Look up the chemical substance or microbiology specimen in the index to find the code number for the individual substances to be tested (i.e, chloride or cytomegalovirus).

Drug Testing

There are four codes in this section used when it is necessary to determine if a drug of a specific classification is present in the blood or urine.

Therapeutic Drug Assays

This section is designed to report tests performed to determine how much of a specific prescribed drug is in the patient's blood.

Evocative/Suppression Testing

This series of codes is used when specific substances are injected for the purpose of confirming or ruling out specific disorders.

Consultations (Clinical Pathology)

These codes are reported by pathologists who, at the request of an attending physician, perform clinical pathology consultations related to specimens and document written reports. These codes are *not* reported for face-to-face patient contact; codes 99241–99275 are reported for examination and evaluation of patients.

Urinalysis, Chemistry, Hematology and Coagulation, and Immunology

Codes in these subsections include laboratory tests on bodily fluids (e.g., urine, blood). The tests are ordered by a physician and are performed by technologists under the supervision of a physician (usually a pathologist).

Transfusion Medicine

These codes are reported for procedures associated with blood transfusions (e.g., blood typing). Codes for the transfusion of blood and blood components are located in the Surgery Section (36430-36460) except for leukocyte transfusion, which is assigned code 86950 from the Pathology and Laboratory Section.

Microbiology

Microbiology codes report procedures for bacteriology, mycology, parasitology, and virology. Procedures performed include taking cultures (e.g., throat culture to test for streptococcus), testing for ova and parasites (e.g., ringworm), and conducting sensitivity studies (e.g., to determine which antibiotic to prescribe).

Anatomic Pathology

This subsection includes codes for postmortem examination (also known as autopsy or necropsy).

Cytopathology and Cytogenic Studies

Cytopathology codes report pathology screening tests (e.g., Pap smear). Cytogenic studies codes report tests that involve obtaining tissue cultures for testing purposes and conducting chromosome analysis studies.

Surgical Pathology

Surgical pathology codes are reported when specimens removed during surgery require pathologic diagnosis. The codes are categorized according to level. Code 88300, Level I, is assigned for the gross (or macroscopic) examination of a specimen; no microscopic examination is performed (e.g., kidney stone). Codes reported for Level II through VI surgical pathology are assigned when gross (or macroscopic) and microscopic examinations of a specimen occur (e.g., appendix, or fallopian tube). The CPT Index contains an entry for Pathology, Surgical along with codes assigned according to level. Carefully review CPT to determine which level categorizes the tissue removed. If multiple specimens were removed that can be classified to more than one level, assign a code for each level.

Transcutaneous Procedures

A new subsection, Transcutaneous Procedures, classifies total bilirubin tests.

Other Procedures

Miscellaneous laboratory procedures are included in the Other Procedures subsection.

EXERCISE 7-12 | **Pathology and Laboratory Coding**

Code the following statements.

1. Hepatic function panel   _____
2. Hepatitis panel   _____
3. TB skin test, PPD   _____
4. UA with micro, automated   _____
5. CBC with Diff, manual   _____
6. Stool for occult blood   _____
7. Wet mount, vaginal smear   _____
8. Glucose/blood sugar, quantitative   _____
9. Sedimentation rate   _____
10. Throat culture, bacterial   _____
11. Urine sensitivity, disk   _____
12. Hematocrit, spun   _____
13. Monospot   _____
14. Strep test, rapid   _____

After completing this exercise, refer to Appendix IV to check your answers.

EVALUATION AND MANAGEMENT SECTION

The **Evaluation and Management (E/M) Section** (codes 99201-99499) is located at the beginning of CPT because these codes describe services most frequently provided by physicians. Accurate assignment of **E/M codes** is essential to the success of a physician's practice because most of the revenue generated by the office is based on provision of these services. Before assigning codes, review the guidelines (located at the beginning of the E/M section) and apply any notes (located below category and subcategory headings).

Assigning Evaluation and Management Codes

CPT 1992 introduced Evaluation and Management (E/M) *level of service* codes, which replaced the *office visit* codes that were included in the Medicine Section of past revisions of CPT. The E/M **level of service** reflects the amount of work involved in providing health care to patients. Between three and five levels of service are included in E/M categories and subcategories, and documentation in the patient's chart must support the level of service reported. CMS often refers to E/M codes by level numbers (e.g., level I or 1, level II or 2, and so on), and the level often corresponds to the CPT fifth digit.

EXAMPLE: Refer to the Office or Outpatient Services category of E/M, and notice that it contains two subcategories (New Patient and Established Patient). The New Patient subcategory contains four codes, while the Established Patient subcategory contains five codes. Each code represents a level of E/M Service, ranked from lowest to highest level. CMS would consider E/M code 99201 a level I code.

Accurate assignment of E/M codes is dependent upon (1) identifying the place and/or type of service provided to the patient, (2) determining whether the patient is new or established to the practice, (3) reviewing the patient's chart for documentation of level of service components, and (4) applying CMS's *Documentation Guidelines for Evaluation and Management Services.*

Place of Service

Place of service refers to the physical location where health care is provided to patients (e.g., office or other outpatient settings, hospitals, nursing facilities, home health care, or emergency departments).

EXAMPLE 1: The provider treated the patient in his office.

Place of Service: Office

E/M Category: Office or Other Outpatient Services

EXAMPLE 2: The patient received care in the hospital's emergency department.

Place of Service: Hospital emergency department

E/M Category: Emergency Department Services

Type of Service

Type of service refers to the kind of health care services provided to patients. It includes critical care, consultation, initial hospital care, subsequent hospital care, confirmatory consultation, and so on.

EXAMPLE 1: The patient underwent an annual physical examination in the provider's office.

Type of Service:	Preventive care
E/M Category:	Preventive Medicine Services

EXAMPLE 2: The hospital inpatient was transferred to the regular Medical-Surgical Unit where he was recovering from surgery. He suddenly stopped breathing and required respirator management by his physician.

Type of Service:	Critical care
E/M Category:	Critical Care Services

NOTE: While this type of care is often administered in a critical care unit, that is not a requirement for code assignment.

Sometimes, both the type and place of service must be identified before the proper code can be assigned.

EXAMPLE 1: Dr. Smith completed Josie Black's history and physical examination on the first day of her inpatient admission.

Place of Service:	Hospital
Type of Service:	Initial care
E/M Category:	Hospital Inpatient Services
E/M Subcategory:	Initial Hospital Care

EXAMPLE 2: Dr. Charles saw Josie Black in her office to render a second opinion.

Type of Service:	Consultation
Place of Service:	Office
E/M Category:	Consultations
E/M Subcategory:	Office or Other Outpatient Consultations

New and Established Patients

A new patient is one who has not received any professional services from the physician or another physician of the same specialty who belongs to the same group practice within the past three years. An established patient is one who has received professional services from the physician or another physician of the same specialty who belongs to the same group practice, within the past three years.

CODING TIP: Professional services may not require a face-to-face encounter with a provider.

● **EXAMPLE 1:** Sally Dunlop had a prescription renewed by Dr. Smith's office on January 1, 2001, but she did not see the physician. She has been Dr. Smith's patient since her initial office visit on March 15, 1998. On December 1, 2001, Dr. Smith treated Sally during an office visit.

New Patient: March 15, 1998

Established Patient: January 1, 2001 & December 1, 2001

Because she received professional services (the prescription renewal) on January 1, 2001, Sally Dunlop is considered an established patient for the December 1, 2001 visit.

● **EXAMPLE 2:** Dr. Charles and Dr. Black share a practice. Dr. Charles is a general surgeon who treated Mary Smith in the office on July 1, 2001. Mary was first seen by the practice on February 15, 2000, when Dr. Black provided preventive care services to her. Mary returned to the practice on November 1, 2001, for her annual physical examination conducted by Dr. Black.

New Patient: February 15, 2000 & July 1, 2001

Established Patient: November 1, 2001 ●

● **NOTE:** Review insurance company policies for definitions of new and established patient visits when provided by different specialties and subspecialties in the same group. ●

CRITICAL THINKING

Dr. Corey left Alfred Medical Group to join Buffalo Physician Group as a family practitioner. At Buffalo Physician Group, when Dr. Corey provides professional services to patients, will those patients be considered new or established?

Answer: Patients who have not received professional services from Dr. Corey or another physician of the same specialty at Buffalo Physician Group would be considered new. If the patients had seen another family practitioner at Buffalo Physician Group within the past three years, the patients would be considered established. If any of Dr. Corey's patients from the Alfred Medical Group choose to seek care from him at the Buffalo Physician Group, they are also considered established patients.

Remember! Definitions of new and established patients include professional services rendered by other physicians of the same specialty in the same group practice.

Key Components

E/M code selection is based on three **key components**: *extent of history, extent of examination,* and *complexity of medical decision making* (terms referenced in CMS's E/M Documentation Guidelines). The CPT E/M guidelines and notes include definitions and instructions for selecting E/M codes. Because they were believed to be insufficient to guarantee consistent coding by providers and reliable medical review by payers, CMS developed **Evaluation and Management Documentation Guidelines**, which explain how E/M codes are assigned according to elements associated with comprehensive multisystem and single system examinations. The first set of guidelines created by CMS in 1995 was criticized by providers as containing unclear criteria for single system examinations. Therefore, CMS created an alternate set of guidelines in 1997, which was also criticized as being confusing and requiring extensive counting of services and other elements. Therefore, CMS instructed Medicare carriers to use both sets of guidelines when reviewing records. Providers could use whichever set of guidelines was most advantageous to their practice reimbursement.

INTERNET LINKS

The 1995 and 1997 E/M Documentation Guidelines can be viewed at
http://cms.hhs.gov/medicare

Specialty exam scoresheets can be downloaded from http://www.hgsa.com

Go to http://www.donself.com and click on Documents to download a variety of forms and scoresheets that can be used to assign E/M codes.

The American Academy of Family Physicians makes available past issues of its *Family Practice Management* journal at http://www.aafp.org, which contains articles about documentation guidelines and other issues.

All three key components must be considered when assigning codes for new patients. For established patients, two of the three key components must be considered. This means that documentation in the patient's chart must support the key components used to determine the E/M code selected.

The E/M code reported to a payer must be supported by documentation in the patient's record (e.g., SOAP or clinic note, diagnostic test results, operative findings). While providers are responsible for selecting the E/M code at the time patient care is rendered, insurance specialists audit records to make sure that the appropriate level of E/M code was reported to the third-party payer.

To assign a code, review documentation in the patient's record and use the *E/M CodeBuilder* (Appendix IV) to record your findings. Then, refer to the CPT coding manual to select the correct E/M code.

It is important to be aware that contributory components *(counseling* and *coordination of care)* also play an important role in selecting the E/M code *when documentation in the patient record indicates that counseling or coordination of care dominated the visit.* In this situation, the contributory component of time can be considered a key or controlling factor in selecting a level of E/M service (code).

NOTE: *Time,* along with *nature of presenting problem,* are listed in some E/M code descriptions to assist in determining which code number to report.

Extent of History

A **history** is an interview of the patient that includes the following components: history of the present illness (HPI) (including the patient's chief complaint), a review of systems (ROS), and a past/family/social history (PFSH). The **extent of history** is categorized according to four types, listed and defined as follows:

Problem focused: chief complaint, brief history of present illness or problem

Expanded problem focused: chief complaint, brief history of present illness, problem pertinent system review

Detailed: chief complaint, extended history of present illness, problem pertinent system review extended to include a limited number of additional systems, pertinent past/family/social history directly related to patient's problem

Comprehensive: chief complaint, extended history of present illness, review of systems directly related to the problem(s) identified in the history of the present illness plus a review of all additional body systems, complete past/family/social history

● **NOTE:** Refer to Figure 7-10A to learn how to determine extent of history. ●

Extent of Examination

A **physical examination** is an assessment of the patient's organ (e.g., extremities) and body systems (e.g., cardiovascular). The **extent of examination** is categorized according to four types, listed and defined as follows:

Problem focused: a limited examination of the affected body area or organ system

Expanded problem focused: a limited examination of the affected body area or organ system and other symptomatic or related organ system(s)

Detailed: an extended examination of the affected body area(s) and other symptomatic or related organ system(s)

Comprehensive: general multisystem examination or a complete examination of a single organ system.

● **NOTE:** Refer to Figure 7-10B to learn how to determine extent of examination. ●

Complexity of Medical Decision Making

Medical decision making refers to the complexity of establishing a diagnosis and/or selecting a management option as measured by the:

- number of diagnoses or management options.
- amount and/or complexity of data to be reviewed.
- risk of complications and/or morbidity or mortality.

Once the key components for extent of history and examination are determined, the medical decision making type can be selected: straightforward, low complexity, moderate complexity, or high complexity. The physician is responsible for determining the complexity of medical decision making, and that decision must be supported by documentation in the patient's chart. CPT includes a table in the E/M Guidelines that can assist in determining complexity of medical decision making (see Table 7-2).

● **NOTE:** Refer to Figure 7-10C to review criteria for determining medical decision making. Level of medical decision making reflects the provider's level of uncertainty, volume of data to review, and risk to the patient. (The criteria in Figure 7-10C can be used to determine the complexity of medical decision making in Table 7-2.) ●

SELECTING EXTENT OF HISTORY: To select extent of history, review the following elements documented in the patient record. If an element is not documented, it cannot be considered when selecting the level of E/M service code.

- History of Present Illness (HPI)
- Review of Systems (ROS)
- Past, Family, and Social History (PFSH)

HISTORY OF PRESENT ILLNESS (HPI): Review the patient's record, and for each documented HPI element listed below place an **x** in the box located in front of the element on this form. Then, count the number of **x**'s, and enter that number in the box located in front of the Total Score (below). Select the level of history based on the total number of elements documented, and place an **x** in the appropriate box.

- ☐ **Location:** of pain/discomfort; is pain diffuse/localized, unilateral/bilateral, does it radiate or refer?
- ☐ **Quality:** a description of the quality of the symptom; e.g., is pain described as sharp, dull, throbbing, stabbing, constant, intermittent, acute or chronic, stable, improving or worsening
- ☐ **Severity:** use of self-assessment scale to measure subjective levels (e.g., "on a scale of 1-10, how severe is the pain?"), or comparison of pain quantitatively with previously experienced pain
- ☐ **Timing:** establishing onset of pain and chronology of pain development; e.g., migraine in the a.m.
- ☐ **Context:** where was the patient and what was he doing when pain begins; was patient at rest or involved in an activity; was pain aggravated or relieved, or does it recur, with a specific activity; did situational stress or some other factor precede or accompanying the pain
- ☐ **Modifying factors:** what has patient attempted to do to relieve pain; e.g., heat vs. cold; does it relieve or exacerbate pain; what makes the pain worse; have over-the-counter drugs been attempted - with what results
- ☐ **Associated signs/symptoms:** clinician's impressions formulated during the interview may lead to questioning about additional sensations or feelings; e.g., diaphoresis associated with indigestion or chest pain, blurred vision accompanying a headache, etc.

_____ **Total Score:** Enter the number of **x**'s selected. Place an **x** in front of the HPI type below.
- ☐ BRIEF HPI (1-3 elements)
- ☐ EXTENDED HPI (4 or more elements)

REVIEW OF SYSTEMS (ROS): Review the clinic or SOAP note in the patient's record, and for each documented ROS element listed below, place an **x** in the box located in front of the element on this form. Then, total **x**'s recorded, and enter that number in the box located in front of the Total Score (below). Finally, select the level of ROS based on the total number of elements documented, and place an **x** in the appropriate box.

- ☐ Constitutional symptoms
- ☐ Allergic or immunologic
- ☐ Cardiovascular
- ☐ Ears
- ☐ Endocrine
- ☐ Eyes, nose, throat, mouth
- ☐ Gastrointestinal
- ☐ Genitourinary
- ☐ Integumentary
- ☐ Musculoskeletal
- ☐ Hematologic/Lymphatic
- ☐ Neurologic
- ☐ Psychiatric
- ☐ Respiratory

_____ **Total Score:** Enter the number of **x**'s selected. Place an **x** in front of the ROS type below.
- ☐ NONE
- ☐ PROBLEM PERTINENT ROS (1 body system documented)
- ☐ EXTENDED ROS (2-9 body systems documented)
- ☐ COMPLETE ROS (all body systems documented)

PAST, FAMILY AND/OR SOCIAL HISTORY (PFSH): Review the clinic or SOAP note in the patient's record, and for each documented PFSH element listed below, place an **x** in the box located in front of the element on this form. Then, total **x**'s recorded, and enter that number in the box located in front of the Total Score (below). Finally, select the level of PFSH based on the total number of elements documented, and place an **x** in the appropriate box.

- ☐ Past history (current medications, drug allergies, immunizations, and prior illnesses/injuries, hospitalizations, surgeries)
- ☐ Family history (health status/cause of death of relatives, specific diseases related to CC, HPI, ROS, hereditary diseases for which patient is at risk)
- ☐ Social history (alcohol use, current employment, illicit drug use, level of education, nutritional status, occupational history, sexual history, tobacco use)

_____ **Total Score:** Enter the number of **x**'s selected. Place an **x** in front of the PFSH type below.
- ☐ NONE
- ☐ PERTINENT PFSH (1 history area documented)
- ☐ COMPLETE PFSH (2 or 3 history areas documented)

Circle the type of HPI, ROS & PFSH. Select the Extent of History. (3 of 3 elements must be met or exceeded.)

HPI	Brief	Brief	Extended	Extended
ROS	None	Problem Pertinent	Extended	Complete
PFSH	None	None	Pertinent	Complete
EXTENT OF HISTORY	PROBLEM FOCUSED	EXPANDED PROBLEM FOCUSED	DETAILED	COMPREHENSIVE

FIGURE 7-10A Extent of history

SELECTING EXTENT OF EXAMINATION: To select the level of examination, first determine whether a *single organ examination* (e.g., specialist exam such as ophthalmologist) or a *general multisystem examination* (e.g., family practitioner) was completed.

SINGLE ORGAN SYSTEM EXAMINATION: Refer to single organ system examination requirements in CMS's *Documentation Guidelines for Evaluation and Management Services.* Place an ✕ in front of the appropriate exam type below.

☐ PROBLEM FOCUSED EXAMINATION (1–5 elements identified by a bullet)

☐ EXPANDED PROBLEM FOCUSED EXAMINATION (at least 6 elements identified by a bullet)

☐ DETAILED EXAMINATION (at least 12 elements identified by a bullet; NOTE: for eye and psychiatric examinations, at least 9 elements in each box with a shaded border and at least one element in each box with an shaded or unshaded border is documented)

☐ COMPREHENSIVE EXAMINATION (all elements identified by a bullet; document every element in each box with a shaded border and at least 1 element in each box with an unshaded border)

GENERAL MULTISYSTEM EXAM: Refer to the general multisystem examination requirements in CMS's *Documentation Guidelines for Evaluation and Management Services.* Place an ✕ in front of the organ system or body area for up to the total number of allowed elements; e.g., up to 2 marks can be made for the Neck exam.

☐ Constitutional (2)   ☐ Gastrointestinal (5)   ☐ Psychiatric (4)
☐ Cardiovascular (7)   ☐ Genitourinary (M–3; F–6)   ☐ Respiratory (4)
☐ Chest (Breasts) (2)   ☐ Musculoskeletal (6)   ☐ Skin (2)
☐ Eyes (3)   ☐ Neck (2)
☐ Ears, nose, mouth, throat (6)   ☐ Neurologic (3)

_____ **Total Score:** Enter the number of ✕'s selected. Place an ✕ in front of the Examination type below.

☐ PROBLEM FOCUSED EXAMINATION (1-5 elements identified by a bullet on CMS's *E/M Documentation Guidelines*)

☐ EXPANDED PROBLEM FOCUSED EXAMINATION (at least 6 elements identified by a bullet on CMS's *E/M Documentation Guidelines*)

☐ DETAILED EXAMINATION (at least 2 elements identified by a bullet from each of 6 organ systems or body areas or at least 12 elements identified by a bullet in two or more systems or areas, on CMS's *E/M Documentation Guidelines*)

☐ COMPREHENSIVE EXAMINATION (documentation of all elements identified by a bullet in at least 9 organ systems or body areas, and documentation of at least 2 elements identified by a bullet from each of 9 organ systems or body areas, on CMS's *E/M Documentation Guidelines*)

FIGURE 7-10B Extent of examination

TABLE 7-2 Complexity of medical decision making

COMPLEXITY OF MEDICAL DECISION MAKING (2 OF 3 ELEMENTS MUST BE MET OR EXCEEDED)			
Number of Diagnoses or Management Options	**Amount/Complexity of Data to be Reviewed**	**Risk of Complications and/or Morbidity/ Mortality**	**Medical Decision Making**
Minimal	Minimal or none	Minimal	Straightforward
Limited	Limited	Low	Low complexity
Multiple	Moderate	Moderate	Moderate complexity
Extensive	Extensive	High	High complexity

Criteria to Determine Minimal, Low, Moderate, and High Levels of Medical Decision Making

	Minimal	Low	Moderate	High
Number of Diagnoses	• One self-limited or minor problem (e.g., cold, insect bite)	• Two or more self-limited minor problems • One stable chronic illness (e.g., controlled hypertension) • Acute, uncomplicated illness or injury (e.g., allergic rhinitis, simple sprain)	• One or more chronic illnesses with mild exacerbation, progression, or side effects of treatment • Two or more stable chronic illnesses • Undiagnosed new problem with uncertain prognosis (e.g., breast lump) • Acute illness with systemic symptoms (e.g., pyelonephritis) • Acute complicated injury (e.g., head injury with unconsciousness)	• One or more chronic illnesses with severe exacerbation, progression, or side effects of treatment • Acute or chronic illnesses or injuries that pose a threat to life or bodily function (e.g., acute myocardial infarction) • An abrupt change in neurologic status (e.g., seizure)
Amount/ Complexity of Data to be Reviewed	• Lab tests requiring venipuncture • Chest X-ray • ECG/EEG • Urinalysis • Ultrasound • KOH prep	• Physiologic tests not under stress (e.g., pulmonary function tests) • Noncardiovascular imaging studies with contrast (e.g., barium enema) • Superficial needle biopsies • Clinical lab tests requiring arterial puncture • Skin biopsies	• Physiologic tests under stress (e.g., cardiac stress test) • Diagnostic endoscopies with no identified risk factors • Deep needle or incisional biopsies • Cardiovascular imaging studies with contrast and no identified risk factors • Obtain fluid from body cavity (e.g., thoracentesis)	• Cardiovascular imaging studies with contrast with identified risk factors • Cardiac electrophysiologic tests • Diagnostic endoscopies with identified risk factors • Discography
Management Options	• Rest • Gargles • Elastic bandages • Superficial dressings	• Over-the-counter drugs • Minor surgery with no identified risk factors • Physical therapy • Occupational therapy • IV fluids without additives	• Minor surgery with identified risk factors • Elective major surgery (open, percutaneous, or endoscopic) with no identified risk factors • Prescription drug management • Therapeutic nuclear medicine • IV fluids with additives • Closed treatment of fracture or dislocation without manipulation	• Elective major surgery (open, percutaneous, or endoscopic) with identified risk factors • Emergency major surgery (open, percutaneous, or endoscopic) • Parenteral controlled substances • Drug therapy requiring intensive monitoring for toxicity • Decision not to resuscitate or to de-escalate care because of poor prognosis

FIGURE 7-10C Criteria to determine medical decision making

Select the E/M code based on selection of extent of history and examination and complexity of medical decision making:					
History	Problem focused	Expanded problem focused	Expanded problem focused	Detailed	Comprehensive
Examination	Problem focused	Expanded problem focused	Expanded problem focused	Detailed	Comprehensive
Medical Decision Making	Straightforward	Low complexity	Moderate complexity	Moderate complexity	High complexity

Go to the appropriate E/M category/subcategory, and select the code based upon the information above

FIGURE 7-10D Selecting the E/M code based on extent of history and examination and complexity of medical decision making

EXAMPLE: Use Figures 7-10A, 7-10B, 7-10C, and 7-10D and Table 7-2 to determine extent of history and examination, and complexity of medical decision making for this patient seen by his general practitioner. (Figure 7-10D summarizes extent of history and examination and complexity of medical decision making so the CPT E/M code can be assigned.)

S: The patient is a 35-year-old established male patient seen today with a chief complaint of severe snoring. He says this has gone on for years, and he's finally ready to do something about it because he awakens during the night from it, and his wife is also losing sleep from his snoring. He says that he wakes up in the morning feeling very tired and notices that he gets very tired during the day. ROS reveals allergies. He denies smoking or alcohol use. He is on no medications

O: Blood pressure is 126/86. Pulse is 82. Weight is 185. EYES: Pupils equal, round, and reactive to light and accommodation; extraocular muscles intact. EARS & NOSE: Tympanic membranes normal; oropharynx benign. NECK: Supple without jugular venous distension, bruits or thyromegaly. RESPIRATORY: Breath sounds are clear to percussion and auscultation. EXTREMITIES: Without edema; pulses intact.

A: Possible sleep apnea.

P: Patient to undergo sleep study in two weeks. Results to be evaluated by Dr. Jones, ENT specialist, to determine whether patient is candidate for laser-assisted uvuloplasty (LAUP) surgery.

To assign the E/M code, the following is determined from the note:

- This patient is a new patient.
- *HISTORY:* HPI elements include quality, severity, timing, and context; extended HPI (4 elements) is documented. ROS elements include allergic; problem pertinent ROS (1 body system) is documented. PFSH elements include documentation of social history; pertinent PFSH (1 history area)) is documented for a score 1. Because 3 out of 3 HPI/ROS/PFHS types must be selected to determine the higher level extent of history, *expanded problem focused history* is assigned.
- *EXAMINATION:* Constitutional (1), Eyes (1), ENT (2), Neck (1), Respiratory (1), Cardiovascular (1); *expanded problem focused examination* (6 elements) is documented.
- *MEDICAL DECISION MAKING:* Undiagnosed new problem with uncertain prognosis is documented (possible sleep apnea). Although physiologic test not

under stress (sleep study) is documented as being ordered, results are not reviewed by this provider. In addition, this provider will not follow through on management options because the patient is referred to an ENT specialist. Therefore, complexity of *medical decision making is straightforward* because 2 of 3 elements are required (and just 1 element is documented).

- *E/M CODE:* 99213 (2 of 3 key components are required).

Contributory Components

Contributory components include counseling, coordination of care, nature of presenting problem, and time. Counseling and/or coordination of care components drive CPT code selection only when they dominate the encounter (e.g., office visit), requiring that more than 50% of the provider's time be spent on such components. In such circumstances, the provider must be sure to carefully document these elements so as to support the higher level code selected.

Counseling

CPT defines **counseling** as it relates to E/M coding as a discussion with a patient and/or family concerning one or more of the following areas:

- diagnostic results, impressions, and/or recommended diagnostic studies
- prognosis
- risks and benefits of management (treatment) options
- instructions for management (treatment) and/or follow-up
- importance of compliance with chosen management (treatment) options
- risk factor reduction
- patient and family education

This counseling is not to be confused with psychotherapy. Psychotherapy codes are located in the Medicine Section of CPT and are reported for behavioral health modification or the treatment of mental illness.

Coordination of Care

When the physician makes arrangements with other providers or agencies for services to be provided to a patient, this is called **coordination of care**.

EXAMPLE: Dr. Smith writes a discharge order for inpatient Carol Kane to be discharged home and to receive home health care. Dr. Smith contacts the home health agency to make the appropriate arrangements for the patient and instructs the hospital to send copies of the patient's record to the home health care agency.

Nature of the Presenting Problem

CPT defines **nature of the presenting problem** as a disease, condition, illness, injury, symptom, sign, finding, complaint, or other reason for the encounter, with or without a diagnosis being established at the time of the encounter. Nature of the presenting problem is considered when determining the number of diagnoses or management options for medical decision making complexity (Table 7-2). Five types of presenting problems are recognized:

- *minimal:* problem may not require the presence of the physician, but service is provided under the physician's supervision (e.g., patient who comes to the office once a week to have blood pressure taken and recorded)

- *self-limited or minor:* a problem that runs a definite and prescribed course, is transient in nature, and is not likely to permanently alter health status; *or* has a good prognosis with management/compliance (e.g., patient diagnosed with adult-onset diabetes mellitus controlled by diet and exercise)

- *low severity:* a problem where the risk of morbidity without treatment is low; there is little to no risk of mortality without treatment; full recovery without functional impairment is expected (e.g., patient diagnosed with eczema that does not respond to over-the-counter medications)

- *moderate severity:* a problem where the risk of morbidity without treatment is moderate; there is moderate risk of mortality without treatment; uncertain prognosis; *or* increased probability of prolonged functional impairment (e.g., 35-year-old male patient diagnosed with chest pain on exertion)

- *high severity:* a problem where the risk of morbidity without treatment is high to extreme; there is a moderate to high risk of mortality without treatment; *or* high probability of severe, prolonged functional impairment (e.g., infant hospitalized with a diagnosis of respiratory syncytial virus)

Time (Face-to-Face vs. Unit/Floor)

Face-to-face time is the amount of time the office or outpatient care provider spends with the patient and/or family. **Unit/floor time** is the amount of time the provider spends at the patient's bedside and managing the patient's care on the unit or floor (e.g., writing orders for diagnostic tests or reviewing test results). Unit/floor time applies to inpatient hospital care, hospital observation care, initial and follow-up inpatient hospital consultations, and nursing facility services.

The key components usually determine the E/M code selected; however, visits that consist *predominantly* of counseling and/or coordination of care are an exception. When counseling and/or coordination of care dominates (more than 50%) the physician-patient and/or family encounter, it can be considered a key factor in selecting a particular E/M code. The extent of counseling must be documented in the patient's chart to support the E/M code selected.

EXAMPLE: Anne Sider sees Dr. Cyrix in the office for her three-month check-up (she has chronic hypertension controlled by diet and exercise). During the visit, Dr. Cyrix notes that the patient seems distracted and stressed, and he asks her about these symptoms. Anne starts to cry and spends 10 minutes telling Dr. Cyrix that her "life is falling apart" and that she wakes up in the middle of the night with a pounding heart, feeling like she's going to die. Dr. Cyrix spends the next 45 minutes counseling Anne about these symptoms. He determines that Anne is suffering from panic attacks, so he prescribes a medication and contacts ABC Counseling Associates to arrange an appointment for mental health counseling.

In this example, a routine three-month check-up (for which code 99212 or 99213 would be selected) evolves into a higher level service (for which code 99215 can be reported).

NOTE: The provider must carefully document all aspects of this visit to include the recheck for hypertension, counseling and coordination of care provided, and length of time spent face-to-face with the patient. ●

CODING TIP: Add V65.4x to the claim when counseling and/or coordination of care dominates the patient encounter, and is documented by the provider.

NOTE: In 2002, The Secretary of HHS's Advisory Committee on Regulatory Reform recommended that CMS eliminate the E/M documentation guidelines. The Committee's E/M Workgroup, which has been reviewing the E/M documentation guidelines, reported that the system is too complicated, has adversely affected medical practice, creates an adversarial billing environment, and suffers from a high error rate. The AMA is working on incorporating the guidelines into the E/M section of CPT. ●

EVALUATION AND MANAGEMENT CATEGORIES

Most of the categories (or subsections), subcategories, and headings in E/M (99201–99499) contain notes that are unique to the category (subsection), subcategory, or heading. *Remember to review instructional notes before assigning an E/M code.*

Office or Other Outpatient Services

Report codes 99201–99215 when E/M services are provided in a physician's office, a hospital outpatient department, or another ambulatory care facility (e.g., stand-alone ambulatory care center). Office or Other Outpatient Services codes contain patient status subcategories (new vs. established patient).

Hospital Observation Services

E/M codes were created to report encounters that are designated as "observation status" in a hospital. Observation services are furnished in a hospital outpatient setting to determine whether further treatment or inpatient admission is needed. When a patient is placed under observation, the patient is treated as an outpatient. If the duration of observation care is expected to be 24 hours or more, the physician must order an inpatient admission. The date the physician orders the inpatient stay is the date of the inpatient admission.

NOTE: The hospital is not required to establish a physical area of observation; however, patients must be designated as "observation status." ●

NOTE: Only one code (an observation service code) is reported on a claim when services are provided to a patient initially seen at another place of service but later designated as observation status. ●

EXAMPLE: A patient seen in the hospital's emergency department and designated as observation status would have just the observation status code reported. ●

The **hospital observation services** E/M category includes subcategories for observation care discharge services and initial observation care, and no differentiation is made as to patient status (new vs. established). The initial observation care codes in this category are reported for patients who are admitted for observation on one date and discharged from observation status on a different date. Thus, the insurance specialist reports multiple codes from this category (e.g., 99218 and 99217). To report codes for patients who are admitted and discharged from observation status on the same date, refer to the Observation or Inpatient Care Services (including Admission and Discharge Services) subcategory of Hospital Inpatient Services category in the E/M Section.

CODING TIPS: Observation services codes may not be reported for postoperative recovery if the "global surgery" (or surgical package) concept applies to the procedure performed.

Patients who are admitted as hospital inpatients from observation status on the same date are reported only as initial hospital care. The code assigned should identify both the observation care provided and the initial hospital care admission service. In this circumstance, a code for observation care discharge services does not apply and is not reported.

 **EXAMPLE:** A patient was treated in the hospital's emergency department (ED) for acute asthmatic bronchitis. The ED physician determines that the patient needed to be observed for a period of 6–8 hours after provision of emergency treatment. The patient received a detailed level of observation services and was discharged from observation services the next day.

In this example, the CPT codes to be reported include 99218 and 99217. If the observation care services rendered had been initiated and concluded on the same day, only code 99234 would be reported. ●

CODING TIP: There is no subsequent day observation code. You must assign a code from Office or Other Outpatient Services, 99212–99215, for a patient who remains designated as observation status for a second calendar day and who is not admitted to inpatient status or discharged from observation services.

Hospital Inpatient Services

Initial hospital care services cover the first inpatient encounter the *admitting/attending physician* has with the patient for each admission. A **hospital inpatient** is someone who is admitted and discharged and has a length of stay (LOS) of one or more days. These codes cover all E/M services performed by that physician as related to the admission, regardless of where other E/M services were performed (e.g., preoperative history and examination performed in the office just days prior to an elective admission). Physicians involved with care of the patient, but not designated as the admitting/attending physician, report services from a different category of E/M depending upon where services were rendered (e.g., emergency department services, and consultations).

Subsequent hospital care includes the review of the patient's chart for changes in the patient's condition, the results of diagnostic studies, and/or the reassessment of the patient's condition since the last assessment performed by the physician.

A code for observation or inpatient care services (including admission and discharge services) is assigned only if the patient was admitted to and discharged from observation/inpatient status on the same day. Do not assign an observation care or inpatient discharge services code.

Assign a code from Observation or Inpatient Care Services, code range 99234–99236, if the patient was admitted and discharged from observation services within the same calendar day. (Medicare requires a minimum 8-hour obervation status.)

Hospital discharge services include the final examination of the patient, discussion of the hospital stay with the patient and/or caregiver; instructions for continuing care provided to the patient and/or caregiver; and preparation of discharge records, prescriptions, and referral forms.

Do not report Subsequent Hospital Care codes (99231–99233) on the day of hospital discharge. Code 99231 describes a stable, recovering, or improving patient. Code 99232 indicates the patient has had an inadequate response to therapy or has developed a complication. Code 99233 is reported for an unstable patient or one who has developed a significant complication or new problem.

Consultations

A consultation is defined (for general coding purposes) as an examination of a patient by a health care provider, usually a specialist, for the purpose of advising the referring or attending physician in the evaluation and/or management of a specific problem with a known diagnosis. Consultants may initiate diagnostic and/or therapeutic services as necessary during the consultative encounter.

The consultation category of E/M allows the following types of consultations to be reported: office or other outpatient, initial and follow-up inpatient, and confirmatory consultations. *Follow-up office or other outpatient consultation services are not reported; if subsequent office or other outpatient consultation services are performed for a patient, these services are reported by the consultant using office or other patient services codes, established patient (99211–99215).*

EXERCISE 7-13 | **E/M Coding I**

Code the following statements. To determine the appropriate level of service codes, refer to the CPT E/M Code Abstract (Table 3) located in Appendix II.

1. Home visit, problem focused, established patient _____

2. ED service, new patient, low complexity;
   DX: low-grade chest pain _____

(continues)

3. Hospital care, new patient, initial, high complexity   _____

4. Hospital care, subsequent, detailed   _____

5. ED care, established patient, problem focused, counseling 15 minutes; DX: bladder infection   _____

6. Patient requested consultation, new patient, moderate complexity, no third-party confirmation required   _____

7. Office consultation, high complexity, established patient, surgery scheduled tomorrow   _____

8. Follow-up consultation, office, problem-focused, counseling 15 minutes, encounter was 25 minutes   _____

9. Follow-up consultation, inpatient, detailed, 35 minutes   _____

After completing this exercise, refer to Appendix IV to check your answers.

Codes 99261–99263 cover follow-up inpatient consultation. To assign code numbers 99241–99245 or 99251–99255 the consultation request must be:

- initiated by the attending physician or other health care provider. (Consultations requested by the patient, the patient's family, or a third party are classified in the Confirmatory Consultation subsection of CPT. See the description on page 239.)

- attending physicians must document all consultation requests in the patient's record.

- the consultant must document a written report that includes the name of the person requesting the consultation, the reason for the consultation, and how the findings were communicated to the referring health care provider.

Any specifically identifiable diagnostic or therapeutic service performed on the same day as the examination may be billed separately. These separate services must be linked to the appropriate diagnosis to ensure that "medical necessity" criteria have been met. Some carriers, including Medicare, may disallow payment when procedures and services are performed during the encounter.

If the consultant assumes responsibility for a portion or all of the management of the case, all subsequent care is to be reported and billed using the appropriate office or other outpatient services, established patient, code or the subsequent hospital care code.

CODING TIP:

Do not confuse a *consultation* with a *referral*. A **referral** is a patient who reports that another provider referred him. Because the referring provider did not schedule the appointment or document a request for referral, this is *not* a consultation. To ensure proper coding of the encounter, call the referring provider to inquire whether a consultation was intended instead of a referral.

Preoperative clearance occurs when a surgeon requests that a specialist or other physician (e.g., general practice) examine a patient and certify whether or not that patient can withstand the expected risks of a specific surgery. This is also considered a consultation, even if the referring physician is the patient's primary care physician. (A written request must be documented in the patient's record.)

Confirmatory Consultation

A **confirmatory consultation** is an E/M service requested by the patient, the patient's family, or a third party for the purpose of rendering a second or third opinion about the necessity or appropriate nature of a previously recommended diagnosis, surgical or medical procedure. The examination setting or site of service does not enter into the selection of the appropriate confirmatory consultation code. When the confirmatory consultation is mandated by a third-party payer, modifier -32 is used for clarification of circumstances surrounding the encounter. Subsequent services rendered to the patient are reported and billed as an established patient office or other outpatient service or a subsequent hospital care.

Emergency Department Services

Emergency department services are defined by CPT as those provided in an organized hospital-based facility, which is open on a 24-hour basis, for the purpose of "providing unscheduled episodic services to patients requiring immediate medical attention." Patients are not designated as new or established in this subsection. Code 99288 is reported when the physician is in two-way voice communication contact with ambulance or rescue crew personnel located outside of the hospital.

Critical Care Services

Critical care services are reported when a physician directly delivers medical care for a critically ill or critically injured patient. Critical care services can be provided on multiple days, even if no changes are made to the treatment rendered to the patient, as long as the patient's condition requires the direct delivery of critical care services by the provider.

NOTE: It is not necessary for a patient to be admitted to a critical care unit or an intensive care unit to receive critical care services. Patients can receive critical care services in the hospital emergency department, medical/surgical unit, and so on.

Critical care service codes are selected according to the total duration of time the provider spent delivering critical care services to the patient, even if the time spent was not continuous. To calculate duration of time, the provider must devote his full attention to the patient and cannot provide services to any other patient during that same period of time.

NOTE: The provider should document the total time spent delivering critical care services.

Critical care service codes include other services and procedures that are not reported as separate codes when critical care service codes are reported. Certain services and procedures are *bundled* with critical care service codes, including chest X-rays, blood gas tests, gastric intubation, interpretation of cardiac output measurements, information stored in computers (e.g., ECGs), temporary transcutaneous pacing, ventilator management, and vascular access procedures. Refer to the notes included under the Critical Care Services subsection of CPT for codes that apply to the "includes services and procedures."

The codes are reported for critical care services that have been rendered to a patient. Likewise, just because patients are located in a critical care unit does not mean they are receiving critical care; if the patient is stable, report the appropriate level of subsequent hospital care or inpatient consultation codes. If, while located in a critical care unit, the patient receives critical care services from a physician in constant attendance, the critical care services codes are reported in addition to hospital care or inpatient consultation codes. Comprehensive documentation of critical care services is crucial.

EXAMPLE: Mary Jones is seen in the hospital emergency department (ED) for trauma as the result of an automobile accident; she also receives one hour of critical care services in the ED. Report the appropriate level ED code *and* code 99291 from the critical care services category of the E/M section. ●

CODING TIP: When critical care services are coded in addition to another E/M service code (e.g., ED care, and initial hospital care), add modifier -25 to the E/M service code to report it as a separately identified service provided to the patient.

Remember! Critical care services are reported based on the total time the physician spends in constant attendance (Table 7-3), and the time does *not* have to be continuous.

EXAMPLE: Dr. Smith delivers critical care services to his patient on June 15th from 8–9 A.M., 10:30–10:45 A.M., and 3–3:45 P.M. To code this case, total the minutes of critical care services directly delivered by the provider (refer to Table 7-3 to select the codes). The answer is 99291 and 99292 x 2. ●

Remember! You may have to report other E/M codes (along with modifier -25).

Neonatal Intensive Care

A physician who directs the care of a critically ill newborn (or the very low birth weight infant) provides **neonatal intensive care** services. Codes 99295–99298 are reported for "neonates (30 days of age or less) admitted to an intensive care unit."

TABLE 7-3 Critical care services

TOTAL DURATION OF CRITICAL CARE	CODES
Less than 30 minutes	Assign appropriate E/M code(s)
30–74 minutes	99291
75–104 minutes	99291, 99292
105–131 minutes	99291, 99292, 99292
135–164 minutes	99291, 99292, 99292, 99292

NOTE: If an infant older than 30 days is admitted to an intensive care unit, report services using codes from the critical care services category of the E/M section. ●

Neonatal intensive care begins on the date of admission, and codes are reported once per day, per patient. The codes are "global 24-hour codes and not reported as hourly services." When the neonate is no longer considered to be critically ill and attains a body weight that exceeds 1500 grams, codes for subsequent hospital care (99231–99233) are reported.

Nursing Facility Services

Nursing facility services are performed at the following sites: skilled nursing facilities (SNFs), intermediate care facilities (ICFs), and long-term care facilities (LTCFs). In addition, E/M services provided to patients in psychiatric residential treatment facilities are also reported from this subsection of CPT.

Each nursing facility providing convalescent, rehabilitative, or long-term care for patients is required to have a **comprehensive assessment** completed on each patient. The comprehensive assessment must include an assessment of the patient's functional capacity, an identification of potential problems, and a nursing plan to enhance, or at least maintain, the patient's physical and psychosocial functions. These assessments are to be written at the time of the patient's admission/readmission to the facility or when a reassessment is necessary owing to a substantial change in the patient's status. Physicians are required to review, amend, and approve these plans. Codes 99301–99303 are used to report this in-depth review.

It is appropriate to report both an acute hospital discharge code (99238–99239), observation discharge (99217), or same day admit/discharge (99221–99223) and a nursing facility services comprehensive assessment code, if a patient is discharged and admitted to a SNF, ICF, or LTCF on the same calendar day.

Subsequent nursing facility care is reported when the evaluation of the patient's assessment plan is not required and/or when the patient has not had a major or permanent change of health status.

For discharge from a nursing facility, refer to codes 99315–99316.

Domiciliary, Rest Home, or Custodial Care Services

Domiciliary care covers E/M services provided to patients who live in custodial care or boarding home facilities that do not provide 24-hour nursing care.

Home Services

Home services are provided in a private residence, and this category of E/M identifies patient status (new vs. established) for the purpose of assigning codes.

Prolonged Services

Prolonged services codes are assigned in addition to other E/M services when treatment exceeds by 30 minutes or more the time included in the CPT description of the service.

This category is divided into three subcategories:

99354–99357	Prolonged physician service with direct (face-to-face) patient contact
99358–99359	Prolonged physician service without direct (face-to-face) patient contact
99360	Physician standby service

Direct patient contact refers to face-to-face patient contact (outpatient or inpatient), and codes 99354–99357 are reported in addition to other physician E/M services provided (e.g., office or other outpatient services).

Without direct patient contact services include non-face-to-face time spent by the physician on an outpatient or inpatient basis and occurring before and/or after direct patient care.

EXAMPLE 1: Review of extensive records and test results. Report 99358 in addition to the appropriate E/M service code.

EXAMPLE 2: Communicating with family members or other professionals. Report 99358 in addition to appropriate E/M service code.

NOTE: Codes 99358 and 99359 are reported in addition to other physician E/M services provided (e.g., subsequent hospital care).

Physician standby services involve a physician spending a prolonged period of time without patient contact waiting for an event to occur that will require the physician's services. Such services must be requested by another physician (e.g., attending physician) and are reported only if they are greater than 30 minutes. In addition, if a physician on standby is called to perform a global surgery service, the standby time is considered part of the surgical package. Examples of standby services include:

- *operative standby:* A surgeon is requested to stand by in the event surgery is required, perhaps for a trauma case.
- *pathology standby:* A pathologist is requested to stand by to perform an evaluation of a frozen section while the patient is in the operating room.
- *diagnostics standby:* A cardiologist is requested to stand by to monitor diagnostics, such as telemetry.
- *obstetrics standby:* A surgeon is requested to stand by in the event that a cesarean section is needed.
- *pediatrics standby:* A pediatrician is requested to stand by in the event that services are needed after the delivery of a high-risk newborn.

CODING TIP: Code 99360 may be reported in addition to codes 99431 (history and examination of normal newborn) and 99440 (newborn resuscitation), but not 99436 (attendance at delivery and initial stabilization of newborn).

Case Management Services

Case management services are defined as the process by which an attending physician coordinates and supervises the care provided to a patient by other health care providers. Community organizations can also be considered part of case management conferences when such events are not attended by the patient. This category is further subdivided for reporting telephone calls either with the patient or with other health care providers for the purpose of altering instructions or initiating new procedures and/or medications.

Care Plan Oversight Services

Care plan oversight services cover the physician's time supervising a complex and multidisciplinary care treatment program for a specific patient who is under the care of a home health agency, hospice, or nursing facility. These codes are classified separately from other E/M codes where the physician is involved in direct patient examinations. The billing covers a 30-day period, and only one physician in a group practice may bill for this service in any given 30-day period.

Preventive Medicine Services

Preventive medicine services consist of routine examinations or risk management counseling for children and adults *exhibiting no overt signs or symptoms of a disorder while presenting to the medical office for a preventive medical physical,* that is, "wellness visits." Discussion of risk factors such as diet and exercise counseling, family problems, substance abuse counseling, injury prevention, and so on, are an integral part of preventive medicine. Great care must be taken to select the proper code according to the age of the patient and the patient's status (new vs. established).

This category is not to be used when the patient under treatment for a specific disorder returns to the office for a "recheck of a known problem."

Both the appropriate preventive medicine code and an office or other outpatient services code (99201–99215) may be reported during one encounter when a significant abnormality or pre-existing problem is addressed during the course of a well child or adult preventive medicine annual physical. To qualify for both codes, the preventive medicine portion of the visit must be complete and comprehensive and the work-up for the significant problem must meet the required key components for assignment of codes 99201–99215.

Modifier -25 should be added to codes 99201–99215, and the diagnosis code reported to justify the 99201–99215 codes must identify the significant problem(s) addressed.

Newborn Care

The CPT definition of **newborn care** covers examinations of normal or high-risk neonates in the hospital or other locations, subsequent newborn care in a hospital, and resuscitation of high-risk babies. Assign code 99436 for a newborn who was assessed and discharged within the same calendar day.

Special E/M Services

Code 99450 may be used when an insurer requests a baseline evaluation on a patient who has applied for life or disability insurance, and the examining provider does not assume active management of the patient's health problems. Codes 99455 and 99456 are used for insurer-requested examinations of a patient with either a work-related or a medical disability problem.

Other E/M Service

Code 99499 is assigned when the E/M service provided is not described in any other listed E/M codes. The use of modifiers with this code is not appropriate. In addition, a special report must be submitted with the CMS-1500 claim.

EXERCISE 7-14   **E/M Coding II**

Code the following services:

1. New patient, routine preventative medicine, age 11. Risk factor discussion, 20 minutes   _____

2. Critical care, 1.5 hours   _____

3. Nursing facility visit, subsequent visit, expanded problem focused H&PE   _____

4. Medical team conference, 50 minutes   _____

5. Follow-up visit, ICU patient, stable, expanded problem focused H&PE   _____

6. Resuscitation of newborn, initial   _____

7. Telephone call with social worker, brief   _____

8. Custodial care, established patient, detailed H&PE, high complexity   _____

9. Pediatrician on standby, high risk birth, 65 minutes   _____

10. Heart risk factor education, group counseling, nonsymptomatic attendees, 65 minutes   _____

11. Prolonged care of subsequent level III inpatient with CPR, 1 hour 45 minutes   _____

After completing this exercise, refer to Appendix IV to check your answers.

Join the CodingPro-L listserv to "talk" with other coders at http://www.codingexpert.com.

SUMMARY

- CPT was developed by the American Medical Association (AMA), which also revises it annually.

- CPT codes reported on claims must be matched to appropriate ICD-9-CM codes to prove *medical necessity* of procedures performed or services rendered. If procedures or services might be found *medically unnecessary*, providers should have the patient sign an Advance Beneficiary Notice (ABN) that acknowledges patient responsibility for payment if Medicare denies the claim.

- CPT consists of three categories, and there are six sections associated with Category I codes.

- CPT's Index is organized according to alphabetical main terms (boldfaced abbreviations, anatomic parts, conditions, eponyms, procedures, or services) and subterms that are indented below main terms.

- To properly assign a CPT code, locate the main term in the Index, apply Index coding conventions (e.g., *See*), and verify the code in the appropriate CPT section. Be sure to review section guidelines and notes found throughout the section.

- Do not forget to assign appropriate modifier(s) when reporting CPT codes.

STUDY CHECKLIST

- ☐ Read the textbook chapter, and highlight key concepts.
- ☐ Create an index card for each key term.
- ☐ Access the chapter Internet links to learn more about concepts.
- ☐ Complete the chapter review, verifying answers in Appendix IV.

- ☐ Complete Web Tutor assignments and take online quizzes.
- ☐ Complete Workbook chapter assignments, verifying answers with your instructor.
- ☐ Form a study group with classmates to discuss chapter concepts in preparation for an exam.

REVIEW

EVALUATION AND MANAGEMENT SECTION

Refer to the CPT coding manual to answer each of the following items.

1. Which category is used to report services for patients seen in stand-alone ambulatory care centers? _____

2. Office or Other Outpatient Services is used to report services rendered by a physician to a patient in a hospital observation area. TRUE or FALSE. _____

3. Which category is used to report services provided to patients in a partial hospital setting? _____

4. What is the name of the service provided by a physician whose opinion is requested? _____

5. The service identified in question #4 must be requested by another physician (e.g. attending physician). TRUE or FALSE. _____

6. Consultations provided in a physician's office are reported using office or other outpatient services codes. TRUE or FALSE. _____

7. Only one initial consultation is to be reported by a consultant per hospital inpatient admission. TRUE or FALSE. _____

8. A consultant who participates in an inpatient's management after conducting an initial consultation will report services using codes from which subcategory? _____

9. Second or third opinions that are mandated by third party payers are reported from which E/M subcategory? What other code would be identified for such cases? _____

10. A distinction is made between new and established patients when reporting E/M Emergency Department Services. TRUE or FALSE. _____

11. Which code would you assign to report for a physician who provides directed emergency care? _____

12. What is meant by the phrase *directed emergency care*? _____

13. Critical care services must be provided in a critical care unit area (e.g. ICU). TRUE or FALSE. _____

14. Which code(s) would be assigned to report 2-1/2 hours of critical care provided by the attending physician? _____

15. SNFs, ICFs, and LTCFs are referred to as _____ .

16. Which category would be used when reporting a physician's visit to a patient residing in a boarding home? _____

17. Services provided by a physician to patients in a private residence are reported using codes from which category? _____

18. Which code would be reported when a physician calls a patient about recent lab test results? _____

19. A physical examination was performed on an 18-year-old who is scheduled to attend college in the fall. Which code(s) would you assign? _____

20. Assign code(s) to well baby care of 9-month-old that includes the administration of DTP and oral polio vaccines.

   ● HINT: You'll also need to refer to the Medicine Section of CPT. ● _____

21. Assign a code for preventive medicine service to a 56 year-old-established-patient. _____

22. Assign code(s) to a patient who was admitted to observation services on June 30th and also discharged from observation services on that date. _____

23. Assign code(s) to a patient who received critical care services for a total of 210 minutes on July 15th. On this date, patient also underwent inpatient comprehensive history and examination with medical decision making of high complexity. _____

24. Identify the code to assign to a patient who underwent a medical disability evaluation by his own physician. _____

25-29: Identify the E/M category and subcategory you would use to code each case below. The key components of history, examination and medical decision making are identified in each case, and you are required to assign the correct code based on that information.

25. Dr. Jones is an Internist who performed a hospital admission, examination, and initiation of treatment program for a 67-year-old male with uncomplicated pneumonia who requires IV antibiotic therapy. Dr. Jones completed a comprehensive history and examination; the medical decision making is of low complexity. Minimal patient counseling was provided. The patient's problem was of low severity.

   Identify the CPT category and subcategory _____ .

   Identify the appropriate CPT code_____ .

26. Dr. Smith completed an office consultation for management of systolic hypertension in a 70-year-old male scheduled for elective prostate resection. Dr. Smith conducted an expanded problem focused history and examination; medical decision making was straightforward. The patient's problem is of low severity. Dr. Smith spent 20 minutes counseling the patient.

   Identify the CPT category and subcategory _____ .

   Identify the appropriate CPT code _____ .

27. Dr. Choi conducted subsequent hospital care for the evaluation and management of a healthy newborn on the second day of inpatient stay.

   Identify the CPT category _____ .

   Identify the appropriate CPT code _____ .

28. Dr. Lange saw an established patient in the office for recent syncopal attacks. Comprehensive history and examination were performed. Medical decision making is of high complexity.

   Identify the CPT category and subcategory _____ .

   Identify the appropriate CPT code _____ .

29. Dr. Doolittle conducted a follow-up hospital visit for a 54-year-old patient, post myocardial infarction, who is out of the CCU but is now having frequent premature ventricular contractions on telemetry. Expanded problem focused interval history and examination were completed. Medical decision making is of moderate complexity. Dr. Doolittle coordinated care with the patient's providers and discussed the case with the patient's immediate family.

Identify the CPT category and subcategory _____ .

Identify the appropriate CPT code _____ .

SURGERY SECTION

Code each procedure using the CPT coding manual.

30. Pneumocentesis; assistant surgeon reporting   _____

31. Electrodesiccation, basal cell carcinoma (1 cm), face   _____

32. Complicated bilateral repair of recurrent inguinal hernia   _____

33. Biopsy of anorectal wall via proctosigmoidoscopy   _____

34. Mastectomy for gynecomastia   _____

35. Open reduction, right tibia/fibula shaft, with insertion of screws   _____

36. Excision, condylomata, penis   _____

37. Replacement of breast tissue expander with breast prosthesis (permanent)   _____

38. Closed reduction of closed fracture, clavicle   _____

39. Incision and drainage infected bursa, wrist   _____

40. Cystourethroscopy with biopsy   _____

41. Endoscopic right maxillary sinusotomy with partial polypectomy   _____

42. Insertion of Hickman catheter (cutdown) (age 70)   _____

43. Avulsion of four nail plates   _____

RADIOLOGY, PATHOLOGY & LABORATORY, AND MEDICINE SECTIONS

Code each procedure/service using the CPT coding manual.

44. Arthrography of the shoulder, supervision and interpretation.   _____

45. Chest X-ray, frontal, single view (professional component only).   _____

46. Complete pelvic echography, pregnant uterus (obstetrics) (B Scan).   _____

47. Application of radioactive needles (radioelement), intracavitary of uterus, intermediate.   _____

48. Lipid panel blood test.   _____

49. Drug screen for opiates (outside laboratory performed drug screen)   _____

50. Hemogram (manual) (complete CBC) _____

51. Papanicolaou smear, cervical _____

52. Gross and microscopic examination of gallbladder _____

53. Echocardiography, complete, M-mode _____

54. Mumps vaccine immunization _____

55. Intermittent positive pressure breathing of a newborn _____

56. Gait training, first 30 minutes _____

57. Medical psychoanalysis _____

58. Ultraviolet light is used to treat a skin disorder _____

59. Chemotherapy, IV infusion technique, 10 hours, requiring use of portable pump (including refill) _____

60. Combined left and right cardiac catheterization and retrograde left heart catheterization _____

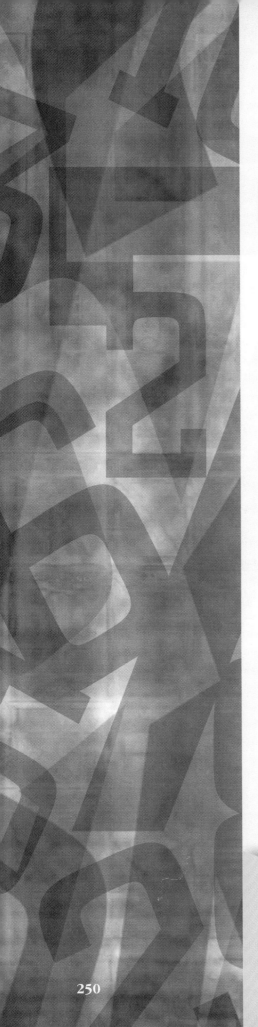

KEY TERMS

Coverage Issues Manual (CIM)

durable medical equipment
  (DME)

durable medical equipment,
  prosthetic and orthotic
  supplies (DMEPOS) dealers

durable medical equipment
  regional carriers
  (DMERC)

HCPCS level II code types:
  dental codes
  miscellaneous codes
  modifiers
  permanent codes
  temporary codes

local Medicare carrier (LMC)

Medicare Carrier Manual (MCM)

pass-through payments

statistical analysis durable medical
  equipment carrier (SADMERC)

Chapter 8 HCPCS Coding System

OBJECTIVES

Upon successful completion of this chapter, you should be able to:

1. Define key terms.

2. Describe the three HCPCS levels.

3. State the characteristics of the HCPCS level II coding system.

4. Differentiate types of HCPCS level II codes.

5. Assign HCPCS level II codes and modifiers.

6. Identify claims to be submitted to DMERC, LMC, or both, according to HCPCS level II code number.

7. Clarify situations in which both HCPCS level I and II codes are assigned.

INTRODUCTION

This chapter presents the procedure/service coding reference developed by CMS, the *Healthcare Common Procedure Coding System* (HCPCS, pronounced "hick-picks"). HCPCS was introduced in 1983 after Medicare found that its payers used over 100 different coding systems, making it difficult to analyze claims data. HCPCS furnishes health care providers and suppliers with a standardized language for reporting professional services, procedures, supplies, and equipment. Most state Medicaid programs also use HCPCS.

 NOTE: HCPCS used to be called the HCFA Common Procedure Coding System when the Centers for Medicare and Medicaid Services (CMS) was titled the Health Care Financing Administration (HCFA). The change to Healthcare Common Procedure Coding System occurred in 2002 when CMS became the new name for HCFA. ●

HCPCS CODING SYSTEM

There are three levels of codes associated with HCPCS, commonly referred to as level I, II, and III codes.

Level I

Level I contains five-digit Current Procedural Terminology (CPT) codes developed and published by the American Medical Association (AMA) as discussed in Chapter 7. The AMA is responsible for the annual update of this coding system and its two-digit modifiers.

Level II

Level II, or national, codes describe common medical services and supplies not included in CPT. These HCPCS codes are also five characters in length, but begin with the letters A–V followed by four numbers. Level II codes identify the services of physician and nonphysician providers (e.g., nurse practitioners and speech therapists) as well as ambulance and durable medical equipment (DME) companies (or durable medical equipment, prosthetic and orthotic supplies [DMEPOS] dealers). **Durable medical equipment (DME)** is defined by Medicare as equipment that:

- can withstand repeated use.
- is primarily used to serve a medical purpose.
- is used in the patient's home.
- would not be used in the absence of illness or injury.

Durable medical equipment, prosthetic and orthotic supplies (DMEPOS) dealers supply patients with **durable medical equipment** (e.g., canes, crutches, walkers, commode chairs, and blood-glucose monitors). DMEPOS claims are submitted to regional **durable medical equipment regional carriers (DMERC)** that were awarded contracts by CMS. Each DMERC covers a specific geographic region of the country and is responsible for processing DMEPOS claims for their specific region. A large section of level II codes, the J codes, list many commonly used medications by name and dosage. Also, when most people refer to HCPCS codes, they are referring to the level II codes. CMS is responsible for the annual updates to HCPCS level II codes and the two-character alphanumeric modifiers. Level II codes are further discussed in this chapter.

INTERNET LINK

View information about HCPCS (including new and deleted codes) at http://www.cms.hhs.gov/medicare/hcpcs

Level III

Effective December 31, 2003, level III HCPCS codes are no longer required. They had the same structure as level II codes but were assigned by the **local Medicare carrier (LMC)**, which is the agent responsible for processing Medicare claims in the local area. Level III codes began with the letters W, X, Y, or Z. Local or level III codes were issued on an as-needed basis, frequently identifying new services or other special procedures. Carriers maintained level III codes and modifiers and notified physicians and other providers and suppliers when the local codes were to be used.

HCPCS LEVEL II CODES

HCPCS level II is a comprehensive and standardized coding system that classifies similar medical products and services according to category for the purpose of efficient claims processing. Each HCPCS code contains a description, and the codes are used primarily for billing purposes.

EXAMPLE: DMEPOS dealers report HCPCS level II codes to identify items on claim forms for which they are billing a private or public health insurer.

HCPCS is *not* a reimbursement methodology or system, and it is important to understand that just because codes exist for certain products or services, coverage (e.g., payment) is not guaranteed. The HCPCS level II coding system has the following characteristics:

- Ensures uniform reporting of medical products or services on claims forms.
- Code descriptors identify similar products or services (rather than specific products or brand/trade names).
- HCPCS is not a reimbursement methodology for making coverage or payment determinations. (Each payer makes determinations on coverage and payment outside this coding process.)

Responsibility for HCPCS Level II Codes

Level II codes are developed and maintained by CMS and do not carry the copyright of a private organization. The national codes are in the public domain and many publishers print annual coding manuals. Each publisher may elect to color code the print or pages, include supplemental explanatory material, or provide reimbursement information from the *Medicare Carriers Manual* (MCM) for Part B or the *Medicare Coverage Issues Manual* (CIM). The *Medicare Carrier Manual* (MCM) provides direction about services and procedures to be reimbursed by the local Medicare Carrier (LMC). The *Coverage Issues Manual* (CIM) advises the LMC whether a service is covered or excluded under Medicare regulations.

INTERNET LINK

The *Medicare Carrier Manual* (MCM) for Part B and the *Medicare Coverage Issues Manual* (CIM) are available at http://cms.hhs.gov/manuals

Some HCPCS level II references contain general instructions or guidelines for each section; an appendix summarizing additions, deletions, and terminology revisions in level II codes (similar to Appendix B in CPT); or separate tables of drugs or deleted codes. Others use symbols to identify codes excluded from Medicare coverage, codes where payment is left to the discretion of the carrier, or codes with special coverage instructions. In addition, most references provide a complete appendix of current HCPCS national modifiers. CMS has stated it is not responsible for any errors that might occur in or from the use of these private printings of HCPCS level II codes.

Types of HCPCS Level II Codes

HCPCS level II codes are organized into type depending on the purpose for the codes and the entity responsible for establishing and maintaining them. The five types are:

- permanent codes.
- dental codes.
- miscellaneous codes.
- temporary codes.
- modifiers.

HCPCS Level II Permanent Codes

HCPCS level II **permanent codes** are maintained by the HCPCS National Panel, which is composed of representatives from the Blue Cross/Blue Shield Association (BCBSA), the Health Insurance Association of America (HIAA), and CMS. The HCPCS National Panel is responsible for making decisions about additions, revisions, and deletions to the permanent national alphanumeric codes. Decisions regarding changes to the national permanent codes are only made by unanimous consent of all three parties. As HCPCS is a national coding system, none of the parties, including CMS, can make unilateral decisions regarding permanent level II national codes. These codes are for the use of all private and public health insurers.

HCPCS Level II Dental Codes

HCPCS level II **dental codes** are actually contained in the *Current Dental Terminology* (CDT-3), a coding manual copyrighted and published by the American Dental Association (ADA) that lists codes for billing for dental procedures and supplies. Decisions regarding the modification, deletion, or addition of CDT-3 codes are made by the ADA and not the HCPCS National Panel. The Department of Health and Human Services' agreement with the ADA is similar to its agreement with the AMA pertaining to the use of CPT codes.

HCPCS Level II Miscellaneous Codes

HCPCS level II **miscellaneous codes** include *miscellaneous/not otherwise classified* codes that are reported when a DMEPOS dealer submits a claim for a product or service for which there is no existing HCPCS level II code. Miscellaneous codes allow DMEPOS dealers to submit a claim for a product or service as soon as it is approved by the Food and Drug Administration (FDA) even though there is no code that describes the product or service. The use of miscellaneous codes also helps avoid the inefficiency of assigning codes for items or services that are rarely furnished or for which carriers expect to receive few claims.

Claims that contain miscellaneous codes are manually reviewed by the payer, and the following must be provided for use in the review process:

- complete description of product or service
- pricing information for product or service
- documentation to explain why the item or service is needed by the beneficiary

Before reporting a miscellaneous code on a claim form, a DMEPOS dealer should check with the payer to determine if a specific code has been identified for use (instead of a miscellaneous code).

NOTE: When claims are to be submitted to one of the four DMERCs, DMEPOS dealers that have coding questions should check with the **statistical analysis durable medical equipment carrier (SADMERC)**, which is responsible for providing suppliers and manufacturers with assistance in determining HCPCS codes to be used. The SADMERC has a toll free helpline for this purpose at (877) 735-1326. ●

HCPCS Level II Temporary Codes

HCPCS level II **temporary codes** are maintained by the CMS and other members of the HCPCS National Panel, independent of permanent level II codes. While permanent codes are updated once a year on January 1, temporary codes allow payers the flexibility to establish codes that are needed before the next January 1 annual update. Approximately 35% of the HCPCS level II codes are temporary codes. Certain sections of the HCPCS level II codes were set aside to allow HCPCS National Panel members to develop temporary codes, and decisions regarding the number and type of temporary codes and how they are used are made independently by each HCPCS National Panel member. Temporary codes serve the purpose of meeting short time frame operational needs of a particular payer.

NOTE: Decisions regarding Medicare carrier temporary codes are made by an internal CMS HCPCS workgroup, and other payers may also use these codes. ●

Although the HCPCS National Panel may decide to replace temporary codes with permanent codes, if permanent codes are not established the temporary codes remain "temporary" indefinitely.

NOTE: Whenever a permanent code is established by the HCPCS National Panel to replace a temporary code, the temporary code is deleted and cross-referenced to the new permanent code. ●

Categories of Temporary Codes

C codes permit implementation of section 201 of the Balanced Budget Refinement Act of 1999, and they identify items that may qualify for **pass-through payments** under the hospital outpatient prospective payment system (OPPS). These are temporary additional payments (over and above the OPPS payment) made for certain innovative medical devices, drugs, and biologicals provided to Medicare beneficiaries. These codes are used exclusively for the OPPS purposes and are only valid for Medicare on claims submitted by hospital outpatient departments.

G codes identify professional health care procedures and services that do not have codes identified in CPT.

H codes are used by state Medicaid agencies that are mandated by state law to establish separate codes for identifying mental health services (e.g., alcohol and drug treatment services).

K codes are used by DMERCs when existing permanent national codes do not include codes needed to implement a DMERC medical review coverage policy.

Q codes identify services that would not ordinarily be assigned a CPT code (e.g., drugs, biologicals, and other types of medical equipment or services).

S codes are used by the BCBSA and the HIAA when no HCPCS level II codes exist to report drugs, services, and supplies, but codes are needed to implement private payer policies and programs or for claims processing.

T codes are used by state Medicaid agencies when no HCPCS level II permanent codes exist, but codes are needed to administer the Medicaid program. (T codes are not used by Medicare but can be used by private payers).

HCPCS Level II Code Modifiers

HCPCS code **modifiers** accompany HCPCS codes (e.g., CPT, level II) to provide additional information regarding the product or service identified. Modifiers are used when the information provided by a HCPCS code descriptor needs to be supplemented to identify specific circumstances that may apply to an item or service.

EXAMPLE: Modifier -UE indicates the product is "used equipment"
Modifier -NU indicates the product is "new equipment"

HCPCS level II modifiers are either alphabetic (two letters) or alphanumeric (one letter followed by one number) (Figure 8-1).

EXAMPLE 1: A patient sees a clinical psychologist for individual psychotherapy (CPT code 90804). Report:

90804-AH

EXAMPLE 2: A Medicare patient undergoes tendon surgery on the right palm (CPT code 26170) and left middle finger (CPT code 26180). Report:

26170-F2
26180-59-RT

HCPCS Level II Modifiers

Bolded modifiers are reported under the Outpatient Prospective Payment System (OPPS).
NOTE: When CPT modifier -50 is reported, do not report modifiers -RT and -LT.

AA	Anesthesia services performed personally by anesthesiologist
AD	Medical supervision by a physician: more than four concurrent anesthesia procedures
AH	Clinical psychologist
AJ	Clinical social worker
AM	Physician, team member service
AP	Determination of refractive state was not performed in the course of diagnostic ophthalmological examination
AS	Physician assistant, nurse practitioner, or clinical nurse specialist services for assistant at surgery
AT	Acute treatment (this modifier should be used when reporting service 98940, 98941, 98942)
BP	The beneficiary has been informed of purchase and rental options and has elected to purchase item
BR	The beneficiary has been informed of the purchase and rental options and has elected to rent the item
BU	The beneficiary has been informed of the purchase and rental options and after 30 days has not informed the supplier of his/her decision
CC	Procedure code change (use CC when the procedure code submitted was changed either for administrative reasons or because an incorrect code was filed)
E1	**Upper left, eyelid**
E2	**Lower left, eyelid**
E3	**Upper right, eyelid**
E4	**Lower right, eyelid**
EJ	Subsequent claims for a defined course of therapy (e.g., sodium, hyaluronate, infliximab)
EM	Emergency reserve supply (for ESRD benefit only)
EP	Service provided as part of Medicaid early periodic screening diagnosis and treatment (EPSDT) program
ET	Emergency services
F1	**Left hand, second digit**

(continues)

FIGURE 8-1 HCPCS level II modifiers (Reprinted according to http://cms.hhs.gov Web Site Content Reuse Policy)

F2	Left hand, third digit
F3	Left hand, fourth digit
F4	Left hand, fifth digit
F5	Right hand, thumb
F6	Right hand, second digit
F7	Right hand, third digit
F8	Right hand, fourth digit
F9	Right hand, fifth digit
FA	Left hand, thumb
FP	Service provided as part of Medicaid family planning program
G1	Most recent URR reading of less than 60
G2	Most recent URR reading of 60 to 64.9
G3	Most recent URR reading of 65 to 69.9
G4	Most recent URR reading of 70 to 74.9
G5	Most recent URR reading of 75 or greater
G6	ESRD patient for whom less than six dialysis sessions have been provided in a month
G7	Pregnancy resulted from rape or incest or pregnancy certified by physician as life threatening
G8	Monitored anesthesia care (MAC) for deep complex, complicated, or markedly invasive surgical procedure
G9	Monitored anesthesia care for patient who has history of severe cardio-pulmonary condition
GA	Waiver of liability statement on file
GB	Claim being re-submitted for payment because it is no longer covered under a global payment demonstration
GC	This service has been performed in part by a resident under the direction of a teaching physician
GE	This service has been performed by a resident without the presence of a teaching physician under the primary care exception
GG	**Performance and payment of a screening mammogram and diagnostic mammogram on the same patient, same day**
GH	**Diagnostic mammogram converted from screening mammogram on same day**
GJ	"Opt out" physician or practitioner emergency or urgent service
GK	Actual item/service ordered by physician, item associated with GA or GZ modifier
GL	Medically unnecessary upgrade provided instead of standard item, no charge, no advance beneficiary notice (ABN)
GM	Multiple patients on one ambulance trip
GN	Service delivered personally by a speech-language pathologist or under an outpatient speech-language pathology plan of care
GO	Service delivered personally by an occupational therapist or under an outpatient occupational therapy plan of care
GP	Service delivered personally by a physical therapist or under an outpatient physical therapy plan of care
GQ	Via asynchronous telecommunications system
GT	Via interactive audio and video telecommunication systems
GU	Procedure performed in non fee schedule place of service
GV	Attending physician not employed or paid under arrangement by the patient's hospice provider
GW	Service not related to the hospice patient's terminal condition
GX	Service not covered by Medicare

(continues)

FIGURE 8-1 *(continued)*

GY	Item or service statutorily excluded or does not meet the definition of any Medicare benefit
GZ	Item or service expected to be denied as not reasonable and necessary
K0	Lower extremity prosthesis functional level 0—does not have the ability or potential to ambulate or transfer safely with or without assistance and a prosthesis does not enhance their quality of life or mobility.
K1	Lower extremity prosthesis functional level 1—has the ability or potential to use a prosthesis for transfers or ambulation on level surfaces at fixed cadence. Typical of the limited and unlimited household ambulator.
K2	Lower extremity prosthesis functional level 2—has the ability or potential for ambulation with the ability to traverse low level environmental barriers such as curbs, stairs or uneven surfaces. Typical of the limited community ambulator.
K3	Lower extremity prosthesis functional level 3—has the ability or potential for ambulation with variable cadence. Typical of the community ambulator who has the ability to transverse most environmental barriers and may have vocational, therapeutic, or exercise activity that demands prosthetic utilization beyond simple locomotion.
K4	Lower extremity prosthesis functional level 4—has the ability or potential for prosthetic ambulation that exceeds the basic ambulation skills, exhibiting high impact, stress, or energy levels, typical of the prosthetic demands of the child, active adult, or athlete.
KA	Add on option/accessory for wheelchair
KH	DMEPOS item, initial claim, purchase or first month rental
KI	DMEPOS item, second or third month rental
KJ	DMEPOS item, parenteral enteral nutrition (pen) pump or capped rental, months four to fifteen
KK	Inhalation solution compounded from an FDA approved formulation
KL	Product characteristics defined in medical policy are met
KM	Replacement of facial prosthesis including new impression/moulage
KN	Replacement of facial prosthesis using previous master model
KO	Single drug unit dose formulation
KP	First drug of a multiple drug unit dose formulation
KQ	Second or subsequent drug of a multiple drug unit dose formulation
KR	Rental item, billing for partial month
KS	Glucose monitor supply for diabetic beneficiary not treated with insulin
KX	Specific required documentation on file
LC	**Left circumflex coronary artery**
LD	**Left anterior descending coronary artery**
LL	Lease/rental (use the 'll' modifier when dme equipment rental is to be applied against the purchase price)
LR	Laboratory round trip
LS	FDA-monitored intraocular lens implant
LT	**Left side (used to identify procedures performed on the left side of the body)**
MS	Six-month maintenance and servicing fee for reasonable and necessary parts and labor which are not covered under any manufacturer or supplier warranty
NR	New when rented (use the 'nr' modifier when dme which was new at the time of rental is subsequently purchased)
NU	New equipment
PL	Progressive addition lenses
Q2	CMS/ORD demonstration project procedure/service

(continues)

FIGURE 8-1 *(continued)*

Q3	Live kidney donor: services associated with postoperative medical complications directly related to the donation
Q4	Service for ordering/referring physician qualifies as a service exemption
Q5	Service furnished by a substitute physician under a reciprocal billing arrangement
Q6	Service furnished by a locum tenens physician
Q7	One class A finding
Q8	Two class B findings
Q9	One class B and two class C findings
QA	FDA investigational device exemption
QB	physician providing service in a rural HPSA
QC	Single channel monitoring
QD	Recording and storage in solid state memory by a digital recorder
QE	Prescribed amount of oxygen is less than 1 liter per minute (LPM)
QF	Prescribed amount of oxygen exceeds 4 liters per minute (LPM) and portable oxygen is prescribed
QG	Prescribed amount of oxygen is greater than 4 liters per minute (LPM)
QH	Oxygen conserving device is being used with an oxygen delivery system
QK	Medical direction of two, three, or four concurrent anesthesia procedures involving qualified individuals
QL	Patient pronounced dead after ambulance called
QM	**Ambulance service provided under arrangement by a provider of services**
QN	**Ambulance service furnished directly by a provider of services**
QP	Documentation is on file showing that the laboratory test(s) was ordered individually or ordered as a CPT-recognized panel other than automated profile codes 80002-80019, G0058, G0059, and G0060.
QQ	Claim submitted with a written statement of intent
QS	Monitored anesthesia care service
QT	Recording and storage on tape by an analog tape recorder
QU	Physician providing service in an urban HPSA
QV	Item or service provided as routine care in a Medicare qualifying clinical trial
QW	CLIA waived test
QX	CRNA service: with medical direction by a physician
QY	Medical direction of one certified registered nurse anesthetist (CRNA) by an anesthesiologist
QZ	CRNA service: without medical direction by a physician
RC	**Right coronary artery**
RP	Replacement and repair -RP may be used to indicate replacement of DME, orthotic and prosthetic devices which have been in use for sometime. The claim shows the code for the part, followed by the RP modifier and the charge for the part.
RR	Rental (use the RR modifier when DME is to be rented)
RT	**Right side (used to identify procedures performed on the right side of the body)**
SA	Nurse practitioner rendering service in collaboration with a physician
SB	Nurse midwife
SC	Medically necessary service or supply
SD	Services provided by registered nurse with specialized, highly technical home infusion training
SE	State and/or federally-funded programs/services
SF	Second opinion ordered by a professional review organization (PRO (100% reimbursement—no Medicare deductible or coinsurance)

(continues)

FIGURE 8-1 *(continued)*

SG	Ambulatory surgical center (ASC) facility service
SH	Second concurrently administered infusion therapy
SJ	Third or more concurrently administered infusion therapy
T1	**Left foot, second digit**
T2	**Left foot, third digit**
T3	**Left foot, fourth digit**
T4	**Left foot, fifth digit**
T5	**Right foot, great toe**
T6	**Right foot, second digit**
T7	**Right foot, third digit**
T8	**Right foot, fourth digit**
T9	**Right foot, fifth digit**
TA	**Left foot, great toe**
TC	Technical component. Under certain circumstances, a charge may be made for the technical component alone. Under those circumstances the technical component charge is identified by adding modifier TC to the usual procedure number. Technical component charges are institutional charges and not billed separately by physicians. However, portable X-ray suppliers only bill for technical component and should utilize modifier TC. The charge data from portable X-ray suppliers will then be used to build customary and prevailing profiles.
TD	RN
TE	LPN/LVN
TF	Intermediate level of care
TG	Complex/high tech level of care
TH	Obstetrical treatment/services, prenatal or postpartum
TJ	Program group, child and/or adolescent
TK	Extra patient or passenger, non-ambulance
TL	Early intervention/individualized family services plan (IFSP)
TM	Individualized education program (IEP)
TN	Rural/outside providers customary service area
TP	Medical transport, unloaded vehicle
TQ	Basic life support (BLS) transport by a volunteer ambulance provider
TR	School-based IEP services provided outside the public school district responsible for the student
U1	Medicaid level of care 1, as defined by each state
U2	Medicaid level of care 2, as defined by each state
U3	Medicaid level of care 3, as defined by each state
U4	Medicaid level of care 4, as defined by each state
U5	Medicaid level of care 5, as defined by each state
U6	Medicaid level of care 6, as defined by each state
U7	Medicaid level of care 7, as defined by each state
U8	Medicaid level of care 8, as defined by each state
U9	Medicaid level of care 9, as defined by each state
UA	Medicaid level of care 10, as defined by each state
UB	Medicaid level of care 11, as defined by each state
UE	Used durable medical equipment
VP	Aphakic patient

FIGURE 8-1 *(continued)*

The alphabetic first character identifies the code sections of HCPCS level II. Some are logical, such as D for dental or R for radiology, while others, such as J for drugs, appear to be arbitrarily assigned. For the 2003 HCPCS, level II code ranges are as follows:

A0000–A0999	Transport Services Including Ambulance
A2000–A2999	Chiropractic Services
A4000–A8999	Medical and Surgical Supplies
A9000–A9999	Administrative, Miscellaneous and Investigational
B4000–B9999	Enteral and Parenteral Therapy
C0000–C9999	Drugs, Biologicals, Devices, and New Technology For Use Only Under the Hospital Outpatient Prospective Payment System (OPPS)
D0100–D9999	Dental Procedures
E0100–E9999	Durable Medical Equipment
G0000–G9999	Procedures/Professional Services (Temporary)
H0001–H0030	Alcohol and/or Drug Services
J0000–J8999	Drugs Other Than Chemotherapy
J9000–J9999	Chemotherapy Drugs
K0000–K9999	Durable Medical Equipment (Temporary)
L0100–L4999	Orthotic Procedures
L5000–L9999	Prosthetic Procedures
M0000–M0399	Medical Services
P2000–P2999	Laboratory Tests
Q0000–Q9999	Temporary Codes
R0000–R5999	Radiology Services
S0009–S9999	Temporary Codes
V0000–V2799	Vision Services
V5000–V5299	Hearing Services
V5300–V5364	Speech-Language Pathology Services

Organization of HCPCS Level II Coding Manual

Because of the wide variety of services and procedures described in HCPCS level II, the alphabetical index (Figure 8-2) is very helpful in finding the correct code. The various publishers of the reference may include an expanded index that lists "alcohol wipes" and "wipes" as well as "Ancef" and "cefazolin sodium," making the search for codes easier and faster. Some references also include a Table of Drugs (Figure 8-3) that lists J codes assigned to medications. Some publishers print brand names beneath the generic description, and some provide a special expanded index of the drug codes. It is important to never code directly from the level II index and to always verify the code in the tabular section of the codebook. You may wish to review the HCPCS references from several publishers and select the one that best meets your needs and is the easiest for you to use.

Index

Abciximab, J0130
Abdomen
dressing holder/binder, A4462
pad, low profile, L1270
supports, pendulous, L0920, L0930
Abduction control, each, L2624
Abduction rotation bar, foot, L3140–L3170
Absorption dressing, A6251–A6256
Access system, A4301
Accessories
ambulation devices, E0153–E0159
artificial kidney and machine (*see also* ESRD), E1510–E1699
beds, E0271–E0280, E0305–E0326
wheelchairs, E0950–E1001, E1050–E1298, K0001–K0109
Acetazolamide sodium, J1120
Acetylcysteine, inhalation solution, J7608
Adenosine, J0150, J0151
Adhesive, A4364
disc or foam pad, A5126
remover, A4365, A4455
support, breast prosthesis, A4280
tape, A4454, A6265
Administrative, Miscellaneous and Investigational, A9000–A9999
Adrenalin, J0170
Aerosol
compressor, E0571, E0572
compressor filter, K0178–K0179
mask, K0180
AFO, E1815, E1830, L1900–L1990, L4392, L4396
Aggrastat, J3245
A-hydroCort, J1710
Air ambulance (*see also* Ambulance), A0030, A0040
Air bubble detector, dialysis, E1530
Air fluidized bed, E0194
Air pressure pad/mattress, E0176, E0186, E0197
Air travel and nonemergency transportation, A0140
Alarm, pressure, dialysis, E1540
Alatrofloxacin mesylate, J0200
Albumin, human, P9041, P9042
Albuterol, all formulations, inhalation solution, concentrated, J7618
Albuterol, all formulations, inhalation solution, unit dose, J7619
Alcohol, A4244
Alcohol wipes, A4245
Aldesleukin (IL2), J9015
Alginate dressing, A6196–A6199
Alglucerase, J0205
Alpha-1-proteinase inhibitor, human, J0256
Alprostadil, injection, J0270
Alprostadil, urethral suppository, J0275
Alteplase recombinant, J2997
Alternating pressure mattress/pad, A4640, E0180, E0181, E0277
Alveoloplasty, D7310–D7320
Amalgam dental restoration, D2110–D2161
Ambulance, A0021–A0999
air, A0430, A0431, A0435, A0436
disposable supplies, A0382–A0398
oxygen, A0422
Ambulation device, E0100–E0159
Aminolevulinic acid HCL, J7308
Aminophylline, J0280
Amiodarone HCl, J0282
Amitriptyline, HCl, J1320

FIGURE 8-2 First page from HCPCS 2003 index (Reprinted according to http://cms.hhs.gov Web Site Content Reuse Policy)

If the service or procedure cannot be found in CPT, the CPT index, or the HCPCS level II index, review the HCPCS level II table of contents and look in the appropriate section (Figure 8-4). Read the descriptions there very carefully. You may need to ask the provider to help select the correct code.

J

J0475 Injection, baclofen, 10 mg
MCM 2049
Use this code for Lioresal.

J0476 Injection, baclofen, 50 mcg for intrathecal trial
MCM 2049

J0500 Injection, dicyclomine HCl, up to 20 mg
MCM 2049
Use this code for Bentyl, Dilomine, Antispas, Dibent, Di-Spaz, Neoquess, Or-Tyl, Spasmoject.

J0510 Injection, benzquinamide HCl, up to 50 mg
MCM 2049
Use this code for Emete-con.

J0515 Injection, benztropine mesylate, per 1 mg
MCM 2049
Use this code for Cogentin.

J0520 Injection, bethanechol chloride mytonachol or urecholine, up to 5 mg
MCM 2049
Use this code for Urecholine.

J0530 Injection, penicillin G benzathine and penicillin G procaine, up to 600,000 units
MCM 2049
Use this code for Bicillin C-R.

J0540 Injection, penicillin G benzathine and penicillin G procaine, up to 1,200,000 units
MCM 2049
Use this code for Bicillin C-R, Bicillin C-R 900/300.

J0550 Injection, penicillin G benzathine and penicillin G procaine, up to 2,400,000 units
MCM 2049
Use this code for Bicillin C-R.

J0560 Injection, penicillin G benzathine, up to 600,000 units
MCM 2049
Use this code for Bicillin L-A, Permapen.

J0570 Injection, penicillin G benzathine, up to 1,200,000 units
MCM 2049
Use this code for Bicillin L-A, Permapen.

J0580 Injection, penicillin G benzathine, up to 2,400,000 units
MCM 2049
Use this code for Bicillin L-A, Permapen.

J0585 Botulinum toxin type A, per unit
MCM 2049

J0590 Injection, ethylnorepinephrine HCl, 1 ml
MCM 2049
Use this code for Bronkephrine

J0600 Injection, edetate calcium disodium, up to 1000 mg
MCM 2049
Use this code for Calcium Disodium Versenate, Calcium EDTA)

J0610 Injection, calcium gluconate, per 10 ml
MCM 2049
Use this code for Kaleinate.

J0620 Injection, calcium glycerophosphate and calcium lactate, per 10 ml
MCM 2049
Use this code for Calphosan.

J0630 Injection, calcitonin-salmon, up to 400 units
MCM 2049
Use this code for Calcimar, Miacalcin.

J0635 Injection, calcitriol, 1 mcg ampule
MCM 2049
Use this code for Calcijex.

J0640 Injection, leucovorin calcium, per 50 mg
MCM 2049
Use this code for Wellcovorin.

J0670 Injection, mepivacaine HCl, per 10 ml
MCM 2049
Use this code for Carbocaine, Polocaine, Isocaine HCl.

J0690 Injection, cefazolin sodium, up to 500 mg
MCM 2049
Use this code for Ancef, Kefzol, Zolicef.

J0694 Injection, cefoxitin sodium, 1 g
MCM 2049
Use this code for Mefoxin.

J0695 Injection, cefonicid sodium, 1 g
MCM 2049
Use this code for Monocid.

J0696 Injection, ceftriaxone sodium, per 250 mg
MCM 2049
Use this code for Rocephin.

J0697 Injection, sterile cefuroxime sodium, per 750 mg
MCM 2049
Use this code for Kefurox, Zinacef.

J0698 Cefotaxime sodium, per g
MCM 2049
Use this code for Claforan.

FIGURE 8-3 Page from HCPCS 2003 J section (Reprinted according to http://cms.hhs.gov Web Site Content Reuse Policy)

Contents

FIGURE 8-4 First page from HCPCS 2003 table of contents (Reprinted according to http://cms.hhs.gov Web Site Content Reuse Policy)

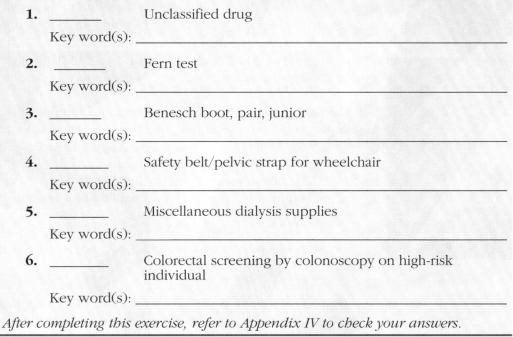

EXERCISE 8–1   **HCPCS INDEX**

Using the Index, find and verify the following codes in the tabular section of the HCPCS coding reference. Indicate the key word(s) used to search the Index.

1. _____   Unclassified drug

   Key word(s): _____

2. _____   Fern test

   Key word(s): _____

3. _____   Benesch boot, pair, junior

   Key word(s): _____

4. _____   Safety belt/pelvic strap for wheelchair

   Key word(s): _____

5. _____   Miscellaneous dialysis supplies

   Key word(s): _____

6. _____   Colorectal screening by colonoscopy on high-risk individual

   Key word(s): _____

After completing this exercise, refer to Appendix IV to check your answers.

DETERMINING CARRIER RESPONSIBILITY

The specific HCPCS level II code determines whether the claim is sent to the local Medicare carrier (LMC) or the DME Regional Carrier (DMERC). HCPCS level II codes beginning with D, G, M, P, or R fall under the jurisdiction of the LMC. The DMERC is responsible for HCPCS level II codes beginning with B, E, K, and L. Codes beginning with A, J, Q, and V may be assigned individually to either the LMC or the DMERC. The Local Medicare Carrier and the DMERC distribute annual lists of valid level II codes. They can also give the provider the complete billing instructions for those services.

EXERCISE 8-2   **RECOGNIZING CARRIER RESPONSIBILITY**

Using the above criteria and the codes and descriptions listed in Exercise 8–1, identify the codes sent to the LMC, the DMERC, or those possibly assigned to either carrier.

Local Medicare Carrier: _____

DMERC: _____

Local Medicare Carrier or DMERC: _____

After completing this exercise, refer to Appendix IV to check your answers.

Because the DMERC is another Medicare carrier, each entity dispensing medical equipment and supplies must register as a provider. When the doctor treats a Medicare patient for a broken ankle and supplies the patient with crutches, two claims are generated. The one for the fracture care, or professional service, is sent to the local Medicare carrier; the claim for the crutches is sent to the DMERC. The physician must register with both carriers, review the billing rules, comply with the claim form instructions, and forward the claims correctly to secure payment for both services. If the doctor is not registered with the DMERC to provide medical equipment and supplies, the patient is given a prescription for crutches to take to a local DMEPOS dealer.

At one time the local Medicare carriers (LMCs) processed all claims for DME. The emphasis on keeping seniors in their own homes led to a rapid expansion in DME services and dealers. Also, many of the larger companies operated in several states and sent their claims to multiple Medicare carriers. Unfortunately, a few companies formed for the sole purpose of collecting as much money as possible from the Medicare program and then closed down. When CMS began to investigate and pursue fraudulent claims, it became apparent that DME billings were out of control, so CMS decided to have all DME claims processed by only four regional carriers, the DMERCs. This allowed the LMCs to concentrate on the familiar, traditional claims of providers billing for services, not equipment.

Some services, such as most dental procedures, are excluded as Medicare benefits by law and will not be covered by either carrier. Splints and casts for traumatic injuries have CPT numbers that would be used to report these supplies or services to the LMC. Because the review procedures for adding new codes to level II is a much shorter process, new medical and surgical services may first be assigned a level II code and then incorporated into CPT at a later date.

ASSIGNING HCPCS LEVEL II CODES

Some services must be reported by assigning both a CPT and a HCPCS code. The most common scenario uses the CPT code for administration of an injection and the HCPCS code to identify the medication. Most drugs have qualifying terms such as dosage limits that could alter the quantity reported (Figure 8-3). If a drug stating "per 50 mg" is administered in a 70-mg dose, the quantity billed would be "2." If you administered only 15 mg of a drug stating "up to 20 mg," the quantity is "1." Imagine how much money providers lose by reporting only the CPT code for injections. Unless the payer or insurance plan advises the provider that they do not pay separately for the medication injected, always report this combination of codes.

It is possible that a particular service would be assigned a CPT code and a level II HCPCS code. Which one should you report? The answer is found in the instructions from the payer. Most commercial payers require the CPT code. Medicare gives HCPCS level II codes the highest priority if the CPT code is general and the HCPCS National (level II) code is more specific.

Most supplies are included in the charge for the office visit or the procedure. CPT provides code 99070 for all supplies and materials exceeding those usually included in the primary service or procedure performed. However, this CPT code may be too general to ensure correct payment. If the office provides additional supplies when performing a service, the HCPCS level II codes may identify the supplies in sufficient detail to secure proper reimbursement.

While CMS developed this system, some HCPCS level I and II services are not payable by Medicare. Medicare may also place qualifications or conditions on payment for some services. As an example, an ECG is a covered service for a cardiac problem but is not covered when performed as part of a routine examination. Also, the payment for some services may be left to the carrier's discretion. Two CMS publications assist the carriers in correctly processing claims. The *Coverage Issues Manual* (CIM) advises the local Medicare carrier (LMC) whether a service is covered or excluded under Medicare regulations. The *Medicare Carriers Manual* (MCM) directs the LMC to pay a service or reject it using a specific "remark" or explanation code.

There are over 4,000 HCPCS level II codes, but you may find that no code exists for the procedure or service you need to report. Unlike CPT, HCPCS level II does not have a consistent method of establishing codes for reporting "unlisted procedure" services. If the LMC does not provide special instructions for reporting these services in HCPCS, report them with the proper "unlisted procedure" code from CPT. Remember to submit documentation explaining the procedure or service when using the "unlisted procedure" codes.

NOTE: CMS developed the level II codes for Medicare, but commercial payers also adopt them.

SUMMARY

- HCPCS is the Healthcare Common Procedure Coding System (formerly the HCFA Common Procedure Coding System).
- The "H" in HCPCS was changed to "Healthcare" (from HCFA) in 2002 when HCFA underwent a name change and became CMS.
- HCPCS contains three levels: level I (CPT codes), level II (national codes), and level III (local codes created by LMCs, discontinued as of December 31, 2003).
- HCPCS level II codes describe durable medical equipment (DME) on claims submitted to DMEPOS dealers and DMERCs.
- Some HCPCS level II coding manuals contain information from the MCM (Medicare reimbursement of services and procedures) and CIM (Medicare coverage for services and procedures).
- HCPCS level II codes classify similar medical products and services according to category for the purpose of efficient claims processing. (HCPCS is *not* a reimbursement methodology.)
- HCPCS level II codes are categorized as: permanent, dental, miscellaneous, and temporary. Two-digit modifiers are also created for use with HCPCS level I and II codes.
- HCPCS level II codes are alphanumeric, starting with A-V, followed by four digits (e.g., A0000).
- The HCPCS level II index is often expanded upon in commercial coding publications (e.g., Ingenix, formerly Medicode/St.Anthony's).
- HCPCS level II codes determine whether claims are submitted to the LMC or the DMERC.
- Both HCPCS level I (CPT) and HCPCS level II codes are often required to completely describe a service or procedure provided to a patient (e.g., specific supply used during an office visit).

STUDY CHECKLIST

☐ Read the textbook chapter, and highlight key concepts.

☐ Create an index card for each key term.

☐ Access the chapter Internet links to learn more about concepts.

☐ Complete the chapter review, verifying answers in Appendix IV.

☐ Complete Web Tutor assignments and take online quizzes.

☐ Complete Workbook chapter, verifying answers with your instructor.

☐ Form a study group with classmates to discuss chapter concepts in preparation for an exam.

REVIEW

FILL-IN-THE-BLANK

1. Using the current edition of a HCPCS level II coding manual, assign the correct codes, HCPCS modifier(s) and quantity to each of the following services.

   a. B-12 injection not covered by Medicare, but patient agrees to pay.

   Code _____ Modifier(s) _____ Quantity _____

   b. Purchase of new rolling chair with 6" wheels. Rental declined.

   Code _____ Modifier(s) _____ Quantity _____

   c. 100 reagent strips for home glucose monitor. Patient not on insulin.

   Code _____ Modifier(s) _____ Quantity _____

   d. Three fecal-occult blood tests, screening for colorectal malignancy at clinic in rural underserved area.

   Code _____ Modifier(s) _____ Quantity _____

   e. Third-month rental oxygen concentrator

   Code _____ Modifier(s) _____ Quantity _____

2. Using the current editions of CPT and HCPCS level II codes, assign the correct code and the HCPCS modifier(s) and quantity to each of the following scenarios.

   a. Metatarsophalangeal synovectomy, third digit, left foot

   Code _____ Modifier(s) _____ Quantity _____

   b. HemoCue 3 sample GTT

   Code _____ Modifier(s) _____ Quantity _____

   c. Closed manipulation, left Potts fracture, by physician who has opted out of Medicare

   Code _____ Modifier(s) _____ Quantity _____

d. Anesthesiologist provides medical direction of his employee for radical nasal surgery (quantity not required)

Code _____ Modifier(s) _____

e. Psychological testing, 2 hours, by clinical psychologist

Code _____ Modifier(s) _____ Quantity _____

KEY TERMS

ambulance fee schedule

ambulatory surgical center (ASC)

balance billing

clinical laboratory fee schedule

conversion factor

DMEPOS fee schedule

employer group health plan (EGHP)

global period

grouper software

Home Assessment Validation and
    Entry (HAVEN)

home health resource groups
    (HHRGs)

incident to

inpatient prospective payment system
    (IPPS)

large group health plan (LGHP)

limiting charge

Medicare Secondary Payer (MSP)

Medicare Summary Notice (MSN)

nurse practitioner (NP)

payment system

physician assistant (PA)

physician fee schedule (PFS)

prospective cost-based rates

prospective price-based rates

relative value units (RVUs)

Resident Assessment Validation and
    Entry (RAVEN)

retrospective reasonable cost system

scope of practice

site of service differential

Chapter 9 — CMS Reimbursement Issues

OBJECTIVES

Upon successful completion of this chapter, you should be able to:

1. Define key terms.
2. Explain the historical development of CMS reimbursement systems.
3. List and define each CMS payment system.
4. Apply special rules for the Medicare physician fee schedule payment system.

INTRODUCTION

Since the Medicare program was implemented in 1966, expenditures have increased at an unanticipated rate, and the news media frequently report that the program will be bankrupt in a few years. In 1983, the Health Care Financing Administration (HCFA, now called CMS) implemented the first Prospective Payment System (PPS) to control the cost of hospital inpatient care.

In subsequent years, similar reimbursement systems were implemented for alternate care (e.g., physician office, long-term care). This chapter details CMS's reimbursement systems and related issues.

HISTORICAL PERSPECTIVE OF CMS REIMBURSEMENT SYSTEMS

In 1964, the Johnson administration avoided opposition from hospitals for passage of the Medicare and Medicaid programs by adopting retrospective reasonable cost-basis payment arrangements previously established by Blue Cross. Reimbursement according to a **retrospective reasonable cost system** meant that hospitals reported actual charges for inpatient care to payers after discharge of the patient from the hospital. Payers then reimbursed hospitals 80% of allowed charges. While this policy helped secure passage of Medicare and Medicaid (by enticing hospital participation), subsequent spiraling reimbursement costs ensued.

NOTE: According to the American Enterprise Institute for Public Policy Research, 1964 projections of Medicare costs in 1990 were $12 billion, but actual costs were $110 billion.

Shortly after the passage of Medicare and Medicaid, Congress began investigating prospective payment systems (PPS), which established predetermined rates based on patient category or the type of facility (with annual increases based on an inflation index and a geographic wage index):

- **Prospective price-based rates** are associated with a particular category of patient (e.g., inpatients), and rates are established by the payer (e.g., Medicare) prior to the provision of health care services. PPS's based on this method include diagnosis-related groups (DRGs) for inpatient care.

- **Prospective cost-based rates** are also established in advance, but they are based on reported health care costs (charges) from which a prospective per diem (Latin meaning "for each day") rate is determined. Annual rates are usually adjusted using actual costs from the prior year. This method may be based on the facility's case mix (patient acuity). PPS's based on this method include resource utilization groups (RUGs) for skilled nursing care facilities.

CMS PAYMENT SYSTEMS

The federal government administers several health care programs, some of which require services to be reimbursed according to a predetermined reimbursement methodology (**payment system**). Federal health care programs (overview of each is located in Chapter 2) include:

- CHAMPVA.
- Indian Health Service (IHS).
- Medicaid (includes State Children's Health Insurance Program, or SCHIP).
- Medicare.
- TRICARE (formerly CHAMPUS).
- Workers' Compensation.

Depending on the type of health care services provided to beneficiaries, the federal government requires that one of the following payment systems be used for the CHAMPVA, Medicaid, Medicare, and TRICARE programs:

- Ambulance Fee Schedule
- Ambulatory Surgical Centers (ASC)
- Clinical Lab Diagnostic Fee Schedule

- Durable Medical Equipment, Prosthetics/Orthotics, and Supplies (DMEPOS) Fee Schedule
- Home Health Prospective Payment System
- Hospital Inpatient Prospective Payment System
- Hospital Outpatient Prospective Payment System
- Inpatient Rehabilitation Facility Prospective Payment System
- Long-Term Care Hospitals Prospective Payment System
- Skilled Nursing Facility (SNF) Prospective Payment System
- Medicare physician fee schedule (PFS)

NOTE: The physician fee schedule (PFS) is listed last among the payment systems (and discussed last in the series within this chapter) because users of this textbook will need to familiarize themselves with the intricacies of this system. ●

INTERNET LINK

Quarterly Medicare provider updates about payment systems can be found at http://cms.hhs.gov/providerupdate

AMBULANCE FEE SCHEDULE

The Balanced Budget Act of 1997 required establishment of an **ambulance fee schedule** payment system for ambulance services provided to Medicare beneficiaries. Starting in April 2002 the ambulance fee schedule was phased in over a 5-year period (Table 9-1), replacing a retrospective reasonable cost payment system for providers and suppliers of ambulance services (because such a wide variation of payment rates resulted for the same service). This schedule requires:

- ambulance suppliers to accept Medicare assignment.
- reporting of HCPCS codes on claims for ambulance services.
- establishment of increased payment under the fee schedule for ambulance services furnished in rural areas based on the location of the beneficiary at the time the beneficiary is placed on board the ambulance.
- revision of the certification requirements for coverage of nonemergency ambulance services.
- Medicare to pay for beneficiary transportation services when other means of transportation are contraindicated. Ambulance services are divided into different levels of ground (land and water transportation) and air ambulance services based on the medically necessary treatment provided during transport.

EXAMPLE: A patient was transported by ambulance from her home to the local hospital for care. Under the retrospective reasonable cost payment system, the ambulance company charged $600, and Medicare paid 80% of that amount or $480. By the end of the 5-year phase-in of the *ambulance fee schedule*, the ambulance company receives just $425, which is an amount equal to the predetermined rate or *fee schedule*. ●

NOTE: For the purpose of this example, the charges and rates remain the same for each year. Medicare will actually adjust ambulance fee schedule rates according to an inflationary formula. ●

TABLE 9-1 Ambulance fee schedule 5-year phase-in (2002–2006)

YEAR	AMBULANCE COMPANY (REASONABLE) CHARGE (a)	% OF REASONABLE CHARGE (b)	AMOUNT (c)	AMBULANCE FEE SCHEDULE RATE (d)	PHASE-IN % (e)	AMOUNT (f)	MEDICARE PAYMENT (g)
Formula: [(a) x (b) = (c)] + [(d) x (e) = (f)] = Medicare payment							
2001	$600	80%	$480	n/a	n/a	n/a	$480
2002	$600	80%	$480	$425	20%	$85	$565
2003	$600	60%	$360	$425	40%	$170	$530
2004	$600	40%	$240	$425	60%	$255	$495
2005	$600	20%	$120	$425	80%	$340	$460
2006	$600	0%	$0	$425	100%	$425	$425

AMBULATORY SURGICAL CENTERS (ASC)

An **ambulatory surgical center (ASC)** is a state-licensed, Medicare-certified supplier (not provider) of surgical health care services that must *accept assignment* on Medicare claims. An ASC must be a separate entity distinguishable from any other entity or facility, and it must have its own employer identifier number (EIN) as well as processes for:

- accreditation.
- administrative functions.
- clinical services.
- financial and accounting systems.
- governance (of medical staff).
- professional supervision.
- recordkeeping.
- state licensure.

NOTE: An ASC can be physically located within a health care organization and still be considered separate for Medicare reimbursement purposes if all the above criteria are met.

Reimbursement for services is based on 80% of the predetermined ASC rate (Table 9-2), adjusted for regional wage variations, and includes approximately 1,500 CPT and HCPCS level II codes. CMS conducts a survey of ASCs based upon a representative sample of procedures and facilities to collect data for the purpose of adjusting ASC payment rates.

NOTE: Hospital outpatient departments that perform surgery are reimbursed under the outpatient prospective payment system (OPPS), which uses ambulatory payment classifications (APCs) as its reimbursement methodology. This system is discussed on page 277.

TABLE 9-2 ASC payment groups and rates—2002

ASC GROUP	REIMBURSEMENT RATE
Group 1 Procedure	$323
Group 2 Procedure	$433
Group 3 Procedure	$495
Group 4 Procedure	$612
Group 5 Procedure	$696
Group 6 Procedure	$806 ($656 + $150 for intraocular lenses)
Group 7 Procedure	$966
Group 8 Procedure	$949 ($799 + $150 for intraocular lenses)

CLINICAL LAB DIAGNOSTIC FEE SCHEDULE

The Deficit Reduction Act of 1984 established the Medicare **clinical laboratory fee schedule**, which is a data set based on local fee schedules (for outpatient clinical diagnostic laboratory services). Medicare reimburses laboratory services according to the (1) submitted charge, (2) national limitation amount, or (3) local fee schedule amount, whichever is lowest. The local fee schedules are developed by Medicare *carriers* (local contractors that process Medicare Part B claims, including claims submitted by independent laboratories and physician office laboratories) and fiscal intermediaries (FIs) (local contractors that process Medicare Part A claims, including outpatient laboratory tests performed by hospitals, nursing homes, and end-stage renal disease centers).

NOTE: The *clinical laboratory fee schedule* contains approximately 1,000 separate clinical laboratory codes currently listed in the 80048–89399 CPT code series along with a small number (less than 50) of HCPCS level II codes.

DURABLE MEDICAL EQUIPMENT, PROSTHETICS/ORTHOTICS, AND SUPPLIES FEE SCHEDULE

The Deficit Reduction Act of 1984 also established the Medicare **durable medical equipment, prosthetics/orthotics, and supplies (DMEPOS) fee schedule**. Medicare reimburses DMEPOS according to either the actual charge *or* the amount calculated according to formulas that use average reasonable charges for items during a base period from 1986 to 1987, whichever is lower. (Fee schedule amounts are annually updated and legislated by Congress.)

HOME HEALTH PROSPECTIVE PAYMENT SYSTEM

The BBA of 1997 called for implementation of a Medicare home health prospective payment system (HHPPS), which uses a classification system called home health resource groups (HHRGs) to establish prospective reimbursement rates for each 60-

day episode of home health care. **Home health resource groups (HHRGs)** (Table 9-3) classify patients into one of 80 groups, which range in severity level according to three domains: clinical, functional, and service utilization. **Grouper software** is used to determine the appropriate HHRG after **Outcomes and Assessment Information Set (OASIS)** data is input on each patient (to measure the outcome of all adult patients receiving home health services). **Home Assessment Validation and Entry (HAVEN)** data entry software is then used to collect OASIS assessment data for transmission to state databases.

⬤ NOTE: ICD-9-CM codes are used to determine the appropriate HHPPS payment level. One principal diagnosis and up to eight additional diagnosis codes are submitted. ⬤

HOSPITAL INPATIENT PROSPECTIVE PAYMENT SYSTEM

Prior to 1983, Medicare payments for hospital inpatient care were based on a *retrospective reasonable cost system*, which meant hospitals received 80% of reasonable charges. Since 1983, when the **inpatient prospective payment system (IPPS)** was implemented, Medicare has reimbursed hospitals for inpatient hospital services according to a predetermined rate for each discharge. Each discharge is categorized into a *diagnosis-related group (DRG)*, which is based on the patient's principal and secondary diagnoses (including comorbidities and complications) as well as principal and secondary procedures (if performed). The DRG determines how much payment the hospital receives.

⬤ NOTE: ICD-9-CM codes directly impact DRG assignment. CPT codes play no role in DRG assignments. ⬤

TABLE 9-3 HHRG severity levels in three domains—clinical, functional, and service utilization (Reprinted according to http://cms.hhs.gov Web Site Content Reuse Policy)

HOME HEALTH RESOURCE GROUPS (HHRGs)

DOMAIN	SCORE	POINTS	SEVERITY LEVEL
Clinical	C0	0–7	Minimal severity
	C1	8–19	Low severity
	C2	20–40	Moderate severity
	C3	41+	High severity
Functional	F0	0–2	Minimal severity
	F1	3–15	Low severity
	F2	16–23	Moderate severity
	F3	24–29	High severity
	F4	30+	Maximum severity
Service Utilization	S0	0–2	Minimum utilization
	S1	3	Low utilization
	S2	4–6	Moderate utilization
	S3	7	High utilization

NOTE: Psychiatric and rehabilitation hospitals and units, long-term care hospitals (defined as those with an average length of stay of at least 25 days), children's hospitals, and cancer hospitals are excluded from the IPPS and continue to be paid on a reasonable cost basis subject to per discharge limits. ●

Because the IPPS payment is based on an adjusted average payment rate, some cases receive Medicare reimbursement in excess of costs (rather than billed charges) while other cases receive payment that is less than costs incurred. The system is designed to provide hospitals with an incentive to manage their operations more efficiently by evaluating those areas in which increased efficiencies can be instituted without affecting the quality of care and by treating a mix of patients to balance cost and payments. It should be noted that a hospital's payment is unaffected by the length of stay prior to discharge (unless the patient is transferred). It is expected that some patients will stay longer than others, and hospitals will offset the higher costs of a longer stay with the lower costs of a reduced stay.

HOSPITAL OUTPATIENT PROSPECTIVE PAYMENT SYSTEM

The BBA of 1997 authorized CMS to implement an outpatient prospective payment system (OPPS) for hospital outpatient services provided to Medicare patients. (The OPPS was implemented in 2000.) Also reimbursed under the OPPS are certain Medicare Part B services furnished to hospital inpatients who have no Part A coverage as well as partial hospitalization services furnished by community mental health centers. All services are paid according to **ambulatory payment classifications (APCs)**, which groups services according to similar clinical characteristics and in terms of resources required. A payment rate is established for each APC and, depending on services provided, hospitals may be paid for more than one APC for a patient encounter. The Medicare beneficiary coinsurance was also recalculated under the OPPS and was based on 20% of the national median charge for services in the APC. (Both the total APC payment and the portion paid as coinsurance amounts are adjusted to reflect geographic wage variations.)

INPATIENT REHABILITATION FACILITY PROSPECTIVE PAYMENT SYSTEM

The BBA of 1997 authorized the implementation of a per discharge prospective payment system (PPS) for inpatient rehabilitation hospitals and rehabilitation units, also called inpatient rehabilitation facilities (IRFs). Implemented in 2002, the IRF PPS utilizes information from a patient assessment instrument to classify patients into distinct groups based on clinical characteristics and expected resource needs. Separate payments are calculated for each group, including the application of case and facility level adjustments.

LONG-TERM CARE HOSPITALS PROSPECTIVE PAYMENT SYSTEM

The Balanced Budget Refinement Act of 1999 (BBRA) authorized the implementation of a per discharge diagnosis related group (DRG) prospective payment system (PPS) for long-term care hospitals (LTCHs) for cost reporting periods beginning on or after October 1, 2002. This new prospective payment system replaced the reasonable cost-based payment system under which the LTCHs were previously paid.

SKILLED NURSING FACILITY (SNF) PROSPECTIVE PAYMENT SYSTEM

The BBA of 1997 modified reimbursement for Medicare Part A (inpatient) skilled nursing facility (SNF) services and, beginning in 1998, SNFs were no longer paid on a reasonable cost basis but rather on the basis of a prospective payment system (PPS). Per diem payments for each SNF admission are case-mix adjusted using a resident classification system called Resource Utilization Groups, which is based on data from resident assessments (called the Minimum Data Set, or MDS) and relative weights developed from staff time data. Computerized data-entry software entitled **Resident Assessment Validation and Entry (RAVEN)** is used to enter MDS data about SNF patients and transmit those assessments in CMS-standard format to individual state databases.

MEDICARE PHYSICIAN FEE SCHEDULE

As of 1992, physicians are reimbursed for services and procedures according to a payment system known as the Resource-Based Relative Value Scale (RBRVS). This system, now called the Medicare **physician fee schedule (PFS)**, divides all services into **relative value units (RVUs)**, which are payment components consisting of:

- *physician work,* which reflects the physician's time and intensity in providing the service (e.g., judgment, technical skill, and physical effort).
- *practice expense,* which reflects overhead costs involved in providing a service (e.g., rent, utilities, equipment, and staff salaries).
- *malpractice expense,* which reflects malpractice expenses (e.g., costs of liability insurance).

Payment limits were also established by adjusting the RVUs for each locality by geographic adjustment factors (GAF) so that Medicare providers are paid differently in each state and also within each state (e.g., New York state has five separate payment localities). An annual **conversion factor** (dollar multiplier) converts RVUs into payments. (The 2003 conversion factor is $36.7856.) The formula for determining the physician fee schedule is:

$$[(RVUw \times GPCIw) + (RVUpe \times GPCIpe) + (RVUm \times GPCIm)] \times CF = payment$$

where: w = work expense pe = practice expense
m = malpractice costs CF = conversion factor

ANESTHESIA, PATHOLOGY/LABORATORY AND RADIOLOGY SERVICES

While the Medicare physician fee schedule is used to determine payment for Medicare Part B (physician) services, other services such as anesthesia, pathology/laboratory, and radiology require special consideration.

- Anesthesia services payments are based on the actual time an anesthesiologist spends with a patient and the American Society of Anesthesiologists' relative value system.
- Radiology services payments vary according to place of service (e.g., hospital radiology department vs. freestanding radiology center).
- Pathology services payments vary according to the number of patients served:
  - Pathology services that include clinical laboratory management and supervision of technologists are covered and paid as hospital services.

• Pathology services that are directed to an individual patient in a hospital setting (e.g., pathology consultation) are paid under the physician fee schedule.

NOTE: The physician fee schedule may list fees for services not commonly provided to Medicare patients (e.g., obstetrical services) because private payers also adopt the schedule. •

Prior to 1992, Medicare required anesthesiologists to submit a CPT surgery code (instead of a code from the anesthesia section of CPT) plus type of service (TOS) code "7" to denote anesthesia services. Medicare discontinued use of the TOS code for any service and replaced that information with a procedure code modifier or expanded two-digit location, or place of service (POS), code. Anesthesiologists now submit the appropriate code from the anesthesia section of CPT with a POS code.

Nonparticipating Physicians

The Medicare physician fee schedule advises nonparticipating physicians (nonPARs) (those who do not accept Medicare assignment) of the **limiting charge** for services (maximum fee the physician may charge), which is calculated as 115% of the physician fee schedule. The nonPAR physician's fee is also subject to a 5% reduction of the Medicare physician fee schedule amount for a particular service on which Medicare reimbursement is based.

Limiting charge information appears on the **Medicare Summary Notice (MSN)** (previously called an *Explanation of Medicare Benefits,* or *EOMB*), which notifies Medicare beneficiaries of actions taken on claims. The limiting charge policy is intended to reduce the amount patients enrolled in Medicare are expected to pay when they receive health care services. If a participating (PAR) and a nonparticipating (nonPAR) physician charge the same fee for an office visit, amounts billed and reimbursement received would be different for each physician.

NOTE: Medicare discounts its physician fee schedule 5% for nonPAR providers. •

EXAMPLE: A PAR and nonPAR physician each charge $50 for an office visit (CPT code 99213). The Medicare physician fee schedule for CPT code 99213 is $40. The nonPAR limiting charge is $46.

The PAR physician is reimbursed:

Medicare payment (80% of $40)	$32.00
Beneficiary coinsurance (20% of $40)	$8.00
TOTAL REIMBURSEMENT TO PAR	$40.00

The nonPAR physician is reimbursed:

Medicare payment (80% of $40 − 5%)	$30.40
Beneficiary is billed the balanced of limiting charge ($46)	$15.60
TOTAL REIMBURSEMENT TO NONPAR	$46.00 •

Generally, participating physicians report their actual fees to Medicare but adjust, or write-off, the uncollectible portion of their charge when they receive payment. NonPAR doctors usually report only the *limiting charge* as their fee. Billing write-off or adjustment amounts to beneficiaries is called **balance billing** and is prohibited by Medicare regulations. In this illustration using CPT code 99213, the write-off amounts are:

Participating physician	$10.00
NonPAR physician	$4.00

The participating/nonparticipating provider difference of $7.60 ($15.60 minus $8 = $7.60) in this illustration can be significant for people living on a fixed income. Beneficiaries frequently ask, "Does the doctor participate with Medicare?" when calling for an appointment. With very few exceptions, people who qualify for Medicare are not allowed to purchase other primary health insurance. CMS must be certain that Medicare beneficiaries are not required to pay excessive amounts out-of-pocket for health care services. To protect Medicare enrollees financially, providers must comply with extensive rules and regulations.

Medicare Secondary Payer

Medicare Secondary Payer (MSP) refers to situations in which the Medicare program does not have primary responsibility for paying a beneficiary's medical expenses. The Medicare beneficiary may be entitled to other coverage that should pay before Medicare. From the time the Medicare program began in 1966, providers of health care grew accustomed to billing Medicare first for services to Medicare beneficiaries. The MSP program was initiated in 1980, and when a Medicare beneficiary also has coverage from one of the following groups, Medicare is a secondary payer:

- automobile medical or no-fault insurance
- disabled individual covered by large group health plan (LGHP) or who has coverage under the LGHP of a family member who is currently employed. A **large group health plan (LGHP)** is provided by an employer who has 100 or more employees *or* a multiemployer plan in which at least one employer has 100 or more full or part-time employees.
- end-stage renal disease program
- federal black lung program
- other liability insurance (e.g., general casualty insurance, homeowner's liability insurance, malpractice insurance, or product liability insurance)
- veterans administration benefits
- workers' compensation
- working aged coverage by an employer group health plan (EGHP), or an individual age 65 or older who is covered by a working spouse's EGHP. (The working spouse can be any age.) An **employer group health plan (EGHP)** is contributed to by an employer or employee pay-all plan and provides coverage to employees and dependents without regard to the enrollee's employment status (i.e., full-time, part-time, or retired). These provisions are applicable regardless of the size of the employer.

Upon claims submission, the amount of secondary benefits payable is the lowest of the:

- actual charge by physician or supplier minus amount paid by the primary payer.
- amount Medicare would pay if services were not covered by the primary payer.
- higher of the Medicare physician fee schedule (or other amount payable under Medicare or the third-party payer's allowable charge) minus the amount actually paid by the primary payer.

To calculate the amount of Medicare secondary benefits payable on a given claim, the following information is required:

- amount paid by the primary payer.
- primary payer's allowable charge.

This information can obtained from the primary payer's transaction notice or the explanation of benefits (EOB) received by the patient.

EXAMPLE: An individual received treatment from a physician who charged $250. The individual's Medicare Part B deductible had previously been met. As primary payer, the employer group health plan's (EGHP) allowed charge was $200, and the EGHP paid 80% of this amount (or $160). The Medicare physician fee schedule amount is $150. The Medicare secondary payment is calculated as follows:

1. Physician charge minus EGHP payment ($250 - $160 = $90)
2. Medicare payment (determined in usual manner) (80% of $150 = $120)
3. EGHP allowable charge minus EGHP payment ($200 - $160 = $40)
4. Medicare pays $40 (lowest of amounts in steps 1, 2, or 3) •

Some Medicare beneficiaries are covered by an employer plan if they are still working or if their spouse is employed and the health plan covers family members. Medicare has very specific rules about payment when another insurance is primary. This billing order is discussed in the Medicare chapter of this text.

"Incident to" Reimbursement

Another example of Medicare regulations that affect the reporting of services involves nurse practitioners (NP) and physician assistants (PA). A **nurse practitioner (NP)** has two or more years of advanced training, has passed a special exam, and often works as a primary care provider along with a physician. A **physician assistant (PA)** has two or more years of advanced training, has passed a special exam, works with a physician, and can do some of the same tasks as the doctor. These health care professionals are licensed by the state, and state law defines their **scope of practice**, which means the state determines the health care services that may be practiced, and Medicare restricts payment for services performed by these practitioners. A PA's state license may permit him or her to care for patients in a hospital, but until recently Medicare did not provide payment when PAs performed hospital services. Medicare now issues special provider numbers for NPs and PAs so that their services can be billed directly to Medicare. NPs and PAs are paid at 100% of the Medicare physician fee schedule.

Before they were issued billing numbers, NP/PA services were billed under the **incident to** provision. This Medicare regulation permitted billing Medicare under the physician's billing number for ancillary personnel services when those services were "incident to" a service performed by a physician. Thus, an ECG performed by a medical assistant in the physician's office is billed under the "incident to" provision. Another regulation states that "incident to" services must be those services typically performed in a doctor's office. This excludes services performed in the hospital, so the hospital services of the NP or PA were not payable by Medicare even though they were within the scope of practice in that state. Medicare does not regulate who can perform a service; that is the responsibility of the individual state. However, the program can and does specify conditions that must be present for payment of services to be rendered.

Location of Service Adjustment

Physicians are usually reimbursed on a fee-for-service basis with payments established by the Medicare physician fee schedule (PFS), based on RBRVS. When office-based services are performed in a facility, such as a hospital or outpatient setting, payments are reduced because the doctor did not provide supplies, utilities, or the costs of running the facility. This is known as the **site of service differential**. Other rules govern the services performed by hospital-based providers and teaching physicians. This chapter discusses rules that affect private practice physicians billing under the PFS.

Managed Care Options

Because of savings associated with **managed care organizations (MCOs)**, Medicare has expanded managed care options to all beneficiaries. Medicare+Choice was established as part of the Balanced Budget Act of 1997 (BBA) and expanded options for health care delivery under Medicare. Medicare beneficiaries can continue to receive their benefits through the original fee-for-service program, but most beneficiaries enrolled in both Hospital Insurance (HI) and Supplementary Medical Insurance (SMI) can choose to participate in a Medicare+Choice plan instead. Organizations that contract as Medicare+Choice plans must meet specific organizational and financial requirements. Medicare+Choice is discussed in greater detail in the Medicare chapter of this text.

CMS must approve a Medicare managed care plan before it is allowed to enroll Medicare beneficiaries. Medicare MCOs must provide coverage that is similar to a fee-for-service program, to include hospital care and office visits. Many plans also offer prescription drug coverage, eyeglasses, hearing aids, and other services that are excluded under the regular Medicare program. These extra features attract patients to managed care plans. The MCO must, however, restrict patient access to a specific provider the patient may choose.

Because Medicare's managed care plan differs from an insurance company's regular product line, there are additional rules to follow for billing purposes. These are very different from the Medicare fee-for-service rules and the payer's regular business billing manuals.

Fee-for-Service Billing Instructions

Medicare sends carriers the *Coverage Issues Manual* (CIM) and the *Medicare Carriers Manual* (MCM) to assist them in paying claims accurately. The CIM identifies services payable by Medicare and conditions eligible for payment. The MCM advises carriers as to the process for paying and denying claims. Portions of these volumes and other CMS instructions are forwarded to providers as part of the provider manual and bulletins distributed by carriers. Many publications from private organizations, as well as those from the Medicare carrier, attempt to organize and clarify the Medicare billing rules.

INTERNET LINK

The *Coverage Issues Manual* (CIM) and the *Medicare Carriers Manual* (MCM) are also available as downloadable files at http://cms.hhs.gov/manuals

Surgery Services

Medicare defines a **global period** for each surgical code as 0, 10, or 90 days. The global period for each surgery includes all services related to that procedure. Suture removal, postoperative office visits, and dressing changes are all included in the surgical payment and are not separately billable. Because 90 days is a lengthy period of time, an office visit or procedure related to any other condition treated by the surgeon must be billed with a modifier to indicate that this procedure or service is not related to the original service. Even if the procedure and diagnosis codes demonstrate that they are unrelated to the surgery, the appropriate modifier must be attached. This extra step serves as the physician's certification that the services are not related.

NOTE: Because these are CPT modifiers, they are printed in CPT and may be reported to other payers to explain how a service was altered in some manner.

SUMMARY

- The *retrospective reasonable cost system* was the methodology used to reimburse hospitals for inpatient care prior to implementation of the inpatient prospective payment system (IPPS), which uses diagnosis-related groups (DRGs).

- Prospective payment systems (PPS) establish predetermined rates based on patient category *(prospective price-based rates)* or type of facility *(prospective cost-based rates)*.

- CMS has implemented numerous *payment systems,* which require services to be paid according to a predetermined reimbursement methodology.

- CMS payment systems include: ambulance fee schedule, ambulatory surgical centers (ASCs), clinical lab diagnostic fee schedule, DMEPOS fee schedule, home health prospective payment system (PPS), hospital inpatient PPS, hospital outpatient PPS, inpatient rehabilitation facility PPS, long-term care hospital PPS, skilled nursing facility PPS, and the physician fee schedule.

- Anesthesia, pathology/laboratory and radiology services require special consideration under the Medicare physician fee schedule.

- Nonparticipating physicians (nonPARs) do not accept Medicare assignment and are subject to a *limiting charge,* which is calculated as 115% of the physician fee schedule. NonPARs are also subject to a 5% reduction of the physician fee schedule for services.

- *Balance billing* (write-off or adjustment amounts) is prohibited by Medicare regulations.

- *Medicare Secondary Payer (MSP)* provisions require other insurance to be billed before Medicare in certain circumstances.

- Nurse practitioners and physician assistants bill Medicare under their own billing number, and are paid at 100% of the Medicare physician fee schedule. They used to be subject to "incident to" billing provisions.

- *Site of service differentials* apply when office-based services are performed in a health care facility (e.g., hospital outpatient department). This means the physician receives reduced payment because no supplies were provided and no costs associated with running the facility were incurred.

- Medicare expanded its managed care options to beneficiaries by implementing the Medicare+Choice program as part of BBA of 1997.
- The Medicare Coverage Issues Manual (CIM) and Medicare Carriers Manual (MCM) contain information about services payable under Medicare as well as conditions that must be met for physicians to be eligible for payment.
- Medicare defines *global period* as 0, 10, or 90 days (depending on the CPT code number) for which all services related to that procedure are included (e.g., suture removal).

STUDY CHECKLIST

- ☐ Read the textbook chapter, and highlight key concepts.
- ☐ Create an index card for each key term.
- ☐ Access the chapter Internet links to learn more about concepts.
- ☐ Complete the chapter review.

- ☐ Complete Web Tutor assignments and take online quizzes.
- ☐ Complete the Workbook chapter, verifying answers with your instructor.
- ☐ Form a study group with classmates to discuss chapter concepts in preparation for an exam.

REVIEW

MATCHING

Match the term with its descriptor.

_____ 1. 0, 10, or days	a. Global period
_____ 2. fee-for-service does not apply	b. Limiting charge
_____ 3. serves as the basis of nonPAR's fee	c. Managed care organization
_____ 4. fee-for-service payment system	d. RBRVS
_____ 5. applies to an office service provided in a hospital	e. Site of service differential

SHORT ANSWER

Complete the following.

6. Name three RBRVS components considered when payments are calculated.

7. Calculate the following amounts for a participating provider who bills Medicare:

Submitted charge (based on provider's regular fee for office visit)	$ 75
Medicare physician fee schedule	$ 60
Coinsurance amount (paid by patient or supplemental insurance)	$ 12
Medicare payment (80% of the allowed amount)	_____
Medicare write-off (not to be paid by Medicare or the beneficiary)	_____

8. Calculate the following amounts for a nonparticipating provider (nonPAR) who bills Medicare:

Submitted charge (based on provider's regular fee)	$ 650
NonPAR Medicare physician fee schedule allowed amount	$ 450
Limiting Charge (115% of Medicare physician fee schedule allowed amount)	_____
Medicare Payment (80% of the Medicare physician fee schedule allowed amount)	_____
Beneficiary is billed 20% plus the balance of the limiting charge	$ 157.50
Medicare write-off (*not* to be paid by Medicare or the beneficiary)	_____

9. Calculate the following amounts for a nurse practitioner (NP) who bills Medicare:

Submitted charge (based on provider's regular fee for office visit)	$ 75
Medicare allowed amount (according to the Medicare physician fee schedule)	$ 60
Nurse practitioner allowed amount (100% of Medicare physician fee schedule)	_____
Medicare payment (80% of the allowed amount)	_____

TRUE/FALSE

Indicate whether each statement is true or false.

10. ☐ T ☐ F To bill Medicare for anesthesia services, providers submit codes from the CPT Surgery Section and include a place of service (POS) code on the claim.

11. ☐ T ☐ F Providers cannot bill for related services during a procedure's global period.

KEY TERMS

assessment

medically managed

narrative clinic note

objective

operative report

plan

SOAP note

subjective

Chapter 10 Coding for Medical Necessity

OBJECTIVES

Upon successful completion of this chapter, you should be able to:

1. Define key terms.
2. Select and code diagnoses and procedures from case studies and sample records.

INTRODUCTION

In Chapters 7-9, coding practice exercises consisted of statements for which diagnosis or procedure/service codes were assigned. The next step in learning to code properly is to select diagnoses and procedure/services from a case and link each procedure/service with the diagnosis code that justifies medical necessity for performing the procedure/service. (Medical necessity of procedures/services is required of payers for reimbursement consideration.) This chapter requires you to review case scenarios and patient records to determine diagnoses and procedure/services to be coded and medical necessity issues.

APPLYING CODING GUIDELINES

In Chapter 6, diagnosis statements were coded according to ICD-9-CM. Now, in preparation for entering codes in the diagnosis blocks on the claim, it is necessary to apply the CMS established *Official Coding Guidelines for Physician and Outpatient Hospital Services,* (page 118), and to understand the limitations of the CMS-1500 claim when billing payers.

Coding may not be a problem when reviewing short, one-line diagnostic statements such as those that appeared in most of the earlier exercises. When working with case scenarios or patient records, you must select the diagnosis and procedure based on provider documentation.

- Code and report only those conditions and procedures that are documented in the record as treated or medically managed.

  NOTE: Medically managed means that a particular diagnosis (e.g., hypertension) may not receive direct treatment during an office visit, but the provider has to consider that diagnosis when determining treatment for other conditions.

- Use the full range of ICD codes from 001 through 999.9 and V01 through V82.9, and supplement with E codes when warranted by circumstances.

- Code to the highest level of specificity any disorder or injury that is known and documented at the time of the encounter.

- Do not code or report tentative (qualified) diagnoses (conditions that are stated as questionable, suspected, or are to be ruled out). Instead, report the documented signs and symptoms.

  NOTE: While signs and symptoms are often documented with a qualified diagnosis, they are not coded when a definitive diagnosis is established.

  EXAMPLE:

  1. Sprained ankle with pain, edema, and discoloration

     Code only the sprained ankle (because it is the definitive diagnosis).

  2. Pharyngitis, with pain on swallowing, and temperature of 101°F of two-day duration.

     Code only the pharyngitis (because it is the definitive diagnosis).

  3. Probable tonsillitis. Patient complains of a sore throat, and redness of the pharynx is noted upon exam.

     Code the sore throat and redness of the pharynx (because the tonsillitis is a qualified diagnosis and is not coded).

- V codes are assigned when there is justification for the patient to seek health care but no disorder currently exists.

- Code only those conditions treated during the encounter or that affect the treatment rendered. Questions to consider include:

  1. Does the problem justify a procedure or service performed during this encounter?

  2. Did the provider prescribe a new medication or change a prescription for a condition?

  3. Are there documented positive results of diagnostic tests?

4. Did the provider have to consider the impact of past treatment (e.g., prescriptions) for a chronic condition when treating a newly diagnosed condition?

- Up to four diagnosis codes can be reported on one CMS-1500 claim. Be careful to match the proper diagnosis with the procedure/service rendered.

- Health care providers often document past conditions that are not currently active problems for the patient. These conditions are not coded as active, but they could be coded with a V code. Do not report codes for inactive problems on the claim (except in cases of medically managed conditions).

  EXAMPLE: Do not assign codes to:

  Status post left ankle fracture

  Strep throat, 6 months ago ●

- Report the primary diagnosis first, and sequence in descending order additional codes for coexisting (secondary) conditions that affect the treatment of the patient.

  The *primary diagnosis* is the major reason the patient sought health care today and is coded and reported on the CMS-1500 claim. Codes for secondary conditions that are treated during the encounter or that influence decisions about managing the primary condition are sequenced below the primary diagnosis. There is no designated order for multiple secondary conditions.

- Link each procedure or service provided with a condition that proves the medical necessity for performing that procedure or service.

  A diagnosis, symptom or sign, or V code should be linked with each procedure or service reported on the CMS-1500 claim. Up to four diagnosis codes are entered next to reference numbers (1–4) in Block 21 of the CMS-1500 claim. The reference number (1–4) is reported in Block 24E for the procedure or service code reported in Block 24D.

  EXAMPLE: Tim Johnson was seen in his primary care physician's office on June 1 where he underwent a detailed history and exam for an upset stomach and vomiting. Mr. Johnson was also evaluated during the visit for his diabetes mellitus. The office drew blood (venipuncture) and performed a blood-glucose test, which was within normal limits. Table 10-1 shows how to link diagnosis and procedure/service codes for entry in the appropriate Blocks (21, 24D, and 24E) on the CMS-1500 claim (Figure 10-1). ●

TABLE 10-1 Linking diagnosis and procedure/service codes for entry in Blocks 21, 24D and 24E of the CMS-1500 claim

DIAGNOSES DOCUMENTED ON PATIENT'S CHART	ICD-9-CM CODE (ENTER IN BLOCK 21 OF CMS-1500 CLAIM)	PROCEDURE OR SERVICE RENDERED TO PATIENT	CPT CODE (ENTER IN BLOCK 24D OF CMS-1500 CLAIM)	REFERENCE NO. (ENTER IN BLOCK 24E OF CMS-1500 CLAIM)
Upset stomach	536.8	Office visit	99213	1
Vomiting	787.03	Office visit	99213	2
Diabetes mellitus	250.00	Venipuncture	36415	3
		Blood-sugar test	82947	3

21. DIAGNOSIS OR NATURE OF ILLNESS OR INJURY. (RELATE ITEMS 1,2,3 OR 4 TO ITEM 24E BY LINE)						22. MEDICAID RESUBMISSION CODE		ORIGINAL REF. NO.		

1. |536.8   3. |250.00

2. |787.03   4. |____.__

23. PRIOR AUTHORIZATION NUMBER

24.	A. DATE(S) OF SERVICE						B. Place of Service	C. Type of Service	D. PROCEDURES, SERVICES, OR SUPPLIES (Explain Unusual Circumstances) CPT/HCPCS MODIFIER		E. DIAGNOSIS CODE	F. $ CHARGES	G. DAYS OR UNITS	H. EPSDT Family Plan	I. EMG	J. COB	K. RESERVED FOR LOCAL USE
	From MM DD YY			To MM DD YY													
1	06 01 YYYY								99213		1,2,3						
2	06 01 YYYY								36415		3						
3	06 01 YYYY								82947		3						
4																	
5																	
6																	

FIGURE 10-1 Completed Blocks 21, 24A, 24D, and 24E of the CMS-1500 claim

EXERCISE 10-1   Choosing the Primary Diagnosis

Review the list of symptoms, complaints, and disorders in each case and underline the primary diagnosis.

1. Occasional bouts of urinary frequency, but symptom-free today
   Sore throat with swollen glands and enlarged tonsils
   Acute pharyngitis with negative, rapid strep test
   Urinalysis test negative

2. Edema, left lateral malleolus
   Limited range of motion due to pain
   Musculoligamentous sprain, left ankle
   X-ray negative for fracture

3. Distended urinary bladder
   Benign prostatic hypertrophy (BPH) with urinary retention
   Enlarged prostate

4. Pale, diaphoretic, and in acute distress
   Bacterial endocarditis
   Limited chest expansion, scattered bilateral wheezes
   Pulse 112 and regular, respirations 22 with some shortness of breath

5. Right leg still weak
   Partial drop foot gait, right
   Tightness in lower back

6. Rule out cervical radiculopathy versus myofascial pain syndrome
   History of pain in both scapular regions
   Spasms, left upper trapezius muscle
   Limited range of motion neck and left arm
   X-rays show significant cervical osteoarthritis

After completing this exercise, refer to Appendix IV to check your answers.

EXERCISE 10-2   Linking Diagnoses with Procedures/Services

Underline the primary diagnosis in each case scenario. Then, link the diagnosis with the procedure/service by entering just one reference number in the **REF #** column.

Reminder: *To link the diagnosis with the procedure/service* means to match up the appropriate diagnosis with the procedure/service that was rendered to treat or manage the diagnosis.

> **EXAMPLE:** The patient was treated by the doctor in the office for a fractured thumb, and X-rays were taken. The following diagnoses and procedures were documented in the patient's chart:
>
> 1. diabetes mellitus, noninsulin dependent, controlled
> 2. benign essential hypertension
> 3. <u>simple fracture, right thumb</u>

REF #	PROCEDURE/SERVICE
3	Office visit
3	X-ray, right thumb

> Based on the procedure and service delivered, the patient was seen for the thumb fracture. Because the diabetes and hypertension are under control, they require no treatment or management during this visit. Therefore, only the fracture is linked to the procedure and service. ●

CASE 1

The patient was treated in the office for abdominal cramping. A hemoccult test was positive for blood in the stool. The patient was scheduled for proctoscopy with biopsy two days later, and Duke's C carcinoma of the colon was diagnosed. The patient was scheduled for proctectomy to be performed in seven days. The following diagnoses were documented on the patient's chart:

1. abdominal cramping
2. blood in the stool
3. Duke's C carcinoma, colon

REF #	PROCEDURE/SERVICE
	Hemoccult lab test
	Proctoscopy with biopsy
	Proctectomy

CASE 2

The patient was treated in the office for urinary frequency with dysuria, sore throat with cough, and headaches. The urinalysis was negative, and the rapid strep test was positive for streptococcus infection. The patient was placed on antiobiotics and was scheduled to be seen in 10 days. The following diagnoses were documented on the patient's chart:

1. urinary frequency with dysuria
2. sore throat with cough
3. headaches
4. strep throat

REF #	PROCEDURE/SERVICE
	Office visit
	Urinalysis
	Rapid strep test

CASE 3

The patient was treated in the office to rule out pneumonia. She had been experiencing wheezing and congestion, and her respirations were labored. The chest X-ray done in the office was positive for pneumonia. The following diagnoses were documented on the patient's chart:

1. pneumonia
2. wheezing
3. congestion
4. labored respirations

REF #	PROCEDURE/SERVICE
	Office visit
	Chest X-ray

CASE 4

The doctor treated the patient in the nursing facility for the second time since she was admitted. The patient complained of malaise and fatigue. It was noted that the patient had a cough as well as a fever of 103°F and that her pharynx was injected. The following diagnoses were documented on the patient's chart:

1. malaise
2. fatigue
3. cough
4. fever of 103°F
5. injected pharynx

REF #	PROCEDURE/SERVICE
	Nursing facility visit

CASE 5

The patient was treated in the emergency department for chills and fever. The physician noted left lower abdominal quadrant pain and tenderness. The physician diagnosed *acute diverticulitis*. The following diagnoses were documented on the patient's chart:

1. chills
2. fever
3. acute diverticulitis

REF #	PROCEDURE/SERVICE
	Emergency department visit

After completing this exercise, refer to Appendix IV to check your answers.

CPT/HCPCS BILLING CONSIDERATIONS

- Locate the CPT or HCPCS level II code.

- Both CPT and HCPCS level II modifiers can be added to CPT codes.

- CPT procedures indicated with asterisks are generally considered minor. This means the asterisked procedure and any subsequent office visits can be reported and billed separately, depending on payer rules.

- Report only those procedures or services performed by the health care provider or staff during the current medical encounter. Do not report diagnostic procedures (lab work and X-rays) ordered for hospital inpatients unless the provider documents that they performed the test. The hospital will bill for all tests performed by hospital staff or employees.

    EXAMPLE: Do not code procedures when the following are documented in the patient's record:

    1. "The following tests were ordered" on a hospitalized patient.

    2. "Patient was referred to Dr. Cardiac for tests."

    3. "Specimens were sent to the Ames Lab for testing."

    4. "Patient will return tomorrow for tests."

CODING FROM CASE SCENARIOS

Case scenarios summarize medical data from patient records and in this text they introduce the student to the process of selecting (or abstracting) diagnoses and procedures. Once this technique is learned, it will be easier to move on to selecting diagnoses and procedures from patient records.

Selecting Diagnoses/Procedures from Case Scenarios

STEP 1 Read the entire case scenario to obtain an overview of the problems presented and procedures/services performed. Research any word or abbreviation not understood.

STEP 2 Reread the problem and highlight the diagnoses, symptoms, or health status that supports, justifies, and/or proves the medical necessity of any procedure or service performed.

   NOTE: Do *not* use a highlighter or other marker on an original document because copies of the document will be illegible. Highlighter marks copy as a thick, black or gray line. Instead, make a copy of the original document for mark-up purposes, and then destroy the copy after the coding process has been completed.

STEP 3 Code the documented diagnoses, symptoms, procedure(s), signs, health status, and/or service(s).

STEP 4 Assign modifiers, if applicable.

STEP 5 Identify the primary condition.

S T E P   6 Link each procedure or service to a diagnosis, symptom, or health status to communicate medical necessity.

Sample Case Scenarios

Case 1

Patient returned to the surgeon's office <u>during postoperative period</u> because of symptoms of <u>shortness of breath, dizzy spells, and pain in the left arm</u>. A level III re-examination (detailed history and examination was documented) of the patient was performed. The wound is healing nicely. There is no abnormal redness or abnormal pain from the incision. A 3-lead ECG rhythm strip was performed which revealed an <u>inversion of the T wave</u>. The <u>abnormal ECG</u> was discussed with the patient and he agreed to an immediate referral to Dr. Cardiac for a cardiac work-up.

Answer

Procedure(s) performed	Code	Diagnosis(es)
1. Office visit, established patient, level III	99213–24	1. During postoperative status
2. 3-lead ECG rhythm strip	93040	2. Shortness of breath and dizziness
		3. Pain in left arm
		4. Abnormal ECG-inverted T wave (794.31)

Rationale

1. The service provided is a level III office visit, established patient.

2. The words "re-examination" and "during postoperative period, by same surgeon" justify the use of the -24 modifier because this examination was conducted during the postoperative period.

3. Abnormal ECG illustrates inversion of T wave, the documented problem.

4. "Shortness of breath, dizzy spells, and pain in the left arm" are symptoms of the abnormal ECG.

Case 2

This 72-year-old man with multiple chronic conditions was scheduled for repair of an initial, uncomplicated left <u>inguinal hernia</u> repair. The patient was cleared for surgery by his primary care physician. General anesthesia was administered by the anesthesiologist, after which the incision was made. At this point the patient went into <u>shock</u>, the surgery was halted, and the wound was closed. Patient was sent to Recovery.

Answer

Procedure(s) performed	Code	Diagnosis(es)
1. Hernia repair, initial	49505–74	1. Inguinal hernia (550.90)
		2. Shock due to surgery (998.0)
		3. Surgery cancelled (V64.1)

Rationale

1. Procedure initiated for uncomplicated, inguinal hernia repair.

2. Modifier -74 indicates surgery was stopped after anesthesia had been administered because of the threat to the patient's well-being from the shock.

3. Primary diagnosis is inguinal hernia, the reason the patient sought health care.

4. Secondary diagnoses include shock resulting from surgery (explains the discontinuation of the surgery) and cancelled surgery.

EXERCISE 10-3   **Coding Case Scenarios**

A. List and code the procedures and diagnosis(es) for each of the following case scenarios.

B. Be sure to include all necessary CPT and/or HCPCS modifiers.

C. Underline the primary condition.

1. A 66-year-old, established Medicare patient came to the office for his annual physical. He had no known health problems and no new complaints. During the course of the examination the physician found BP of 160/130. A detailed history and exam of this established patient was performed in addition to the preventive medicine encounter. Lab work done in the office included automated CBC, automated dipstick UA with microscopy, and chest X-ray, 2 views. A screening flexible sigmoidoscopy was performed with negative findings. Patient also received an IM influenza vaccination.

Procedures	Diagnoses

2. A 67-year-old woman came to the surgery center for a scheduled diagnostic arthroscopy of her right shoulder because of constant pain on rotation of the shoulder. Prior to entering the operating room she told the nurse "I have been feeling weak, depressed, and tired ever since my last visit." The surgeon performs a re-examination with a detailed history, expanded problem-focused physical, and moderate complexity decision-making prior to the surgery. The operative findings were negative and the procedure uneventful.

Procedures	Diagnoses

(continued)

3. The patient was seen in the emergency department (ED) at 10 A.M. for right lower quadrant pain; the ED physician performed an expanded problem focused history and exam. Laparoscopic appendectomy was performed at 1 P.M. for ruptured appendix with abscess, and the patient was discharged at 9 A.M. the next morning.

Procedures	Diagnoses

4. An emergency department (ED) physician performs a level III evaluation on a patient who complains of severe abdominal pain, nausea, and vomiting. An ultrasound reveals enlarged gallbladder. A surgeon is called in to perform evaluation/management of the patient (level III), and the decision for surgery is made. The surgeon performs a laparoscopic cholecystectomy, which reveals acute cholecystitis.

Procedures	Diagnoses

5. Dr. B performed an expanded problem focused, postoperative examination on an established patient. He also removed the sutures on the patient who returned to her hometown on the opposite coast immediately after discharge from the hospital following an open appendectomy.

Procedures	Diagnoses

After completing this exercise, refer to Appendix IV to check your answers.

Additional scenarios are found at the end of this chapter and in the Workbook that accompanies this text.

CODING FROM CLINIC NOTES AND DIAGNOSTIC TEST RESULTS

Diagnoses, procedures, and services are selected and coded from clinic notes, consultation reports, and diagnostic reports. This process is the same as that used for case scenarios. The major difference is that clinic notes, consultations, and diagnostic reports contain more detail. In addition, abbreviations are commonly used by providers, for example:

Chief complaint (cc)	By mouth (po)
Every day (qd)	Three times a day (tid)
Follow-up (FU)	Return to clinic (RTC)

Types of Clinic Notes

There are two major formats that health care providers use for documenting clinic notes. Diagnoses, procedures, and services can be selected and coded from either format. Both require documentation to support the level of Evaluation and Management (E/M) service coded and reported on the CMS-1500 claim, even if the provider selects the E/M code from a preprinted encounter form (e.g., superbill).

EXAMPLE: Portion of encounter form containing E/M service, date, code, and charge

01-01-YYYY	New Patient E/M Service	☑	99203	$70.00

Narrative Clinic Note

A **narrative clinic note** is written in paragraph format.

EXAMPLE: Narrative Style Clinic Note

A 21-year-old female patient comes to the office today having been referred by Dr. Bandaid, M.D. for pain in the RLQ of the abdomen, 2 days duration. Temp: 102°F. Detailed history and physical examination revealed rebound tenderness over McBurney's point with radiation to the RUQ and RLQ. The remainder of the physical examination was normal. For additional information see the complete History and Physical in this chart. Laboratory data ordered by Dr. Bandaid (oral report given by Goodtechnique Lab) is as follows: WBC 19.1; RBC 4.61; platelets 234,000; hematocrit 42; hemoglobin 13.5; bands 15%, and PMNs 88%. UA and all other blood work were within normal limits. Patient is to be admitted to Goodmedicine Hospital for further work-up and possible appendectomy.

T.J. Stitcher, M.D.

SOAP Notes

SOAP notes are written in outline format ("SOAP" is an acronym derived from the first letter of the topic headings used in the note: Subjective, Objective, Assessment, and Plan).

The **subjective** part of the note contains the chief complaint and the patient's description of the presenting problem. It can also include the response to treatment prescribed earlier, past history, review of symptoms, and relevant family and social history. The documentation may appear in quotes because it represents the patient's statement verbatim.

The **objective** part of the note contains documentation of measurable or objective observations made during physical examination and diagnostic testing. Some health care providers may also include historical information obtained from previous encounters in this section.

The **assessment** contains the diagnostic statement and may include the physician's rationale for the diagnosis. If this section is missing from the report, look for positive diagnostic test results documented in the objective data or code the symptoms presented in either the subjective or objective data.

The **plan** is the statement of the physician's future plans for the work-up and medical management of the case. This includes plans for medications, diet, and therapy, future diagnostic tests to be performed, suggested lifestyle changes, items covered in the informed consent discussions, items covered in patient education sessions, and suggested follow-up care.

EXAMPLE: SOAP Note

3/29/YYYY

    S: Pt states "no complaints, no new symptoms since last visit."

    O: T 98.6°F; P 80; R 20; BP 120/86, right arm, sitting, WT 120 lb.

        Incision, inner aspect of left breast, healing well. No sign of inflammation or infection.

    A: Papilloma with fibrocystic changes, no malignancy.

        Size 3.0 x 1.5 x 0.2 cm.

    P: 1. Suture removal today.

        2. Return visit, 3 months for follow-up.

        3. Note dictated to Dr. Neckhurts.

Janet B. Surgeon, M.D.

In this example, the chief complaint (S:) and the vital signs (O:) were documented by the medical assistant (or nurse). The provider then performed an examination (O:), documented her findings (A:), and established a plan for the patient (P:). Because this note documents a postoperative follow-up office visit, no diagnoses or procedures/services are selected and coded. ●

EXERCISE 10-4 **Coding SOAP Notes**

Review the following SOAP notes, then select and code the diagnoses.

    1. S: Patient complains of stomach pain, 3 days duration. She also stated that her legs still get cold and painful from the knees down.

          O: Ht 5' 6"; Wt 164; BP 122/86; pulse 92 and regular; Temp 97.0°F, oral; chest normal; heart normal. The Doppler arteriogram of lower extremities taken last week at the hospital is reported as within normal limits bilaterally.

          A: Another episode of atrophic gastritis.

(continues)

(continued)

P: Carafate 1 g. Take 1 tablet qid before meals and at bedtime, #120 tabs.

DIAGNOSES	ICD-9-CM CODE NUMBERS

2. S: Patient seems to be doing quite well; however, the pain that he had prior to his surgery is not gone. He is currently being evaluated for what appears to be metastatic pancreatic carcinoma of his liver. His diabetes is now under control.

O: Incision is well healed. Abdomen is soft and nontender.

A: Pathology revealed chronic cholecystitis and cholelithiasis. Liver biopsy revealed metastatic adenocarcinoma.

P: 1. Lengthy discussion with patient and his wife about treatment in the future. Asked that they call any time they have questions.

2. Return visit here on a prn basis.

DIAGNOSES	ICD-9-CM CODE NUMBERS

3. S: The patient complains of generalized stiffness and being tired. She also notes that her left knee was swollen and felt hot to the touch last week. She was last seen 18 months ago on Penicillamine and 2 mg prednisone bid. Her other meds are loperamide for loose stool and Tagamet 300 mg bid.

O: Examination reveals some swelling of the left knee with active synovitis and minimal fluid. Her present weight is 134 lb, BP 116/72. The hematocrit performed today is 37.5 and her sed rate is 65.

A: This patient has active rheumatoid arthritis.

P: 1. Increase prednisone to 5 mg bid, and Penicillamine to 500 mg bid.

2. X-ray of left knee tomorrow.

3. Recheck CBC, sed rate, and urinalysis in 4 weeks.

4 Discussed with her the possibility of injecting steroids into the knee if she shows no improvement.

DIAGNOSES	ICD-9-CM CODE NUMBERS

(continues)

(continued)

4. S: Patient returns today for follow-up of chronic angina and dyspnea. She says the angina still appears mainly when she is resting, and particularly just as she is waking up in the morning. This is accompanied by some dyspnea and pain occasionally radiating into the left jaw, but no palpitations. The angina is relieved by nitroglycerin. She continues to take Inderal 40 mg qid.

O: BP, left arm, sitting, 128/72; weight is 150 lb. Chest is clear. No wheezing or rales.

A: Unstable angina. Patient again refused to consider a heart catheterization.

P: New RX: Isordil Tembids 40 mg.

Refill nitroglycerin.

DIAGNOSES	ICD-9-CM CODE NUMBERS

5. S: This 17-year-old, single, white female presents to the office with a sore throat, fever, and swollen glands, 2 days duration.

O: Oral temp 102.4°F; pulse 24; respiration 18; BP 118/78; Wt 138 lb. The throat is markedly erythematous with evidence of exudative tonsillitis. Ears show normal TMs bilaterally. Few tender, submandibular nodes, bilaterally.

A: Exudative tonsillitis.

P: 1. Obtained throat culture that was sent to the lab.

2. Patient started on an empiric course of Pen Vee K 250 mg #40 to be taken qid X 10 days

3. Encouraged patient to increase oral fluid intake.

4. Patient to call office in 48 hours to obtain culture results and report her progress.

DIAGNOSES	ICD-9-CM CODE NUMBERS

6. S: This is a 50-year-old widow who comes to the office following a possible seizure. Her friend reports she was seated at her desk, and after a crash was heard, they found her lying on the floor. She had urinary

(continued)

incontinence, and now complains of confusion and headache. Patient says this was her first episode and denies ever having chest pain, palpitations, or paresthesias. She cannot recall any recent head trauma or auras. She reports no allergies to medication and currently denies taking a medication.

She does have a history of well-differentiated nodular lymphoma, which was treated successfully by a course of radiation at the Goodmedicine Hospital in Anywhere, USA. She has had no clinical evidence of recurrence. She reports no hospitalizations except for normal delivery of her son 25 years ago. She does admit to mild COPD. Her family history is negative for seizures.

O: Review of systems is noncontributory. Wt 155 lb; BP 116/72, both arms; pulse 72 and regular; respirations 18 and unlabored. Head is normocephalic and atraumatic. PERRLA. EOMs are intact. The sclerae are white. Conjunctivae are pink. Funduscopic examination is benign. The ears are normal bilaterally. No evidence of Battle sign. Mouth and throat are normal; tongue is midline and normal. The neck is supple and negative. Chest is clear. Heart rate and rhythm are regular with a grade II/IV systolic ejection murmur along the left sternal border without gallop, rub, click, or other adventitious sounds. Abdomen is soft, nontender, and otherwise negative. Bowel sounds are normal. Pelvic was deferred. There is good rectal sphincter tone. No masses are felt. Hemoccult test was negative. Extremities and lymphatics are noncontributory.

Neurologic exam shows normal mental status. Cranial nerves II–XII are intact. Motor, sensory, cerebellar function, and Romberg are normal. Babinski is absent. Reflexes are 2+ and symmetric in both upper and lower extremities.

A: New-onset seizure disorder. Rule out metabolic versus vascular etiologies.

P: The patient will be scheduled for MRI of the brain and EEG at Goodmedicine Hospital. Obtain electrolytes, calcium, albumin, LFTs, and CBC with platelet and sed rate at the same visit.

DIAGNOSES	ICD-9-CM CODE NUMBERS

Documentation of Diagnostic Test Results

Diagnostic test results are documented in two locations:

- clinic notes
- laboratory reports (e.g., generated by an independent laboratory)

MILLION, IMA   **Patient No.** 12345   **PROVIDER:** Erin Helper, M.D.

Specimen: Blood (collected 03/03/YYYY).   Test completed: 03/03/YYYY at 04:50 P.M.   Technician: 099

Test	Result	Normal Values
Sodium	142 mEq/L	(135–148)
Potassium	4.4 mEq/L	(3.5–5.1)
Chloride	105 mEq/L	(97–107)
Glucose	176 mg/dL**H	(70–110)
BUN	14 mg/dL	(5–20)
Creatinine	1.0 mg/dL	(0.8–1.5)

FIGURE 10-2 Sample laboratory report with abnormal glucose level

Laboratory reports usually quantify data, and diagnostic implications are summarized in clinic notes documented by the provider. Other diagnostic tests (e.g., X-ray and pathology reports) include an interpretation by the responsible physician (e.g., radiologist or pathologist).

The laboratory report in Figure 10-2 documents a high glucose level (denoted by the "**H" on the report). Upon review of the clinic note, if the insurance specialist finds documentation of signs and symptoms, the provider should be asked whether a diagnosis is to be coded to justify performing this group of laboratory tests.

The X-ray in Figure 10-3 was justified by the diagnosis of mild fibrocystic changes of the breast. (If the diagnosis is not documented in the patient's record, be sure to check with the provider before coding this as the diagnosis.)

CODING OPERATIVE REPORTS

Operative reports will vary from a short narrative description of a minor procedure that is performed in the physician's office (Figure 10-4) to more formal reports dictated by the surgeon in a format required by hospitals and ambulatory surgical centers (ASCs) (Figure 10-5).

MILLION, IMA   **Patient No.** 12345   **PROVIDER:** Erin Helper, M.D.

Baseline Mammogram

There are mild fibrocystic changes in both breasts but without evidence of a dominant mass, grouped microcalcifications, or retractions. Density on the left side is slightly greater and thought to be simply asymmetric breast tissue. There are some small axillary nodes bilaterally.

IMPRESSION: Class 1 (normal or clinically insignificant findings).

Follow-up in 1 year is suggested to assess stability in view of the fibrocystic asymmetric findings. Thereafter, biannual follow-up if stable. No dominant mass is present particularly in the upper inner quadrant of the left breast.

Maryanne Iona, M.D.

FIGURE 10-3 Sample radiology report

MILLION, IMA   **Patient No.** 12345   **PROVIDER:** Erin Helper, M.D.

12/5/YYYY

Reason for Visit: Postpartum exam and colposcopy.

Vital Signs: Temperature 97.2°F. Blood pressure 88/52. Weight 107.

Labs: Glucose negative; Albumin, trace.

Patient seems to be doing fine, thinks the bleeding has just about stopped at this point. Her daughter is apparently doing fine; she is to get back chromosomal analysis in a couple of days. No other system defects have been found yet.

Examination: *Breasts:* Negative. Patient is breastfeeding. *Abdomen:* Soft, flat, no masses, nontender. *Pelvic:* Cervix appeared clear, no bleeding noted. Uterus anteverted, small, nontender. Adnexa negative. Vagina appeared atrophic. Episiotomy healing well.

Procedure: Colposcopy of cervix performed with staining of acetic acid. Entire squamocolumnar junction could not be visualized even with aid of endocervical speculum. Exam was made more difficult because of very thick cervical mucus, which could not be completely removed, and because the vagina and cervix were somewhat atrophic appearing. Whitening of epithelium around entire circumference of cervix noted, but no abnormal vasculature noted. Numerous biopsies were taken from posterior and anterior lip of cervix. Endocervical curettage done. Repeat Pap smear of cervix also done.

Plan: Patient to call at the end of this week for biopsy results. Patient told she could have intercourse after five days, to use condoms, or to come back to office first to have size of diaphragm checked.

Erin Helper, M.D.

FIGURE 10-4 Sample physician's office operative report

MILLION, IMA   **Patient No.** 12345   **PROVIDER:** Gail R. Bones, M.D.
Room #: 101B   **DATE OF SURGERY:** 01/01/YYYY

Preoperative Diagnosis: Displaced supracondylar fracture, left humerus
Postoperative Diagnosis: Same
Procedure: Closed reduction and casting, left humeral fracture
Surgeon: Gail R. Bones, M.D.
Assistant Surgeon: T.J. Stitcher, M.D.

Findings and Procedure:
After adequate general anesthesia, the patient's left elbow was gently manipulated and held at 110 degrees of flexion, at which point continued to maintain a good radial pulse. X-rays revealed a good reduction; therefore, a plaster splint was applied, care being taken not to put any constriction in the antecubital fossa. X-rays were taken again, and showed excellent reduction has been maintained. Patient maintained good radial pulse, was awake, and was taken to Recovery in good condition.

Gail R. Bones, M.D.

FIGURE 10-5 Sample hospital or ASC operative report

Hospital and ASC formats may vary slightly but all contain the following information in outline form:

- date of the surgery
- patient identification
- pre- and postoperative diagnosis(es)
- list of the procedure(s) performed
- name of primary and secondary surgeons who performed surgery.

The body of the report contains a detailed narrative of:

- positioning and draping of the patient for surgery
- achievement of anesthesia
- detailed description of how the procedure(s) was performed, identification of the incision made, and instruments, drains, dressings, special packs, and so on used during surgery
- identification of abnormalities found during the surgery
- description of how hemostasis was obtained and the closure of the surgical site(s)
- condition of the patient when (s)he left the operating room.
- signature of surgeon

Procedure for Coding Operative Reports

STEP 1 Make a copy of the operative report.

This will allow you to freely make notations in the margin and highlight special details without marking up the original (which must remain in the patient's record).

STEP 2 Carefully review the listing of procedures performed.

STEP 3 Read the body of the report and make a note of procedures to be coded.

Key words to look for include:

Simple versus complicated
Partial, complete, total, or incomplete
Unilateral versus bilateral
Initial versus subsequent
Incision versus excision
Open versus closed treatment, surgery, or fracture
Reconstructive surgery, ___ plasty,
___ plastic repair
Repair, ___ pexy
Endoscopy
Biopsy
Ligation
Debridement
Complex, simple, intermediate, repair
Micronerve repair

Reconstruction

Graft (bone, nerve, or tendon needing additional code)

Diagnostic versus surgical procedure

Be alert to the following:

1. Additional procedures documented in the body of the report that are not listed in the heading of the report (e.g., Procedures Performed:).

🔘 EXAMPLE:

Postoperative Diagnosis: Chronic cholecystitis and cholelithiasis without obstruction

Procedures Performed: Laparoscopic cholecystectomy with cholangiography

In the body of the operative report the surgeon describes the laparoscopic cholecystectomy and a cholangiogram. The surgeon also documents the operative findings and a biopsy of a suspicious liver nodule. The insurance specialist should contact the surgeon so that the liver biopsy is added to the *Procedures Performed* statement, and then assign a CPT code to it (in addition to the laparoscopic cholecystectomy and cholangiogram). ●

2. The *Procedures Performed* heading lists procedures performed that are not described in the body of the operative report. In these cases, the surgeon will have to add a written addendum to the operative report documenting the performance of any listed procedure that should be coded.

🔘 EXAMPLE:

Procedures Performed: Arthroscopy, right knee. Open repair, right knee, collateral and cruciate ligaments

Upon review of the body of the report, the insurance specialist notes that the surgeon did not document removal of the scope. Even though the removal of a scope is not coded, the insurance specialist should instruct the surgeon to document this as an addendum to the operative report. ●

S T E P 4 Identify main term(s) and subterms for the procedure(s) to be coded.

S T E P 5 Underline and research any terms in the report that you cannot define.

Many coding errors are made when the coder does not understand critical medical terms in the report.

S T E P 6 Locate the main term(s) in the CPT Index.

Check for the proper anatomic site or organ.

S T E P 7 Research all suggested codes.

Read all notes and guidelines pertaining to the codes you are investigating. Watch for "add on" procedures described in any notes/guidelines.

S T E P 8 Return to the index and research additional codes if you cannot find a particular code(s) that matches the description of the procedure(s) performed in the operative report.

Because there is a monetary value for each CPT code and to avoid bundling, never assign multiple, separate codes to describe a procedure if CPT has a single code that classifies all the individual components of the procedure described by the physician.

Key Words Associated With Global Surgeries (*Remember!* Global surgery includes preoperative assessment, the surgery, and normal uncomplicated postoperative care.)

Exploratory	Anastomosis
Exploration of _____	Transection
Minor lysis of adhesions	Bisection
Temporary _____	Blunt bisection (dissection)
Electrocautery	Sharp dissection
Simple closure	Take down (to take apart)
Minor debridement	Undermining of tissue (to
Wound culture	cut at a horizontal angle)
Intraoperative photo	

Never assign a code number described in CPT as a "separate procedure" when it is performed within the same incision as the primary procedure and is an integral part of a greater procedure.

STEP 9 Investigate the possibility of adding modifiers to a specific code description to fully explain the procedure(s) performed.

Key Word Indicators for Use of Modifier -22

Extensive debridement/lysis or adhesions

Excessive bleeding (>500 cc)

Friable tissue

Prolonged procedure due to _____

Unusual anatomy, findings or circumstances

Very difficult

STEP 10 Code the postoperative diagnosis. This should explain the medical necessity for performing the procedure(s). If the postoperative diagnosis does not support the procedure performed, be sure the patient's chart contains documentation to justify the procedure.

EXAMPLE: Patient seen in the emergency department (ED) with right lower quadrant pain, and evaluation reveals elevated temperature and increased white blood count. Preoperative diagnosis is *appendicitis*, and the patient undergoes *appendectomy*, however, the postoperative diagnosis is *normal appendix*. In this situation the documentation of the patient's signs and symptoms in the ED chart justifies the surgery performed. ●

Look for additional findings in the body of the report if the postoperative diagnosis listed on the operative report does not completely justify the medical necessity for the procedure.

Compare the postoperative diagnosis with the biopsy report on all excised neoplasms to determine whether the tissue is benign or malignant.

When working with the exercises in this text and workbook, use any stated pathology report to determine whether or not excised tissue is benign or malignant if it is not covered in the postoperative diagnosis(es).

When working in a medical practice do not code an excision until the pathology report is received.

S T E P 11 Review code options with the physician who performed the procedure if the case is unusual.

Before assigning an "unlisted CPT procedure" code, review HCPCS level II codes. Remember that a description of the procedure performed must accompany the claim if an unlisted CPT code is reported.

S T E P 12 Assign final code numbers for procedures verified in Steps 3 and 4 and any addendum the physician added to the original report.

S T E P 13 Properly sequence the codes listing first the most significant procedure performed during the episode.

S T E P 14 Be sure to destroy the copy of the operative report (e.g., shred it) after the abstracting and coding process is completed.

EXERCISE 10-5   **Coding Operative Reports**

When working with the case studies in this text, rank the procedures as listed on the encounter form. When working in a medical practice, refer to the Medicare Physician Fee Schedule or the payer's fee schedule to determine which surgical procedure receives the highest reimbursement.

CASE 1

Preoperative Diagnosis:	Questionable recurrent basal cell carcinoma, frontal scalp.
Postoperative Diagnosis:	Benign lesion, frontal scalp.
Operation:	Biopsy of granulating area with electrodessication of possible recurrent basal cell carcinoma of frontal scalp.

History: About 1 year ago, the patient had an excision and grafting of a very extensive basal cell carcinoma of the forehead at the edge of the scalp. The patient now has a large granular area at 12 o'clock on the grafted area. This may be a recurrence of the basal cell carcinoma.

Procedure: The patient was placed in the dorsal recumbent position and draped in the usual fashion. The skin and subcutaneous tissues at the junction of the skin grafts of the previous excision and the normal scalp were infiltrated with 1/2% xylocaine containing epinephrine. An elliptical excision of the normal skin and the granulating area was made. After hemostasis was obtained, the entire area of granulating tissue was thoroughly electrodesiccated.

Pathology Report: The entire specimen measures 0.7 x 0.4 x 0.3 cm depth. Part of the specimen is a slightly nodular hemorrhagic lesion measuring 0.3 cm in diameter.

Resected piece of skin shows partial loss of epithelium accompanied by acute and chronic inflammation of granulation tissue from a previous excision of basal cell carcinoma.

Diagnosis: This specimen is benign; there is no evidence of tumor.

CASE 2

Preoperative Diagnosis:	Tumor of the skin of the back with atypical melanocyte cells

(continues)

(continued)

Postoperative Diagnosis:	Same
Operation Performed:	Wide excision
Anesthesia:	General

Indications: The patient had a previous biopsy of a nevus located on the back. The pathology report indicated atypical melanocyte cells in the area close to the margin of the excision. The pathologist recommended that a wide re-excision be performed. The patient was informed of the situation during an office visit last week, and he agreed to be readmitted for a wider excision of the tumor area.

Procedure: The patient was placed on his left side, and general anesthesia was administered. The skin was prepped and draped in a usual fashion. A wide excision, 5.0 cm in length and 4.0 cm wide, was made. The pathologist was alerted and the specimen was sent to the lab. The frozen section was reported as negative for melanocytes on the excisional margin at this time. After the report was received, the wound was closed in layers and a dressing was applied. The patient tolerated the procedure well and was sent to Recovery in good condition.

CASE 3

Preoperative Diagnosis:	Colonic polyps
Postoperative Diagnosis:	Benign colonic polyps
	Melanosis coli
Operation Performed:	Colonoscopy

Anesthesia: An additional 25 mg of Demerol and 2.5 mg of Valium were administered for sedation.

Procedure: The Olympus CF-100 L video colonoscope was passed into the rectum and slowly advanced. The cecum was identified by the ileocecal valve. The prep was suboptimal.

The colonic mucosa had diffuse dark pigmentation suggestive of melanosis coli. The ascending colon, transverse colon, and proximal descending colon appeared unremarkable. There were two polyps which were about 8 mm in size adjacent to each other in the sigmoid colon. One was removed for biopsy, and the other was fulgurated with hot wire biopsy forceps. After this, the colonoscope was gradually withdrawn. The patient tolerated the procedure well and was sent to Recovery.

Because of the suboptimal prep, small polyps or arteriovenous malformations could have been missed.

CASE 4

Preoperative Diagnosis:	Serous otitis media
Postoperative Diagnosis:	Same
Operation Performed:	Bilateral myringotomy with insertion of ventilating tubes
Anesthesia:	General

Procedure: The patient was placed in a supine position and induction of general anesthesia was achieved by face mask. The ears were examined bilaterally using an operating microscope. An incision was made in the anteroinferior quadrants. A large amount of thick fluid was aspirated from both ears, more so from the left side. Ventilating tubes were introduced with no difficulties. Patient tolerated the procedure well and was sent to Recovery in satisfactory condition.

(continues)

(continued)

CASE 5

Preoperative Diagnosis: Lesion, buccal mucosa, left upper lip.
Postoperative Diagnosis: Same
Operation Performed: Excisional biopsy of lesion, left buccal mucosa
Anesthesia: Local

Procedure: The patient was placed in the supine position, and a 3 X 4 mm hard lesion could be felt under the mucosa of the left upper lip. After application of 1% xylocaine with 1:1000 epinephrine, the lesion was completely excised. The surgical wound was closed using #4-00 chromic catgut.

    The patient tolerated the procedure well and returned to the Outpatient Surgery Unit in satisfactory condition.

CASE 6

Preoperative Diagnosis: Pilonidal cyst
Postoperative Diagnosis: Same
Operation Performed: Pilonidal cystectomy
Anesthesia: Local with 4 cc of 1/2% xylocaine.
Estimated Blood Loss: Minimal
Fluids: 550 cc intraoperatively

Procedure: The patient was brought to the operating room and placed in a jack-knife position. After sterile prepping and draping, 40 cc of 1/2% xylocaine was infiltrated into the surrounding tissue of the pilonidal cyst that had a surface opening on the median raphe over the sacrum. After adequate anesthesia was obtained and 1 gram of IV Ancef administered intraoperatively, the surface opening was probed. There were no apparent tracks demonstrated upon probing. Next, a scalpel was used to make an approximately 8 X 8 cm elliptical incision around the pilonidal cyst. The incision was carried down through subcutaneous tissue to the fascia and the tissue was then excised. Attention was turned to achieving hemostasis with Bovie electrocautery. The pilonidal cyst was then opened and found to contain fibrous tissue. The wound was closed with 0 Prolene interrupted vertical mattress. Estimated blood loss was minimal, and the patient received 550 cc of crystalloid intraoperatively. The patient tolerated the procedure well and was sent to the Recovery Room in stable condition.

CASE 7

Preoperative Diagnosis: Incarcerated right femoral hernia.
Postoperative Diagnosis: Same
Operation Performed: Right femoral herniorrhaphy
Anesthesia: General

Procedure: Patient is a 37-year-old male. Initially, the patient was placed in the supine position, and the abdomen was prepped and draped with Betadine in the appropriate manner. Xylocaine (1%) was infiltrated into the skin and subcutaneous tissue. Because of the patient's reaction to pain, general anesthesia was also administered. An oblique skin incision was performed from the anterior superior iliac spine to the pubic tubercle. The skin and subcutaneous tissues were sharply incised. Dissection was carried down until the external oblique was divided in the line of its fibers with care taken to identify the ilioinguinal nerve to avoid injury. Sharp and blunt dissection were used to free the inguinal cord. The cremasteric muscle was transected. Attempts at reduction of the incarcerated femoral hernia from below were unsuccessful.

(continues)

(continued)

The femoral canal was opened in an inferior to superior manner, and finally this large incarcerated hernia was reduced. The conjoint tendon was then sutured to Cooper's ligament with 0 Prolene interrupted suture. The conjoint tendon was somewhat attenuated and of poor quality. A transition suture was placed from the conjoint tendon to Cooper's ligament and then to the inguinal ligament with care taken to obliterate the femoral space without stenosis of the femoral vein. The conjoint tendon was then sutured laterally to the shelving border or Poupart's ligament. The external oblique was closed over the cord with 0 chromic running suture. 3-0 plain was placed in the subcutaneous tissue and the skin was closed with staples. Sterile dressings were applied. The patient tolerated the operative procedure well and was gently taken to Recovery in satisfactory condition.

After completing this exercise, refer to Appendix IV to check your answers.

SUMMARY

- Payers require medical necessity of procedures/services for consideration of payment; linking procedures/services to diagnoses justifies medical necessity.

- *Official Coding Guidelines for Physician and Outpatient Hospital Services* must be followed when reporting codes on the CMS-1500 claim.

- The primary diagnosis is the major reason the patient sought health care and is reported on the CMS-1500 claim (along with secondary diagnoses that are treated or medically managed during the same visit).

- It is appropriate to report diagnoses that are medically managed during an office visit, which means the diagnosis was not actively treated but considered by the provider when determining treatment for other conditions.

- When a CPT code cannot be located for a procedure or service, identify the HCPCS level II code instead.

- Case scenarios summarize medical data from patient records and are often used for coding practice.

- Carefully review case scenarios and patient records to select and code diagnoses, procedures, and services for reporting on the CMS-1500 claim.

- Narrative style clinic notes are documented by the provider in paragraph format.

- SOAP notes are documented by the provider in outline format, as subjective (S), objective (O), assessment (A), and plan (P) data.

- Diagnostic tests results are documented in clinic notes as well as on separate reports generated by a laboratory.

- Operative reports are documented as a short narrative description of minor office procedures and as formal reports dictated by hospital/ASC surgeons.

STUDY CHECKLIST

- ☐ Read the textbook chapter, and highlight key concepts.
- ☐ Create an index card for each key term.
- ☐ Complete the chapter review.
- ☐ Complete Web Tutor assignments and take online quizzes.

- ☐ Complete the Workbook chapter, verifying answers with your instructor.
- ☐ Form a study group with classmates to discuss chapter concepts in preparation for an exam.

REVIEW

COMPREHENSIVE CODING PRACTICE

A. Code all diagnoses, procedures, and services in the following case scenarios, and link the diagnoses to the appropriate procedure/service.

1. A 42-year-old white male was referred to a gastroenterologist by his primary care physician because of a 2-month history of gross rectal bleeding. The new patient was seen, and the doctor performed a comprehensive history and exam. Medical decision making was of moderate complexity. The patient was scheduled for a complete diagnostic colonoscopy 4 days later. The patient was given detailed instructions for the bowel prep that was to be started at home on Friday at 1 P.M. On Friday, conscious sedation was administered and the colonoscopy started. The examination had to be halted at the splenic flexure because of inadequate bowel preparation. The patient was rescheduled for Monday and given additional instructions for bowel prep to be performed starting at 3 P.M. on Sunday. On Monday, conscious sedation was again administered and a successful total colonoscopy was performed. Diverticulosis was noted in the ascending colon and 2 polyps were excised from the descending colon. The pathology report indicated the polyps were benign.

2. Patient underwent an upper GI series, which included both a KUB and delayed films. The request form noted severe esophageal burning daily for the past 6 weeks. The radiology impression was Barrett's esophagus.

3. Patient was referred to a cardiologist for transesophageal echocardiography. Patient suffered a stroke 3 days after a 3-hour session of cardiac arrhythmia. The cardiologist performed conscious sedation and supervised and interpreted the echocardiography. The report stated the "transesophageal echocardiogram showed normal valvular function with no intra-atrial or intraventicular thrombus, and no significant aortic atherosclerosis."

4. The patient had been seen in the office on the morning of May 5th and a diagnosis of sinusitis was made. Her husband called at 8 P.M. that same evening to report his wife had become very lethargic and her speech was slightly slurred. The patient was admitted to the hospital at 8:30 P.M. by the primary care physician. The doctor performed a comprehensive history and examination, and medical decision making was of high complexity. At 9 A.M. the next day, the patient was comatose and was transferred to the critical care unit. The doctor was in constant attendance from 8:10 A.M. until the patient expired at 9:35 A.M. The attending physician listed CVA as the diagnosis.

B. Determining Medical Necessity

5. Make several copies of the Coding Case Study Form located in Appendix III.

6. Refer to Appendix I, and review the case studies located there.

7. In the appropriate column enter each case study number (e.g., 1-1), procedure/service code(s), and diagnosis code(s).

8. Match the appropriate diagnosis code with procedure/service code to establish medical necessity for each.

C. Coding and Determining Medical Necessity

9. Make several copies of the Coding Case Studies worksheet located in Appendix III.

10. Refer to Appendix II, and review the case studies located there.

11. In the appropriate column enter each case study number (e.g., 2-1).

12. Assign codes to diagnoses and procedures/services documented on each encounter form.

13. In the appropriate column enter each procedure/service code(s), and diagnosis code(s).

14. Match the appropriate diagnosis code with procedure/service code to establish medical necessity for each.

EVALUATION AND MANAGEMENT CODING PRACTICE

Review each case, and select the appropriate level of history, examination, and medical decision making (key components) before referring to the CPT E/M Section to assign the code. To assist in the process of selecting the correct level of history, examination, and medical decision making, refer to CMS's E/M Documentation Guidelines, located in Appendix II.

15. Mary Adams was initially seen by her physician, Dr. Thompson, as an inpatient on May 1 with the chief complaint of having taken an overdose of Ornade. She had been suffering from flu-like symptoms for one week and had been taking the prescribed drug, Ornade, for several days. She states that she apparently took too many pills this morning and started exhibiting symptoms of dizziness and nausea. She called the office complaining of these symptoms and was told to meet Dr. Thompson at the hospital emergency department. From the emergency department, she was admitted to the hospital.

Past History revealed no history of hypertension, diabetes, or rheumatic fever. The patient denies any chest pain or past history of previously having taken an overdose of Ornade as mentioned above. Social history reveals she does not smoke or drink. She has two healthy children. Family history is unremarkable.

Systemic Review revealed HEENT within normal limits. Review of the CNS revealed headache and dizziness. She had a fainting spell this morning. No paresthesias. Cardiorespiratory revealed cough but no chest pain or hemoptysis. GI revealed nausea; she had one episode of vomiting early this morning. No other abdominal distress noted. GU revealed no frequency, dysuria or hematuria.

Physical Examination revealed the patient to be stable without any major symptoms upon arrival to the telemetry area. Head & Neck Exam revealed pupil reaction normal to light and accommodation. Funduscopic examination is normal. Thyroid is not palpable. ENT normal. No lymphadenopathy noted. Cardiovascular Exam revealed the point of maximum impulse is felt in the left fifth intercostal space in the midclavicular line. No S_3 or S_4 gallop. Ejection click was heard and grade 2/6 systolic murmur in the left third and fourth intercostal space was heard. No diastolic murmur. Chest is clear to auscultation. Abdomen reveals no organomegaly. Neurologic Exam is normal. Peripheral Vascular System is intact.

ECG reveals a sinus tachycardia and there was no evidence of myocardial ischemia. A pattern of early repolarization syndrome was noted.

Assessment: Will be briefly observed in the telemetry area to rule out any specific evidence of cardiac arrhythmia. She will also have a routine biochemical and hematologic profile, chest X-ray, and cardiogram. Estimated length of stay will be fairly short.

Impression: Rule out dizziness. Rule out cardiac arrhythmias.

Identify the E/M category/subcategory _____

Determine the extent of history obtained _____

Determine the extent of examination performed _____

Determine the complexity of medical decision making _____

CPT E/M code number: _____

16. Sandy White is a 52-year-old white female who was seen in the office by Dr. Kramer on January 15 with the chief complaint of low back pain. The patient has complained of lumbosacral pain off and on for many months, but it has been getting worse for the last two to three weeks. The pain is constant and gets worse with sneezing and coughing. There is no radiation of the pain to the legs.

Past History reveals no history of trauma, no history of urinary symptoms and no history of weakness or numbness in the legs. Had measles during childhood. She's had high blood pressure for a few years. Also has a previous history of rectal bleeding from hemorrhoids. She had appendectomy and cholecystectomy in 1975. She also has diabetes mellitus, controlled by diet alone.

Family History: Mother died postoperatively at the age 62 of an abdominal operation, the exact nature of which is not known. She had massive bleeding. Father died at the age of 75 of a myocardial infarction. He also had carcinoma of the bladder and diabetes mellitus. One sister has high blood pressure. Social History: She is widowed. Smokes and drinks just socially. Works at the Evening Tribune which involves heavy lifting.

Systemic Review reveals no history of cough, expectoration, or hemoptysis. No history of weight loss or loss of appetite. No history of thyroid or kidney disease. The patient has been overweight for many years. HEENT is unremarkable; hearing and vision are normal. Cardiorespiratory reveals no known murmurs. GI reveals no food allergies or chronic constipation. GU reveals no nocturia, enuresis or GI infection. Neuromuscular reveals no history of paralysis or numbness in the past.

Physical Examination in the office reveals a slightly obese, middle-aged female in acute distress with lower back pain. Pulse is 80, blood pressure is 140/85, respirations 16, temperature 98.4°F. HEENT: PERRLA. Conjunctivae are not pale. Sclerae not icteric. Fundi show arteriolar narrowing. Neck: No thyroid or lymph node palpable. No venous engorgement. No bruit heard in the neck. Chest: PMI is not palpable. S_1, S_2 normal. No gallop or murmur heard. Chest moves equally on both sides with respirations. Breath sounds are diminished. No adventitious sounds heard. Abdomen: She has scars from her previous surgery. There is no tenderness. Liver, spleen, kidneys not palpable. Bowel sounds normal. Extremities: Leg raising sign is negative on both sides. Both femorals and dorsalis pedis are palpable and equal bilaterally. There is no ankle edema. Central Nervous System: Speech is normal. Cranial nerves are intact. Motor system is normal. Sensory system is normal. Reflexes are equal bilaterally.

Impression: The impression is lumbosacral pain. The patient is being referred for physical therapy treatment twice per week. Darvocet-N will be prescribed for the pain.

Identify the E/M category/subcategory _____

Determine the extent of history obtained _____

Determine the extent of examination performed _____

Determine the complexity of medical decision making _____

CPT E/M code number: _____

17. S: Monica Sullivan was seen in the office by Dr. White on 12/13 for the second time. She presents with a chief complaint of dizziness and weakness; she stated that she wanted to have her blood pressure checked.

O: Patient has been on Vasotec 5 mg and Hydrodiuril 25 mg. B/P has been going up at home. Patient has felt ill, weak, and dizzy, with headache for three days. Cardiovascular exam reveals a B/P of 130/110 and pulse rate of 84. Her temperature is 98.6°F and normal.

A: Accelerated hypertension. Bell's palsy.

P: Increase Vasotec to 5 mg A.M. and 2.5 mg P.M. SMA & CBC.

Identify the E/M category/subcategory _____

Determine the extent of history obtained _____

Determine the extent of examination performed _____

Determine the complexity of medical decision making _____

CPT E/M code number: _____

18. Ginny Tallman is a 73-year-old female who is followed in the Alfred State Medical Clinic for COPD. Her medications include Theo-Dur 300 mg p.o. q A.M. History of present illness reveals that she seems to have adequate control of bronchospasm using this medication. She also uses an Albuterol inhaler two puffs p.o. q6h. She has no recent complaints of acute shortness of breath, no chest tightness. She has a chronic, dry cough, productive of scanty sputum. At this time she is complaining of shortness of breath.

PE reveals an elderly female in no real distress. BP in the left arm sitting is 110/84, pulse 74 per minute and regular, respiratory rate 12 per minute and somewhat labored. Lungs reveal scattered wheezes in both lung fields. There is also noted an increased expiratory phase. CV exam reveals no S_3, S_4, or murmurs.

The impression is COPD with asthmatic bronchitis. The patient will have present medications increased to Theo-Dur 300 mg p.o. q A.M. and 400 mg p.o. q P.M. She should receive follow-up care in the clinic in approximately two months time.

Identify the E/M category/subcategory _____

Determine the extent of history obtained _____

Determine the extent of examination performed _____

Determine the complexity of medical decision making _____

CPT E/M code number: _____

19. Dr. Linde telephoned established patient Mark Jones to discuss the results of his blood-glucose level test. The doctor spent a great deal of time discussing the test results and proposed therapy regimen. Mr. Jones had numerous questions that Dr. Linde took the time to answer completely.

Identify the E/M category/subcategory _____

Identify the appropriate code(s) _____

CORRECTING CLAIMS SUBMISSION ERRORS

Review each case scenario and identify the coding error(s).

   a. Code is inappropriate for patient's age

   b. Code is incomplete (e.g., missing digits)

   c. Code reported is incorrect (e.g., wrong code)

   d. Medical necessity justification not met

   e. Procedure codes are unbundled

   EXAMPLE: A patient was treated for excision of a 1-cm skin lesion on her arm. The pathology diagnosis was benign nevus.

Coding Error	Procedure Code	Diagnosis Code
c	11401	709.9

Select "**c**" because the coder referred to Lesion, Skin in the ICD-9-CM Index to Diseases to assign 709.9, which is incorrect. The pathology diagnosis documents "benign nevus." The Index to Diseases term "Nevus" instructs the coder to "*see also* Neoplasm, skin, benign." The neoplasm table entry for "skin, benign" assigns code 216.6 to the "benign nevus" pathology diagnosis. ●

20. The physician performed an automated urinalysis without microscopy in the office on a patient who complained of dysuria. The urinalysis revealed greater than 100,000 white cells and was positive for bacteria.

Coding Error	Procedure Code	Diagnosis Code
	81003	599.0
		041.4

21. An office single view frontal chest X-ray was performed on a patient referred for shortness of breath. The radiologist reported no acute findings, but an incidental note was made of a small hiatal hernia.

Coding Error	Procedure Code	Diagnosis Code
	71010	553.3

22. A healthy 20-year-old male underwent a physical examination, performed by his family physician, prior to starting soccer training.

Coding Error	Procedure Code	Diagnosis Code
	99394	V70.3

23. The patient was diagnosed with incipient cataract, and on March 5 underwent extracapsular cataract removal using microsurgery technique with insertion of intraocular lens prosthesis.

Coding Error	Procedure Code	Diagnosis Code
	66984	366.12
	69990-51	

24. Patient underwent physical therapy evaluation for hemiplegia due to CVA.

Coding Error	Procedure Code	Diagnosis Code
	97001	438.2

KEY TERMS

billing entity

claim attachment

diagnosis reference number

Medigap

optical character reader (OCR)

optical scanning

supplemental plan

Chapter 11 Essential CMS-1500 Claim Instructions

OBJECTIVES

Upon successful completion of this chapter, you should be able to:

1. Define key terms.

2. Discuss billing guidelines for the following cases: inpatient medical, inpatient/outpatient global surgery, medical/surgical, and minor surgery.

3. Apply optical scanning guidelines when completing claims.

4. Discuss reporting guidelines and restrictions covering the following claim items: accept assignment, assignment of benefits, diagnoses, date entry, procedures, modifiers, charges, diagnostic reference numbers, and units (on Line 24 of the CMS-1500 claim).

5. Explain why the billing entity's employer tax identification number (EIN) should appear on the claim rather than the provider's Social Security Number.

6. State the processing steps that must occur before a completed claim can be submitted to the payer.

7. Create a "tickler" filing system for completed claims.

INTRODUCTION

This chapter presents universal instructions that must be considered before entering data on the CMS-1500 claim. In addition, there is a discussion of common errors made on claims, guidelines for maintaining the practice's insurance claim files, processing assigned claims, and the Federal Privacy Act of 1974.

Remember! To prevent breach of patient confidentiality, all health care professionals involved with processing insurance claims should check to be sure the patient has signed an "Authorization for Release of Medical Information" statement before completing the claim. The release can be obtained in one of two ways:

- Ask the patient to sign Block 12, Patient's or Authorized Person's Signature, of the CMS-1500 claim.

- Ask the patient to sign a special release form that is customized by each practice and specifically names the patient's insurance carrier, and enter SIGNATURE ON FILE in Block 12 of the CMS-1500 claim.

Don't forget! HIPAA privacy standards require providers to notify patients about their right to privacy, and providers should obtain their patients' written acknowledgement of receipt of this notice. Patients will be also required to authorize in advance the nonroutine use or disclosure of information. In addition, state or other applicable laws govern the control of health information about minor children and provide parents with new rights to control that information.

EXAMPLE: Before Aetna will pay the claim submitted for Mary Sue Patient's office visit, the provider is required to submit a copy of the patient's entire medical record. HIPAA regulations specify that providers can disclose protected health information for payment activities. Typically, this information includes just the patient's diagnosis and procedures/services rendered. Therefore, the provider should require Mary Sue Patient to sign an authorization to release medical information before sending a copy of her record to Aetna.

Distinguish between a patient's primary and secondary insurance policies as determined during the Preclinical Interview and Check-In Procedures discussed in Chapter 4.

Remember! The development of an insurance claim begins when the patient contacts a health care provider's office and schedules an appointment. At this time, it is important to determine whether the patient is requesting an initial appointment or is returning to the practice for additional services. (The preclinical interview and check-in of a new patient is more extensive than that of an established patient.)

NOTE: Federal and state regulations also determine primary and secondary insurance coverage.

EXAMPLE: Section 1862 of Title XVIII—Health Insurance for the Aged and Disabled of the Social Security Act specifies that for an individual covered by both workers' compensation (WC) and Medicare, WC is primary. For an individual covered by both Medicare and Medicaid, Medicare is primary.

GENERAL BILLING GUIDELINES

General billing guidelines common to most carriers include:

1. Provider services for *inpatient medical cases* are billed on a fee-for-service basis. Each physician service results in a unique and separate charge designated by a CPT/HCPCS service/procedure code.

   EXAMPLE: The patient was admitted on June 1 with a diagnosis of bronchopneumonia. The doctor sees the patient each morning until the patient is discharged on June 5. The billing for this patient will show:

6/1	Initial hospital visit (99xxx)
6/2–6/4	3 subsequent hospital visits (99xxx X 3)
6/5	Discharge visit (99xxx)

NOTE: Members of the same practice *cannot* bill for inpatient services on the same day unless circumstances are documented that justify medical necessity and modifiers are assigned to reported code number(s). This is considered duplication of services. ●

EXAMPLE: Dr. Adams and Dr. Lowry are partners in an internal medicine group practice. Dr. Adams' patient, Irene Ahearn, was admitted on May 1 with chief complaint of severe chest pain, and Dr. Adams provided E/M services at 11 A.M. at which time the patient was stable. (Dr. Lowry is on call as of 5 P.M. on May 1.) At 7 P.M., Dr. Lowry was summoned to provide critical care because the patient's condition became unstable. Dr. Adams reports an initial hospital care CPT code, and Dr. Lowry reports appropriate E/M critical care code(s) with modifier -25 attached. ●

2.   Appropriately report observation services. Section 230.6 of the Medicare hospital manual defines *observation services* as "those furnished by a hospital on the hospital's premises, including use of a bed and periodic monitoring by a hospital's nursing or other staff, which are reasonable and necessary to evaluate an outpatient's condition or determine the need for possible admission to the hospital as an inpatient. Such services are covered only when provided by the order of a physician or another individual authorized by State licensure law and hospital staff bylaws to admit patients to the hospital or to order outpatient tests."

NOTE: Observation services are reimbursed under the Outpatient Prospective Payment System (OPPS) and are an alternative to inpatient admission. Medicare coverage is limited to not more than 48 hours unless the fiscal intermediary grants an exception. While outpatient observation care can progress to inpatient admission, an inpatient admission *cannot* be converted to outpatient observation. If an inpatient admission is warranted, *observation services are not billed separately and are reported on the inpatient claim!* ●

EXAMPLE: A 66-year old male experiences 3–4 annual episodes of mild lower substernal chest pressure after meals. The condition is unresponsive to nitroglycerin and usually subsides after 15–30 minutes. The patient's physician has diagnosed stable angina versus gastrointestinal pain. While in recovery following outpatient bunion repair, the patient experiences an episode of lower substernal chest pressure. The patient's physician is contacted and seven hours of observation services are provided after which the patient is released. ●

3.   Inpatient or outpatient *major surgery cases* designated by CPT surgery code numbers without an asterisk (*) are billed on a global fee (all-inclusive surgery fee) basis that covers the presurgical work-up, initial and subsequent hospital visits, surgery, the discharge visit, and uncomplicated postoperative follow-up care in the physician's office.

4.   Postoperative complications requiring a return to the operating room for surgery related to the original procedure are billed as an additional procedure. (Be sure to use the correct modifier, and link the additional procedure to a new diagnosis that describes the complication.)

5.   *Minor surgery cases* are designated in CPT by an asterisk (or star) and are billed on a fee-for-service basis. The preoperative service, surgery, and all postoperative care are individually itemized and billed. Coding of starred procedures is explained in CPT guidelines in the surgery section.

6. *Combined medical/surgical cases* in which the patient is admitted to the hospital as a medical case but, after testing, requires surgery, are billed according to the instructions in items 3 through 5.

EXAMPLE: Patient is admitted on June 1 for suspected pancreatic cancer. Tests are performed on June 2 and 3. On June 4 the decision is made to perform surgery. Surgery is performed on June 5. The patient is discharged on June 10.

This case begins as a medical admission.

The billing will show:

6/1	Initial hospital visit (99xxx)
6/2 and 6/3	2 subsequent hospital visits (99xxx X 2)
6/4	1 subsequent hospital visit with modifier -57 (99xxx-57) (indicating the decision for surgery was made on this day)

At this point this becomes a surgery case.

The billing continues with:

6/5	Pancreatic surgery (48xxx)

NOTE: No subsequent hospital visits or discharge day codes are reported because the global surgery concept applies.

7. Some claims require attachments such as operative reports, discharge summaries, clinic notes, or letters to aid in the determination of the fee to be paid by the insurance company. Attachments are also required when unlisted codes are reported. Each **claim attachment** (medical report substantiating the medical condition) should include patient and policy identification information. Instructions are different for *electronic media claims (EMC)* and paper-generated claims:

- With EMC processing, wait for the carrier to request additional information.

- For paper-generated claims, required attachments should accompany the original claim.

Any *letter* written by the provider should contain clear and simple English rather than "medicalese." The letter can describe an unusual procedure, special operation, or a patient's medical condition that warranted performing surgery in a setting different from the CMS-stipulated site for that surgery. It should be used in any of the following circumstances:

- Surgery defined as an inpatient procedure that is performed at an *Ambulatory Surgical Center (ASC)* or physician's office.

- Surgery typically categorized as an office procedure that is performed in an ASC or hospital.

- A patient's stay in the hospital prolonged because of medical or psychological complications.

- An outpatient or office procedure performed as an inpatient procedure because patient is a high-risk case.

- Explanation of why a fee submitted to an insurance company is higher than the health care provider's normal fee for the coded procedure. (Modifier -22 should be added to the procedure code number.)

- A procedure submitted with an "unlisted procedure" code number or a procedure requiring an explanation or report before reimbursement can be determined.

A claim that requires attachments for clarification has not traditionally been submitted electronically. Such claims were generated on paper and sent by mail. Due to HIPAA regulations effective October 2003, all payers must be able to accept electronic attachments (e.g., notes, reports, referrals).

8. For paper-generated claims, great care must be taken to ensure that the data prints well within the boundaries of the properly designated blocks on the form. Data that run over into the adjacent blocks or appears in the wrong block will cause rejection of claims.

Most computer programs have a claim form test pattern to assist with the alignment of paper in printers. Print this test pattern before printing claims. If claims must be completed on a typewriter, each must be meticulously aligned in both the horizontal and vertical planes.

OPTICAL SCANNING GUIDELINES

The CMS-1500 claim was designed to accommodate optical scanning of paper claims, which uses a device (e.g., scanner) to convert printed or handwritten characters into text that can be viewed by an **optical character reader (OCR)** (a device used for optical character recognition). Entering data into the computer using this technology greatly increases productivity associated with claims processing because the need to manually enter data from the claim into a computer is eliminated. OCR guidelines were established when the HCFA-1500 (now called CMS-1500) claim was developed and are now used by all payers that process claims using the official CMS-1500 claim.

NOTE: If entering patient claim data directly into practice management software, such as Medical Manager®, the software may require that all data be entered using upper and lower case and other data to be entered without regard to OCR guidelines. In these cases, the computer program converts the data to the OCR format when claims are printed or electronically transmitted to a carrier. ●

All claims for case studies in this text are prepared according to OCR standards.

- All data must be entered on the claim within the borders of the data field. "X"s must be contained completely within the boxes, and no letters or numbers should be printed on vertical solid or dotted lines (Figure 11-1).

  Computer-generated paper claims: Software programs should have a test pattern program that fills the claim with "X"s so that you can test the alignment of forms. This is a critical operation with a pin-fed printer. Check the alignment and make any necessary adjustments each time a new batch of claims is inserted into the printer.

  Typewritten claims: Proper alignment in the typewriter is critical. The claim has two test strips printed at the right and left margins of the HEALTH INSURANCE CLAIM FORM line. To check the horizontal alignment, it is necessary to type "X"s in both the left and the right test patterns.

- Use pica type (10 characters per inch). The equivalent computer font is Courier 10 or OCR 10.

1) Correct placement of "X" in box   1)

2) Incorrect placement   2)

FIGURE 11-1 Correct placement of the X within a box on the CMS-1500 claim

- Type all alpha characters in uppercase (capital letters).
- Do not interchange a zero (0) with the alpha character "O."
- *Substitute a space* for the following key strokes:
  Dollar sign or decimal in all charges or totals
  Decimal point in a diagnosis code number
  Dash in front of a procedure code modifier
  Parentheses surrounding the area code in a telephone number
  Hyphens in social security numbers
- Enter one blank space between the patient or policyholder's last name, first name, and middle initial.
- *Do not* use any punctuation in a patient's, policyholder's, or provider's name, except for a hyphen in a compound name.

    EXAMPLE: Gardner-Bey ●

- *Do not* use a person's title or other designations such as Sr., Jr., II, or III on a claim unless they appear on the patient's insurance ID card.

    EXAMPLE: The name on the ID card reads:
    Wm F. Goodpatient, IV
    Name on claim is written:
    GOODPATIENT IV WILLIAM F ●

- Enter two zeros in the cents column when a fee or a monetary total is expressed in whole dollars. *Do not* enter any leading zeros in front of the dollar amount.

    EXAMPLES:

    Six dollars is entered as 6 00

    Six thousand dollars is entered as 6 000 00

- All birth dates should be entered using eight digits with spaces between the digits representing the month, day, and the *four-digit year (MM DD YYYY)*. Care should be taken to ensure that none of the digits fall on the vertical separations within the block (Figure 11-2). Two-digit code numbers for the months are:

Jan—01	Apr—04	July—07	Oct—10
Feb—02	May—05	Aug—08	Nov—11
Mar—03	June—06	Sept—09	Dec—12

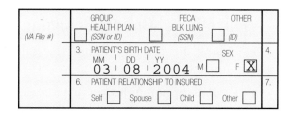

FIGURE 11-2 Proper entry for birth date

- All corrections to typewriter-generated claims must be made using permanent, not removable or lift-off, correction tape and should be typed/printed using pica type. For an electronic media claim, all corrections must be made within the computer data set. On a computer-generated paper claim, for errors caught before mailing, correct the data in the computer and reprint the form. If a paper claim with insufficient or incorrect data is returned by the payer or contains payer processing numbers or markings, corrections should be made by typewriter directly on the returned form. Errors should then be corrected in the computer database.

- *Handwritten claims:* Claims that contain handwritten data, with the exception of the blocks that require signatures, must be manually processed because they cannot be processed by scanners. This will cause a delay in payment of the claim.

    NOTE: Typewritten and handwritten claims have higher error rates, resulting in payment delays. •

- Extraneous data such as handwritten notes, printed material, or special stamps should be placed on an attachment to the claim.

- The borders of pin-fed claims should be removed evenly at the side perforations, and the claim forms should be separated.

- Nothing should be written or typed in the upper right-hand half of the claim. Place the name and address of the insurance company in the upper left-hand corner of the form. The words "Do not write in this space" were added for clarification (Figure 11-3).

- List only one procedure per line starting with line one of Block 24. Do not skip lines between dates of service (Blocks 24A–K on page 330).

- Photocopies of claims are not allowed because they cannot be optically scanned. All resubmissions must also be prepared on an original (red print) claim form. (In addition, information located on the reverse of the claim must be present.)

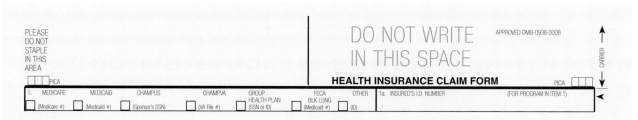

FIGURE 11-3 Top of CMS-1500 claim

EXERCISE 11-1 **Application of Optical Scanning Guidelines**

On a blank sheet of paper enter the following items according to optical scanning guidelines.

1. Patient name: Jeffrey L. Green, D.D.S.
2. Total charge of three hundred dollars
3. Procedure code 12345 with modifiers -22 and -51
4. Your phone number with area code
5. ID number 123-45-6789.
6. Your birth date.
7. Illustrate improper marking of boxes.
8. Enter the birth date for a person who was born on March 8, 2000.

Answer the following questions.

9. Your computer always writes the name of the payer and its mailing address on the claim. Where should this be placed?
10. Your computer uses pin-fed paper. You just ran a batch of 50 claims that will be mailed to one insurance company. All claims are properly processed. What must be done to the claims before they are placed in the envelope for mailing?
11. What is the rule for placing handwritten material on the claim?
12. Name the computer/typewriter font style and print size requirements acceptable for optical scanning of claims.

ASSIGNMENT OF BENEFITS/ ACCEPT ASSIGNMENT

An area of confusion for health insurance specialists is differentiating between *assignment of benefits* and *accept assignment*. Patients sign Block 13 of the CMS-1500 claim to instruct the payer to directly reimburse the provider. This is called assignment of benefits. If the patient does not sign Block 13, the payer sends reimbursement to the patient. The patient is then responsible for reimbursing the provider.

When the YES box in Block 27 contains an X, the provider agrees to accept as payment whatever the payer reimburses. This is called accept assignment. The provider can still collect deductible, copayment, and coinsurance amounts from the patient. If the NO box in Block 27 contains an X, the provider does not accept assignment. The provider can bill patient for the amount not paid by the payer.

REPORTING DIAGNOSES: ICD-9-CM CODES
Block 21

Diagnosis codes are entered in Block 21 on the claim. A maximum of *four* ICD-9-CM codes may be entered on a single claim.

21. DIAGNOSIS OR NATURE OF ILLNESS OR INJURY. (RELATE ITEMS 1, 2, 3, OR 4 TO ITEM 24E BY LINE)
1. L___ . __   3. L___ . __
2. L___ . __   4. L___ . __

If more than four diagnoses are required to justify the procedures and/or services on a claim, generate additional claims. In such cases, be sure that the diagnoses justify the medical necessity for performing the procedures/services reported on each claim. Diagnoses must be documented in the patient's record to validate medical necessity of procedures or services billed.

Sequencing Multiple Diagnoses

The first code reported should be the *primary diagnosis* or the major reason the patient came to the health care provider. *Secondary diagnoses codes are entered in numbers 2 through 4 of Block 21 and should be included on the claim only if they are necessary to justify procedures/services listed in Block 24.* Do not enter any diagnoses stated in the patient record that were not treated or medically managed during the encounter.

Be sure code numbers are placed within the designated field on the claim. The decimal point needed to separate the third and fourth digits is preprinted on the form. Enter a space; do not enter decimal points.

Accurate Coding

For physician office and outpatient claims processing, *never* report a code for diagnoses that include such terms as "rule out," "suspicious for," "probable," "ruled out," "possible," or "questionable." Code either the patient's symptoms or complaints, or do not complete this block until a definitive diagnosis is determined.

Be sure all diagnosis codes are reported to the highest degree of specificity known at the time of the treatment. Verify fourth and fifth digits in the coding manual. Do not assign unspecified codes (xxx.9).

If the computerized billing system displays a default diagnosis code (e.g., condition last treated) when entering a patient's claim information, determine if the code validates the current procedure/service reported. It may be necessary to frequently edit this code because, although the diagnosis may still be present, it may not have been treated or medically managed during each encounter.

NOTE: Coders should be aware that some chronic conditions always affect patient care and should, therefore, be coded and reported on the CMS-1500 claim. Examples include diabetes mellitus and hypertension. ●

When completing case studies in this text and Workbook, code the signs and/or symptoms documented in the record instead of tentative diagnoses.

REPORTING PROCEDURES AND SERVICES: HCPCS

Instructions in this section are for those blocks that are universally required. All other blocks are discussed individually in Chapters 12 through 17.

Block 24A—Dates of Service

When the claim was designed, space was allotted for a 6-digit date pattern with spaces between the month, day, and two-digit year (MM DD YY). No allowance was made for the year 2000 or beyond and the need for a 4-digit year. Therefore, an 8-digit date is entered *without spaces* in Blocks 24A and 32 (MMDDYYYY). All other blocks that require dates have room for the OCR required MM DD YYYY pattern as illustrated in Figure 11-2.

	DATE(S) OF SERVICE					
	From			To		
MM	DD	YY	MM	DD	YY	
1	01 02 2004					

NOTE: All third-party payers require entry of the 8-digit date in the *From* column of Block 24A. A few payers (e.g., Blue Cross/Blue Shield) require entry of the 8-digit date in both the *From* and *To* columns, even when a service was performed on one date.

Block 24B—Place of Service

All payers require entry of a Place of Service (POS) code (Appendix II) on the claim. The POS code reported must be consistent with the CPT procedure/service code description, and it will be one or two-digits, depending on the payer.

Blue Shield POS Codes	Medicare POS Codes	Description
1	21	Hospital as Inpatient
2	22	Hospital as Outpatient
3	11	Physician's Office
4	12	Patient's Home

Block 24C—Type of Service

Medicare providers are not required to enter Type of Service (TOS) codes (Appendix II). Be sure to contact individual payers to determine whether TOS codes are to be reported.

Block 24D—Procedures and Services

Procedure codes and modifiers are reported in Block 24D. A maximum of six procedures may be submitted on one claim. If the reporting of additional procedure and/or service codes is necessary, generate additional CMS-1500 claim(s).

NOTE: Do not report procedure and/or service codes if no fee was charged.

Below the heading in Block 24D is a parenthetical instruction that says *(Explain Unusual Circumstances)*. This is followed by reporting official CPT or

HCPCS modifiers, attaching documentation from the patient's record, or including a letter written by the provider.

When reporting more than one code on a CMS-1500 claim, enter the code with the highest fee in line 1 of Block 24, and then enter additional codes (and modifiers) in descending order of charges. Be sure to completely enter data on each horizontal line before beginning to enter data on another line.

Identical procedures or services can be reported on the same line *if* the following circumstances apply:

- Procedures were performed on consecutive days in the same month.
- The same code is assigned to the procedures/services reported.
- Identical charges apply to the assigned code.
- Block 24G (Days or Units) is completed.

EXAMPLE: Patient is admitted to the hospital on June 1. The doctor reports detailed subsequent hospital visits on June 2, 3, and 4.

Date of service 06012004 (no spaces) is entered on a separate line in Block 24 because the CPT code assigned for initial inpatient care (on the day of admission) is different from subsequent hospital visits (reported for June 2, 3, and 4 as 0602004 through 06042004).

DATE(S) OF SERVICE					
From			To		
MM	DD	YY	MM	DD	YY
06	02	2004	06	04	2004

If identical consecutive procedures fall within a 2-month span, use two lines, one for the first month and one for the second. •

EXAMPLE: Patient is admitted to the hospital on May 29. The doctor reports expanded problem focused visits on May 30, May 31, June 1, and June 2.

24. A						G
DATE(S) OF SERVICE						DAYS OR UNITS
From			To			
MM	DD	YY	MM	DD	YY	
05	29	2004	05	29	2004	1
05	30	2004	05	31	2004	2
06	01	2004	06	02	2004	2

When reporting consecutive days on one line, the first date is reported in 24A in the "From" column and the last day in the "To" column. The "DAYS OR UNITS" column (24G) should reflect the number of days reported in 24A. •

Modifiers

To accurately report a procedure or service, up to three CPT/HCPCS modifiers can be entered to the right of the solid vertical line in Block 24D on the claim. The first modifier is entered between the solid vertical line and the dotted line. If additional modifier(s) are added, enter two blank spaces between modifiers. *Do not* enter a dash in front of the modifier.

D		
PROCEDURES, SERVICES, OR SUPPLIES		
(Explain Unusual Circumstances)		
CPT/HCPCS	MODIFIER	
99221	57	
44960	22	47 60

Block 24E—Diagnosis Code

The title of column 24E (Diagnosis Code) is misleading because the diagnosis reference number(s) from Block 21 is to be entered, not the ICD code number. **Diagnosis reference numbers** are item numbers 1 through 4 preprinted in Block 21 of the CMS-1500 claim. While reporting diagnosis reference numbers rather than ICD code numbers is required, some payers require just one reference number to be entered in Block 24E and others will allow multiple reference numbers (separated by one blank space) to be entered in Block 24E. Be sure to consult individual payers for specific instructions on how many reference numbers can be reported in Block 24E.

Remember! If more than one reference number is reported, the first number must represent the primary diagnosis.

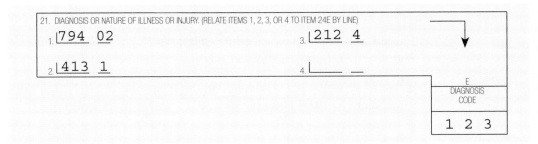

When working with the case studies in this text, follow the Block 24E instruction for each plan as directed in Chapters 12 through 17.

Block 24F Charges

Careful alignment of the charges in Block 24F as well as the totals in Blocks 28 through 30 is critical. Precise entry of dollars and cents is also critical. The block has room for five characters in the dollar column and three in the cents column. Dollar amounts and cents must be typed in their own blocks with only one blank space between them (Figure 11-4).

Block 24G Days/Units

Block 24G requires reporting the number of encounters, units of service or supplies, amount of drug injected, and so on, for the procedure reported on the same line in Block 24D. This block has room for only three digits.

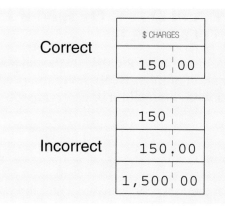

FIGURE 11-4 Correct entry of charges in Blocks 24F and 28–30

The most common number entered in Block 24G is "1" to represent the delivery of a single procedure/service.

The entry of a number greater than "1" is required if identical procedures are reported on the same line. Do not confuse the number of units assigned on one line with the number of days the patient is in the hospital.

EXAMPLE: Patient is in the hospital 3 days following an open cholecystectomy. The number of units assigned to the line reporting the surgery is "1" (only one cholecystectomy was performed).

Remember! When a procedure is performed more than once a day, enter appropriate modifier(s) in Block 24D and attach a copy of supporting documentation to the claim.

Rules to follow when reporting multiple days/units include:

- *Anesthesia time:* Report elapsed time. Convert all hours to minutes.

  EXAMPLE: Elapsed time 3 hours and 15 minutes, reported as 195 units.

- *Multiple procedures:* Enter the primary procedure code first and then enter secondary procedure codes. Enter a "1" in the units column for each procedure entered. Then enter any required modifiers to the secondary procedures in Block 24D (e.g., 51 for multiple procedures).

- *Inclusive dates of similar services:* Report the number of days indicated in the "From" and "To" blocks (Block 24A); the number of days is reported as units in Block 14G.

  EXAMPLE: Physician treated Mr. Greenstalk on 01/02 through 01/04 and performed a detailed inpatient subsequent exam each day. This equals 3 units if reported on one line in Block 24.

- *Radiology services:* Enter a number greater than "1" when the same radiology study is performed more than once on the same day. *Do not report the number of X-ray views taken for a specific study.*

  EXAMPLE: 71030 Chest, four views equals one unit
  Enter 1 in Block 24G.

NATIONAL STANDARD EMPLOYER IDENTIFIER NUMBER

Block 25 requires entry of either the social security number (SSN) or the employer tax identification number (EIN). Enter the practice's EIN in this block. In most cases it is entered with the hyphen (e.g., 11-123456).

25. FEDERAL TAX I.D. NUMBER	SSN	EIN
11-123341	☐	☒

NOTE: If the EIN is unavailable, enter the provider's SSN.

NOTE: Reporting correct EIN and/or SSN information is crucial because payers report reimbursement to the Internal Revenue Service (IRS) according to EIN or SSN.

EXERCISE 11-2 **Entering Procedures on Line 24**

Review the following unrelated scenarios and enter the data into columns A, D, F, and G of Block 24.

If a procedure is performed on consecutive dates enter on one line.

1.	10/10	OV, est pt, detailed	99213	$65.00
2.	10/10	Subsequent hosp visit, expanded problem focused	99232	$45.00
	10/10	Subsequent hosp visit, expanded problem focused	99232	$45.00
	10/12	Subsequent hosp visit, problem focused	99231	$35.00
3.	10/11	Anesthesia, 1 hour 36 minutes		
4.	10/10	X-ray, pelvis, 4 views	72170	$150.00
5.	11/09	Cholecystectomy, open	47600	$900.00
	11/09	Diagnostic Arthroscopy, knee	29871-51	$500.00

24. A DATE(S) OF SERVICE From MM DD YY	To MM DD YY	B Place of Service	C Type of Service	D PROCEDURES, SERVICES, OR SUPPLIES (Explain Unusual Circumstances) CPT/HCPCS | MODIFIER	E DIAGNOSIS CODE	F $ CHARGES	G DAYS OR UNITS	H EPSDT Family Plan	I EMG	J COB	K RESERVED FOR LOCAL USE
1											
2											
3											
4											
5											
6											

REPORTING THE BILLING ENTITY

Block 33 requires entry of the name, address, and telephone number of the billing entity. The **billing entity** is the legal business name of the practice (e.g., Goodmedicine Clinic). In the case of a solo practitioner, the name of the practice may be entered as the name of the physician followed by initials that designate how the practice is incorporated (e.g., Irvin M. Gooddoc, M.D., PA). The phone number, including area code, should be entered on the same line as the printed words "& phone #." Below this line is a blank space for a three-line billing entity mailing address.

The last line of Block 33 is for entering the provider and/or group practice numbers, if one is assigned by the payer.

When working with case studies in this text, follow the specific PIN and/or GRP instructions for each plan as directed in the step-by-step instructions in Chapters 12 through 17.

Remember! Consult the payer for specific instructions as to whether or not a *PIN (provider identification number)* and *group practice identification number (GRP#)* are required.

EXERCISE 11-3 | **Completing the Billing Entity Block**

What is the name of the billing entity in these cases?

1. Dr. Cardiac is employed by Goodmedicine Clinic.

2. Dr. Blank is a solo practitioner. The official name of his practice is Timbuktu Orthopedics.

3. Dr. Jones shares office space with Dr. Blank at Timbuktu Orthopedics; Dr. Jones, PA and Timbuktu Orthopedics have separate EIN numbers.

PROCESSING SECONDARY CLAIMS

The secondary insurance claim is filed only after the transaction notice generated as a result of processing the primary claim has been received by the medical practice. As a general rule, the secondary claim cannot be filed electronically because the transaction notice must be attached to the claim sent to the secondary payer.

Many payers require primary insurance information to be entered in Blocks 11 through 11c. The secondary policy is identified in Blocks 1 and 1a. In addition, payers require the secondary policy to be identified in Blocks 9–9d (Figure 11-5).

When generating claims from this text and the Workbook, multiple claims are completed when the patient is covered by multiple insurance policies. For example, if the patient has both primary and secondary insurance, two claims are generated. The primary claim is completed according to step-by-step instructions, and the secondary claim is completed by following special instructions included in each chapter.

Supplemental Plans

Supplemental plans usually cover the deductible and copay or coinsurance of a primary health insurance policy. Some plans may also cover additional benefits not

PLEASE
DO NOT
STAPLE
IN THIS
AREA

SAMPLE ONLY - NOT APPROVED FOR USE

UNDERSTANDING HEALTH INSURANCE FORM

Secondary insurance is marked

Secondary insurance policy number

Secondary insurance information

Primary insurance information

FIGURE 11-5 Secondary policy information is entered in Blocks 1, 1a, and 9 (primary policy information is entered in Block 11)

included in the primary policy. The best known supplemental plans are the **Medigap** plans, which are supplemental plans designed by the federal government but sold by private commercial insurance companies to "cover the gaps in Medicare." *Supplemental plan information is entered in Blocks 9–9D on the primary insurance claim (Figure 11-6).*

Block 10 (Figure 11-7) indicates whether the condition treated is related to employment, auto accident, or other accident. Information reported in this block affects which payer is considered primary.

FIGURE 11-6 Supplemental plan information is entered in Block 9

FIGURE 11-7 Block 10 of CMS-1500 claim

COMMON ERRORS THAT DELAY PROCESSING

After the claim has been completed, check for these common errors:

1. Typographic errors or incorrect information, as follows:
   - Procedure code number
   - Diagnosis code number
   - Policy identification numbers
   - Dates of service
   - Federal Employer Tax ID Number (EIN)
   - Total amount due on a claim
   - Incomplete or incorrect name of the patient or policyholder (names must match the name on the policy; no nicknames).

2. Omission of the following:
   - Current diagnosis (because of failure to change the patient's default diagnosis in the computer program)
   - Required fourth and/or fifth ICD-9-CM digits
   - Procedure service dates
   - Hospital admission and/or discharge dates
   - Name and required identification numbers of the referring provider
   - Required prior treatment authorization numbers
   - Units of service

3. Attachments without patient and policy identification information on each page.

4. Staples or other defacement of the bar code area on the form.

   NOTE: CMS-1500 claims can be ordered with or without a bar code.

5. Failure to properly align the claim form in the printer to ensure that each item fits within the proper field on the claim.

6. Handwritten items or messages on the claim other than required signatures.

7. Failure to properly link each procedure with the correct diagnosis (Block 24E).

FINAL STEPS IN PROCESSING PAPER CLAIMS

STEP 1 Double check each paper claim for errors and omissions.

STEP 2 Add any necessary attachments.

STEP 3 If required by the payer, obtain the provider's signature on claims.

STEP 4 Post the filing of the claim on the patient's account/ledger.

STEP 5 File a copy of the claim in the practice's claims files.

STEP 6 Mail the claim to the payer.

MAINTAINING INSURANCE CLAIM FILES FOR THE PRACTICE

The federal *Omnibus Budget Reconciliation Act (OBRA) of 1987* requires physicians to keep copies of any government insurance claims and copies of all attachments filed by the provider for a period of five years. As of March 1992, "providers and billing services filing claims electronically can comply with the federal regulation by retaining the source documents (routing slip, charge slip, encounter form, superbill) from which they generated the claim and the daily summary of claims transmitted and received for the five years."

Although there are no specific laws covering retention of commercial or Blue Cross/Blue Shield claims, health care provider contracts with specific insurance carriers may stipulate a specific time frame for all participating providers. It is good business practice to keep these claims until you are sure all transactions have been completed.

Insurance File Set-up

Paper claim files should be organized in the following manner:

1. File *open assigned cases* by month and payer. (These claims have been sent to the payer, but processing is not complete.)

2. File *closed assigned cases* by year and payer.

3. File *batched transmittal notices.*

4. File *unassigned or nonparticipating claims* by year and payer.

Processing Assigned Paid Claims

When the transmittal notice arrives from the payer, pull the claim(s) and review the payment(s). Make a notation of the amount of payment, transmittal notice processing date, and applicable EOB batch number on the claim. Claims with no processing errors and payment in full are marked "closed." They are moved to the Closed Assigned Claims file. Single-payment transmittal notices may be stapled to the claim before filing in the Closed Assigned Claims file. Batched transmittal notices are refiled and if, after comparing the transmittal notice and the claim, an error in processing is found, the following steps should be taken:

STEP 1 Write an immediate appeal for reconsideration of the payment.

STEP 2 Make a copy of the original claim, the transmittal notice, and the written appeal.

STEP 3 Generate a new CMS-1500 claim, and attach it to the transmittal notice and the appeal. (Black and white copies cannot be read by the insurance carrier's optical scanner.) Make sure the date in Block 31 matches the date on the original claim.

STEP 4 Mail the appeal and claim to the payer.

STEP 5 Make a notation of the payment (including the check number) on the office copy of the claim.

STEP 6 Refile the claim and attachments in the "Open claims file."

Federal Privacy Act

The Federal Privacy Act of 1974 prohibits a payer from notifying the provider about payment or rejections of unassigned claims or payments sent directly to the patient/policyholder. If the provider is to assist the patient with the appeal of a claim, the patient must provide a copy of the EOB received from the payer and a letter that explains the error. The letter is to be signed by the patient and policyholder giving the payer permission to allow the provider to appeal the unassigned claim. The EOB and letter must accompany the provider's request for reconsideration of the case. If the policyholder writes the appeal, the provider must supply the policyholder with the supporting documentation required to have the claim reconsidered.

In recent years, Congress has increased efforts to prevent submission of fraudulent claims to government programs. Congress is now considering repealing the legislation that prohibits sending EOBs to the provider on unassigned claims. This would allow the provider to appeal processing errors on unassigned government claims.

SUMMARY

- The patient must either sign Block 12 of the CMS-1500 claim or a special release form (and SIGNATURE ON FILE is entered in Block 12).

- Billing guidelines vary according to whether the patient is an inpatient medical or surgical case and whether major or minor surgery was performed. Combined medical/surgical cases also have special guidelines.

- Claims attachments include operative reports, discharge summaries, clinic notes, and even letters written by providers.

- Data entered on paper-generated claims must be within the boundaries of properly designated blocks on the form.

- The CMS-1500 claim allows for optical scanning to facilitate claims processing.

- Enter a space on the CMS-1500 claim instead of entering a dollar sign, decimal point (for codes), dash (in front of modifiers), parentheses, or hyphens (in SSNs). The hyphen in the EIN is entered.

- Dates are entered using eight digits in MM DD YYYY format (with spaces), *except* for dates entered in Block 24A, which are entered in MMDDYYY format (no spaces).

- Diagnosis codes are entered in Block 21, and the item number (1, 2, 3, or 4) is entered in Block 24E. Some payers allow more than one item number to be entered in Block 24E, each separated by a space.

- Code the patient's signs or symptoms instead of qualified (tentative) diagnoses when processing medical practice claims. (Inpatient claims can contain codes for qualified diagnoses.)

- If more than six procedures or services are entered for an encounter, generate a second CMS-1500 claim.

- If no fee was charged for a procedure or service provided to the patient during an encounter, do not report the procedure/service on the CMS-1500 claim.

- When reporting multiple procedures/services for one encounter, enter the code for the highest paying procedure/service on line 1 of Block 24, followed by additional codes in descending order according to payment.

- If an identical procedure or service was performed multiple times during the same encounter (e.g., office visit or inpatient stay), enter the code once in Block 24 and indicate the number of units (e.g., number of times the same service was provided) in Block 24G.

- If multiple modifiers describe a procedure or service, enter them in Block 24D separated by 2 spaces. *Do not enter a dash in front of the modifier(s).*

- Reporting a modifier on the CMS-1500 claim may require a claims attachment (e.g., clinic note).

- Enter the EIN in Block 25 (including the hyphen). If the SSN is entered instead (because the provider does not have an EIN), do not enter hyphens.

- The billing entity entered in Block 33 is the legal business name of the practice, along with address and telephone number.

- Prior to submitting the CMS-1500 claim to a payer, be sure to check for errors that would delay processing and carefully follow the final steps for processing the claim.

- OBRA of 1987 requires medical practices to maintain insurance claim files for a period of five years, including claims attachments.

- Organize paper claims according to: open assigned cases, closed assigned cases, batched EOBs, and unassigned or nonparticipating claims. All should be filed according to year and payer.

- Prepare an appeal for each denied claim, including a new CMS-1500 claim, copy of transaction notice, appeal letter, and any supporting documentation.

- The Federal Privacy Act of 1974 prohibits payers from notifying providers about payment or rejections of unassigned claims. If providers assist patients with appeals, the patient and policyholder must provide a copy of the EOB and a letter explaining the error and giving permission to the provider to appeal the unassigned claim. If the patient chooses to appeal the claim, the provider must supply supporting documentation required for claims reconsideration.

STUDY CHECKLIST

- ☐ Read the textbook chapter, and highlight key concepts.
- ☐ Create an index card for each key term.
- ☐ Complete the chapter review.
- ☐ Complete Web Tutor assignments and take online quizzes.

- ☐ Complete the Workbook chapter, verifying answers with your instructor.
- ☐ Form a study group with classmates to discuss chapter concepts in preparation for an exam.

REVIEW

SHORT ANSWER

Briefly respond to each.

1. Describe the billing rules for the following:

    a. Inpatient medical case

    b. Major surgery case

    c. Minor surgery case

2. Define the following abbreviations:

    a. ASC

    b. GRP

    c. EIN

    d. PIN

3. A patient is admitted on 10/10 and had an appendectomy on the same day. After postoperative complications, the patient was discharged on 10/12. How many units would appear on the claim for the surgery entry?

4. The doctor performed a subsequent hospital visit, expanded problem focused (99232), each day on October 29 through November 1. Illustrate the consecutive date entry for Block 24, for this case, showing only the proper entry for dates, procedure code, charge, and units.

5. The social security number for Erin A. Helper, M.D. is 222-26-9865. Her Blue Cross provider number is EAH1234. She is employed by Goodmedicine Clinic. The clinic's Employer Identification Number is 52-1256789 and the Blue Cross group number is GC1145. Which number should be entered in Block 25 on the CMS-1500 claim?

6. What is meant by the "diagnosis reference number?"

7. What is the meaning of the phrase "billing entity?"

8. Compare the difference between a secondary and a supplemental insurance plan.

ORDERING

9. Listed below are steps required for the final processing of paper claims before they are mailed to the carriers. It is important that the steps be performed in proper sequence.

    Arrange the steps in proper sequence by placing the correct step number to the left of the statement.

    _____ Post the filing of the insurance claim on the patient's account/ledger

    _____ File a copy of the claim in the practice's claims file

    _____ Obtain the provider's signature on the claim

    _____ Add any necessary attachments

    _____ Double-check each paper claim for errors and omissions

Chapter 12 | Filing Commercial Claims

OBJECTIVES

OBJECTIVES

Upon successful completion of this chapter, you should be able to:

1. Differentiate between primary and secondary commercial claims.

2. Complete commercial primary and secondary fee-for-service claims accurately.

3. Complete commercial primary supplemental fee-for-service claims accurately.

4. Create a comparison chart as an aid to mastering the details of completing claims.

INTRODUCTION

This chapter contains step-by-step instructions for completing fee-for-service claims that are generally accepted nationwide by most commercial health insurance companies, including Aetna, United Health Care, Prudential, Mailhandler's, Cigna, and others. (Instructions for filing Blue Cross/Blue Shield, Medicare, Medicaid, TRICARE/ CHAMPUS, CHAMPVA, and Workers' Compensation claims are found in later chapters.)

These step-by-step instructions apply to *all primary commercial and HMO fee-for-service (noncapitated) claims.* Separate instructions are provided when the patient has secondary health insurance coverage.

⬤ NOTE: Information presented in this chapter builds on the claim completion instructions presented in Chapter 11, Essential CMS-1500 Claim Instructions. ⬤

To assist in learning how to process commercial claims, this chapter includes:

- separate instructions for primary and secondary commercial insurance plans.

- step-by-step instructions broken down into four distinct learning sections with an exercise after each section:

- Blocks 1–13: Entering Patient and Policy Information
- Blocks 14–23: Entering Dates of Service and Diagnostic Data
- Block 24: Entering Procedures, Services, and Supplies
- Blocks 25–33: Entering Provider Information

- A case study and completed claim to illustrate each section of the instructions.
- An Insurance Plan Comparison Chart exercise to help the student master claims completion instructions and to draw attention to variations in requirements among payers (as seen in Chapters 12 through 17.)

NOTE: The portion of the Insurance Plan Comparison Chart (Figure 12-4) illustrates how step-by-step instructions will be entered according to part of the first of four learning sections (mentioned above). The finished Chart allows you to compare CMS-1500 claims completion requirements for commercial, Blue Cross/Blue Shield, TRICARE, and Workers' Compensation programs. (A separate chart will be created for Medicare and Medicaid claims completion.)

Permission is granted by the publisher to print unlimited copies of the Comparison Chart.

COMMERCIAL CLAIMS

The step-by-step commercial claims completion instructions in this chapter are generally recognized nationwide. Some payers may require variations in a few of the blocks, and their requirements should be followed accordingly. Throughout the year, commercial payers implement changes to claims completion requirements that are discovered by providers when claims are denied—commercial payers do not typically make available their billing manual or updates.

Primary claims submission is covered in this chapter's step-by-step instructions, as determined by one of the following criteria:

- The patient is covered by just one plan.

- The patient is covered by a large employer group health plan (EGHP), and patient is also a Medicare beneficiary.

- The patient is covered by a small or large employer group health plan (EGHP) on which the patient is designated as policyholder (or insured), and the patient is also listed as a dependent on another EGHP.

- The patient is a child covered by two or more plans; the primary policyholder is the parent whose birthday occurs first in the year. *Remember!* The birthday rule states that the policyholder whose birth month and day occurs earlier in the calendar year holds the primary policy when each parent subscribes to a different health insurance plan.

NOTE: The instructions that follow have been divided into four sections to allow for introduction and mastery of small sections of the claim. An illustration of a completed section of the claim is found at the end of each section of instructions.

STEP-BY-STEP CLAIM INSTRUCTIONS—BLOCKS 1–13—ENTERING PATIENT AND POLICY INFORMATION

The instructions below are based on general commercial claims completion and optical scanning guidelines located in Chapter 11, Essential CMS-1500 Claim Instructions. When reviewing the step-by-step instructions below, refer to Figure 12-1 for a sample of the CMS-1500 claim, Blocks 1–13. After review of the instructions, refer to the John Q. Public encounter form in Figure 12-2 and the completed CMS-1500 claim, Blocks 1–13, in Figure 12-3.

NOTE: Encounter forms used in actual practice will not look like those included in this text, which provide all the information needed to generate CMS-1500 claims.

NOTE: Remember to press the Caps Lock key on your keyboard before entering claims data.

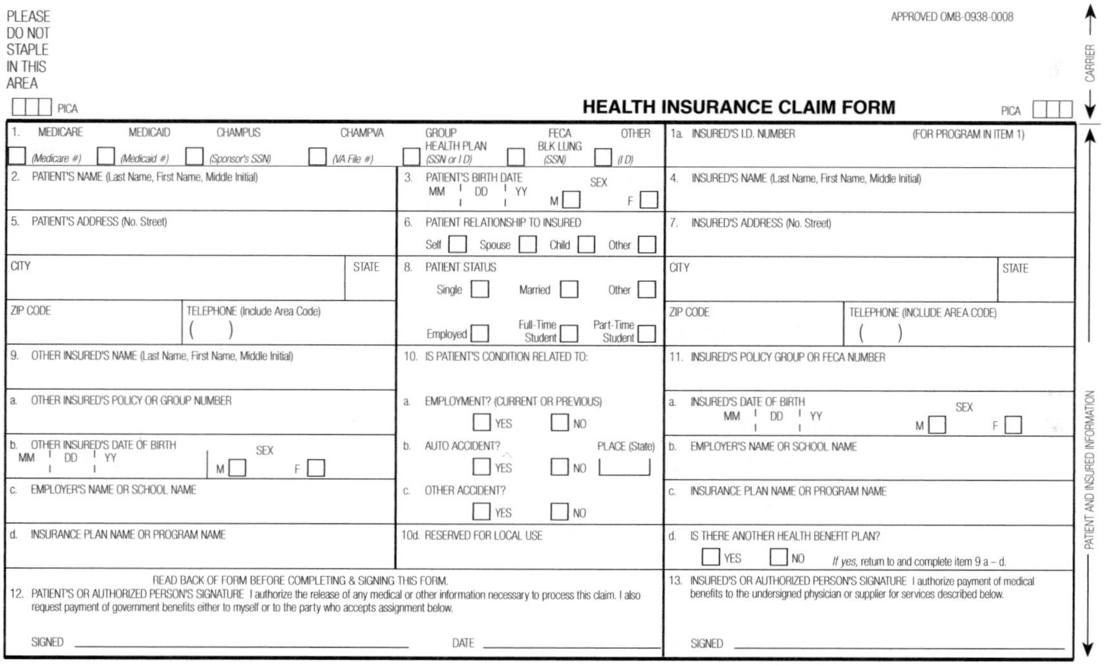

PLEASE DO NOT STAPLE IN THIS AREA

APPROVED OMB-0938-0008

CARRIER

PICA **HEALTH INSURANCE CLAIM FORM** PICA

1. MEDICARE (Medicare #) MEDICAID (Medicaid #) CHAMPUS (Sponsor's SSN) CHAMPVA (VA File #) GROUP HEALTH PLAN (SSN or I D) FECA BLK LUNG (SSN) OTHER (I D)

1a. INSURED'S I.D. NUMBER (FOR PROGRAM IN ITEM 1)

2. PATIENT'S NAME (Last Name, First Name, Middle Initial)

3. PATIENT'S BIRTH DATE MM DD YY SEX M F

4. INSURED'S NAME (Last Name, First Name, Middle Initial)

5. PATIENT'S ADDRESS (No. Street)

6. PATIENT RELATIONSHIP TO INSURED Self Spouse Child Other

7. INSURED'S ADDRESS (No. Street)

CITY STATE

8. PATIENT STATUS Single Married Other

CITY STATE

ZIP CODE TELEPHONE (Include Area Code) ( )

Employed Full-Time Student Part-Time Student

ZIP CODE TELEPHONE (INCLUDE AREA CODE) ( )

9. OTHER INSURED'S NAME (Last Name, First Name, Middle Initial)

10. IS PATIENT'S CONDITION RELATED TO:

11. INSURED'S POLICY GROUP OR FECA NUMBER

a. OTHER INSURED'S POLICY OR GROUP NUMBER

a. EMPLOYMENT? (CURRENT OR PREVIOUS) YES NO

a. INSURED'S DATE OF BIRTH MM DD YY SEX M F

b. OTHER INSURED'S DATE OF BIRTH MM DD YY SEX M F

b. AUTO ACCIDENT? PLACE (State) YES NO

b. EMPLOYER'S NAME OR SCHOOL NAME

c. EMPLOYER'S NAME OR SCHOOL NAME

c. OTHER ACCIDENT? YES NO

c. INSURANCE PLAN NAME OR PROGRAM NAME

d. INSURANCE PLAN NAME OR PROGRAM NAME

10d. RESERVED FOR LOCAL USE

d. IS THERE ANOTHER HEALTH BENEFIT PLAN? YES NO *If yes,* return to and complete item 9 a – d.

READ BACK OF FORM BEFORE COMPLETING & SIGNING THIS FORM.

12. PATIENT'S OR AUTHORIZED PERSON'S SIGNATURE I authorize the release of any medical or other information necessary to process this claim. I also request payment of government benefits either to myself or to the party who accepts assignment below.

SIGNED DATE

13. INSURED'S OR AUTHORIZED PERSON'S SIGNATURE I authorize payment of medical benefits to the undersigned physician or supplier for services described below.

SIGNED

PATIENT AND INSURED INFORMATION

FIGURE 12-1 Blocks 1 through 13 of the CMS-1500 claim

Block 1

Enter an X in the *Other* box.

Block 1A

Enter the insurance identification number as it appears on the patient's insurance card. *Do not enter dashes.*

Block 2

Enter the patient's name as it appears on the patient's insurance identification form. *Be sure to enter last name first, followed by the first name and middle initial. Do not enter nicknames or make errors in data entry because this may result in rejection of the claim.*

Block 3

Enter the patient's birth date in the MM DD YYYY (with spaces) format. Enter an X in the appropriate box to indicate the patient's gender.

Block 4

Enter SAME if the patient and policyholder are the same person. *If the patient is not the policyholder, enter the policyholder's name (last name first, followed by the first name and middle initial).*

Block 5

Enter the patient's mailing address on lines 1 and 2. Enter the five-digit zip code, area code, and telephone number on line 3. *Do not enter the parentheses for the area code because they are preprinted on the CMS-1500 claim.*

Block 6

Enter an X in the appropriate box to indicate the patient's relationship to the policyholder (or insured).

Block 7

Enter SAME if the patient and policyholder are the same person. *If the patient is not the policyholder, enter the policyholder's address.*

Block 8

Enter an X in the appropriate boxes to indicate the patient's marital, employment, and/or student status.

> **NOTE:** If the patient is between 19 and 23, is a dependent on a family policy, and is a full-time student, the claim will not be paid unless the patient can prove full-time student status at the time of the encounter (obtained from an academic advisor, department chairperson, or registrar). Be sure to file written acknowledgment of the student's status with the first claim of each semester. ●

Block 9

Enter NONE. *Block 9 is completed if the patient has secondary insurance, discussed later in this chapter.*

Blocks 9a through 9d

Leave blank. *Blocks 9a–9d are completed if the patient has secondary insurance, discussed later in this chapter.*

Blocks 10a through 10c

Enter an X in the appropriate boxes to indicate whether the patient's condition is related to employment or an auto or other accident.

> **NOTE:** Entering an X in any of the YES boxes alerts the commercial payer that another insurance plan might be liable for payment. The commercial payer will not consider the claim unless the provider submits a transmittal notice from the liable party (e.g., workers' compensation, auto insurance). For employment-related conditions, another

option is to attach a letter from workers' compensation rejecting payment for an on-the-job injury. ●

Block 10d

Leave blank. *This block is reserved for local use.*

NOTE: Check commercial payer billing manuals or contact the payers to determine if any information is to be entered. ●

Block 11

Enter the group policy name or number if provided on the patient's insurance card.

Block 11a

If Block 4 contains a name other than the patient's, this is considered the policyholder (or subscriber). Enter the policyholder's birth date in MM DD YYYY (with spaces) format, and enter an X to indicate the policyholder's gender.

NOTE: Leave blank if Block 4 contains the word SAME, which means the patient and policyholder are the same person. (Birth date and gender information have already been entered in Block 3.) ●

Block 11b

Enter the name of the employer if commercial insurance coverage is provided by an employer-sponsored group policy (EGHP). *Check the patient's insurance card for EGHP designation.*

Block 11c

Enter the name of the patient's commercial insurance payer.

Block 11d

Enter an X in the NO box to indicate that the patient has no other health insurance coverage. *Block 11d is completed if the patient has secondary insurance, discussed later in this chapter.*

Block 12

Enter SIGNATURE ON FILE, and leave the date blank.

NOTE: Entering SIGNATURE ON FILE means that the patient has signed an authorization to release medical information to the payer. If the patient has not signed an authorization, the patient must sign and date Block 12. ●

Block 13

Enter SIGNATURE ON FILE to authorize direct payment to the provider for benefits due the patient.

NOTE: Entering SIGNATURE ON FILE means that the patient has signed an assignment of benefits authorization statement, which allows the payer to directly reimburse the provider. ●

ERIN A. HELPER, M.D.
101 Medic Dr, Anywhere US 12345
(101) 111-1234 (Office) • (101) 111-9292 (Fax)
EIN: 11-123452 **MCD:** EBH8881
UPIN: EH8888 **BCBS:** EH11881

Encounter Form

PATIENT INFORMATION:

Name:	Public, John Q.
Address:	10A Senate Avenue
City:	Anywhere
State:	US
Zip Code:	12345
Telephone:	(101) 201-7891
Gender:	Male
Date of Birth:	03-09-1945
Occupation:	Supervisor
Employer:	Legal Research, Inc.

INSURANCE INFORMATION:

Patient Number:	12-2
Place of Service:	Office
Primary Insurance Plan:	Metropolitan (EGHP)
Primary Insurance Plan ID #:	225120661W
Group #:	A15
Primary Policyholder:	Public, John Q.
Policyholder Date of Birth:	03-09-1945
Relationship to Patient:	Self
Secondary Insurance Plan:	
Secondary Insurance Plan ID #:	
Secondary Policyholder:	

Patient Status ☐ Married ☐ Divorced ☒ Single ☐ Student

DIAGNOSIS INFORMATION

	Diagnosis	Code		Diagnosis	Code
1.	Bronchiopneumonia	485	5.		
2.	Urinary frequency	788.41	6.		
3.			7.		
4.			8.		

PROCEDURE INFORMATION

	Description of Procedure or Service	Date	Code	Charge
1.	Established patient office visit, level III	01-09-YYYY	99213	75.00
2.	Urinalysis, dipstick, automatic microscopy	01-09-YYYY	81001	10.00
3.	Chest X-ray, 2 views	01-09-YYYY	71020	50.00
4.				
5.				

SPECIAL NOTES: Recheck 01-19-YYYY. Referring Physician: Ivan Gooddoc, M.D. (SSN 777707070).
Authorization Number: IGI23-45

FIGURE 12-2 John Q. Public encounter form

EXERCISE 12-1 Preparing the Insurance Plan Comparison Chart (Blocks 1–13)

The objective of this assignment is to create a useful reference that will help to master the details of claims completion for different payers. Refer to the sample chart in Figure 12-4.

1. Make five copies of the Insurance Plan Comparison Chart located in Appendix III.

(continues)

PLEASE
DO NOT
STAPLE
IN THIS
AREA

APPROVED OMB-0938-0008

CARRIER

☐☐☐ PICA

HEALTH INSURANCE CLAIM FORM

PICA ☐☐☐

| 1. MEDICARE ☐ (Medicare #) | MEDICAID ☐ (Medicaid #) | CHAMPUS ☐ (Sponsor's SSN) | CHAMPVA ☐ (VA File #) | GROUP HEALTH PLAN ☐ (SSN or I D) | FECA BLK LUNG ☐ (SSN) | OTHER ☒ (I D) | 1a. INSURED'S I.D. NUMBER (FOR PROGRAM IN ITEM 1) 225120661W |

| 2. PATIENT'S NAME (Last Name, First Name, Middle Initial) PUBLIC JOHN Q | 3. PATIENT'S BIRTH DATE MM DD YY 03 09 1945 SEX M ☒ F ☐ | 4. INSURED'S NAME (Last Name, First Name, Middle Initial) SAME |

| 5. PATIENT'S ADDRESS (No. Street) 10A SENATE AVENUE | 6. PATIENT RELATIONSHIP TO INSURED Self ☒ Spouse ☐ Child ☐ Other ☐ | 7. INSURED'S ADDRESS (No. Street) SAME |

| CITY ANYWHERE | STATE US | 8. PATIENT STATUS Single ☒ Married ☐ Other ☐ | CITY | STATE |

| ZIP CODE 12345 | TELEPHONE (Include Area Code) (101) 201 7891 | Employed ☒ Full-Time Student ☐ Part-Time Student ☐ | ZIP CODE | TELEPHONE (INCLUDE AREA CODE) ( ) |

| 9. OTHER INSURED'S NAME (Last Name, First Name, Middle Initial) NONE | 10. IS PATIENT'S CONDITION RELATED TO: | 11. INSURED'S POLICY GROUP OR FECA NUMBER A15 |

| a. OTHER INSURED'S POLICY OR GROUP NUMBER | a. EMPLOYMENT? (CURRENT OR PREVIOUS) ☐ YES ☒ NO | a. INSURED'S DATE OF BIRTH MM DD YY SEX M ☐ F ☐ |

| b. OTHER INSURED'S DATE OF BIRTH MM DD YY SEX M ☐ F ☐ | b. AUTO ACCIDENT? ☐ YES ☒ NO PLACE (State) | b. EMPLOYER'S NAME OR SCHOOL NAME LEGAL RESEARCH INC |

| c. EMPLOYER'S NAME OR SCHOOL NAME | c. OTHER ACCIDENT? ☐ YES ☒ NO | c. INSURANCE PLAN NAME OR PROGRAM NAME METROPOLITAN |

| d. INSURANCE PLAN NAME OR PROGRAM NAME | 10d. RESERVED FOR LOCAL USE | d. IS THERE ANOTHER HEALTH BENEFIT PLAN? ☐ YES ☒ NO If yes, return to and complete item 9 a – d. |

READ BACK OF FORM BEFORE COMPLETING & SIGNING THIS FORM.
12. PATIENT'S OR AUTHORIZED PERSON'S SIGNATURE I authorize the release of any medical or other information necessary to process this claim. I also request payment of government benefits either to myself or to the party who accepts assignment below.

SIGNED SIGNATURE ON FILE   DATE _____

13. INSURED'S OR AUTHORIZED PERSON'S SIGNATURE I authorize payment of medical benefits to the undersigned physician or supplier for services described below.

SIGNED SIGNATURE ON FILE

PATIENT AND INSURED INFORMATION

FIGURE 12-3 Completed Blocks 1 through 13 for John Q. Public encounter form in Figure 12-2

ITEM	COMMERCIAL
1	X IN OTHER BOX
1a	ID NUMBER
2	PATIENT NAME (NO PUNCTUATION)
3	PT DOB/GENDER
4	NAME OF INSURED OR SAME
5	PT ADDRESS
6	RELAT TO INSURED
7	INSURED ADDRESS OR SAME
8	PATIENT STATUS
9	NONE
9a	BLANK
9b	↓
9c	
9d	

FIGURE 12-4 Sample Insurance Plan Comparison Chart (Blocks 1–9d)

2. Enter the following titles in each column of the first row:

- Commercial
- BCBS
- TRICARE
- Workers' Compensation

3. Enter the following block numbers in the first column on each page of the chart:

- Page 1—Blocks 1 through 9d
- Page 2—Blocks 10 through 16
- Page 3—Blocks 17 through 23
- Page 4—Blocks 24A through 24K
- Page 5—Blocks 25 through 33

4. Review the step-by-step instructions for Blocks 1 through 13 (above), and enter abbreviated instructions on the chart.

5. Upon completion, save the chart because it will be used for additional exercises in this and other chapters.

EXERCISE 12-2 **CMS-1500 Blocks 1 through 13**

This exercise requires two copies of a blank CMS-1500 claim. You may either make photocopies of the form in Appendix III of the text, or print copies of the blank form using the CD-ROM. (Instructions for installing the computer program are located in Appendix V.)

1. Obtain two copies of the CMS-1500 claim, and review instructions for Blocks 1 through 13 on your comparison chart.

2. On the first claim, complete Blocks 1 through 13 using your own personal data for filing an employer-sponsored claim with a commercial policy. If you do not have a commercial insurance policy, or lack any of the required data use the following information:

Policy ID: 123-45-6789

Group number: ZZ34

Policyholder: Yourself

Name of the insurance carrier: MetLife

Employer: Employee International

Other Insurance: None

4. Save this form for use in Exercise 12-8.

5. Review the Mary Sue Patient encounter form (Figure 12-5). Place a page marker (e.g., Post-It Note) at the encounter form.

(continues)

6. Select the information needed for Blocks 1 through 13 from Figure 12-5, and enter the required information on a blank claim using Optical Scanning Guidelines. This may be completed by handwriting the information, using the Blank Form Mode on the disk found in the text, or entering the data using a typewriter. Instructions for installing the disk are found in Appendix V.

7. Review Blocks 1 through 13 of the claim to be sure all required blocks are properly completed.

NOTE: This same encounter form and claim will be used for Exercise 12-4. ●

ERIN A. HELPER, M.D.
101 Medic Dr, Anywhere US 12345
(101) 111-1234 (Office) • (101) 111-9292 (Fax)
EIN: 11-123452 **MCD:** EBH8881
UPIN: EH8888 **BCBS:** EH11881

Encounter Form

PATIENT INFORMATION:

Name:	Patient, Mary Sue
Address:	91 Home Street
City:	Nowhere
State:	US
Zip Code:	12367
Telephone:	(101) 201-8989
Gender:	Female
Date of Birth:	10-10-1959
Occupation:	Homemaker
Employer:	

INSURANCE INFORMATION:

Patient Number:	12-5
Place of Service:	Hospital Inpatient
Primary Insurance Plan:	Conn General (EGHP)
Primary Insurance Plan ID #:	222017681
Group #:	
Primary Policyholder:	James W. Patient
Policyholder Date of Birth:	03-01-1948
Relationship to Patient:	Spouse
Secondary Insurance Plan:	
Secondary Insurance Plan ID #:	
Secondary Policyholder:	

Patient Status ☒ Married ☐ Divorced ☐ Single ☐ Student

DIAGNOSIS INFORMATION

Diagnosis		Code	Diagnosis		Code
1.	Abnormal ECG	794.31	5.		
2.	Prinzmetal angina	413.1	6.		
3.	Alpha-lipoproteinemia	272.4	7.		
4.			8.		

PROCEDURE INFORMATION

Description of Procedure or Service		Date	Code	Charge
1.	Initial hospital visit, level III	01-07-YYYY	99223	150.00
2.	Subsequent hospital visit, level I	01-08-YYYY	99221	75.00
3.	Discharge visit, 30 minutes	01-09-YYYY	99238	75.00
4.				
5.				

SPECIAL NOTES: See Dr. Cardiac for Thallium Stress Test on 01-10-YYYY, and follow-up with Dr. Helper on 01-17-YYYY.

FIGURE 12-5 Mary Sue Patient encounter form

STEP-BY-STEP CLAIM INSTRUCTIONS—BLOCKS 14–23—DATES OF SERVICE AND DIAGNOSIS CODES

When reviewing the step-by-step instructions below, refer to Figure 12-6 for a sample of the CMS-1500 claim, Blocks 14 through 23. After review of the instructions, refer to the John Q. Public encounter form in Figure 12-2 and the completed CMS-1500 claim, Blocks 14 through 23, in Figure 12-7.

Block 14

The arrow in this block indicates that the date refers to either illness, injury, or pregnancy. For illness or injury, enter the date the patient first experienced signs or symptoms. For obstetric visits, enter the date of last menstrual period if available in the documentation. In cases where the history does not document a starting date, but provides an approximation, simply count back to the approximated date and record it on the claim. Enter the date in MM DD YYYY (with spaces) format.

EXAMPLE: Encounter date: 03/08/2004, record says "injured 3 months ago." Enter date in Block 14 as 12 08 2003. ●

Block 15

Enter the date that a prior episode of the same or similar illness began if documented in the patient's record. Date format is MM DD YYYY (with spaces).

Block 16

Enter the dates the patient was unable to work if documented in the record or on the encounter form. Date format is MM DD YYYY (with spaces).

Block 17

Enter the full name and credentials of the referring/ordering physician(s) or other health care provider if any of the following services are to be entered in Block 24D: consultation, surgery, diagnostic testing, physical or occupational therapy, home health care, or durable medical equipment. For Assistant Surgeon claims, enter the name of the attending surgeon. Otherwise, leave Block 17 blank.

NOTE: If the health care provider has assumed total care of the patient for an illness/injury, complete Block 17 on the initial claim filed for the condition. ●

14. DATE OF CURRENT: ILLNESS (First symptom) OR INJURY (Accident) OR PREGNANCY (LMP) MM DD YY	15. IF PATIENT HAS HAD SAME OR SIMILAR ILLNESS, GIVE FIRST DATE MM DD YY	16. DATES PATIENT UNABLE TO WORK IN CURRENT OCCUPATION MM DD YY MM DD YY FROM TO
17. NAME OF REFERRING PHYSICIAN OR OTHER SOURCE	17a. I.D. NUMBER OF REFERRING PHYSICIAN	18. HOSPITALIZATION DATES RELATED TO CURRENT SERVICES MM DD YY MM DD YY FROM TO
19. RESERVED FOR LOCAL USE		20. OUTSIDE LAB? $ CHARGES ☐ YES ☐ NO
21. DIAGNOSIS OR NATURE OF ILLNESS OR INJURY. (RELATE ITEMS 1, 2, 3, OR 4 TO ITEM 24E BY LINE) 1. ⌊___ . __ 3. ⌊___ . __ 2. ⌊___ . __ 4. ⌊___ . __		22. MEDICAID RESUBMISSION CODE ORIGINAL REF. NO.
		23. PRIOR AUTHORIZATION NUMBER

FIGURE 12-6 Blocks 14 through 23 of the CMS-1500 claim

Block 17a

PAR providers: Enter the payer assigned PIN (provider identification number).

NonPAR providers: Enter the Social Security Number or Medicare UPIN of the provider, with no spaces or hyphens.

Block 18

Enter the admission date and the discharge date if any procedure/service is rendered to a patient with inpatient status. If the patient is still hospitalized, leave the "TO" block blank. Date format is MM DD YYYY (with spaces).

Block 19

Leave blank. This block has been reserved for local use.

NOTE: Check with the payer to determine if any action is required. ●

Block 20

Enter an X in the NO box if all laboratory procedures reported on this claim were performed in the provider's office.

Enter an X in the YES box if laboratory procedures reported on the claim were performed by an outside laboratory and billed to the referring health care provider. Enter the total amount charged for all tests performed by the outside laboratory. The charge for each test should be entered as a separate line in Block 24D and the name and address of the outside laboratory entered in Block 32.

NOTE: Some payers may have other specific instructions for completion of this block. ●

Block 21

Enter the ICD-9-CM code number for the diagnoses or conditions treated. Do not enter the decimal. Enter a space instead because the decimal is preprinted on the CMS-1500 claim.

NOTE: Detailed instructions for entering codes in this block appear in Chapter 11. ●

Block 22

Leave blank. (Pertains to Medicaid claims only.)

Block 23

Enter the precertification or authorization number assigned by the payer. Some payers may require copies of written authorization to be attached to the claim.

FIGURE 12-7 Completed Blocks 14 through 23 for John Q. Public encounter form in Figure 12-2

EXERCISE 12-3 **Continuation of Exercise 12-1**

Review the instructions for completing Blocks 14 through 23, and enter a concise description of the instructions in the appropriate block in the Commercial column of the Comparison Chart.

EXERCISE 12-4 **Continuation of Exercise 12-2**

1. Review the Mary Sue Patient encounter form in Figure 12-5 for diagnostic and treatment data.

2. Select the information needed for Blocks 14 through 23, and enter the required information on a claim using Optical Scanning Guidelines. This may be completed by handwriting the information, using the Blank Form Mode on the disk or entering the data using a typewriter. Instructions for installing the disk are found in Appendix V.

3. Review Blocks 14 through 23 of the claim to be sure all required blocks are properly completed.

4. Compare your claim with Figure 12-8.

NOTE: This same claim will be used for Exercise 12-6. ●

STEP-BY-STEP INSTRUCTIONS— BLOCK 24—PROCEDURES, SERVICES, AND SUPPLIES

While reviewing the step-by-step instructions below, refer to Figure 12-9 for a sample of the CMS-1500 claim, Block 24. After review of the instructions, refer to the John Q. Public encounter form in Figure 12-2 and the completed CMS-1500 claim, Block 24, in Figure 12-10.

Block 24A

Enter the date the procedure was performed in the FROM column. *Do not* enter a date in the TO column for a single procedure entry unless you are entering a range of dates for consecutive dates of service. Date format is MMDDYYYY with no spaces.

To report procedures or services that are assigned the same codes and charges because they were performed on consecutive days, indicate the last day the procedure was performed in the TO column. Also, enter the number of consecutive days or units in the DAYS OR UNITS column (Block 24G).

Block 24B

Enter the appropriate Place of Service (POS) code (Appendix II) that identifies where the service reported was performed. Note that POS code numbers vary by carrier. (Refer to Appendix II for POS codes.)

PLEASE
DO NOT
STAPLE
IN THIS
AREA

CARRIER

(SAMPLE ONLY - NOT APPROVED FOR USE)

☐☐ PICA

UNDERSTANDING HEALTH INSURANCE CLAIM FORM PICA ☐☐

| 1. MEDICARE ☐ (Medicare #) MEDICAID ☐ (Medicaid #) CHAMPUS ☐ (Sponsor's SSN) CHAMPVA ☐ (VA File #) GROUP HEALTH PLAN ☐ (SSN or ID) FECA BLK LUNG ☐ (SSN) OTHER ☒ (ID) | 1a. INSURED'S I.D. NUMBER (FOR PROGRAM IN ITEM 1) 222017681 |

2. PATIENT'S NAME (Last Name, First Name, Middle Initial)
PATIENT MARY SUE

3. PATIENT'S BIRTH DATE MM 10 DD 10 YY 1959 SEX M ☐ F ☒

4. INSURED'S NAME (Last Name, First Name, Middle Initial)
PATIENT JAMES W

5. PATIENT'S ADDRESS (No. Street)
91 HOME STREET

6. PATIENT RELATIONSHIP TO INSURED
Self ☐ Spouse ☒ Child ☐ Other ☐

7. INSURED'S ADDRESS (No. Street)

CITY
NOWHERE   STATE US

8. PATIENT STATUS
Single ☐ Married ☒ Other ☐
Employed ☐ Full-Time Student ☐ Part-Time Student ☐

CITY   STATE

ZIP CODE 12367   TELEPHONE (Include Area Code) (101) 201 8989

ZIP CODE   TELEPHONE (INCLUDE AREA CODE) ( )

9. OTHER INSURED'S NAME (Last Name, First Name, Middle Initial)
NONE

10. IS PATIENT'S CONDITION RELATED TO:

11. INSURED'S POLICY GROUP OR FECA NUMBER

a. OTHER INSURED'S POLICY OR GROUP NUMBER

a. EMPLOYMENT? (CURRENT OR PREVIOUS)
☐ YES ☒ NO

a. INSURED'S DATE OF BIRTH MM 03 DD 01 YY 1948 SEX M ☒ F ☐

b. OTHER INSURED'S DATE OF BIRTH MM DD YY   SEX M ☐ F ☐

b. AUTO ACCIDENT?   PLACE (State)
☐ YES ☒ NO

b. EMPLOYER'S NAME OR SCHOOL NAME

c. EMPLOYER'S NAME OR SCHOOL NAME

c. OTHER ACCIDENT?
☐ YES ☒ NO

c. INSURANCE PLAN NAME OR PROGRAM NAME
CONN GENERAL

d. INSURANCE PLAN NAME OR PROGRAM NAME

10d. RESERVED FOR LOCAL USE

d. IS THERE ANOTHER HEALTH BENEFIT PLAN?
☐ YES ☒ NO If yes, return to and complete item 9 a – d.

READ BACK OF FORM BEFORE COMPLETING & SIGNING THIS FORM.
12. PATIENT'S OR AUTHORIZED PERSON'S SIGNATURE I authorize the release of any medical or other information necessary to process this claim. I also request payment of government benefits either to myself or to the party who accepts assignment below.
SIGNED SIGNATURE ON FILE   DATE _____

13. INSURED'S OR AUTHORIZED PERSON'S SIGNATURE I authorize payment of medical benefits to the undersigned physician or supplier for services described below.
SIGNED SIGNATURE ON FILE

PATIENT AND INSURED INFORMATION

14. DATE OF CURRENT: MM 01 DD 07 YY YYYY ☐ ILLNESS (First symptom) OR INJURY (Accident) OR PREGNANCY (LMP)

15. IF PATIENT HAS HAD SAME OR SIMILAR ILLNESS, GIVE FIRST DATE MM DD YY

16. DATES PATIENT UNABLE TO WORK IN CURRENT OCCUPATION FROM MM DD YY TO MM DD YY

17. NAME OF REFERRING PHYSICIAN OR OTHER SOURCE

17a. I.D. NUMBER OF REFERRING PHYSICIAN

18. HOSPITALIZATION DATES RELATED TO CURRENT SERVICES FROM MM 01 DD 07 YY YYYY TO MM 01 DD 09 YY YYYY

19. RESERVED FOR LOCAL USE

20. OUTSIDE LAB? ☐ YES ☒ NO $ CHARGES

21. DIAGNOSIS OR NATURE OF ILLNESS OR INJURY. (RELATE ITEMS 1, 2, 3, OR 4 TO ITEM 24E BY LINE)
1. 794.31   3. 272.4
2. 413.1   4. ___.___

22. MEDICAID RESUBMISSION CODE   ORIGINAL REF. NO.

23. PRIOR AUTHORIZATION NUMBER

24. A DATE(S) OF SERVICE From MM DD YY To MM DD YY	B Place of Service	C Type of Service	D PROCEDURES, SERVICES, OR SUPPLIES (Explain Unusual Circumstances) CPT/HCPCS MODIFIER	E DIAGNOSIS CODE	F $ CHARGES	G DAYS OR UNITS	H EPSDT Family Plan	I EMG	J COB	K RESERVED FOR LOCAL USE
1 01 07 YYYY	21		99223	1	150 00	1				
2 01 08 YYYY	21		99221	1	75 00	1				
3 01 09 YYYY	21		99238	1	75 00	1				
4										
5										
6										

25. FEDERAL TAX I.D. NUMBER SSN ☐ EIN ☒
11-123452

26. PATIENT'S ACCOUNT NO.
12-2

27. ACCEPT ASSIGNMENT? (For govt. claims, see back) ☒ YES ☐ NO

28. TOTAL CHARGE $ 300 00

29. AMOUNT PAID $

30. BALANCE DUE $ 300 00

31. SIGNATURE OF PHYSICIAN OR SUPPLIER INCLUDING DEGREES OR CREDENTIALS
(I certify that the statements on the reverse apply to this bill and are made a part thereof.)
ERIN A HELPER MD
SIGNED   DATE MMDDYYYY

32. NAME AND ADDRESS OF FACILITY WHERE SERVICES WERE RENDERED (If other than home or office)
GOODMEDICINE HOSPITAL
ANYWHERE STREET
ANYWHERE US 12345

33. PHYSICIAN'S SUPPLIER'S BILLING NAME, ADDRESS, ZIP CODE & PHONE #
(101) 111 1234
ERIN A HELPER MD
101 MEDIC DRIVE
ANYWHERE USA 12345
PIN#   GRP#

PHYSICIAN OR SUPPLIER INFORMATION

(SAMPLE ONLY - NOT APPROVED FOR USE)   PLEASE PRINT OR TYPE   SAMPLE FORM 1500
SAMPLE FORM 1500 SAMPLE FORM 1500

FIGURE 12-8 Completed Mary Sue Patient primary claim

24.	A						B	C	D		E	F	G	H	I	J	K
	DATE(S) OF SERVICE						Place	Type	PROCEDURES, SERVICES, OR SUPPLIES		DIAGNOSIS	$ CHARGES	DAYS	EPSDT	EMG	COB	RESERVED FOR LOCAL
	From			To			of	of	(Explain Unusual Circumstances)		CODE		OR	Family			USE
	MM	DD	YY	MM	DD	YY	Service	Service	CPT/HCPCS	MODIFIER			UNITS	Plan			
1																	
2																	
3																	
4																	
5																	
6																	

FIGURE 12-9 Blocks 24A through 24K of the CMS-1500 claim

Block 24C

Leave blank.

Block 24D

Enter the five-digit CPT or HCPCS level II code and any required CPT or HCPCS modifiers for services or procedure reported. *Enter a blank space, not a dash, to separate the code number from the modifier or multiple modifiers.*

Block 24E

Enter the *diagnosis reference number* (1 through 4) for the ICD code number reported in Block 21 that justifies the medical necessity for each procedure or service reported in Block 24D.

NOTE: Some payers will accept more than one reference number on each line. If more than one reference number is entered, the first number must represent the primary diagnosis that justifies the medical necessity for performing the procedures on that line. Unless otherwise directed by the payer, multiple reference numbers should be separated by blank spaces, not commas or dashes. ●

Block 24F

Enter the fee charged to the patient's account for the procedure/service performed. If identical, consecutive services or procedures are reported, enter the total fee charged for the combined services or procedures.

Block 24G

Enter the number of units/days of services or procedures reported in 24D. (Review the discussion on units in Chapter 11, page 328, if necessary.)

Block 24H

Leave blank. (This pertains to Medicaid claims only.)

Block 24I

Enter an X in this box when the service was provided in a hospital emergency department.

NOTE: Place of service in Block 24B must match. ●

Block 24J

Leave blank.

⬤ **NOTE:** If the patient has secondary insurance, payers require an X to be entered in this block to indicate coordination of benefits (COB). ●

Block 24K

Leave blank.

24. A DATE(S) OF SERVICE						B Place of Service	C Type of Service	D PROCEDURES, SERVICES, OR SUPPLIES (Explain Unusual Circumstances)		E DIAGNOSIS CODE	F $ CHARGES	G DAYS OR UNITS	H EPSDT Family Plan	I EMG	J COB	K RESERVED FOR LOCAL USE
From			To					CPT/HCPCS	MODIFIER							
MM	DD	YY	MM	DD	YY											
1	0109YYYY					11		99213		1	75 00	1				
2	0109YYYY					11		81001		2	10 00	1				
3	0109YYYY					11		71020		1	50 00	1				
4																
5																
6																

FIGURE 12-10 Completed Block 24 for John Q. Public encounter form in Figure 12-2

EXERCISE 12-5 | **Continuation of Exercise 12-3**

Review the step-by-step instructions for completing Blocks 24A through 24K, and enter a concise description of the instructions in the appropriate block in the Commercial column of the Comparison Chart.

EXERCISE 12-6 | **Continuation of Exercise 12-4**

1. Review the procedure data on the Mary Sue Patient encounter form in Figure 12-5.

2. Select the information needed for Blocks 24A through 24K and enter the required information on a claim using Optical Scanning Guidelines. This may be completed by handwriting the information, using the Blank Form Mode on the disk, or entering the data using a typewriter. Instructions for installing the disk are found in Appendix V.

3. Review Blocks 24A through 24K of the claim to be sure all required blocks are properly completed.

4. Compare your claim with Figure 12-8.

⬤ **NOTE:** This same claim will be used for Exercise 12-8. ●

STEP-BY-STEP INSTRUCTIONS—BLOCKS 25–33—PROVIDER INFORMATION

While reviewing the step-by-step instructions below, refer to Figure 12-11 for a sample of the CMS-1500 claim, Blocks 25 through 33. After review of the instructions, refer to the John Q. Public encounter form in Figure 12-2 and the completed CMS-1500 claim, Blocks 25 through 33, in Figure 12-12, page 356.

Block 25

Enter the billing entity's Employer Tax Identification Number (EIN). In addition, be sure to enter an X in the EIN box.

NOTE: While third-party payers will accept the number with or without hyphens, when completing claims in this text (and when using the CD-ROM), be sure to enter hyphens. ●

Block 26

Enter the patient's account number.

Block 27

To *accept assignment* means that the provider agrees to accept the carrier-determined allowed fee for services performed. This statement is different from the *assignment of benefits* (Block 13) statement signed by the patient to indicate that payment is to be made directly to the provider. Some payers, however, use Block 27 to indicate whether the patient or provider receives the reimbursement. Enter an X in the YES box if the provider has a participating provider contract with the payer. Enter an X in the NO box if the provider has not signed a participating provider contract with the payer. (Enter an X in the YES box when completing textbook CMS-1500 claims.)

Block 28

Total the charges on this claim, and enter the total in this block. This figure should *never* reflect negative charges or show that a credit is due the patient. If multiple claims for one patient are generated by the computer because more than six services were reported, be sure the total charge recorded on each claim accurately represents the total of the items on each separate claim submitted.

Block 29

Enter the amount the patient has paid toward the required annual deductible, or any copayment/coinsurance payments collected from the patient for procedures or services listed on this claim. Leave this block blank if no payment is made.

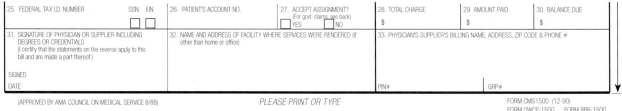

FIGURE 12-11 Blocks 25 through 33 of the CMS-1500 claim

Block 30

Subtract the figure in Block 29 from the figure in Block 28 and enter the total here.

Block 31

Enter the provider's complete name and credential (e.g., MARY SMITH MD) and the date the claim was generated in MMDDYYYY (no spaces) format.

NOTE: Payers usually allow providers to use a signature stamp or enter their complete name and credential in Block 30. If not, the provider must sign each claim. For electronic claims transmission, a certification letter is filed with the payer. ●

Block 32

Enter information in this block when the services listed on the claim were performed at a site other than the provider's office or the patient's home.

NOTE: If Block 18 contains hospitalization dates of service and/or Block 20 contains an X in the YES box, enter the name and address of the facility that provided services. ●

Block 33

Enter the provider's telephone number, including area code, and then the official name of the billing entity and the mailing address. The zip code is entered on the same line as the city and state.

PAR provider: Enter the payer-assigned provider identification number (PIN) and/or group practice identification number (GRP#).

NonPAR provider: Leave PIN and GRP# blank.

EXERCISE 12-7 | **Continuation of Exercise 12-5**

Review the step-by-step instructions for completing Blocks 25 through 33, and enter a concise description of the instructions in the appropriate block in the Commercial column of the Comparison Chart.

EXERCISE 12-8 | **Continuation of Exercise 12-6**

Additional information needed for this case:

Dr. Helper is on the medical staff and admits patients at Goodmedicine Hospital, Anywhere Street, Anywhere, US 12345.

1. Review the Mary Sue Patient encounter form (Figure 12-5).

2. Select the information needed for Blocks 25 through 33 from the encounter form and the additional data provided above and enter it on the claim. This may be completed by handwriting the information, using the Blank Form Mode on the disk, or entering the data using a typewriter. Instructions for installing the disk are found in Appendix V.

3. Review Blocks 25 through 33 of the claim to be sure all required blocks are properly completed.

4. Compare your claim with the completed claim in Figure 12-8.

FIGURE 12-12 Completed Blocks 25 through 33 of CMS-1500 claim. The claim is shown with all information provided.

Additional commercial claim case studies are found in Appendix I of this text.

Case studies in Appendix II require coding of the diagnostic procedure information. Necessary clinic, hospital, and physician data are included in the case study encounter forms located in Appendix II.

COMMERCIAL SECONDARY COVERAGE

Modifications are made to the CMS-1500 claim when patients are covered by primary and secondary or supplemental health insurance plans. Secondary health insurance plans provide similar coverage to primary plans, while supplemental health insurance plans usually cover just deductible, copayment, and coinsurance expenses.

When the same payer issues the primary and secondary or supplemental policies, submit just one CMS-1500 claim. If the payers for the primary and secondary or supplemental policies are different, submit a CMS-1500 claim to the primary payer. When the primary payer has processed the claim (e.g., provider is reimbursed), generate a second CMS-1500 claim to send to the secondary carrier, and include a copy of the primary payer's transmittal notice.

MODIFICATIONS TO PRIMARY CMS-1500 CLAIMS

Block 9

Enter the name of the *secondary* or *supplemental policyholder*, if different from the patient; otherwise, enter SAME.

Block 9a

Enter the ID and group number of the secondary or supplemental policy.

Block 9b

Enter the secondary or supplemental policyholder's date of birth, and enter an X in the appropriate box to indicate the insured's gender.

Block 9c

Enter the name of the employer, school, or organization if the secondary or supplemental policy is an EGHP policy.

Block 9d

Enter the name of the secondary or supplemental health insurance plan.

Block 11d

Enter an X in the YES box.

MODIFICATIONS TO SECONDARY CMS-1500 CLAIMS

The instructions below are applicable only when the secondary or supplemental policy payer is different from the primary payer.

🔘 **NOTE:** If the payer is the same for the primary and secondary or supplemental policies, do not generate a second CMS-1500 claim. ●

Block 1a

Enter the ID number of the *secondary* or *supplemental policy*.

Block 4

Enter the name of the secondary or supplemental policyholder, if different from the patient; otherwise, enter SAME.

Block 7

Enter the address of the secondary or supplemental policyholder, if different from the patient; otherwise, enter SAME.

Block 9

Enter the name of the primary policyholder, if different from the patient; otherwise, enter SAME.

Block 9a

Enter the ID and group number of the primary policy.

Block 9b

Enter the primary policyholder's date of birth, and enter an X in the appropriate box to indicate the insured's gender.

Block 9c

Enter the name of the employer or school, if the primary policy is an EGHP policy; otherwise, leave blank.

Block 9d

Enter the name of the *primary insurance plan*.

Block 11

Enter the group number of the secondary or supplemental policy, if applicable.

Block 11a

Enter the secondary or supplemental policyholder's date of birth, and enter an X in the appropriate box to indicate the insured's gender, if different from the patient; otherwise, leave blank.

Block 11b

Enter the name of the employer or school.

Block 11c

Enter the name of the secondary or supplemental insurance plan.

Block 11d

Enter an X in the YES box.

EXERCISE 12-9　**Filing Commercial Secondary Claims**

1. Obtain a blank claim.

2. Underline Blocks 9 through 9d and 11d on the new claim.

3. Refer to the encounter form for Mary Sue Patient (Figure 12-5). Enter the following information in the appropriate blocks for the secondary policy (as highlighted above):

   Conn General ID # 22233544 Group # AA2

   Policyholder: James W. Patient

   Birth date: 03/01/48

   Relationship: Spouse

   Employer: Anywhere Water Company

   Add an "S" to the Patient's Account Number in Block 26 (e.g., 12-2S).

4. Review the completed claim to be sure all required blocks are properly completed. Compare your claim with the completed claim in Figure 12-13.

PLEASE DO NOT STAPLE IN THIS AREA

EOB ATTACHED

(SAMPLE ONLY - NOT APPROVED FOR USE)

CARRIER

[ ] [ ] PICA

HEALTH INSURANCE CLAIM FORM

PICA [ ] [ ]

| 1. MEDICARE (Medicare #) | MEDICAID (Medicaid #) | CHAMPUS (Sponsor's SSN) | CHAMPVA (VA File #) | GROUP HEALTH PLAN (SSN or ID) | FECA BLK LUNG (SSN) | OTHER [X] (ID) | 1a. INSURED'S I.D. NUMBER (FOR PROGRAM IN ITEM 1) 222017681 |

2. PATIENT'S NAME (Last Name, First Name, Middle Initial)
PATIENT MARY SUE

3. PATIENT'S BIRTH DATE   MM 10 | DD 10 | YY 1959   SEX   M [ ]   F [X]

4. INSURED'S NAME (Last Name, First Name, Middle Initial)
PATIENT JAMES W

5. PATIENT'S ADDRESS (No. Street)
91 HOME STREET

6. PATIENT RELATIONSHIP TO INSURED
Self [ ]   Spouse [X]   Child [ ]   Other [ ]

7. INSURED'S ADDRESS (No. Street)
SAME

CITY NOWHERE   STATE US

8. PATIENT STATUS
Single [ ]   Married [X]   Other [ ]

CITY   STATE

ZIP CODE 12367   TELEPHONE (Include Area Code) 101 201 8989

Employed [ ]   Full-Time Student [ ]   Part-Time Student [ ]

ZIP CODE   TELEPHONE (INCLUDE AREA CODE) (   )

9. OTHER INSURED'S NAME (Last Name, First Name, Middle Initial)
PATIENT JAMES W

10. IS PATIENT'S CONDITION RELATED TO:

11. INSURED'S POLICY GROUP OR FECA NUMBER

a. OTHER INSURED'S POLICY OR GROUP NUMBER
22335544   AA2

a. EMPLOYMENT? (CURRENT OR PREVIOUS)   YES [ ]   NO [X]

a. INSURED'S DATE OF BIRTH   MM 03 | DD 01 | YY 1948   SEX   M [X]   F [ ]

b. OTHER INSURED'S DATE OF BIRTH   MM 03 | DD 01 | YY 1948   SEX   M [X]   F [ ]

b. AUTO ACCIDENT?   PLACE (State)   YES [ ]   NO [X]

b. EMPLOYER'S NAME OR SCHOOL NAME

c. EMPLOYER'S NAME OR SCHOOL NAME
ANYWHERE WATER COMPANY

c. OTHER ACCIDENT?   YES [ ]   NO [X]

c. INSURANCE PLAN NAME OR PROGRAM NAME
CONN GENERAL

d. INSURANCE PLAN NAME OR PROGRAM NAME
CONN GENERAL

10d. RESERVED FOR LOCAL USE

d. IS THERE ANOTHER HEALTH BENEFIT PLAN?
[X] YES   [ ] NO   If yes, return to and complete item 9 a - d.

READ BACK OF FORM BEFORE COMPLETING & SIGNING THIS FORM.
12. PATIENT'S OR AUTHORIZED PERSON'S SIGNATURE I authorize the release of any medical or other information necessary to process this claim. I also request payment of government benefits either to myself or to the party who accepts assignment below.

SIGNED SIGNATURE ON FILE   DATE

13. INSURED'S OR AUTHORIZED PERSON'S SIGNATURE I authorize payment of medical benefits to the undersigned physician or supplier for services described below.

SIGNED SIGNATURE ON FILE

PATIENT AND INSURED INFORMATION

14. DATE OF CURRENT: MM 01 | DD 07 | YY YYYY   ILLNESS (First symptom) OR INJURY (Accident) OR PREGNANCY (LMP)

15. IF PATIENT HAS HAD SAME OR SIMILAR ILLNESS, GIVE FIRST DATE   MM | DD | YY

16. DATES PATIENT UNABLE TO WORK IN CURRENT OCCUPATION   FROM MM | DD | YY   TO MM | DD | YY

17. NAME OF REFERRING PHYSICIAN OR OTHER SOURCE

17a. I.D. NUMBER OF REFERRING PHYSICIAN ★

18. HOSPITALIZATION DATES RELATED TO CURRENT SERVICES   FROM MM 01 | DD 07 | YY YYYY   TO MM 01 | DD 09 | YY YYYY

19. RESERVED FOR LOCAL USE

20. OUTSIDE LAB?   [ ] YES   [X] NO $ CHARGES

21. DIAGNOSIS OR NATURE OF ILLNESS OR INJURY. (RELATE ITEMS 1, 2, 3, OR 4 TO ITEM 24E BY LINE)
1. 794.31
2. 413.1
3. 272.4
4.

22. MEDICAID RESUBMISSION CODE   ORIGINAL REF. NO.

23. PRIOR AUTHORIZATION NUMBER

24. A. DATE(S) OF SERVICE From MM DD YY To MM DD YY	B. Place of Service	C. Type of Service	D. PROCEDURES, SERVICES, OR SUPPLIES (Explain Unusual Circumstances) CPT/HCPCS MODIFIER	E. DIAGNOSIS CODE	F. $ CHARGES	G. DAYS OR UNITS	H. EPSDT Family Plan	I. EMG	J. COB	K. RESERVED FOR LOCAL USE
1 01 07 YYYY	21		99223	1	150 00	1				
2 01 08 YYYY	21		99221	1	75 00	1				
3 01 09 YYYY	21		99238	1	75 00	1				
4										
5										
6										

25. FEDERAL TAX I.D. NUMBER   11-123452   SSN [ ]   EIN [X]

26. PATIENT'S ACCOUNT NO.   12-2S

27. ACCEPT ASSIGNMENT? (For govt. claims, see back)   [X] YES   [ ] NO

28. TOTAL CHARGE $ 300 00

29. AMOUNT PAID $

30. BALANCE DUE $ 300 00

31. SIGNATURE OF PHYSICIAN OR SUPPLIER INCLUDING DEGREES OR CREDENTIALS (I certify that the statements on the reverse apply to this bill and are made a part thereof.)
ERIN A HELPER MD
SIGNED   DATE MMDDYYYY

32. NAME AND ADDRESS OF FACILITY WHERE SERVICES WERE RENDERED (If other than home or office)
GOODMEDICINE HOSPITAL
ANYWHERE STREET
ANYWHERE US 12345

33. PHYSICIAN'S SUPPLIER'S BILLING NAME, ADDRESS, ZIP CODE & PHONE #
(101) 111 1234
ERIN A HELPER MD
101 MEDIC DRIVE
ANYWHERE USA 12345
PIN#   GRP#

PHYSICIAN OR SUPPLIER INFORMATION

(SAMPLE ONLY - NOT APPROVED FOR USE)

PLEASE PRINT OR TYPE

SAMPLE FORM 1500
SAMPLE FORM 1500   SAMPLE FORM 1500

FIGURE 12-13 Completed secondary claim

SUMMARY

- The Insurance Plan Comparison Chart that you created is a helpful tool for accurately completing CMS-1500 commercial claims.
- While the step-by-step commercial claims instructions in this chapter are generally recognized nationwide, some payers may require variations in some of the blocks.
- Primary claims submission is determined when the patient is covered:
  - by just one health insurance plan.
  - by a large EHGP and is also a Medicare beneficiary.
  - by a small or large EHGP on which the patient is designated the policyholder, and the patient is also listed as a dependent on another EGHP.
  - as a child on two or more plans. The primary policyholder is determined according to the *birthday rule*.
- This chapter organizes CMS-1500 claim instructions in sections:
  - Blocks 1 through 13 (patient and policy information)
  - Blocks 14 through 23 (dates of service and diagnosis data)
  - Block 24 (procedures, services, and supplies)
  - Blocks 25 through 33 (provider information)

  (Subsequent chapters do not separate instructions in sections.)
- When a patient is covered by primary *and* secondary and/or supplemental health insurance plans, modifications are made to the CMS-1500 claim:
  - If the same payer provides both primary and secondary coverage, just one claim is submitted, and information is entered in Blocks 9 through 11d.
  - If the secondary payer is different from the primary payer, a primary claim is submitted to the primary payer and a new claim is generated and submitted to the secondary payer, with information entered in Blocks 1a, 4, 7, 9 through 9d, and 11 through 11d.
- When completing CMS-1500 commercial claims for case studies in this text and the Workbook, the following special instructions apply:
  - Block 10d—Leave blank
  - Block 12—Enter SIGNATURE ON FILE
  - Block 13—Enter SIGNATURE ON FILE
  - Block 17a—Enter the payer assigned PIN, if applicable
  - Block 19—Leave blank
  - Block 20—Enter an X in the NO box
  - Block 23—Leave blank
  - Block 24E—Enter just one diagnosis reference number on each line
  - Block 25—Enter the EIN with a hyphen
  - Block 26—Enter the case study number (e.g., 12-2). If the patient has both primary and secondary coverage, enter a P (for primary) next to the number (on the primary claim) and an S (for secondary) next to the number (on the secondary claim)
  - Block 27—Enter an X in the YES box (because all providers are PARs for commercial plans)

- Block 31—Enter provider's complete name with credentials (instead of a signature as indicated in the chapter instructions). This will allow you to completely generate claims using the student software (instead of having to print the claim and sign it)
- Block 32—If Block 18 contains dates and/or Block 20 contains an X in the YES box, enter the name and address of the responsible provider in Block 32 (e.g., hospital, outside laboratory)
- Block 33—Leave PIN and GRP# blank

STUDY CHECKLIST

☐ Read the textbook chapter, and prepare the Insurance Plan Comparison Chart.

☐ Install the software from the disk (instructions are in Appendix V), and become familiar with the software.

☐ Complete CMS-1500 claims for each chapter encounter form.

☐ Complete the chapter review.

☐ Complete Web Tutor assignments, and take online quizzes.

☐ Complete commercial claims for cases located in Appendices I and II.

☐ Complete the Workbook chapter, verifying answers with your instructor.

☐ Form a study group with classmates to discuss chapter concepts in preparation for an exam.

REVIEW

TRUE/FALSE

Enter a T if the statement is true. Enter an F if the statement is false.

1. ☐ T ☐ F   When the patient signs Block 13 of the CMS-1500 to "assign benefits," the provider accepts, as payment in full, whatever the payer reimburses for the service provided.

2. ☐ T ☐ F   Commercial supplemental policies cover deductibles and copayments/coinsurances associated with primary policies.

3. ☐ T ☐ F   SIGNATURE ON FILE in Blocks 12 or 13 indicates that the patient has signed a special form that has been placed in the financial or medical record.

4. ☐ T ☐ F   A *place of service* code identifies the classification of the procedure or medical service.

5. ☐ T ☐ F   To *accept assignment* means that the patient has authorized the provider to be directly reimbursed for services rendered.

6. ☐ T ☐ F   When entering ICD-9-CM codes in Block 21, it is appropriate to enter the decimal.

7. ☐ T ☐ F   When entering modifiers in Block 24D, do not enter the hyphen between the CPT code and the modifier.

8. ☐ T ☐ F   In Block 24E, it is acceptable to enter either the reference number from Block 21 or the ICD-9-CM code number.

9. ☐ T ☐ F   When totaling the charges in Block 28, if a credit is due the patient, it is appropriate to indicate this on the claim.

SHORT ANSWER

Briefly respond to each.

10. Explain how claims are handled for patients between the ages of 19 and 23, who are full-time students, and are listed as dependents on their family's insurance policy.

11. What is the significance of entering an X in the YES box in Block 10B?

12. What does the abbreviation EGHP mean?

13. What does it mean when a patient signs Block 12

14. In what circumstances would Block 18 be completed?

15. What does it mean when an X is entered in the YES box in Block 20?

16. What do the abbreviations POS and TOS mean?

17. How is Block 24F completed when a patient receives identical services during the same encounter (e.g., on the same date)?

18. What does placing an X in Block 24I indicate?

19. What does COB mean?

20. What date is entered in Block 14?

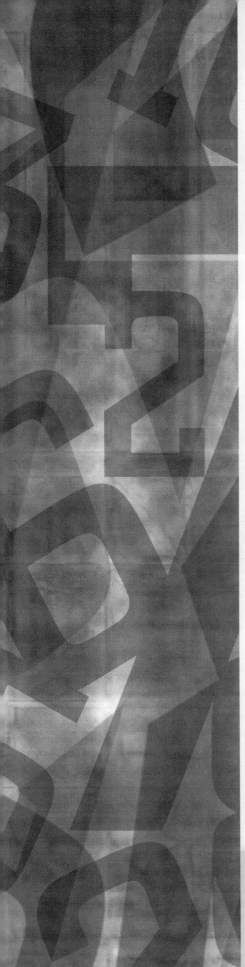

KEY TERMS

American Hospital Association (AHA)

Away From Home Care®

BCBS basic coverage

BCBS major medical (MM) coverage

BlueCard® PPO

BlueCard® Program

BlueCard® Worldwide

BluesCONNECT®

Blue Cross (BC)

Blue Cross/Blue Shield (BCBS)

Blue Shield (BS)

coordinated home health and hospice
care

Federal Employee Health Benefits
Program (FEHBP)

Federal Employee Program (FEP)

for-profit corporations

Government-Wide Service Benefit
Plan

host plan

indemnity coverage

medical emergency care rider

Medicare supplemental plans

member

member hospitals

nonprofit corporations

outpatient pretreatment authorization
plan (OPAP)

PPN provider

precertification

preferred provider network (PPN)

prospective authorization

rider

second surgical opinion (SSO)

service location

special accidental injury rider

third-party administrator (TPA)

usual, customary, and reasonable
(UCR)

Chapter 13 | Blue Cross and Blue Shield Plans

OBJECTIVES

Upon successful completion of this chapter, you should be able to:

1. Define key terms.

2. Explain the function of the national Blue Cross and Blue Shield Association.

3. List four features that make BCBS plans different from other commercial plans.

4. List the advantages of being a BCBS participating provider.

5. Describe the features of BCBS basic benefits.

6. List typical services found in Major Medical coverage.

7. Explain the benefits of special accidental injury riders/clauses.

8. Explain the benefits of a medical emergency rider.

9. Describe the purpose of the BlueCard Program.

10. Explain how a BlueCard patient is identified.

11. Compare how PARs and nonPARs process BlueCard claims.

12. Compare the major differences between BCBS, PPA, and POS plans.

13. State the deadline for filing BCBS claims.

14. Complete BCBS claims accurately.

INTRODUCTION

Blue Cross (BC) and *Blue Shield (BS)* plans are perhaps the best known medical insurance programs in the United States. They began as two separate *prepaid health plans* selling contracts to individuals or groups for coverage of specified medical expenses as long as the premiums were paid.

Instructions for completing claims in this chapter are devoted to fee-for-service BCBS claims only.

HISTORY OF BLUE CROSS AND BLUE SHIELD

Origin of Blue Cross

The forerunner of what is known today as the **Blue Cross** plan began in 1929 when Baylor University Hospital in Dallas, Texas, approached teachers in the Dallas school district with a plan that would guarantee up to 21 days of hospitalization per year for subscribers and each of their dependents in exchange for a $6 annual premium. This plan was accepted by the teachers and worked so well that the concept soon spread across the country. Early plans specified which hospital subscribers and their dependents could use for care. By 1932, some plans modified this concept and organized community-wide programs that allowed the subscriber to be hospitalized in one of several **member hospitals**, which had signed contracts to provide services for special rates.

The blue cross symbol was first used in 1933 by the St. Paul, Minnesota plan and was adopted in 1939 by the **American Hospital Association (AHA)** when it became the approving agency for accreditation of new prepaid hospitalization plans. In 1948, the need for additional national coordination among plans arose, and the Blue Cross Association was created. In 1973, the AHA deeded the right to both the name and the use of the blue cross symbol to the Blue Cross Association. At that time, the symbol was updated to the trademark in use today.

Origin of Blue Shield

The **Blue Shield** plans began as a resolution passed by the House of Delegates at an American Medical Association meeting in 1938. This resolution supported the concept of voluntary health insurance that would encourage physicians to cooperate with prepaid health care plans. The first known plan was formed in Palo Alto, California, in 1939 and was called the California Physicians' Service. This plan stipulated that physicians' fees for covered medical services would be paid in full by the plan if the subscriber earned less than $3,000 a year. When the subscriber earned more than $3,000 a year, a small percentage of the physician's fee would be paid by the patient. This patient responsibility for a small percentage of the health care fee is the forerunner of today's industry-wide required patient coinsurance or copay.

The blue shield design was first used as a trademark by the Buffalo, New York plan in 1939. The name and symbol were formally adopted by the Associated Medical Care Plans, formed in 1948, as the approving agency for accreditation of new Blue Shield plans adopting programs created in the spirit of the California Physicians' Service program. In 1951, this accrediting organization changed its name to the National Association of Blue Shield Plans. Like the Blue Cross plans, each Blue Shield plan in the association was established as a separate, nonprofit corporate entity, that issued its own contracts and plans within a specific geographic area.

Blue Cross/Blue Shield Joint Ventures

Blue Cross plans originally covered only hospital bills, and Blue Shield plans covered fees for physician services. Over the years, both programs increased their coverage to include almost all health care services. In many areas of the country, there was close cooperation between Blue Cross and Blue Shield plans that resulted in the formation of joint ventures in some states where the two corporations were housed in one building. In these joint ventures, the **Blue Cross/Blue Shield (BCBS)** corporations shared one building and computer services but maintained separate corporate identities.

BCBS Association

In 1977, the membership of the separate Blue Cross and Blue Shield national associations voted to combine personnel under the leadership of a single president, responsible to both Boards of Directors. Further consolidation occurred in 1986 when the Boards of Directors of the separate national Blue Cross and Blue Shield associations merged into a single corporation named the **Blue Cross Blue Shield Association (BCBSA)**.

Today, BCBSA consists of over 450 independent, locally operated Blue Cross and Blue Shield Plans that collectively provide health care coverage to more than 80 million Americans and serve more than one million enrolled in the Medicare+Choice program (discussed in Chapter 14). The BCBSA is located in Chicago, Illinois, and performs the following functions:

- establishes standards for new plans and programs
- assists local plans with enrollment activities, national advertising, public education, professional relations, and statistical and research activities
- serves as the primary contractor for processing Medicare hospital, hospice, and home health care claims
- coordinates nationwide BCBS plans

The association is also the registered owner of the BC and BS trademarks (Figure 13-1).

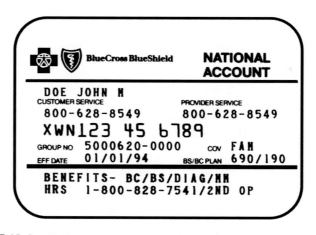

FIGURE 13-1 BCBS National Account identification card (Courtesy of Care First Blue Cross Blue Shield)

The Changing Business Structure

Strong competition among all health insurance companies in the United States emerged during the 1990s and resulted in the following:

- Mergers occurred among BCBS regional corporations (within a state or with neighboring states) and names no longer had regional designations.

    EXAMPLE: Care First BCBS is the name for the corporation that resulted from a merger between BCBS of Maryland and Washington, D.C. BCBS.

- Blue Cross Blue Shield Association no longer requires plans to be nonprofit (as of 1994).

Regional corporations that needed additional capital to compete with commercial for-profit insurance carriers, petitioned their respective state legislatures to allow conversion from their nonprofit status to for-profit corporations. **Nonprofit corporations** are charitable, educational, civic, or humanitarian organizations whose profits are returned to the program of the corporation rather than distributed to shareholders and officers of the corporation. Because no profits of the organization are distributed to shareholders, the government does not tax the organization's income. **For-profit corporations** pay taxes on profits generated by the corporation's for-profit enterprises and pay dividends to shareholders on after-tax profits.

Some BCBS nonprofit to for-profit conversions include:

- Blue Cross Blue Shield of Missouri (1994), which transferred 80% of managed care business to RightChoice, a for-profit HMO subsidiary.
- Blue Cross of California (1996), now called WellPoint Health Networks.
- Blue Cross Blue Shield of Georgia (1996).
- Trigon Blue Cross Blue Shield of Virginia (1997), now called Anthem.
- Triple-S (1999) (Seguros de Servicio de Salud de Puerto Rico, Inc.).

While some BCBS plans have converted to for-profit companies, state regulators and courts are scrutinizing these transactions, some on a retroactive basis, to ensure that charitable assets are preserved. Some organizations such as Blue Cross Blue Shield of Missouri are engaged in litigation over whether *restructuring* (e.g., placing assets in a for-profit subsidiary) is actually a conversion. Other organizations, such as Empire BCBS in New York State, publicly acknowledge its nonprofit obligations and agree to preserve 100% of its assets for nonprofit charitable purposes as part of proposed conversions to for-profit corporations.

BCBS Distinctive Features

The "Blues" were pioneers in nonprofit, prepaid health care, and they possessed features that distinguished them from other commercial health insurance groups.

1. They maintain negotiated contracts with providers of care. In exchange for such contracts, BCBS agrees to perform the following services:
   - make prompt, direct payments of claims
   - maintain regional professional representatives to assist participating providers with claim problems
   - provide educational seminars, workshops, billing manuals, and newsletters to keep participating providers up-to-date on BCBS insurance procedures

2. BCBS plans, in exchange for tax relief for their nonprofit status, are forbidden by state law from canceling coverage for an individual because he or she is in poor health or if BCBS payments to providers have far exceeded the average. Policies issued by the nonprofit entity can only be canceled or an individual disenrolled:
   - when premiums are not paid.
   - if the plan can prove that fraudulent statements were made on the application for coverage.

For-profit commercial plans have the right to cancel a policy at renewal time if the patient moves into a region of the country in which the company is not licensed to sell insurance or if the person is a high user of benefits and has purchased a plan that does not include a noncancellation clause.

3. BCBS plans must obtain approval from their respective state insurance commissioner for any rate increases and/or benefit changes that affect all BCBS members within the state. For-profit commercial plans have more freedom to increase rates and modify general benefits without state approval when the premium is due for annual renewal (if there is no clause restricting such action in the policy).

4. BCBS plans must allow conversion from group to individual coverage and guarantee the transferability of membership from one local plan to another when a change in residency moves a policyholder into an area served by a different BCBS corporation.

Participating Providers

As mentioned earlier, the "Blues" were pioneers in negotiating contracts with providers of care. A *participating provider (PAR)* is a health care provider who enters into a contract with a BCBS corporation and agrees to:

- submit insurance claims for all BCBS subscribers.
- provide access to the Provider Relations Department, which assists the PAR provider in resolving claims or payment problems.
- write off (make a fee adjustment) for the difference or balance between the amount charged by the provider and the approved fee established by the insurer.
- bill patients for only the deductible and copay/coinsurance amounts that are based on BCBS allowed fees and the full charged fee for any uncovered service.

In return, BCBS corporations agreed to:

- make direct payments to PARs.
- conduct regular training sessions for PAR billing staff.
- provide free billing manuals and PAR newsletters.
- maintain a provider representative department to assist with billing/payment problems.
- publish the name, address, and specialty of all PARs in a directory distributed to BCBS subscribers and PARs.

Preferred Providers

PARs can also contract to participate in the plan's **preferred provider network (PPN)**, a program that requires providers to adhere to managed care provisions. In this contractual agreement, the **PPN provider** (a provider who has signed a PPN contract) agrees to accept the PPN allowed rate, which is generally 10% lower than the PAR allowed rate. The provider further agrees to uphold all cost containment, utilization, and quality assurance programs of the PPN program. In return for a PPN agreement, the "Blues" agree to notify PPN providers in writing of new employer groups and hospitals that have entered into PPN contracts and to maintain a PPN directory.

Nonparticipating Providers

Nonparticipating providers (nonPAR) have not signed participating provider contracts, and they expect to be paid the full fee charged for services rendered. In these cases, the patient may be asked to pay the provider in full and then be reimbursed by BCBS the allowed fee for each service minus the patient's deductible and copayment obligations. When the provider agrees to file the claim for the patient, the insurance company will send the payment for the claim directly to the patient and not to the provider.

BLUE CROSS BLUE SHIELD PLANS

Blue Cross Blue Shield (BCBS) coverage includes the following programs:

- Fee-for-Service
- Indemnity
- Managed Care Plans
    - Coordinated Home Health and Hospice Care
    - Exclusive Provider Organization (EPO)
    - Health Maintenance Organization (HMO)
    - Outpatient Pretreatment Authorization Plan (OPAP)
    - Point-of-Service (POS) plan
    - Preferred Provider Organization (PPO)
    - Second Surgical Opinion (SSO)
- Away From Home Care®
- Federal Employee Program (FEP)
- Medicare Supplemental Plans

INTERNET LINK

The http://www.bcbshealthissues.com Web site contains health care news about BCBS and general health care issues.

Fee-for-Service Coverage

BCBS *fee-for-service* coverage is selected by (1) individuals who do not have access to a group plan, and (2) many small business employers. These contracts are divided into two types of coverage within one policy:

- basic coverage
- major medical (MM) benefits

Minimum benefits under **BCBS basic coverage** routinely include the following services:

- Hospitalizations
- Diagnostic laboratory services
- X-rays
- Surgical fees
- Assistant surgeon fees
- Obstetric care
- Intensive care
- Newborn care
- Chemotherapy for cancer

BCBS major medical (MM) coverage includes the following services in addition to basic coverage:

- Office visits
- Outpatient nonsurgical treatment
- Physical and occupational therapy
- Purchase of durable medical equipment (DME)
- Mental health visits
- Allergy testing and injections
- Prescription drugs
- Private duty nursing (when medically necessary)
- Dental care required as a result of a covered accidental injury

Major medical services are usually subject to patient deductible and copayment requirements, and in a few cases the patient may be responsible for filing claims for these benefits.

Some of the contracts also include one or more **riders**, which are special clauses stipulating additional coverage over and above the standard contract. Common riders include special accidental injury and medical emergency care coverage.

The **special accidental injury rider** covers 100 % of nonsurgical care sought and rendered within 24 to 72 hours (varies according to the policy) of the accidental injury. Surgical care is subject to any established contract basic plan deductible and patient copayment requirements. Outpatient follow-up care for these accidental injuries is not included in the accidental injury rider, but will be covered if the patient has supplemental coverage.

The **medical emergency care rider** covers *immediate treatment sought and received for sudden, severe, and unexpected conditions* that if not treated would place the patient's health in permanent jeopardy or cause permanent impairment or dysfunction of an organ or body part. Chronic or subacute conditions do not qualify for treatment under the medical emergency rider unless the symptoms suddenly become acute and require immediate medical attention. Special attention must be paid to the ICD-9-CM coding (Blocks 21 and 24D) on the CMS-1500 claim to ensure that services rendered under the medical emergency rider are linked to diagnoses or reported symptoms generally accepted as conditions that require immediate care. Nonspecific conditions such as "acute upper respiratory infection" or "bladder infection" would not be included on the medical emergency diagnosis list.

Indemnity Coverage

BCBS **indemnity coverage** offers choice and flexibility to subscribers who want to receive a full range of benefits along with the freedom to use any licensed health care provider. Coverage includes hospital-only or comprehensive hospital and medical coverage. Subscribers share the cost of benefits through coinsurance options, do not have to select a primary care provider, and do not need a referral to see a provider.

Managed Care Plans

Managed care is a health care delivery system that provides health care and controls costs through a network of physicians, hospitals, and other health care providers. BCBS managed care plans include the coordinated home health and hospice care program, exclusive provider organizations, health maintenance organizations, outpatient pretreatment authorization plans, point-of-service plans, preferred provider organizations, and second surgical opinions.

The **coordinated home health and hospice care** program allows patients with this option to elect an alternative to the acute care setting. The patient's physician must file a treatment plan with the case manager assigned to review and coordinate the case. All authorized services must be rendered by personnel from a licensed home health agency or approved hospice facility.

An *exclusive provider organization (EPO)* is similar to a health maintenance organization that provides health care services through a network of doctors, hospitals and other health care providers, except that members are not required to select a primary care provider (PCP), and they do not need a referral to see a specialist. However, they must obtain services from EPO providers only or the patient is responsible for the charges. A *primary care provider (PCP)* is a physician or other medical professional that serves as a subscriber's first contact with a plan's health care system. The PCP is also known as a personal care physician or personal care provider.

All BCBS corporations now offer at least one *health maintenance organization (HMO)* plan that assumes or shares the financial and health care delivery risks associated with providing comprehensive medical services to subscribers in return for a fixed, prepaid fee. Some plans were for-profit acquisitions; others were developed as separate nonprofit plans. Examples of plan names are *Capital Care* and *Columbia Medical Plan*. Because familiar BCBS names are not always used in the plan name, some HMOs may not be easily recognized as BCBS plans. The BCBS trademarks, however, usually appear on the plan's ID cards and advertisements.

The **outpatient pretreatment authorization plan (OPAP)** requires preauthorization of outpatient physical, occupational, and speech therapy services. In addition, OPAP requires periodic treatment/progress plans to be filed. OPAP is a requirement for the delivery of certain health care services and is issued prior to the provision of services. OPAP is also known as **prospective authorization** or **precertification**.

A *point-of-service (POS) plan* allows subscribers to choose, at the time medical services are needed, whether they will go to a provider within the plan's network or outside the network. When subscribers go outside the network to seek care, out-of-pocket expenses and copayments generally increase. POS plans provide a full range of inpatient and outpatient services, and subscribers choose a primary care provider (PCP) from the carrier's PCP list. The PCP assumes responsibility for coordinating subscriber and dependent medical care, and the PCP is often referred to as the *gatekeeper* of the patient's medical care. The name and telephone number of the PCP appears on POS Plan ID cards, and written referral notices issued by the PCP are usually mailed to the appropriate local processing address following the transmission of an electronic claim. Because the PCP is responsible for authorizing all inpatient hospitalizations, a specialist's office should contact the PCP when hospitalization is necessary and follow up that call with one to the utilization control office at the local BCBS plan office.

NOTE: When subscribers go outside the network for health care, the approval of the PCP is not required, and costs are usually higher.

A *preferred provider organization (PPO)* offers discounted health care services to subscribers who use designated health care providers (who contract with the PPO) but also provides coverage for services rendered by health care providers who are not part of the PPO network. The BCBS PPO plan is sometimes described as a subscriber-driven program, and BCBS substitutes the terms *subscriber* (or **member**) for *policyholder* (used by other commercial carriers). In this type of plan, the subscriber (member) is responsible for remaining within the network of PPO providers and must request referrals to PPO specialists whenever possible. The subscriber must also adhere to the managed care requirements of the PPO policy, such as obtaining required second surgical opinions and/or hospital admission review. Failure to adhere to these requirements will result in denial of the surgical claim or reduced payment to the provider. In such cases, the patient is responsible for the difference or balance between the reduced payment and the normal PPO allowed rate.

The mandatory **second surgical opinion (SSO)** requirement is necessary when a patient is considering elective, nonemergency surgical care. The initial surgical recommendation must be made by a physician qualified to perform the anticipated surgery. If a second surgical opinion is not obtained prior to surgery, the patient's out-of-pocket expenses may be greatly increased. The patient or surgeon should contact the subscriber's BCBS local plan for instructions. In some cases, the second opinion must be obtained from a member of a select surgical panel. In other cases, the concurrence of the need for surgery from the patient's PCP may suffice.

Away From Home Care®

Blue Cross and Blue Shield organizations typically offer **Away From Home Care®** (Table 13-1) through guest membership programs that provide continuous care for subscribers who will be out of their service area for more than 90 consecutive days. In addition, subscribers can also receive care while traveling outside their service area (e.g., urgent care through BluesCONNECT®). Subscribers who travel outside the United States are typically covered for life-threatening and accidental injury emergencies only.

The **BlueCard® Program** allows Blue Cross and Blue Shield subscribers to receive local Blue Plan health care benefits while traveling or living outside their plan's area. More than 85% of U.S. hospitals and physicians contract with independent Blue Cross and Blue Shield Plans, and this program links health care professionals so that claim information can be electronically processed. Subscribers first call BlueCard Access® (800-810-BLUE) to obtain names and addresses of participating doctors and hospitals, then call their Blue Cross and/or Blue Shield Plan for precertification or prior authorization (telephone number is on subscriber's Plan ID card). When they arrive at the participating doctor's office or hospital, patients present their Plan ID card. Providers view the Plan ID card and call the BlueCard® eligibility number (800-676-BLUE) to provide the member's three-character alpha prefix (located at the beginning of the subscriber's ID number) so eligibility and coverage information can be verified. After providing care to the subscriber, the provider submits the claim (including alpha prefix) to the local Blue plan for reimbursement. The claim is electronically

TABLE 13-1 Sample coverage limitations in an Away From Home Care® program

BCBS PLAN	BLUECARD® PROGRAM	BLUECARD® PPO	BLUECARD® WORLDWIDE	BLUESCONNECT®
Traditional Indemnity	X		X	
EPO		X	X	
PPO		X	X	
HMO				X

routed to the subscriber's local plan for processing. The local plan pays the provider, and the subscriber's plan sends an explanation of benefits (EOB) to the subscriber.

NOTE: Subscribers do not pay for medical services other than usual out-of-pocket expenses (noncovered services, deductible, copayment, and coinsurance). •

BlueCard® PPO provides subscribers with access to a large national health care network of participating hospitals and physicians, specialists, and other health care practitioners. Subscribers call toll-free for network access and can receive low-cost care anywhere in the United States.

NOTE: Subscribers select a PPO that provides benefits similar to those available from their **host plan** (the plan in which the subscriber originally enrolled). The subscriber's identification card contains a "suitcase logo" (Figure 13-2). •

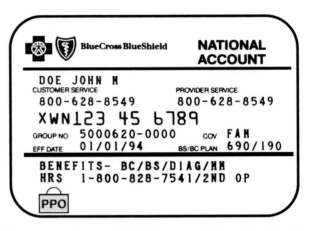

FIGURE 13-2 BCBS National Account PPO (Courtesy of Care First Blue Cross Blue Shield)

BlueCard® Worldwide is a program that allows subscribers who travel or live abroad to receive covered inpatient hospital care and physician services from a network of hospitals and doctors around the world. For emergencies, the subscriber should go directly to the nearest hospital. For referrals, subscribers call BlueCard Access® (800-810-BLUE) to locate names and addresses of participating doctors and hospitals. A medical assistance coordinator, in conjunction with a medical professional, schedules an appointment with a doctor or arranges hospitalization, if necessary. Subscribers contact their Blue Plan for precertification or prior authorization, where necessary, and show their Plan ID card to avoid up-front payment for inpatient participating hospital services. Subscribers are responsible for paying out-of-pocket expenses (deductible, copayment, coinsurance, and noncovered services). For outpatient hospital care or physician services, subscribers pay the provider, complete an international claim form, and send it to the BlueCard® Worldwide Service Center.

BluesCONNECT® allows subscribers to access a national network of physicians and hospitals and provides the following services:

- Urgent care for sudden illnesses or injuries that require immediate attention while traveling
- Guest membership for subscribers living in another city for at least 90 days
- Follow-up care while traveling

Federal Employee Program

The **Federal Employee Health Benefits Program (FEHBP)** (or **Federal Employee Program, FEP**) is an employer-sponsored health benefits program established by an Act of Congress in 1959. The FEP began covering federal employees on July 1, 1960, and now provides benefits to over nine million federal enrollees and dependents through contracts with about 300 insurance carriers. FEP is underwritten and administered by participating insurance plans (e.g., Blue Cross and Blue Shield Plans) that are called local plans. Claims are submitted to local plans that serve the location where the patient was seen (called a **service location**) regardless of the member's FEP Plan affiliation.

NOTE: The federal government's Office of Personnel Management (OPM) oversees administration of the FEHBP, and BCBS is just one of several payers who reimburse health care services. Others include the Alliance Health Plan (AHP), American Postal Workers Union (APWU) Health Plan, Government Employee Hospital Association (GEHA), Mail Handlers Benefit Plan (MHPB), National Association of Letter Carriers (NALC), and People Before Profit (PBP) Health Plan sponsored by the National League of Postmasters. ●

FEP cards contain the phrase **Government-Wide Service Benefit Plan** under the BCBS trademark. FEP enrollees have identification numbers that begin with the letter "R" followed by eight numeric digits (Figure 13-3). All ID cards contain the name of the government employee. Dependents' names do *not* appear on the card. A three-digit enrollment code is located on the front of the card to specify the option(s) elected when the government employee enrolled in the program. This code should be entered as the group ID number on BCBS claims.

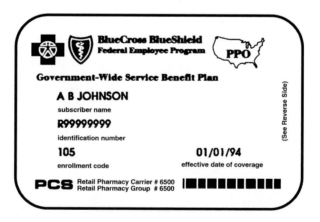

FIGURE 13-3 BCBS FEP PPO plan ID (Courtesy of Care First Blue Cross Blue Shield)

The four enrollment options are:
- 101—Individual, High Option Plan.
- 102—Family, High Option Plan.
- 104—Individual Standard (Low) Option Plan.
- 105—Family Standard (Low) Option Plan.

The FEP is considered a "managed fee-for-service program" and has generally operated as a PPO plan. The patient is responsible for ensuring that precertification is obtained for all hospitalizations except routine maternity care, home health and hospice care, and emergency hospitalization within 48 hours of admission. In 1997, a POS product was introduced in specific geographic sections of the country, and gradual expansion to a nationwide POS program is planned. The federal POS program requires that the subscriber select a PCP. This plan offers enhanced benefits and reduced out-of-pocket expenses when PCP referrals are obtained for specialty care.

Medicare Supplemental Plans

BCBS corporations offer several federally-designed and regulated **Medicare supplemental plans** (described in Chapter 14), which augment the Medicare program by paying for Medicare deductibles and copayments. These plans are better known throughout the industry as *Medigap Plans* and are usually identified by the word *Medigap* on the patient's plan ID card.

BILLING INFORMATION SUMMARY

A summary follows of nationwide billing issues for traditional BCBS fee-for-service claims. PAR providers are required to submit claims for subscribers.

Claims Processing

BCBS plans process their own claims. (CMS contracts with carriers and fiscal intermediaries to process claims for Medicare and Medicaid.)

Deadline for Filing Claims

The deadline is customarily one year from the date of service, unless otherwise specified in the subscriber's or provider's contracts.

Forms Used

Most corporations currently accept the CMS-1500 claim.

Inpatient and Outpatient Coverage

Inpatient and outpatient coverage may vary according to the plan. Many plans require second surgical opinions and prior authorization for elective hospitalizations. Information on the individual program requirements can be found in the BCBS local plan manual.

Deductible

The deductible will vary according to the BCBS plan. Consult the local corporation billing manual or eligibility status computerized phone bank for specific patient requirements. Patients enrolled in PPO plans may have no applicable deductibles for certain preventive medicine services.

Copayment/Coinsurance

Patient copayment/coinsurance requirements will vary according to the patient plan. The most common coinsurance amounts are 20% or 25%, although they may be as high as 50% for mental health services on some policies.

Allowable Fee Determination

The allowable fee will vary according to the program. Many corporations have begun to use the physician fee schedule to determine the allowed fees for each procedure. Other plans use a **usual, customary, and reasonable (UCR)** basis, which is the amount commonly charged for a particular medical service by providers within a particular geographic region for establishing their allowable rates. Participating providers must accept the allowable rate on all covered services and write off or adjust the difference or balance between the plan determined allowed amount and the amount billed. Patients are responsible for any deductible and copay/coinsurance described in their policy as well as full charges for uncovered services.

The transmittal notice sent to PAR and PPN providers clearly states the patient's total deductible and copayment/coinsurance responsibility for each claim submission.

NonPARs may collect the full fee from the patient. BCBS payments are then sent directly to the patient.

Assignment of Benefits

All claims filed by participating providers qualify for an **assignment of benefits** to the provider. This means that payment is made directly to the provider by BCBS.

Special Handling

1. Make it a habit and priority to retain a current photocopy of the front and back of all patient ID cards in the patient's file.

2. Claims for BlueCard patients with more than one insurance policy must be billed directly to the plan from which the program originated. Use the CMS-1500 claim.

3. NonPARs must bill the patient's plan for all non-national account patients with BlueCards.

4. Rebill claims not paid within 30 days.

5. Some mental health claims are forwarded to a **third-party administrator (TPA)**, a company that provides administrative services to health care plans and specializes in mental health case management. Check the back of the ID card and billing manual for special instructions.

Before working with BCBS claims, turn to page 399 in this chapter and complete the Review.

STEP-BY-STEP CLAIM INSTRUCTIONS

When working with case studies in this text, primary, secondary, and supplemental insurance information is included on each case study encounter form (Figure 13-5).

The step-by-step claim instructions in this section are used for completing primary BCBS claims. (At the end of the chapter, you will find instructions for completing secondary and supplemental claims.) Blocks 1 through 13 of the CMS-1500 claim contain patient identification and policy information. When reviewing the instructions, refer to Figure 13-4 for a sample of the CMS-1500 claim, Blocks 1 through 13. After review of the instructions, refer to the John Q. Public encounter form in Figure 13-5 and the completed CMS-1500 claim, Blocks 1 through 13, in Figure 13-6.

BCBS primary claim status is determined when the patient is:

- covered by only one BCBS policy.
- covered by both a government-sponsored plan and an employer-sponsored BCBS plan.
- covered by a non-BCBS plan that is not employer-sponsored.

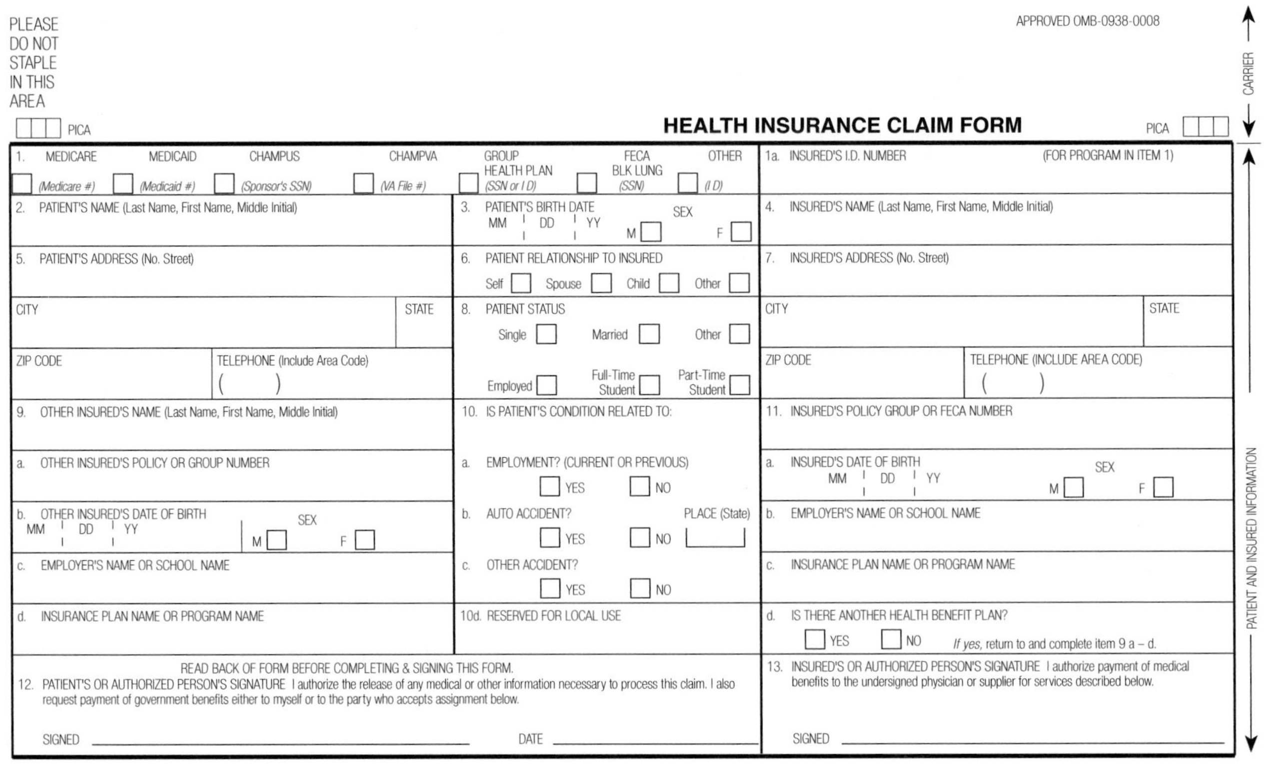
PLEASE DO NOT STAPLE IN THIS AREA

APPROVED OMB-0938-0008

CARRIER

PICA — HEALTH INSURANCE CLAIM FORM — PICA

1. MEDICARE (Medicare #) MEDICAID (Medicaid #) CHAMPUS (Sponsor's SSN) CHAMPVA (VA File #) GROUP HEALTH PLAN (SSN or I D) FECA BLK LUNG (SSN) OTHER (I D)

1a. INSURED'S I.D. NUMBER (FOR PROGRAM IN ITEM 1)

2. PATIENT'S NAME (Last Name, First Name, Middle Initial)

3. PATIENT'S BIRTH DATE MM DD YY SEX M F

4. INSURED'S NAME (Last Name, First Name, Middle Initial)

5. PATIENT'S ADDRESS (No. Street)

6. PATIENT RELATIONSHIP TO INSURED Self Spouse Child Other

7. INSURED'S ADDRESS (No. Street)

CITY STATE

8. PATIENT STATUS Single Married Other

CITY STATE

ZIP CODE TELEPHONE (Include Area Code) ( )

Employed Full-Time Student Part-Time Student

ZIP CODE TELEPHONE (INCLUDE AREA CODE) ( )

9. OTHER INSURED'S NAME (Last Name, First Name, Middle Initial)

10. IS PATIENT'S CONDITION RELATED TO:

11. INSURED'S POLICY GROUP OR FECA NUMBER

a. OTHER INSURED'S POLICY OR GROUP NUMBER

a. EMPLOYMENT? (CURRENT OR PREVIOUS) YES NO

a. INSURED'S DATE OF BIRTH MM DD YY SEX M F

b. OTHER INSURED'S DATE OF BIRTH MM DD YY SEX M F

b. AUTO ACCIDENT? YES NO PLACE (State)

b. EMPLOYER'S NAME OR SCHOOL NAME

c. EMPLOYER'S NAME OR SCHOOL NAME

c. OTHER ACCIDENT? YES NO

c. INSURANCE PLAN NAME OR PROGRAM NAME

d. INSURANCE PLAN NAME OR PROGRAM NAME

10d. RESERVED FOR LOCAL USE

d. IS THERE ANOTHER HEALTH BENEFIT PLAN? YES NO *If yes,* return to and complete item 9 a – d.

READ BACK OF FORM BEFORE COMPLETING & SIGNING THIS FORM.

12. PATIENT'S OR AUTHORIZED PERSON'S SIGNATURE I authorize the release of any medical or other information necessary to process this claim. I also request payment of government benefits either to myself or to the party who accepts assignment below.

SIGNED ______ DATE ______

13. INSURED'S OR AUTHORIZED PERSON'S SIGNATURE I authorize payment of medical benefits to the undersigned physician or supplier for services described below.

SIGNED ______

PATIENT AND INSURED INFORMATION

FIGURE 13-4 Blocks 1 through 13 of the CMS-1500 claim

- designated as the policyholder of one employer-sponsored plan and is also listed as a dependent on another employer-sponsored plan.

NOTE: Insurance carriers frequently change billing rules and instructions. Coding and insurance specialists should be made aware of all changes and can obtain updates from a variety of sources (e.g., professional publications, Internet-based listservs, and payer Web sites). Providers also receive publications that contain valuable information pertaining to coding and claims processing rules, regulations, and changes. Be sure these publications are circulated among staff members to ensure proper updating of databases, comparison charts, and billing/coding manuals.

Your instructor may substitute local requirements for specific CMS-1500 blocks. *Write these local instructions in the margins of this text for quick reference when working with case study assignments that are to be graded by the instructor.*

Block 1

Enter an X in the OTHER box.

Block 1a

Enter the BCBS ID number, two spaces, and the group identifier if provided.

Block 2

Enter the patient's name (last name first, followed by the first name and middle initial) as it is listed on the patient's insurance identification card. *Be sure to enter the last name first, followed by the first name and middle initial. Do not enter nick-*

ERIN A. HELPER, M.D.
101 Medic Dr, Anywhere US 12345
(101) 111-1234 (Office) • (101) 111-9292 (Fax)
EIN: 11-123341 **MCD:** EBH8881
UPIN: EH8888 **BCBS:** EH11881
BCBS GRP: 1204-P

Encounter Form

PATIENT INFORMATION:

Name:	Public, John Q.	
Address:	10A Senate Avenue	
City:	Anywhere	
State:	US	
Zip Code:	12345	
Telephone:	(101) 201-7891	
Gender:	Male	
Date of Birth:	03-09-1945	
Occupation:	Supervisor	
Employer:	Legal Research, Inc.	

INSURANCE INFORMATION:

Patient Number:	13-5
Place of Service:	Office
Primary Insurance Plan:	Blue Cross Blue Shield US
Primary Insurance Plan ID #:	WW123456
Group #:	A1
Primary Policyholder:	Public, John Q.
Policyholder Date of Birth:	03-09-1945
Relationship to Patient:	Self
Secondary Insurance Plan:	
Secondary Insurance Plan ID #:	
Secondary Policyholder:	

Patient Status ☒ Married ☐ Divorced ☐ Single ☐ Student

DIAGNOSIS INFORMATION

	Diagnosis	Code		Diagnosis	Code
1.	Bronchiopneumonia	485	5.		
2.	Urinary frequency	788.41	6.		
3.			7.		
4.			8.		

PROCEDURE INFORMATION

	Description of Procedure or Service	Date	Code	Charge
1.	Established patient office visit, level III	01-12-YYYY	99213	75.00
2.	Urinalysis, dipstick, automatic microscopy	01-12-YYYY	81001	10.00
3.	Chest X-ray, 2 views	01-12-YYYY	71020	50.00
4.				
5.				

SPECIAL NOTES: Recheck 01-19-YYYY. Referring Physician: Ivan Gooddoc, M.D. (UPIN IG7777).

FIGURE 13-5 John Q. Public encounter form

names or make errors in data entry because this may result in rejection of the claim.

Block 3

Enter the patient's birth date in the format MM DD YYYY (with spaces). Enter an X in the appropriate box to indicate the patient's gender.

Block 4

Enter SAME if the patient and policyholder are the same person. *If the patient is not the policyholder, enter the policyholder's name (last name first, followed by the first name and middle initial).*

Block 5

Enter the patient's mailing address on lines 1 and 2. Enter the five-digit zip code, area code, and telephone number on line 3. *Do not enter the parentheses for the area code because they are preprinted on the CMS-1500 claim. Do not enter the hyphen in the telephone number.*

Block 6

Enter an X in the appropriate box to indicate the patient's relationship to the policyholder (or insured).

Block 7

Enter SAME if the patient and policyholder are the same person. *If the patient is not the policyholder, enter the policyholder's address.*

Block 8

Enter an X in the appropriate boxes to indicate the patient's marital, employment, and/or student status.

> **NOTE:** If the patient is between 19 and 23, is a dependent on a family policy, and is a full-time student, the claim will not be paid unless the patient can prove full-time student status at the time of the encounter (obtained from an academic advisor, department chairperson, or registrar). Be sure to file written acknowledgment of the student's status with the first claim of each semester. ●

Block 9 through 9d

Leave blank. *Block 9 is completed if the patient has secondary insurance, discussed later in this chapter.*

Blocks 10a through 10c

Enter an X in the appropriate boxes to indicate whether the patient's condition is related to employment or an auto or other accident.

> **NOTE:** Entering an X in any of the YES boxes alerts the BCBS payer that another insurance plan might be liable for payment. The BCBS payer will not consider the claim unless the provider submits a copy of the transmittal notice from the liable party (e.g., workers' compensation, auto insurance). For employment-related conditions, another option is to attach a letter from workers' compensation rejecting payment for an on-the-job injury. ●

Block 10d

Leave blank.

Block 11

Leave blank.

Block 11a

If Block 4 contains a name other than the patient's, this is considered the policyholder (or subscriber). Enter the policyholder's birth date in MM DD YYYY format (with spaces), and enter an X to indicate the policyholder's gender.

> **NOTE:** Leave blank if Block 4 contains the word SAME, which means the patient and policyholder are the same person. (Birth date and gender information have already been entered in Block 3.) ●

Block 11b

Enter the name of the employer if BCBS insurance coverage is provided by an employer-sponsored group policy (EGHP). *Check the patient's insurance card for EGHP designation.*

Block 11c

Enter the name of the patient's BCBS carrier.

Block 11d

Enter an X in the NO box to indicate that the patient has no other health insurance coverage. *An X is entered in the YES box in Block 11d if the patient has secondary insurance, discussed later in this chapter.*

Block 12

Enter SIGNATURE ON FILE, and leave the date blank.

> **NOTE:** BCBS recommends that patients annually sign an authorization to release medical information. If the patient has not signed an authorization, the patient must sign and date Block 12. ●

Block 13

Leave blank.

FIGURE 13-6 Completed Blocks 1 through 13 for John Q. Public encounter form in Figure 13-5

NOTE: Assignment of benefits is a provision of the BCBS contract (signed by the patient) that authorizes BCBS to directly reimburse the provider for benefits due the patient.

EXERCISE 13-1 | Preparing the Insurance Plan Comparison Chart (Blocks 1 through 13)

NOTE: Complete all the steps in this exercise if you have not completed Exercise 12-1 prior to working in this chapter. If you have already completed Exercise 12-1 on page 344, use that Chart and proceed to Step 4 below.

OBJECTIVE: To create a useful reference as an aid to mastering the details of completing claims for six major insurance programs.

1. Make five copies of the Insurance Plan Comparison Chart located in Appendix II.

2. Enter the following titles in each column of the first row:
   - Commercial
   - BCBS
   - TRICARE STANDARD
   - Workers' Compensation

3. Enter the following block numbers in the first column of each page as follows:
   - Page 1—Blocks 1 through 9d
   - Page 2—Blocks 10 through 16
   - Page 3—Blocks 17 through 23
   - Page 4—Blocks 24A through 24K
   - Page 5—Blocks 25 through 33

4. Review the step-by-step instructions for Blocks 1 through 13, and enter abbreviated instructions on the chart.

5. Upon completion, save the chart because it will be used for additional exercises in this and other chapters.

EXERCISE 13-2 | BCBS Claim Blocks 1 through 13

This exercise requires two copies of a blank CMS-1500 claim. You may either make photocopies of the form in Appendix III of this text or print copies of the blank form using the CD-ROM in the back of the text. Instructions for installing the CD-ROM and printing blank forms are included in Appendix V.

1. Obtain two copies of the CMS-1500 claim, and review the instructions for Blocks 1 through 13 on your comparison chart.

2. On the first claim, complete Blocks 1 through 13 using your personal data for filing an employer-sponsored claim with a BCBS policy. If you do not have a BCBS insurance policy, or lack any of the required data use the following information:

   Policy ID: 123-45-6789

   Group number: ZZ34

   Policyholder: Yourself

   Name of the insurance carrier: BCBS

(continues)

Employer: Employee International
Other insurance: None

3. Save this form for use in Exercise 13-8.

4. Review the Mary Sue Patient encounter form (Figure 13-7).

5. Select the information needed for Blocks 1 through 13 from Figure 13-7, and enter the required information on the claim using Optical Scanning Guidelines. This may be completed by handwriting the information, using the Blank Form Mode on the disk found in the text, or entering

(continues)

ERIN A. HELPER, M.D.
101 Medic Dr, Anywhere US 12345
(101) 111-1234 (Office) • (101) 111-9292 (Fax)

EIN:	11-123341	**MCD:**	EBH8881
UPIN:	EH8888	**BCBS:**	EH11881
		BCBS GRP:	1204-P

Encounter Form

PATIENT INFORMATION:

Name:	Patient, Mary Sue
Address:	91 Home Street
City:	Nowhere
State:	US
Zip Code:	12367
Telephone:	(101) 201-8989
Gender:	Female
Date of Birth:	10-10-1959
Occupation:	Manager
Employer:	Happy Farm's Day Care

INSURANCE INFORMATION:

Patient Number:	13-7
Place of Service:	Office
Primary Insurance Plan:	BCBS US
Primary Insurance Plan ID #:	WWW1023456
Group #:	HFD6
Primary Policyholder:	Mary Sue Patient
Policyholder Date of Birth:	10-10-1959
Relationship to Patient:	Self
Secondary Insurance Plan:	
Secondary Insurance Plan ID #:	
Secondary Policyholder:	

Patient Status [X] Married   ☐ Divorced   ☐ Single   ☐ Student

DIAGNOSIS INFORMATION

Diagnosis		Code	Diagnosis		Code
1.	Strep throat	034.0	5.		
2.	IDDM	250.01	6.		
3.			7.		
4.			8.		

PROCEDURE INFORMATION

	Description of Procedure or Service	Date	Code	Charge
1.	Office visit, level II	01-12-YYYY	99212	65.00
2.	Strep test	01-12-YYYY	87880	12.00
3.				
4.				
5.				

SPECIAL NOTES:

FIGURE 13-7 Mary Sue Patient encounter form

the data using a typewriter. Instructions for installing the disk are found in Appendix V.

6. Review Blocks 1 through 13 of the claim to be sure all required blocks are properly completed.

NOTE: This same encounter form and claim will be used for Exercise 13-4. ●

Refer to Figure 13-5 (John Q. Public encounter form) and Figure 13-8 (Blocks 14 through 23 of the CMS-1500 claim.)

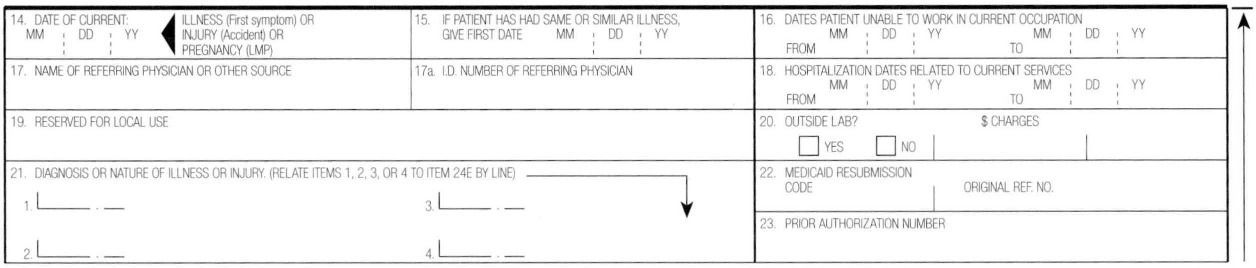

FIGURE 13-8 Blocks 14 through 23 of the CMS-1500 claim

Block 14

Enter the date of illness, injury, or pregnancy as MM DD YYYY (with spaces). If known, enter the date of the first symptoms or injury. For obstetric visits, enter the date of last menstrual period (if available in the documentation).

If the patient's history provides only an approximation of the date, count back from the approximated date and enter it on the claim.

EXAMPLE: Current date: 03/08/2004, and patient's record documents "injury 3 months ago." Enter the date in Block 14 as: 12 08 2003. ●

Block 15

Leave blank.

Block 16

Leave blank.

Block 17

Enter the *full name and credentials* of the referring/ordering physician(s) or other health care provider if any of the following services are to be entered in Block 24D: consultation, surgery, diagnostic testing, physical or occupational therapy, home health care, or durable medical equipment.

For Assistant Surgeon claims, enter the name of the attending surgeon.

NOTE: If the health care provider has assumed total care of the patient for an illness/injury, complete only block 17 for the first claim filed for the condition. ●

Block 17a

PAR Providers: Enter the payer assigned PIN (provider identification number).

NonPAR providers: Enter the social security number of the provider with no spaces or dashes.

Block 18

Enter the admission date and the discharge date *if* any procedure/service is rendered to a patient with inpatient status.

If the patient is still hospitalized, leave the TO box blank. Date format is MM DD YYYY (with spaces).

Block 19

Enter the name of the lab, procedures performed, and charges if the provider was directly billed for clinical analysis of specimens by an outside laboratory. An entry in this block requires an X to be entered in the YES box in Block 20 and laboratory codes reported in Blocks 24A through G.

Block 20

Enter an X in the YES box if the name of a lab is entered in Block 19; otherwise enter an X in the NO box.

Block 21

Enter the ICD-9-CM code number for the diagnoses or conditions treated. Do not enter the decimal. Enter a space instead because the decimal is preprinted on the CMS-1500 claim.

NOTE: Detailed instructions for entering codes in this block appear in Chapter 11.

Block 22

Leave blank. (Pertains to Medicaid claims only.)

Block 23

Enter the assigned authorization number when the patient's insurance plan requires specific services to be authorized by the patient's primary physician or the carrier's managed care department prior to the procedure being performed.

Refer to Figure 13-9 for completed Blocks 14 through 23 of the CMS-1500 claim.

EXERCISE 13-3 Continuation of Exercise 13-1

Review the instructions for completing Blocks 14 through 23, and enter in the appropriate block in the BCBS column of the Chart.

14. DATE OF CURRENT: ILLNESS (First symptom) OR INJURY (Accident) OR PREGNANCY (LMP) MM DD YY 01 12 YYYY	15. IF PATIENT HAS HAD SAME OR SIMILAR ILLNESS, GIVE FIRST DATE MM DD YY	16. DATES PATIENT UNABLE TO WORK IN CURRENT OCCUPATION MM DD YY MM DD YY FROM TO
17. NAME OF REFERRING PHYSICIAN OR OTHER SOURCE IVAN GOODDOC MD	17a. I.D. NUMBER OF REFERRING PHYSICIAN 1G7777	18. HOSPITALIZATION DATES RELATED TO CURRENT SERVICES MM DD YY MM DD YY FROM TO
19. RESERVED FOR LOCAL USE		20. OUTSIDE LAB? $ CHARGES ☐ YES ☒ NO
21. DIAGNOSIS OR NATURE OF ILLNESS OR INJURY. (RELATE ITEMS 1, 2, 3, OR 4 TO ITEM 24E BY LINE) 1. 485 . ___ 3. ___ . ___		22. MEDICAID RESUBMISSION CODE ORIGINAL REF. NO.
2. 788 41 4. ___ . ___		23. PRIOR AUTHORIZATION NUMBER

FIGURE 13-9 Completed blocks 14 through 23 for the John Q. Public encounter form in Figure 13-5

EXERCISE 13-4 | **Continuation of Exercise 13-2**

1. Review the Mary Sue Patient encounter form in Figure 13-7 for the diagnostic and treatment data.

2. Select the information needed for Blocks 14 through 23 and enter the required information on a new claim using Optical Scanning Guidelines.

   This may be completed by handwriting the information, using the Blank Form Mode on the disk found in the text, or entering the data using a typewriter. Instructions for installing the disk are found in Appendix V.

3. Review Blocks 14 through 23 of the claim to be sure all required blocks are properly completed.

4. Compare your claim with Figure 13-14.

   NOTE: This same claim will be used for Exercise 13-6. ●

Refer to Figure 13-10 for Block 24 of the CMS-1500 claim.

Block 24A

Enter eight-digit dates (MMDDYYYY without spaces) in both the FROM and the TO columns.

NOTE: The same date is entered in the FROM and TO columns if the same procedure or service was not performed on consecutive dates or the patient was treated on one date. ●

Block 24B

Enter the proper Place of Service (POS) code (Appendix II).

Block 24C

Leave blank.

24.	A DATE(S) OF SERVICE						B Place of Service	C Type of Service	D PROCEDURES, SERVICES, OR SUPPLIES (Explain Unusual Circumstances)		E DIAGNOSIS CODE	F $ CHARGES	G DAYS OR UNITS	H EPSDT Family Plan	I EMG	J COB	K RESERVED FOR LOCAL USE
	From MM	DD	YY	To MM	DD	YY			CPT/HCPCS	MODIFIER							
1																	
2																	
3																	
4																	
5																	
6																	

FIGURE 13-10 Block 24 of the CMS-1500 claim

Block 24D

Enter the five-digit CPT code or HCPCS level II code number and any required CPT or HCPCS modifier(s) for the procedure or service being reported. *Enter a space, not a hyphen, to separate the code number from the modifier or multiple modifiers.*

Block 24E

Enter the diagnosis *reference number* (1 through 4) for the ICD code number reported in Block 21 that justifies the medical necessity for each procedure reported in Block 24D.

This reference number should be followed by up to three reference numbers for any secondary or concurrent condition that applies to the procedure or service reported in Block 24D. Do not use commas to separate any multiple reference numbers.

Block 24F

Enter the fee charged to the patient's account for the procedure or service performed.

If identical, consecutive procedures are reported on this line, enter the total fee charged for the combined procedures.

Block 24G

Enter the number of units/days in this column. Some BCBS corporations require a three-digit number in this column; others do not.

The three-digit numbers are created by adding zeros in front of any single- or double-digit number (e.g., a unit of 1 becomes 001; a unit of 10 becomes 010). Special instructions are needed for computer systems not programmed to place three digits in this block. The BCBS manuals from the carriers that require the three-digit numbers say to disregard Optical Scanning Guidelines for this block by placing the first two digits in block 24G and the third digit on the upright line defining the border between blocks 24G and 24H.

When working with case studies in this text, enter a three-digit number for all entries.

Block 24H

Leave blank.

Block 24I

Leave blank.

Block 24J

Leave blank. (COB is the abbreviation for coordination of benefits.)

Block 24K

Leave blank.

● **NOTE:** This may be a local field required by some state carriers. ●

Refer to Figure 13-11 for completed Blocks 24A through 24K of the CMS-1500 claim.

24. A				B	C	D		E	F	G	H	I	J	K
DATE(S) OF SERVICE				Place of Service	Type of Service	PROCEDURES, SERVICES, OR SUPPLIES (Explain Unusual Circumstances)		DIAGNOSIS CODE	$ CHARGES	DAYS OR UNITS	EPSDT Family Plan	EMG	COB	RESERVED FOR LOCAL USE
From MM DD YY		To MM DD YY				CPT/HCPCS	MODIFIER							
1 0112YYYY		0112YYYY		11		99213		1	75 00	001				
2 0112YYYY		0112YYYY		11		71020		1	50 00	001				
3 0112YYYY		0112YYYY		11		81001		2	10 00	001				
4														
5														
6														

FIGURE 13-11 Completed Block 24 for John Q. Public encounter form in Figure 13-5

EXERCISE 13-5 **Continuation of Exercise 13-3**

Review the instructions for completing Blocks 24A through 24K, and enter a brief description of the instructions in the appropriate block in the BCBS column of the chart.

EXERCISE 13-6 **Continuation of Exercise 13-2**

1. Review the procedure data on the Mary Sue Patient encounter form (Figure 13-7).
2. Select the information needed for Blocks 24A through 24K and enter the required information on a claim using Optical Scanning Guidelines. This may be completed by handwriting the information, using the Blank Form Mode on the disk found in the text, or entering the data using a typewriter. Instructions for installing the disk are found in Appendix V.
3. Review Blocks 24A through 24K of the claim to be sure all required blocks are properly completed.
4. Compare your claim with Figure 13-14.

NOTE: This same claim will be used for Exercise 13-8.

Refer to Figure 13-12 for Blocks 25 through 33 of the CMS-1500 claim.

Block 25

Enter the billing entity's Employer Tax Identification Number (EIN) with the hyphen, and enter an X in the EIN box. If the provider does not have an EIN, enter the social security number (with hyphens), and enter an X in the SSN box.

Block 26

Enter the patient's account number.

Block 27

To *accept assignment* means the provider has negotiated a participating provider contract and has agreed to accept the carrier-determined, allowed fee for all services performed. Enter an X in the YES box if the provider has a participating provider

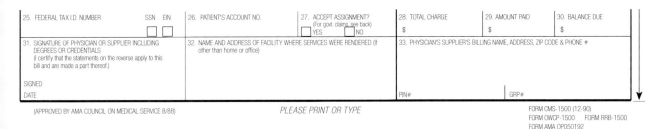

FIGURE 13-12 Blocks 25 through 33 of CMS-1500 claim

contract with the carrier. Enter an X in the NO box if the provider has not signed a participating provider contract with the carrier.

Block 28

Total all charges on the claim and enter in this block. This figure should never reflect negative charges or show a credit due to the patient.

If multiple claims for one patient are generated by the computer because more than six services must be reported, be sure the total charge recorded on each claim accurately represents the total of the items on each separate claim submitted.

Block 29

Leave blank.

Block 30

Leave blank.

Block 31

Enter the provider's complete name and credential (e.g., MARY SMITH MD) and the date the claim was generated in MMDDYYYY (no spaces) format.

NOTE: Payers usually allow providers to use a signature stamp or enter their complete name and credential in Block 31. If not, the provider must sign each claim. For electronic claims transmission, a certification letter is filed with the payer. ●

Block 32

Complete this item when the services listed on the claim were performed at a site other than the provider's office or the patient's home.

NOTE: If Block 18 contains hospitalization dates of service and/or Block 20 contains an X in the YES box, enter the name and address of the facility that provided services. ●

Block 33

Enter the provider's telephone number, including area code, and then the official name of the billing entity and the mailing address. The zip code is entered on the same line as the city and state.

PAR provider: Enter the payer-assigned provider identification number (PIN) and/or group practice identification number (GRP#).

NonPAR provider: Leave PIN and GRP# blank.

EXERCISE 13-7 | **Continuation of Exercise 13-5**

Review the instructions for completing Blocks 25 through 33, and enter a brief description of the instructions in the appropriate block in the BCBS column of the Chart.

EXERCISE 13-8 | **Continuation of Exercise 13-6**

Additional information you need for this case:

Dr. Helper is a BCBS PAR provider. The billing entity is Erin A. Helper, M.D. She is on the medical staff and admits patients at Goodmedicine Hospital, Anywhere Street, Anywhere US 12345.

1. Review the Mary Sue Patient encounter form (Figure 13-7).

2. Select the information needed for Blocks 25 through 33 from the encounter form and the additional data above, and enter it on the claim. This may be completed by handwriting the information, using the Blank Form Mode on the disk, or entering the data using a typewriter. Instructions for installing the disk are found in Appendix V.

   Refer to Figure 13-13 to review the completed claim for the John Q. Public encounter form in Figure 13-5.

3. Review Blocks 25 through 33 of the claim to be sure all required blocks are properly completed.

4. Compare your claim with the completed claim in Figure 13-14.

BCBS SECONDARY COVERAGE

Modifications are made to the CMS-1500 claim when patients are covered by primary and secondary or supplemental health insurance plans. Secondary health insurance plans provide similar coverage to primary plans, while supplemental health plans usually cover just deductible, copayment, and coinsurance expenses.

When the same BCBS payer issues the primary and secondary or supplemental policies, submit just one CMS-1500 claim. If BCBS payers for the primary and secondary or supplemental policies are different, submit a CMS-1500 claim to the primary carrier. After the primary payer processes the claim, generate a second CMS-1500 claim to send to the secondary or supplemental carrier and include a copy of the primary payer's transmittal notice.

Modifications to CMS-1500 Primary Claims

The following modifications are made to the primary claim when the patient is covered by the same BCBS plan for primary and secondary or supplemental coverage (Figure 13-15).

Block 9

Enter the secondary or supplementary policyholder's name, if different from the patient; otherwise, enter SAME.

Block 9a

Enter the ID number of the secondary or supplemental policy.

PLEASE
DO NOT
STAPLE
IN THIS
AREA

(SAMPLE ONLY - NOT APPROVED FOR USE)

CARRIER

PICA

UNDERSTANDING HEALTH INSURANCE CLAIM FORM PICA

1. MEDICARE (Medicare #) ☐ MEDICAID (Medicaid #) ☐ CHAMPUS (Sponsor's SSN) ☐ CHAMPVA (VA File #) ☐ GROUP HEALTH PLAN (SSN or ID) ☐ FECA BLK LUNG (SSN) ☐ OTHER (ID) ☒

1a. INSURED'S I.D. NUMBER (FOR PROGRAM IN ITEM 1)
WWW123456 A1

2. PATIENT'S NAME (Last Name, First Name, Middle Initial)
PUBLIC JOHN Q

3. PATIENT'S BIRTH DATE MM 03 DD 09 YY 1945 SEX M ☒ F ☐

4. INSURED'S NAME (Last Name, First Name, Middle Initial)
SAME

5. PATIENT'S ADDRESS (No. Street)
10A SENATE AVENUE

6. PATIENT RELATIONSHIP TO INSURED Self ☒ Spouse ☐ Child ☐ Other ☐

7. INSURED'S ADDRESS (No. Street)
SAME

CITY ANYWHERE   STATE US

8. PATIENT STATUS Single ☐ Married ☒ Other ☐
Employed ☒ Full-Time Student ☐ Part-Time Student ☐

CITY   STATE

ZIP CODE 12345   TELEPHONE (Include Area Code) (101)201 7891

ZIP CODE   TELEPHONE (INCLUDE AREA CODE) (   )

9. OTHER INSURED'S NAME (Last Name, First Name, Middle Initial)

10. IS PATIENT'S CONDITION RELATED TO:

11. INSURED'S POLICY GROUP OR FECA NUMBER

a. OTHER INSURED'S POLICY OR GROUP NUMBER

a. EMPLOYMENT? (CURRENT OR PREVIOUS) YES ☐ NO ☒

a. INSURED'S DATE OF BIRTH MM DD YY SEX M ☐ F ☐

b. OTHER INSURED'S DATE OF BIRTH MM DD YY SEX M ☐ F ☐

b. AUTO ACCIDENT? PLACE (State) YES ☐ NO ☒

b. EMPLOYER'S NAME OR SCHOOL NAME
LEGAL RESEARCH INC

c. EMPLOYER'S NAME OR SCHOOL NAME

c. OTHER ACCIDENT? YES ☐ NO ☒

c. INSURANCE PLAN NAME OR PROGRAM NAME
BLUE CROSS BLUE SHIELD US

d. INSURANCE PLAN NAME OR PROGRAM NAME

10d. RESERVED FOR LOCAL USE

d. IS THERE ANOTHER HEALTH BENEFIT PLAN? YES ☐ NO ☒ If yes, return to and complete item 9 a – d.

READ BACK OF FORM BEFORE COMPLETING & SIGNING THIS FORM.
12. PATIENT'S OR AUTHORIZED PERSON'S SIGNATURE I authorize the release of any medical or other information necessary to process this claim. I also request payment of government benefits either to myself or to the party who accepts assignment below.

SIGNED SIGNATURE ON FILE   DATE

13. INSURED'S OR AUTHORIZED PERSON'S SIGNATURE I authorize payment of medical benefits to the undersigned physician or supplier for services described below.

SIGNED

14. DATE OF CURRENT: MM 01 DD 12 YY YYYY ILLNESS (First symptom) OR INJURY (Accident) OR PREGNANCY (LMP)

15. IF PATIENT HAS HAD SAME OR SIMILAR ILLNESS, GIVE FIRST DATE MM DD YY

16. DATES PATIENT UNABLE TO WORK IN CURRENT OCCUPATION FROM MM DD YY TO MM DD YY

17. NAME OF REFERRING PHYSICIAN OR OTHER SOURCE
IVAN GOODDOC MD

17a. I.D. NUMBER OF REFERRING PHYSICIAN 1G7777

18. HOSPITALIZATION DATES RELATED TO CURRENT SERVICES FROM MM DD YY TO MM DD YY

19. RESERVED FOR LOCAL USE

20. OUTSIDE LAB? YES ☐ NO ☒ $ CHARGES

21. DIAGNOSIS OR NATURE OF ILLNESS OR INJURY. (RELATE ITEMS 1, 2, 3, OR 4 TO ITEM 24E BY LINE)
1. 485 . ___   3. ___ . ___
2. 788 . 41   4. ___ . ___

22. MEDICAID RESUBMISSION CODE   ORIGINAL REF. NO.

23. PRIOR AUTHORIZATION NUMBER

24. DATE(S) OF SERVICE From MM DD YY	To MM DD YY	B Place of Service	C Type of Service	D PROCEDURES, SERVICES, OR SUPPLIES (Explain Unusual Circumstances) CPT/HCPCS MODIFIER	E DIAGNOSIS CODE	F $ CHARGES	G DAYS OR UNITS	H EPSDT Family Plan	I EMG	J COB	K RESERVED FOR LOCAL USE
0112YYYY	0112YYYY	11		99213	1	75 00	001				
0112YYYY	0112YYYY	11		71020	1	50 00	001				
0112YYYY	0112YYYY	11		81001	2	10 00	001				

25. FEDERAL TAX I.D. NUMBER 11-123341 SSN ☐ EIN ☒

26. PATIENT'S ACCOUNT NO. 13-5

27. ACCEPT ASSIGNMENT? (For govt. claims, see back) YES ☒ NO ☐

28. TOTAL CHARGE $ 135 00

29. AMOUNT PAID $

30. BALANCE DUE $

31. SIGNATURE OF PHYSICIAN OR SUPPLIER INCLUDING DEGREES OR CREDENTIALS (I certify that the statements on the reverse apply to this bill and are made a part thereof.)
ERIN A HELPER MD
SIGNED   DATE MMDDYYYY

32. NAME AND ADDRESS OF FACILITY WHERE SERVICES WERE RENDERED (If other than home or office)

33. PHYSICIAN'S SUPPLIER'S BILLING NAME, ADDRESS, ZIP CODE & PHONE #
(101) 111 1234
ERIN A HELPER MD
101 MEDIC DRIVE
ANYWHERE, US 12345
PIN# EH11881   GRP# 1204-P

(SAMPLE ONLY - NOT APPROVED FOR USE)   PLEASE PRINT OR TYPE   SAMPLE FORM 1500 SAMPLE FORM 1500 SAMPLE FORM 1500

PATIENT AND INSURED INFORMATION
PHYSICIAN OR SUPPLIER INFORMATION

FIGURE 13-13 Completed claim for the John Q. Public encounter form in Figure 13-5

PLEASE
DO NOT
STAPLE
IN THIS
AREA

(SAMPLE ONLY - NOT APPROVED FOR USE)

| | PICA

HEALTH INSURANCE CLAIM FORM   PICA | | |

1. MEDICARE MEDICAID CHAMPUS CHAMPVA GROUP HEALTH PLAN FECA BLK LUNG OTHER	1a. INSURED'S I.D. NUMBER (FOR PROGRAM IN ITEM 1)
(Medicare #) (Medicaid #) (Sponsor's SSN) (VA File #) (SSN or ID) (SSN) [X] (ID)	WWW1023456 HFD6

2. PATIENT'S NAME (Last Name, First Name, Middle Initial)	3. PATIENT'S BIRTH DATE SEX	4. INSURED'S NAME (Last Name, First Name, Middle Initial)
PATIENT MARY SUE	MM 10 DD 10 YY 1959 M [ ] F [X]	SAME

5. PATIENT'S ADDRESS (No. Street)	6. PATIENT RELATIONSHIP TO INSURED	7. INSURED'S ADDRESS (No. Street)
91 HOME STREET	Self [X] Spouse [ ] Child [ ] Other [ ]	SAME

CITY	STATE	8. PATIENT STATUS	CITY	STATE
NOWHERE	US	Single [ ] Married [X] Other [ ]		

ZIP CODE	TELEPHONE (Include Area Code)		ZIP CODE	TELEPHONE (INCLUDE AREA CODE)
12367	(101)201 8989	Employed [X] Full-Time Student [ ] Part-Time Student [ ]		( )

9. OTHER INSURED'S NAME (Last Name, First Name, Middle Initial)	10. IS PATIENT'S CONDITION RELATED TO:	11. INSURED'S POLICY GROUP OR FECA NUMBER
a. OTHER INSURED'S POLICY OR GROUP NUMBER	a. EMPLOYMENT? (CURRENT OR PREVIOUS) [ ] YES [X] NO	a. INSURED'S DATE OF BIRTH MM DD YY SEX M [ ] F [ ]
b. OTHER INSURED'S DATE OF BIRTH MM DD YY SEX M [ ] F [ ]	b. AUTO ACCIDENT? PLACE (State) [ ] YES [X] NO	b. EMPLOYER'S NAME OR SCHOOL NAME HAPPY FARM'S DAY CARE
c. EMPLOYER'S NAME OR SCHOOL NAME	c. OTHER ACCIDENT? [ ] YES [X] NO	c. INSURANCE PLAN NAME OR PROGRAM NAME BCBS US
d. INSURANCE PLAN NAME OR PROGRAM NAME	10d. RESERVED FOR LOCAL USE	d. IS THERE ANOTHER HEALTH BENEFIT PLAN? [ ] YES [X] NO If yes, return to and complete item 9 a – d.

READ BACK OF FORM BEFORE COMPLETING & SIGNING THIS FORM.
12. PATIENT'S OR AUTHORIZED PERSON'S SIGNATURE I authorize the release of any medical or other information necessary to process this claim. I also request payment of government benefits either to myself or to the party who accepts assignment below.

13. INSURED'S OR AUTHORIZED PERSON'S SIGNATURE I authorize payment of medical benefits to the undersigned physician or supplier for services described below.

SIGNED   SIGNATURE ON FILE   DATE _____

SIGNED _____

14. DATE OF CURRENT: ILLNESS (First symptom) OR INJURY (Accident) OR PREGNANCY (LMP) MM 01 DD 12 YY YYYY	15. IF PATIENT HAS HAD SAME OR SIMILAR ILLNESS, GIVE FIRST DATE MM DD YY	16. DATES PATIENT UNABLE TO WORK IN CURRENT OCCUPATION FROM MM DD YY TO MM DD YY
17. NAME OF REFERRING PHYSICIAN OR OTHER SOURCE	17a. I.D. NUMBER OF REFERRING PHYSICIAN	18. HOSPITALIZATION DATES RELATED TO CURRENT SERVICES FROM MM DD YY TO MM DD YY
19. RESERVED FOR LOCAL USE		20. OUTSIDE LAB? [ ] YES [X] NO $ CHARGES

21. DIAGNOSIS OR NATURE OF ILLNESS OR INJURY. (RELATE ITEMS 1, 2, 3, OR 4 TO ITEM 24E BY LINE)	22. MEDICAID RESUBMISSION CODE ORIGINAL REF. NO.
1. 034 0 3.	
2. 250 01 4.	23. PRIOR AUTHORIZATION NUMBER

24. A. DATE(S) OF SERVICE		B. Place of Service	C. Type of Service	D. PROCEDURES, SERVICES, OR SUPPLIES (Explain Unusual Circumstances) CPT/HCPCS MODIFIER	E. DIAGNOSIS CODE	F. $ CHARGES	G. DAYS OR UNITS	H. EPSDT Family Plan	I. EMG	J. COB	K. RESERVED FOR LOCAL USE
From MM DD YY	To MM DD YY										
01 12 YYYY	01 12 YYYY	11		99212	1	65 00	001				
01 12 YYYY	01 12 YYYY	11		87880	1	12 00	001				

25. FEDERAL TAX I.D. NUMBER SSN EIN	26. PATIENT'S ACCOUNT NO.	27. ACCEPT ASSIGNMENT? (For govt. claims, see back)	28. TOTAL CHARGE	29. AMOUNT PAID	30. BALANCE DUE
11-123341 [X]	13-7	[X] YES [ ] NO	$ 72 00	$	$

31. SIGNATURE OF PHYSICIAN OR SUPPLIER INCLUDING DEGREES OR CREDENTIALS (I certify that the statements on the reverse apply to this bill and are made a part thereof.) ERIN A HELPER MD SIGNED DATE MMDDYYYY	32. NAME AND ADDRESS OF FACILITY WHERE SERVICES WERE RENDERED (If other than home or office)	33. PHYSICIAN'S SUPPLIER'S BILLING NAME, ADDRESS, ZIP CODE & PHONE # (101) 111 1234 ERIN A HELPER MD 101 MEDIC DRIVE ANYWHERE, US 12345 PIN# EH1181 GRP# 1204-P

(SAMPLE ONLY - NOT APPROVED FOR USE)   PLEASE PRINT OR TYPE   SAMPLE FORM 1500 SAMPLE FORM 1500 SAMPLE FORM 1500

CARRIER

PATIENT AND INSURED INFORMATION

PHYSICIAN OR SUPPLIER INFORMATION

FIGURE 13-14 Completed claim for Mary Sue Patient encounter form in Figure 13-7

Block 9b

Enter secondary policyholder's eight-digit birth date (MM DD YYYY with spaces), and enter an X in the appropriate box to indicate the secondary subscriber's gender.

Block 9c

Enter the secondary policyholder's employer name if the policy is an employer-sponsored group (EGHP) policy. Otherwise, leave blank.

Block 9d

Enter the name of the secondary plan.

Block 11d

Enter an X in the YES box.

EXERCISE 13-9 **Filing a Claim When a Patient Has Two BCBS Policies**

1. Obtain a blank claim.

2. Underline Blocks 9 through 9d and 11d identifiers on the new claim.

3. Refer to the encounter form for Mary Sue Patient (Figure 13-7). Enter the following information in the blocks for the secondary policy (9–9d):

   BC/BS FEDERAL R1527418 GROUP 101

   Policyholder: James W. Patient

   Birth date: 03/01/48

   Relationship: Spouse

   Employer: NAVAL STATION

   Add a BB to the patient account number when entering data in Block 26. (BB means BCBS/BCBS)

4. Complete the secondary claim on Mary Sue Patient using the data from the encounter form and placing the secondary information in the blocks highlighted in Step 2.

5. Review the completed claim to be sure all required blocks are properly completed. Compare your claim with Figure 13-15.

Modifications to CMS-1500 Secondary Claims

These instructions are for claims in which the primary payer is a commercial or government plan, and the patient is also covered by a BCBS secondary policy. The primary carrier EOB must be attached to the secondary claim.

These instructions do not apply to BCBS policies that are purchased as a supplement to primary Medicare coverage. Instructions for billing these policies are covered in the Medicare chapter (Chapter 14).

Block 1a

Enter the patient's BCBS ID and group plan numbers.

FIGURE 13-15 Completed claim for a patient with two BCBS policies

Block 11

Enter the *policy group number (GRP#)*, if known.

Block 11a

Enter *policyholder's birth date* in MM DD YYYY format (with spaces), and enter an X in the appropriate box for gender.

Block 11b

Enter *either* the name of the primary subscriber's employer *or* the name of the school the patient attends (if the patient is a full-time student between age 19–24 *and* is covered by a school plan).

Block 11c

Enter the name of the *payer*.

Block 29

Enter only payments made by the *primary payer*.

EXERCISE 13-10 | **Filing BCBS Secondary Claims**

1. Obtain a blank claim.
2. Underline Blocks 1a, 11 through 11c, and 29 identification numbers for the changes discussed above.
3. Review Figure 13-16. Complete the BCBS secondary claim for this case using data from the encounter form.
4. Review the completed claim to be sure all required blocks are properly completed.
5. Compare your claim with Figure 13-17.

Additional BCBS claim case studies are found in Appendix I and Appendix II.

Case studies in Appendix II require reading the case study chart entries and selecting and coding diagnostic/procedural information. Necessary clinic, hospital, and physician data are included in the case study encounter forms in Appendix II.

SUMMARY

- Blue Cross plans were initiated in 1929 and originally provided coverage for hospital bills.
- Blue Shield was created in 1938 and originally covered fees for physician services.
- Blue Cross and Blue Shield (BCBS) plans entered into joint ventures that increased coverage of almost all health care services.
- The Blue Cross Blue Shield Association (BSBSA) was created in 1986 when the separate Blue Cross association merged with the Blue Shield association.
- The BCBS plans were pioneers in nonprofit, prepaid health care. Competition among all health insurance payers in the United States resulted in further mergers and the BCBSA no longer requiring plans to be nonprofit.

ERIN A. HELPER, M.D.
101 Medic Dr, Anywhere US 12345
(101) 111-1234 (Office) • (101) 111-9292 (Fax)
EIN: 11-123341 **MCD:** EBH8881
UPIN: EH8888 **BCBS:** EH11881
BCBS GRP: 1204-P

Encounter Form

PATIENT INFORMATION:

		INSURANCE INFORMATION:	
Name:	Cross, Janet B.	**Patient Number:**	13-16
Address:	1901 Beach Head Drive	**Place of Service:**	Hospital Inpatient
City:	Anywhere	**Primary Insurance Plan:**	Medicare
State:	US	**Primary Insurance Plan ID #:**	191266844A
Zip Code:	12345	**Group #:**	
Telephone:	(101) 201-1991	**Primary Policyholder:**	Cross, Janet B.
Gender:	Female	**Policyholder Date of Birth:**	11-01-1934
Date of Birth:	11-01-1934	**Relationship to Patient:**	Self
Occupation:	Retired	**Secondary Insurance Plan:**	BCBS US
Employer:		**Secondary Insurance Plan ID #:**	WWW191266844
		Secondary Policyholder:	Cross, Janet B.
		Relationship to Patient:	Self

Patient Status ☒ Married   ☐ Divorced   ☐ Single   ☐ Student

DIAGNOSIS INFORMATION

Diagnosis		**Code**	**Diagnosis**		**Code**
1.	Intracranial hemorrhage	432.9	5.		
2.	Dysphasia	784.5	6.		
3.			7.		
4.			8.		

PROCEDURE INFORMATION

Description of Procedure or Service		**Date**	**Code**	**Charge**
1.	Initial hospital visit, level III	01-13-YYYY	99223	150.00
2.	Discharge management, 60 minutes	01-14-YYYY	99239	100.00
3.				
4.				
5.				

SPECIAL NOTES: Patient transferred to University Medical Center via ambulance. Place of service: Goodmedicine Hospital, Anywhere US 12345

FIGURE 13-16 Janet B. Cross encounter form

- BCBS negotiates contracts with providers that result in the *participating provider* (PAR) designation. PARs are eligible to contract with preferred provider networks (PPNs), which is considered managed care. PARs also qualify for assignment of benefits, which means payment is made directly to the provider.
- Nonparticipating providers do not sign such contracts, and they expect to be reimbursed their complete fee. They collect payment from the patient, and the patient receives reimbursement from BCBS.
- BCBS plans include fee-for-service, indemnity, managed care, Away From Home Care®, Federal Employee Program (FEP), and Medicare supplemental plans.
- BCBS managed care plans include coordinated home health and hospice care, exclusive provider organizations (EPOs), health maintenance organizations

PLEASE
DO NOT
STAPLE
IN THIS
AREA

TRANSMITTAL NOTICE ATTACHED

(SAMPLE ONLY - NOT APPROVED FOR USE)

CARRIER

PICA

HEALTH INSURANCE CLAIM FORM   PICA

1.						1a. INSURED'S I.D. NUMBER	(FOR PROGRAM IN ITEM 1)
MEDICARE	MEDICAID	CHAMPUS	CHAMPVA	GROUP HEALTH PLAN	FECA BLK LUNG	OTHER	WWW191266844
☐ (Medicare #)	☐ (Medicaid #)	☐ (Sponsor's SSN)	☐ (VA File #)	☐ (SSN or ID)	☐ (SSN)	☒ (ID)	

2. PATIENT'S NAME (Last Name, First Name, Middle Initial)
CROSS JANET B

3. PATIENT'S BIRTH DATE   MM 11 DD 01 YY 1934   SEX M☐ F☒

4. INSURED'S NAME (Last Name, First Name, Middle Initial)
SAME

5. PATIENT'S ADDRESS (No. Street)
1901 BEACH HEAD DRIVE

6. PATIENT RELATIONSHIP TO INSURED
Self ☒ Spouse ☐ Child ☐ Other ☐

7. INSURED'S ADDRESS (No. Street)
SAME

CITY
ANYWHERE   STATE US

8. PATIENT STATUS
Single ☐ Married ☒ Other ☐

CITY   STATE

ZIP CODE
12345   TELEPHONE (Include Area Code)
(101) 201 1991

Employed ☐ Full-Time Student ☐ Part-Time Student ☐

ZIP CODE   TELEPHONE (INCLUDE AREA CODE)
( )

9. OTHER INSURED'S NAME (Last Name, First Name, Middle Initial)

10. IS PATIENT'S CONDITION RELATED TO:

11. INSURED'S POLICY GROUP OR FECA NUMBER

a. OTHER INSURED'S POLICY OR GROUP NUMBER

a. EMPLOYMENT? (CURRENT OR PREVIOUS)
☐ YES ☒ NO

a. INSURED'S DATE OF BIRTH   MM DD YY   SEX M☐ F☐

b. OTHER INSURED'S DATE OF BIRTH   MM DD YY   SEX M☐ F☐

b. AUTO ACCIDENT?   PLACE (State)
☐ YES ☒ NO

b. EMPLOYER'S NAME OR SCHOOL NAME

c. EMPLOYER'S NAME OR SCHOOL NAME

c. OTHER ACCIDENT?
☐ YES ☒ NO

c. INSURANCE PLAN NAME OR PROGRAM NAME
BCBS US

d. INSURANCE PLAN NAME OR PROGRAM NAME

10d. RESERVED FOR LOCAL USE

d. IS THERE ANOTHER HEALTH BENEFIT PLAN?
☐ YES ☒ NO   If yes, return to and complete item 9 a – d.

READ BACK OF FORM BEFORE COMPLETING & SIGNING THIS FORM.
12. PATIENT'S OR AUTHORIZED PERSON'S SIGNATURE I authorize the release of any medical or other information necessary to process this claim. I also request payment of government benefits either to myself or to the party who accepts assignment below.

SIGNED   SIGNATURE ON FILE   DATE

13. INSURED'S OR AUTHORIZED PERSON'S SIGNATURE I authorize payment of medical benefits to the undersigned physician or supplier for services described below.

SIGNED

14. DATE OF CURRENT: MM 01 DD 13 YY YYYY   ◀ ILLNESS (First symptom) OR INJURY (Accident) OR PREGNANCY (LMP)

15. IF PATIENT HAS HAD SAME OR SIMILAR ILLNESS, GIVE FIRST DATE   MM DD YY

16. DATES PATIENT UNABLE TO WORK IN CURRENT OCCUPATION   FROM MM DD YY   TO MM DD YY

17. NAME OF REFERRING PHYSICIAN OR OTHER SOURCE

17a. I.D. NUMBER OF REFERRING PHYSICIAN

18. HOSPITALIZATION DATES RELATED TO CURRENT SERVICES   FROM MM 01 DD 13 YY YYYY   TO MM 01 DD 14 YY YYYY

19. RESERVED FOR LOCAL USE

20. OUTSIDE LAB?   ☐ YES ☒ NO $ CHARGES

21. DIAGNOSIS OR NATURE OF ILLNESS OR INJURY. (RELATE ITEMS 1, 2, 3, OR 4 TO ITEM 24E BY LINE)
1. 432.9
2. 784.5
3. └─ . ─┘
4. └─ . ─┘

22. MEDICAID RESUBMISSION CODE   ORIGINAL REF. NO.

23. PRIOR AUTHORIZATION NUMBER

24. A DATE(S) OF SERVICE From MM DD YY	To MM DD YY	B Place of Service	C Type of Service	D PROCEDURES, SERVICES, OR SUPPLIES (Explain Unusual Circumstances) CPT/HCPCS | MODIFIER	E DIAGNOSIS CODE	F $ CHARGES	G DAYS OR UNITS	H EPSDT Family Plan	I EMG	J COB	K RESERVED FOR LOCAL USE
1 0113YYYY	0113YYYY	21		99233	2	150 00	001				
2 0114YYYY	0114YYYY	21		99239	1	100 00	001				
3											
4											
5											
6											

25. FEDERAL TAX I.D. NUMBER   SSN☐ EIN☒
11-123341

26. PATIENT'S ACCOUNT NO.
13-16S

27. ACCEPT ASSIGNMENT? (For govt. claims, see back)
☒ YES ☐ NO

28. TOTAL CHARGE $ 250 00

29. AMOUNT PAID $

30. BALANCE DUE $

31. SIGNATURE OF PHYSICIAN OR SUPPLIER INCLUDING DEGREES OR CREDENTIALS (I certify that the statements on the reverse apply to this bill and are made a part thereof.)
ERIN A HELPER MD
SIGNED   DATE MMDDYYYY

32. NAME AND ADDRESS OF FACILITY WHERE SERVICES WERE RENDERED (If other than home or office)
GOODMEDICINE HOSPITAL
ANYWHERE STREET
ANYWHERE US 12345

33. PHYSICIAN'S SUPPLIER'S BILLING NAME, ADDRESS, ZIP CODE & PHONE #
(101) 111 1234
ERIN A HELPER MD
101 MEDIC DRIVE
ANYWHERE, US 12345
PIN# EH11811   GRP# 1204-P

(SAMPLE ONLY - NOT APPROVED FOR USE)   PLEASE PRINT OR TYPE   SAMPLE FORM 1500   SAMPLE FORM 1500 SAMPLE FORM 1500

PATIENT AND INSURED INFORMATION

PHYSICIAN OR SUPPLIER INFORMATION

FIGURE 13-17 Completed claim for the BCBS secondary coverage

(HMOs), outpatient pretreatment authorization plans (PAP), point-of-service plans (POS), preferred provider organizations (PPOs), and secondary surgical opinion plans (SSOs).

- BCBS plans process their own claims using the CMS-1500 claim, and the deadline for claims submission is one year from the date of service (unless otherwise specified in the subscriber's or provider's contract).

- Inpatient and outpatient care, copayment/coinsurance, and deductible amounts vary according to a plan's contract.

- The allowable fee determination is usually based on the physician fee schedule but is sometimes based on usual, customary, and reasonable (UCR) charges.

- Patient BCBS identification cards are copied (front/back) and filed in the patient's financial record.

- Third-party administrators provide administrative services to payers, and they often specialize in mental health care claims processing.

- When completing BCBS CMS-1500 claims for case studies in this text and the Workbook, the following special instructions apply:
  - Block 12—Enter SIGNATURE ON FILE (patients have signed a customized authorization that is filed in the patient's record)
  - Block 19—Leave blank
  - Block 20—Enter an X in the NO box
  - Block 23—Leave blank
  - Block 24G—Enter 3-digit days or units (e.g., 001 instead of 1)
  - Block 25—Enter the EIN with a hyphen
  - Block 26—Enter the case study number (e.g., 13-4). If the patient has both primary and secondary coverage, enter a P (for primary) next to the case study number (on the primary claim) and an S (for secondary) next to the number (on the secondary claim); if the same BCBS plan provides both primary and secondary coverage, enter a BB next to the case study number
  - Block 27—Enter an X in the YES box
  - Block 31—Enter provider's complete name with credentials (instead of a signature as indicated in the chapter instructions). This will allow you to completely generate claims using the UHI software (instead of having to print the claim and sign it).
  - Block 32—If Block 18 contains dates and/or Block 20 contains an X in the YES box, enter the name and address of the responsible provider in Block 32 (e.g., hospital, outside laboratory)
  - When completing secondary claims, enter TRANSMITTAL NOTICE ATTACHED in the top margin of the CMS-1500 claim (to simulate the attachment of a primary payer's transmittal notice with a claim submitted to a secondary payer)

STUDY CHECKLIST

- ☐ Read the textbook chapter, and prepare the Insurance Plan Comparison Chart.

- ☐ Install the UHI software from the disk (instructions are in Appendix V), and become familiar with the software.

- ☐ Complete CMS-1500 claims for each chapter encounter form.

- ☐ Complete the chapter review.

- ☐ Complete the chapter CD-ROM activities.

- ☐ Complete Web Tutor assignments, and take online quizzes.

- ☐ Complete BCBS claims for cases located in Appendices I and II.

☐ Complete the Workbook chapter, verifying answers with your instructor.

☐ Form a study group with classmates to discuss chapter concepts in preparation for an exam.

REVIEW

TRUE/FALSE

Indicate whether the definition is true or false.

1. ☐ T ☐ F Participating provider (PAR): A physician or other health care provider of medical care who has entered into a contract with BCBS to accept the carrier-determined allowed amount as payment in full.

2. ☐ T ☐ F Nonparticipating provider (nonPAR): A health care provider who expects full payment from the carrier for fees charged to patients.

3. ☐ T ☐ F FEHBP: Federal Employee Health Benefit Program.

4. ☐ T ☐ F Medical emergency care: Treatment sought and received at any time for sudden, severe, and unexpected conditions that, if not treated, would place the patient's health in jeopardy or lead to impairment or permanent dysfunction of an organ or body part.

5. ☐ T ☐ F Preferred Provider Network (PPN): A program that requires subscribers to adhere to managed care provisions.

SHORT ANSWER

Answer each of the following.

6. State the purpose of the Baylor University plan, which was the precursor of what is now known as Blue Cross.

7. Discuss how the California Physicians' Service Program, established in 1938, differed from the Baylor University plan.

8. BCBS corporations function as independent corporations serving specific regions of the country. Discuss the function of the national BCBSA.

9. List the advantages to the consumer when they select a Blue Shield participating provider.

10. List the advantages of being a Blue Shield participating provider.

11. List the nine distinct types of benefits normally covered by the Blue Shield basic policy.

12. Describe two policy riders that are often added to Blue Shield basic benefits.

13. List eight types of benefits that may appear as Blue Shield major medical benefits.

14. Describe two policy riders that are often added to major medical benefits.

15. Explain how BCBS PARs determine what the deductible, copay/coinsurance, and plan benefits are for a BlueCard patient.

16. State the usual filing deadline for BCBS plans.

17. Indicate where completed paper claims are sent for processing in the following situations:

    PAR PROVIDER

    a. Patient ID # XYW12345678

    b. Patient ID # 332124433

    c. Patient has out-of-area BCBS ID XYW12345678 and is also covered by an Aetna full-benefit policy.

    d. Patient ID # R12345678

    e. The "home plan" is located in California; the "host plan" is located in Virginia.

KEY TERMS

allogeneic bone marrow transplant

aplastic anemia

autologous bone marrow transplant

benefit period

Clinical Laboratory Improvement Act
(CLIA) certification number

conditional primary payer status

coordinated care plans

cost-based HMO

dialysis

disability

employer-sponsored retirement plan

end-stage renal disease (ESRD)

extra coverage plans

general enrollment period (GEP)

hemodialysis

hospice

initial enrollment period (IEP)

kidney transplant

leukemia

lifetime reserve days

limited license practitioner (LLP)

lock-in provision

medical necessity denial

Medicare Part A

Medicare Part B

Medicare private contract

Medicare SELECT

Medicare-Medicaid crossover

multiple myeloma

nonphysician provider

Original Medicare Plan

peritoneal dialysis

plan identification number (planID)

Privacy Act of 1974

private fee-for-service (PFFS)

provider identifying number (PIN)

provider-sponsored organization (PSO)

qualified Medicare beneficiary (QMB)

religious fraternal benefit society
plans

remission

respite care

risk-based HMO

roster billing

severe combined immunodeficiency
disease (SCID)

Social Security Administration (SSA)

special enrollment period (SEP)

specified low-income Medicare
beneficiary (SLMB)

spell of illness

Sunshine Law

TRICARE For Life

TRICARE Senior Pharmacy Program

unique provider identification number
(UPIN)

Wiskott-Aldrich syndrome

Chapter 14 Medicare

OBJECTIVES

Upon successful completion of this chapter, you should be able to:

1. Define key terms.
2. List six categories of persons eligible for Medicare coverage.
3. Describe coverage for each of the following:

Medicare Part A	hospice care
Medicare Part B	heart transplant
ESRD dialysis cases	kidney donor

4. List and describe six incentives developed by Congress to encourage providers to become Medicare participating providers.
5. List and describe six restrictions placed on Medicare nonPAR providers.
6. Explain the requirements for use of the Medicare medical necessity statement.
7. Explain requirements governing use of the surgery financial disclosure statement.
8. List and define seven types of insurance programs that are primary to Medicare.
9. List and define two types of programs that are classified as Medicare supplemental plans.
10. Explain how a policy falls into the extra coverage category and how it affects Medicare billing.
11. Explain how a Medicare claim is filed for Medicare patients enrolled in Medicare risk-restricted or cost-based HMOs.
12. Explain the billing sequence for Medicare patients with employer-sponsored plans, Medigap, Medicare-Medicaid crossover plans, and Medicare as secondary coverage.
13. Explain how Medicare's liability as a secondary payer is calculated.
14. State the deadline for filing Medicare claims.
15. Discuss the provider's legal responsibility for collecting the patient's deductible and coinsurance obligations.
16. Explain the procedure health care providers must follow to "opt out" of Medicare.
17. Describe the features of Medicare+Choice with regard to the following: private fee-for-service plan, provider-sponsored organizations, and Medicare Savings Accounts.
18. File traditional Medicare or Medicare HMO fee-for-service claims properly.

INTRODUCTION

Medicare, the largest single medical benefits program in the United States, is a federal program authorized by Congress and administered by the Centers for Medicare and Medicaid Services (CMS, formerly HCFA). CMS is responsible for the operation of the Medicare program and for selecting a *fiscal intermediary (FI)* to process Part A claims and a *carrier* to process Part B claims. Medicare is a two-part program:

- **Medicare Part A** reimburses institutional providers for inpatient, hospice, and some home health services.
- **Medicare Part B** reimburses institutional providers for outpatient services and physicians for inpatient services.

The billing instructions in this chapter cover the filing of Medicare Part B services only. Part A claims are not filed by insurance specialists working in health care provider offices; they are filed by hospitals, hospices, and home health care providers.

MEDICARE ELIGIBILITY

General Medicare eligibility requires individuals to:

1. Have worked at least 10 years in Medicare-covered employment.
2. Be a minimum age of 65 years old.
3. Be a citizen or permanent resident of the United States.

Individuals can also qualify for coverage if they are younger than 65 years old *and* have a disability or chronic kidney disease. The **Social Security Administration (SSA)** (an agency of the Federal Government) bases their definition of **disability** on an individual's inability to work; an individual can be considered disabled if unable to do work as before and it is determined that adjustments cannot be made to do other work because of a medical condition(s). In addition, the disability must last or be expected to last a year or to result in death. There is no premium for Part A if individuals meet one of the above conditions; however, they do pay for Part B coverage. The Part B monthly premium changes annually and is deducted from Social Security, Railroad Retirement, or Civil Service Retirement checks.

Medicare Part A coverage is available to individuals *age 65 and over* who:

- are already receiving retirement benefits from Social Security or the Railroad Retirement Board (RRB).
- are eligible to receive Social Security or Railroad benefits but who have not yet filed for them.
- had Medicare-covered government employment.

Medicare Part A coverage is available to individuals *under age 65* who:

- are disabled per SSA or RRB guidelines.
- have received SSA or RRB disability benefits for 24 months.
- are kidney dialysis or kidney transplant patients.

Provider Telephone Inquiries for Medicare Eligibility Information

The standard method for obtaining eligibility information is through electronic data interchange (EDI). EDI is the most efficient and cost-effective way to make eligibility information available because provider agreements ensure privacy safeguards. Instructions regarding provider EDI access to limited eligibility information can be found in Part 3 of the Medicare Carriers Manual (MCM).

Eligibility information is also available over the telephone, subject to ensuring the protection of the beneficiary's privacy rights. The eligibility information that can be released by telephone is limited to *that information available via EDI.* The provider's name and identification number must be verified and the following information must be obtained about each beneficiary:

- last name and first initial
- date of birth
- HICN (health insurance claim number)
- gender

NOTE: The Privacy Act prohibits release of information unless all the above required information is accurately provided.

MEDICARE ENROLLMENT

Medicare enrollment is handled in two ways: individuals are either enrolled automatically or they apply for coverage. In addition, individuals age 65 and over and who do not qualify for Social Security benefits may "buy in" to Medicare Part A by paying monthly premiums. The "buy in" premiums for 2003 are $316/month (Part A with less than 30 quarters SSA coverage) or $174/month (Part A with more than 30 quarters SSA coverage), and $58.70 (Part B optional coverage).

Automatic Enrollment

Individuals not yet age 65 who already receive Social Security, Railroad Retirement Board, or disability benefits are automatically enrolled in Part A and Part B effective the month of their 65th birthday. About three months prior to their 65th birthday, or 24th month of disability, individuals are sent an initial enrollment package that contains information about Medicare, a questionnaire, and a Medicare card. If the individual wants both Medicare Part A (hospital insurance) and Part B (supplemental medical insurance), they just sign their Medicare card and keep it in a safe place.

Individuals who do not want Part B coverage (because there is a monthly premium associated with it) must follow the instructions that accompany their Medicare card requiring the individual to mark an "X" in the refusal box on the back of the Medicare card form, sign the form, and return it *with* the Medicare card to the address indicated. The individual is then sent a new Medicare card showing coverage for Part A only.

Applying for Medicare

Individuals who do not receive Social Security, Railroad Retirement Board, or disability benefits must apply for Medicare Part A and Part B by contacting the Social Security Administration (or Railroad Retirement Board) approximately three months before the month in which they turn 65 or 24th month of disability. Upon applying for Medicare Part A and Part B, a seven month **initial enrollment period (IEP)** begins that provides an opportunity for the individual to enroll in Medicare Part A and/or Part B. Those who wait until they turn 65 to apply for Medicare will cause a delay in the start of Part B coverage because they will have to wait until the next **general enrollment period (GEP)**, which is held January 1 through March 31 of each year; Part

B coverage starts on July 1 of that year. The Part B premium is also increased by 10% for each 12-month period that an individual was eligible for Part B coverage but did not participate.

Under certain circumstances, individuals can delay their Part B enrollment without having to pay higher premiums. Examples include individuals age 65 or older who have group health insurance based on their own or their spouse's current employment or disabled individuals who have group health insurance based on their own or any family member's current employment. If Part B enrollment is delayed for one of these reasons, individuals can enroll anytime during the **special enrollment period (SEP)**. The Special Enrollment Period is a set time when individuals can sign up for Medicare Part B if they did not enroll in Part B during the Initial Enrollment Period.

Qualified Medicare Beneficiary Program

Under the **qualified Medicare beneficiary (QMB)** program, the federal government requires state Medicaid programs to pay Medicare premiums, patient deductibles, and coinsurance for individuals who have Medicare Part A, a low monthly income, limited resources, and who are not otherwise eligible for Medicaid. See Table 14-1 for programs that help pay Medicare expenses for individuals and couples. In addition to income and assets, an individual or couple may have financial resources and/or own items valued at or below $4,000 for an individual and $6,000 for a couple. Financial resources include bank accounts, stocks, and bonds. Items that are not counted as financial resources include the house the individual/couple lives in, one car, burial plots, furniture, and some life insurance.

Specified Low-Income Medicare Beneficiary Program

Another federally mandated program, the **specified low-income Medicare beneficiary (SLMB)** program, requires states to cover just the Medicare Part B premium for persons whose income is slightly above the poverty level. See Table 14-1 for monthly income limits for individuals and couples. Assets, house, car, and burial plan requirements are the same as for QMBs.

TABLE 14-1 Programs that help pay Medicare expenses

MONTHLY INCOME LIMIT (2003) *		NAME OF PROGRAM**	PROGRAM WILL PAY:
$759	Individual (or)	Qualified Medical Beneficiary (QMB)	Medicare Part A and Part B premiums, deductibles, and coinsurance
$1015	Couple		
$906	Individual (or)	Special Low-income Medicare Beneficiary (SLMB)	Medicare Part B premiums
$1214	Couple		
$1017	Individual (or)	Qualifying Individual (QI-1)	Medicare Part B premiums
$1364	Couple		
$3039	Individual (or)	Qualified Disabled Working Individual (QDWI)	Medicare Part B premiums
$4065	Couple		

*Alaska and Hawaii income limits are slightly higher, and all income limits will increase slightly next year.
**Qualifying Individual (QI-2) program that paid a small part of Medicare Part B premiums ended in 2003.

MEDICARE PART A COVERAGE
Hospitalizations

Medicare pays only a portion of a patient's acute care hospitalization expenses, and the patient's out-of-pocket expenses are calculated on a "benefit period basis." A **benefit period** begins with the first day of hospitalization and ends when the patient has been out of the hospital for 60 consecutive days. (Some Medicare literature uses the term **spell of illness**, formerly called "spell of sickness," in place of "benefit period.") After 90 continuous days of hospitalization, the patient may elect to use some or all of the allotted lifetime reserve days, or pay the full daily charges for hospitalization. **Lifetime reserve days** (60 days) may be used only once during a patient's lifetime and are usually reserved for use during the patient's final, terminal hospital stay. The 2003 Part A deductibles per benefit period are:

Days 1–60	$840 total
Days 61–90	$210/day
Days 91–150	Patient pays total charges, or elects to use lifetime reserve days at $420/day
150+ continuous days	Patient pays total charges

A person who has been out of the hospital for a period of 60 consecutive days will enter a new benefit period if rehospitalized, and the expenses for the first 90 days under this new benefit period are the same as stated above. Persons confined to a psychiatric hospital are allowed 190 lifetime reserve days instead of the 60 days allotted for a stay in an acute care hospital.

Skilled Nursing Facility Stays

Individuals who become inpatients at a skilled nursing facility after a 3-day-minimum acute hospital stay and who meet Medicare's qualified diagnosis and comprehensive treatment plan requirements pay 2003 rates of:

Days 1–20	Nothing
Days 21–100	$105 per day
Days 101+	Full daily rate

Home Health Services

Individuals receiving physician-prescribed, Medicare-covered home health services have no deductible or coinsurance responsibilities for services provided. Patients must be confined to the home, but they do not have to be hospitalized in an acute care hospital before qualifying for home health benefits. The patient is responsible for a 20% deductible of the approved amount for durable medical equipment.

Hospice Care

All terminally ill patients qualify for hospice care. **Hospice** is an autonomous, centrally administered program of coordinated inpatient and outpatient palliative (relief of symptoms) services for terminally ill patients and their families. This program is for patients for whom there is nothing further the provider can do to stop the progression of disease, and the patient is treated only to relieve pain or other discomfort. In addition to medical care, a physician-directed interdisciplinary team provides psychological, sociological, and spiritual care. Medicare limits hospice care to four benefit periods:

- Two periods of 90 days each
- One 30-day period
- A final "lifetime" extension of unlimited duration

The hospice patient is responsible for:

- 5% of the cost of each prescription for symptom management or pain relief, but not more than $5 for any prescription.
- 5% of the Medicare payment amount for inpatient respite care for up to five consecutive days at a time.

Respite care is the temporary hospitalization of a hospice patient for the purpose of providing relief from duty for the nonpaid person who has the major day-to-day responsibility for the care of the terminally ill, dependent patient.

Patients who withdraw from the hospice program during the final benefit period are considered to have exhausted their hospice benefits. A patient receiving hospice benefits is not eligible for Medicare Part B services except for those services that are totally unrelated to their terminal illness. When a patient chooses Medicare hospice benefits, all other Medicare benefits stop with the exception of physician services or treatment for conditions not related to the patient's terminal diagnosis.

End-Stage Renal Disease (ESRD) Coverage

For Medicare purposes, **end-stage renal disease (ESRD)** refers to that stage of kidney impairment that appears irreversible and permanent and requires a regular course of dialysis or kidney transplantation to maintain life. **Dialysis** involves a process by which waste products are removed from the body; two types of renal dialysis are commonly performed:

- **Hemodialysis** involves passing the patient's blood through an artificial kidney machine to remove waste products; cleansed blood is subsequently returned to the patient's body.
- **Peritoneal dialysis** involves the passage of waste products from the patient's body through the peritoneal membrane into the peritoneal (abdominal) cavity where a solution is introduced and periodically removed.

A **kidney transplant** involves surgically inserting a healthy kidney from another person (a kidney donor) into the patient who has ESRD; the new kidney does the work that the patient's kidneys cannot.

This special coverage is available for Medicare-eligible persons in need of renal dialysis or transplant due to ESRD. Medicare coverage for ESRD cases begins with:

- the fourth month of dialysis treatments for (1) individuals who enrolled in Medicare based on their ESRD diagnosis and for (2) individuals who are covered by an employer group health plan (the employer group plan pays first and Medicare pays second for a 30-month coordination period).
- the first month of dialysis treatment for (1) individuals who take part in a home dialysis training program at a Medicare-approved training facility that teaches how to administer dialysis treatments at home, (2) individuals who begin home dialysis training before the third month of dialysis, (3) individuals who expect to finish home dialysis training and self-administer dialysis treatments.
- the month an individual is admitted to a Medicare-approved hospital for a kidney transplant or for health care services needed prior to the transplant

if the transplant takes place in that same month or within the two following months.

- two months prior to the month of the transplant if the transplant is delayed more than two months after admission to the hospital for the transplant or for health care services needed before the transplant.

EXAMPLE: Mr. Small was admitted to the hospital on January 5 for tests needed prior to a kidney transplant. He was to undergo the transplant on February 5, but it was delayed until June 25. Medicare coverage for Mr. Small starts in April, two months prior to the month of his scheduled kidney transplant.

Coverage continues for individuals who have Medicare because of ESRD for:

- 12 months after the month the patient stops dialysis treatments, or
- 36 months after the month of a successful kidney transplant.

Medicare coverage does not end if:

- the patient starts dialysis again or receives a kidney transplant within 12 months after the month the patient stopped receiving dialysis, or
- the patient continues to receive dialysis or undergoes another kidney transplant within 36 months after a transplant.

Special circumstances can occur for individuals with ESRD and who need a pancreas transplant. Medicare covers pancreas transplants:

- when done at the same time as a kidney transplant, or after a kidney transplant.
- if the pancreas transplant is performed after the kidney transplant, Medicare will pay for immunosuppressive drug therapy for 36 months after the month of the pancreas transplant.

Kidney Donor Coverage

Medicare Parts A and B cover the cost of medical care for a person donating a kidney to a Medicare-eligible ESRD patient. This coverage includes all preoperative testing, surgery, postoperative services, and any treatment for complications arising from the surgery. Medicare rules state that services furnished to the kidney donor are to be treated as services furnished to the kidney recipient. This stipulation allows Medicare to become the secondary payer when the kidney recipient has *large group health plan (LGHP)* coverage for the kidney donor's medical expenses. If the donor's medical expenses are not a covered benefit of the recipient's plan, Medicare will cover the donor's medical expenses for the organ donation. The donor, qualifying under this special Medicare kidney donation program, is not entitled to medical coverage for expenses not directly related to the donation of the kidney. If donors sell their kidneys for transplantation, the purchase price of the donated kidney is not covered by Medicare. All payments for medical expenses incurred by the donor are made directly to the hospital and health care providers.

Heart and Heart-Lung Transplant Coverage

Until 1987, ESRD coverage was the only specified disease and/or transplant coverage in the Medicare program. Heart and heart-lung transplants are now covered if the person is eligible for Medicare and the transplant takes place in a Medicare-certified regional transplant center.

Lung Transplants

The national policy for Medicare coverage of lung transplants was established in 1995 for hospitals with documented experience and success in performing the procedure. Medicare had been paying for the procedure when approved by Medicare contractors in individual cases. To become an approved Medicare Lung Transplant Center, a hospital must present data (based on CMS-established criteria) on its lung transplants and outcomes for patients along with documentation of survival rates. In addition, a hospital is required to perform a minimum number of lung transplants each year to retain its status in the Medicare program. This mandate is designed to ensure that the transplant team maintains the skills needed for quality performance. Combined heart-lung transplantation is also covered when performed in a hospital approved for either heart or lung transplants.

Liver Transplants

Liver transplants for adults are covered if the person is eligible for Medicare, does not have a malignancy, and the surgery takes place in a Medicare-certified regional liver transplant center (until 2000, Medicare had not covered liver transplants for patients with hepatitis B). Follow-up care for patients who have received noncovered liver transplants is also available.

Children are covered if they have a diagnosis of biliary atresia or any other form of end-stage liver disease *except* when caused by malignancy that has extended beyond the margins of the liver or those diagnosed with persistent viremia. All transplants must take place in Medicare-certified pediatric liver transplant facilities.

Bone Marrow Transplants

Autologous bone marrow transplants use the patient's own (previously stored) cells and are covered for patients diagnosed with (1) acute leukemia in remission, (2) resistant non-Hodgkin lymphomas, (3) recurrent or refractory neuroblastomas, or (4) advanced Hodgkin disease, only if conventional therapy has failed or there is no HLA-matched (human leukocyte antigen) donor available. Coverage is denied for the following diagnoses: (1) chronic granulocytic leukemia, (2) acute leukemia in relapse, and (3) any solid tumors other than neuroblastoma.

Allogeneic bone marrow transplants use a portion of a healthy donor's stem cell or bone marrow as obtained and prepared for intravenous infusion; patients are covered for the treatment of:

- **Leukemia** (progressive proliferation of abnormal white blood cells).
- Leukemia in **remission** (symptoms lessen in severity).
- **Aplastic anemia** (decreased formation of red blood cells and hemoglobin) when it is reasonable and necessary.
- **Severe combined immunodeficiency disease (SCID)** (defective immune system due to a defect in the immune mechanism or another disease process).
- **Wiskott-Aldrich syndrome** (X-linked immunodeficiency disorder that occurs in male children).

Allogeneic bone marrow transplants are *not* covered as treatment for **multiple myeloma** (a form of bone marrow cancer).

MEDICARE PART B COVERAGE

Medicare Part B is designed to cover outpatient services and professional services provided to inpatients including:

- physician services, but not routine physicals or strictly cosmetic surgery, unless the result of an injury.
- professional services provided to inpatients.
- services of nonphysician professionals such as nurses, certified registered nurse anesthetists, nurse practitioners, clinical nurse specialists, certified nurse midwives, and physicians assistants.
- services of *limited* license personnel such as institutional and independent physical, occupational, and speech therapists; podiatrists; chiropractors; and clinical psychologists.
- diagnostic testing.
- radioactive isotope therapy.
- drugs that are not self-administered.
- ambulance services.
- durable medical equipment (DME) and supplies used in the home and certified by a physician.
- influenza, hepatitis B, and pneumonococcal vaccines (over deductibles).
- therapeutic shoes and shoe inserts for diabetic patients.
- home health services for persons enrolled only in Medicare Part B (the benefits, deductible, and coinsurance match those available under Part A).

The following preventive screening services were added to the benefits under the Balanced Budget Act of 1997:

- annual mammogram screening for women over age 39
- annual colorectal screening/fecal–occult blood for patients age 50 and over, if ordered in writing by a physician
- colorectal screening/flexible sigmoidoscopies every four years for patients age 50 and over (barium enemas may be substituted for the flexible sigmoidoscopy if a physician writes the order)
- colorectal screening/colonoscopies every two years if the patient is at high risk for colorectal cancer (barium enemas may be substituted for the colonscopy if the attending physician determines it is a more appropriate test and issues a written order)
- screening pelvic and clinical breast examinations every three years for women (these tests may be performed annually for certain women of child bearing age or women at high risk for cervical or vaginal cancer)

Deductible and Coinsurance Expenses

Medicare Part B costs to the patient include:

- a $100 deductible (payable annually).
- 20% of Medicare allowed fees on all covered benefits, except in the outpatient setting.
- 50% of Medicare allowed fees for most outpatient mental health care.
- 20% of the first $1,500 for all physical or occupational therapy services, and all related charges thereafter.
- 20% of Medicare allowed fees for home health care durable medical equipment.
- no less than 20% of the Medicare allowed fees (after the deductible) for hospital outpatient services.
- the first three pints of blood plus 20% of the Medicare allowed fees for additional pints of blood (after the deductible).

Providers who routinely refrain from collecting the patient's deductible and coinsurance are in violation of Medicare regulations and are subject to large fines and exclusion from the Medicare program.

Special Outpatient Mental Health Benefits

Outpatient mental health treatments are subject to the following special rules. The coinsurance is 50% of allowable charges; however, this is reduced to 20% of allowable outpatient hospital charges if the patient would have required admission to a psychiatric facility if outpatient treatments were not available.

Physician Fee Schedule

Since 1992, Medicare has reimbursed provider services according to a *physician fee schedule* (also called the *Resource Based Relative Value Scale, RBRVS*), which also limits amounts nonparticipating providers (nonPARs) can charge beneficiaries. Reimbursement under the fee schedule is based on relative value units (RVUs) that consider resources used in providing a service (physician work, practice expense, and malpractice expense). The schedule is revised annually and is organized in a table format that includes HCPCS/CPT code numbers and the Medicare allowed fee for each.

EXAMPLE: CPT E/M codes would be listed in the physician fee schedule as:

99201	$ 35.68	99211	$ 21.47
99202	$ 64.48	99212	$ 38.02
99203	$ 96.32	99213	$ 52.76
99204	$ 136.57	99214	$ 82.57
99205	$ 173.30	99215	$ 120.93

INTERNET LINKS

Click on the Medicare link at http://cms.hhs.gov to access current physician fee schedules according to regional carrier. RBRVS and related information can be found at http://www.rbrvs.com

PARTICIPATING PROVIDERS

Medicare has established a **participating provider (PAR)** agreement in which the provider contracts to *accept assignment* on all claims submitted to Medicare. By 2000, more than 85% of all physicians, practitioners, and suppliers in the United States were PARs. Congress mandated special incentives to increase the number of health care providers signing PAR agreements with Medicare, including:

- direct payment of all claims.
- a 5% higher fee schedule than that for nonparticipating providers.
- bonuses provided to carriers for recruitment and enrollment of PARs.
- publication of an annual, regional PAR directory (MedPARD) made available to all Medicare patients.
- a special message printed on all unassigned explanation of benefits (EOB) forms mailed to patients, reminding them of the reduction in out-of-pocket

expenses if they use PARs and stating how much they would save with PARs.

- hospital referrals for outpatient care that provide the patient with the name and full address of at least one PAR provider each time the hospital provides a referral for care.
- faster processing of assigned claims.

Regardless of the type of Medicare Part B services billed, PARs have "one stop" billing for beneficiaries who have nonemployment-related Medigap coverage and who assign both Medicare and Medigap payments to participants. After Medicare has made payment, the claim will be automatically sent to the Medigap insurer for payment of all coinsurance and deductible amounts due under the Medigap policy. The Medigap insurer must pay the participant directly.

NONPARTICIPATING PROVIDER RESTRICTIONS

Medicare **nonparticipating providers (nonPAR)** may elect to accept assignment on a claim-by-claim basis, but several restrictions must be adhered to:

- NonPARs must file all Medicare claims.
- Fees are restricted to not more than the "limiting charge" on nonassigned claims.
- Balance billing of the patient by a nonPAR is forbidden.
- Collections are restricted to only the deductible and coinsurance due at the time of service on an assigned claim.
- Patients must sign a Surgical Disclosure Notice for all nonassigned surgical fees over $500.
- NonPARs must accept assignment on clinical laboratory charges.

Limiting Charge

Nonparticipating physicians who do not accept assignment on their Medicare claims are subject to a limit (established by federal law) on what can be charged to beneficiaries for covered services. The Medicare allowed fee for nonPARs is 5% below the PAR fee schedule, but the nonPAR physician may charge a maximum of 15% above the nonPAR approved rate (or 10% above the PAR fee schedule). The *limiting charge (LC)* or *limiting fee* is the maximum fee a nonPAR may charge for a covered service. It applies regardless of who is responsible for payment and whether Medicare is primary or secondary.

EXAMPLE:

NonPAR limiting charge for office visit	$110
Medicare allowed fee (5% below PAR schedule)	$95
Medicare pays 80% of allowed fee	$ 76
Patient owes provider:	$34
The difference between limiting charge and Medicare allowed fee	$ 15
plus	
20% (copay) of Medicare allowed fee of $95	$19
Total payment to nonPAR ($76 + $34)	$110

Compare the previous example to the following example of a patient who is seen by a PAR provider for the same service.

EXAMPLE:

PAR usual fee for office visit	$110
PAR Medicare allowed fee	$99.75
Medicare pays 80% of allowed fee	$79.80
PAR adjusts the difference between the usual charge and Medicare allowed fee	$10.25
Patient pays PAR 20% of $99.75 allowed fee	$19.95
Total payment to PAR	$99.75

Although it appears that the nonPAR is paid more than the PAR ($110 versus $99.75), the nonPAR has to collect $34 from the patient while the PAR has to collect just $19.95 from the patient. (It is also more cost-effective for patients to seek treatment from PARs.)

HIPAA ALERT: With the passage of the Health Insurance Portability and Accountability Act (HIPAA) of 1996, Congress increased the potential fine from $2,000 to $10,000 if a nonPAR does not heed the carrier's warnings to desist from flagrant abuse of the "limiting charge" rules.

Accepting Assignment on a Claim

A nonparticipating provider who agrees to accept assignment on a claim will be reimbursed the Medicare allowed fee. The nonPAR may also collect any unpaid deductible and the 20% coinsurance determined from the Medicare Physician Fee Schedule (PFS). If the nonPAR collects the entire charge at the time of the patient's visit, the assigned status of the claim is voided and the nonPAR limiting fee is then in effect. The nonPAR may also be subject to a fine or may be in violation of PFS requirements.

The nonPAR cannot revoke the agreement for an assigned claim *unless* it is by mutual written consent of the provider and the beneficiary. Even then, such an agreement must be communicated to the carrier *before* the carrier has determined the allowed amount. Providers who repeatedly violate the assignment agreement could be charged and found guilty of a misdemeanor, which is punishable by a fine, imprisonment, or both. In addition, a criminal violation may result in suspension from Medicare participation.

Mandatory Assignment

Providers who are *required* to accept assignment on *all* Medicare covered services include:

- **non-physician providers** (physician assistants, nurse practitioners, nurse midwives, clinical nurse specialists, clinical psychologists, clinical social workers, and Certified Registered Nurse Anesthetists).
- **limited license practitioners (LLPs)** (psychologists, clinical psychologists, and clinical social workers).

In addition, the following Medicare covered services are paid *only* on an assigned basis:

- clinical diagnostic laboratory services
- physician services provided to Medicaid eligible recipients
- Ambulatory Surgical Center (ASC) facility fees

EXAMPLE: A patient undergoes laboratory procedures and sees the physician during an office visit (evaluation and management service). If the nonPAR accepts assignment for just the laboratory procedures, two claims must be submitted: one for the laboratory services and another for the office visit. ●

Surgery Disclosure Notice

Nonparticipating providers must notify beneficiaries in writing of projected out-of-pocket expenses for elective surgery and nonassigned procedures when the charge for surgery is $500 or more. This notification is required of both surgeons and assistant surgeons. For Medicare purposes, "elective surgery" is defined as a surgery that:

- can be scheduled in advance;
- is not an emergency; and
- if delayed, *would not* result in death or permanent impairment of health.

The Omnibus Budget Reconciliation Act (OBRA) of 1986 requires the following information to be provided in writing to the patient:

- estimated actual charge for surgery
- estimated Medicare payment
- excess of the provider's actual charge as compared with the approved charge
- applicable coinsurance amount
- beneficiary's out-of-pocket expenses

NonPARs must document the receipt and acknowledgment of the above information by having the beneficiary or his/her representative sign and date a Surgical Disclosure Notice (Figure 14-1). A copy of the signed and dated notice must be maintained and provided upon request from the carrier. If the nonPAR fails to properly notify the beneficiary prior to performing surgery, any money collected from the beneficiary that exceeds the Medicare approved amount must be refunded. Failure to make the appropriate refund could result in civil monetary penalties and/or exclusion from the Medicare program.

Mandatory Claims Submission

Federal law requires that all providers and suppliers submit claims to Medicare if they provide a Medicare-covered service to a patient enrolled in Medicare Part B. This regulation does not apply if the:

- patient is not enrolled in Part B.
- patient disenrolled before the service was furnished.
- patient or the patient's legal representative refuses to sign an authorization for release of medical information.
- provider opts out of the Medicare program, and those patients enter into private contracts with the provider (see Private Contracting on page 415).

An exception may occur if a patient refuses to sign an authorization for the release of medical information to Medicare. However, if the patient later opts to sign a Medicare authorization and requests that claims for all prior services be filed with Medicare, the request must be honored.

Waiver of Medicare Billing Contracts

Medicare law specifically states that nonPARs are subject to sanctions, including fines and exclusions from the Medicare program, if they require patients to sign

---

Goodmedicine Clinic ■ 1 Provider St ■ Anywhere US 12345 ■ (101)111-2222

_____   _____
Name of Medicare Beneficiary   Date

As previously discussed, I am not accepting Medicare assignment for reimbursement of your surgery. Medicare regulations require that I provide the following information to patients who are considering surgery that will cost $500 or more.

Type of surgery   _____

Name of provider   _____

Estimated actual charge $ _____

Estimated Medicare payment $ _____

Patient's estimated payment (includes coinsurance) $ _____

ACKNOWLEDGED AND AGREED BY:

_____   _____
Signature of Medicare Beneficiary   Date   Signature of Provider   Date
or Legal Representative

FIGURE 14-1 Sample nonPAR surgery disclosure notice

---

agreements stating that the patient waives the right to have the nonPAR provider file the patient's Medicare claims or that the patient agrees to pay for services that are in excess of the nonPAR charge limits.

Privacy Act

In addition to the above restrictions, the **Privacy Act of 1974** forbids the regional carrier from disclosing the status of any unassigned claim beyond the following:

- Date the claim was received by the carrier.
- Date the claim was paid, denied, or suspended.
- General reason the claim was suspended.

The nonPAR provider will *not* be told payment amounts or approved charge information.

State Law Bans Balance Billing

Many states have passed legislation restricting **balance billing** (or *hold harmless*) of patients, which is the act of billing the patient for the difference between the charged fee and the Medicare allowed fee. Balance billing does not affect the patient's deductible and coinsurance obligations. It should be noted that state law takes precedence over CMS rules.

- Connecticut and Vermont require providers to accept assignment for patients with incomes below the state-established amount.
- Arizona, Florida, Georgia, Massachusetts, Ohio, Pennsylvania, and Rhode Island prohibit balance billing.
- New York restricts billing to 110% above the nonPAR fee schedule amount.

In all other states, the nonPAR may collect the difference between the nonPAR approved amount and the limiting fee.

EXAMPLE: A provider charges $150 for an office visit, and upon submission of the bill to Medicare it is determined that the Medicare allowed fee is $100 for that visit. Medicare reimburses the provider $80 (80% of the allowed fee), and the patient reimburses the provider $20 (20% of the allowed fee). In states where balance billing is prohibited, the patient cannot be billed the difference between the Medicare allowed fee of $100 and the provider's charges of $150. The provider must absorb this loss. *If the patient paid the $150 charge at the time of the office visit, the patient is entitled to a $50 refund.* (In states where balance billing is allowed, the patient can be billed according to *limiting charge* rules. Refer to page 411 for limiting charge calculations.)

PRIVATE CONTRACTING

Under the Balanced Budget Act of 1997, physicians were provided the option of dropping out of Medicare and entering into a private contract with their Medicare patients. This **Medicare private contract** is an agreement between the Medicare beneficiary and a physician or other practitioner who has "opted out" of Medicare for two years for *all* covered items and services furnished to Medicare beneficiaries. This means that the physician/practitioner will not bill for any service or supplies provided to any Medicare beneficiary for at least 2 years.

Under a private contract:

- no Medicare payment will be made for services or procedures provided to a patient.
- the patient is required to pay whatever the physician/practitioner charges, and there is no limit on what the physician/practitioner can charge for Medicare approved services (the *limiting charge* will not apply).
- Medicare Managed Care Plans will not pay for services rendered under a private contract.
- no claim is to be submitted to Medicare, and Medicare will not pay if a claim is submitted.
- Supplemental Insurance (Medigap) will not pay for services or procedures rendered.
- other insurance plans may not pay for services or procedures rendered.

The private contract applies only to services and procedures rendered by the physician or practitioner with whom you signed an agreement. Patients cannot be asked to sign a private contract when facing an emergency or urgent health situation. If patients want to pay for services that the Original Medicare Plan does not cover, the physician does not have to leave Medicare or ask the patient to sign a private contract. The patient is welcome to obtain noncovered services and to pay for those services.

A physician who enters into a Medicare private contract with one patient will be unable to bill Medicare for any patient for a period of 2 years with the exception of emergency or urgent care provided to a patient who has not signed an agreement with the provider to forego Medicare benefits. In these cases, the claim for urgent or emergency care must be accompanied by an attachment explaining the following: (1) the nature of the emergency or urgent problem, and (2) a statement affirming that this patient has not signed an agreement with the provider to forego Medicare. If a provider submits a nonemergency or urgent care claim for any patient before the "opt out agreement" becomes effective, the provider must submit claims for all Medicare patients thereafter and abide by the "limiting fee" rules. If, however, the patient files the claim, the provider will not be penalized.

ADVANCE BENEFICIARY NOTICE

An **Advance Beneficiary Notice (ABN)** is a written document provided to a Medicare beneficiary by a supplier, physician, or provider prior to rendering a service (Figure 14-2). The ABN indicates that the service is unlikely to be reimbursed by Medicare, specifies why Medicare denial is anticipated, and requests the beneficiary to sign an agreement that guarantees personal payment for services. A beneficiary who signs an ABN agreement will be held responsible for payment of the bill if Medicare denies payment. ABNs should be generated whenever the supplier or provider believes that a claim for the services is likely to receive a Medicare **medical necessity denial** (a denial of otherwise covered services that were found to be not "reasonable and necessary").

Patient's Name: _____   Medicare # (HICN): _____

ADVANCE BENEFICIARY NOTICE (ABN)

NOTE: You need to make a choice about receiving these health care items or services.

We expect that Medicare will not pay for the item(s) or service(s) that are described below. Medicare does not pay for all of your health care costs. Medicare only pays for covered items and services when Medicare rules are met. The fact that Medicare may not pay for a particular item or service does not mean that you should not receive it. There may be a good reason your doctor recommended it. Right now, in your case, **Medicare probably will not pay for –**

Items or Services:

Because:

The purpose of this form is to help you make an informed choice about whether or not you want to receive these items or services, knowing that you might have to pay for them yourself. Before you make a decision about your options, you should **read this entire notice carefully.**

- Ask us to explain, if you don't understand why Medicare probably won't pay.
- Ask us how much these items or services will cost you (**Estimated Cost: $_____**), in case you have to pay for them yourself or through other insurance.

PLEASE CHOOSE **ONE** OPTION. CHECK **ONE** BOX. **SIGN & DATE** YOUR CHOICE.

☐ **Option 1. YES. I want to receive these items or services.**

I understand that Medicare will not decide whether to pay unless I receive these items or services. Please submit my claim to Medicare. I understand that you may bill me for items or services and that I may have to pay the bill while Medicare is making its decision. If Medicare does pay, you will refund to me any payments I made to you that are due to me. If Medicare denies payment, I agree to be personally and fully responsible for payment. That is, I will pay personally, either out of pocket or through any other insurance that I have. I understand I can appeal Medicare's decision.

☐ **Option 2. NO. I have decided not to receive these items or services.**

I will not receive these items or services. I understand that you will not be able to submit a claim to Medicare and that I will not be able to appeal your opinion that Medicare won't pay.

_____   _____
Date   **Signature of patient or person acting on patient's behalf**

NOTE: Your health information will be kept confidential. Any information that we collect about you on this form will be kept confidential in our offices. If a claim is submitted to Medicare, your health information on this form may be shared with Medicare. Your health information, which Medicare sees, be will kept confidential by Medicare.

OMB Approval No. 0938-0566   Form No. CMS-R-131-G   (June 2002)

FIGURE 14-2 Advance Beneficiary Notice (ABN) form approved for use by CMS (Reprinted according to http://cms.hhs.gov Web Site Content Reuse Policy)

The purpose of obtaining the ABN is to ensure payment for a procedure or service that might not be reimbursed under Medicare.

ABNs are unnecessary for Medicare's "categorically noncovered services" (e.g., cosmetic surgery, hearing aids, routine physicals, and screening tests). In addition, cost estimates are unnecessary when an ABN is generated because the purpose of the ABN is to document that the beneficiary has received notice that a service is unlikely to be reimbursed by Medicare. Hospital ABNs are called "Hospital-Issued Notices of Noncoverage" (HINN) or "Notices of Noncoverage" (NONC).

CAUTION: Do not obtain ABNs on every procedure or service to be rendered to a patient "just in case" Medicare denies the claim. To do so is considered fraudulent. ●

Experimental and Investigational Procedures

Medicare law allows payment only for services or supplies that are considered reasonable and necessary for the stated diagnosis. Medicare will not cover procedures deemed to be experimental in nature. There are cases in which the provider determines that treatments or services are fully justified and such treatment options are then explained to the patient, who must pay the full cost of the uncovered procedure.

Medicare regulations specify that the provider must refund any payment received from a patient for a service denied by Medicare as investigational, unnecessary, unproved, or experimental, unless the patient agreed in writing prior to receiving the services to personally pay for such services. Figure 14-3 shows a CMS-approved Medical Necessity Statement. An appeal of the denial of payment must be made in writing, and if the appeal is not granted, a refund must be paid to the patient within 30 days. A refund is not required if the provider "could not have known a specific treatment would be ruled unnecessary."

NOTE: CMS has announced that it will consider, for Medicare coverage, certain devices with an FDA-approved Investigational Device (IDE) that are considered nonexperimental or investigational. The FDA categorizes all FDA-approved IDEs into either Category A (experimental) or Category B (nonexperimental/investigational) for Medicare reimbursement consideration. Only those IDEs placed in Category B by the FDA are eligible for Medicare coverage consideration. ●

MEDICARE AS A SECONDARY PAYER

A clarification of the **Medicare Secondary Payer (MSP)** rules was published in 1996 stating that Medicare is secondary when the patient is eligible for Medicare and is also covered by one or more of the following plans:

- An employer-sponsored group health plan (EGHP) that has more than 20 covered employees.
- Disability coverage through an employer-sponsored group health plan that has more than 100 covered employees.
- An ESRD case covered by an employer-sponsored group plan of any size during the first 18 months of the patient's eligibility for Medicare.
- A third-party liability policy, if the Medicare-eligible person is seeking treatment for an injury covered by such a policy (this category includes automobile insurance, no-fault insurance, and self-insured liability plans).

Goodmedicine Clinic ■ 1 Provider St ■ Anywhere US 12345 ■ (101)111-2222

To My Medicare Patients:

My primary concern as your physician is to provide you with the best possible care. Medicare does not pay for all services and will only allow those which it determines, under the guidelines spelled out in the Omnibus Budget Reconciliation Act of 1986 Section 1862(a)(1), to be reasonable and necessary. Under this law, a procedure or service deemed to be medically unreasonable or unnecessary will be denied. Since I believe each scheduled visit or planned procedure is both reasonable and necessary, I am required to notify you in advance that the following procedures or services listed below, which we have mutually agreed on, may be denied by Medicare.

Date of Service _____

Description of Service   Charge

_____   _____

_____   _____

_____   _____

Denial may be for the following reasons:
1. Medicare does not usually pay for this many visits or treatments,
2. Medicare does not usually pay for this many services within this period of time, and/or
3. Medicare does not usually pay for this type of service for your condition.

I, however, believe these procedures/services to be both reasonable and necessary for your condition, and will assist you in collecting payment from Medicare. In order for me to assist you in this matter, the law requires that you read the following agreement and sign it.

I have been informed by <u>(fill in the name and title of the provider)</u> that he/she believes, in my case, Medicare is likely to deny payment for the services and reasons stated above. If Medicare denies payment, I agree to be personally and fully responsible for payment.

Beneficiary's Name: _____ Medicare ID# _____ or

Beneficiary's Signature: _____

or

Authorized Representative's Signature _____

FIGURE 14-3 Sample letter of medical necessity

- A Workers' Compensation program; if the claim is contested, the provider should file a Medicare primary claim and include a copy of the workers' compensation notice declaring that the case is "pending a Compensation Board decision."
- Veterans Administration (VA) preauthorized services for a beneficiary who is eligible for both VA benefits and Medicare.
- Federal Black Lung Program that covers currently or formerly employed coal miners.

All primary plans, which are collectively described in the Medicare literature as MSP plans, must be billed first. Medicare is billed only after the EOB from the primary plan or plans has been received. (The EOBs must be attached to the Medicare claim when the claim is submitted.)

NOTE: Providers are required to collect or verify Medicare as Secondary Payer (MSP) information during the initial beneficiary encounter instead of each time the patient is seen. Providers are also encouraged to retain MSP questionnaires for at least ten years, even though five years is the required retention period. ●

To avoid fines and penalties for routinely billing Medicare as primary when it is the secondary payer, a more detailed Medicare Secondary Payer (MSP) questionnaire (Figure 14-4) should be provided to all Medicare patients when they register/reregister (update demographic and/or insurance information) with the practice. This form is used to clarify primary and secondary insurance payers.

Goodmedicine Clinic ■ 1 Provider St ■ Anywhere US 12345 ■ (101)111-2222

To: All Medicare Patients
In order for us to comply with the Medicare as Secondary Payer laws you must complete this form before we can properly process your insurance claim.

Please complete this questionnaire and return it to the front desk. We will also need to make photocopies of all your insurance identification cards. Do not hesitate to ask for clarification of any item on this form.

CHECK ALL ITEMS THAT DESCRIBE YOUR HEALTH INSURANCE COVERAGE
1. I am working full time _____ part time_____ I retired on ___/___/___.
2. _____ I am enrolled in a Medicare HMO Plan.
   _____ I am entitled to Black Lung Benefits.
   _____ I had a job-related injury on ___/___/___.
   _____ I have a fee service card from the VA.
   _____ I had an organ transplant on ___/___/___.
   _____ I have been on kidney dialysis since ___/___/___.
   _____ I am being treated for an injury received in a car accident _____.
   _____ Other vehicle (please identify)
   _____ Other type of accident (please identify) _____
   _____.
3. _____ I am employed/My spouse is employed and I am covered by an employer-sponsored health care program covering more than 20 employees. Name of policy:
   _____
4. _____ I/My spouse has purchased a private insurance policy to supplement Medicare.
   Name of policy:
   _____
5. _____ I have health insurance through my/my spouse's previous employer or union. Name of previous employer or union:
   _____
6. _____ I am covered by Medicaid and my ID number is: _____
7. _____ I am retired and covered by an employer-sponsored retiree health care plan.
   Name of plan:
   _____
8. _____ I am retired, but have been called back temporarily and have employee health benefits while I am working. Name of plan:
   _____

Patient Signature _____ Date _____/_____/_____

FIGURE 14-4 Sample Medicare secondary payer questionnaire

MSP Fee Schedule Rules

- The primary insurance fee schedule overrules the Medicare schedule on *assigned claims only.*
- NonPARs who do not accept assignment are prohibited from collecting amounts above the applicable limiting charge.
- Providers are not required to file Medicare secondary claims unless the patient specifically requests it.

Medicare Primary Rules

Medicare is considered the primary payer under the following circumstances.

- The employee is eligible for a group health plan but has declined to enroll or recently dropped coverage.
- The employee is currently employed, but is not yet eligible for group plan coverage or has exhausted benefits under the plan.
- The health insurance plan is only for self-employed individuals.
- The health insurance plan was purchased as an individual plan and not obtained through a group.
- The patient is also covered by TRICARE (formerly known as CHAMPUS), which provides health benefits to retired members of the uniformed services and spouses/children of active duty, retired, and deceased service members.
- The patient is under 65 and has Medicare due to a disability or ESRD and is not also covered by an employer-sponsored plan.
- The patient is under 65, has ESRD, and has an employer-sponsored plan but has been eligible for Medicare for more than 30 months.
- The patient has left a company and has elected to continue coverage in the group health plan under federal COBRA rules.
- The patient has both Medicare and Medicaid (crossover patient).

The Consolidated Omnibus Budget Reconciliation Act of 1985 (COBRA) requires employers with 20 or more employees to allow employees and their dependents to keep their employer-sponsored group health insurance coverage for up to 18 months for any of the following occurrences:

- death of the employed spouse
- loss of employment or reduction in work hours
- divorce

The employee or dependents may have to pay their share as well as the employer's share of the premium.

Medicare Conditional Primary Payer Status

Medicare will award an assigned claim **conditional primary payer status** and process the claim under the following circumstances:

- A plan that is normally considered to be primary to Medicare issues a Status denial of payment that is under appeal.
- A patient who is physically or mentally impaired failed to file a claim to the primary carrier.
- A workers' compensation claim has been denied, and the case is slowly moving through the appeal process.

- There is no response from a liability carrier within 120 days of filing the claim.

Medicare is to be immediately reimbursed if payment is received from the primary carrier at a later date.

MEDICARE PLANS

Depending on where a Medicare beneficiary lives, up to three Medicare plans are available:

- Original Medicare plan, which is offered by the Federal government and available throughout the United States.
- Medicare managed care plans are available in many areas of the country and often require beneficiaries to seek care from providers on the plan's list; the advantage is that other benefits such as drug plans are usually offered.
- Private fee-for-service plan, in which Medicare pays a pre-established, monthly rate to a private insurance company that provides health care coverage to Medicare beneficiaries on a pay-per-visit arrangement.

NOTE: The private insurance company, not Medicare, determines how much beneficiaries pay for services received. •

Original Medicare Plan

The **Original Medicare Plan** is also known as "fee-for-service" or "traditional pay-per-visit." Beneficiaries are usually charged a fee for each health care service or supply received. Medicare beneficiaries satisfied with receiving health care in this manner do not have to join a Medicare managed care plan or private fee-for-service plan; they can remain in the Original Medicare Plan. To help cover costs that the Original Medicare Plan does not cover, beneficiaries often purchase supplemental insurance plans (e.g., Medigap or employer-sponsored supplemental plans, explained on page 423).

Beneficiaries of the Original Medicare Plan:

- may go to any doctor, specialist, or hospital that accepts Medicare.
- pay a monthly Part B premium.
- pay an annual deductible before Medicare reimbursement is generated.
- pay a coinsurance (copayment) amount for each health care service received.
- receive a Medicare Summary Notice (MSN) in the mail.
- can obtain additional information about the Original Medicare Plan by calling 1-800-MEDICARE.

INTERNET LINK

Visit http://www.medicare.gov to obtain consumer information about the Original Medicare Plan. CMS's Web site for Medicare is http://cms.hhs.gov/medicare and includes downloadable files.

Medicare Summary Notice (MSN)

The *Medicare Summary Notice (MSN)* (Figure 14-5) is an easy-to-read, monthly statement that clearly lists health insurance claims information. It replaced the

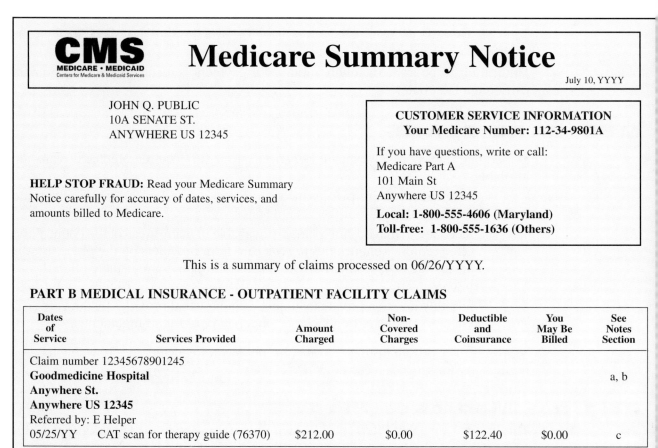

CMS
MEDICARE · MEDICAID
Centers for Medicare & Medicaid Services

Medicare Summary Notice

July 10, YYYY

JOHN Q. PUBLIC
10A SENATE ST.
ANYWHERE US 12345

CUSTOMER SERVICE INFORMATION
Your Medicare Number: 112-34-9801A

If you have questions, write or call:
Medicare Part A
101 Main St
Anywhere US 12345

Local: 1-800-555-4606 (Maryland)
Toll-free: 1-800-555-1636 (Others)

HELP STOP FRAUD: Read your Medicare Summary
Notice carefully for accuracy of dates, services, and
amounts billed to Medicare.

This is a summary of claims processed on 06/26/YYYY.

PART B MEDICAL INSURANCE - OUTPATIENT FACILITY CLAIMS

Dates of Service	Services Provided	Amount Charged	Non-Covered Charges	Deductible and Coinsurance	You May Be Billed	See Notes Section
Claim number 12345678901245 **Goodmedicine Hospital** **Anywhere St.** **Anywhere US 12345** Referred by: E Helper						a, b
05/25/YY	CAT scan for therapy guide (76370)	$212.00	$0.00	$122.40	$0.00	c

Notes Section:

  a. This information is being sent to your private insurer(s). Send any questions regarding your benefits to them.
  b. $100.00 of the money approved by your primary insurer has been credited to your Medicare Part B deductible. You do not have to pay this amount.
  c. $100.00 of this approved amount has been applied toward your deductible.

Your Medicare Number: 112-34-9801A

Deductible Information:

  You have met the Part B deductible for 2000.

General Information:

  Who pays? You pay. Report Medicare fraud by calling 1-800-447-8477. An example of fraud would be claims for Medicare items or services you did not receive. If you have any other questions about your claim, please contact the Medicare contractor telephone number shown on this notice.

  You can protect yourself from some pneumococcal infections by getting a pneumococcal vaccination. Medicare Part B will pay for your vaccination. One pneumococcal vaccination may be all you ever need.

Appeals Information - Part B (Outpatient)

If you disagree with any claims decision on this notice, you can request an appeal by **January 10, YYYY**. Follow the instructions below:

  1. Circle the item(s) you disagree with and explain why you disagree.

  2. Send this notice, or a copy, to the address in the "Customer Service Information" box on Page 1.

  3. Sign here _____ Phone number (_____) _____

THIS IS NOT A BILL - Keep this notice for your records.

FIGURE 14-5 Sample Medicare Summary Notice (MSN)

Explanation of Medicare Benefits (EOMB), the Medicare Benefits Notice (Part A), and benefit denial letters.

INTERNET LINK

Go to http://www.medicare.gov/Basics/SummaryNotice_HowToReadB.asp to view a sample Medicare Summary Notice (MSN) that also explains its components.

Medicare Supplemental Plans

Beneficiaries often purchase one or more of the following Medicare supplementary plans (MSP) to cover the Medicare deductible and coinsurance requirements:

1. Medigap plan
2. Employer-sponsored retirement plan
3. Extra coverage plan

NOTE: If Medicare does not accept liability for a particular claim, the MSP has no obligation to provide coverage.

Medigap Plans

A **Medigap policy** is a private, commercial plan that meets the federal government standards for Medigap coverage and collects the premiums directly from the patient. It provides coverage to patients for health care costs not paid by Medicare to "fill the gap". The federal government approved 10 different types of coverage for Medigap policies (Table 14-2). While Plan A is restricted to the basic benefit package with no additions, all the other plans (B–J) include the basic package plus one or more additional benefits. In the basic package, the coinsurance coverage begins on the 61st day but does not cover the initial inpatient deductible, the coinsurance for posthospital skilled nursing facility stays, or the Part B deductible. Other plans cover additional benefits including the Part A deductible, Part B deductible, and so forth, depending on the plan chosen by the subscriber.

It is important to note that the federal government has standard benefits, not premiums. The premiums can vary widely even within the same geographic area. Beneficiaries should shop around before enrolling in coverage. Patients thinking of enrolling in Medigap coverage are urged to call their local area Council Office on Aging to get a listing of Medigap carriers in a given county or state.

Medigap claims are handled in one of two ways:

1. *PAR claims:* The Medicare carrier electronically transfers the billing and Medicare payment information to the Medigap carrier when the Medigap carrier and policyholder information appears on the Medicare claim in Blocks 9 through 9d and 13. If no response from the Medigap carrier with electronic transfer capability has been received within 30 days of receiving the Medicare MSN, a copy of the Medicare/Medigap claim form with a photocopy of the Medicare MSN attached should be filed with the Medigap insurer.

2. *NonPAR claims:* NonPAR providers are not required to include Medigap information on the claim form. If the nonPAR extends a courtesy to the patient by filing a Medigap claim, the patient must provide a copy of the Medicare MSN to the provider. (MSNs for nonassigned claims go directly to the patient; the provider does not receive an MSN directly from Medicare.)

TABLE 14-2 Medigap plans

BASIC BENEFITS REQUIRED BY ALL MEDIGAP PLANS	A	B	C	D	E	F	G	H	I	J
Part A Hospital (Days 61–90)	✔	✔	✔	✔	✔	✔	✔	✔	✔	✔
Lifetime Reserve Days (91–150)	✔	✔	✔	✔	✔	✔	✔	✔	✔	✔
365 Life Hospital Days—100%	✔	✔	✔	✔	✔	✔	✔	✔	✔	✔
Parts A & B Blood	✔	✔	✔	✔	✔	✔	✔	✔	✔	✔
Part B Coinsurance—20%	✔	✔	✔	✔	✔	✔	✔	✔	✔	✔

ADDITIONAL BENEFITS	A	B	C	D	E	F	G	H	I	J
Skilled Nursing Facility Coinsurance (Days 21–90)			✔	✔	✔	✔	✔	✔	✔	✔
Part A Deductible		✔	✔	✔	✔	✔	✔	✔	✔	✔
Part B Deductible			✔			✔				✔
Part B Excess Charges						100%	80%		100%	100%
Foreign Travel Emergency			✔	✔	✔	✔	✔	✔	✔	✔
At-Home Recovery				✔			✔		✔	✔
Prescription Drugs								$1,250	$1,250	$3,000
Preventive Medical Care					✔					✔

Employer-Sponsored Retirement Plan

An **employer-sponsored retirement plan** is a conversion plan offered to employees by certain companies at the time of retirement. These plans are intended to complement the retiree's Medicare coverage, are not regulated by the federal government, and are subject to limitations established in the employer's regular health insurance plans. The premiums are paid to the insurance carrier either by or through the employer. If the employer's regular group plan does not cover office visits, these visits may be excluded by the conversion plan.

These plans do *not* qualify for designation as a Medigap policy and health care providers are not required to file employer-sponsored retirement plan claims. Some employers send the Medicare carrier monthly data on retirement plan eligibility, which is incorporated into Medicare's database for the purpose of an automatic electronic transfer of Medicare claims data to the retirement plan carrier. If the employer-sponsored retirement claim is not forwarded electronically, the patient will need to file for benefits after the MSN is received.

Medicare-Medicaid Crossover

The **Medicare-Medicaid crossover** program is a combination of the Medicare and Medicaid (or MediCal in California) programs. The designation "MCD" is entered in

Block 10d of the CMS-1500 claim. This plan is available to Medicare-eligible persons with incomes below the federal poverty level. These cases are generally known as Medi/Medi claims, Care/Caid claims, or 18/19 claims, depending on the individual state's designation. ("18/19" refers to Medicare and Medicaid designations as Title 18 and 19, respectively, of the Social Security Act Amendments of 1965.) Persons who are eligible for the SLMB program are also considered eligible for Medicare-Medicaid crossover claims.

The Medicare carrier electronically transfers the Medicare claim and the payment information to Medicaid for processing of the patient's Medicare deductible and coinsurance responsibilities and for payment of any service covered by Medicaid/MediCal but not Medicare. The Medicaid/MediCal payment should be received within 2 to 4 weeks after the Medicare payment. Care must be taken to submit a Medi/Medi claim before the Medicaid/MediCal deadline for filing claims, referred to as the *timely filing period.*

Patients who might qualify for the crossover program should be directed to the local Medicaid/MediCal office to apply for the program. Care must be taken to accept assignment on these claims. If not done, the Medicare payment may be sent to the patient and the Medicaid payment, depending on state policy, may either go to the patient or be denied.

Extra Coverage Plans

Extra coverage plans are specialized insurance plans that cover specific diagnoses or fall into the special hospital indemnity class. The specified-diseases plan pays only if the provider certifies that the patient has a specified disorder, such as cancer or AIDS. Special hospital indemnity plans are usually advertised in magazines and on the radio and television as a plan that "pays $200 per day for every day hospitalized." Any payment for these claims goes directly to the patient and is not reportable to Medicare or any other primary health insurance plan.

EXERCISE 14-1 ## Medicare Plan Review

1. Review the five cases in the following example.
2. Determine the CMS-prescribed billing order for each case.

● **EXAMPLE:** Patient retired; covered by Medicare, an employer-sponsored retirement plan, and the spouse's employer-sponsored large group plan.

Billing order is: Employer-sponsored large group plan, Medicare, employer-sponsored retirement plan. ●

CASE 1 Patient is the policyholder in an employer-sponsored large group plan, has Medicare, a Medigap policy, and a $100/day extra coverage hospital plan.

Billing order is:

CASE 2 Patient has Medicare, an employer-sponsored retirement plan, and is a dependent on the spouse's employer-sponsored large group plan. The claim is for an injury received in a car accident.

Billing order is:

(continues)

CASE 3 The patient has a retirement plan through his former employer, Medicare, and a cancer policy. The spouse is deceased.

Billing order is:

CASE 4 Patient is 67, working full-time, and covered by Medicare, an employer-sponsored large group plan, and a Medigap plan. The spouse is retired, 62, and covered by an employer-sponsored plan for 18 employees.

Billing order is:

CASE 5 Patient is 50 and disabled, and has Medicare and an employer-sponsored group health plan for 50 employees.

Billing order is:

Medicare Managed Care

The Balanced Budget Act of 1997 established the *Medicare+Choice Program*, which provides Medicare beneficiaries with the choice to receive benefits through the original fee-for-service program (Original Medicare Program) or through one of the following:

- Health Maintenance Organizations (HMOs)
- Provider-Sponsored Organizations (PSOs)
- Preferred Provider Organizations (PPOs)
- Medical Savings Accounts (MSAs)
- Religious fraternal benefit plans
- Department of Defense (DoD)/TRICARE (demo)
- Private Fee-for-Service Plan

NOTE: Medicare categorizes HMOs, PSOs, and PPOs as **coordinated care plans.**

Newly eligible enrollees who do not choose a Medicare+Choice plan are considered to have selected the Original Medicare plan.

Beneficiaries can select a Medicare+Choice plan at initial eligibility or during an enrollment period. As of 1999, coordinated enrollment periods occur each November, and enrollments are effective the following January 1. Individuals remain enrolled in the option of their choice until they choose another plan. Beginning in 2002, beneficiaries enroll or disenroll from plans during the first six months of the year (or the first six months of eligibility in a year), but they can only change plans once during the six-month period. Also, beginning in 2002, newly eligible beneficiaries who elect a Medicare+Choice option are able to choose to go back to the original Medicare fee-for-service plan any time during the first twelve months of their enrollment. After 2002, beneficiaries will be able to change their enrollment options during the first three months of the year (or the first three months of eligibility in a year) and/or during the annual enrollment period.

Each year prior to the November coordinated enrollment period, beneficiaries will be mailed general information about Medicare and comparative information on the Medicare+Choice plans available in their area. General information includes covered benefits, cost sharing, and balanced billing liability under the original fee-for-service program; election procedures; grievances and appeals; and information on Medigap plans and Medicare SELECT. **Medicare SELECT** is a type of Medigap policy available in some states, and beneficiaries can choose from one of the 10 standardized Medigap plans, A through J. With a Medicare SELECT plan, beneficiaries must use specific hospitals and, in some cases, specific doctors in order to receive full benefits (except in an emergency). For this reason, Medicare SELECT plans generally cost less. If beneficiaries do not use a Medicare SELECT hospital or doctor for nonemergency services, they have to pay what the Original Medicare Plan does not pay. (The Original Medicare Plan will pay its share of approved charges no matter what hospital or doctor the beneficiary chooses.) Comparative information includes extensive information on benefits and beneficiary liability, premiums, service areas, quality and performance, and supplemental benefits. Plans may only disenroll beneficiaries for cause (i.e., failure to pay premiums) or plan termination in the beneficiary's geographic area. Beneficiaries terminated for cause are automatically enrolled in the Original Medicare Plan.

Health Maintenance Organizations (HMOs)

A *health maintenance organization (HMO)* is a provider and insurer of health care. A Medicare HMO is a Medicare-approved, contracted, organized, community-based network of physicians, hospitals, and other health care providers. They provide all Medicare-covered services and receive payment directly from Medicare for the beneficiary's care. All Medicare HMOs offer preventive care, and some offer prescription drugs, dental care, hearing aids, and/or eyeglasses.

Medicare beneficiaries are eligible to enroll if they:

- live in or are willing to travel to the HMO's service area.
- are enrolled in Medicare Part B.
- do not have permanent kidney failure before joining or have not had a kidney transplant within the past 36 months.
- have not selected the Medicare hospice program.

Beneficiaries who join Medicare HMOs usually must obtain services from the health care professionals and facilities that are part of the HMO's community-based network. A primary care physician is selected to coordinate care by either providing health care or arranging for beneficiaries to see other providers when necessary.

Enrollees must continue to pay the Medicare Part B monthly premium and a monthly premium to the HMO, and they may also be required to make copayments when seeking services. In return, the HMO provides all Medicare hospital and medical benefits, if the beneficiary is enrolled in Medicare Part A *and* Part B.

Advantages of Joining a Medicare HMO. According to Medicare, enrollment in an HMO can result in:

- *additional benefits* (e.g., preventive care, dental care, prescription drugs, hearing aids, and eyeglasses at very little or no additional cost).
- *lower costs.* (HMOs are expected to minimize out-of-pocket payments and charge predictable premium amounts; beneficiaries do not need Medicare Supplemental Insurance.)
- *less paperwork.* (There are no claims to complete for services provided by the HMO as beneficiaries usually just show their enrollment card, pay any required copayment, and receive services. The Medicare Summary Form is not mailed to Medicare HMO enrollees.)
- *no "accepting assignment" problems.* (Enrollees do not worry about finding a doctor who accepts Medicare assignment.)

- *no health screening requirement.* (Enrollment is approved despite health problems, and beneficiaries cannot be denied membership because of a pre-existing medical condition.)
- *access and convenience.* (Care is available on a 24-hour basis through the community-based network.)
- *preventive care.* (There is an emphasis on preventive care, including mammograms, flu shots, and diabetes and hypertension screening.)
- *educational services.* (Health education classes and information are available to encourage healthier lifestyles.)
- *quality.* (Medicare HMOs must meet standards to maintain eligibility; the primary care physician coordinates health care services from other providers, which helps reduce inappropriate care and prevent adverse prescription drug interactions.)
- *flexibility.* (Beneficiaries can return to the Original Medicare Plan, which would be effective the first day of the month following the month in which the request is received.)

Disadvantages of Joining a Medicare HMO. Medicare also lists the following associated with Medicare HMO enrollment:

- *lack of freedom* (Patients cannot choose any provider from which to seek health care, except perhaps for emergency or out-of-area urgent care).
- *prior approval required* (Patients need to obtain prior approval of the primary care provider before seeking care from a specialist, scheduling elective surgery, or obtaining equipment or other medical services.)
- *disenrollment can be lengthy* (Length of time to disenroll from the plan can take up to 30 days, and the patient must continue to use HMO providers until disenrollment is finalized.)

Types of Medicare HMO Plans. There are two types of Medicare HMO plans:

- The **risk-based HMO** (also known as a risk plan), a type of Medicare HMO, is a capitated plan, which requires the HMO to provide all Medicare benefits but may offer additional benefits not available to regular Medicare patients. A **lock-in provision** may be associated with the risk-restricted HMO, which means that neither the HMO nor Medicare will pay for non-emergency services provided by health care providers who are not part of the HMO's community-based network unless referred outside the network by the primary care physician. The regular Medicare carrier is not responsible for processing risk-restricted HMO claims, and such claims will be forwarded to the HMO for processing. An MSN will be generated, alerting the practice that the patient is in a risk-restricted HMO plan and that the claim was forwarded to the HMO.
- The **cost-based HMO**, a type of Medicare HMO, allows beneficiaries to receive care through an HMO without the loss of traditional Medicare benefits. When the patient receives care from an HMO provider, the HMO is responsible for paying the claim. If the patient seeks care outside the HMO's community-based network, the claim is submitted to the regular Medicare carrier for processing.

Special Medicare HMO Billing Situations. Medicare HMO patients do not have special Medicare cards that indicate a Medicare HMO; however, they may be issued an HMO card in addition to their regular Medicare card. Be sure to ask Medicare patients at each visit whether they are currently enrolled in an HMO program. The practice must be aware of the type of HMO plans offered in the area (risk-restricted versus cost-based).

Capitated providers do not file claims to a Medicare-HMO unless special book-keeping procedures are required for tracking Medicare patients. In these cases, the HMO's special instructions are followed.

HMO-Authorized Fee-for-Service (FFS) Specialty Care. For HMO-authorized FFS specialty care, the claim is sent directly to the HMO. Medicare has no responsibility for making direct payments to providers for patients enrolled in a risk-based HMO. Medicare providers who perform unauthorized, nonemergency medical care to a risk-based HMO beneficiary may bill the patient directly. NonPARs may charge up to the "limiting fee" for covered services. PARs are instructed to use the regular Medicare Fee Schedule.

All services for emergency care should be billed directly to the HMO on the CMS-1500 claim. Because HMOs fall into a commercial claim category, the rules for filing regular commercial claims are followed, not the Medicare claims instructions. (These instructions are found in Chapter 12.) The patient may be responsible for a copayment (e.g., $5 or $10), and all providers may bill normal, non-Medicare fees for any noncovered service.

Medicare *will* make payment if the patient receives unauthorized care from a cost-based HMO. *The deadline for filing Medicare-HMO claims is established by the HMO. It may be as short as 45 days after the service is rendered. It is important that the practice's billing department be aware of each HMO's timely filing restrictions.*

HMO Primary Plans. All employer-sponsored group health HMO plans covering 25 or more employees are primary to Medicare when the beneficiary meets Medicare Secondary Payer (MSP) provisions. Medicare secondary payments are possible depending on the amount of payment from the HMO primary insurer. Contact the patient's HMO to determine how to bill the HMO. MSP payments are filed using the normal rules for filing MSP claims (see page 000.)

HMO Supplemental Plan. Medicare recognizes employer-sponsored retiree plans as Medicare supplemental plans. Medicare will pay 80% of the allowed amount after the regular annual deductible has been met. Medicare billing rules discussed on page 452 are followed.

Provider-Sponsored Organizations (PSOs)

Provider-sponsored organizations (PSOs) are managed care organizations owned and operated by a network of physicians and hospitals rather than by an insurance company.

Preferred Provider Organizations (PPOs)

Preferred provider organizations (PPOs) provide care through a network of doctors and hospitals. The beneficiary does not usually have to select a primary care physician and can go to any doctor in the plan's network. Insurance claims are processed first by Medicare, then the PPO pays the portion of the Medicare-allowed amount that Medicare does not pay, including Medicare deductibles.

NOTE: Beneficiaries can also receive care from doctors and hospitals outside the plan's network if they are willing to pay out-of-pocket costs.

Medical Savings Accounts (MSAs)

Medicare's *medical savings accounts (MSAs)* were authorized by the Balanced Budget Act of 1997 and are offered on a first-come, first-served basis to beneficiaries; they contain two parts:

- *Medicare MSA* (referred to as an *Account* by Medicare) is a special savings account that is used by the beneficiary to pay medical bills. This money is deposited annually by Medicare into a savings account offered through an insurance company or other qualified company. It is not taxed if used for qualified medical expenses and may earn interest or dividends.

- *Medicare MSA health policy* (referred to as a *Policy* by Medicare) is a special insurance policy that has a high deductible. Currently, the deductible cannot exceed $6,000.

Together, the *Medicare MSA* and *Medicare MSA health policy* comprise a Medicare MSA plan.

EXAMPLE: Jill selects the Medicare MSA plan option and establishes an Account. She also selects a Policy with a $5,000 deductible. For this Policy, Medicare deposits $1,200 per year into her Account on January 1.

During the first year of the MSA plan, Jane has an annual physical exam and fills her regular prescriptions (these benefits are not covered by the Original Medicare Plan). She pays for these services using $300 of the $1,200 in her Account. At the end of the year, Jill has $900 remaining in her Account.

On January 1 of the next year, Medicare deposits another $1,200 into her Account; now, Jill has $2,100 for medical expenses. During this year, Jill undergoes surgery that costs $8000. She uses the $2,100 in her Account to pay part of the cost; she pays $2,900 of her own money to meet the policy's deductible of $5,000; and the remaining $3,000 is partially paid by the Policy. Jill pays any remaining amount after the Policy has covered some of the costs.

NOTE: MSA plan beneficiaries are required to pay the monthly Part B premium.

Religious Fraternal Benefit Society Plans

Religious fraternal benefit society plans may restrict enrollment to members of the church, convention, or group with which the society is affiliated. Payments to such plans may be adjusted, as appropriate, to take into consideration the actuarial characteristics and experience of plan enrollees.

TRICARE Health Care and Pharmacy Benefits Program

The National Defense Authorization Act of 2001 created two TRICARE programs:

- **TRICARE Senior Pharmacy Program** authorizes uniformed services beneficiaries 65 years of age and over to obtain low-cost prescription medications from the National Mail Order Pharmacy (NMOP) and TRICARE network and non-network civilian pharmacies. (Beneficiaries can also continue to use military hospital and clinic pharmacies.)

- **TRICARE For Life** is a permanent health care benefit that provides expanded medical coverage for uniformed service beneficiaries who are age 65 or older, are Medicare-eligible, and have purchased Medicare Part B.

Private Fee-for-Service

A **private fee-for-service (PFFS)**, health care plan is offered by private insurance companies and is available in some areas of the country. Medicare pays a pre-established amount of money each month to a private insurance company. The insurance company, not Medicare, decides how much it will pay for services. Private fee-for-service plans reimburse providers on a fee-for-service basis and are authorized to charge enrolled beneficiaries up to 115% of the plan's payment schedule (which may be different from the Medicare physician fee schedule).

Private fee-for-service plans are also required to meet most of the same requirements of other Medicare+Choice plans and will be capitated in exchange for providing enrollees with the full package of Medicare benefits. Unlike coordinated care Medicare+Choice plan options, PFFS plans are prohibited from placing the health care provider at financial risk or from varying payment based on utilization experience.

BILLING NOTES

Following is a summary of nationwide billing information for Original Medicare Plan claims submission.

Medicare Carriers

The regional carrier for traditional Medicare claims is selected by CMS through a competitive bidding process. Obtain the name and mailing address of the carrier for your region.

INTERNET LINK

CMS's Intermediary-Carrier Directory can be found on their Web site at http://cms.hhs.gov/manuals

Durable Medical Equipment Claims

Durable Medical Equipment (DME) claims must be sent to one of the Medicare *Durable Medical Equipment Regional Carriers (DMERC)* in the country. Check the Medicare manual for the carrier responsible for processing DME claims for your region. The four DMERCs are referred to as DMERCA, DMERCB, DMERCC, and DMERCD.

Coal Miner's Claim

Coal Miner's claims are sent to the:
Federal Black Lung Program
P.O. Box 828
Lanham-Seabrook, MD 20703-0828

Deadline for Filing Claims

The claim filing deadline for both regular Medicare and Railroad Retirement claims is December 31 of the year following the date of service. For example, a claim for services performed late in January of 2001 must be postmarked on or before December 31, 2002. To expedite claims filing, CMS has directed carriers to apply a 10% penalty for any initial claim filed 13 or more months after services were performed.

Forms Used

All paper claims must be filed on the CMS-1500 claim. A minimum of 45 days should pass before an unpaid paper claim is resubmitted. A surgery disclosure notice is required for all nonassigned surgeries totaling $500.00 or more. A letter of medical necessity is required if the provider is to collect fees from the patient for procedures deemed by Medicare to be unreasonable, experimental, unproved, or investigational.

Medicare does not differentiate between basic and major medical benefits. Medicare is not the primary carrier for accidental injuries covered by any third-party liability program.

Special Handling

All providers are required to file Medicare claims for their patients. Noncompliance with MSP rules and regulations may result in a substantial penalty or fine. For each infraction, when Medicare is the secondary payer, a copy of the primary carrier's transmittal notice must be attached to the Medicare claim.

Two claims may be needed to describe one encounter in the following circumstances:

- when multiple referring, ordering, or supervising names and provider identifier numbers are required in Blocks 17 through 17a.
- when multiple facility names and addresses are required in Block 32.
- when DME is charged to the patient at the same time the patient had a reimbursable medical or surgical encounter
- when the patient has had covered lab services and other medical or surgical services during an encounter with a nonPAR provider

When more than one claim is needed to describe an encounter, be sure that the diagnoses on each claim prove the medical necessity for performing the service, and the proper names and numbers required in Blocks 17, 17a, and 32 appear on the correct claims.

Before continuing with the information in this chapter complete the Short Answer questions on page 463.

STEP-BY-STEP CLAIM INSTRUCTIONS

The law requires that all Medicare claims be filed using Optical Scanning Guidelines. Practices must make certain that forms generated by computer software follow Medicare claim guidelines. Extraneous data on the claims or data appearing in blocks not consistent with Medicare guidelines will cause the claim to be rejected.

Chapter 11, Essential CMS-1500 Claim Instructions, should be studied before working with Medicare claim instructions.

Read the following instructions carefully. Medicare requires many details that are not required for other programs in this text.

Primary Fee-for-Service Medicare

These instructions are for filing primary, Original Medicare Plan claims when the patient is not covered by additional insurance. (Instructions for filing Medicare-HMO fee-for-service claims are found in Chapter 12, Filing Commercial Claims.)

When reviewing the step-by-step instructions below, refer to Figure 14-6 for a sample of the CMS-1500 claim, Blocks 1 through 13. After review of the instructions,

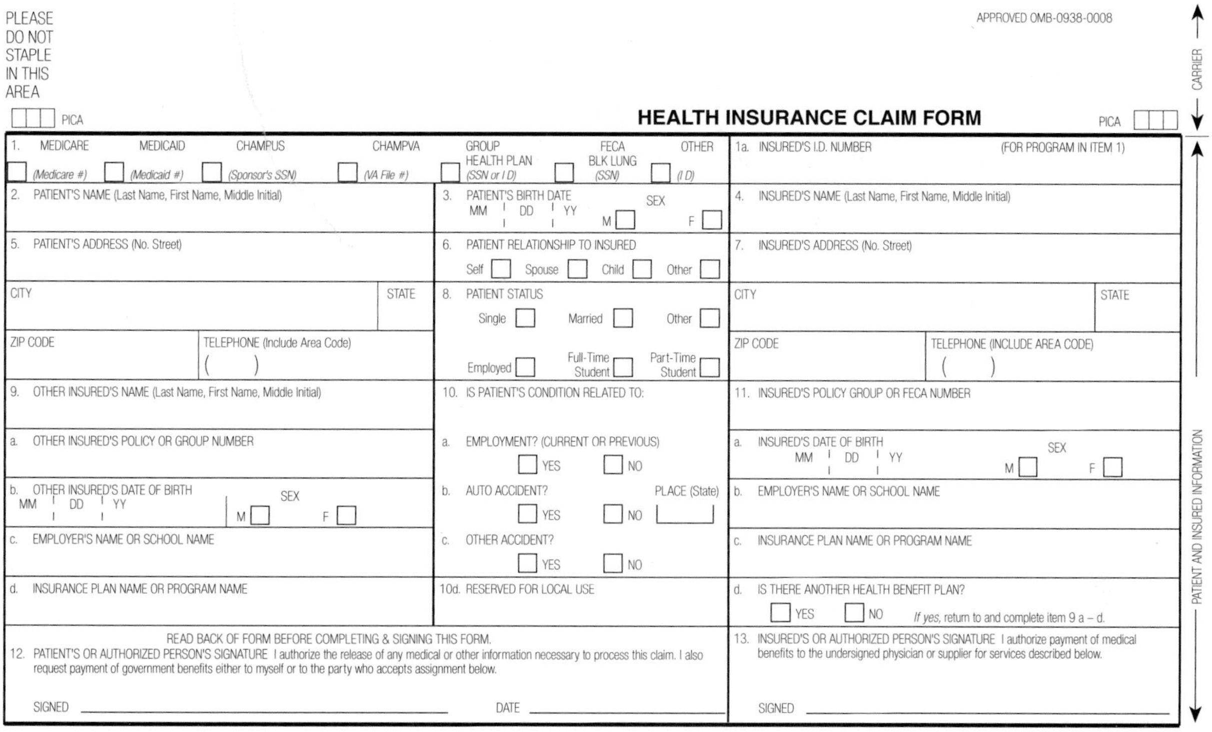

FIGURE 14-6 Blocks 1 through 13 of the CMS-1500 claim

refer to the John Q. Public encounter form in Figure 14-7 and the completed CMS-1500 claim, Blocks 1 through 13, in Figure 14-8.

Block 1

Enter an X in the MEDICARE box.

Block 1a

Enter the Medicare ID number with its proper numeric/alphanumeric prefix or suffix as it appears on the patient's Medicare Health Insurance Card.

> **NOTE:** Traditional Medicare ID numbers contain nine digits followed by an alpha one-character suffix. Some ID numbers will contain two additional characters that are either numeric or alphabetic. Patients who are retired railway workers have special Railroad Retirement cards with ID numbers containing an alpha prefix. These claims are to be sent to the regional Railroad Retirement carrier, which is different from the carrier for the regular Medicare cases.

Block 2

Enter the patient's name (last name, first name, and middle initial) exactly as it appears on the patient's Medicare card.

Block 3

Enter the patient's birth date (MM DD YYYY, with spaces format). Enter an X in the appropriate box to indicate gender.

Block 4

Leave blank.

Block 5

Enter the patient's current street address on the first line, the city and state on the second line, and the zip code and phone number on the third line.

Block 6

Leave blank.

Block 7

Leave blank.

Block 8

Enter an X in the appropriate marital and employment status boxes if known. "Single" is selected if the patient is widowed or divorced. Indicate if the patient is employed or a student.

NOTE: Young children who are disabled are often covered by Medicare. ●

Block 9 through 9d

Leave blank. These blocks are completed if the patient has Medigap coverage.

Block 10a

Enter an X in the NO box.

NOTE: If any of Blocks 10a, 10b, or 10c contain an "X" in the "YES" box, Medicare is secondary and not primary. Submit a CMS-1500 claim to the proper third-party liability or workers' compensation carrier first. ●

Block 10b

Enter an X in the NO box.

Block 10c

Enter an X in the NO box.

Block 10d

Leave blank. This block is used exclusively for Medicaid information. If the patient is entitled to Medicaid, enter the patient's Medicaid number preceded by the abbreviation, *MCD.*

Block 11

Enter NONE. *Exception:* If there has been a recent change from Medicare Secondary status to Medicare Primary status, proceed to Block 11b.

Block 11a

Leave blank.

Block 11b

If applicable, enter a brief description of the change from Medicare secondary to Medicare primary status and the date the change was effective.

 EXAMPLES: Retired 12/31/99.

Spouse employer plan cancelled 12/31/99 ●

Block 11c

Leave blank.

Block 11d

Leave blank.

Block 12

The patient must either sign and date (MM DD YYYY, with spaces format) the actual claim or a separate "Authorization for Release of Medicare Information" must be on file.

If the authorization for release of Medicare information is on file, enter SIGNATURE ON FILE or SOF in this block. This block also authorizes payment of Medicare benefits to any provider who accepts assignment in Block 27.

DME supplier assigned claims only: Enter PATIENT'S REQUEST FOR PAYMENT ON FILE if the patient is receiving special rentals or purchases and has signed special authorization statements required by CMS and outlined in the DMERC manual.

Block 13

PAR providers only: Enter SIGNATURE ON FILE or SOF if the patient has signed the special Medigap authorization on file. Be sure to complete Blocks 9 through 9d.

NonPAR providers: Leave blank.

Refer to Figure 14-8 showing completed Blocks 1 through 13 for the encounter form in Figure 14-7.

EXERCISE 14-2   **Medicare/Medicaid Comparison Chart**

OBJECTIVE: To create a useful reference that will help you master the details of completing claims for major insurance programs.

● **NOTE:** This is a new chart as compared to those completed in Exercises 12-1 and 13-1. ●

1. Make five copies of the Insurance Plan Comparison Chart in Appendix III.
2. Enter the following titles in each column of the first row:
   - Medicare Primary
   - Medicare Primary/Medigap
   - Medicare Secondary
   - Medicare/Medicaid
   - Medicaid

(continues)

Encounter Form

ERIN A. HELPER, M.D.
101 Medic Dr, Anywhere US 12345
(101) 111-1234 (Office) • (101) 111-9292 (Fax)

EIN:	11-123452	**MCD:**	EBH8881
UPIN:	EH8888	**BCBS:**	EH11881
PIN:	A09293	**MC GRP:**	G1515

PATIENT INFORMATION:

Name:	Public, John Q.
Address:	10A Senate Avenue
City:	Anywhere
State:	US
Zip Code:	12345
Telephone:	(101) 201-7891
Gender:	Male
Date of Birth:	09-25-1930
Occupation:	
Employer:	
Spouse's Employer:	

INSURANCE INFORMATION:

Patient Number:	14-7
Place of Service:	Office/Hospital Inpatient
Primary Insurance Plan:	Medicare
Primary Insurance Plan ID #:	112349801A
Group #:	
Primary Policyholder:	Public, John Q.
Policyholder Date of Birth:	09-25-1930
Relationship to Patient:	Self
Secondary Insurance Plan:	
Secondary Insurance Plan ID #:	
Secondary Policyholder:	

Patient Status   ☐ Married   ☐ Divorced   ☒ Single   ☐ Student

DIAGNOSIS INFORMATION

Diagnosis		Code	Diagnosis		Code
1.	Acute appendicitis with rupture	540.0	5.		
2.			6.		
3.			7.		
4.			8.		

PROCEDURE INFORMATION

	Description of Procedure or Service	Date	Code	Charge
1.	New patient office visit, level III	01-20-YYYY	99203	75.00
2.	Open appendectomy	01-21-YYYY	44960	1,200.00
3.				
4.				
5.				

SPECIAL NOTES: Referring physician: Ivan Gooddoc, M.D. (UPIN IG7777). Patient admitted 01/21 and discharged 01/23. Recheck in office on 01/25.

FIGURE 14-7 John Q. Public encounter form

3. Enter the following numbers in the first column:

Page 1	Blocks	1	through	9d
Page 2	Blocks	10	through	16
Page 3	Blocks	17	through	23
Page 4	Blocks	24A	through	24K
Page 5	Blocks	25	through	33

4. Review the step-by-step instructions for Blocks 1 through 13 (above), and enter abbreviated instructions on the chart.

5. Upon completion, save this chart because it will be used for additional exercises in this chapter and in Chapter 15.

APPROVED OMB-0938-0008

PLEASE
DO NOT
STAPLE
IN THIS
AREA

HEALTH INSURANCE CLAIM FORM

| | PICA | | | | | PICA | |

1. MEDICARE [X] (Medicare #)   MEDICAID [ ] (Medicaid #)   CHAMPUS [ ] (Sponsor's SSN)   CHAMPVA [ ] (VA File #)   GROUP HEALTH PLAN [ ] (SSN or I.D.)   FECA BLK LUNG [ ] (SSN)   OTHER [ ] (I.D.)   1a. INSURED'S I.D. NUMBER (FOR PROGRAM IN ITEM 1)   112349801A

2. PATIENT'S NAME (Last Name, First Name, Middle Initial)   PUBLIC JOHN Q

3. PATIENT'S BIRTH DATE MM 09 DD 25 YY 1930   SEX M [X] F [ ]

4. INSURED'S NAME (Last Name, First Name, Middle Initial)

5. PATIENT'S ADDRESS (No. Street)   10A SENATE AVENUE

6. PATIENT RELATIONSHIP TO INSURED   Self [ ] Spouse [ ] Child [ ] Other [ ]

7. INSURED'S ADDRESS (No. Street)

CITY   ANYWHERE   STATE US

8. PATIENT STATUS   Single [X] Married [ ] Other [ ]

CITY   STATE

ZIP CODE   12345   TELEPHONE (Include Area Code) (101) 201 7891

Employed [ ] Full-Time Student [ ] Part-Time Student [ ]

ZIP CODE   TELEPHONE (INCLUDE AREA CODE) ( )

9. OTHER INSURED'S NAME (Last Name, First Name, Middle Initial)

10. IS PATIENT'S CONDITION RELATED TO:

11. INSURED'S POLICY GROUP OR FECA NUMBER   NONE

a. OTHER INSURED'S POLICY OR GROUP NUMBER

a. EMPLOYMENT? (CURRENT OR PREVIOUS)   YES [ ] NO [X]

a. INSURED'S DATE OF BIRTH MM DD YY   SEX M [ ] F [ ]

b. OTHER INSURED'S DATE OF BIRTH MM DD YY   SEX M [ ] F [ ]

b. AUTO ACCIDENT?   PLACE (State)   YES [ ] NO [X]

b. EMPLOYER'S NAME OR SCHOOL NAME

c. EMPLOYER'S NAME OR SCHOOL NAME

c. OTHER ACCIDENT?   YES [ ] NO [X]

c. INSURANCE PLAN NAME OR PROGRAM NAME

d. INSURANCE PLAN NAME OR PROGRAM NAME

10d. RESERVED FOR LOCAL USE

d. IS THERE ANOTHER HEALTH BENEFIT PLAN?   YES [ ] NO [ ]   If yes, return to and complete item 9 a – d.

READ BACK OF FORM BEFORE COMPLETING & SIGNING THIS FORM.
12. PATIENT'S OR AUTHORIZED PERSON'S SIGNATURE I authorize the release of any medical or other information necessary to process this claim. I also request payment of government benefits either to myself or to the party who accepts assignment below.

SIGNED   SIGNATURE ON FILE   DATE

13. INSURED'S OR AUTHORIZED PERSON'S SIGNATURE I authorize payment of medical benefits to the undersigned physician or supplier for services described below.

SIGNED   SIGNATURE ON FILE

FIGURE 14-8 Completed Blocks 1 through 13 for John Q. Public encounter form in Figure 14-7

EXERCISE 14-3   **Medicare Primary Only Claim Blocks 1 through 13**

This exercise requires one copy of a blank CMS-1500 claim. You may either make photocopies of the form in Appendix III of the text, or print copies of the blank form using the CD-ROM in the back of the text. Instructions for installing the CD-ROM and printing blank forms are included in Appendix V.

1. Obtain a copy of the CMS-1500 claim.

2. Review the instructions for Blocks 1 through 13 in the Medicare primary column of the comparison chart created in Exercise 14-2.

3. Review the Mary Sue Patient encounter form (Figure 14-9).

4. Select the information needed for Blocks 1 through 13 from the encounter form (Figure 14-9) and enter the required information on the second claim using Optical Scanning Guidelines. This may be completed by handwriting the information, using the Blank Form Mode on the CD-ROM found in the text, or entering the data with a typewriter.

5. Review Blocks 1 through 13 of the claim to be sure all required blocks are properly completed.

⬤ NOTE: This same encounter form and claim will be used for Exercise 14-5. ⬤

Refer to Figure 14-10 for Blocks 14 through 23 of the CMS-1500 claim.

ERIN A. HELPER, M.D.
101 Medic Dr, Anywhere US 12345
(101) 111-1234 (Office) • (101) 111-9292 (Fax)
EIN: 11-123341 **MCD:** EBH8881
UPIN: EH8888 **BCBS:** EH11881
PIN: A09293 **MC GRP:** G1515

Encounter Form

PATIENT INFORMATION:

Name:	Patient, Mary Sue
Address:	91 Home Street
City:	Nowhere
State:	US
Zip Code:	12367
Telephone:	(101) 201-8989
Gender:	Female
Date of Birth:	03-08-1933
Occupation:	
Employer:	

INSURANCE INFORMATION:

Patient Number:	14-9
Place of Service:	Office
Primary Insurance Plan:	Medicare
Primary Insurance Plan ID #:	001287431D
Group #:	
Primary Policyholder:	Mary Sue Patient
Policyholder Date of Birth:	03-08-1933
Relationship to Patient:	Self
Secondary Insurance Plan:	
Secondary Insurance Plan ID #:	
Secondary Policyholder:	

Patient Status ☐ Married ☐ Divorced ☒ Single ☐ Student

DIAGNOSIS INFORMATION

Diagnosis		Code	Diagnosis		Code
1.	Pleurisy	511.0	5.		
2.	Atrial tachycardia	427.89	6.		
3.	History of pulmonary embolism	V12.51	7.		
4.			8.		

PROCEDURE INFORMATION

	Description of Procedure or Service	Date	Code	Charge
1.	Office consultation, Level III	01-30-YYYY	99243	150.00
2.	Chest X-ray, two views (frontal and lateral)	01-30-YYYY	71020	50.00
3.	12-lead ECG with interpretation and report	01-30-YYYY	93000	50.00
4.				
5.				

SPECIAL NOTES: Date of onset 01-28-YYYY. X-ray and ECG ordered by Dr. Gooddoc (UPIN IG7777).

FIGURE 14-9 Mary Sue Patient encounter form

14. DATE OF CURRENT: ILLNESS (First symptom) OR INJURY (Accident) OR PREGNANCY (LMP) MM DD YY	15. IF PATIENT HAS HAD SAME OR SIMILAR ILLNESS, GIVE FIRST DATE MM DD YY	16. DATES PATIENT UNABLE TO WORK IN CURRENT OCCUPATION MM DD YY MM DD YY FROM TO
17. NAME OF REFERRING PHYSICIAN OR OTHER SOURCE	17a. I.D. NUMBER OF REFERRING PHYSICIAN	18. HOSPITALIZATION DATES RELATED TO CURRENT SERVICES MM DD YY MM DD YY FROM TO
19. RESERVED FOR LOCAL USE		20. OUTSIDE LAB? $ CHARGES ☐ YES ☐ NO
21. DIAGNOSIS OR NATURE OF ILLNESS OR INJURY. (RELATE ITEMS 1, 2, 3, OR 4 TO ITEM 24E BY LINE) 1.___.___ 2.___.___	3.___.___ 4.___.___	22. MEDICAID RESUBMISSION CODE ORIGINAL REF. NO.
		23. PRIOR AUTHORIZATION NUMBER

FIGURE 14-10 Blocks 14 through 23 of the CMS-1500 claim

Block 14

All providers except chiropractors: Enter the date (MM DD YYYY, with spaces format) of the beginning of the spell of illness reported on this claim or the date the accident or injury occurred. If the claim includes treatment for an accident or injury, one of Blocks 10a through 10c should contain an X in the YES box.

Chiropractors only: Enter the date (MM DD YYYY, with spaces format) the course of treatment was initiated. (Also requires an entry in Block 19.)

NOTE: Medicare requires uniformity in the date format in Blocks 14, 16, 18, and 31. Use eight-digit with spaces format in all of these blocks.

Block 15

Leave blank.

Block 16

Leave blank. An entry in this block may indicate employment-related insurance coverage, if the patient is employed and is unable to work. If so, enter the start date (MM DD YYYY, with spaces format) the patient was unable to work.

Block 17

Enter the full name, but not the credentials, of the referring, ordering, or supervising physician if a service on this claim falls into one of the categories below. (An *ordering physician* is a physician who orders diagnostic or clinical laboratory tests, pharmaceutical services, or durable medical equipment.)

Physician Services

Physician services include:

- consultation.
- surgery.
- independent diagnostic radiology providers.
- independent diagnostic laboratory providers.

Enter the name of the referring physician in Block 17.

Nonphysician Services

Nonphysician services include:

- physical therapy.
- audiology.
- occupational therapy.
- DME
- prosthesis.
- orthotic devices.
- parenteral and enteral nutrition.
- immunosuppressive drug claims.
- portable X-ray services.

Enter the name of the ordering physician in Block 17.

Nonphysician Providers/Limited License Practitioners

Nonphysician providers/limited license practitioners include:

- physician assistants (PA).
- nurse practitioners (NP).
- clinical nurse specialists (CNS).

Limited license practitioners (LLP) include:

- clinical psychologists.
- licensed clinical social workers (LCS).
- dentists.
- oral surgeons.
- oral/maxillofacial surgeons.
- podiatrists.
- chiropractors.
- optometrists.
- physical and occupational therapists.

Enter the name of the supervising physician in Block 17.

NOTE: If multiple names are required in this block, a separate claim must be generated for each service requiring a name in Block 17.

A name entered in Block 17 requires entry of the UPIN in Block 17a.

Block 17a

Enter the Medicare assigned *unique provider identification number (UPIN)* of the physician named in Block 17. The UPIN is a 6-character (2 alpha, 4 digit) number. Medicare issues the **unique provider identification number (UPIN)** during processing of a provider's application; the UPIN which is reported in Block 17a by providers who order services *or* refer patients. Regional carriers issue the **provider identifying number (PIN)**, which is reported in Block 33 to identify the provider who rendered services. The PIN begins with an alpha character and is followed by 5 numbers.

NOTE: CMS continues to work on implementing the national provider identifier (NPI) for Medicare certified physicians, which is intended to replace both the Medicare PIN and UPIN. The scheduled date for NPI implementation has not yet been announced.

Block 18

Enter the admission and discharge dates when services relate to hospitalization or skilled nursing facility stays (MM DD YYYY, with spaces format).

Block 19

Routine Foot Care claims: Enter the date (MM DD YYYY, with spaces format) the patient was last seen and the UPIN of his/her attending physician when an independent physical or occupational therapist or physician providing routine foot care submits claims. For physical and occupational therapists, entering this information certifies that the required physician certification (or recertification) is on file.

Chiropractor Services: Enter the date (MM DD YYYY, with spaces format) an X-ray was taken, for chiropractor services.

○ **NOTE:** Chiropractors are no longer mandated by federal law to perform X-rays to document the level of subluxation. ●

Pharmaceuticals: Enter the name and dosage of the drug when submitting a claim for "not otherwise classified" (NOC) drugs.

Unlisted Procedure Codes: Enter a concise description of an "unlisted procedure code" if it will fit within the 45 spaces provided in the block. Otherwise, submit an attachment with the claim.

Modifiers: Enter all applicable modifiers when modifier -99 (multiple modifiers) is entered in block 24D. If modifier -99 is reported more than once on a single claim, enter the line number from block 24 followed by an "equals sign" and the modifiers that apply to the referenced line.

○ **EXAMPLES:** 1 = 20 50 80   (1 refers to line 1 of block 24, and 20 50 80 are the modifiers reported in block 24D of that line)

3 = 20 51 80   (3 refers to line 3 of block 24, and 20 51 80 are the modifiers reported in block 24D of that line) ●

Homebound: Enter the word HOMEBOUND when an independent laboratory performs an ECG on or obtains a specimen from a homebound or institutionalized patient.

Patient Refuses to Assign Benefits: Enter the statement PATIENT REFUSES TO ASSIGN BENEFITS when the beneficiary absolutely refuses to assign benefits to a participating provider. In this case, no payment may be made on the claim until the situation is resolved.

Testing for Hearing Aid: Enter the statement, TESTING FOR HEARING AID when billing services involve the testing of a hearing aid(s); this is done to obtain intentional denials when other payers are involved.

Dental Examinations: When dental examinations are billed, enter the specific surgery for which the exam is performed.

Low Osmolar Contrast Material: Enter the specific name and dosage amount when low osmolar contrast material is billed only if HCPCS codes do not cover them.

Global Surgery: Enter the date (MM DD YYYY) for a global surgery claim when providers share postoperative care.

Hospice Service: Enter the statement ATTENDING PHYSICIAN, NOT HOSPICE EMPLOYEE when a physician renders services to a hospice patient but the hospice providing the patient's care does not employ the attending physician.

National Emphysema Treatment Trial: Enter demonstration ID number "30" for all national emphysema treatment trial claims.

Block 20

A NO indicates that no purchased laboratory services are reported on the claim. A YES indicates that some diagnostic tests listed on this claim were performed by an outside laboratory. The provider filing this claim was billed for them and is passing the fee on to the patient. The total purchase price of the tests should be entered in the charge column of this block. (The name and address of the clinical laboratory that performed the test must appear in Block 32.)

Separate claims must be generated when billing for multiple purchased diagnostic services.

○ **NOTE:** NonPAR providers must accept assignment on all diagnostic laboratory services. ●

Block 21

Enter up to four diagnosis codes, beginning with the primary diagnosis. *Space through the place a decimal point usually appears.*

Block 22

Leave blank.

Block 23

Enter the preauthorization number *if* one was assigned.

If billing for physician care plan oversight services, enter the six-digit Medicare provider number of the home health agency or hospice program that is providing services for the patient.

If clinical laboratory services performed by the practice are reported on this claim, enter the 10-digit CMS assigned **Clinical Laboratory Improvement Act (CLIA) certification number**.

Enter the Investigational Device Exemption (IDE) number for the nonexperimental/investigational device used in an FDA-approved clinical trial. Refer to page 417 for clarification of investigational procedures.

Refer to Figure 14-11 for completed Blocks 14 through 23 based on the encounter form in Figure 14-7.

EXERCISE 14-4   **Continuation of Exercise 14-2**

Review the instructions for completing Blocks 14 through 23. As you read each block, enter a brief description of the instructions in the appropriate block in Medicare Primary column of the Chart.

EXERCISE 14-5   **Continuation of Exercise 14-3**

1. Review the Mary Sue Patient encounter form in Figure 14-9 for the diagnostic and treatment data.

2. Select the information needed for Blocks 14 through 23, and complete the required information on the claim using Optical Scanning Guidelines. This may be completed using the CD-ROM found in the back of the text, or by handwriting or typing the data.

(continues)

FIGURE 14-11   Completed Blocks 14 through 23 for John Q. Public encounter form in Figure 14-7

3. Review Blocks 14 through 23 of the claim to be sure all required blocks are properly completed.
4. Compare your claim with Figure 14-16.

NOTE: This same claim will be used for Exercise 14-7.

Refer to Figure 14-12 for Block 24 of the CMS-1500 claim.

24.	A DATE(S) OF SERVICE From MM	DD	YY	To MM	DD	YY	B Place of Service	C Type of Service	D PROCEDURES, SERVICES, OR SUPPLIES (Explain Unusual Circumstances) CPT/HCPCS	MODIFIER	E DIAGNOSIS CODE	F $ CHARGES	G DAYS OR UNITS	H EPSDT Family Plan	I EMG	J COB	K RESERVED FOR LOCAL USE
1																	
2																	
3																	
4																	
5																	
6																	

FIGURE 14-12 Block 24 of the CMS-1500 claim

Block 24A

Enter the date of service in the FROM column in MMDDYYYY format (no spaces).

Complete the TO column only if reporting consecutive dates for the same service. If the consecutive services extend from one month to the next, make separate line entries for each month.

EXAMPLE: The patient receives subsequent hospital care from January 25 through February 5. (The patient was admitted January 24 and discharged February 6.) Report the subsequent hospital care FROM and TO dates on lines 1 and of Block 24A as:

0125YYYY	0131YYYY
0201YYYY	0205YYYY

Block 24B

Enter the proper two-digit Place of Service code from the list in Appendix II to indicate the location where the item was used or the service performed.

Block 24C

Leave blank. Not required by Medicare.

Block 24D

Enter the CPT/HCPCS procedure code of the service rendered along with appropriate CPT/HCPCS modifiers if applicable. If more than two modifiers apply to one line, enter the modifier "99" and follow the instructions in Block 19 for describing multiple modifiers.

Block 24E

Enter the *one diagnosis reference number* from Block 21 that best justifies the medical necessity for the service on this line.

Block 24F

PAR claim: Enter the amount charged by the PAR provider for the service on this line.
NonPAR claim: Enter the amount charged by the nonPAR provider. This must be no more than the Medicare *limiting fee.*
For consecutive services reported on one line on either PAR or nonPAR claims: Enter the charge for a single service and indicate the number of units in 24G. Do not bill a combined fee for the multiple services.

Block 24G

Enter the number of days or units.

Block 24H

Leave blank. Not required by Medicare.

Block 24I

Leave blank. Not required by Medicare.

Block 24J

Solo practices: Leave blank.
Group practices: When the NPI is eventually implemented, enter the first two digits of the NPI of the performing provider of service/supplier if they are a member of a group practice (the remaining six digits of the NPI are entered in Block 24K). When several different service providers or suppliers within a group are billing on the same CMS-1500 claim, enter the individual NPI in Blocks 24J and 24K of the corresponding line item.

Block 24K

Solo practices: Leave blank.
Group practices: Enter the carrier assigned Medicare *provider identification number (PIN)* of the provider who performed the service.
When the NPI is eventually implemented, enter the last six digits of the NPI (including the 2-digit location identifier) for the service provider or supplier, if a member of a group practice.

⬤ NOTE: This may be a local field required by some state carriers or fiscal intermediaries. ●

Refer to Figure 14-13 for completed Block 24 based on the encounter form in Figure 14-7.

EXERCISE 14-6 **Continuation of Exercise 14-4**

Review the instructions for completing Blocks 24A through 24K. As you read each block, enter a concise description of the instructions in the appropriate block in the Medicare Primary column of the chart.

---

24. A DATE(S) OF SERVICE						B Place of Service	C Type of Service	D PROCEDURES, SERVICES, OR SUPPLIES (Explain Unusual Circumstances) CPT/HCPCS | MODIFIER		E DIAGNOSIS CODE	F $ CHARGES		G DAYS OR UNITS	H EPSDT Family Plan	I EMG	J COB	K RESERVED FOR LOCAL USE
From MM	DD	YY	To MM	DD	YY												
1 0120YYYY						11		99203	57	1	75	00	1				
2 0121YYYY						21		44960		1	1200	00	1				
3																	
4																	
5																	
6																	

FIGURE 14-13 Completed Block 24 for John Q. Public encounter form in Figure 14-7

EXERCISE 14-7 **Continuation of Exercise 14-3**

1. Review the Procedure Data on the Mary Sue Patient encounter form found in Figure 14-9.

2. Select the information needed for Blocks 24A through 24K and complete the required information on the claim using Optical Scanning Guidelines. This may be completed using the CD-ROM found in the back of the text, or handwriting or typing the data.

3. Review Blocks 24A through 24K of the claim to be sure all required blocks are properly completed.

NOTE: This same claim will be used for Exercise 14-9. ●

Refer to Figure 14-14 for Blocks 25 through 33 of the CMS-1500 claim.

Block 25

Enter the billing entity's Employer Tax Identification Number (EIN), if available. Otherwise, enter the provider's Social Security Number. In addition, be sure to enter an X in the appropriate box to indicate which is being reported.

Block 26

Optional: Enter the patient account number, if applicable. The number will appear on the MSN and make it easier to identify the patient account when files are indexed numerically rather than alphabetically.

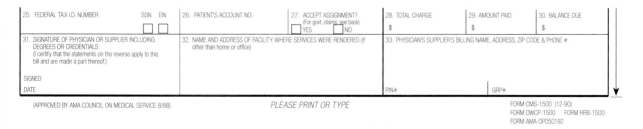

FIGURE 14-14 Blocks 15 through 33 of the CMS-1500 claim

Block 27

Indicate YES or NO on the accept assignment option.

PAR claim: Enter an X in the YES box.

NonPAR claim: An X may be entered in either the YES or NO box. If an X is entered in the YES box, the patient is not billed for the balance due.

Assignment must also be accepted on the following claims:

- Clinical diagnostic laboratory services
- Medicare-Medicaid crossover claims
- Participating physician/supplier services
- Services of physician assistants, nurse practitioners, clinical nurse specialists, nurse midwives, certified registered nurse anesthetists, clinical psychologists, and clinical social workers
- Ambulatory surgical center (ASC) services for covered procedures
- Home dialysis supplies and equipment; check with the local Durable Medical Equipment Regional Carrier (DMERC) for exceptions

Block 28

Enter the total of all charges on this claim.

NOTE: Claims will be returned as "unprocessable" if the total on the claim is incorrect.

Block 29

Enter the total amount the patient paid for covered services reported on this claim.

Block 30

Leave blank.

Block 31

The provider must either sign or use a signature stamp on Medicare CMS-1500 claims. Enter the date the claim was processed (MMDDYYYY, without spaces format) on the bottom line.

Block 32

If Block 18 contains dates of service *and/or* Block 20 contains an X in the YES box, enter the facility's name, mailing address, and PIN.

NOTE: When the facility is a hospital, precede the hospital's PIN with the abbreviation HSP.

If the Place of Service (POS) code entered in Block 24B is *other than* 11, 12, 23, or 53, enter the facility's (or supplier's) name, mailing address, and PIN.

Block 33

Enter the provider's telephone number, including area code, and then the official name of the billing entity and the mailing address. The zip code is entered on the same line as the city and state.

Individual PAR provider: Enter the provider's Medicare PIN (provider identifying number). Enter the GRP# (group practice identification number) if one has been assigned to the provider.

Group Practice PAR provider: Enter the billing entity's Medicare PIN and GRP #.

NOTE: Do not confuse PIN with UPIN. The referring provider's UPIN is entered in Block 17a.

NonPAR provider: Leave PIN and GRP# blank.

Refer to Figure 14-15 for the completed CMS-1500 claim based on the encounter form in Figure 14-7.

FIGURE 14-15 Completed CMS-1500 claim for John Q. Public encounter form in Figure 14-7

EXERCISE 14-8 | **Continuation of Exercise 14-6**

Review the instructions for completing Blocks 25 through 33. As you read each block enter a brief description of the instructions in the appropriate block in the Medicare Primary column of the chart.

EXERCISE 14-9 | **Continuation of Exercise 14-3**

Additional information needed for this case:
Dr. Helper is a Medicare PAR. The billing entity is Erin Helper, M.D.

1. Review Mary Sue Patient encounter form (Figure 14-9).

2. Select the information needed for Blocks 25 through 33 from the encounter form and the additional data given above, and enter it on the claim.

3. Review Blocks 25 through 33 of the claim to be sure all required blocks are properly completed.

4. Compare your claim with the completed claim in Figure 14-16.

MEDICARE WITH MEDIGAP CLAIMS

The following modifications must be made to the Medicare primary claim when the health care provider is a Medicare PAR, the patient has a Medigap policy in addition to Medicare, and the patient has signed an Authorization for Release of Medigap Benefits. If a separate Medigap release is on file, the words SIGNATURE ON FILE must appear in Block 13. No benefits will be paid to the PAR if Block 27, Accept Assignment, contains an X in the NO box.

The following modifications are not to be made when the patient is covered by an employer-sponsored supplemental or retirement plan, or when the provider is a nonPAR.

Block 9

Enter the last name, first name, and middle initial of the enrollee in the Medigap policy if it is different from the name listed in Block 2. If the patient is the policyholder, enter SAME.

Block 9a

Enter MEDIGAP followed by the policy and/or group number. (The abbreviations MG or MGAP may be entered instead of MEDIGAP.)

Block 9b

Enter the Medigap enrollee's birth date (MM DD YYYY, with spaces format) and gender.

Block 9c

Disregard the heading in this block. Leave this block blank if the **Medigap plan identification number (PlanID)** assigned by the payer is known. (A Medigap policy is iden-

PLEASE
DO NOT
STAPLE
IN THIS
AREA

(SAMPLE ONLY - NOT APPROVED FOR USE)

CARRIER

| | PICA |

HEALTH INSURANCE CLAIM FORM

PICA | | |

1. MEDICARE	MEDICAID	CHAMPUS	CHAMPVA	GROUP HEALTH PLAN	FECA BLK LUNG	OTHER	1a. INSURED'S I.D. NUMBER	(FOR PROGRAM IN ITEM 1)
[X] (Medicare #)	(Medicaid #)	(Sponsor's SSN)	(VA File #)	(SSN or ID)	(SSN)	(ID)	001287431D	

2. PATIENT'S NAME (Last Name, First Name, Middle Initial)
PATIENT MARY SUE

3. PATIENT'S BIRTH DATE
MM | DD | YY   SEX
03 | 08 | 1933 M [ ] F [X]

4. INSURED'S NAME (Last Name, First Name, Middle Initial)

5. PATIENT'S ADDRESS (No. Street)
91 HOME STREET

6. PATIENT RELATIONSHIP TO INSURED
Self [ ] Spouse [ ] Child [ ] Other [ ]

7. INSURED'S ADDRESS (No. Street)

CITY
NOWHERE

STATE
US

8. PATIENT STATUS
Single [X] Married [ ] Other [ ]

CITY

STATE

ZIP CODE
12367

TELEPHONE (Include Area Code)
(101) 201 8989

Employed [ ] Full-Time Student [ ] Part-Time Student [ ]

ZIP CODE

TELEPHONE (INCLUDE AREA CODE)
( )

9. OTHER INSURED'S NAME (Last Name, First Name, Middle Initial)

10. IS PATIENT'S CONDITION RELATED TO:

11. INSURED'S POLICY GROUP OR FECA NUMBER
NONE

a. OTHER INSURED'S POLICY OR GROUP NUMBER

a. EMPLOYMENT? (CURRENT OR PREVIOUS)
YES [ ] [X] NO

a. INSURED'S DATE OF BIRTH
MM | DD | YY   SEX
M [ ] F [ ]

b. OTHER INSURED'S DATE OF BIRTH
MM | DD | YY   SEX
M [ ] F [ ]

b. AUTO ACCIDENT?   PLACE (State)
YES [ ] [X] NO | |

b. EMPLOYER'S NAME OR SCHOOL NAME

c. EMPLOYER'S NAME OR SCHOOL NAME

c. OTHER ACCIDENT?
YES [ ] [X] NO

c. INSURANCE PLAN NAME OR PROGRAM NAME

d. INSURANCE PLAN NAME OR PROGRAM NAME

10d. RESERVED FOR LOCAL USE

d. IS THERE ANOTHER HEALTH BENEFIT PLAN?
YES [ ] NO [ ]   If yes, return to and complete item 9 a – d.

READ BACK OF FORM BEFORE COMPLETING & SIGNING THIS FORM.
12. PATIENT'S OR AUTHORIZED PERSON'S SIGNATURE I authorize the release of any medical or other information necessary to process this claim. I also request payment of government benefits either to myself or to the party who accepts assignment below.

SIGNED   SIGNATURE ON FILE

DATE _____

13. INSURED'S OR AUTHORIZED PERSON'S SIGNATURE I authorize payment of medical benefits to the undersigned physician or supplier for services described below.

SIGNED   SIGNATURE ON FILE

14. DATE OF CURRENT: ► ILLNESS (First symptom) OR
MM | DD | YY   INJURY (Accident) OR
01 | 28 | YYYY   PREGNANCY (LMP)

15. IF PATIENT HAS HAD SAME OR SIMILAR ILLNESS, GIVE FIRST DATE   MM | DD | YY

16. DATES PATIENT UNABLE TO WORK IN CURRENT OCCUPATION
MM | DD | YY   MM | DD | YY
FROM   TO

17. NAME OF REFERRING PHYSICIAN OR OTHER SOURCE
I M GOODDOC

17a. I.D. NUMBER OF REFERRING PHYSICIAN
IG7777

18. HOSPITALIZATION DATES RELATED TO CURRENT SERVICES
MM | DD | YY   MM | DD | YY
FROM   TO

19. RESERVED FOR LOCAL USE

20. OUTSIDE LAB? $ CHARGES
YES [ ] [X] NO

21. DIAGNOSIS OR NATURE OF ILLNESS OR INJURY. (RELATE ITEMS 1, 2, 3, OR 4 TO ITEM 24E BY LINE)

1. 511.0

3. V12.51

2. 427.89

4. ___.___

22. MEDICAID RESUBMISSION
CODE   ORIGINAL REF. NO.

23. PRIOR AUTHORIZATION NUMBER

24. A. DATE(S) OF SERVICE From MM DD YY	To MM DD YY	B. Place of Service	C. Type of Service	D. PROCEDURES, SERVICES, OR SUPPLIES (Explain Unusual Circumstances) CPT/HCPCS	MODIFIER	E. DIAGNOSIS CODE	F. $ CHARGES	G. DAYS OR UNITS	H. EPSDT Family Plan	I. EMG	J. COB	K. RESERVED FOR LOCAL USE
1	0130YYYY		11		99243		1	150 00	1				
2	0130YYYY		11		71020		1	50 00	1				
3	0130YYYY		11		93000		2	50 00	1				
4													
5													
6													

25. FEDERAL TAX I.D. NUMBER   SSN EIN
11-123341   [ ] [X]

26. PATIENT'S ACCOUNT NO.
14-9

27. ACCEPT ASSIGNMENT? (For govt. claims, see back)
[X] YES [ ] NO

28. TOTAL CHARGE
$ 250 00

29. AMOUNT PAID
$

30. BALANCE DUE
$

31. SIGNATURE OF PHYSICIAN OR SUPPLIER INCLUDING DEGREES OR CREDENTIALS
(I certify that the statements on the reverse apply to this bill and are made a part thereof.)

Erin A Helper MD

SIGNED   DATE MMDDYYYY

32. NAME AND ADDRESS OF FACILITY WHERE SERVICES WERE RENDERED (If other than home or office)

33. PHYSICIAN'S SUPPLIER'S BILLING NAME, ADDRESS, ZIP CODE & PHONE #
(101) 111 1234
ERIN A HELPER MD
101 MEDIC DRIVE
ANYWHERE US 12345
PIN# A09293   GRP# G1515

(SAMPLE ONLY - NOT APPROVED FOR USE)

PLEASE PRINT OR TYPE

SAMPLE FORM 1500
SAMPLE FORM 1500 SAMPLE FORM 1500

PATIENT AND INSURED INFORMATION

PHYSICIAN OR SUPPLIER INFORMATION

FIGURE 14-16 Completed Mary Sue Patient primary CMS-1500 claim

tifiable by the numbers "99" in the seventh and eighth positions of the nine-digit ID number.)

If the PlanID is not known, enter an abbreviated mailing address of the Medigap carrier.

● **EXAMPLE:** 111 Anyplace Street, Anywhere, MD 12345 is entered as:

111 ANYPLACE ST MD 12345 ●

The **National Health PlanID** is being developed by CMS, as authorized by the Health Insurance Portability and Accountability Act of 1996, to enumerate health plans and provide a standard plan identifier for efficient electronic data interchange (EDI) and health care administrative operations.

Block 9d

Enter the Medigap PlanID number. If no PlanID number is available, enter the Medigap plan name.

Block 13

The patient's signature or SIGNATURE ON FILE statement authorizes direct payment of Medigap to the PAR providers.

● **NOTE:** A special authorization with the designated Medigap carrier must be signed. The wording on the claim is not acceptable to CMS. ●

EXERCISE 14-10 **Continuation of Exercise 14-8**

1. Review the instructions for changes to a primary claim when the patient is also covered by a Medigap policy.

2. Enter brief instructions in the Medigap column of the chart.

3. Draw a horizontal arrow from any block in the Medicare Primary column that remains the same in the Medigap column.

EXERCISE 14-11 **Medicare Primary and Medigap Claims Processing**

Additional information needed for this case:
Dr. Helper is a Medicare PAR and her Medicare PIN number is A09293. The billing entity is Erin Helper, M.D. The Medicare group identifier number is G1515.

1. Obtain a blank CMS-1500 claim.

2. Underline the block identifiers on the new claim for the blocks discussed in the Medigap claim form instructions.

3. Refer to the encounter form for John Q. Public (Figure 14-7). Enter the following information in the blocks for the secondary policy:

Aetna Medigap ID # 22233544   Group # AA2

PlanID: 11543299

Policyholder: John Q. Public

Employer: Retired

(continues)

4. Complete the Medicare/Medigap claim using the data from the encounter form.

5. Compare the completed claim to the claim in Figure 14-17 to be sure all required blocks are properly completed.

FIGURE 14-17 Completed John Q. Public Medicare/Medigap CMS-1500 claim

MEDICARE-MEDICAID CROSSOVER CLAIMS

The following modifications must be added to the Medicare Primary claim when the patient is covered by Medicare and also has Medicaid coverage for services rendered on a fee-for-service basis.

Block 1a

Enter an X in both the Medicare and the Medicaid boxes.

Block 10d

Enter the abbreviation MCD followed by the patient's Medicaid/MediCal ID number.

Block 27

Enter an X in the YES box. NonPAR must accept assignment on this claim.

EXERCISE 14-12 Continuation of Exercise 14-10

1. Review the instructions for completing a Medicare-Medicaid crossover claim.
2. Enter brief instructions in the Medicare-Medicaid crossover column of the chart.
3. Draw a horizontal arrow from any block in the Medicare Primary and Medigap columns that remain the same in the Medicare crossover column.

EXERCISE 14-13 Medicare-Medicaid Crossover Claims Processing

Additional information needed for this case:
Dr. Helper is a Medicare PAR. The billing entity is Erin Helper, M.D.

1. Obtain a blank CMS-1500 claim.
2. Underline the Block identifiers on the new claim for the blocks discussed in the Medicare-Medicaid crossover claim instructions.
3. Refer to the Mary Sue Patient encounter form in Figure 14-9, and enter the additional Medicaid information in the Secondary Policy blocks:
   Insurance policy: Medicaid
   ID #: 101234591XT
   Relationship: Self
4. Complete the Medicare/Medicaid claim.
5. Compare the completed claim with the claim in Figure 14-18.

MEDICARE SECONDARY PAYER (MSP) CLAIMS

Block 1

Enter an X in the MEDICARE and OTHER boxes.

(SAMPLE ONLY - NOT APPROVED FOR USE)

CARRIER

PLEASE
DO NOT
STAPLE
IN THIS
AREA

☐ PICA

HEALTH INSURANCE CLAIM FORM

PICA ☐☐☐

1. MEDICARE	MEDICAID	CHAMPUS	CHAMPVA	GROUP HEALTH PLAN	FECA BLK LUNG	OTHER	1a. INSURED'S I.D. NUMBER (FOR PROGRAM IN ITEM 1)
[X] (Medicare #)	[X] (Medicaid #)	☐ (Sponsor's SSN)	☐ (VA File #)	☐ (SSN or ID)	☐ (SSN)	☐ (ID)	001287431D

2. PATIENT'S NAME (Last Name, First Name, Middle Initial)
PATIENT MARY SUE

3. PATIENT'S BIRTH DATE MM | DD | YY SEX
03 | 08 | 1933 M ☐ F [X]

4. INSURED'S NAME (Last Name, First Name, Middle Initial)

5. PATIENT'S ADDRESS (No. Street)
91 HOME STREET

6. PATIENT RELATIONSHIP TO INSURED
Self ☐ Spouse ☐ Child ☐ Other ☐

7. INSURED'S ADDRESS (No. Street)

CITY NOWHERE   STATE US

8. PATIENT STATUS
Single [X] Married ☐ Other ☐
Employed ☐ Full-Time Student ☐ Part-Time Student ☐

CITY   STATE

ZIP CODE 12367   TELEPHONE (Include Area Code) (101) 201 8989

ZIP CODE   TELEPHONE (INCLUDE AREA CODE) ( )

9. OTHER INSURED'S NAME (Last Name, First Name, Middle Initial)

10. IS PATIENT'S CONDITION RELATED TO:

11. INSURED'S POLICY GROUP OR FECA NUMBER
NONE

a. OTHER INSURED'S POLICY OR GROUP NUMBER

a. EMPLOYMENT? (CURRENT OR PREVIOUS) ☐ YES [X] NO

a. INSURED'S DATE OF BIRTH MM | DD | YY SEX M ☐ F ☐

b. OTHER INSURED'S DATE OF BIRTH MM | DD | YY SEX M ☐ F ☐

b. AUTO ACCIDENT? PLACE (State) ☐ YES [X] NO

b. EMPLOYER'S NAME OR SCHOOL NAME

c. EMPLOYER'S NAME OR SCHOOL NAME

c. OTHER ACCIDENT? ☐ YES [X] NO

c. INSURANCE PLAN NAME OR PROGRAM NAME

d. INSURANCE PLAN NAME OR PROGRAM NAME

10d. RESERVED FOR LOCAL USE
MCD 101234591XT

d. IS THERE ANOTHER HEALTH BENEFIT PLAN? ☐ YES ☐ NO If yes, return to and complete item 9 a – d.

READ BACK OF FORM BEFORE COMPLETING & SIGNING THIS FORM.
12. PATIENT'S OR AUTHORIZED PERSON'S SIGNATURE I authorize the release of any medical or other information necessary to process this claim. I also request payment of government benefits either to myself or to the party who accepts assignment below.

SIGNED SIGNATURE ON FILE   DATE _____

13. INSURED'S OR AUTHORIZED PERSON'S SIGNATURE I authorize payment of medical benefits to the undersigned physician or supplier for services described below.

SIGNED SIGNATURE ON FILE

14. DATE OF CURRENT: MM | DD | YY ILLNESS (First symptom) OR INJURY (Accident) OR PREGNANCY (LMP)
01 | 28 | YYYY

15. IF PATIENT HAS HAD SAME OR SIMILAR ILLNESS, GIVE FIRST DATE MM | DD | YY

16. DATES PATIENT UNABLE TO WORK IN CURRENT OCCUPATION MM | DD | YY FROM   TO MM | DD | YY

17. NAME OF REFERRING PHYSICIAN OR OTHER SOURCE
I M GOODDOC

17a. I.D. NUMBER OF REFERRING PHYSICIAN
IG7777

18. HOSPITALIZATION DATES RELATED TO CURRENT SERVICES MM | DD | YY FROM   TO MM | DD | YY

19. RESERVED FOR LOCAL USE

20. OUTSIDE LAB? ☐ YES [X] NO $ CHARGES

21. DIAGNOSIS OR NATURE OF ILLNESS OR INJURY. (RELATE ITEMS 1, 2, 3, OR 4 TO ITEM 24E BY LINE)
1. 511 0
2. 427 89
3. V12 51
4. _____

22. MEDICAID RESUBMISSION CODE   ORIGINAL REF. NO.

23. PRIOR AUTHORIZATION NUMBER

24. A. DATE(S) OF SERVICE From MM DD YY	To MM DD YY	B. Place of Service	C. Type of Service	D. PROCEDURES, SERVICES, OR SUPPLIES CPT/HCPCS	MODIFIER	E. DIAGNOSIS CODE	F. $ CHARGES	G. DAYS OR UNITS	H. EPSDT Family Plan	I. EMG	J. COB	K. RESERVED FOR LOCAL USE
1 0130YYYY		11		99243		1	150 00	1				
2 0130YYYY		11		71020		1	50 00	1				
3 0130YYYY		11		93000		2	50 00	2				
4												
5												
6												

25. FEDERAL TAX I.D. NUMBER SSN ☐ EIN [X]
11-123452

26. PATIENT'S ACCOUNT NO.
14-9MM

27. ACCEPT ASSIGNMENT? (For govt. claims, see back) [X] YES ☐ NO

28. TOTAL CHARGE $ 250 00

29. AMOUNT PAID $

30. BALANCE DUE $

31. SIGNATURE OF PHYSICIAN OR SUPPLIER INCLUDING DEGREES OR CREDENTIALS (I certify that the statements on the reverse apply to this bill and are made a part thereof.)
Erin A Helper MD
SIGNED   DATE MMDDYYYY

32. NAME AND ADDRESS OF FACILITY WHERE SERVICES WERE RENDERED (If other than home or office)

33. PHYSICIAN'S SUPPLIER'S BILLING NAME, ADDRESS, ZIP CODE & PHONE #
(101) 111 1234
ERIN A HELPER MD
1201 MEDIC DRIVE
ANYWHERE US 12345
PIN# A09293   GRP# G1515

(SAMPLE ONLY - NOT APPROVED FOR USE)

PLEASE PRINT OR TYPE

SAMPLE FORM 1500
SAMPLE FORM 1500 SAMPLE FORM 1500

PATIENT AND INSURED INFORMATION

PHYSICIAN OR SUPPLIER INFORMATION

FIGURE 14-18 Completed Mary Sue Patient Medicare/Medicaid CMS-1500 claim

Block 4

Enter the primary insurance policyholder's name. If the policyholder is the patient, enter SAME.

Block 6

Indicate the relationship of the patient to the primary insurance policyholder named.

Block 7

Enter the address and telephone number of the policyholder named in Block 4, if different from the patient. If the patient is the policyholder or the address of the policyholder is the same as that in Block 5, enter SAME.

Block 10

Enter an X in the appropriate boxes to indicate whether the patient's condition is related to employment or an auto or other accident.

NOTE: Entering an X in any of the YES boxes alerts the Medicare carrier that another insurance plan might be liable for payment. Medicare payer will not consider the claim unless the provider submits an explanation of benefits (EOB) from the liable party (e.g., workers' compensation, auto insurance).

Block 11

Enter the complete policy/group number of the primary plan. (Blocks 4 and 7 must also be completed.)

Block 11a

Enter the primary policyholder's date of birth (MM DD YYYY, with spaces format) and gender.

Block 11b

Enter the employer's name for any large group health plan that is primary to Medicare. If the policyholder is retired, enter RETIRED and the date of retirement (MM DD YYYY, with spaces format).

Block 11c

Enter the primary insurance plan name or the PlanID number. The primary EOB must be attached to this claim.

NOTE: The EOB must contain the name and address of the payer.

Block 16

Enter dates if patient is employed full time and unable to work.

Block 29

Enter only patient payment for services on this claim. The attached transmittal notice from primary insurers will indicate the primary carrier's payments.

EXERCISE 14-14 Continuation of Exercise 14-12

1. Review the instructions for completing a Medicare-Medicaid crossover claim.

2. Enter brief instructions in the Medicare Secondary column of the chart.

3. Draw a horizontal arrow from any block in the Medicare Primary, Medigap, and Medicare/Medicaid columns that remains the same in the Medicare Secondary column.

EXERCISE 14-15 Medicare Secondary Claims Processing

Additional information needed for this case:
Dr. Helper is a Medicare PAR. The billing entity is Erin Helper, M.D. The PIN for the Ambulatory Surgical Center is ASC1000.

1. Obtain a blank CMS-1500 claim.

2. Underline the Block numbers for the changes discussed above.

3. Refer to the Jackie L. Neely encounter form (Figure 14-19) and complete the Medicare Secondary claim for this case using the data from the encounter form.

4. Review the completed claim to be sure all required blocks are filled in.

5. Compare your claim with Figure 14-20.

Additional Medicare case studies are found in Appendix I and Appendix II.

Case Studies require reading the case study chart entries and selecting and coding the diagnostic information. Necessary hospital and physician data are included in the case study encounter forms in Appendix II.

ROSTER BILLING FOR MASS VACCINATION PROGRAMS

The simplified **roster billing** process was developed to enable Medicare beneficiaries to participate in mass PPV (pneumococcal pneumonia virus) and influenza virus vaccination programs offered by Public Health Clinics (PHCs) and other entities that bill Medicare carriers. (Medicare has not yet developed roster billing for hepatitis B vaccinations.) Properly licensed individuals and entities conducting mass immunization programs may submit claims using a simplified claims filing procedure to bill for the PPV and influenza virus vaccine benefit for multiple beneficiaries if they agree to accept assignment for these claims. Entities that submit claims on roster bills (and therefore must accept assignment) may not collect any donations or other cost-sharing of any kind from Medicare beneficiaries for PPV or influenza vaccinations. However, the entity may bill Medicare for the amount not subsidized from its own budget.

EXAMPLE: A public health clinic (PHC) sponsors an influenza vaccination virus clinic for Medicare beneficiaries. The cost is $12.50 per vaccination, and the PHC pays $2.50 of the cost from its budget. The PHC is therefore eligible to roster bill Medicare

ERIN A. HELPER, M.D.
101 Medic Dr, Anywhere US 12345
(101) 111-1234 (Office) • (101) 111-9292 (Fax)
EIN: 11-123452 **MCD:** EBH8881
UPIN: EH8888 **BCBS:** EH11881
PIN: A09293 **MC GRP#** G1515

Encounter Form

PATIENT INFORMATION:

Name:	Jack L. Neely
Address:	329 Water Street
City:	Nowhere
State:	US
Zip Code:	12367
Telephone:	(101) 201-1278
Gender:	M
Date of Birth:	09-09-1929
Occupation:	Retired
Employer:	
Spouse's Employer:	Federal Investigative Services

INSURANCE INFORMATION:

Patient Number:	14-19
Place of Service:	Anywhere Surgical Center
Primary Insurance Plan:	BCBS Federal
Primary Insurance Plan ID #:	R1234567
Group #:	103
Primary Policyholder:	Mary Neely
Policyholder Date of Birth:	03-19-1935
Relationship to Patient:	Spouse
Secondary Insurance Plan:	Medicare
Secondary Insurance Plan ID #:	111223344A
Secondary Policyholder:	Jackie L. Neely

Patient Status   [X] Married   [ ] Divorced   [ ] Single   [ ] Student

DIAGNOSIS INFORMATION

	Diagnosis	Code		Diagnosis	Code
1.	Rectal bleeding (3 days)	569.3	5.		
2.	Hx polyps, ascending colon	V10.05	6.		
3.			7.		
4.			8.		

PROCEDURE INFORMATION

	Description of Procedure or Service	Date	Code	Charge
1.	Colonoscopy, flexible to ileum	01-08-YYYY	45378	700.00
2.				
3.				
4.				
5.				

SPECIAL NOTES: Anywhere Surgical Center, 101 Park St, Anywhere US 12345 (PIN: ASC 1000)
Referring physician: Arnold Younglove M.D. (PIN: AY9999)

FIGURE 14-19 Jackie L. Neely encounter form

the $10 cost difference for each beneficiary. The PHC submits both a CMS-1500 claim (Figure 14-21) as a cover sheet and the roster billing form (Figure 14-22).

NOTE: There is no minimum requirement as to the number of beneficiaries to be reported on the same date (the rule used to be a minimum of five beneficiaries reported on the same date to qualify for roster billing). *However, the date of service for each vaccination administered must be entered.*

NOTE: Roster billing is not used to submit single patient bills.

PLEASE
DO NOT
STAPLE
IN THIS
AREA

TRANSMITTAL NOTICE ATTACHED

(SAMPLE ONLY - NOT APPROVED FOR USE)

CARRIER

| | PICA

HEALTH INSURANCE CLAIM FORM PICA | | |

1. MEDICARE	MEDICAID	CHAMPUS	CHAMPVA	GROUP HEALTH PLAN (SSN or ID)	FECA BLK LUNG (SSN)	OTHER	1a. INSURED'S I.D. NUMBER (FOR PROGRAM IN ITEM 1)
[X] (Medicare #)	[ ] (Medicaid #)	[ ] (Sponsor's SSN)	[ ] (VA File #)	[ ]	[ ]	[ ] (ID)	111223344A

2. PATIENT'S NAME (Last Name, First Name, Middle Initial)
NEELY JACK L

3. PATIENT'S BIRTH DATE MM | DD | YY SEX
09 | 09 | 1929 M [X] F [ ]

4. INSURED'S NAME (Last Name, First Name, Middle Initial)
NEELY MARY

5. PATIENT'S ADDRESS (No. Street)
329 WATER STREET

6. PATIENT RELATIONSHIP TO INSURED
Self [ ] Spouse [ ] Child [ ] Other [ ]

7. INSURED'S ADDRESS (No. Street)
SAME

CITY
NOWHERE

STATE
US

8. PATIENT STATUS
Single [ ] Married [X] Other [ ]

CITY

STATE

ZIP CODE
12367

TELEPHONE (Include Area Code)
(101) 201 1278

Employed [ ] Full-Time Student [ ] Part-Time Student [ ]

ZIP CODE

TELEPHONE (INCLUDE AREA CODE)
( )

9. OTHER INSURED'S NAME (Last Name, First Name, Middle Initial)

10. IS PATIENT'S CONDITION RELATED TO:

11. INSURED'S POLICY GROUP OR FECA NUMBER
R1234567   103

a. OTHER INSURED'S POLICY OR GROUP NUMBER

a. EMPLOYMENT? (CURRENT OR PREVIOUS)
[ ] YES [X] NO

a. INSURED'S DATE OF BIRTH MM | DD | YY SEX
03 | 19 | 1935 M [ ] F [X]

b. OTHER INSURED'S DATE OF BIRTH MM | DD | YY SEX M [ ] F [ ]

b. AUTO ACCIDENT? PLACE (State)
[ ] YES [X] NO

b. EMPLOYER'S NAME OR SCHOOL NAME
FEDERAL INVESTIGATIVE SERVICES

c. EMPLOYER'S NAME OR SCHOOL NAME

c. OTHER ACCIDENT?
[ ] YES [X] NO

c. INSURANCE PLAN NAME OR PROGRAM NAME
BCBS FEDERAL

d. INSURANCE PLAN NAME OR PROGRAM NAME

10d. RESERVED FOR LOCAL USE

d. IS THERE ANOTHER HEALTH BENEFIT PLAN?
[ ] YES [X] NO If yes, return to and complete item 9 a – d.

READ BACK OF FORM BEFORE COMPLETING & SIGNING THIS FORM.
12. PATIENT'S OR AUTHORIZED PERSON'S SIGNATURE I authorize the release of any medical or other information necessary to process this claim. I also request payment of government benefits either to myself or to the party who accepts assignment below.

SIGNED SIGNATURE ON FILE DATE _____

13. INSURED'S OR AUTHORIZED PERSON'S SIGNATURE I authorize payment of medical benefits to the undersigned physician or supplier for services described below.

SIGNED SIGNATURE ON FILE

PATIENT AND INSURED INFORMATION

14. DATE OF CURRENT: MM | DD | YY ILLNESS (First symptom) OR INJURY (Accident) OR PREGNANCY (LMP)
01 | 05 | YYYY

15. IF PATIENT HAS HAD SAME OR SIMILAR ILLNESS, GIVE FIRST DATE MM | DD | YY

16. DATES PATIENT UNABLE TO WORK IN CURRENT OCCUPATION MM | DD | YY FROM TO MM | DD | YY

17. NAME OF REFERRING PHYSICIAN OR OTHER SOURCE
ARNOLD YOUNGLOVE

17a. I.D. NUMBER OF REFERRING PHYSICIAN
AY9999

18. HOSPITALIZATION DATES RELATED TO CURRENT SERVICES MM | DD | YY FROM TO MM | DD | YY

19. RESERVED FOR LOCAL USE

20. OUTSIDE LAB? $ CHARGES
[ ] YES [X] NO

21. DIAGNOSIS OR NATURE OF ILLNESS OR INJURY. (RELATE ITEMS 1, 2, 3, OR 4 TO ITEM 24E BY LINE)
1. 569 3
2. V10 05
3. ____ . ____
4. ____ . ____

22. MEDICAID RESUBMISSION CODE ORIGINAL REF. NO.

23. PRIOR AUTHORIZATION NUMBER

24. A. DATE(S) OF SERVICE						B. Place of Service	C. Type of Service	D. PROCEDURES, SERVICES, OR SUPPLIES (Explain Unusual Circumstances)		E. DIAGNOSIS CODE	F. $ CHARGES	G. DAYS OR UNITS	H. EPSDT Family Plan	I. EMG	J. COB	K. RESERVED FOR LOCAL USE
From MM	DD	YY	To MM	DD	YY			CPT/HCPCS	MODIFIER							
01	08	YYYY				24		45378		1	700 00	1				

PHYSICIAN OR SUPPLIER INFORMATION

25. FEDERAL TAX I.D. NUMBER SSN [ ] EIN [X]
11-123452

26. PATIENT'S ACCOUNT NO.
14-19S

27. ACCEPT ASSIGNMENT? (For govt. claims, see back)
[X] YES [ ] NO

28. TOTAL CHARGE
$ 700 00

29. AMOUNT PAID
$

30. BALANCE DUE
$

31. SIGNATURE OF PHYSICIAN OR SUPPLIER INCLUDING DEGREES OR CREDENTIALS (I certify that the statements on the reverse apply to this bill and are made a part thereof.)
Erin A Helper MD
SIGNED DATE MMDDYYYY

32. NAME AND ADDRESS OF FACILITY WHERE SERVICES WERE RENDERED (If other than home or office)
ANYWHERE SURGICAL CENTER
101 PARK STREET
ANYWHERE US 12345
ASC1000

33. PHYSICIAN'S SUPPLIER'S BILLING NAME, ADDRESS, ZIP CODE & PHONE #
(101) 111 1234
ERIN A HELPER MD
101 MEDIC DRIVE
ANYWHERE US 12345
PIN# A09293 GRP# G1515

(SAMPLE ONLY - NOT APPROVED FOR USE)

PLEASE PRINT OR TYPE

SAMPLE FORM 1500
SAMPLE FORM 1500 SAMPLE FORM 1500

FIGURE 14-20 Completed Jackie L. Neely Medicare secondary CMS-1500 claim

PLEASE
DO NOT
STAPLE
IN THIS
AREA

ROSTER ATTACHED

(SAMPLE ONLY - NOT APPROVED FOR USE)

CARRIER

| | PICA | | **HEALTH INSURANCE CLAIM FORM** | PICA | | |

| 1. MEDICARE | MEDICAID | CHAMPUS | CHAMPVA | GROUP HEALTH PLAN | FECA BLK LUNG | OTHER | 1a. INSURED'S I.D. NUMBER | (FOR PROGRAM IN ITEM 1) |
| [X] (Medicare #) | (Medicaid #) | (Sponsor's SSN) | (VA File #) | (SSN or ID) | (SSN) | (ID) | SEE ATTACHED ROSTER | |

2. PATIENT'S NAME (Last Name, First Name, Middle Initial)

3. PATIENT'S BIRTH DATE MM DD YY   SEX M F

4. INSURED'S NAME (Last Name, First Name, Middle Initial)

5. PATIENT'S ADDRESS (No. Street)

6. PATIENT RELATIONSHIP TO INSURED Self Spouse Child Other

7. INSURED'S ADDRESS (No. Street)

CITY STATE

8. PATIENT STATUS Single Married Other

CITY STATE

ZIP CODE TELEPHONE (Include Area Code) ( )

Employed Full-Time Student Part-Time Student

ZIP CODE TELEPHONE (INCLUDE AREA CODE) ( )

9. OTHER INSURED'S NAME (Last Name, First Name, Middle Initial)

10. IS PATIENT'S CONDITION RELATED TO:

11. INSURED'S POLICY GROUP OR FECA NUMBER NONE

a. OTHER INSURED'S POLICY OR GROUP NUMBER

a. EMPLOYMENT? (CURRENT OR PREVIOUS) YES NO

a. INSURED'S DATE OF BIRTH MM DD YY   SEX M F

b. OTHER INSURED'S DATE OF BIRTH MM DD YY SEX M F

b. AUTO ACCIDENT? PLACE (State) YES NO

b. EMPLOYER'S NAME OR SCHOOL NAME

c. EMPLOYER'S NAME OR SCHOOL NAME

c. OTHER ACCIDENT? YES NO

c. INSURANCE PLAN NAME OR PROGRAM NAME

d. INSURANCE PLAN NAME OR PROGRAM NAME

10d. RESERVED FOR LOCAL USE

d. IS THERE ANOTHER HEALTH BENEFIT PLAN? YES NO If yes, return to and complete item 9 a – d.

READ BACK OF FORM BEFORE COMPLETING & SIGNING THIS FORM.
12. PATIENT'S OR AUTHORIZED PERSON'S SIGNATURE I authorize the release of any medical or other information necessary to process this claim. I also request payment of government benefits either to myself or to the party who accepts assignment below.

SIGNED _____ DATE _____

13. INSURED'S OR AUTHORIZED PERSON'S SIGNATURE I authorize payment of medical benefits to the undersigned physician or supplier for services described below.

SIGNED _____

14. DATE OF CURRENT: MM DD YY ILLNESS (First symptom) OR INJURY (Accident) OR PREGNANCY (LMP)

15. IF PATIENT HAS HAD SAME OR SIMILAR ILLNESS, GIVE FIRST DATE MM DD YY

16. DATES PATIENT UNABLE TO WORK IN CURRENT OCCUPATION MM DD YY FROM TO MM DD YY

17. NAME OF REFERRING PHYSICIAN OR OTHER SOURCE

17a. I.D. NUMBER OF REFERRING PHYSICIAN

18. HOSPITALIZATION DATES RELATED TO CURRENT SERVICES MM DD YY FROM TO MM DD YY

19. RESERVED FOR LOCAL USE

20. OUTSIDE LAB? YES [X] NO $ CHARGES

21. DIAGNOSIS OR NATURE OF ILLNESS OR INJURY. (RELATE ITEMS 1, 2, 3, OR 4 TO ITEM 24E BY LINE)

1. V04.8   3. |___.___|

2. |___.___| 4. |___.___|

22. MEDICAID RESUBMISSION CODE ORIGINAL REF. NO.

23. PRIOR AUTHORIZATION NUMBER

24. A DATE(S) OF SERVICE						B Place of Service	C Type of Service	D PROCEDURES, SERVICES, OR SUPPLIES (Explain Unusual Circumstances) CPT/HCPCS MODIFIER	E DIAGNOSIS CODE	F $ CHARGES	G DAYS OR UNITS	H EPSDT Family Plan	I EMG	J COB	K RESERVED FOR LOCAL USE
From MM	DD	YY	To MM	DD	YY										
1115YYYY						60		90659		1	50 00					
1115YYYY						60		G0008		1	0 00					

25. FEDERAL TAX I.D. NUMBER SSN EIN 12-3456789 [X]

26. PATIENT'S ACCOUNT NO.

27. ACCEPT ASSIGNMENT? (For govt. claims, see back) [X] YES NO

28. TOTAL CHARGE $

29. AMOUNT PAID $ 0 00

30. BALANCE DUE $

31. SIGNATURE OF PHYSICIAN OR SUPPLIER INCLUDING DEGREES OR CREDENTIALS (I certify that the statements on the reverse apply to this bill and are made a part thereof.)
PROVIDER SIGNATURE STAMP
SIGNED _____ DATE 1115YYYY

32. NAME AND ADDRESS OF FACILITY WHERE SERVICES WERE RENDERED (If other than home or office)

33. PHYSICIAN'S SUPPLIER'S BILLING NAME, ADDRESS, ZIP CODE & PHONE #
(101) 555 1111
ALLEGANY PUBLIC HEALTH CLINIC
101 MAIN ST
ANYWHERE US 12345
PIN# B23868 GRP#

(SAMPLE ONLY - NOT APPROVED FOR USE)

PLEASE PRINT OR TYPE

SAMPLE FORM 1500
SAMPLE FORM 1500 SAMPLE FORM 1500

PATIENT AND INSURED INFORMATION

PHYSICIAN OR SUPPLIER INFORMATION

FIGURE 14-21 CMS-1500 claim as cover sheet for roster billing form

HICN	Name	DOB	Sex	Address	Signature

Provider	Allegany Public Health Clinic
	100 Main St, Anywhere US 12345
	(101) 555-1111
EIN	12-456789
Date of Service	November 15, YYYY
Type of Service	Flu vaccine (ICD code V04.8) (CPT code 90659)
	(HCPCS code G0008)
Cost	$12.50 ($10.00 to be billed to Medicare)

Patient Information

HICN	Name	DOB	Sex	Address	Signature
215659849	Doe, John A	02/05/34	M	1 Hill, Anywhere US 12345	*John A. Doe*
236595428	Doe, Jane M	12/24/30	F	5 Main, Anywhere US 12345	*Jane M. Doe*
236595214	Smith, May J	02/18/32	F	8 Roe, Anywhere US 12345	*May J Smith*
956325954	Brown, Lou	05/15/20	F	2 Sims, Anywhere US 12345	*Lou Brown*
596524854	Green, Julie	09/30/25	F	6 Pine, Anywhere US 12345	*Julie Green*

FIGURE 14-22 Sample roster billing form (to be attached to CMS-1500 claim)

Provider Enrollment Criteria

All individuals and entities that submit PPV and influenza virus vaccination benefit claims to Medicare on roster bills must complete Form CMS-855, the Provider/Supplier Enrollment Application. Specialized instructions must be followed to simplify the enrollment process, and providers may not bill Medicare for any services other than PPV and influenza virus vaccinations.

NOTE: Providers should establish a computer edit to identify individuals and entities that plan to participate in the Medicare program only for the purpose of mass immunizing beneficiaries. ●

Completing the CMS-1500 Claim for Roster Billing Purposes

Providers that qualify for roster billing may use a preprinted CMS-1500 claim that contains standardized information about the entity and the benefit. Providers that submit roster bills to carriers must complete the following blocks on a single modified CMS-1500 claim, which serves as the cover sheet for the roster bill:

- Block 1   Enter an X in the Medicare box
- Block 2   Enter SEE ATTACHED ROSTER
- Block 11   Enter NONE
- Block 20   Enter an X in the NO box

NOTE: During a mass immunization clinic, beneficiaries receive either the PPV *or* the Influenza virus vaccination, not both. (This note applies to Blocks 21 and 24D.) ●

- Block 21   On line 1, enter V03.82 for PPV *or* V04.8 for influenza virus
- Block 24B   Enter 60

- Block 24D On line 1, enter 90732 for PPV *or* 90659 for influenza virus

  On line 2, enter G0009 (administration code for PPV) *or* G0008 (administration code for influenza)

- Block 24E On lines 1 and 2, enter the diagnosis code reference number from Block 21

- Block 24F Enter the total charges for each listed service

NOTE: If the provider is not charging for the vaccine or its administration, enter 0 00 or NC (for "no charge") on the appropriate line for that item. This information is required for both paper claims and electronic submissions.

- Block 25   Enter the provider's EIN
- Block 27   Enter X in the YES box
- Block 29   Enter the total amount paid by the beneficiaries
- Block 31   Have the provider either sign the claim *or* use a signature stamp
- Block 33   If the provider's PIN and GRP# (if the provider has one) does not appear on the roster billing form (which is attached to the CMS-1500 claim), enter the provider's PIN and GRP#

SUMMARY

- *Medicare Part A* reimburses institutional providers for inpatient hospital and skilled nursing facility stays, home health and hospice services, ESRD and kidney donor coverage, and heart/heart-lung, liver, and bone marrow transplants.

- A Medicare Part A *benefit period* (or *spell of illness*) begins with the first day of hospitalization and ends when the patient has been out of the hospital for 60 consecutive days. Medicare Part A *lifetime reserve days* (60 days) may be used only once during a patient's lifetime and are usually reserved for use during the patient's final, terminal hospital stay.

- *Medicare Part B* reimburses noninstitutional health care providers for all outpatient services such as physician services (e.g., office visits, inpatient visits), diagnostic testing, ambulance services, DME and supplies used in the home and certified by a physician, and so on.

- The Medicare *Physician Fee Schedule* is part of the *Resource Based Relative Value Scale (RBRVS)* system implemented in 1992, and the schedule is revised annually.

- Medicare Part B costs to patients include:
  - $100 annual deductible.
  - 20% of Medicare allowed fees on covered benefits (except in outpatient setting).
  - 50% of Medicare allowed fees for most outpatient mental health care.
  - 20% of the first $1,500 for all physical/occupational therapy services and related charges thereafter.
  - 20% of Medicare allowed fees for home health care DME.
  - not less than 20% of Medicare allowed fees (after deductible) for hospital outpatient services.
  - first three pints of blood plus 20% of Medicare allowed fees for additional pints of blood, after the deductible.

- Medicare eligibility requires individuals or spouses to have worked at least 10 years in Medicare-covered employment, be a minimum age of 65 years old, and be a citizen or permanent resident of the United States.

- Individuals who are younger than age 65 can qualify for Medicare coverage through the SSA if they are disabled or have chronic kidney disease.

- Medicare enrollment is handled in two ways: (1) *automatic enrollment* for individuals about three months prior to their 65th birthday or 24th month of disability, whichever applies, and (2) *application process* through the SSA for individuals who do not receive Social Security, Railroad Retirement Board, or disability benefits.

- For those who are eligible for Social Security benefits, there is no cost for Medicare Part A coverage, but individuals pay monthly premiums for Medicare Part B coverage. Individuals who do not qualify for Social Security benefits can *buy in* to Medicare Part A and B.

- The *QMB program* requires state Medicaid programs to pay Medicare premiums, patient deductibles, and coinsurance for individuals who have Medicare Part A, a low monthly income, and limited resources, but who are otherwise not eligible for Medicaid. The *SLMB program* requires states to cover just Medicare Part B premiums for individuals whose incomes are slightly above the poverty level.

- Participating providers (PARs) agree to *accept assignment* on all Medicare claims submitted, and PARs receive special incentives as part of the agreement.

- Nonparticipating providers (nonPARs) may elect to *accept assignment* on a claim-by-claim basis, and restrictions apply. NonPARS restrictions include the limiting charge, surgical disclosure notice, mandatory claims submission, Privacy Act of 1979 (or Sunshine Law), and prohibition on balance billing (depending on state law).

- The BBA of 1997 provided for a *private contracting* option, which means providers can "drop out" of Medicare and enter into private agreements with Medicare patients. Restrictions apply!

- Providers and suppliers must have patients sign an *advance beneficiary notice (ABN)* when services rendered are unlikely to be reimbursed by Medicare (e.g., providers believes Medicare will issue a *medical necessity denial).*

- *Medicare Secondary Payer (MSP)* rules state that Medicare is the secondary payer when one of several rules applies (e.g., patient is covered by EGHP that has more than 20 covered employees). The provider must obtain MSP information to comply (e.g., have the patient complete an MSP questionnaire).

- Medicare plans include the (1) Original Medicare Plan, (2) Medicare managed care plans (e.g., Medicare+Choice), and (3) private fee-for-service plans.

- The *Medicare Summary Notice (MSN)* replaced the Explanation of Medicare Benefits (EOMB) in 2001, and provides an easy-to-read monthly statement that lists health insurance claims information.

- Medicare beneficiaries purchase supplemental plans to cover the deductible and coinsurance amounts, including: (1) Medigap, (2) employer-sponsored retirement plans, and (3) extra coverage plans.

- The *Medicare-Medicaid crossover* program is available to Medicare beneficiaries who have incomes below the federal poverty level. Beneficiaries have both Medicare and Medicaid coverage, and Medicare is billed first.

- When completing Medicare CMS-1500 claims for case studies in this text and the workbook, the following special instructions apply:
  - Block 9a—Enter MEDIGAP followed by the policy and/or group number. (This instruction applies to Medigap claims only.)
  - Block 12—Enter SIGNATURE ON FILE (patients have signed a customized authorization that is filed in the patient's record)
  - Block 13—Enter SIGNATURE ON FILE (because all providers are PARs)
  - Block 19—Leave blank
  - Block 20—Enter an X in the NO box
  - Block 23—Leave blank
  - Block 25—Enter the EIN with a hyphen.
  - Block 26—Enter the case study number (e.g., 14-7). If the patient has both primary and secondary coverage, enter a P (for primary) next to the case study number (on the primary claim) and an S (for secondary) next to the number (on the secondary claim); if the patient is eligible for the Medicare-Medicaid crossover plan, enter MM next to the case study number.
  - Block 27—Enter an X in the YES box.
  - Block 31—Enter provider's complete name with credentials (instead of a signature as indicated in the chapter instructions). This will allow you to completely generate claims using the UHI software (instead of having to print the claim and sign it).
  - Block 32—If Block 18 contains dates and/or Block 20 contains an X in the YES box, enter the name and address of the responsible provider in Block 32 (e.g., hospital, outside laboratory)
  - When completing secondary claims, enter EOB ATTACHED in the top margin of the CMS-1500 claim (to simulate the attachment of a primary payer's EOB with a claim submitted to a secondary payer)
- The simplified *roster billing* process was developed to enable Medicare beneficiaries to participate in mass PPV (pneumococcal pneumonia virus) and influenza virus vaccination programs offered by Public Health Clinics (PHCs) and other entities that bill Medicare carriers.

STUDY CHECKLIST

- ☐ Read the textbook chapter, and prepare the Insurance Plan Comparison Chart.
- ☐ Install the UHI software from the disk (instructions are in Appendix V), and become familiar with the software.
- ☐ Complete CMS-1500 claims for each chapter encounter form.
- ☐ Complete the chapter review.
- ☐ Complete the chapter CD-ROM activities.

- ☐ Complete Web Tutor assignments, and take online quizzes.
- ☐ Complete the Workbook chapter, verifying answers with your instructor.
- ☐ Complete Medicare claims for cases located in Appendices I and II.
- ☐ Form a study group with classmates to discuss chapter concepts in preparation for an exam.

REVIEW

TRUE/FALSE

Indicate whether each definition is true or false.

1. ☐ T ☐ F Specified Low-Income Medicare Beneficiary Program: A Medicare program that requires states to cover premiums, deductibles, and copayments for Medicare-eligible persons with incomes that are slightly above the federal poverty line.

2. ☐ T ☐ F Medicare Part B: Covers services provided by institutions and outpatient health care providers.

3. ☐ T ☐ F Medicare Part A: Covers inpatient hospital, hospice, skilled nursing facility, and home health care services.

4. ☐ T ☐ F Balance Billing: Billing the patient for the entire amount included on the Medical claim.

5. ☐ T ☐ F Hospice: Autonomous, centrally-administered program coordinating inpatient and outpatient services for terminally ill patients and their families.

6. ☐ T ☐ F ESRD: End-stage renal disorder.

7. ☐ T ☐ F Limiting Charge: The maximum charge a PAR provider may charge a Medicare patient.

8. ☐ T ☐ F MCD: The initials indicating the Medicare-Medicaid crossover program.

SHORT ANSWER

Briefly answer each of the following.

9. List six *separate and distinct classifications* of persons who are automatically eligible for full Medicare coverage.

10. List two classifications of persons who could qualify for Medicare coverage under special circumstances.

11. Explain how persons over age 65, who otherwise do not qualify for Medicare coverage, may buy into the program.

12. Describe six *distinctly different* categories of coverage a person can receive under Medicare Part B.

13. Discuss the limitations in Medicare coverage for a kidney donor.

14. Explain how a Medicare-eligible person, who needs a heart or liver transplant, can obtain Medicare to cover the cost of the transplant.

15. List seven incentives developed by the federal government to encourage health care providers to become PARS.

16. List five insurance programs that are considered primary to Medicare.

17. List the advantages for a Medicare beneficiary to sign up for a Medicare-HMO plan.

18. Explain the steps a provider must take to "opt out" of Medicare.

19. Explain how a patient would use a Medicare Savings Account/high deductible insurance plan combination.

20. List four combinations of services performed during one encounter that would require two separate claims to fully report the encounter when only two diagnoses and four services were performed.

adjusted claim

dual eligibles

Early and Periodic Screening,
Diagnostic, and Treatment
(EPSDT) services

Federal Medical Assistance
Percentage (FMAP)

federal poverty level (FPL)

Medicaid eligibility verification system
(MEVS)

Medicaid remittance advice

medical assistance program

mother/baby claim

recipient eligibility verification system
(REVS)

State Children's Health Insurance
Program (SCHIP)

surveillance and utilization review
system (SURS)

Temporary Assistance to Needy
Families (TANF)

voided claim

Chapter 15 | Medicaid

Upon successful completion of this chapter, you should be able to:

1. Define key terms.

2. List Medicaid federal guidelines.

3. List services covered under the federal portion of Medicaid assistance.

4. List services covered in your state that are not federally mandated services.

5. Explain how to verify a patient's Medicaid eligibility.

6. State the deadline for filing claims (timely filing period).

7. Explain the importance of the spousal impoverishment protection legislation.

8. Describe the preauthorization procedure for services.

9. File a Medicaid claim using the rules for the CMS-1500 claim.

INTRODUCTION

In 1965, Congress passed Title 19 of the Social Security Act establishing a federally-mandated, state-administered **medical assistance program** for individuals with incomes below the federal poverty level. The federal name for this program is *Medicaid*; several states assign local designations (e.g., California uses the title *MediCal*). Unlike Medicare, a nationwide entitlement program, the federal government mandated national requirements for Medicaid and gave the states latitude to develop eligibility rules and additional benefits if they assumed responsibility for the program's support.

Medicaid provides medical assistance to certain individuals and families with low incomes and limited resources (the "medically indigent"). It is jointly funded by the federal and state governments to assist states in providing adequate medical care to qualified individuals. Within broad federal guidelines, each state:

- establishes its own eligibility standards.
- determines the type, amount, duration, and scope of services.

- sets rates of payment for services.
- administers its own program.

Thus, Medicaid varies considerably from state to state, and each state has modified its program over time.

INTERNET LINK

Go to http://cms.hhs.gov/publications to download and view Medicaid publications, including Medicare manuals.

FEDERAL ELIGIBILITY REQUIREMENTS FOR MEDICAID

States have some discretion in determining Medicaid coverage policies as well as establishing financial criteria for Medicaid eligibility. To be eligible for federal funds, however, states must provide Medicaid coverage to most individuals who receive federally assisted income maintenance payments, as well as to related groups who do not receive cash payments. Federal funds are not provided for state-only programs.

Mandatory Eligibility Groups

The following represents **mandatory eligibility groups** for which federal matching funds are provided:

- recipients of the Temporary Assistance to Needy Families (TANF) program, which replaced the Aid to Families with Dependent Children (AFDC) program in 1996. The **Temporary Assistance to Needy Families (TANF)** makes cash assistance available on a time-limited basis for children deprived of support because of a parent's death, incapacity, absence, or unemployment.
- infants born to Medicaid-eligible pregnant women. Medicaid eligibility continues throughout the first year of life as long as the infant remains in the mother's household and she remains eligible or would be eligible if she were still pregnant.
- children under age 6 and pregnant women whose family income is at or below 133% of the **federal poverty level (FPL)** (income guidelines established annually by the federal government).
- **Supplemental Security Income (SSI)** recipients in most states (some states use more restrictive Medicaid eligibility requirements).
- recipients of adoption assistance or foster care assistance under Title IV-E of the Social Security Act.
- special protected groups (typically individuals who lose their cash assistance due to earnings from work or from increased Social Security benefits, but who may keep Medicaid for a period of time).
- certain Medicare beneficiaries (described later in this chapter).

Optional Eligibility Groups

States can provide Medicaid coverage to **optional eligibility groups**, which share characteristics with the mandatory groups (that is, they fall within defined categories), but eligibility criteria are more liberally defined. Optional eligibility groups for which states will receive federal matching funds include:

- infants up to age 1 and pregnant women not covered under the mandatory rules whose family income is not more than 185% of the FPL (this percent can be modified by each state).

- children under age 21 who meet TANF income and resources requirements but who otherwise are not eligible for TANF.

- institutionalized individuals with income and resources below specified limits.

- individuals who would be eligible if institutionalized, but who are receiving care under home- and community-based services waivers.

- certain aged, blind, or disabled adults who have incomes above those requiring mandatory coverage, but below the FPL.

- recipients of state supplementary payments.

- TB-infected persons who would be financially eligible for Medicaid at the SSI income level if they were within a Medicaid-covered category (coverage is limited to TB-related ambulatory services and TB drugs).

- optional targeted low-income children included within the State Children's Health Insurance Program (SCHIP) established by the Balanced Budget Act of 1997 (BBA).

- "medically needy" individuals (discussed next).

- low-income, uninsured women screened and diagnosed through the *Centers for Disease Control and Prevention's National Breast and Cervical Cancer Early Detection Program* and determined to be in need of treatment for breast or cervical cancer.

Medically Needy Eligibility Groups

Medically needy eligibility groups include individuals who may have too much income to qualify for Medicaid under the mandatory or optional eligibility groups. Individuals are allowed to *spend down* to Medicaid eligibility by incurring medical expenses that reduce excess income to or below their state's medically needy income level. States may also allow families to establish eligibility as medically needy by paying monthly premiums in an amount equal to the difference between family income (reduced by unpaid expenses, if any, incurred for medical care in previous months) and the income eligibility standard.

NOTE: States that opt to include a medically needy eligibility group in their Medicaid program are required to include certain children under age 18 and pregnant women who, except for income and resources, would otherwise be eligible.

Spousal Impoverishment Protection

The *Medicare Catastrophic Coverage Act of 1988 (MCCA)* implemented *Spousal Impoverishment Protection Legislation* in 1989 to prevent married couples from being required to *spend down* income and other *liquid assets* (cash and property) before one of the partners could be declared eligible for Medicaid coverage for nursing facility care. The spouse residing at home is called the *community spouse* (which has nothing to do with community property), and before monthly income is used to pay nursing facility costs, a minimum monthly maintenance needs allowance (MMMNA) is deducted.

To determine whether the spouse residing in a facility meets the state's resource standard for Medicaid, a *Protected Resource Amount (PRA)* is subtracted from the couple's combined resources. The PRA is the greatest of:

- spousal share, up to a maximum of $89,280 in 2002.
- state spousal resource standard, which a state can set at any amount between $17,856 and $89,280 in 2002.
- amount transferred to the community spouse for her/his support as directed by a court order.
- amount designated by a state officer to raise the community spouse's protected resources up to the minimum monthly maintenance needs standard.

After the PRA is subtracted from the couple's combined countable resources, the remainder is considered available as resources to the spouse residing in the facility. If the amount of resources is below the state's resource standard, the individual is eligible for Medicaid. Once resource eligibility is determined, any resources belonging to the community spouse are no longer considered available to the spouse in the facility.

NOTE: The couple's home, household goods, automobile, and burial funds are *not* included in the couple's combined resources. ●

NOTE: The community spouse's income is *not* available to the spouse who resides in the facility, and the two individuals are not considered a couple for income eligibility purposes. The state uses the income eligibility standard for one person rather than two, and the standard income eligibility process for Medicaid is used. ●

EXAMPLE: John Q. Public is required to reside in a nursing facility. His wife, Nancy Public, resides in the family home. At the time of Mr. Public's Medicaid application they have $160,000 in resources (not including the family home, which is not included in resources as long as the spouse is in residence). John Q. Public's monthly Social Security income (SSI) is $1,000, and Nancy Public's monthly SSI is $500, totaling $1,500.

Under the income-first approach, the state attributes one-half of the resources (or $80,000) to Mrs. Public as her community spouse resource allowance (CSRA). This allows Mr. Public to retain $80,000, which must be reduced to $2,000 before he becomes eligible for Medicaid. This means the Publics are expected to convert the $78,000 in resources (e.g., stocks, bonds, summer home) to cash and spend it on nursing facility care for Mr. Public. Because the state's minimum monthly maintenance needs allowance (MMMNA) is $1,450, Mrs. Public keeps all her monthly SSI in addition to $950 of her husband's monthly SSI. The remaining $50 must be expended on nursing facility care for Mr. Public.

Under the resources-first approach, Mr. Public is expected to expend his $1,000 monthly SSI on nursing facility care. This means that Mrs. Public has a monthly income of only $500 and because the state's MMMNA is $1,450, Mr. Public can transfer his $80,000 in resources to Mrs. Public. This increases her CSRA to an amount that generates an additional $950/month (the difference between the state's $1,450 MMMNA and her $500 SSI). As a result, Mr. Public becomes immediately eligible for Medicaid, and Mrs. Public is allowed to retain all $160,000 in resources. ●

The **State Children's Health Insurance Program (SCHIP)** (also abbreviated as CHIP) provides health insurance coverage to uninsured children whose family income is up to 200% of the federal poverty level (monthly income limits for a family of four also apply). Under federal law, SCHIP must provide health coverage to targeted uninsured children who must:

- be less than 19 years of age.
- have family income at or below 200% of the federal poverty level.
- not be covered by any other health insurance.
- not have been covered by a group health plan in the prior three months.
- not be otherwise eligible for Medicaid.
- meet certain other nonfinancial criteria, such as state residency and citizenship.

NOTE: Some states provide SCHIP coverage to children who already have private health insurance to cover the costs of deductibles, copayments, and medical services not covered by the private policy.

Confirming Medicaid Eligibility

Any time patients state that they receive Medicaid, a valid Medicaid identification card must be presented. Eligibility, in many cases, will depend on the monthly income of the patient. As eligibility may fluctuate from one month to the next, most states have a dedicated telephone line for verification of eligibility. Confirmation of eligibility should be obtained for each visit; failure to do so may result in a denial of payment. If residing in one of these states, be sure to access the Medicaid verification line. Some states have a point-of-sale device similar to those used by credit card companies. Beneficiaries carry plastic cards containing encoded data strips. When the card is swiped, the printout indicates eligibility or noneligibility data.

Retroactive eligibility is sometimes granted to patients whose income has fallen below the state-set eligibility level and who had high medical expenses prior to filing for Medicaid. When patients notify the practice that they have become retroactively eligible for Medicaid benefits, confirm this information before proceeding. A refund of any payments made by the patient during the retroactive period must be made and Medicaid billed for these services.

INTERNET LINK

State Medicaid toll-free numbers can be found at http://cms.hhs.gov/medicaid/tollfree.asp

MEDICAID COVERED SERVICES

Medicaid allows considerable flexibility within state plans, but some federal requirements are mandatory if federal matching funds are to be received. A state's Medicaid program *must* offer medical assistance for certain *basic* services to eligible groups.

Mandatory Services

To receive federal matching funds, states must offer the *mandatory eligibility group* the following basic services:

- inpatient hospital services
- outpatient hospital services
- physician services
- medical and surgical dental services
- nursing facility (NF) services for individuals aged 21 or older
- home health care for persons eligible for nursing facility services
- family planning services and supplies

- rural health clinic and ambulatory services offered by a rural health clinic, otherwise covered under the state plan
- laboratory and X-ray services
- pediatric and family nurse practitioner services
- federally-qualified health center and ambulatory services offered by a federally-qualified health center, otherwise covered under the state plan
- nurse-midwife services (to the extent authorized by state law).
- early and periodic screening, diagnosis, and treatment (EPSDT) services for individuals under age 21.

If a state chooses to provide to the *medically needy* population, the following services must be offered:

- prenatal care and delivery services for pregnant women
- ambulatory services to individuals under age 18 and individuals entitled to institutional services
- home health services to individuals entitled to nursing facility services

States that include services in mental health facilities or intermediate care facilities for the mentally retarded (ICF/MRs) must offer:

- inpatient and outpatient hospital services.
- laboratory and X-ray services.
- Early and Periodic Screening, Diagnostic, and Treatment (EPSDT) items and services.
- physician services.
- medical and surgical services of a dentist.
- home health services.
- nurse-midwife services.

States have the option to also offer the following:

- prescribed drugs
- medical and other remedial care recognized under state law furnished by licensed practitioners
- private-duty nursing services
- clinic services
- physical therapy
- occupational therapy
- services for individuals with speech, hearing, and language disorders
- other diagnostic screening, preventive, and rehabilitative services
- inpatient psychiatric hospital services
- durable medical equipment
- prosthetic devices

Optional Services

To receive federal funding for the provision of optional services, states commonly offer the following:

- clinic services
- nursing facility services for those under age 21
- intermediate care facility/mentally retarded services

- optometrist services and eyeglasses
- prescribed drugs
- TB-related services for TB infected persons
- prosthetic devices
- dental services

Waiver Services

States may provide home- and community-based care waiver services to certain individuals who are eligible for Medicaid. The services to be provided to these persons may include case management, personal care services, respite care services, adult day health services, homemaker/home health aide, rehabilitation, and other requested services that are approved by CMS.

Breast and Cervical Cancer Early Detection Program

The Centers for Disease Control and Prevention's National Breast and Cervical Cancer Early Detection Program (NBCCEDP) gives states the option to provide medical services to certain women who have been found to have breast or cervical cancer or precancerous conditions. States may also receive enhanced funding for this new option. In order for a woman to be eligible for Medicaid under this option, she must:

- have been screened for and found to have breast or cervical cancer, including precancerous conditions, through NBCCEDP.
- be under age 65.
- be uninsured and otherwise not eligible for Medicaid.

NOTE: Some states implement *presumptive eligibility*, a Medicaid option that allows women to be enrolled in Medicaid for a limited period of time before full Medicaid applications are filed and processed. This facilitates immediate access to services for women who are in need of treatment for breast or cervical cancer. ●

EPSDT Services

In 1989, Congress updated the **Early and Periodic Screening, Diagnostic, and Treatment (EPSDT)** services, which was originally launched in 1967. Original EPSDT legislation mandated that if states were to receive federal funds, they would be required to provide routine pediatric checkups to all children enrolled in Medicaid. The Omnibus Budget Reconciliation Act of 1989 strengthened the program by providing a statutory definition of such terms as "screening services," "vision services," "dental services," and "hearing services," considered a regular part of a routine pediatric checkup. A new requirement was added that states,

> Such other necessary health care, diagnostic services, treatment, and other measures . . . to correct or ameliorate defects and physical and mental illnesses and conditions discovered by the screening services, whether or not such services are covered under the State plan.

Preauthorized Services

Most states that have not placed all Medicaid beneficiaries into a prepaid HMO have some form of prior approval or preauthorization for recipients. Examples of preauthorization guidelines include:

1. Elective inpatient admission
   a. Medical necessity justification of inpatient treatment
   b. Admission diagnosis and treatment plan

2. Emergency inpatient admission
   a. Medical necessity justification for inpatient treatment
   b. Admission diagnosis and treatment plan

3. More than one preoperative day
   a. Reason(s) surgery cannot be performed within 24 hours of indication for surgery
   b. Number of additional preoperative day(s) requested

4. Outpatient procedure(s) to be performed in an inpatient setting
   a. Code and description of surgical procedure
   b. Medical necessity justification for performing surgery on an inpatient basis

5. Days exceeding state hospital stay limitation due to complication(s)
   a. Diagnosis stated on original preauthorization request
   b. Beginning and ending dates originally preauthorized
   c. Statement describing the complication(s)
   d. Date complication(s) presented
   e. Principal diagnosis
   f. Complication(s) diagnosis

6. Extension of inpatient days
   a. Medical necessity justification for the extension
   b. Number of additional days requested

   EXAMPLE 1: The performance of multiple procedures that, when combined, necessitate a length of stay in excess of that required for any one individual procedure.

   EXAMPLE 2: The development of postoperative complication(s) or a medical history that dictates longer-than-usual postoperative observation by skilled medical staff.

Payment for Medicaid Services

Medicaid makes payment directly to providers, and those participating in Medicaid must accept the reimbursement level as payment in full. States determine their own reimbursement methodology and rates for services, with three exceptions: (1) for institutional services, payment may not exceed amounts that would be paid under Medicare payment rates; (2) for disproportionate share hospitals (DSHs), different limits apply; and (3) for hospice care services, rates cannot be lower than Medicare rates.

States can require deductibles, coinsurance, or copayments for certain services performed for some Medicaid recipients. Emergency services and family planning services are exempt from copayments. Certain Medicaid recipients are also excluded from this cost sharing, including pregnant women, children under age 18, and hospital or nursing home patients who are expected to contribute most of their income to institutional care.

The portion of the Medicaid program paid by the federal government is known as the **Federal Medical Assistance Percentage (FMAP)** and is determined annually for each state using a formula that compares the state's average per capita income level with the national average. Wealthier states receive a smaller share of reimbursed costs, and the federal government shares in administration expenses (50% match).

MEDICARE-MEDICAID RELATIONSHIP

Certain eligible Medicare beneficiaries may also receive help from the Medicaid program. For those eligible for *full* Medicaid coverage, Medicare coverage is supplemented by services available under a state's Medicaid program. These additional services may include, for example, nursing facility care beyond the 100-day limit covered by Medicare, prescription drugs, eyeglasses, and hearing aids.

NOTE: When an individual has both Medicare and Medicaid coverage, covered services are paid by Medicare first before any payments are made by the Medicaid program. The reason for this is because Medicaid is always the *payer of last resort.*

Dual Eligibles

Medicare beneficiaries with low incomes and limited resources may receive help with out-of-pocket medical expenses from state Medicaid programs. Various benefits are available to **dual eligibles**, individuals entitled to Medicare and eligible for some type of Medicaid benefit. Individuals eligible for full Medicaid coverage receive program supplements to their Medicare coverage via services and supplies available from the state's Medicaid program. Services covered by both programs are paid first by Medicare and the difference by Medicaid, up to the state's payment limit. Medicaid also covers the following additional services:

- nursing facility care beyond the 100-day limit covered by Medicare
- prescription drugs
- eyeglasses
- hearing aids

Qualified Medicare Beneficiaries

Limited Medicaid benefits are also available to pay for out-of-pocket Medicare cost-sharing expenses for certain other Medicare beneficiaries *Qualified Medicare Beneficiaries (QMBs)* have resources at or below twice the standard allowed under the SSI program and incomes at or below 100% of the federal poverty level (FPL); they do not have to pay monthly Medicare premiums, deductibles, and coinsurance.

Specified Low-Income Medicare Beneficiaries

Specified Low-Income Medicare Beneficiaries (SLMBs) have incomes that exceed the QMB level, but are less than 120% of the FPL; they do not have to pay monthly Medicare Part B premiums.

Qualifying Individuals

Qualifying Individuals (QIs), not otherwise eligible for full Medicaid benefits and with resources at or below twice the standard allowed under the SSI program, receive assistance with all or a small part of their monthly Medicare Part B premiums, depending on whether their income exceeds 120% of the FPL, but less than 175% of the FPL.

Qualified Disabled and Working Individuals

Individuals eligible for Medicare due to disability but who lost Medicare entitlement because they returned to work may purchase Part A of Medicare. If the individual's income is below 200% of the FPL and they are not otherwise eligible for Medicaid benefits, they may qualify for Medicaid to pay their monthly Medicare Part A premiums as *Qualified Disabled and Working Individuals (QDWIs)*.

MEDICAID AS A SECONDARY PAYER

Medicaid is always the *payer of last resort*. If the patient is covered by another medical or liability policy, including Medicare, TRICARE (formerly CHAMPUS), CHAMP-VA, or Indian Health Services (IHS), this coverage must be billed first. Medicaid is billed only if the other coverage denies responsibility for payment, pays less than the Medicaid fee schedule, or if Medicaid covers procedures not covered by the other policy.

PARTICIPATING PROVIDERS

Any provider who accepts a Medicaid patient must accept the Medicaid-determined payment as payment in full. Providers are forbidden by law to bill (*balance billing*) patients for Medicaid-covered benefits. A patient may be billed for any service that is not a covered benefit; however, some states have historically required providers to sign formal participating Medicaid contracts. Other states do not require contracts.

MEDICAID AND MANAGED CARE

Between 1991 and 1997, the percent of Medicaid beneficiaries enrolled in some form of managed care grew from 10% to almost 50%. By 1998, CMS announced that the percent of Medicaid beneficiaries enrolled in a managed care program had increased to almost 54% (or 16,573,996 people). Medicaid *managed care* does not always mean a comprehensive health care plan that requires a monthly premium and is at financial risk for the cost of care provided to all enrollees. Medicaid beneficiaries are also enrolled in *primary care case management (PCCM)* plans, which are similar to fee-for-service plans except that each PCCM enrollee has a primary care provider who authorizes access to specialty care but is not at risk for the cost of care provided.

MEDICAID ELIGIBILITY VERIFICATION SYSTEM (MEVS)

The **Medicaid eligibility verification system (MEVS)** (sometimes called **recipient eligibility verification system**, or **REVS**) allows providers to electronically access the state's eligibility file through:

- *Point-of-sale device:* The patient's medical identification card contains a magnetic strip, and when the provider "swipes" the card through a reader, accurate eligibility information is displayed. (The provider purchases magnetic card reader equipment.)
- *Computer software:* When the provider enters a Medicaid recipient's identification number into special computer software, accurate eligibility information is displayed.

●   *Automated voice response:* Providers can call the state's Medicaid office to receive eligibility verification information through an automated voice response.

   NOTE: The provider receives a "receipt ticket" upon eligibility verification through the MEVS (Figure 15-1). ●

MEDICAID REMITTANCE ADVICE

Providers receive reimbursement from Medicaid on a lump-sum basis, which means they will receive payment for several claims at once. A **Medicaid remittance advice** is sent to the provider, which serves as a transmittal notice from Medicaid and contains the current status of all claims (including adjusted and voided claims). An **adjusted claim** has a payment correction, resulting in additional payment(s) to the provider. A **voided claim** is one that Medicaid should not have originally paid, and results in a deduction from the lump-sum payment made to the provider. If a year-to-date negative balance appears on the Medicaid remittance advice as a result of voided claims, the provider receives no payment until the amount of paid claims exceeds the negative balance amount.

US MEDICAID
Eligibility

05/15/YYYY	14:44:58
Date of Service:	05/15/YYYY
Provider ID #:	1236526

Individual Status

Verification Number:	23659856236541
Name:	John Q. Public
RID #:	562365951
Card Generation #:	001
DOB/(age):	03/09/1945
Sex:	M
Restriction:	None
Co-Pay:	N

Managed Care

Managed Care:	N
PCP Name:	Dr. Erin Helper
PCP Telephone #:	101-111-1234

Third-Party Liability

Coverage Code:	LDO–4
Policy #:	DD1234
Carrier Name:	Any Insurance
Address:	111 Main St
City/State/Zip:	Anywhere, US 12345
Phone #:	101 555-1234

FIGURE 15-1 Sample Medicaid eligibility verification system (MEVS) "receipt ticket"

NOTE: The provider should compare content on the remittance advice to claims submitted to determine whether proper payment was received. If improper payment was issued, the provider has the option to appeal the claim. ●

NOTE: Remittance advice documents should be maintained according to the statute of limits of the state in which the provider practices. ●

UTILIZATION REVIEW

The federal government requires states to verify the receipt of Medicaid services, which means a sample of Medicaid recipients is sent a monthly survey letter requesting verification of services paid the previous month on their behalf. (Such services are identified in nontechnical terms, and confidential services are omitted.) Federal regulations also required Medicaid to establish and maintain a **surveillance and utilization review system (SURS)**, which safeguards against unnecessary or inappropriate use of Medicaid services or excess payments and assesses the quality of those services. A postpayment review process monitors both the use of health services by recipients and the delivery of health services by providers. Overpayments to providers may be recovered by the SURS unit, regardless of whether the payment error was caused by the provider or by the Medicaid program.

FRAUD AND ABUSE

The SURS unit is also responsible for identifying possible fraud or abuse, and most states organize the unit under the state's Office of Attorney General, which is certified by the federal government to detect, investigate, and prosecute fraudulent practices or abuse against the Medicaid program.

MEDICAL NECESSITY

Medicaid covered services are payable only when the service is determined by the provider to be medically necessary. Covered services must be:
- consistent with the recipient's symptoms, diagnosis, condition, or injury.
- recognized as the prevailing standard and consistent with generally accepted professional medical standards of the provider's peer group.
- provided in response to a life-threatening condition; to treat pain, injury, illness, or infection; to treat a condition that could result in physical or mental disability; or to achieve a level of physical or mental function consistent with prevailing community standards for diagnosis or condition.

In addition, medically necessary services are:
- not furnished primarily for the convenience of the recipient or the provider.
- furnished when there is no other equally effective course of treatment available or suitable for the recipient requesting the service that is more conservative or substantially less costly.

BILLING INFORMATION NOTES

Following is information on nationwide fee-for-service billing. Consult the HMO billing manual to bill for noncapitated HMO services.

Fiscal Agent

The name of the state's Medicaid fiscal agent will vary from state to state. Contact the local county government for information about the Medicaid program in your area.

Underwriter

Underwriting responsibility is shared between state and federal governments. Federal responsibility rests with CMS. The name of the state agency will vary according to state preference.

Form Used

The CMS-1500 claim is the required form.

Timely Filing Deadline

Deadlines vary from state to state. Check with your local Medicaid office. It is important to file a Medicaid fee-for-service claim as soon as possible. The only time a claim should be delayed is when the patient does not identify Medicaid eligibility or if the patient has applied for retroactive Medicaid coverage.

Medicare-Medicaid crossover claims follow the Medicare, not Medicaid, deadlines for claims. (See page 431 for details of the Medicare claim filing deadline.)

Allowable Determination

The state establishes the maximum reimbursement payable for each nonmanaged care service. It is expected that Medicaid programs will use the new Medicare Physician Fee Schedule for these services, with each state establishing its own conversion factor. Medicaid recipients can be billed for any noncovered procedure performed. However, because most Medicaid patients have incomes below the poverty level, collection of fees for uncovered services is difficult.

Accept Assignment

Accept assignment must be selected on the CMS-1500 claim or reimbursement (depending on state policy) may be denied. It is illegal to attempt collection of the difference between the Medicaid payment and the fee the provider charged, even if the patient did not reveal Medicaid status at the time services were rendered.

NOTE: Medicaid patients must "assign benefits" to providers.

Deductibles

There may be a deductible for persons in the **medically needy** classification. In such cases, eligibility cards usually are not issued until after the stated deductible has been met. No other eligibility classifications have deductible requirements.

Copayments

Copayments are required for some categories of Medicaid recipients.

Premiums

The Medicaid recipient does not pay a premium for medical coverage.

Inpatient Benefits

All nonemergency hospitalizations must be preauthorized. If the patient's condition warrants an extension of the authorized inpatient days, the hospital must seek an authorization for additional inpatient days.

Major Medical/Accidental Injury Coverage

There is no special treatment for either of these categories. Medicaid will conditionally subrogate claims when there is liability insurance to cover a person's injuries. *Subrogation* is the assumption of an obligation for which another party is primarily liable.

Because Medicaid eligibility is determined by income, patients can be eligible one month and not the next. Check eligibility status on each visit. New work requirements may change this, as beneficiaries will continue coverage for a specific time even if their income exceeds the state eligibility levels. Prior authorization is required for many procedures and most nonemergency hospitalizations. Consult the current Medicaid Handbook for a listing of the procedures that must have prior authorization. When in doubt, contact the state agency for clarification.

Cards may be issued for the "Unborn child of . . . " (the name of the pregnant woman is inserted in the blank space). These cards are good only for services that promote the life and good health of the unborn child.

Because other health and liability programs are primary to Medicaid, the EOB from the primary coverage must be attached to the Medicaid claim.

A combined Medicare-Medicaid claim should be filed by the Medicaid deadline on the CMS-1500 claim.

STEP-BY-STEP CLAIM INSTRUCTIONS

NOTE: The instructions in this section are for filing primary Medicaid fee-for-service claims when the patient is not covered by additional insurance. If the patient is covered by Medicare and Medicaid, follow the instructions for Medicare-Medicaid crossover claims on page 452.

Refer to Figure 15-2 for Blocks 1 through 13 of the CMS-1500 claim.

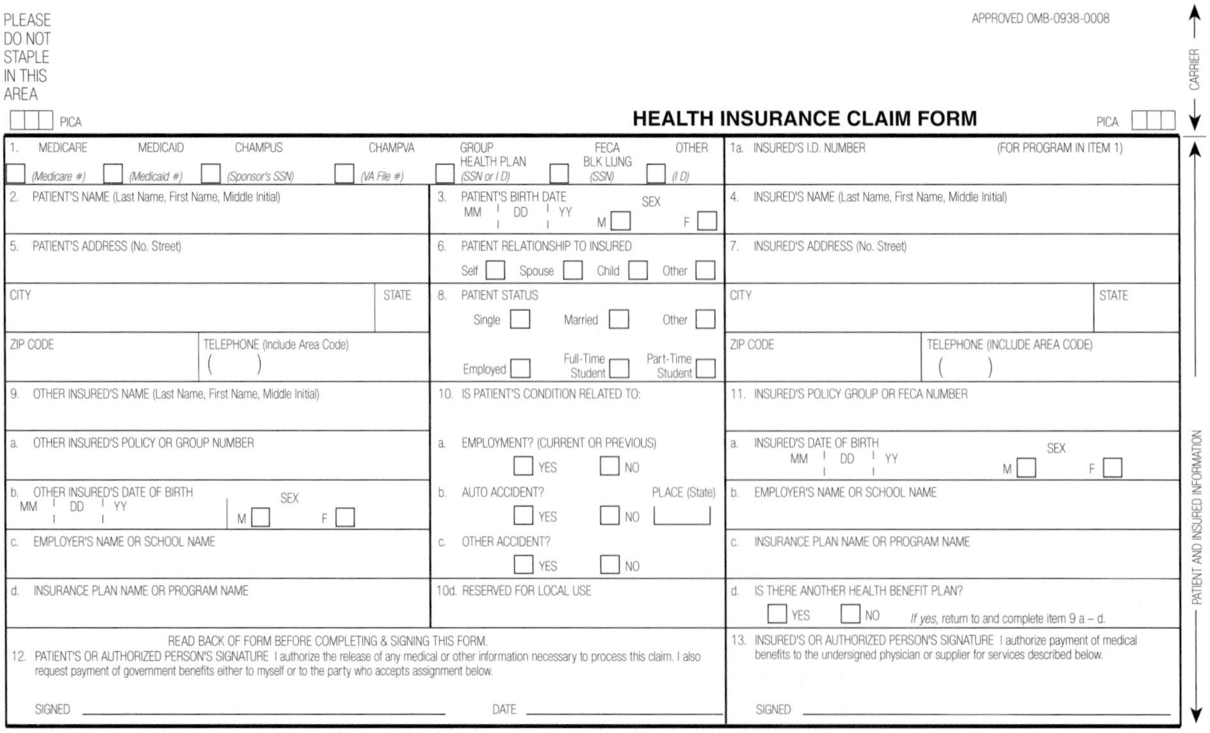

PLEASE DO NOT STAPLE IN THIS AREA

APPROVED OMB-0938-0008

CARRIER

PICA HEALTH INSURANCE CLAIM FORM PICA

1. MEDICARE (Medicare #) MEDICAID (Medicaid #) CHAMPUS (Sponsor's SSN) CHAMPVA (VA File #) GROUP HEALTH PLAN (SSN or I D) FECA BLK LUNG (SSN) OTHER (I D)

1a. INSURED'S I.D. NUMBER (FOR PROGRAM IN ITEM 1)

2. PATIENT'S NAME (Last Name, First Name, Middle Initial)

3. PATIENT'S BIRTH DATE MM DD YY SEX M F

4. INSURED'S NAME (Last Name, First Name, Middle Initial)

5. PATIENT'S ADDRESS (No. Street)

6. PATIENT RELATIONSHIP TO INSURED Self Spouse Child Other

7. INSURED'S ADDRESS (No. Street)

CITY STATE

8. PATIENT STATUS Single Married Other Employed Full-Time Student Part-Time Student

CITY STATE

ZIP CODE TELEPHONE (Include Area Code) ( )

ZIP CODE TELEPHONE (INCLUDE AREA CODE) ( )

9. OTHER INSURED'S NAME (Last Name, First Name, Middle Initial)

10. IS PATIENT'S CONDITION RELATED TO:

11. INSURED'S POLICY GROUP OR FECA NUMBER

a. OTHER INSURED'S POLICY OR GROUP NUMBER

a. EMPLOYMENT? (CURRENT OR PREVIOUS) YES NO

a. INSURED'S DATE OF BIRTH MM DD YY SEX M F

b. OTHER INSURED'S DATE OF BIRTH MM DD YY SEX M F

b. AUTO ACCIDENT? YES NO PLACE (State)

b. EMPLOYER'S NAME OR SCHOOL NAME

c. EMPLOYER'S NAME OR SCHOOL NAME

c. OTHER ACCIDENT? YES NO

c. INSURANCE PLAN NAME OR PROGRAM NAME

d. INSURANCE PLAN NAME OR PROGRAM NAME

10d. RESERVED FOR LOCAL USE

d. IS THERE ANOTHER HEALTH BENEFIT PLAN? YES NO *If yes,* return to and complete item 9 a – d.

READ BACK OF FORM BEFORE COMPLETING & SIGNING THIS FORM.

12. PATIENT'S OR AUTHORIZED PERSON'S SIGNATURE I authorize the release of any medical or other information necessary to process this claim. I also request payment of government benefits either to myself or to the party who accepts assignment below.

SIGNED DATE

13. INSURED'S OR AUTHORIZED PERSON'S SIGNATURE I authorize payment of medical benefits to the undersigned physician or supplier for services described below.

SIGNED

PATIENT AND INSURED INFORMATION

FIGURE 15-2 Blocks 1 through 13 of the CMS-1500 claim

Block 1

Enter an X in the MEDICAID box.

Block 1a

Enter the insured's Medicaid ID number.

Block 2

Enter the complete name (last name first, followed by the first name and middle initial) of the patient as listed on the patient's insurance identification card. Use of nicknames or typographic errors will cause rejection of the claim.

Block 3

Enter the patient's birth date in the MM DD YYYY format (with spaces). Enter an X in the appropriate box to indicate the patient's gender.

Block 4

Leave blank.

Block 5

Enter the patient's mailing address on lines 1 and 2. Enter the zip code, area code, and telephone number on line 3. *Do not type parentheses around the area code or a dash in the telephone number.*

Blocks 6 through 9d

Leave blank.

Block 10a through 10c

Enter an X in the appropriate boxes to indicate whether the patient's condition is related to employment or an auto or other accident.

NOTE: Entering an X in any of the YES boxes alerts Medicaid that another insurance plan might be liable for payment. Medicaid will not consider the claim unless the provider submits an explanation of benefits (EOB) from the liable party (e.g., workers', auto insurance). For employment-related conditions, another option is to attach a letter from workers' compensation rejecting payment for an on-the-job injury. ●

Block 10d

Leave blank.

NOTE: For Medicaid managed care programs, enter an E for emergency or U for urgent care if instructed to do so by the fiscal agent. ●

Blocks 11 through 11d

Leave blank.

Block 12

Leave blank. The patient's signature or the statement, SIGNATURE ON FILE, is not required on Medicaid claims.

NOTE: If Medicaid *waiver services* are provided, enter SIGNATURE ON FILE, and maintain the original patient signature on file. ●

Block 13

Leave blank.

Refer to Figure 15-3 for the John Q. Public encounter form and Figure 15-4 for completed Blocks 1 through 13 (based on the encounter form in Figure 15-3) of the CMS-1500 claim.

ERIN A. HELPER, M.D.
101 Medic Dr, Anywhere US 12345
(101) 111-1234 (Office) • (101) 111-9292 (Fax)

EIN:	11-123341	**MCD:**	EBH8881
UPIN:	EH8888	**BCBS:**	EH1188
PIN:	A09293	**BCBS GRP:**	1204P

Encounter Form

PATIENT INFORMATION:

Name:	Public, John Q.
Address:	10A Senate Avenue
City:	Anywhere
State:	US
Zip Code:	12345
Telephone:	(101) 201-7891
Gender:	Male
Date of Birth:	10-10-1959
Occupation:	
Employer:	

INSURANCE INFORMATION:

Patient Number:	15-3
Place of Service:	Office
Primary Insurance Plan:	Medicaid
Primary Insurance Plan ID #:	99811948
Group #:	
Primary Policyholder:	Public, John Q.
Policyholder Date of Birth:	10-10-1959
Relationship to Patient:	Self
Secondary Insurance Plan:	
Secondary Insurance Plan ID #:	
Secondary Policyholder:	

Patient Status   [X] Married   [ ] Divorced   [ ] Single   [ ] Student

DIAGNOSIS INFORMATION

Diagnosis		Code	Diagnosis		Code
1.	Benign cyst, sebaceous	706.2	5.		
2.	Malignant lesion, trunk	173.5	6.		
3.			7.		
4.			8.		

PROCEDURE INFORMATION

	Description of Procedure or Service	Date	Code	Charge
1.	Excision, 2.1 cm benign cyst, skin of back	01-21-YYYY	11403-51	50.00
2.	Excision, 1.4 cm malignant lesion, skin of trunk, with intermediate repair	01-21-YYYY	11602	75.00
			12031-51	75.00
3.				
4.				
5.				

SPECIAL NOTES: Preauthorization No. YY8301

FIGURE 15-3 John Q. Public encounter form

PLEASE
DO NOT
STAPLE
IN THIS
AREA

APPROVED OMB-0938-0008

CARRIER

| | PICA | **HEALTH INSURANCE CLAIM FORM** | PICA | | | |

HEALTH INSURANCE CLAIM FORM

MEDICARE	MEDICAID	CHAMPUS	CHAMPVA	GROUP HEALTH PLAN	FECA BLK LUNG	OTHER	1a. INSURED'S I.D. NUMBER	(FOR PROGRAM IN ITEM 1)
☐ (Medicare #)	☒ (Medicaid #)	☐ (Sponsor's SSN)	☐ (VA File #)	☐ (SSN or I.D)	☐ (SSN)	☐ (I.D)	99811948	

2. PATIENT'S NAME (Last Name, First Name, Middle Initial)
PUBLIC JOHN Q

3. PATIENT'S BIRTH DATE
MM 10 DD 10 YY 1959   SEX M ☒ F ☐

4. INSURED'S NAME (Last Name, First Name, Middle Initial)

5. PATIENT'S ADDRESS (No. Street)
10A SENATE AVENUE

6. PATIENT RELATIONSHIP TO INSURED
Self ☐ Spouse ☐ Child ☐ Other ☐

7. INSURED'S ADDRESS (No. Street)

CITY
ANYWHERE   STATE US

8. PATIENT STATUS
Single ☐   Married ☐   Other ☐

CITY   STATE

ZIP CODE
12345   TELEPHONE (Include Area Code)
(101) 201 9871

Employed ☐   Full-Time Student ☐   Part-Time Student ☐

ZIP CODE   TELEPHONE (INCLUDE AREA CODE)
( )

9. OTHER INSURED'S NAME (Last Name, First Name, Middle Initial)

10. IS PATIENT'S CONDITION RELATED TO:

11. INSURED'S POLICY GROUP OR FECA NUMBER

a. OTHER INSURED'S POLICY OR GROUP NUMBER

a. EMPLOYMENT? (CURRENT OR PREVIOUS)
☐ YES ☒ NO

a. INSURED'S DATE OF BIRTH
MM DD YY   SEX M ☐ F ☐

b. OTHER INSURED'S DATE OF BIRTH
MM DD YY   SEX M ☐ F ☐

b. AUTO ACCIDENT?   PLACE (State)
☐ YES ☒ NO

b. EMPLOYER'S NAME OR SCHOOL NAME

c. EMPLOYER'S NAME OR SCHOOL NAME

c. OTHER ACCIDENT?
☐ YES ☒ NO

c. INSURANCE PLAN NAME OR PROGRAM NAME

d. INSURANCE PLAN NAME OR PROGRAM NAME

10d. RESERVED FOR LOCAL USE

d. IS THERE ANOTHER HEALTH BENEFIT PLAN?
☐ YES ☐ NO   If yes, return to and complete item 9 a – d.

READ BACK OF FORM BEFORE COMPLETING & SIGNING THIS FORM.
12. PATIENT'S OR AUTHORIZED PERSON'S SIGNATURE I authorize the release of any medical or other information necessary to process this claim. I also request payment of government benefits either to myself or to the party who accepts assignment below.

SIGNED _____   DATE _____

13. INSURED'S OR AUTHORIZED PERSON'S SIGNATURE I authorize payment of medical benefits to the undersigned physician or supplier for services described below.

SIGNED _____

PATIENT AND INSURED INFORMATION

FIGURE 15-4   Completed Blocks 1 through 13 for the John Q. Public encounter form in Figure 15-3

EXERCISE 15-1 — Continuation of Medicare/Medicaid Comparison Chart

OBJECTIVE: To create a useful reference that will help you master the details of claims completion for Medicare and Medicaid.

1. Obtain the chart created in Chapter 14.

2. Review the step-by-step instructions for Blocks 1 through 13, and enter abbreviated instructions on the chart.

3. Upon completion, save the chart because it will be used for additional exercises in this chapter.

EXERCISE 15-2 — Medicaid Primary Blocks 1 through 13

This exercise requires one copy of a blank CMS-1500 claim. You may either make photocopies of the form in Appendix III of the text or print copies of a blank form using the computer disk in the Workbook. (Instructions for installing the computer program and printing blank forms are in Appendix V.)

1. Obtain a copy of the CMS-1500 claim.

2. Review the instructions for Blocks 1 through 13 in the Medicaid primary column of the chart created in Exercise 14-2.

3. Review Figure 15-5, the Mary Sue Patient encounter form.

(continues)

4. Select the information needed for Blocks 1 through 13 from Figure 15-5. Enter the required information on the claim using Optical Scanning Guidelines. This may be completed by handwriting the information, using the Blank Form Mode on the computer disk, or typing the data.

5. Review Blocks 1 through 13 of the claim to be sure all required blocks are properly completed.

NOTE: This same encounter form and claim will be used for Exercise 15-4.

Refer to Figure 15-6 for Blocks 14 through 23 of the CMS-1500 claim.

ERIN A. HELPER, M.D.
101 Medic Dr, Anywhere US 12345
(101) 111-1234 (Office) • (101) 111-9292 (Fax)
EIN: 11-123341 **TRICARE:** EBH8881
UPIN: EH8888 **BCBS:** EH11881
PIN: A09293 **BCBS GRP:** 1204-P

Encounter Form

PATIENT INFORMATION:

Name:	Patient, Mary Sue
Address:	91 Home Street
City:	Nowhere
State:	US
Zip Code:	12367
Telephone:	(101) 201-8989
Gender:	Female
Date of Birth:	10-10-1959
Occupation:	
Employer:	

INSURANCE INFORMATION:

Patient Number:	15-5
Place of Service:	Office
Primary Insurance Plan:	Medicaid
Primary Insurance Plan ID #:	99811765
Group #:	
Primary Policyholder:	
Policyholder Date of Birth:	
Relationship to Patient:	
Secondary Insurance Plan:	
Secondary Insurance Plan ID #:	
Secondary Policyholder:	

Patient Status [X] Married ☐ Divorced ☐ Single ☐ Student

DIAGNOSIS INFORMATION

Diagnosis	Code	Diagnosis	Code
1. Annual Exam	V70.0	5.	
2. Hypertension	401.9	6.	
3.		7.	
4.		8.	

PROCEDURE INFORMATION

Description of Procedure or Service	Date	Code	Charge
1. Preventive Medicine Office Visit	01-05-YYYY	99386	150.00
2. Established Patient Office Visit, Level III	01-05-YYYY	99213-25	75.00
3. Urinalysis, with microscopy	01-05-YYYY	81001	10.00
4. Venipuncture, routine	01-05-YYYY	36415	8.00
5.			

SPECIAL NOTES: Patient scheduled for outpatient chest X-ray and mammogram at RadioDiagnostics. Blood work is to be done at American Labs.

FIGURE 15-5 Mary Sue Patient encounter form

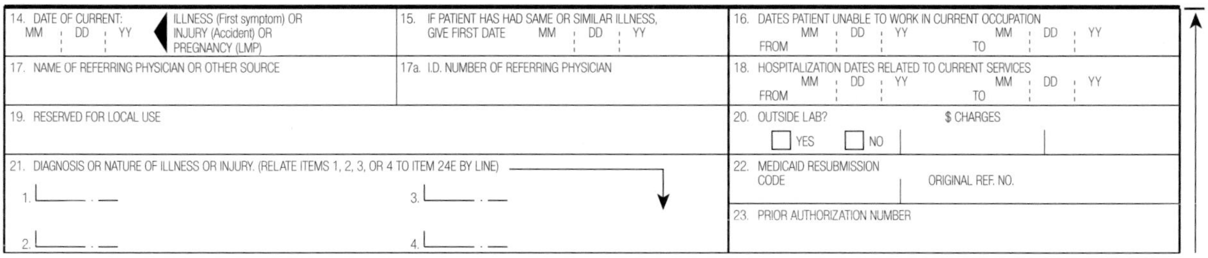

FIGURE 15-6 Blocks 14 through 23 of the CMS-1500 claim

Blocks 14 through 16

Leave blank.

Block 17

Enter the complete name and credentials of the referring provider, if applicable.

Block 17a

Enter the Medicaid ID number of the provider named in Block 17, if any.

> **NOTE:** Medicaid will eventually switch from using a state ID number to using the NPI (national provider identifier) when required by CMS. ●

Block 18

Enter the admission date and the discharge date as MM DD YYYY (with spaces), if a procedure/service is rendered to the patient with inpatient status.

If the patient is still hospitalized, leave the TO box blank.

Block 19

Reserved for local use.

Some Medicaid programs require entry of the Medicaid provider number of the practitioner rendering the service. Others require a description to be entered if an unlisted procedure or service code is reported.

> **NOTE:** If the description does not fit in Block 19, attach documentation to the claim describing unlisted services/procedures and enter SEE ATTACHMENT. ●

Block 20

Enter an X in the appropriate box to indicate whether lab work was sent out to be processed.

> **NOTE:** Medicaid law forbids billing for services rendered by another provider. Providers should bill only for services they performed. ●

Block 21

Enter the ICD-9-CM code for up to four diagnoses or conditions treated. Do not enter the decimal. Enter a space instead because the decimal is preprinted on the CMS-1500 claim.

Block 22

Enter the Medicaid Resubmission code if it applies to this claim.

Block 23

Enter the preauthorization number if applicable. If written authorization was obtained, attach a copy to the claim.

Refer to Figure 15-7 for completed Blocks 14 through 23 for the encounter form in Figure 15-3.

14. DATE OF CURRENT: ILLNESS (First symptom) OR INJURY (Accident) OR PREGNANCY (LMP) MM DD YY	15. IF PATIENT HAS HAD SAME OR SIMILAR ILLNESS, GIVE FIRST DATE MM DD YY	16. DATES PATIENT UNABLE TO WORK IN CURRENT OCCUPATION MM DD YY MM DD YY FROM TO
17. NAME OF REFERRING PHYSICIAN OR OTHER SOURCE	17a. I.D. NUMBER OF REFERRING PHYSICIAN	18. HOSPITALIZATION DATES RELATED TO CURRENT SERVICES MM DD YY MM DD YY FROM TO
19. RESERVED FOR LOCAL USE EBH8881		20. OUTSIDE LAB? $ CHARGES ☐ YES ☒ NO
21. DIAGNOSIS OR NATURE OF ILLNESS OR INJURY. (RELATE ITEMS 1, 2, 3, OR 4 TO ITEM 24E BY LINE) 1. 706.2 3.		22. MEDICAID RESUBMISSION CODE ORIGINAL REF. NO.
2. 173.5 4.		23. PRIOR AUTHORIZATION NUMBER YY8301

FIGURE 15-7 Completed Blocks 14 through 23 for the John Q. Public encounter form in Figure 15-3

EXERCISE 15-3 | ## Continuation of Exercise 15-1

Review the instructions for completing Blocks 14 through 23 and enter a concise description of the instructions in the appropriate block in the Medicaid column of the chart.

EXERCISE 15-4 | ## Continuation of Exercise 15-2

1. Review the Mary Sue Patient encounter form found in Figure 15-5 and locate the diagnostic and treatment data.

2. Select the information needed for Blocks 14 through 23 and enter the required information on a claim using Optical Scanning Guidelines. This may be completed using the disk, or by handwriting or typing the data.

3. Review Blocks 14 through 23 of the claim to be sure all required blocks are properly completed.

4. Compare your claim with the completed claim in Figure 15-12.

 NOTE: This same claim will be used for Exercise 15-6. ●

Refer to Figure 15-8 for Block 24 of the CMS-1500 claim.

Block 24A

Medicaid rules do not permit the billing of consecutive dates. Enter the date as MMDDYYYY (without spaces format) for each service rendered.

Block 24B

Enter the appropriate CMS Place of Service (POS) code from the list in Appendix II.

FIGURE 15-8 Block 24 of the CMS-1500 claim

Block 24C

Enter the appropriate Type of Service (TOS) code from the list in Appendix II.

Block 24D

Enter the CPT/HCPCS code for the service rendered and applicable CPT/HCPCS modifiers.

Block 24E

Enter the *one diagnosis reference number* from Block 21 that best proves the medical necessity for the service rendered.

Block 24F

Enter the amount charged for the service reported in 24D.

Block 24G

Enter the number of units. Units represent the number furnished in a single visit or day. Services listed on different days must be listed on separate lines in Block 24.

Block 24H

Enter an E if the service is rendered under the Early and Periodic Screening, Diagnosis, and Treatment (EPSDT) program. Enter an F if the service is known to be for family planning. Enter B if service(s) rendered can be categorized as both EPSDT and family planning. Otherwise, leave blank.

Block 24I

Enter an X or an E (depending on which is required by the Medicaid carrier) if the service was for a medical emergency, regardless of where it was rendered.

Blocks 24J and 24K

Leave blank.

Refer to Figure 15-9 for completed Block 24 based on the encounter form in Figure 15-3.

24. A DATE(S) OF SERVICE						B Place of Service	C Type of Service	D PROCEDURES, SERVICES, OR SUPPLIES (Explain Unusual Circumstances)		E DIAGNOSIS CODE	F $ CHARGES		G DAYS OR UNITS	H EPSDT Family Plan	I EMG	J COB	K RESERVED FOR LOCAL USE
From MM	DD	YY	To MM	DD	YY			CPT/HCPCS	MODIFIER								
1 0121YYYY						11	2	11602		2	75	00	1				
2 0121YYYY						11	2	12031	51	2	75	00	1				
3 0121YYYY						11	1	11403	51	1	50	00	1				
4																	
5																	
6																	

FIGURE 15-9 Completed Block 24 for the John Q. Public encounter form in Figure 15-3

EXERCISE 15-5 | **Continuation of Exercise 15-3**

Review the instructions for completing Blocks 24A through 24K, and enter a concise description of the instructions in the appropriate block in the Medicaid column of the chart.

EXERCISE 15-6 | **Continuation of Exercise 15-4**

1. Review the procedure data on the Mary Sue Patient encounter form in Figure 15-5.

2. Select the information needed for Blocks 24A through 24K and enter the required information on a new claim using Optical Scanning Guidelines. This may be completed using the disk, or by handwriting or typing the data.

3. Review Blocks 24A through 24K of the claim to be sure all required blocks are properly completed.

NOTE: This same claim will be used for Exercise 15-8.

Refer to Figure 15-10 for Blocks 25 through 33 of the CMS-1500 claim.

Block 25

Enter the billing entity's EIN (with hyphen), if available. Otherwise, enter the provider's Social Security Number. Be sure to enter an X in the appropriate box to indicate which is being reported.

Block 26

Enter the patient's account.

Block 27

Enter an X in the YES box.

Block 28

Total the charges on the claim and enter the total in this block. This figure should *never* reflect negative charges or show that a credit is due to the patient.

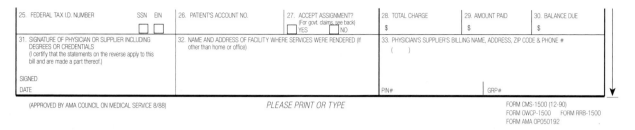

FIGURE 15-10 Blocks 25 through 33 of the CMS-1500 claim

> **NOTE:** If multiple claims for one patient are generated by the computer because more than six services were reported, be sure the total charge entered on each claim accurately represents the total of the items on each separate claim submitted. •

Blocks 29 and 30

Leave blank.

Block 31

Enter the provider's complete name and credential (e.g., MARY SMITH MD) and the date the claim was generated in MMDDYYYY (without spaces) format.

> **NOTE:** Payers usually allow providers to use a signature stamp or enter their complete name and credential in Block 31. If not, the provider must sign each claim. For electronic claims transmission, a certification letter is filed with the payer. •

Block 32

If Block 18 contains hospitalization dates of service and/or Block 20 contains an X in the YES box, enter the name and address of the facility that provided services. Enter the Medicaid provider number on the last line of this block.

Block 33

Enter the provider's telephone number, including area code, and then the official name of the billing entity and the mailing address. The zip code is entered on the same line as the city and state. Enter the Medicaid provider identification number (PIN).

> **NOTE:** Leave GRP# blank. •

Refer to Figure 15-11 for completed Blocks 25 through 33 for the encounter form in Figure 15-3.

EXERCISE 15-7 **Continuation of Exercise 15-5**

Review the instructions for completing Blocks 25 through 33, and enter a concise description of the instructions in the appropriate block in the Medicaid column of the chart.

FIGURE 15-11 Completed Blocks 25 through 33 for the John Q. Public encounter form in Figure 15-3. The form is shown in its entirety with all information entered.

EXERCISE 15-8   Continuation of Exercise 15-6

> *Additional information needed for this case:*
> The billing entity is Erin A. Helper, M.D. She is on the medical staff and admits patients at Anywhere General Hospital, 222 Hospital Drive, in Anywhere, US.
>
> **1.** Review the Mary Sue Patient encounter form in Figure 15-5.
>
> **2.** Select the information needed for Blocks 25 through 33 from the encounter form and the additional data provided above, and enter it on the claim.
>
> **3.** Review Blocks 25 through 33 of the claim to be sure all required blocks are properly completed.
>
> **4.** Compare your claim with the completed claim in Figure 15-12.

Additional Medicaid case studies are provided in Appendix II.

Case studies require reading the case study chart entries and diagnoses and coding the procedures/services.

MEDICAID AS SECONDARY CLAIMS

These instructions are for cases when the patient is covered by a commercial or liability insurance policy.

> **NOTE:** Some individuals who have health insurance coverage may meet Medicaid criteria established by states for *medically needy eligibility groups*. The individual's health insurance is primary and Medicaid is secondary.

The instructions *do not* apply to Medicare-Medicaid crossover cases discussed in the Medicare chapter on page 424.

These instructions modify the primary Medicaid instructions.

Block 4

Enter the name of the primary policyholder.

Block 9

Enter the name of the primary policyholder. If the name of the primary policyholder is the patient, enter SAME.

Block 9a

Enter the primary policy number. Enter a space and the policy's group number if assigned.

Block 9b

If other than the patient, enter the primary policyholder's date of birth.

Block 9d

Enter the name of the primary policy.

Blocks 10a through 10c

Enter an X in the appropriate boxes.

PLEASE
DO NOT
STAPLE
IN THIS
AREA

(SAMPLE ONLY - NOT APPROVED FOR USE)

CARRIER

HEALTH INSURANCE CLAIM FORM

1.	MEDICARE	MEDICAID	CHAMPUS	CHAMPVA	GROUP HEALTH PLAN	FECA BLK LUNG	OTHER	1a. INSURED'S I.D. NUMBER	(FOR PROGRAM IN ITEM 1)
	(Medicare #)	[X] (Medicaid #)	(Sponsor's SSN)	(VA File #)	(SSN or ID)	(SSN)	(ID)	99811765	

2. PATIENT'S NAME (Last Name, First Name, Middle Initial)
PATIENT MARY SUE

3. PATIENT'S BIRTH DATE   MM 10 | DD 10 | YY 1959 SEX M   F [X]

4. INSURED'S NAME (Last Name, First Name, Middle Initial)

5. PATIENT'S ADDRESS (No. Street)
91 HOME STREET

6. PATIENT RELATIONSHIP TO INSURED
Self [ ]   Spouse [ ]   Child [ ]   Other [ ]

7. INSURED'S ADDRESS (No. Street)

CITY
NOWHERE

STATE
US

8. PATIENT STATUS
Single [ ]   Married [ ]   Other [ ]

Employed [ ]   Full-Time Student [ ]   Part-Time Student [ ]

CITY   STATE

ZIP CODE
12367

TELEPHONE (Include Area Code)
(101) 201 8989

ZIP CODE   TELEPHONE (INCLUDE AREA CODE)
(   )

9. OTHER INSURED'S NAME (Last Name, First Name, Middle Initial)

10. IS PATIENT'S CONDITION RELATED TO:

11. INSURED'S POLICY GROUP OR FECA NUMBER

a. OTHER INSURED'S POLICY OR GROUP NUMBER

a. EMPLOYMENT? (CURRENT OR PREVIOUS)
YES [ ]   NO [X]

a. INSURED'S DATE OF BIRTH   MM | DD | YY   SEX   M [ ]   F [ ]

b. OTHER INSURED'S DATE OF BIRTH   MM | DD | YY   SEX   M [ ]   F [ ]

b. AUTO ACCIDENT?   PLACE (State)
YES [ ]   NO [X]

b. EMPLOYER'S NAME OR SCHOOL NAME

c. EMPLOYER'S NAME OR SCHOOL NAME

c. OTHER ACCIDENT?
YES [ ]   NO [X]

c. INSURANCE PLAN NAME OR PROGRAM NAME

d. INSURANCE PLAN NAME OR PROGRAM NAME

10d. RESERVED FOR LOCAL USE

d. IS THERE ANOTHER HEALTH BENEFIT PLAN?
YES [ ]   NO [ ]   If yes, return to and complete item 9 a – d.

READ BACK OF FORM BEFORE COMPLETING & SIGNING THIS FORM.
12. PATIENT'S OR AUTHORIZED PERSON'S SIGNATURE I authorize the release of any medical or other information necessary to process this claim. I also request payment of government benefits either to myself or to the party who accepts assignment below.

SIGNED _____   DATE _____

13. INSURED'S OR AUTHORIZED PERSON'S SIGNATURE I authorize payment of medical benefits to the undersigned physician or supplier for services described below.

SIGNED _____

PATIENT AND INSURED INFORMATION

14. DATE OF CURRENT: MM | DD | YY   ILLNESS (First symptom) OR INJURY (Accident) OR PREGNANCY (LMP)

15. IF PATIENT HAS HAD SAME OR SIMILAR ILLNESS, GIVE FIRST DATE   MM | DD | YY

16. DATES PATIENT UNABLE TO WORK IN CURRENT OCCUPATION   MM | DD | YY   FROM   TO   MM | DD | YY

17. NAME OF REFERRING PHYSICIAN OR OTHER SOURCE

17a. I.D. NUMBER OF REFERRING PHYSICIAN

18. HOSPITALIZATION DATES RELATED TO CURRENT SERVICES   MM | DD | YY   FROM   TO   MM | DD | YY

19. RESERVED FOR LOCAL USE
EBH8881

20. OUTSIDE LAB? $ CHARGES
YES [ ]   NO [X]

21. DIAGNOSIS OR NATURE OF ILLNESS OR INJURY. (RELATE ITEMS 1, 2, 3, OR 4 TO ITEM 24E BY LINE)
1. V70 0   3. |___._
2. 401 9   4. |___._

22. MEDICAID RESUBMISSION CODE   ORIGINAL REF. NO.

23. PRIOR AUTHORIZATION NUMBER
YY8345

24. A. DATE(S) OF SERVICE From MM DD YY	To MM DD YY	B. Place of Service	C. Type of Service	D. PROCEDURES, SERVICES, OR SUPPLIES (Explain Unusual Circumstances) CPT/HCPCS	MODIFIER	E. DIAGNOSIS CODE	F. $ CHARGES	G. DAYS OR UNITS	H. EPSDT Family Plan	I. EMG	J. COB	K. RESERVED FOR LOCAL USE
1	0105YYYY		11	1	99386		1	150 00	1				
2	0105YYYY		11	1	99213	25	2	75 00	1				
3	0105YYYY		11	5	81001		2	10 00	1				
4	0105YYYY		11	1	36415		1	8 00	1				
5													
6													

25. FEDERAL TAX I.D. NUMBER   SSN [ ]   EIN [X]
11-123341

26. PATIENT'S ACCOUNT NO.
15-5

27. ACCEPT ASSIGNMENT? (For govt. claims, see back)
YES [X]   NO [ ]

28. TOTAL CHARGE
$ 243 00

29. AMOUNT PAID
$

30. BALANCE DUE
$

31. SIGNATURE OF PHYSICIAN OR SUPPLIER INCLUDING DEGREES OR CREDENTIALS
(I certify that the statements on the reverse apply to this bill and are made a part thereof.)
Erin A Helper MD
SIGNED   DATE MMDDYYYY

32. NAME AND ADDRESS OF FACILITY WHERE SERVICES WERE RENDERED (If other than home or office)

33. PHYSICIAN'S SUPPLIER'S BILLING NAME, ADDRESS, ZIP CODE & PHONE #
(101) 111 1234
ERIN A HELPER MD
101 MEDIC DRIVE
ANYWHERE US 12345
PIN# EBH8881   GRP#

PHYSICIAN OR SUPPLIER INFORMATION

(SAMPLE ONLY - NOT APPROVED FOR USE)

PLEASE PRINT OR TYPE

SAMPLE FORM 1500
SAMPLE FORM 1500 SAMPLE FORM 1500

FIGURE 15-12 Completed Mary Sue Patient claim for the encounter form in Figure 15-5

Block 11

Enter the rejection code if the patient has other third-party payer coverage and the claim was rejected.

Block 11d

Enter an X in the YES box.

Block 29

Enter any payment from the primary insurer. If the other insurance denied the claim, enter 0 00.

ERIN A. HELPER, M.D.
101 Medic Dr, Anywhere US 12345
(101) 111-1234 (Office) • (101) 111-9292 (Fax)
EIN: 11-123341 **MCD:** EBH8881
UPIN: EH8888 **BCBS:** EH11881
PIN: A09293 **BCBS:** 1204-P

Encounter Form

PATIENT INFORMATION:

Name:	Connelly, Jennifer
Address:	45 Main Street
City:	Nowhere
State:	US
Zip Code:	12367
Telephone:	(101) 555-5624
Gender:	Female
Date of Birth:	05-05-1955
Occupation:	
Employer:	

INSURANCE INFORMATION:

Patient Number:	15-13
Place of Service:	Office
Primary Insurance Plan:	Aetna
Primary Insurance Plan ID #:	56265897
Group #:	
Primary Policyholder:	Thomas Connelly
Policyholder Date of Birth:	05-25-1956
Relationship to Patient:	Spouse
Secondary Insurance Plan:	Medicaid
Secondary Insurance Plan ID #:	56215689
Secondary Policyholder:	Jennifer Connelly

Patient Status [X] Married ☐ Divorced ☐ Single ☐ Student

DIAGNOSIS INFORMATION

Diagnosis	Code	Diagnosis	Code
1. Hypertension	401.9	5.	
2.		6.	
3.		7.	
4.		8.	

PROCEDURE INFORMATION

Description of Procedure or Service	Date	Code	Charge
1. New patient, office visit, Level III	01-07-YYYY	99203	150.00
2.			
3.			
4.			
5.			

SPECIAL NOTES: Aetna paid $105.00 as primary payer.

FIGURE 15-13 Jennifer Connelly encounter form

Block 30

Enter the balance due.

Refer to Figure 15-14 for a completed secondary Medicaid CMS-1500 claim for the encounter form in Figure 15-13.

FIGURE 15-14 Completed Jennifer Connelly claim for the encounter form in Figure 15-13

MOTHER/BABY CLAIMS

These instructions are for mother/baby claims and are for reference purposes. They modify the primary Medicaid instructions. Refer to Figures 15-15 and 15-16.

The infant of a Medicaid recipient is automatically eligible for Medicaid for the entire first year of life. Individual state Medicaid programs determine reimbursement procedures for services provided to newborns. When claims are submitted under the mother's Medicaid identification number, coverage is usually limited to the baby's first 10 days of life (during which time an application is made so the baby is assigned its own identification number). Medicaid usually covers babies through the end of the month of its first birthday (e.g., baby born January 5, 2004 is covered until

---

KIM A. CARRINGTON, M.D.
900 Medic Dr, Anywhere US 12345
(101) 111-2365 (Office) • (101) 111-5625 (Fax)
EIN: 11-562356   **MCD:** KAC5558
UPIN: KC5558   **BCBS:** EH11881
PIN: A56235   **BCBS GRP:** 2356-P

Encounter Form

PATIENT INFORMATION:

Name:	Muracek, Newborn
Address:	515 Hill Street
City:	Anywhere
State:	US
Zip Code:	12367
Telephone:	(101) 555-5598
Gender:	Female
Date of Birth:	06-01-2004
Occupation:	
Employer:	

INSURANCE INFORMATION:

Patient Number:	15-15
Place of Service:	Inpatient Hospital
Primary Insurance Plan:	Medicaid
Primary Insurance Plan ID #:	56265987
Group #:	
Primary Policyholder:	Yvonne Muracek
Policyholder Date of Birth:	12-24-1970
Relationship to Patient:	Mother
Secondary Insurance Plan:	
Secondary Insurance Plan ID #:	
Secondary Policyholder:	

Patient Status   ☐ Married   ☐ Divorced   ☒ Single   ☐ Student

DIAGNOSIS INFORMATION

Diagnosis	Code	Diagnosis	Code
1. Healthy single liveborn infant	V30.00	5.	
2.		6.	
3.		7.	
4.		8.	

PROCEDURE INFORMATION

Description of Procedure or Service	Date	Code	Charge
1. History and examination of normal newborn	06-01-2004	99431	150.00
2. Attendance at delivery	06-01-2004	99436	400.00
3. Subsequent care for normal newborn	06-02-2004	99432	100.00
4.			
5.			

SPECIAL NOTES: Inpatient care provided at Goodmedicine Hospital, Anywhere St, Anywhere, US 12345. Medicaid PIN GHA123. Application for infant's Medicaid ID number has been submitted.

FIGURE 15-15 Newborn Muracek encounter form

FIGURE 15-16 Completed Newborn Muracek claim for the encounter form in Figure 15-15

January 31, 2005). The baby must continuously live with its mother to be eligible for the full year, and the baby remains eligible for Medicaid even if changes in family size or income occur and the mother is no longer eligible for Medicaid.

A **mother/baby claim** is submitted for services provided to a baby under the mother's Medicaid identification number. (The mother's services are *not* reimbursed on the *mother/baby claim*; they are submitted on a separate CMS-1500 claim according to the step-by-step instructions starting on page 478 of this chapter.)

NOTE: Medicaid *Baby Your Baby* programs cover the mother's prenatal care only. ●

Block 1a

Enter the mother's Medicaid ID number.

Block 2

Enter the mother's last name followed by the word NEWBORN.

EXAMPLE: VANDERMARK NEWBORN ●

Block 3

Enter the infant's date of birth and gender.

Block 4

Enter the mother's name, followed by (MOM), as the responsible party.

EXAMPLE: VANDERMARK JOYCE (MOM) ●

Block 21

Enter secondary diagnosis codes in fields 2, 3, and/or 4.

SUMMARY

- Title 19 of the SSA was passed in 1965, creating Medicaid, a medical assistance program for individuals with incomes below the FPL. (Medicaid is called MediCal in California.)
- The federal government establishes Medicaid eligibility requirements, and individual states have discretion in determining coverage policies as well as establishing financial criteria for eligibility.
- Medicaid eligibility criteria depends into which of the following a recipient is categorized: mandatory eligibility groups, optional eligibility groups, medically needy eligibility groups, and SCHIP.
- Medicaid coverage is categorized as mandatory, optional, waiver, and EPSDT services.
- Preauthorized services are used by Medicaid programs that have not implemented managed care (e.g., HMOs).
- Dual eligibles are individuals covered by both Medicare and Medicaid with Medicare billed as primary payer.

- Medicaid is always *payer of last resort* when a recipient is covered by other insurance (e.g., Medicare, TRICARE, IHS or commercial health insurance).
- Participating providers accept Medicaid payments as payment in full, and balance billing is illegal.
- The MEVS (or REVS) allowed providers to electronically verify a recipient's eligibility for Medicaid coverage via a point-of-sale device, computer software, or an automated voice response system.
- A Medicaid remittance advice sent to providers contains the status of claims submitted, including paid, adjusted, and voided claims.
- Medicaid's surveillance utilization review system (SURS) assesses unnecessary or inappropriate use of Medicaid services or excess payments, as well as the quality of services rendered.
- Each state's Office of Attorney General is certified by the federal government to detect, investigate, and prosecute fraudulent practices or abuse against Medicaid.
- Medicaid services are reimbursed only when determined to be medically necessary.
- When completing Medicaid CMS-1500 claims for case studies in this text and the Workbook, the following special instructions apply:
  - Block 20–Enter an X in the NO box
  - Block 22–Leave blank
  - Block 23–Leave blank
  - Block 24C–Leave blank
  - Block 24H–Leave blank
  - Block 24I–Leave blank
  - Block 25–Enter the EIN with a hyphen
  - Block 26–Enter the case study number (e.g., 15-5). If the patient has Medicaid as secondary coverage, enter an S (for secondary) next to the number (on the secondary claim)
  - Block 27–Enter an X in the YES box
  - Block 31–Enter provider's complete name with credentials (instead of a signature as indicated in the chapter instructions). This will allow you to completely generate claims using the UHI software (instead of having to print the claim and sign it)
  - Block 32–If Block 18 contains dates and/or Block 20 contains an X in the YES box, enter the name, address, and Medicaid PIN of the responsible provider (e.g., hospital, outside laboratory)
  - When completing secondary claims, enter TRANSMITTAL NOTICE ATTACHED in the top margin of the CMS-1500 claim (to simulate the attachment of a primary payer's EOB with a claim submitted to a secondary payer)

STUDY CHECKLIST

☐ Read the textbook chapter, and prepare the Insurance Plan Comparison Chart.

☐ Install the UHI software from the disk (instructions are in Appendix V), and become familiar with the software.

☐ Complete CMS-1500 claims for each chapter encounter form.

☐ Complete the chapter review.

☐ Complete the chapter CD-ROM activities.

☐ Complete Web Tutor assignments, and take online quizzes.

☐ Complete Medicaid claims for cases located in Appendices I and II.

☐ Complete the Workbook chapter, verifying answers with your instructor.

☐ Form a study group with classmates to discuss chapter concepts in preparation for an exam.

REVIEW

TRUE/FALSE

Indicate whether the definition is true or false.

1. ☐ T ☐ F Medicaid: Local government program designed to help the poor with medical expenses.

2. ☐ T ☐ F MediCal: Title the state of California assigns to its Medicare program.

3. ☐ T ☐ F Medically needy: Special medical coverage to persons who have extremely high medical bills but can cover some of their other expenses.

4. ☐ T ☐ F Medical assistance: Medical coverage provided by Medicare programs.

5. ☐ T ☐ F SSI (Social Security Income): Government program for the aged, blind, and disabled.

SHORT ANSWER

Briefly answer the following:

6. List and define four *distinct and separate* categories of individuals eligible for Medicaid coverage as stated in the federal guidelines.

7. List six medical services covered by federal funding for Medicaid.

8. State the range of timely filing deadlines for Medicaid claims.

9. Explain how to verify a patient's Medicaid eligibility.

10. Explain the meaning of the abbreviation TANF.

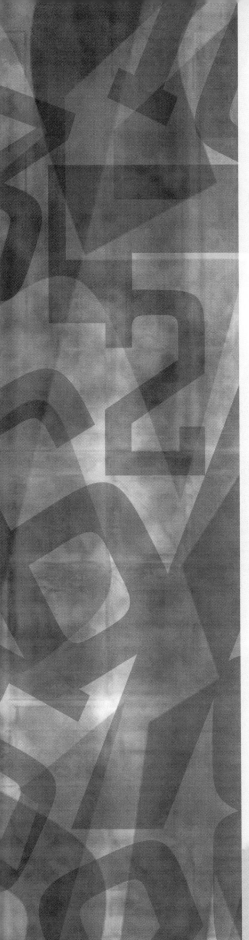

KEY TERMS

beneficiary services representative
(BSR)

catastrophic cap benefit

catchment area

CHAMPUS Reform Initiative (CRI)

clinical trials

critical pathway

Defense Enrollment Eligibility
Reporting System (DEERS)

demonstration project

Department of Defense (DoD) Cancer
Treatment Clinical Trials

DSM *(Diagnostic & Statistical
Manual)*

emergency care

fiscal year

Health Affairs (HA)

health care finder (HCF)

Lead Agent (LA)

Military Health Services System
(MHSS)

nonavailability statement (NAS)

nurse advisor

other health insurance (OHI)

practice guidelines

primary care manager (PCM)

Program Integrity (PI) Office

TRICARE

TRICARE beneficiary

TRICARE Dental Program (TDP)

TRICARE Extra

TRICARE Management Activity
(TMA)

TRICARE Pharmacy Plan

TRICARE Prime

TRICARE Program Management
Organization (PMO)

TRICARE Retiree Dental Program
(TRDP)

TRICARE Service Center (TSC)

TRICARE sponsor

TRICARE Standard

uniformed services

Chapter 16 TRICARE

OBJECTIVES

Upon successful completion of this chapter, you should be able to:

1. Define key terms.

2. List TRICARE eligibility categories.

3. State TRICARE definitions for "medical emergency" and "urgent medical problem."

4. State TRICARE outpatient coverage for mental health and substance abuse.

5. Explain the meaning of TRICARE catastrophic coverage.

6. List six services not covered by TRICARE.

7. List types of health insurance primary to the TRICARE program.

8. List and define the three levels of TRICARE coverage.

9. State deductibles and cost-shares for TRICARE Extra, Standard, and Point-of-Service options.

10. File TRICARE Standard and Extra claims properly.

INTRODUCTION

TRICARE is a health care program for (1) active duty members of the military and their qualified family members, (2) CHAMPUS-eligible retirees and their qualified family members, and (3) eligible survivors of members of the uniformed services. **CHAMPUS** (now called TRICARE Standard) is an abbreviation for the **Civilian Health and Medical Program of the Uniformed Services**, a federal program created in 1966 (and implemented in 1967) as a benefit for dependents of personnel serving in the **uniformed services** (U.S. military branches that include the Army, Navy, Air Force, Marines, and Coast Guard), Public Health Service, and the North Atlantic Treaty Organization (NATO). TRICARE was created to expand health care access, ensure quality of care, control health care costs, and improve medical readiness.

TRICARE BACKGROUND

CHAMPUS (now called TRICARE) was implemented in 1967 as the result of an initiative to provide military medical care for families of active-duty members. The original budget was $106 million, and the current budget is more than $24 billion (*2002 Tricare Stakeholders' Report,* Volume IV). In the 1980s, the Department of Defense (DoD) began researching ways to improve access to quality care while controlling costs, and demonstration projects were authorized. One demonstration project, the **CHAMPUS Reform Initiative (CRI)** carried out in California and Hawaii, offered military families a choice of how their health care benefits could be used. The DoD noted the successful operation and high levels of patient satisfaction associated with the CRI, and it was determined that its concepts should be expanded to a nationwide uniform program.

TRICARE

This new program became known as TRICARE, a regionally managed health care program that joins the health care resources of the uniformed services (e.g., Army) and supplements them with networks of civilian health care professionals to provide access and high quality service while maintaining the capability to support military operations. TRICARE is a health care program for active duty members of the uniformed services and their families, retirees and their families, and survivors of all uniformed services who are not eligible for Medicare.

There are eleven TRICARE Regions in the United States plus TRICARE Europe, Pacific (includes Hawaii and Westpac), Puerto Rico/Virgin Islands, and Canada/Latin America (Figure 16-1). Each is managed by a Lead Agent staff that is responsible for the military health system in that region. Commanders of selected military treatment facilities (MTFs) are selected as **Lead Agents (LA)** for the TRICARE regions. The Lead Agent staff serves as a federal health care team created to work with regional military treatment facility commanders, uniformed service headquarters' staffs, and Health Affairs (HA) to support the mission of the Military Health Services System (MHSS). The **Military Health Services System (MHSS)** is the entire health care system of the U.S. uniformed services and includes military treatment facilities (MTFs) as well as various programs in the civilian health care market, such as TRICARE. **Health Affairs (HA)** refers to the Office of the Assistant Secretary of Defense for Health Affairs, which is responsible for both military readiness and peacetime health care.

TRICARE ADMINISTRATION

The **TRICARE Management Activity (TMA)** (formerly called OCHAMPUS) is the office that coordinates and administers the TRICARE program and is accountable for quality health care provided to members of the uniformed services and their families. The TMA also serves as arbitrator for denied claims submitted for consideration by TRICARE sponsors and beneficiaries; its offices are located in Aurora, Colorado. **TRICARE sponsors** are uniformed service personnel who are either active duty, retired, or deceased. (Dependents of deceased sponsors are eligible for TRICARE benefits.) Sponsor information (e.g., SSN, DOB, and last name) can be verified in the **Defense Enrollment Eligibility Reporting System (DEERS)**, which is a computer system that contains up-to-date Defense Department Workforce personnel information. **TRICARE beneficiaries** include sponsors and dependents of sponsors.

NOTE: Do not submit TRICARE claims to the TMA; claims are processed by TRICARE contractors (similar to Medicare carriers and fiscal intermediaries) for different regions of the country and overseas.

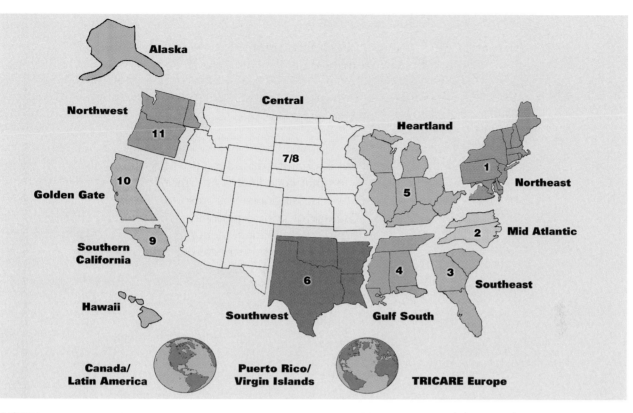

FIGURE 16-1 Map of TRICARE regions

TRICARE manuals can be downloaded from http://www.tricare.osd.mil.

TRICARE Service Centers

TRICARE regions are served by one or more **TRICARE Service Centers (TSC)**, which are business offices staffed by one or more beneficiary services representatives and health care finders who assist TRICARE sponsors with health care needs and answer questions about the program.

Beneficiary Services Representatives

A **beneficiary services representative (BSR)** is employed at a TRICARE Service Center, provides information about using TRICARE, and assists with other matters affecting access to health care (e.g., appointment scheduling).

Health Care Finders

A **health care finder (HCF)** is a registered nurse or physician assistant who assists primary care providers with preauthorizations and referrals to health care services in a military treatment facility or civilian provider network. A *preauthorization* is formal approval obtained from a health care finder before certain specialty procedures and inpatient care services are rendered. A *referral* is a request for a member to receive treatment from another provider.

Nurse Advisors

In most TRICARE regions, **nurse advisors** are also available 24/7 for advice and assistance with treatment alternatives and to discuss whether a sponsor should see a provider based on a discussion of symptoms. Nurse advisors will also discuss preventive care and ways to improve a family's health.

Case Management

TRICARE *case management* is organized under TRICARE utilization management, and is a collaborative process that coordinates and monitors a beneficiary's health care options and services by assessing available resources to promote quality and cost-effective outcomes. The use of critical pathways, practice guidelines, and discharge planning can enhance the case management process. A **critical pathway** is the sequence of activities that can normally be expected to result in the most cost-effective clinical course of treatment. **Practice guidelines** are decision-making tools used by providers to determine appropriate health care for specific clinical circumstances. They offer the opportunity to improve health care delivery processes by reducing unwanted variation. The Institute of Medicine specifies that practice guidelines should be valid, reliable and reproducible, clinically applicable and flexible, a multidisciplinary process, reviewed on a scheduled basis, and well-documented. *Discharge planning* assesses requirements so that arrangements can be made for the appropriate and timely discharge of patients from acute care or outpatient settings.

EXAMPLE: Inpatient records undergo quarterly review (using predetermined screening criteria) to identify individuals whose frequency of services or cost of services make them candidates for case management. ●

Program Integrity Office

The TMA **Program Integrity (PI) Office** is responsible for the surveillance of fraud and abuse activities worldwide involving purchased care for beneficiaries in the Military Health Care System. PI develops policies and procedures for the prevention, detection, investigation, and control of TRICARE fraud, waste, and program abuse, monitoring contractor program integrity activities, coordinating with the Department of Defense (DoD) and external investigative agencies, and initiating administrative remedies as required. TRICARE authorized providers can be excluded from program participation if one of the following conditions applies:

- any criminal conviction or civil judgment involving fraud
- fraud or abuse under TRICARE
- exclusion or suspension by another federal, state, or local government agency
- participation in a conflict of interest situation
- when it is in the best interest of the TRICARE program or its beneficiaries

EXAMPLE: A Colorado psychologist pled guilty to two felony counts of health care fraud, one felony count of conspiracy to defraud with respect to claims, and one felony count of criminal forfeiture. This culminated a six-year investigation of a counseling center where a billing-fraud scam involved filing claims for services not provided as well as using an authorized provider's identification number to submit claims for services that were provided by an unauthorized provider. TRICARE will recover almost $500,000 in damages. The psychologist received a sentence of 21 months of imprisonment and three years of released supervision. ●

CHAMPVA

Although similar to TRICARE Standard with regard to coverage, the *Civilian Health and Medical Program of the Department of Veterans Affairs (CHAMPVA)* is a separate program from TRICARE Standard. CHAMPVA is a health care benefits program for:

- dependents of veterans who have been rated by VA as having a total and permanent disability.
- survivors of veterans who died from VA-rated, service-connected conditions, or who at the time of death were rated permanently and totally disabled from a VA-rated, service-connected condition.
- survivors of veterans who died in the line of duty and not from misconduct.

Under CHAMPVA, the VA shares the cost of covered health care services and supplies with eligible beneficiaries. The administration of CHAMPVA is centralized at the Health Administration Center in Denver, Colorado.

INTERNET LINK

More information about CHAMPVA can be found at http://www.va.gov/hac (click on the CHAMPVA link).

TRICARE Eligibility

TRICARE-eligible individuals include:

- active duty and retired service members.
- eligible family members of active duty and retired service members.
- eligible family members of deceased active duty or retired service members.
- eligible family members of active duty service members who were court-martialed and separated for spouse or child abuse.
- Congressional Medal of Honor recipients and their family members.
- children placed in the custody of a service member or former member by a court of law or by a recognized adoption agency in anticipation of legal adoption by the member.
- certain abused spouses, former spouses, and dependent children of service members who were eligible for retirement but had that eligibility taken away as a result of abuse of the spouse or child.
- former spouses of active or retired military who were married to a service member or former member who had performed at least 20 years of creditable service for retirement purposes at the time the divorce or annulment occurred.
- spouses and children of NATO and Partners for Peace (PFP) national representatives who officially accompany representatives while stationed in, or passing through, the United States on official business. Family members are eligible for outpatient benefits only.
- spouses and unmarried children of reservists and National Guard ordered to active duty for more than 30 consecutive days (covered only during the reservist's active duty tour) *or* who died while on active duty *or* who are injured or aggravate an injury, illness, or disease during, or on the way to, active duty training for a period of 30 days or less, or a period of inactive duty training, and who die as a result of the specific injuries, illnesses, or diseases.

TRICARE OPTIONS

TRICARE offers three health care options:

1. *TRICARE Prime:* Military treatment facilities are the principal source of health care under this option.

2. *TRICARE Extra:* A preferred provider organization (PPO) option that costs less when compared to TRICARE Prime and TRICARE Standard.

    NOTE: This option is not offered in all regions because of the limited availability of PPOs in some civilian markets; instead, TRICARE Standard is available. ●

3. *TRICARE Standard:* A fee-for-service option (formerly CHAMPUS).

TRICARE Prime

TRICARE Prime is a managed care option similar to a civilian health maintenance organization (HMO). Enrollment in TRICARE Prime guarantees priority access to care at the Military Treatment Facilities (MTF).

Features of TRICARE Prime

- Guaranteed access to timely medical care
- Priority for care at military treatment facilities
- Assignment of a primary care manager
- Lowest cost option of the three TRICARE options
- Requires enrollment for one year
- Retired military pay annual enrollment fee
- Care sought outside of TRICARE Prime network is costly
- May be unavailable in some TRICARE regions

TRICARE Prime provides comprehensive health care benefits at the lowest cost of the three options. *Eligible individuals are required to enroll in TRICARE Prime so that adequate professional staffing and resources are available in military treatment facilities and supporting civilian facilities.* Individuals eligible for TRICARE Prime include (1) active duty military personnel, (2) family members of active duty sponsors (no enrollment fee), and (3) retirees and their family members, all of whom are under 65. See Tables 16-1 and 16-2, which contain out-of-pocket costs for TRICARE Prime.

A **primary care manager (PCM)** is a doctor assigned to a sponsor and is part of the TRICARE provider network. The PCM guides TRICARE Prime members through the health care system and coordinates all specialty medical needs. Prime members can choose a PCM from the Military Treatment Facility (MTF) or the TRICARE provider directory. TRICARE Prime beneficiaries also receive care if they reside and work outside an MTF **catchment area**, which is the region defined by code boundaries within a 40-mile radius of an MTF. Note that certain TRICARE regions only allow a military doctor or medical clinic to serve as a PCM.

The PCM provides nonemergency care to eligible beneficiaries and arranges referrals for specialty care if needed, usually through a military hospital. If military specialty care is unavailable, the PCM authorizes care from a civilian specialist. For

TABLE 16-1 TRICARE deductible, copayment, and coinsurance amounts

	TRICARE PRIME	TRICARE EXTRA/STANDARD
Annual deductible	$0	$50 individual $100 family
Civilian outpatient visit	$0	Extra: 15% Standard: 20%
Civilian inpatient admission	$0	$11.90 per day
Civilian inpatient mental health	$0	$20 per day or $25.00 minimum, whichever is greater.

TABLE 16-2 TRICARE out-of-pocket expenses for retirees and their family members

	TRICARE PRIME	TRICARE EXTRA	TRICARE STANDARD
Annual deductible	$0	$150 individual $300 family	$150 individual $300 family
Annual enrollment fees	$230 individual $460 family	$0	$0
Civilian Provider Copays			
Outpatient visit	$12	20% of negotiated fees	25% of allowed charges
Emergency care	$30	20% of negotiated fees	25% of allowed charges
Mental health visit	$25	20% of negotiated fees	25% of allowed charges
Mental health visit (family or group therapy)	$17	20% of negotiated fees	25% of allowed charges
Civilian inpatient cost share	$11 per day ($25 minimum)	Lesser of $250/day or 25% of billed charges; plus 20% of negotiated professional fees	Lesser of $414/day or 25% of billed charges; plus 25% of allowed professional charges
Civilian inpatient mental health	$40 per day	20% of institutional charges; plus 25% of professional charges	Lesser of $154 per day or 25% of institutional; plus 25% of professional charges

(Reprinted according to Security and Provide Notice at http://www.tricare.osd.mil/main/privacy.html)

beneficiaries to receive coverage for specialty care, the PCM must make these arrangements. TRICARE Prime guarantees enrollees access to care, and urgent care is rendered within one day while less urgent care is provided within one week. In addition, travel is limited to no more than 30 minutes to the PCM. Preventive care is emphasized, and the following services are provided at no additional charge: eye exams, immunizations, hearing screenings, mammograms, Pap smears, prostate exams, and other cancer-prevention and early diagnosis exams.

TRICARE Prime covers nonemergency care if the beneficiary is away from home and receives prior approval from the PCM. Such authorization is required for all routine medical care provided out of the area or at another facility. If the beneficiary seeks medical care without prior approval, the *point-of-service option* is activated, requiring payment of an annual deductible plus 50% or more of visit or treatment fees.

Beneficiaries who require emergency care should seek that care at the nearest civilian or military treatment facility.

Catastrophic Cap Benefit

The **catastrophic cap benefit** protects TRICARE beneficiaries from devastating financial loss due to serious illness or long-term treatment by establishing limits over which payment is not required. Under TRICARE Prime, the maximum out-of-pocket cost per year for covered medical services is $1,000 for active duty family members and $3,000 for retirees and their families per enrollment year.

TRICARE Extra

TRICARE Extra allows TRICARE Standard users to save 5% of their TRICARE Standard cost-shares by using health care providers in the TRICARE network. No enrollment is required to be covered by TRICARE Extra; enrollees simply go to any network doctor, hospital, or other provider and show a military ID card. Care is also available at an MTF on a space-available basis.

Features of TRICARE Extra

- Choice of any physician in the network
- Less costly than TRICARE Standard
- May be more expensive than TRICARE Prime
- Annual enrollment is not required
- Lower priority for care provided at MTFs

Unlike for TRICARE Prime, individuals eligible for TRICARE Extra do not have to enroll or pay an enrollment fee. They can use the option whenever they choose by selecting any health care provider from within the TRICARE Extra provider network. When a TRICARE Extra network provider renders care, it is just like using TRICARE Standard (formerly CHAMPUS), with the bonus of a 5% discount on most cost-shares (e.g., copayments).

TRICARE Extra offers enrollees the choice of receiving health care services from participating civilian hospitals, physicians, and other medical providers who have agreed to charge an approved fee for medical treatment and procedures. Two groups that usually prefer TRICARE Extra include (1) individuals and families whose regular physician is a participating member of the TRICARE Extra network, and (2) individuals who do not have convenient access to MTFs and want reduced health care costs as compared with TRICARE Standard.

Those eligible for TRICARE Extra coverage include: (1) family members of active duty sponsors (no enrollment fee), and (2) retirees (except most Medicare-eligible beneficiaries) and their family members under 65.

NOTE: All active duty members are enrolled in TRICARE Prime and are not eligible for TRICARE Extra.

TRICARE Extra Coverage

Individuals eligible to enroll in TRICARE Extra are not required to pay an annual fee, can seek care from a network provider, receive a discount on services, and usually pay reduced copayments (5% less than TRICARE Standard; participating providers are reimbursed the approved rate plus 5%). In addition, network providers file insurance claims for enrollees and are prohibited from balance billing. **Balance billing** refers to the practice of a provider billing a patient for all charges not reimbursed by a health plan.

TRICARE Extra enrollees can also seek health care services from an MTF on a space-available basis, and they can select between TRICARE Extra and TRICARE Standard options on a visit-by-visit basis. Tables 16-1 and 16-2 contain out-of-pocket costs for TRICARE Extra.

Catastrophic Cap Benefit

Under TRICARE Extra, active duty family members are responsible for up to $1,000 and retirees for up to $3,000 per year in out-of-pocket costs for covered services.

TRICARE Standard

TRICARE Standard is the new name for traditional CHAMPUS. To use this option, enrollees either make an appointment at an MTF or seek care from any TRICARE-certified civilian health care provider (fee-for-service option). Enrollees are responsible for annual deductibles and copayments. It provides beneficiaries with the greatest freedom in selecting civilian providers; however, it has the highest out-of-pocket costs of the three plans. There is no enrollment requirement for TRICARE Standard.

Features of TRICARE Standard

- Greatest flexibility in selecting health care providers
- Most convenient when traveling or away from home
- Potentially most expensive of all options
- Enrollment not required
- TRICARE Extra can be used
- Space-available care in MTFs is a provision (low priority is assigned to TRICARE Standard enrollees)

NOTE: A **nonavailability statement (NAS)** is a certificate issued by an MTF that cannot provide needed care to TRICARE Standard beneficiaries. This means the beneficiary can seek care from a civilian provider and reimbursement will be approved. NAS certificates are not required for **emergency care**, which is defined by TRICARE as the sudden and unexpected onset of a medical or mental health condition that is threatening to life, limb, or sight.

Individuals who meet TRICARE eligibility criteria are covered by TRICARE Standard, *except* for active duty service members (who are covered by TRICARE Prime). ●

TRICARE Standard Coverage

Annual deductibles, cost-shares, and benefits are the same as they were for CHAMPUS. Under TRICARE Standard, enrollees can select their health care provider; however, out-of-pocket costs are higher when compared with other TRICARE options.

Also, enrollees who seek care from nonparticipating providers may have to file their own claim forms and, perhaps, pay more for care (up to 15% more than the allowable charge). Participating providers accept the TRICARE Standard allowable charge as payment in full for care rendered and they will file insurance claims for enrollees.

NOTE: TRICARE Standard does not enroll participating providers; they participate voluntarily and may do so on a case-by-case basis. When using TRICARE Standard, enrollees should ask the selected provider whether they participate in TRICARE Standard. ●

Catastrophic Cap Benefit

Under TRICARE Standard, active duty family members are responsible for up to $1,000 and retirees for up to $3,000 per year in out-of-pocket costs for covered services.

TRICARE PROGRAMS AND DEMONSTRATION PROJECTS

The **TRICARE Program Management Organization (PMO)** manages TRICARE programs and demonstration projects. A **demonstration project** tests and establishes the feasibility of implementing a new program during a trial period, after which the program is evaluated, modified, and/or abandoned. If, upon evaluation, it is determined that program implementation criteria are met (e.g., cost-effectiveness and meets intended needs of a population), the demonstration project is approved as a program, and enrollment is expanded to include all eligible individuals.

Programs include:
- TRICARE For Life (Medicare Eligibles)
- TRICARE Dental Program
- TRICARE Retiree Dental Program
- TRICARE Pharmacy Plan

Demonstration projects include:
- Department of Defense (DoD) Cancer Treatment Clinical Trials
- Other Demonstrations

TRICARE For Life (Medicare Eligibles)

TRICARE For Life (previously discussed in Chapter 15) provides Medigap-like wraparound coverage for Medicare beneficiaries. As secondary payer, TRICARE reimburses out-of-pocket expenses. (The only cost to the beneficiary is payment of Medicare Part B premiums.) Those eligible include uniformed service retirees and family members age 65 or over who are enrolled in Medicare Part B. Enrollment is automatic with Medicare enrollment.

TRICARE Dental Program

The **TRICARE Dental Program (TDP)** is a voluntary, comprehensive dental program offered worldwide by the Department of Defense to family members of all active duty uniformed service members and to Selected Reserve and Individual Ready Reserve (IRR) members and/or their family members. Single and family plans are available, and costs include low monthly premiums and copayments based on a sponsor's pay grade.

INTERNET LINK

Visit the administrator of TDP at http://www.ucci.com, and click on the TRICARE (TDP) link.

TRICARE Retiree Dental Program

The **TRICARE Retiree Dental Program (TRDP)** provides comprehensive dental benefits program to uniformed services retirees and their family members. Eligibility criteria include:

- retired uniformed services regardless of age.
- retired National Reserve/Guard who would be entitled to retired pay, but are under age 60.
- current spouses and children of enrolled members.
- un-remarried surviving spouses and children of deceased active duty and retired uniformed service members.

INTERNET LINK

Visit the administrator of TDRP at http://www.ddpdelta.org

TRICARE Pharmacy Plan

The **TRICARE Pharmacy Plan** allows active duty military members to fill prescriptions for reduced costs.

FILLING PRESCRIPTIONS AT:	WILL COST:
Military Treatment Facilities	$0
National Mail Order Pharmacy	$3 for generic for 90-day supply $9 for brand name for 90-day supply
Civilian Retail Network Pharmacy	$3 for generic for 30-day supply $9 for brand name for 30-day supply
Civilian Retail Non-Network Pharmacy	$9 or 20% of the cost for a 30-day supply

INTERNET LINK

Visit the TRICARE Pharmacy Web site at http://www.tricare.osd.mil/pharmacy/ for more information.

DoD/NCI Cancer Clinical Trials Demonstration Project

The **Department of Defense (DoD)/Cancer Treatment Clinical Trials** offer TRICARE beneficiaries the latest in cancer preventive care and treatment. **Clinical trials** are research studies that help find ways to prevent, diagnose, or treat illnesses and improve health care. The Department of Defense (DoD) joined forces with the

National Cancer Institute (NCI) through an interagency agreement in which beneficiaries can participate in NCI-sponsored cancer prevention and treatment studies as part of their TRICARE health care benefits. For some TRICARE beneficiaries with cancer, the DoD/NCI Clinical Trials project offers choices when few treatment options exist.

Other Demonstrations

Various TRICARE regions also implement demonstration projects that involve tests of alternative health care delivery methods. Coverage in demonstration areas may differ from usual TRICARE policies, and providers should contact appropriate regional contractors to find out about any demonstration projects affecting their area.

TRICARE SUPPLEMENTAL PLANS

TRICARE supplemental insurance policies are offered by most military associations and by some private firms. They are designed to reimburse patients for the civilian medical care expenses that must be paid after TRICARE reimburses the government's share of health care costs. Each TRICARE supplemental policy has its own rules concerning pre-existing conditions, eligibility requirements for family members, deductibles, mental health limitations, long-term care illnesses, well-baby care, disability care, claims processed under the diagnosis-related group (DRG) payment system for inpatient hospital charges, and rules concerning allowable charges.

NOTE: Because there is no direct transfer of claims information between TRICARE and supplemental carriers, do not enter supplemental policy information on TRICARE claims. ●

INTERNET LINK

TRICARE/CHAMPUS Supplemental Plan can be researched at
http://www.tricare.osd.mil/supplementalinsurance/plans.cfm

TRICARE BILLING INFORMATION

The following is a summary of the nationwide billing information for TRICARE Standard and TRICARE Extra out-of-network services. Providers of services are required to file these claims.

TRICARE Carriers

In recent years, TRICARE carrier contracts were grouped in large regional districts covering many states. Each regional carrier assigned post office box numbers and an associated nine-digit zip code for each state served. Be sure to use and proofread carefully both the post office box number and its associated zip code when submitting claims or correspondence to the carrier. Contact the nearest military facility to obtain the current address of the carrier assigned to your area, or access the TRICARE Web site of the U.S. Department of Defense Military Health System at http://www.tricare.osd.mil.

Underwriter

TRICARE is based in Colorado. Changes in general benefits are enacted by the United States Congress.

Forms Used

1. CMS-1500 claim.

2. A *nonavailability statement* must be obtained for all civilian nonemergency inpatient care.

3. *Mental health cases only:* A TRICARE Treatment Report must be filed with a claim for more than twenty-three outpatient visits in any calendar year. Inpatient care requires a Treatment Report every thirty days.

4. *Personal injury claims:* A "Personal Injury–Possible Third-Party Liability Statement" must accompany a claim for treatment of personal injury covering services rendered for diagnosis codes between 800 and 959.

Filing Deadline

Claims will be denied if they are filed more than one year after the date of service for outpatient care or more than one year from the date of discharge for inpatient care.

Allowable Fee Determination

TRICARE follows the principles of the RBRVS system but has made some adjustments to the geographic regions and assigned a slightly higher conversion factor. Fee schedules are available from regional carriers. The TRICARE fee schedule must still be followed when TRICARE is a secondary payer.

Enrollment Fees

There is an enrollment fee for TRICARE Prime but not for TRICARE Standard or TRICARE Extra (Table 16-2).

Deductibles

All deductibles are applied to the government's **fiscal year**, which runs from October 1 of one year to September 30 of the next. This is different from other insurance programs, for which deductibles are usually calculated on a calendar year basis (Tables 16-1 and 16-2).

Confirmation of Eligibility

Confirmation of TRICARE eligibility and nonavailability statement requirements is obtained from the nationwide computerized Defense Enrollment Eligibility Reporting System (DEERS).

Accepting Assignment

Accepting assignment for nonPARs is determined on a claim-by-claim basis. Be sure to indicate the provider's choice in Block 27 of the claim. All deductibles and cost-shares may be collected at the time service is rendered. When assignment is elected, the local beneficiary services representative (BSR) can assist if there are problems collecting the deductible and cost-share (copayment) from the patient. The carrier's provider representative can assist with claims review or intervene when a claim payment is overdue.

TRICARE has established a "good faith policy" for assigned claims when the copy of the front and back of the patient's ID card on file turns out to be invalid. If copies of the card are on file and TRICARE provides notification that the patient is ineligible for payment, the local BSR can help in the investigation of the claim. If the investigation reveals that the ID card is invalid, refile the claim with a note stating: "We treated this patient in good faith. Please note the enclosed copy of the ID that was presented at the time the treatment was rendered." *Do not send* your file copy of the ID card. You should receive payment of the TRICARE-approved fee for these services.

TRICARE Limiting Charges

All TRICARE nonPAR providers are subject to a limiting charge of 15% above the TRICARE Fee Schedule for PAR providers. Patients can no longer be billed for the difference between the provider's normal fee and the TRICARE limiting charge (called *balance billing*). Exceptions to the 15% limiting charge are claims from independent laboratory and diagnostic laboratory companies, durable medical equipment, and medical supply companies.

Major Medical or Special Accidental Injury Benefits

There is no separate billing procedure necessary for accidental injury claims. There is no differentiation between basic benefits and major medical benefits.

Special Handling

1. Always make a copy of the front and back of the patient's ID card.

2. Check to determine whether the patient knows the date of his or her next transfer. If it is within six months, it would be wise to accept assignment on the claim to avoid interstate collection problems.

3. Make sure the patient has obtained the necessary nonavailability statement for all nonemergency civilian inpatient care and specified outpatient surgeries if the sponsor lives within a catchment area.

4. Nonemergency inpatient mental health cases require preauthorization, and a nonavailability statement must be obtained.

5. TRICARE Mental Health Treatment Reports should be submitted to TRICARE every 30 days for inpatient cases and on or about the 48th outpatient visit and every 24th visit thereafter. This report should cover the following points:
   - date treatment began
   - age, sex, and marital status of patient
   - diagnosis and DSM axis information

     NOTE: DSM is the *Diagnostic & Statistical Manual,* published by the American Psychiatric Association, which classifies mental health disorders and is based on ICD. ●
   - presenting symptoms
   - historical data
   - prior treatment episodes

- type and frequency of therapy
- explanation of any deviation from standard treatment for the diagnosis
- mental status and psychological testing
- progress of patient
- physical examination and/or pertinent laboratory data
- future plans and treatment goals

6. A *Personal Injury–Possible Third-Party Liability Statement* is required for all injuries that have been assigned ICD codes in the 800 to 959 range. If there is no third-party liability, call the BSR for information on how to file the claim.
7. When filing a claim for services that fall under the special handicap benefits, enter DEPENDENT DISABILITY PROGRAM at the top of the claim.
8. Contact the regional carrier representative if there has been no response within 45 days of filing the claim.
9. For hospice claims, enter HOSPICE CLAIMS on the envelope to ensure the claim arrives at the regional carrier's hospice desk.

TRICARE PRIMARY CLAIM INSTRUCTIONS

The following instructions are for claims submitted to TRICARE Extra and TRICARE Standard regional carriers. When reviewing the step-by-step instructions, refer to Figure 16-2 for a sample of the CMS-1500 claim, Blocks 1 through 13. After review of the instructions, refer to the John Q. Public encounter form in Figure 16-3 and the completed CMS-1500 claim, Blocks 1 through 13, in Figure 16-4.

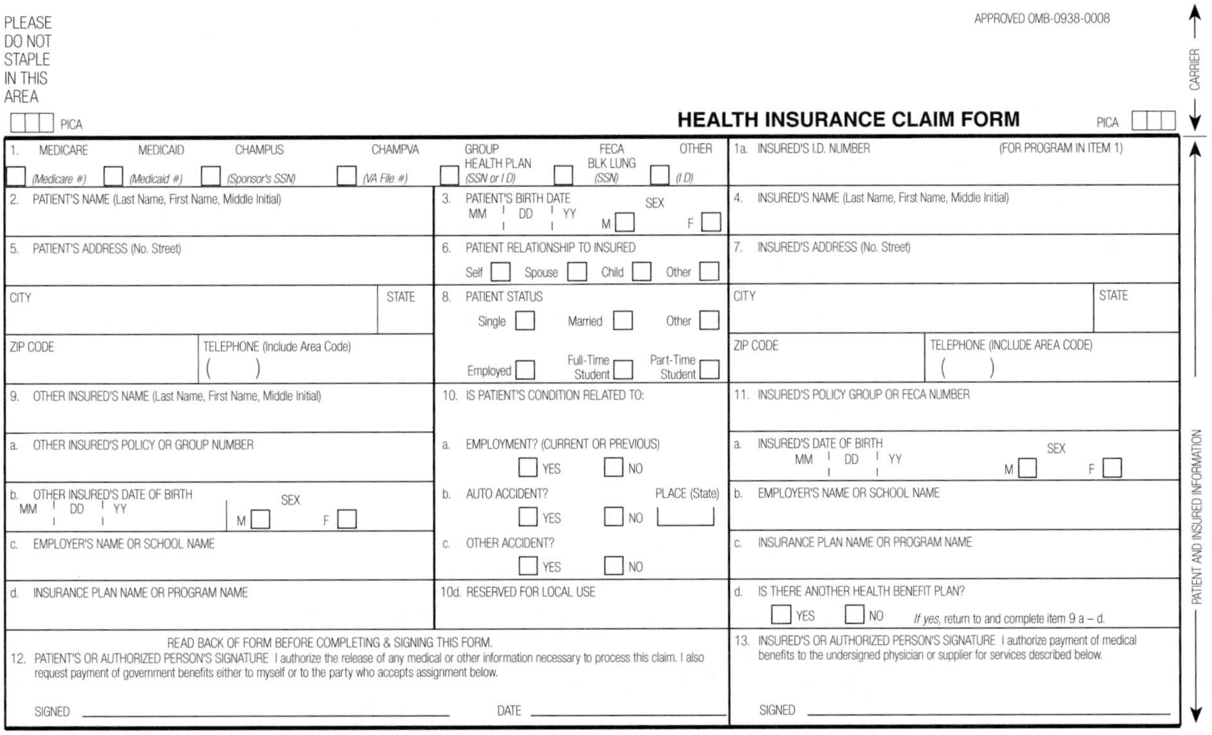

PLEASE DO NOT STAPLE IN THIS AREA

APPROVED OMB-0938-0008

PICA — HEALTH INSURANCE CLAIM FORM — PICA

CARRIER

1. MEDICARE (Medicare #) MEDICAID (Medicaid #) CHAMPUS (Sponsor's SSN) CHAMPVA (VA File #) GROUP HEALTH PLAN (SSN or I D) FECA BLK LUNG (SSN) OTHER (I D)

1a. INSURED'S I.D. NUMBER (FOR PROGRAM IN ITEM 1)

2. PATIENT'S NAME (Last Name, First Name, Middle Initial)

3. PATIENT'S BIRTH DATE MM DD YY SEX M F

4. INSURED'S NAME (Last Name, First Name, Middle Initial)

5. PATIENT'S ADDRESS (No. Street)

6. PATIENT RELATIONSHIP TO INSURED Self Spouse Child Other

7. INSURED'S ADDRESS (No. Street)

CITY STATE

8. PATIENT STATUS Single Married Other

CITY STATE

ZIP CODE TELEPHONE (Include Area Code) ( )

Employed Full-Time Student Part-Time Student

ZIP CODE TELEPHONE (INCLUDE AREA CODE) ( )

9. OTHER INSURED'S NAME (Last Name, First Name, Middle Initial)

10. IS PATIENT'S CONDITION RELATED TO:

11. INSURED'S POLICY GROUP OR FECA NUMBER

a. OTHER INSURED'S POLICY OR GROUP NUMBER

a. EMPLOYMENT? (CURRENT OR PREVIOUS) YES NO

a. INSURED'S DATE OF BIRTH MM DD YY SEX M F

b. OTHER INSURED'S DATE OF BIRTH MM DD YY SEX M F

b. AUTO ACCIDENT? PLACE (State) YES NO

b. EMPLOYER'S NAME OR SCHOOL NAME

c. EMPLOYER'S NAME OR SCHOOL NAME

c. OTHER ACCIDENT? YES NO

c. INSURANCE PLAN NAME OR PROGRAM NAME

d. INSURANCE PLAN NAME OR PROGRAM NAME

10d. RESERVED FOR LOCAL USE

d. IS THERE ANOTHER HEALTH BENEFIT PLAN? YES NO *If yes,* return to and complete item 9 a – d.

READ BACK OF FORM BEFORE COMPLETING & SIGNING THIS FORM.

12. PATIENT'S OR AUTHORIZED PERSON'S SIGNATURE I authorize the release of any medical or other information necessary to process this claim. I also request payment of government benefits either to myself or to the party who accepts assignment below.

SIGNED DATE

13. INSURED'S OR AUTHORIZED PERSON'S SIGNATURE I authorize payment of medical benefits to the undersigned physician or supplier for services described below.

SIGNED

PATIENT AND INSURED INFORMATION

FIGURE 16-2 Blocks 1 through 13 of the CMS-1500 claim

Block 1

Enter an X in the CHAMPUS box.

Block 1a

Enter the sponsor's Social Security Number (SSN).

> **NOTE:** If the sponsor is an active duty security agent, enter SECURITY next to the social security number (SSN). If the sponsor is a NATO beneficiary, enter NATO next to the SSN. ●

Block 2

Enter the patient's complete name (last name first, followed by the first name and middle initial) as listed on the insurance identification card. Use of nicknames or typographic errors will cause rejection of the claim.

Block 3

Enter the patient's birth as MM DD YYYY (with spaces format).
Enter an X in the appropriate box to indicate the patient's gender.

Block 4

Enter the sponsor's complete name (last name, first name, middle initial). Enter SAME if the patient is the sponsor.

Block 5

Enter the patient's mailing residence address at the time services were rendered along with phone numbers; if a rural address, include route and box number.

> **NOTE:** An APO/FPO address should not be used for a patient's mailing address unless that person resides overseas. Be sure to include both daytime and evening telephone numbers so the claims processor can contact the patient if necessary. ●

Block 6

Enter an X in the appropriate box to indicate patient's relationship to the sponsor.

Block 7

Enter the sponsor's mailing address. Enter SAME if the sponsor's address is the same as the patient's. If the sponsor resides overseas, enter the APO/FPO address.

Block 8

Enter an X in the appropriate box to indicate marital, employment, and/or student status.

Blocks 9 through 9d

Leave blank. Blocks 9 through 9d are completed only if the patient has supplemental or secondary insurance, discussed later in this chapter.

Blocks 10a through 10c

Enter an X in the appropriate boxes to indicate whether the patient's condition is related to employment or an auto or other accident.

NOTE: If YES is selected for any of these boxes submit DD Form 2527, *Statement of Personal Injury-Possible Third-Party Liability*, with the CMS-1500 claim. ●

Block 10d

Leave blank.

NOTE: If a DD Form 2527 is attached to the CMS-1500 claim, enter DD FORM 2527 ATTACHED in Block 10d. ●

ERIN A. HELPER, M.D.
101 Medic Dr, Anywhere US 12345
(101) 111-1234 (Office) • (101) 111-9292 (Fax)
EIN: 11-123452   **TRICARE:** 123456789
UPIN: EH8888   **BCBS:** EH1188
PIN: A09293   **BCBS GRP:** 1204-P

Encounter Form

PATIENT INFORMATION:

		INSURANCE INFORMATION:	
Name:	Public, John Q.	**Patient Number:**	16-3
Address:	10A Senate Avenue	**Place of Service:**	Inpatient Hospital
City:	Anywhere	**Primary Insurance Plan:**	Tricare Standard
State:	US	**Primary Insurance Plan ID #:**	100 23 9678
Zip Code:	12345	**Group #:**	
Telephone:	(101) 201-7891	**Primary Policyholder:**	Public, John Q.
Gender:	Male	**Policyholder Date of Birth:**	03-09-1945
Date of Birth:	03-09-1945	**Relationship to Patient:**	Self
Occupation:	Retired	**Secondary Insurance Plan:**	
Employer:		**Secondary Insurance Plan ID #:**	
		Secondary Policyholder:	

Patient Status ☒ Married   ☐ Divorced   ☐ Single   ☐ Student

DIAGNOSIS INFORMATION

Diagnosis		Code	Diagnosis		Code
1.	Mycoplasma pneumonia	483.0	5.		
2.	IDDM, uncontrolled	250.03	6.		
3.			7.		
4.			8.		

PROCEDURE INFORMATION

	Description of Procedure or Service	Date	Code	Charge
1.	Initial hospital visit, level III	01-09-YYYY	99223	150.00
2.	Subsequent hospital visit, level II	01-10-YYYY	99232	75.00
3.	Subsequent hospital visit, level II	01-11-YYYY	99232	75.00
4.	Subsequent hospital visit, level I	01-12-YYYY	99231	50.00
5.	Discharge, 30 minutes	01-13-YYYY	99238	50.00

SPECIAL NOTES: Goodmedicine Hospital, Anywhere St, Anywhere US 12345. Return visit one week.

FIGURE 16-3 John Q. Public encounter form

Blocks 11 through 11c

Leave blank.

NOTE: Blocks 11 through 11c are completed only if the patient is covered by Medicare or another insurance policy, discussed later in this chapter.

Block 11d

Enter an X in the appropriate box to indicate whether the patient is covered by another primary health care plan.

Block 12

Enter SIGNATURE ON FILE.

Block 13

Leave blank.

EXERCISE 16-1 Preparing the Insurance Plan Comparison Chart

NOTE: Complete all steps in this exercise if you have not completed Exercise 12-1 or 13-1 prior to working with this chapter. If you have already completed Exercise 12-1 and/or 13-1, refer to the Comparison Chart you used in that exercise and proceed to Step 4.

(continues)

PLEASE DO NOT STAPLE IN THIS AREA

APPROVED OMB-0938-0008

CARRIER

PICA

HEALTH INSURANCE CLAIM FORM

PICA

1. MEDICARE (Medicare #) ☐ MEDICAID (Medicaid #) ☐ CHAMPUS (Sponsor's SSN) [X] CHAMPVA (VA File #) ☐	GROUP HEALTH PLAN (SSN or I D) ☐ FECA BLK LUNG (SSN) ☐ OTHER (I D) ☐	1a. INSURED'S I.D. NUMBER (FOR PROGRAM IN ITEM 1) 100239678
2. PATIENT'S NAME (Last Name, First Name, Middle Initial) PUBLIC JOHN Q	3. PATIENT'S BIRTH DATE MM DD YY 03 09 1945 SEX M [X] F ☐	4. INSURED'S NAME (Last Name, First Name, Middle Initial) SAME
5. PATIENT'S ADDRESS (No. Street) 10A SENATE AVENUE	6. PATIENT RELATIONSHIP TO INSURED Self [X] Spouse ☐ Child ☐ Other ☐	7. INSURED'S ADDRESS (No. Street) SAME
CITY ANYWHERE STATE US	8. PATIENT STATUS Single ☐ Married [X] Other ☐	CITY STATE
ZIP CODE 12345 TELEPHONE (Include Area Code) (101) 201 7891	Employed ☐ Full-Time Student ☐ Part-Time Student ☐	ZIP CODE TELEPHONE (INCLUDE AREA CODE) ( )
9. OTHER INSURED'S NAME (Last Name, First Name, Middle Initial)	10. IS PATIENT'S CONDITION RELATED TO:	11. INSURED'S POLICY GROUP OR FECA NUMBER
a. OTHER INSURED'S POLICY OR GROUP NUMBER	a. EMPLOYMENT? (CURRENT OR PREVIOUS) ☐ YES [X] NO	a. INSURED'S DATE OF BIRTH MM DD YY SEX M ☐ F ☐
b. OTHER INSURED'S DATE OF BIRTH MM DD YY SEX M ☐ F ☐	b. AUTO ACCIDENT? ☐ YES [X] NO PLACE (State)	b. EMPLOYER'S NAME OR SCHOOL NAME
c. EMPLOYER'S NAME OR SCHOOL NAME	c. OTHER ACCIDENT? ☐ YES [X] NO	c. INSURANCE PLAN NAME OR PROGRAM NAME
d. INSURANCE PLAN NAME OR PROGRAM NAME	10d. RESERVED FOR LOCAL USE	d. IS THERE ANOTHER HEALTH BENEFIT PLAN? ☐ YES [X] NO *If yes, return to and complete item 9 a – d.*
READ BACK OF FORM BEFORE COMPLETING & SIGNING THIS FORM. 12. PATIENT'S OR AUTHORIZED PERSON'S SIGNATURE I authorize the release of any medical or other information necessary to process this claim. I also request payment of government benefits either to myself or to the party who accepts assignment below. SIGNED SIGNATURE ON FILE	DATE	13. INSURED'S OR AUTHORIZED PERSON'S SIGNATURE I authorize payment of medical benefits to the undersigned physician or supplier for services described below. SIGNED

PATIENT AND INSURED INFORMATION

FIGURE 16-4 Completed Blocks 1 through 13 for John Q. Public encounter form in Figure 16-3

OBJECTIVE: To create a useful reference that will help you master the details of completing claims for different payers.

1. Make five copies of the Insurance Plan Comparison Chart in Appendix III.

2. Enter the following titles in each column of the first row:
   Commercial
   BCBS
   TRICARE Standard
   Workers' Compensation

3. Enter the following numbers in the first column on each page of the chart:

Page 1	Blocks	1	through	9d
Page 2	Blocks	10	through	16
Page 3	Blocks	17	through	23
Page 4	Blocks	24A	through	24K
Page 5	Blocks	25	through	33

4. Review the step-by-step instructions for Blocks 1 through 13, and enter abbreviated instructions on the chart.

5. Upon completion, save the chart because it will be used for additional exercises in this and other chapters.

EXERCISE 16-2   CMS-1500 Claim Blocks 1 through 13

This exercise requires a copy of a blank CMS-1500 claim. You may either make photocopies of the form in Appendix III of the text or print copies of the blank form using the computer disk located at the back of the text. Instructions for installing the computer program and printing blank forms are located in Appendix V.

1. Obtain a copy of the CMS-1500 claim.

2. Review instructions for Blocks 1 through 13 on your comparison chart.

3. Review Figure 16-5, Mary Sue Patient encounter form.

4. Select the information needed for Blocks 1 through 13 from Figure 16-5, and enter the required information on the claim using Optical Scanning Guidelines. This may be completed by handwriting the information, using the Blank Form Mode on the disk, or enter the data using a type-writer.

5. Review Blocks 1 through 13 of the claim to be sure all required blocks are properly completed.

6. Compare your claim with the completed claim in Figure 16-12.

NOTE: This same encounter form and claim will be used for Exercise 16-4.

ERIN A. HELPER, M.D.
101 Medic Dr, Anywhere US 12345
(101) 111-1234 (Office) • (101) 111-9292 (Fax)
EIN: 11-123452   **TRICARE:** 123456789
UPIN: EH8888   **BCBS:** EH11881
PIN: A09293   **BCBS GRP:** 1204-P

Encounter Form

PATIENT INFORMATION:

Name:	Patient, Mary Sue
Address:	91 Home Street
City:	Nowhere
State:	US
Zip Code:	12367
Telephone:	(101) 201-8989
Gender:	Female
Date of Birth:	10-10-1959
Occupation:	Homemaker
Employer:	

INSURANCE INFORMATION:

Patient Number:	16-5
Place of Service:	Office
Primary Insurance Plan:	TRICARE Standard
Primary Insurance Plan ID #:	101 23 9945
Group #:	
Primary Policyholder:	James L. Patient
Policyholder Date of Birth:	08-22-1944
Relationship to Patient:	Spouse
Secondary Insurance Plan:	US Navy
Secondary Insurance Plan ID #:	Dept 07 Naval Station Nowhere US 12367
Secondary Policyholder:	

Patient Status   [X] Married   [ ] Divorced   [ ] Single   [ ] Student

DIAGNOSIS INFORMATION

Diagnosis	Code	Diagnosis	Code
1. Fracture, distal radius	813.42	5.	
2. Fell at home	E849.0	6.	
3. Fell down stairs	E880.9	7.	
4.		8.	

PROCEDURE INFORMATION

Description of Procedure or Service	Date	Code	Charge
1. Closed manipulation, distal radius	01-10-YYYY	25600	300.00
2. X-ray, wrist, 3 views	01-10-YYYY	73110-51	50.00
3. X-ray, forearm, 1 view	01-10-YYYY	73090-51	25.00
4.			
5.			

SPECIAL NOTES: Fell down stairs at home today.

FIGURE 16-5 Mary Sue Patient encounter form

Refer to Figure 16-6 for Blocks 14 through 23 of the CMS-1500 claim.

Block 14

Enter the date in MM DD YYYY (with spaces) format of current illness, injury, or pregnancy, if known.

Block 15

Enter the first date in MM DD YYYY (with spaces) format that the patient had same or similar illness/injury, if known.

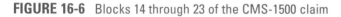

14. DATE OF CURRENT: ILLNESS (First symptom) OR	15. IF PATIENT HAS HAD SAME OR SIMILAR ILLNESS,	16. DATES PATIENT UNABLE TO WORK IN CURRENT OCCUPATION

FIGURE 16-6 Blocks 14 through 23 of the CMS-1500 claim

Block 16

Enter dates in MM DD YYYY (with spaces) format that the patient was unable to work, if known.

Block 17

Enter the name of the referring provider. If the patient was referred from a military treatment facility, enter the name of the facility.

NOTE: If the patient was referred from a Military Treatment Facility (MTF), enter the name of the MTF and attach DD Form 2161 *(Referral for Civilian Medical Care)* or SF 513 *(Print Referral).* ●

Block 17a

Enter the referring physician's EIN or SSN.

Block 18

Enter the admission and discharge dates in MM DD YYYY (with spaces) format if any procedure/service is rendered to a patient with inpatient status.

If the patient is still hospitalized when the claim is submitted, leave the TO box blank.

Block 19

Leave blank.

Block 20

Enter an X in the NO box if all laboratory procedures reported on this claim were performed in the provider's office.

Enter an X in the YES box if laboratory procedures reported on the claim were performed by an outside laboratory and billed to the health care provider. Enter the total amount charged for all tests performed by the outside laboratory. The charge for each test should be entered as a separate line in Block 24D and the name and address of the outside laboratory entered in Block 32.

Block 21

Enter up to four ICD-9-CM codes in priority order. Do not enter the decimal point.

Block 22

Leave blank.

Block 23

Enter prior authorization (or preauthorization) number. Attach a copy of any preauthorization required (e.g., heart-lung transplant authorization).

Refer to Figure 16-7 for completed Blocks 14 through 23 for the encounter form in Figure 16-3.

FIGURE 16-7   Completed Blocks 14 through 23 for John Q. Public encounter form in Figure 16-3

EXERCISE 16-3 | **Continuation of Exercise 16-1**

Review the instructions for completing Blocks 14 through 23. As you review each block, enter a concise description of the instructions in the appropriate block in the TRICARE column of the Comparison Chart.

EXERCISE 16-4 | **Continuation of Exercise 16-2**

1. Review the Mary Sue Patient encounter form in Figure 16-5 to locate diagnostic and treatment data.

2. Select the information needed for Blocks 14 through 23, and enter the required information on a new claim using Optical Scanning Guidelines. This may be completed using the disk, or handwriting, or typing the data.

3. Review Blocks 14 through 23 of the claim to be sure all required blocks are properly completed.

4. Compare your claim with the completed claim in Figure 16-12.

   NOTE: This same claim will be used for Exercise 16-5. ●

Refer to Figure 16-8 for Block 24 of the CMS-1500 claim.

Block 24A

Enter the date with in MMDDYYYY (no spaces) format for the procedure performed in the FROM column. Do not complete the TO column for a single procedure entry.
    To list procedures with the same codes and charges performed on consecutive days, enter the last day the procedure was performed in the TO column. Also, enter the number of consecutive days or units in Block 24G.

24.	A							B	C	D		E	F	G	H	I	J	K
	\multicolumn{6}{c}{DATE(S) OF SERVICE}						Place of Service	Type of Service	\multicolumn{2}{c}{PROCEDURES, SERVICES, OR SUPPLIES (Explain Unusual Circumstances)}		DIAGNOSIS CODE	$ CHARGES	DAYS OR UNITS	EPSDT Family Plan	EMG	COB	RESERVED FOR LOCAL USE
	\multicolumn{3}{c}{From}	\multicolumn{3}{c}{To}						CPT/HCPCS	MODIFIER							
	MM	DD	YY	MM	DD	YY													
1																		
2																		
3																		
4																		
5																		
6																		

FIGURE 16-8 Block 24 of the CMS-1500 claim

Block 24B

Enter the appropriate Place-of-Service code from the list in Appendix II.

Block 24C

Enter the appropriate Type of Service code from the list in Appendix II.

Block 24D

Enter the five-digit CPT code or HCPCS level II code and any required CPT or HCPCS modifiers for the procedure reported in this block. *Enter a blank space, not a hyphen, to separate the code number from the modifier or multiple modifiers.*

Block 24E

Enter the *diagnosis reference number* (1 through 4) for the ICD code number reported in Block 21 that justifies the medical necessity for each procedure reported in Block 24D.

NOTE: Some carriers will accept more than one reference number on each line. If more than one reference number is used, the first number stated must represent the primary diagnosis that justifies the medical necessity for performing the procedures on that line. Unless otherwise directed by the carrier, multiple reference numbers should be separated by a blank space, not commas or dashes. ●

Block 24F

Enter the fee charged for procedures/services reported in Block 24D.

If identical, consecutive procedures are reported on this line, enter the total fee charged for combined procedures.

Block 24G

Enter the number of units/days for services reported in 24D. (Review the discussion on units in Chapter 11, if necessary.)

Block 24H

Leave blank.

Block 24I

Enter an X in this block to indicate services were provided in a hospital emergency department.

Block 24J

Leave blank.

Block 24K

Leave blank if all services on this claim are performed by one provider.

Multiple providers from group practice: Enter the provider's name and specialty in Blocks 24H through 24K.

Refer to Figure 16-9 for completed Block 24 for the John Q. Public encounter form in Figure 16-3.

24. A DATE(S) OF SERVICE						B Place of Service	C Type of Service	D PROCEDURES, SERVICES, OR SUPPLIES (Explain Unusual Circumstances)		E DIAGNOSIS CODE	F $ CHARGES		G DAYS OR UNITS	H EPSDT Family Plan	I EMG	J COB	K RESERVED FOR LOCAL USE
MM	From DD	YY	MM	To DD	YY			CPT/HCPCS	MODIFIER								
1	0109YYYY					21	1	99223		1 2	150	00	1				
2	0110YYYY		0111YYYY			21	1	99232		1 2	150	00	2				
3	0112YYYY					21	1	99231		1 2	50	00	1				
4	0113YYYY					21	1	99238		1 2	50	00	1				
5																	
6																	

FIGURE 16-9 Completed Block 24 for John Q. Public encounter form in Figure 16-3

EXERCISE 16-5 | **Continuation of Exercise 16-3**

Review the instructions for completing Blocks 24A through 24K. As you review each block, enter a concise description of the instructions in the appropriate block in the TRICARE column of the Comparison Chart.

Refer to Figure 16-10 for Blocks 25 through 33 of the CMS-1500 claim.

Block 25

Enter the billing entity's Employer Tax Identification Number (EIN), if available. Otherwise, enter the provider's Social Security Number. In addition, be sure to enter an X in the appropriate box to indicate which is reported.

Block 26

Enter the patient's account number.

Block 27

Enter an X in the appropriate box. The nonPAR provider may elect to accept assignment on a case-by-case basis.

Block 28

Total all charges on this claim and enter in this block. This figure should never reflect negative charges or show a credit is due the patient.

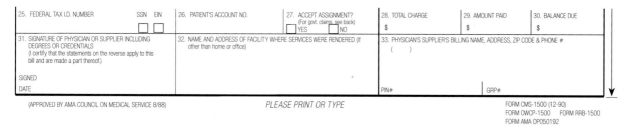

FIGURE 16-10 Blocks 25 through 33 of the CMS-1500 claim

If multiple claims for one patient are generated by the computer because more than six services were reported, be sure the total charge recorded on each claim accurately represents the total of the items indicated on each separate claim submitted.

Block 29

Enter the amount received from **other health insurance (OHI)**; attach the other insurance EOB. Do not include payment from patient or beneficiary.

Block 30

Enter the balance due.

Block 31

TRICARE requires the provider/supplier to personally sign and date the claim unless special arrangements have been made with the carrier.

Block 32

Enter information in this block when the services reported on the claim were performed at a site other than the provider's office or the patient's home.

If the YES box in Block 20 contains an X, enter the name and address of the laboratory that performed the laboratory procedures.

Block 33

Enter the billing entity's name, mailing address, and phone number. Enter the TRICARE provider identification number (PIN).

Refer to Figure 16-11 for completed CMS-1500 claim based on the encounter form in Figure 16-3.

EXERCISE 16-6 **Continuation of Exercise 16-2**

1. Review the Mary Sue Patient encounter form found in Figure 16-5.
2. Select the information needed for Blocks 24 through 33 and enter the required information on a new claim using Optical Scanning Guidelines. This may be completed using the Blank Form Mode on the disk, or by handwriting or typing the data.
3. Review Blocks 24 through 33 of the claim to be sure all required blocks are properly completed.
4. Compare your claim with the completed claim in Figure 16-12.

FIGURE 16-11 Completed John Q. Public CMS-1500 claim

FIGURE 16-12 Completed Mary Sue Patient CMS-1500 claim

PRIMARY TRICARE WITH A SUPPLEMENTAL POLICY

The following modifications must be made to the TRICARE primary claim when the health care provider is a TRICARE participating provider and the patient has a supplemental policy in addition to TRICARE.

Block 9

Enter the complete name of the insured (last name, first name, middle initial) if different from that in Block 2.

Block 9a

Enter the policy and/or group number of other insured's policy.

Block 9b

Enter the other insured's date of birth in MM DD YYYY (with spaces) format, and enter an X in the appropriate box for gender.

Block 9c

Enter the name of the patient's employer or school.

Block 9d

Enter the name of the insurance plan of the patient's other insurance coverage. On an attached sheet, provide a complete mailing address for the insurance plan or program.

Block 10d

Enter the word ATTACHMENT.

Block 11c

Enter the name of the supplemental insurance plan.

TRICARE AS SECONDARY PAYER

Block 11

Enter the beneficiary's policy, group, or FECA number if the patient has other insurance that is primary to TRICARE. If the patient is covered by Medicare, enter MEDICARE in this block after the number.

Block 11a

If different from information in Block 3, enter the insured's date of birth in MM DD YYYY (with spaces) format, and enter an X in the appropriate box to indicate gender.

Block 11b

Enter the name of the patient's employer or school, if applicable.

Block 11c

Enter the name of the insurance plan.

⬤ **NOTE:** For patients covered by a health maintenance organization (HMO), attach a copy of the HMO brochure showing that services submitted on this claim are not covered by the HMO. TRICARE will be able to process the claim more quickly if provided with this information. ⬤

Block 11d

Enter an X in the YES or NO box to indicate if there is, or is not, another primary insurance or health plan (e.g., patient may be covered by spouse's health plan).

⬤ **NOTE:** Blocks 9a through 9d are also completed to report additional insurance coverage. For example, the patient may have primary insurance coverage through an employer, insurance coverage through the spouse's employer, and TRICARE Standard coverage. TRICARE Standard pays last in this situation because the spouse's insurance is considered primary to TRICARE Standard. ⬤

Block 29

Enter only direct payments from other insurances, not from the patient.

⬤ **NOTE:** All secondary claims must be accompanied by the primary EOB, worksheet, or denial. Add the name of the policyholder to the EOB if is not included on the form. ⬤

EXERCISE 16-7 **Completion of TRICARE Secondary CMS-1500 Claim**

1. Obtain a blank claim.

2. Refer to Figure 16-13, the John R. Neely encounter form.

3. Complete the TRICARE secondary claim for this case.

4. Review the completed claim to be sure all required blocks are properly completed. Refer to Figure 16-14.

Additional TRICARE case studies are found in Appendix I and II of this text and in the Workbook.

ERIN A. HELPER, M.D.
101 Medic Dr, Anywhere US 12345
(101) 111-1234 (Office) • (101) 111-9292 (Fax)
EIN: 11-123452   **TRICARE:** 123456789
UPIN: EH8888   **BCBS:** EH11881

Encounter Form

PATIENT INFORMATION:

Name:	John R. Neely
Address:	1 Military Drive
City:	Nowhere
State:	US
Zip Code:	12345
Telephone:	(101) 111-9941
Gender:	M
Date of Birth:	10-25-1945
Occupation:	Retired Navy Captain
Employer:	
Spouse's Employer:	

INSURANCE INFORMATION:

Patient Number:	16-13
Place of Service:	Office
Primary Insurance Plan:	Blue Cross Blue Shield
Primary Insurance Plan ID #:	WXY7031
Group #:	AS101
Primary Policyholder:	Janet B. Neely
Policyholder Date of Birth:	09-09-1945
Relationship to Patient:	Spouse
Secondary Insurance Plan:	TRICARE Standard
Secondary Insurance Plan ID #:	0010670198
Secondary Policyholder:	John R. Neely

Patient Status   ☒ Married   ☐ Divorced   ☐ Single   ☐ Student

---

DIAGNOSIS INFORMATION

	Diagnosis	Code		Diagnosis	Code
1.	Abnormal ECG	794.31	5.		
2.	Coronary Artery Disease	414.00	6.		
3.	Family History, Heart Disease	V17.4	7.		
4.			8.		

PROCEDURE INFORMATION

	Description of Procedure or Service	Date	Code	Charge
1.	Established patient office visit, level III	03-10-YYYY	99213	75.00
2.	ECG, 12-lead with interpretation and report	03-10-YYYY	93000	60s.00
3.				
4.				
5.				

SPECIAL NOTES: Schedule stress test for tomorrow.

FIGURE 16-13 John R. Neely encounter form

SUMMARY

- TRICARE is a regionally managed health care program for active duty and retired military members and qualified family members, as well as eligible survivors of deceased uniformed services members.
- CHAMPUS is the former name of TRICARE and was created in 1966 as a benefit for dependents of personnel serving in the uniformed services.
- TRICARE regions are managed by Lead Agent staff, responsible for the military health system in their region. *Lead Agents* serve as a federal health care team to support the mission of the *Military Health Services System (MHSS),* which is the entire health care system of the U.S. uniformed services.

PLEASE
DO NOT
STAPLE
IN THIS
AREA

(SAMPLE ONLY - NOT APPROVED FOR USE)

CARRIER

| | PICA

HEALTH INSURANCE CLAIM FORM   PICA | |

1. MEDICARE   MEDICAID   CHAMPUS   CHAMPVA   GROUP HEALTH PLAN   FECA BLK LUNG   OTHER
(Medicare #)   (Medicaid #)   [X] (Sponsor's SSN)   (VA File #)   (SSN or ID)   (SSN)   (ID)

1a. INSURED'S I.D. NUMBER   (FOR PROGRAM IN ITEM 1)
0010670198

2. PATIENT'S NAME (Last Name, First Name, Middle Initial)
NEELY JOHN R

3. PATIENT'S BIRTH DATE   SEX
MM DD YY
10 25 1945 M [X] F [ ]

4. INSURED'S NAME (Last Name, First Name, Middle Initial)
NEELY JANET B

5. PATIENT'S ADDRESS (No. Street)
1 MILITARY DRIVE

6. PATIENT RELATIONSHIP TO INSURED
Self [ ] Spouse [X] Child [ ] Other [ ]

7. INSURED'S ADDRESS (No. Street)

CITY
ANYWHERE

STATE
US

8. PATIENT STATUS
Single [ ] Married [X] Other [ ]

Employed [ ] Full-Time Student [ ] Part-Time Student [ ]

CITY

STATE

ZIP CODE
12345

TELEPHONE (Include Area Code)
(101) 111 9941

ZIP CODE

TELEPHONE (INCLUDE AREA CODE)
(   )

9. OTHER INSURED'S NAME (Last Name, First Name, Middle Initial)

10. IS PATIENT'S CONDITION RELATED TO:

11. INSURED'S POLICY GROUP OR FECA NUMBER
WXY7031 AS101

a. OTHER INSURED'S POLICY OR GROUP NUMBER

a. EMPLOYMENT? (CURRENT OR PREVIOUS)
YES [ ] [X] NO

a. INSURED'S DATE OF BIRTH   SEX
MM DD YY
09 09 1945   M [ ] F [X]

b. OTHER INSURED'S DATE OF BIRTH   SEX
MM DD YY   M [ ] F [ ]

b. AUTO ACCIDENT?   PLACE (State)
YES [ ] [X] NO

b. EMPLOYER'S NAME OR SCHOOL NAME

c. EMPLOYER'S NAME OR SCHOOL NAME

c. OTHER ACCIDENT?
YES [ ] [X] NO

c. INSURANCE PLAN NAME OR PROGRAM NAME
BLUE CROSS BLUE SHIELD

d. INSURANCE PLAN NAME OR PROGRAM NAME

10d. RESERVED FOR LOCAL USE

d. IS THERE ANOTHER HEALTH BENEFIT PLAN?
YES [ ] [X] NO   If yes, return to and complete item 9 a – d.

READ BACK OF FORM BEFORE COMPLETING & SIGNING THIS FORM.
12. PATIENT'S OR AUTHORIZED PERSON'S SIGNATURE I authorize the release of any medical or other information necessary to process this claim. I also request payment of government benefits either to myself or to the party who accepts assignment below.

SIGNED   SIGNATURE ON FILE   DATE

13. INSURED'S OR AUTHORIZED PERSON'S SIGNATURE I authorize payment of medical benefits to the undersigned physician or supplier for services described below.

SIGNED

PATIENT AND INSURED INFORMATION

14. DATE OF CURRENT: ILLNESS (First symptom) OR   INJURY (Accident) OR   PREGNANCY (LMP)
MM DD YY

15. IF PATIENT HAS HAD SAME OR SIMILAR ILLNESS, GIVE FIRST DATE   MM DD YY

16. DATES PATIENT UNABLE TO WORK IN CURRENT OCCUPATION
MM DD YY   MM DD YY
FROM   TO

17. NAME OF REFERRING PHYSICIAN OR OTHER SOURCE

17a. I.D. NUMBER OF REFERRING PHYSICIAN

18. HOSPITALIZATION DATES RELATED TO CURRENT SERVICES
MM DD YY   MM DD YY
FROM   TO

19. RESERVED FOR LOCAL USE

20. OUTSIDE LAB? $ CHARGES
YES [ ] [X] NO

21. DIAGNOSIS OR NATURE OF ILLNESS OR INJURY. (RELATE ITEMS 1, 2, 3, OR 4 TO ITEM 24E BY LINE)
1. 794 31
2. 414 00
3. V17 4
4.

22. MEDICAID RESUBMISSION
CODE   ORIGINAL REF. NO.

23. PRIOR AUTHORIZATION NUMBER

24. A DATE(S) OF SERVICE						B Place of Service	C Type of Service	D PROCEDURES, SERVICES, OR SUPPLIES (Explain Unusual Circumstances) CPT/HCPCS MODIFIER		E DIAGNOSIS CODE	F $ CHARGES		G DAYS OR UNITS	H EPSDT Family Plan	I EMG	J COB	K RESERVED FOR LOCAL USE
From MM DD YY			To MM DD YY														
03 10 YYYY						11	1	99213		1 2 3	75 00		1				
03 10 YYYY						11	9	93000		1	60 00		1				

25. FEDERAL TAX I.D. NUMBER   SSN EIN
11-123452   [ ] [X]

26. PATIENT'S ACCOUNT NO.
16-3S

27. ACCEPT ASSIGNMENT? (For govt. claims, see back)
[X] YES   [ ] NO

28. TOTAL CHARGE
$ 135 00

29. AMOUNT PAID
$

30. BALANCE DUE
$ 135 00

31. SIGNATURE OF PHYSICIAN OR SUPPLIER INCLUDING DEGREES OR CREDENTIALS
(I certify that the statements on the reverse apply to this bill and are made a part thereof.)
ERIN A HELPER MD
SIGNED   DATE MMDDYYYY

32. NAME AND ADDRESS OF FACILITY WHERE SERVICES WERE RENDERED (If other than home or office)

33. PHYSICIAN'S SUPPLIER'S BILLING NAME, ADDRESS, ZIP CODE & PHONE #
(101) 111 1234
ERIN A HELPER MD
101 MEDIC DRIVE
ANYWHERE US 12345
PIN# 123456789   GRP#

PHYSICIAN OR SUPPLIER INFORMATION

(SAMPLE ONLY - NOT APPROVED FOR USE)

PLEASE PRINT OR TYPE

SAMPLE FORM 1500
SAMPLE FORM 1500 SAMPLE FORM 1500

FIGURE 16-14 Completed TRICARE secondary claim for John R. Neely encounter form in Figure 16-13

- TRICARE Management Activity (TMA) (formerly OCHAMPUS) coordinates and administers the TRICARE program.
- TRICARE options include TRICARE Prime, TRICARE Extra, and TRICARE Standard. All active military duty personnel are enrolled in TRICARE Prime.
- CHAMPVA is a health care benefits program for dependents of veterans who have been rated by Veterans Affairs (VA) as having a total and permanent disability, survivors of veterans who died from VA-rated service-connected conditions, and survivors of veterans who died in the line of duty and not from misconduct.
- TRICARE programs include TRICARE For Life (Medicare Eligibles), TRICARE Dental Program, TRICARE Retiree Dental Program, and TRICARE Pharmacy Plan.
- TRICARE demonstration projects include Department of Defense (DoD) Cancer Treatment Clinical Trials and other demonstrations implemented in various TRICARE regions.
- TRICARE beneficiaries who have *other health insurance (OHI)* that is primary to TRICARE must submit documentation (e.g., EOB) when filing TRICARE claims.
- TRICARE is the secondary payer to civilian insurance plans, workers' compensation, liability insurance plans, and employer-sponsored HMO plans.
- TRICARE is the primary payer to Medicaid and TRICARE supplemental plans.
- When completing TRICARE CMS-1500 claims for case studies in this text and the Workbook, the following special instructions apply:
  - Blocks 9 through 9d—Complete if TRICARE beneficiary has a supplemental plan; otherwise, leave blank
  - Blocks 11 through 11c—Complete if TRICARE beneficiary has a health plan that is primary to TRICARE; otherwise, leave blank
  - Block 14—Leave blank
  - Block 15—Leave blank
  - Block 16—Leave blank
  - Block 18—Enter dates for inpatient care only
  - Block 20—Enter an X in the NO box
  - Block 23—Leave blank
  - Block 24E—Enter one or more diagnosis reference number(s) from Block 21, as appropriate (separate numbers with a space)
  - Blocks 24H through Block 24K—Leave blank
  - Block 25—Enter the EIN with a hyphen
  - Block 26—Enter the case study number (e.g., 16-5). If the patient has TRICARE as secondary coverage, enter an S (for secondary) next to the number (on the secondary claim)
  - Block 27—Enter an X in the YES box
  - Block 31—Enter provider's complete name with credentials (instead of a signature as indicated in the chapter instructions). This will allow you to completely generate claims using the UHI software (instead of having to print the claim and sign it)
  - Block 32—If Block 18 contains dates, enter the name, address of the responsible provider (e.g., hospital)
  - When completing secondary claims, enter EOB ATTACHED in the top margin of the CMS-1500 (to simulate the attachment of a primary payer's EOB with a claim submitted to a secondary payer)

STUDY CHECKLIST

☐ Read the textbook chapter, and prepare the Insurance Plan Comparison Chart.

☐ Install the UHI software from the disk (instructions are in Appendix V), and become familiar with the software.

☐ Complete CMS-1500 claims for each chapter encounter form.

☐ Complete the chapter review.

☐ Complete the chapter CD-ROM activities.

☐ Complete Web Tutor assignments, and take online quizzes.

☐ Complete TRICARE claims for cases located in Appendices I and II.

☐ Complete the Workbook chapter, verifying answers with your instructor.

☐ Form a study group with classmates to discuss chapter concepts in preparation for an exam.

REVIEW

TRUE/FALSE

Indicate whether the definition is true or false.

1. ☐ T ☐ F CHAMPUS: Civilian Health and Medical Program for the Uniformed Services. This program covers medical care for the members of the Armed Services when they need health care in the civilian community.

2. ☐ T ☐ F OCHAMPUS: Administrative headquarters of the TRICARE program and the fiscal agent responsible for processing claims.

3. ☐ T ☐ F Uniformed services: Army, Navy, Air Force, Marines, and Coast Guard only.

4. ☐ T ☐ F Armed forces: Army, Navy, Marines, Coast Guard, Air Force, and NOAA.

5. ☐ T ☐ F TRICARE sponsor: Uniformed service personnel, either active duty, retired, or deceased.

6. ☐ T ☐ F Catchment area: An area defined by postal zip codes that fits roughly within a 40-mile radius of a government treatment facility.

7. ☐ T ☐ F Nonavailability statement: A form authorizing dependent medical care by the nearest military or public health treatment facility when the needed care is not available in the catchment area.

8. ☐ T ☐ F Active duty personnel: Service personnel on current assignment with one of the Armed Forces.

9. ☐ T ☐ F Fiscal year: January 1 through December 31 of a given year.

10. ☐ T ☐ F BSR: Basic Services Representative.

SHORT ANSWER

Briefly respond to the following:

11. State the TRICARE Standard outpatient deductibles for the following categories:
    a. Retired person   b. Dependent child   c. Spouse of active duty sponsor

12. State the inpatient deductible for the following categories:
    a. Spouse of a retired person   c. Dependent child of a retired sponsor
    b. Dependent child of an active duty sponsor   d. Active duty personnel

13. Explain how a health care provider can check on the TRICARE eligibility of a military dependent.

14. State the requirements for filing a treatment report for mental health cases.

15. Explain the circumstances that require a Nonavailability Statement before claims will be processed for services rendered in the civilian community.

16. Explain why the government established the TRICARE program.

KEY TERMS

adjudication

arbitration

Energy Employees Occupational
   Illness Compensation Program

Federal Black Lung Program

Federal Employment Liability Act
   (FELA)

First Report of Injury

Longshore and Harbor Workers'
   Compensation Program

Material Safety Data Sheets
   (MSDS)

Medical treatment

Merchant Marine Act (Jones Act)

Mine Safety and Health Administration

(MSHA)

Occupational Safety and Health
   Administration (OSHA)

Office of Workers' Compensation
   Programs (OWCP)

on-the-job injury

permanent disability

State Insurance Fund (or State
   Compensation Fund)

survivor benefits

temporary disability

vocational rehabilitation

Workers' Compensation Board
   (Commission)

Chapter 17 Workers' Compensation

OBJECTIVES

Upon successful completion of this chapter, you should be able to:

1. Define key terms.

2. List the categories of workers covered by the federal compensation program.

3. List and describe the types of workers' compensation available at the state level.

4. List and describe the classifications of workers' compensation cases as stipulated by federal law.

5. Select proper terminology to describe employee's " diminished capacity."

6. Identify final destinations for the required copies of the *First Report of Injury* form.

7. Describe correct billing procedures for workers' compensation cases.

8. Explain the necessity for separating treatment data for work-related injuries and illnesses from those not related to the patient's employment.

9. List the forms necessary to properly file compensation claims.

10. File *First Report of Injury* reports and claims accurately.

INTRODUCTION

Federal and state laws require workers' compensation coverage to meet minimum standards, covering a majority of employees for work-related illnesses and injuries (as long as the employee was not negligent in performing assigned duties). Employees receive health care and monetary awards (if applicable), and dependents of workers killed on-the-job receive benefits. Workers' compensation laws also protect employers and fellow workers by limiting the award an injured employee can recover from an employer and by eliminating the liability of coworkers in most accidents. Federal workers' compensation statutes (laws) apply to federal employees or workers employed in a significant aspect of interstate commerce. Individual state workers' compensation laws provide for comprehensive programs and are applicable to most employers. For example, California laws (1) limit the liability of employer and fellow employees for work-related illness and injuries, (2) require employers to obtain workers' compensation coverage for potential claims, and (3) establish a state fund to pay claims when employers have illegally failed to obtain coverage.

● **NOTE:** *Workers' compensation* is sometimes mistakenly referred to by its previous name, *workmans' compensation.* The name change occurred years ago to reflect an increase in the number of women in the workforce. ●

FEDERAL WORKERS' COMPENSATION PROGRAMS

The U.S. Department of Labor's (DOL) **Office of Workers' Compensation Programs (OWCP)** administers programs that provide wage replacement benefits, medical treatment, vocational rehabilitation, and other benefits to federal workers (or eligible dependents) who are injured at work or acquire an occupational disease. The four programs include:

- Energy Employees Occupational Illness Compensation Program.
- Federal Black Lung Program.
- Federal Employees' Compensation Act (FECA) Program.
- Longshore and Harbor Workers' Compensation Program.

The Department of Labor also manages the following programs designed to prevent work-related injuries and illnesses:

- Mine Safety and Health Administration (MSHA).
- Occupational Safety and Health Administration (OSHA).

Other federal programs include:

- Federal Employment Liability Act (FELA).
- Merchant Marine Act (Jones Act).

Energy Employees Occupational Illness Compensation Program

Effective July 31, 2001, the **Energy Employees Occupational Illness Compensation Program** started providing benefits to eligible employees and former employees of the Department of Energy, its contractors and subcontractors or to certain survivors of such individuals, and to certain beneficiaries of the Radiation Exposure Compensation Act. The Department of Labor's Office of Workers' Compensation Programs is responsible for adjudicating and administering claims filed by employees or former employees or certain qualified survivors.

Federal Black Lung Program

The **Federal Black Lung Program** was enacted in 1969 as part of the *Black Lung Benefits Act* and provides medical treatment and other benefits for respiratory conditions related to former employment in the nation's coal mines. The *Division of Coal Mine Workers' Compensation* administers and processes claims filed by coal miners (and their surviving dependents) who are or were employed in or around

U.S. coal mines. Monthly benefit checks are sent to coal miners (or their eligible surviving dependents) who are totally disabled by *pneumoconiosis* (black lung disease) arising from their employment in or around the nation's coal mines.

Federal Employees' Compensation Act (FECA) Program

Enacted in 1908, the *Federal Employees' Compensation Act (FECA)* is administered by the *Office of Workers' Compensation Programs (OWCP)* and provides workers' compensation coverage to all federal and postal workers throughout the world for employment-related injuries and occupational diseases. Benefits include wage replacement, payment for medical care, and where necessary, medical and vocational rehabilitation assistance in returning to work. The OWCP's *Division of Federal Employees' Compensation (DFEC)* processes new claims for benefits and manages ongoing cases, pays medical expenses and compensation benefits to injured workers and survivors, and helps injured employees return to work when they are medically able to do so.

NOTE: Federal agencies reimburse FECA for workers' compensation expenses through an annual *budget chargeback process,* which transfers funds from a responsible federal agency's budget (e.g., U.S. Postal Service) to the DFEC. ●

Longshore and Harbor Workers' Compensation Program

The **Longshore and Harbor Workers' Compensation Program**, administered by the U.S. Department of Labor, provides medical benefits, compensation for lost wages, and rehabilitation services to longshoremen, harbor workers, and other maritime workers who are injured during the course of employment or suffer from diseases caused or worsened by conditions of employment. The Program also covers private-industry workers who are engaged in the extraction of natural resources from the outer continental shelf, employees on American defense bases, and those working under contract with the U.S. government for defense or public-works projects outside the continental United States.

NOTE: The program is also responsible for over $2 billion in negotiable securities, cash, and bonds maintained for the payment of benefits in the event that an employer or insurance carrier goes out of business. ●

Mine Safety and Health Administration (MSHA)

The U.S. Labor Department's **Mine Safety and Health Administration (MSHA)** helps to reduce deaths, injuries, and illnesses in U.S. mines through a variety of activities and programs. MSHA develops and enforces safety and health rules that apply to all U.S. mines, helps mine operators who have special compliance problems, and makes available technical, educational, and other types of assistance. MSHA works cooperatively with industry, labor, and other federal and state agencies toward improving safety and health conditions for all miners. MSHA's responsibilities are delineated in the *Federal Mine Safety and Health Act of 1977.*

NOTE: U.S. federal mine safety laws were first enacted in 1911 and have since become increasingly stronger, culminating in the 1977 law. ●

INTERNET LINK

Visit http://www.msha.gov for more information.

Occupational Safety and Health Administration (OSHA)

The *Occupational Safety and Health Act of 1970* created the **Occupational Safety and Health Administration (OSHA)** to protect employees against injuries from occupational hazards in the workplace. OSHA and its state partners (of approximately 2,100 inspectors) establish protective standards, enforce those standards, and reach out to employers and employees by providing technical assistance and consultation programs. OSHA has special significance for those employed in health care because employers are required to obtain and retain manufacturers' **Material Safety Data Sheets (MSDS)**, which contain information about chemical and hazardous substances used on site. Training employees in the safe handling of these substances is also required.

Health care workers who might come into contact with human blood and infectious materials must be provided specific training in their handling (including use of Standard Precautions) to avoid contamination. Health care workers who might be exposed to infectious materials must be offered hepatitis B vaccinations.

NOTE: Comprehensive records of all vaccinations administered and any accidental exposure incidences (e.g., needle sticks) must be retained for 20 years.

Federal Employment Liability Act (FELA)

The **Federal Employment Liability Act (FELA)** is not a workers' compensation statute, but it provides railroad employees with protection from employer negligence, and makes railroads engaged in interstate commerce liable for injuries to employees if the railroad was negligent.

Merchant Marine Act (Jones Act)

The **Merchant Marine Act** (or **Jones Act**) is also not a workers' compensation statute, but it provides seamen with the same protection from employer negligence as FELA provides railroad workers.

INTERNET LINK

Visit http://www.osha.gov and http://www.dol.gov/dol/topic/workcomp/index.htm for additional information federal workers' compensation programs.

STATE WORKERS' COMPENSATION PROGRAM

Workers' compensation insurance provides weekly cash payments and reimburses health care costs for covered employees who develop a work-related illness or sustain an injury while on the job. It also provides payments to qualified dependents of a worker who dies from a compensable illness or injury. Each state establishes a **Workers' Compensation Board** or **Commission**, which is a state agency responsible for administering workers' compensation laws and handling appeals for denied claims or cases in which a worker feels compensation was too low.

State workers' compensation legislation resulted in the following types of coverage:

- **State Insurance** (or **Compensation**) **Fund**: a quasi-public agency that provides workers' compensation insurance coverage to private and public employers and acts as an agent in state workers' compensation cases involving state employees.

  ● NOTE: The *State Insurance Fund* must offer workers' compensation insurance to any employer requesting it, thereby making the Fund an *insurer of last resort* for employers otherwise unable to obtain coverage. ●

- *Self-insurance plans:* employers with sufficient capital to qualify can self-insure, which means they are required to set aside a state-mandated percentage of capital funds to cover medical expenses, wage compensation, and other benefits (e.g., death benefit to an employee's dependents) payable to employees who develop on-the-job illnesses and/or incur injuries.

- *Commercial workers' compensation insurance:* employers are permitted to purchase policies from commercial insurance companies that meet state mandates for workers' compensation coverage.

- *Combination programs:* employers in some states are allowed to choose a combination of any of the above to comply with workers' compensation coverage requirements (e.g., companies with a majority of employees who are at high risk for injury participate in the State Insurance Fund but may purchase commercial insurance coverage for office workers).

ELIGIBILITY FOR COVERAGE

To qualify for workers' compensation benefits, the employee is either injured while working within the scope of the job description, injured while performing a service required by the employer, or succumbs to a disorder that can be directly linked to employment, such as asbestosis or mercury poisoning. In some states, coverage has been awarded for stress-related disorders to workers in occupations that include emergency services personnel, air traffic controllers, and persons involved in hostage situations at work.

The worker does not have to be physically on company property to qualify for workers' compensation. An **on-the-job injury** would include, for example, a medical assistant who is injured while picking up reports for the office at the local hospital or a worker who is making a trip to the bank to deposit checks. These both qualify as job-related assignments. An employee sent to a workshop in another state who falls during the workshop would also be eligible for compensation, but not if they were injured while sightseeing.

● NOTE: In a workers' compensation case, no one party is determined to be at fault, and the amount a claimant receives is not decreased by proof of carelessness (nor increased by proof of employer's fault). A worker will lose the right to workers' compensation coverage if injury results solely from intoxication from drugs or alcohol or from the intent to injure him/herself or someone else. ●

CLASSIFICATION OF WORKERS' COMPENSATION CASES

The injured employee's health care provider determines the extent of disability, and cash benefits are directly related to established disability classifications. Federal law mandates the following classification of workers' compensation cases:

- Medical treatment
- Temporary disability
- Permanent disability
- Vocational rehabilitation
- Survivor benefits

NOTE: The term *disability* associated with the following classifications does not refer to *disability insurance* (or *benefits*), which are temporary cash benefits paid to an eligible wage earner when he/she is disabled by an off-the-job injury or illness. This concept was discussed in Chapter 2.

Medical Treatment

Medical treatment claims are the easiest to process because they are filed for minor illness or injuries that are treated by a health care provider, and result in the employee continuing to work or returning to work within a few days.

Temporary Disability

Temporary disability claims cover health care treatment for illness and injuries, as well as payment for lost wages. They are further subclassified as:

- *Temporary total disability* in which the employee's wage-earning capacity is totally lost, but only on a temporary basis.
- *Temporary partial disability* in which the employee's wage-earning capacity is partially lost, but only on a temporary basis.

Permanent Disability

Permanent disability refers to an ill or injured employee's diminished capacity to return to work. In this case, a provider has determined that although the employee's illness or injury has stabilized, the employee has been permanently impaired. The employee is therefore unable to return to the position held prior to the illness or injury. Subclassifications include:

- *Permanent total disability* in which the employee's wage-earning capacity is permanently and totally lost. (There is no limit on the number of weeks payable and an employee may continue to engage in business or employment if his/her wages, combined with the weekly benefit, do not exceed the maximums established by law.)
- *Permanent partial disability* in which part of the employee's wage-earning capacity has been permanently lost. Benefits are payable as long as the partial disability exists, except in the following circumstances:
  - *Schedule loss of use* in which the employee has a loss of eyesight, hearing, or a part of the body or its use. Compensation is limited to a certain number of weeks, according to a schedule set by law.
  - *Disfigurement* in which serious and permanent disfigurement to the face, head, or neck may entitle the employee to compensation (up to a maximum benefit, depending upon the date of the accident).

Vocational Rehabilitation

Vocational rehabilitation claims cover expenses for vocational retraining for both temporary and permanent disability cases. Retraining allows an ill or injured employee to return to the work force, although the employee may be incapable of resuming the position held prior to the illness or injury.

Survivor Benefits

Survivor benefits claims provide death benefits to eligible dependents, which are calculated according to the employee's earning capacity at the time of illness or injury.

SPECIAL HANDLING OF WORKERS' COMPENSATION CASES

Providers are required to accept the workers' compensation–allowable fee as payment in full for covered services rendered on cases involving on-the-job illnesses and injuries. An adjustment to the patient's account must be made if the amount charged for the treatment is greater than the approved reimbursement for the treatment.

State Compensation Boards/Commissions and insurance carriers are entitled by law to review only history and treatment data pertaining to a patient's on-the-job injury.

NOTE: Providers who treat established patients for work-related disorders should create a compensation file (separate from the established medical record). Caution must be used to ensure that treatment data, progress notes, diagnostic test reports, and other pertinent chart entries pertaining to non-work-related disorders or injuries are not combined with notes and reports covering work-related disorders. ●

EXAMPLE: Patient A has been treated for diabetes by his doctor for the past 2 years. The patient was then treated by the same doctor for a broken ankle after falling at his place of employment. The patient was told to return in 5 days for a recheck. Three days after the original treatment for the broken ankle, the patient was seen in the office for "strep throat." The doctor also checks on the ankle. The treatment for the throat condition should be reported in the patient's medical record; the progress report on the broken ankle will be recorded in the workers' compensation record. ●

Out-of-State Treatment

Billing regulations vary from state to state. Contact the workers' compensation Board/Commission in the state where the injury occurred for billing instructions if an injured worker presents for treatment of a work-related injury that occurred in another state.

INTERNET LINK

State workers' compensation Web sites can be found at
http://www.dol.gov/esa/regs/compliance/owcp/wc.htm

WORKERS' COMPENSATION AND MANAGED CARE

Both employees and employers have benefited from incorporating managed care into workers' compensation programs, thereby improving the quality of medical benefits and services provided. For employers, managed care protects human resources and reduces workers' compensation costs. For employees, the benefits include:

- more comprehensive coverage because states continue to eliminate exemptions under current law (e.g., small businesses and temporary workers).

- expanded health care coverage if the injury or illness is work-related and the treatment/service is reasonable and necessary.
- provision of appropriate medical treatment to facilitate healing and promote prompt return-to-work (as lack of treatment can result in increased permanent disability, greater wage replacement benefits, and higher total claim costs).
- internal grievance and dispute resolution procedures involving the care and treatment provided by the workers' compensation program along with an appeals process to the state workers' compensation agency.
- coordination of medical treatment and services with other services designed to get workers back to work (research by the Florida Division of workers' compensation suggests that managed care may reduce the time it takes an injured worker to return to work).
- no out-of-pocket costs for coverage or provision of medical services and treatment, and cost/time limits do not apply when an injury or illness occurs.

FIRST REPORT OF INJURY

First Report of Injury forms should be completed when the patient first seeks treatment for a work-related illness or injury (Figure 17-1). This report must be completed in quadruplicate with one copy distributed to each of the following parties.

- State Workers' Compensation Board/Commission
- Employer-designated compensation carrier
- Ill or injured party's employer
- Patient's work-related injury chart

NOTE: There is no patient signature line on this form. The law says that when a patient requests treatment for a work-related injury or disorder the patient has given consent for the filing of compensation claims and reports. The required state forms may be obtained from the state Compensation Board/Commission. Necessary forms for filing federal forms may be obtained from the personnel office where the employee works or from the workers' compensation Federal District Office listed under the United States Government listings in the phone book.

The time limit for filing this form varies from 24 hours to 14 calendar days, depending on state requirements. It is best to make a habit of completing the form immediately, thus ensuring that the form is filed on time and not overlooked.

The *First Report of Injury* form requires some information that is not automatically furnished by a patient. When the patient tells you this was a work-related injury, it will be necessary to obtain the following information:

- name and address of present employer
- name of immediate supervisor
- date and time of the accident or onset of the disease
- site where injury occurred
- patient's description of the onset of the disorder; if the patient is claiming injury due to exposure to hazardous chemicals or compounds, these should be included in the patient's description of the problem.

In addition, the patient's employer must be contacted to obtain the name and mailing address of the compensation carrier. Ask for a faxed confirmation from the employer of the worker with the on-the-job injury. If the employer disputes the

INSTRUCTIONS

1. Type answers to ALL questions and file original with the Workers' Compensation Commission within 72 hours after first treatment.

2. DO NOT FAIL to forward to the Workers' Compensation Commission PROGRESS REPORTS and FINAL REPORT upon discharge of patient.

WORKERS' COMPENSATION COMMISSION
6 NORTH LIBERTY STREET, BALTIMORE, MD 21201-3785
SURGEON'S REPORT

This is   First Report ☐   Progress Report ☐   Final Report ☐

DO NOT WRITE IN THIS SPACE

WCC CLAIM #

EMPLOYER'S REPORT Yes ☐   No ☐

1. Name of Injured Person:	Soc. Sec. No. / D.O.B. / Sex M ☐ F ☐

2. Address: (No. and Street)   (City or Town)   (State)   (Zip Code)

3. Name and Address of Employer:

4. Date of Accident or Onset of Disease: Hour: A.M. ☐   P.M. ☐   5. Date Disability Began:

6. Patient's Description of Accident or Cause of Disease:

7. Medical Description of Injury or Disease:

8. Will Injury result in:

(a) Permanent defect? Yes ☐ No ☐   If so, what?   (b) Disfigurement? Yes ☐ No ☐

9. Causes, other than injury, contributing to patient's condition:

10. Is patient suffering from any disease of the heart, lungs, brain, kidneys, blood, vascular system or any other disabling condition not due to this accident? Give particulars.

11. Is there any history or evidence present of previous accident or disease? Give particulars.

12. Has normal recovery been delayed for any reason? Give particulars.

13. Date of first treatment: Who engaged your services?

14. Describe treatment given by you:

15. Were X-rays taken? By whom? — (Name and Address)   Date:
Yes ☐   No ☐

16. X-ray Diagnosis:

17. Was patient treated by anyone else? By whom? — (Name and Address)   Date:
Yes ☐   No ☐

18. Was patient hospitalized? Name and Address of Hospital   Date of Admission: Date of Discharge:
Yes ☐   No ☐

19. Is further treatment needed? For how long?   20. Patient was ☐ will be ☐ able resume regular work on:
Yes ☐   No ☐   Patient was ☐ will be ☐ able resume light work on:

21. If death ensued give date: 22. Remarks: (Give any information of value not included above.)

23. I am a qualified specialist in: I am a duly licensed Physician in the State of: I graduated from Medical School: (Name)   Year:

Date of this report: (Signed)

(This report must be signed PERSONALLY by Physician.)

Address: Phone:

EVERY QUESTION MUST BE ANSWERED AND FORM SIGNED

FIGURE 17-1 *First Report of Injury* form (Courtesy of Maryland Workers' Compensation Commission)

legitimacy of the claim, you should still file the *First Report of Injury*. The employer must also file an injury report with the Compensation Commission/Board.

Completing the *First Report of Injury* Form

NOTE: The *physician* is responsible for completing this form. •

Item 1

Enter the employee's full name as shown on personnel files (last, first, middle). Enter the employee's social security number and date of birth (MMDDYYYY). Indicate the employee's gender by entering an X in the appropriate box.

Item 2

Enter the employee's complete home address. This is very important as workers' compensation disability payments, when due, will be mailed to this address. An incorrect address will delay their receipt.

Item 3

Enter the complete name and address of the employer.

Item 4

Enter the date (MMDDYYYY) on which the accident or onset of disease occurred. Enter the time of the day at which the accident or onset of disease occurred, and check the appropriate box to indicate A.M. or P.M.

NOTE: The date of the claimed accident must be specific. For example, if an employee was lifting heavy boxes on Tuesday (11/6) and called in sick on Thursday (11/8) because of a sore back, the date that is entered in Item 4 is 11/6. •

Item 5

Enter the last date the employee worked after having the accident. If no time was lost from work, enter STILL WORKING.

Item 6

Enter the employee's, word-for-word description of the accident. A complete description of the accident is required. Attach an additional page if space provided on the *First Report of Injury* is insufficient.

Item 7

Enter the description of the injury or disease. Explain the physical injuries or disease (e.g.,laceration, fracture, or contusion). Enter the anatomic part(s) of the body that required medical attention. Be specific, and indicate the location of the injured part when necessary (e.g., left middle finger, right thumb, or left shoulder). Enter the location and address where the accident occurred.

Items 8 through 12

Enter as appropriate.

Item 13

Enter the date (MMDDYYYY) the patient initially received services and/or treatment.

Items 14 through 19

Enter as appropriate.

Item 20

Enter an X in the appropriate box.

Item 21

If the employee died as a result of the injury sustained, enter the date of death (MMDDYYYY). Notify the appropriate state agency immediately upon the work-related death of an employee.

Item 22

Enter additional information of value that was not previously documented on the form.

Item 23

Enter the physician's specialty (e.g., internal medicine), the state in which the physician is licensed, the name of the medical school from which the physician graduated, along with the year of graduation (YYYY).

Be sure the physician dates (MMDDYYYY) and signs the report. Enter the physician's office address and telephone number.

PROGRESS REPORTS

A detailed narrative progress/supplemental report (Figure 17-2) should be filed to document any significant change in the worker's medical or disability status. This report should include the following information:

- patient's name and compensation file/case number
- treatment and progress report
- work status at the present time
- statement of further treatment needed
- estimate of the future status with regard to work or permanent loss or disability
- copies of substantiating X-ray, laboratory, or consultation reports

The physician should personally sign the original and all photocopies of these reports. No patient signature is required for the release of any report to the compensation carrier or Commission/Board. These reports should be generated in duplicate because:

- one copy is sent to the compensation carrier.
- one copy is retained in the patient's file.

The physician is required to answer all requests for further information sent from the compensation carrier or the Commission/Board. Acknowledgment of receipt of a claim will be made by the carrier or the Commission/Board. This acknowledgment will contain the file or case number assigned to the claim. This file/claim number should be written on all further correspondence forwarded to the employer, the carrier, the Commission/Board, and, of course, on all billings sent to the carrier.

| Employee Name (First, Middle, Last) | | | | Workers' Compensation # _____ |

Employee Name (First, Middle, Last)

Name of Employer:

Workers' Compensation # _____

Social Security Number: _____

Date of Injury: _____

Disability Date: _____

Type of Report ☐ Initial ☐ Supplement ☐ Final ☐ Reopened

Treatment Now Being Administered:

Diagnosis:

Patient is under my care.	☐ Yes ☐ No	If no, care was transferred to: _____
Patient is totally disabled.	☐ Yes ☐ No	**Patient is partially disabled.** ☐ Yes ☐ No
Patient is working.	☐ Yes ☐ No	**Date patient returned to work:** _____
Patient may be able to return to work.	☐ Yes ☐ No	**Date patient may be able to return to work:** _____

Work Limitations:

☐ None: _____

☐ Cannot Work: _____

☐ Light Work: _____

☐ Weightlifting limit: _____

Present Condition:

☐ Improved: _____

☐ Unchanged: _____

☐ Worsening: _____

Anticipated Date of Maximum Medical Improvement or Discharge:

☐ Weeks: _____

☐ Months: _____

☐ Specific Date: _____

☐ Undetermined: _____

Signature of Provider: _____   **EIN:** _____

FIGURE 17-2 Sample workers' compensation narrative progress (supplemental) report

APPEALS AND ADJUDICATION

When a workers' compensation claim is denied, the employee (or eligible dependents) can appeal the denial to the state Workers' Compensation Board (or Commission) and undergo a process called **adjudication**, a judicial dispute resolution process in which an appeals board makes a final determination. All applications for appeal should include supporting medical documentation of the claim when there is a dispute about medical issues. During the appeal process, involved parties will undergo a *deposition*, a legal proceeding during which a party answers questions under oath (but not in open court). If the appeal is successful, the Board (Commission) will notify the health care provider to submit a claim to the employer's compensation carrier and refund payments made by the patient to cover medical expenses for the on-the-job illness or injury.

⬤ **NOTE:** Adjudication is different from **arbitration**, which is a dispute resolution process in which a final determination is made by an impartial person who may not have judicial powers. ●

FRAUD AND ABUSE

Workers' compensation fraud occurs when individuals knowingly obtain benefits for which they are not eligible (e.g., provider who submits a false claim for workers' compensation coverage of patient treatment). *Workers' compensation abuse* occurs when the workers' compensation system is used in a way that is contrary to its intended purpose or to the law; fraud is a form of abuse. Penalties include fines and imprisonment, and most states offer a toll-free hotline to report fraud and abuse. Categories of fraud include:

- *Employer fraud:* committed by an employer who misrepresents payroll amounts or employee classification or who attempts to avoid higher insurance risk by transferring employees to a new business entity that is rated a lower risk category.
- *Employee fraud:* committed when an employee lies or provides a false statement, intentionally fails to report income from work, or willfully misrepresents a physical condition to obtain benefits from the state compensation fund.
- *Provider fraud:* committed by health care providers and attorneys who inflate their bills for services or bill for treatment of nonwork-related illnesses and/or injuries.

INTERNET LINK

State workers' compensation Web sites can be found at
http://www.dol.gov/esa/regs/compliance/owcp/wc.htm

BILLING INFORMATION NOTES

The following is a summary of the general nationwide billing information for workers' compensation claims. Local requirements will vary by state. Be sure to follow all the regulations established by your state commission.

Eligibility

For-profit company/corporation or state employees with a work-related injury are eligible for workers' compensation benefits. Coal miners, longshoremen, harbor workers, and all federal employees except those in the uniformed services with a work-related injury are eligible for federal compensation plans.

Fiscal Agent

State Plans

Any one of the following can be designated the fiscal agent by state law and the corporation involved.

1. State Insurance or Compensation Fund (Do not confuse this with the states' Compensation Board or Commission.)

2. A private, commercial insurance carrier

3. The employer's special company capital funds set aside for compensation cases

Federal Plans

Information may be obtained from the human resources officer at the agency where the patient is employed.

Underwriter

The federal or state government is the plan's underwriter, depending on the case.

Forms Used

The forms used include:
- *First Report of Injury* form.
- CMS-1500 claim.

Filing Deadline

The filing deadline for the first injury report is determined by state law. The deadline for filing of the claim for services performed will vary from carrier to carrier.

Deductible

There is no deductible for workers' compensation claims.

Copayment

There is no copayment for workers' compensation cases.

Premium

The employer pays all premiums.

Approved Fee Basis

The State Compensation Board or Commission establishes a schedule of approved fees. Many states use a Relative Value Study (RVS) unit value scale. Contact the State Commission/Board for information.

Accept Assignment

All providers must accept the compensation payment as payment in full.

Special Handling

Contact the employer immediately when an injured worker presents for the first visit without a written or personal referral from the employer. Contact the Workers' Compensation Board/Commission of the state where the work-related injury occurred if treatment is sought in another state.

No patient signature is needed on the *First Report of Injury, Progress Report,* or billing forms. If an established patient seeks treatment of a work-related injury, a separate compensation chart and ledger/account must be established for the patient.

The *First Report of Injury* requires a statement from the patient describing the circumstances and events surrounding the injury. Progress Reports should be filed when there is any significant change in the patient's condition and when the patient is discharged. Prior authorization may be necessary for nonemergency treatment.

Private Payer Mistakenly Billed

When a patient fails to inform a provider that an illness or injury is work-related, the patient's primary payer is billed for services or procedures rendered. If the patient subsequently requests that the workers' compensation carrier be billed instead, the claim will probably be denied. The patient must then initiate the appeal process (and the provider will be responsible for submitting appropriate documentation to support the workers' compensation claim). Any reimbursement paid by the primary payer must be returned.

WORKERS' COMPENSATION CLAIM INSTRUCTIONS—PATIENT AND POLICY IDENTIFICATION

Refer to Figure 17-3 for Blocks 1 through 13 of CMS-1500 claim.

Block 1

Enter an X in the FECA box for all work-related illness or injury claims.

NOTE: FECA refers to the Federal Employee Compensation Act.

Block 1a

First claim: Enter the patient's social security number.

Subsequent claims: Enter the workers' compensation assigned claim number if it is known. Otherwise, enter the patient's social security number.

Block 2

Enter the complete name (last name first, followed by the first name and middle initial). Use of nicknames or typographic errors will cause rejection of the claim.

Block 3

Enter the patient's name, birth date, (MM DD YYYY, with spaces format), and enter an X in the appropriate box to indicate gender.

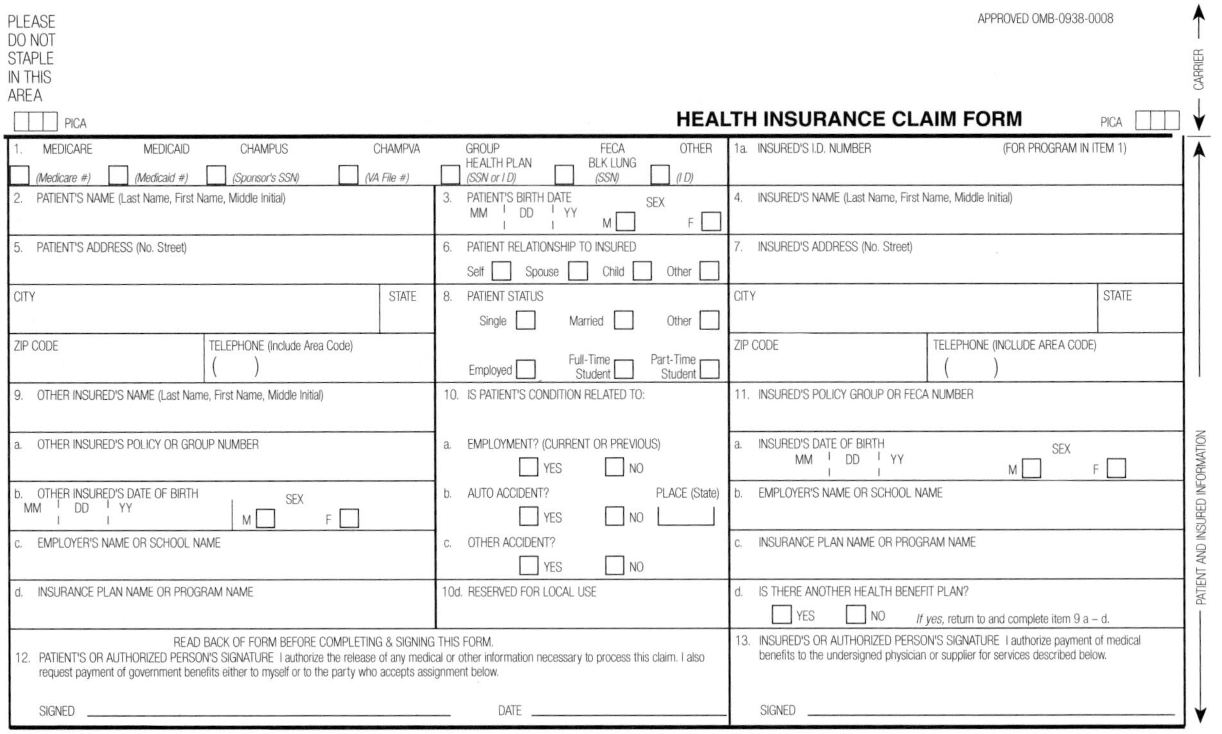

FIGURE 17-3 Blocks 1 through 13 of the CMS-1500 claim

Block 4

Enter the employer's name, if known.

Block 5

Enter patient's home address and phone number.

Block 6

Enter an X in the OTHER box.

Block 7

Enter address and telephone number of employer, if known.

Block 8

Enter an X in the EMPLOYED box.

Blocks 9 through 9d

Leave blank.

Blocks 10a through 10c

Enter an X in the YES box in Block 10a. Enter an X in the appropriate boxes in 10b and 10c.

Block 10d

Leave blank.

Blocks 11 through 11a

Leave blank.

Block 11b

Enter the name of the patient's employer.

Block 11c

Enter the name of the workers' compensation carrier.

Block 11d

Leave blank.

Block 12

Leave blank. (The patient's signature and date are not required for workers' compensation claims.)

Block 13

Leave blank.

Refer to the John Q. Public encounter form in Figure 17-4 and then review the completed CMS-1500 claim in Figure 17-5 (Blocks 1 through 13).

EXERCISE 17-1 | **Completing the Comparison Chart**

⬤ **NOTE:** Complete all the steps in this exercise if you have not completed Exercise 12-1 prior to working in this chapter. If you have already completed Exercise 12-1, use the Comparison Chart from that exercise and proceed to Step 4. ⬤

OBJECTIVE: To create a useful reference sheet as an aid to mastering the details of completing claims for major insurance plans.

STEP 1 Make five copies of the Comparison Chart in Appendix III.

STEP 2 Enter the following titles in the first row of each page:

Commercial

BCBS

TRICARE Standard

Workers' Compensation

STEP 3 Enter the following numbers in the first column of each page:

Page 1	Blocks	1 through 9d
Page 2	Blocks	10 through 16
Page 3	Blocks	17 through 23
Page 4	Blocks	24A through 24K
Page 5	Blocks	25 through 33

(continues)

ERIN A. HELPER, M.D.
101 Medic Dr, Anywhere US 12345
(101) 111-1234 (Office) • (101) 111-9292 (Fax)

EIN:	11-123452	**MCD:**	12345678
UPIN:	EH8888	**BCBS:**	EH1188
PIN:	A09293	**BCBS GRP:**	1204P

Encounter Form

PATIENT INFORMATION:

Name:	Public, John Q.
Address:	10A Senate Avenue
City:	Anywhere
State:	US
Zip Code:	12345
Telephone:	(101) 201-7891
Gender:	Male
Date of Birth:	10-10-1959
Occupation:	Technician
Employer:	BIO Laboratory

INSURANCE INFORMATION:

Patient Number:	17-4
Place of Service:	Office
Primary Insurance Plan:	BCBS
Primary Insurance Plan ID #:	252 45 9568
Group #:	A123
Primary Policyholder:	Public, John Q.
Policyholder Date of Birth:	10-10-1959
Relationship to Patient:	Self
Workers' Compensation Plan:	High Risk, Inc
Workers' Compensation Plan ID #:	BL3638B

Patient Status   [X] Married   ☐ Divorced   ☐ Single   ☐ Student

DIAGNOSIS INFORMATION

Diagnosis	Code	Diagnosis	Code
1. Whiplash	847.0	5.	
2. Motor vehicle accident	E819.0	6.	
3.		7.	
4.		8.	

PROCEDURE INFORMATION

Description of Procedure or Service	Date	Code	Charge
1. Established visit office visit, level III	01-03-YYYY	99213	40.00
2.			
3.			
4.			
5.			

SPECIAL NOTES: Originally injured driving delivery car while working 12/29/YYYY. Return to work 01/04/YYYY. NOTE: Submit claim to Workers' Compensation payer.

FIGURE 17-4 John Q. Public encounter form

 **STEP   4** Enter abbreviated instructions in Blocks 1 through 13 of the workers' compensation column.

STEP   5 Save this form. It is used for additional exercises in this chapter and other chapters mentioned in Step 2.

PLEASE
DO NOT
STAPLE
IN THIS
AREA

APPROVED OMB-0938-0008

CARRIER

☐☐☐ PICA

HEALTH INSURANCE CLAIM FORM   PICA ☐☐☐

1. MEDICARE MEDICAID CHAMPUS CHAMPVA	GROUP HEALTH PLAN FECA BLK LUNG OTHER	1a. INSURED'S I.D. NUMBER (FOR PROGRAM IN ITEM 1)
☐ (Medicare #) ☐ (Medicaid #) ☐ (Sponsor's SSN) ☐ (VA File #)	(SSN or I D) ☒ (SSN) ☐ (I D)	BL3638B

2. PATIENT'S NAME (Last Name, First Name, Middle Initial)	3. PATIENT'S BIRTH DATE SEX	4. INSURED'S NAME (Last Name, First Name, Middle Initial)
PUBLIC JOHN Q	MM DD YY 10 10 1959 M ☒ F ☐	BIO LABORATORY

5. PATIENT'S ADDRESS (No. Street)	6. PATIENT RELATIONSHIP TO INSURED	7. INSURED'S ADDRESS (No. Street)
10A SENATE AVENUE	Self ☐ Spouse ☐ Child ☐ Other ☒	

CITY	STATE	8. PATIENT STATUS	CITY	STATE
ANYWHERE	US	Single ☐ Married ☐ Other ☐		

ZIP CODE	TELEPHONE (Include Area Code)		ZIP CODE	TELEPHONE (INCLUDE AREA CODE)
12345	(101) 201 7891	Employed ☒ Full-Time Student ☐ Part-Time Student ☐		( )

9. OTHER INSURED'S NAME (Last Name, First Name, Middle Initial)	10. IS PATIENT'S CONDITION RELATED TO:	11. INSURED'S POLICY GROUP OR FECA NUMBER
a. OTHER INSURED'S POLICY OR GROUP NUMBER	a. EMPLOYMENT? (CURRENT OR PREVIOUS) ☒ YES ☐ NO	a. INSURED'S DATE OF BIRTH SEX MM DD YY M ☐ F ☐
b. OTHER INSURED'S DATE OF BIRTH SEX MM DD YY M ☐ F ☐	b. AUTO ACCIDENT? PLACE (State) ☒ YES ☐ NO US	b. EMPLOYER'S NAME OR SCHOOL NAME BIO LABORATORY
c. EMPLOYER'S NAME OR SCHOOL NAME	c. OTHER ACCIDENT? ☐ YES ☒ NO	c. INSURANCE PLAN NAME OR PROGRAM NAME HIGH RISK INC
d. INSURANCE PLAN NAME OR PROGRAM NAME	10d. RESERVED FOR LOCAL USE	d. IS THERE ANOTHER HEALTH BENEFIT PLAN? ☐ YES ☐ NO If yes, return to and complete item 9 a – d.

PATIENT AND INSURED INFORMATION

READ BACK OF FORM BEFORE COMPLETING & SIGNING THIS FORM.
12. PATIENT'S OR AUTHORIZED PERSON'S SIGNATURE I authorize the release of any medical or other information necessary to process this claim. I also request payment of government benefits either to myself or to the party who accepts assignment below.

SIGNED _____ DATE _____

13. INSURED'S OR AUTHORIZED PERSON'S SIGNATURE I authorize payment of medical benefits to the undersigned physician or supplier for services described below.

SIGNED _____

FIGURE 17-5 Completed Blocks 1 through 13 for John Q. Public encounter form in Figure 17-4

EXERCISE 17-2 CMS-1500 Claim Blocks 1 through 13

This exercise requires one blank copy of a CMS-1500 claim. You may either make photocopies of the form in Appendix III or print copies of the blank form using the CD-ROM in the back of the text. (Instructions for installing the CD-ROM are printed in Appendix V.)

S T E P 1 Obtain one copy of the CMS-1500 claim.

S T E P 2 Review the instructions for Blocks 1 through 13 on your comparison chart.

S T E P 3 Review the Mary Sue Patient encounter form (Figure 17-6).

S T E P 4 Select the information needed for Blocks 1 through 13 from the encounter form and enter the required information on the claim using Optical Scanning Guidelines. This may be completed by handwriting the information, using the Blank Form Mode on the disk, or typing the data.

S T E P 5 Review Blocks 1 through 13 of the claim to be sure all required blocks are properly completed.

⬤ NOTE: This same encounter form and claim will be used for Exercise 17-4. ⬤

```
ERIN A. HELPER, M.D.                          Encounter Form
101 Medic Dr, Anywhere US 12345
(101) 111-1234 (Office) • (101) 111-9292 (Fax)
EIN:    11-123452    TRICARE:    12345678
UPIN:   EH8888       BCBS:       EH11881
PIN:    A09293       BCBS GRP:   1204-P
```

PATIENT INFORMATION:		INSURANCE INFORMATION:	
Name:	Patient, Mary Sue	Patient Number:	17-6
Address:	91 Home Street	Place of Service:	Office
City:	Nowhere	Primary Insurance Plan:	
State:	US	Primary Insurance Plan ID #:	
Zip Code:	12367	Group #:	
Telephone:	(101) 201-8989	Primary Policyholder:	
Gender:	Female	Policyholder Date of Birth:	
Date of Birth:	10-10-1959	Relationship to Patient:	
Occupation:	Clerk	Workers' Compensation Plan:	State Insurance Fund
Employer:	Al Grocery	Workers' Compensation Plan ID #:	MSP9761

Patient Status [X] Married ☐ Divorced ☐ Single ☐ Student

DIAGNOSIS INFORMATION

Diagnosis		Code	Diagnosis		Code
1.	Muscle spasms, trapezius m.	728.85	5.		
2.	Weakness, both arms	728.9	6.		
3.	Cervical osteoarthritis	721.90	7.		
4.			8.		

PROCEDURE INFORMATION

Description of Procedure or Service		Date	Code	Charge
1.	Office visit, established patient, level II	01-27-YYYY	99212	45.00
2.	Trigger point injections (upper and medial trapezius muscles)	01-27-YYYY	20552	75.00
3.				
4.				
5.				

SPECIAL NOTES: Injured at work 01-20-YYYY.

FIGURE 17-6 Mary Sue Patient encounter form

Refer to Figure 17-7 for Blocks 14 through 23 of the CMS-1500 claim.

Block 14

Enter the date the symptoms began or the on-the-job injury occurred.

Block 15

Enter the date a prior episode of the same or similar illness began, if documented in the patient's record.

FIGURE 17-7 Blocks 14 through 23 of the CMS-1500 claim

Block 16

Enter the dates the patient was unable to work, if documented in the patient's record..

Block 17

Enter the name and title of any referring health care provider, if applicable.

Block 17a

Enter the Social Security Number (SSN), with no spaces or hyphens, of the provider named in Block 17. If there is no referring provider, leave blank.

Block 18

Enter the admission date and the discharge date (MM DD YYYY) if any procedure/service is rendered to a patient with inpatient status. If the patient is still hospitalized, leave the TO box blank.

Block 19

Leave blank.

Block 20

Enter an X in the NO box if all laboratory procedures included on this claim were performed in the provider's office.

Enter an X in the YES box if laboratory procedures listed on the claim were performed by an outside laboratory and billed to the referring health care provider.

Enter the total amount charged for all tests performed by the outside laboratory. The charge for each test should be entered as a separate line in Block 24D, and the name and address of the outside laboratory is entered in Block 32.

Block 21

Enter the ICD-9-CM code number for the diagnoses or conditions treated.

NOTE: Detailed instructions for data entry in this block appear in Chapter 11.

Block 22

Leave blank.

Block 23

Enter any assigned managed care preauthorization number. Some carriers may also require that copies of any written authorization the provider received be attached to the claim.

Refer to Figure 17-8 for completed Blocks 14 through 23 for the encounter form in Figure 17-4.

14. DATE OF CURRENT:	ILLNESS (First symptom) OR	15. IF PATIENT HAS HAD SAME OR SIMILAR ILLNESS,	16. DATES PATIENT UNABLE TO WORK IN CURRENT OCCUPATION
MM DD YY	INJURY (Accident) OR	GIVE FIRST DATE MM DD YY	MM DD YY MM DD YY
12 29 YYYY	PREGNANCY (LMP)		FROM 12 29 YYYY TO 01 04 YYYY

17. NAME OF REFERRING PHYSICIAN OR OTHER SOURCE 17a. I.D. NUMBER OF REFERRING PHYSICIAN 18. HOSPITALIZATION DATES RELATED TO CURRENT SERVICES FROM MM DD YY TO MM DD YY

19. RESERVED FOR LOCAL USE 20. OUTSIDE LAB? $ CHARGES ☐ YES ☒ NO

21. DIAGNOSIS OR NATURE OF ILLNESS OR INJURY. (RELATE ITEMS 1, 2, 3, OR 4 TO ITEM 24E BY LINE) 22. MEDICAID RESUBMISSION CODE ORIGINAL REF. NO.

1. 847.0   3.

2. E819.0   4.   23. PRIOR AUTHORIZATION NUMBER

FIGURE 17-8 Completed Blocks 14 through 23 for John Q. Public encounter form in Figure 17-4

EXERCISE 17-3 | ## Continuation of Exercise 17-1

Review the instructions for completing Blocks 14 through 23. As you review each block, enter a description of the instructions in the appropriate block in the "workers' compensation" column of the Comparison Chart.

EXERCISE 17-4 | ## Continuation of Exercise 17-2

STEP 1 Review the Mary Sue Patient encounter form in Figure 17-6 to locate diagnostic and treatment data.

STEP 2 Select the information needed for Blocks 14 through 23 and enter the required information on a new claim using Optical Scanning Guidelines. This may be done using the disk, or handwriting or typing the data.

STEP 3 Review Blocks 14 through 23 of the claim to be sure all required blocks are properly completed.

STEP 4 Compare your claim with the completed claim in Figure 17-13.

● **NOTE:** The same claim will be used for Exercise 17-6. ●

Refer to Figure 17-9 for Block 24 of the CMS-1500 claim.

Block 24A

Enter the date the procedure was performed in the FROM column. Do not enter a date in the TO column for a single procedure entry unless you have special instructions to do so from a specific carrier. Use the MMDDYYYY (no spaces) date format.

FIGURE 17-9 Blocks 24A through 24K of the CMS-1500 claim

To report identical procedures and charges performed on consecutive days, indicate the last day the procedure was performed in the TO column. Also, enter the number of consecutive days or units in the DAYS OR UNITS column, Block 24G.

Block 24B

Enter the appropriate two-digit code from the list in Appendix II.

Block 24C

Enter the appropriate code from the list Appendix II.

Block 24D

Enter the appropriate five-digit CPT code or HCPCS level II code and any required CPT or HCPCS modifiers for the procedure being reported in this block. Enter a blank space, not a hyphen, to separate the code from the modifier or multiple modifiers.

Block 24E

Enter the *reference number* (1 through 4) for the ICD-9 code reported in Block 21 that justifies medical necessity for each procedure reported in Block 24D.

Block 24F

Enter the fee for the procedure charged to the patient's account. If identical, consecutive procedures are reported on this line, enter the total fee for the combined procedures.

Block 24G

Enter the number of units/days for services reported in Block 24D.

Block 24H

Leave blank.

Block 24I

Enter an X if the patient received emergency care before any required authorization was obtained.

Blocks 24J through 24K

Leave blank.

Refer to Figure 17-10 for completed Blocks 24A through 24K for the encounter form in Figure 17-4.

24. A DATE(S) OF SERVICE From			To			B Place of Service	C Type of Service	D PROCEDURES, SERVICES, OR SUPPLIES (Explain Unusual Circumstances) CPT/HCPCS MODIFIER		E DIAGNOSIS CODE	F $ CHARGES		G DAYS OR UNITS	H EPSDT Family Plan	I EMG	J COB	K RESERVED FOR LOCAL USE
MM	DD	YY	MM	DD	YY												
01	09	YYYY				21	1	99223		1 2	150	00	1				
01	10	YYYY	01	11	YYYY	21	1	99232		1 2	150	00	2				
01	12	YYYY				21	1	99231		1 2	50	00	1				
01	13	YYYY				21	1	99238		1 2	50	00	1				

FIGURE 17-10 Completed Blocks 24A through 24K for John Q. Public encounter form in Figure 17-4

EXERCISE 17-5 | ## Continuation of Exercise 17-3

Review the instructions for completing Blocks 24A through 24K. As you review each block, enter a concise description of the instructions in the appropriate block in the "workers' compensation" column of the Comparison Chart.

EXERCISE 17-6 | ## Continuation of Exercise 17-2

STEP 1 Review the procedure data on the Mary Sue Patient encounter form in Figure 17-6.

STEP 2 Select the information needed for Blocks 24A through 24K, and enter the required information on a new claim using Optical Scanning Guidelines. This may be completed by using the disk, or handwriting or typing the data.

STEP 3 Review Blocks 24A through 24K of the claim to be sure all required blocks are properly completed.

STEP 4 Compare your claim with the completed claim in Figure 17-13.

NOTE: This same claim will be used for Exercise 17-8. ●

Refer to Figure 17-11 for Blocks 25 through 33 of the CMS-1500 claim.

Block 25

Enter the billing entity's Employer Tax Identification Number, if available. Otherwise, enter the provider's Social Security Number. In addition, be sure to enter an X in the appropriate box to indicate which is being reported.

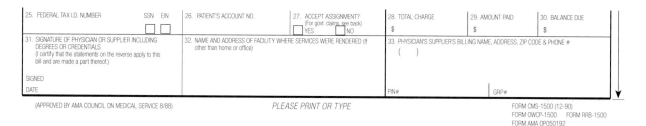

FIGURE 17-11 Blocks 25 through 33 of the CMS-1500 claim

Block 26

Enter the number assigned to the patient's account.

Block 27

Leave blank.

Block 28

Total all charges on this claim and enter in this block. This figure should never reflect negative charges or show a credit due the patient.

If multiple claims for one patient are generated by the computer because more than six services were reported, be sure the total charge recorded on each claim accurately represents the total of the items on each separate claim submitted.

Blocks 29 and 30

Leave blank.

Block 31

Paper claims: Most health care providers have arranged with major health insurance carriers to permit use of either a signature stamp or a typed name and professional credential. If these special arrangements have not been made, the provider must sign each claim.

NOTE: When arrangements are made to transmit claims electronically to an insurance company, a certification letter must be filed with the insurance company to replace the signature usually required in this space. ●

Block 32

When a date is reported in Block 18 or charges are reported in Block 20, enter the name and address of the facility that performed the procedures.

Block 33

Enter the telephone number, including area code, to the right of the phrase "& PHONE #." It may overlap into the above printing.
Enter the provider's name.

Out-of-network provider claims: Leave blank.

In-network provider claims: Enter payer-assigned PIN and/or GRP #.

Refer to Figure 17-12 for the completed Blocks 25 through 33 for the encounter form in Figure 17-4.

FIGURE 17-12 Completed John Q. Public CMS-1500 claim

EXERCISE 17-7 **Continuation of Exercise 17-5**

Review the instructions for completing Blocks 25 through 33. As you review each block, enter a concise description of the instructions in the appropriate block of the "workers' compensation" column of the Comparison Chart.

EXERCISE 17-8 **Continuation of Exercise 17-2**

S T E P **1** Review the Mary Sue Patient encounter form in Figure 17-6.

S T E P **2** Select the information needed for Blocks 25 through 33 from the encounter form and enter it on the claim.

S T E P **3** Review Blocks 25 through 33 of the claim to be sure all required blocks are properly completed.

S T E P **4** Compare your claim with the completed claim in Figure 17-13.

Additional workers' compensation case studies are found in Appendix II.

SUMMARY

- The U.S. DOL Office of Workers' Compensation Programs (OWCP) administers programs that provide wage replacement benefits, medical treatment, vocational rehabilitation, and other benefits to federal workers (or eligible dependents) who are injured at work or acquire an occupational disease.

- Federal programs include the following:
  - Energy Employees Occupational Illness Compensation Program
  - Federal Black Lung Program
  - Federal Employees' Compensation Program (FECA)
  - Longshore and Harbor Workers' Compensation Program
  - Mine Safety and Health Administration (MSHA)
  - Occupational Safety and Health Administration (OSHA)

- State programs include the following types of coverage:
  - State Insurance (or Compensation) Fund
  - Employer Self-Insured Programs
  - Private, Commercial Workers' Compensation Programs
  - Combination Programs

- To qualify for workers' compensation, employees must either be injured while working within the scope of their job description, injured while performing a service required of the employer, or succumb to an illness that can be directly linked to employment.

- Workers' compensation cases are classified as:
  - Medical claims with no disability

PLEASE
DO NOT
STAPLE
IN THIS
AREA

(SAMPLE ONLY - NOT APPROVED FOR USE)

CARRIER

| | PICA | | **HEALTH INSURANCE CLAIM FORM** | PICA | |

1. MEDICARE ☐ (Medicare #) MEDICAID ☐ (Medicaid #) CHAMPUS ☐ (Sponsor's SSN) CHAMPVA ☐ (VA File #) GROUP HEALTH PLAN [X] (SSN or ID) FECA BLK LUNG ☐ (SSN) OTHER ☐ (ID)

1a. INSURED'S I.D. NUMBER (FOR PROGRAM IN ITEM 1)
MSP9761

2. PATIENT'S NAME (Last Name, First Name, Middle Initial)
PATIENT MARY SUE

3. PATIENT'S BIRTH DATE   MM 10 | DD 10 | YY 1959   SEX M ☐ F [X]

4. INSURED'S NAME (Last Name, First Name, Middle Initial)

5. PATIENT'S ADDRESS (No. Street)
91 HOME STREET

6. PATIENT RELATIONSHIP TO INSURED
Self ☐ Spouse ☐ Child ☐ Other [X]

7. INSURED'S ADDRESS (No. Street)

CITY
NOWHERE

STATE
US

8. PATIENT STATUS
Single ☐ Married ☐ Other ☐

CITY

STATE

ZIP CODE
12367

TELEPHONE (Include Area Code)
(101) 201 8989

Employed [X] Full-Time Student ☐ Part-Time Student ☐

ZIP CODE

TELEPHONE (INCLUDE AREA CODE)
( )

9. OTHER INSURED'S NAME (Last Name, First Name, Middle Initial)

10. IS PATIENT'S CONDITION RELATED TO:

11. INSURED'S POLICY GROUP OR FECA NUMBER

a. OTHER INSURED'S POLICY OR GROUP NUMBER

a. EMPLOYMENT? (CURRENT OR PREVIOUS)
[X] YES ☐ NO

a. INSURED'S DATE OF BIRTH   MM | DD | YY   SEX M ☐ F ☐

b. OTHER INSURED'S DATE OF BIRTH   MM | DD | YY   SEX M ☐ F ☐

b. AUTO ACCIDENT?   PLACE (State)
☐ YES [X] NO

b. EMPLOYER'S NAME OR SCHOOL NAME
A1 GROCERY

c. EMPLOYER'S NAME OR SCHOOL NAME

c. OTHER ACCIDENT?
☐ YES [X] NO

c. INSURANCE PLAN NAME OR PROGRAM NAME
STATE INSURANCE FUND

d. INSURANCE PLAN NAME OR PROGRAM NAME

10d. RESERVED FOR LOCAL USE

d. IS THERE ANOTHER HEALTH BENEFIT PLAN?
☐ YES ☐ NO   If yes, return to and complete item 9 a – d.

READ BACK OF FORM BEFORE COMPLETING & SIGNING THIS FORM.
12. PATIENT'S OR AUTHORIZED PERSON'S SIGNATURE I authorize the release of any medical or other information necessary to process this claim. I also request payment of government benefits either to myself or to the party who accepts assignment below.

SIGNED _____ DATE _____

13. INSURED'S OR AUTHORIZED PERSON'S SIGNATURE I authorize payment of medical benefits to the undersigned physician or supplier for services described below.

SIGNED _____

PATIENT AND INSURED INFORMATION

14. DATE OF CURRENT: MM 01 | DD 20 | YY YYYY   ILLNESS (First symptom) OR INJURY (Accident) OR PREGNANCY (LMP)

15. IF PATIENT HAS HAD SAME OR SIMILAR ILLNESS, GIVE FIRST DATE   MM | DD | YY

16. DATES PATIENT UNABLE TO WORK IN CURRENT OCCUPATION   FROM MM | DD | YY TO MM | DD | YY

17. NAME OF REFERRING PHYSICIAN OR OTHER SOURCE

17a. I.D. NUMBER OF REFERRING PHYSICIAN

18. HOSPITALIZATION DATES RELATED TO CURRENT SERVICES   FROM MM | DD | YY TO MM | DD | YY

19. RESERVED FOR LOCAL USE

20. OUTSIDE LAB?   ☐ YES [X] NO $ CHARGES

21. DIAGNOSIS OR NATURE OF ILLNESS OR INJURY. (RELATE ITEMS 1, 2, 3, OR 4 TO ITEM 24E BY LINE)
1. 728 85
2. 728 9
3. 721 90
4.

22. MEDICAID RESUBMISSION CODE   ORIGINAL REF. NO.

23. PRIOR AUTHORIZATION NUMBER

24. A. DATE(S) OF SERVICE						B. Place of Service	C. Type of Service	D. PROCEDURES, SERVICES, OR SUPPLIES (Explain Unusual Circumstances)		E. DIAGNOSIS CODE	F. $ CHARGES		G. DAYS OR UNITS	H. EPSDT Family Plan	I. EMG	J. COB	K. RESERVED FOR LOCAL USE
From MM	DD	YY	To MM	DD	YY			CPT/HCPCS	MODIFIER								
01	27	YYYY				11	1	99212		1	45	00	1				
01	27	YYYY				11	2	20552		1	75	00	1				

25. FEDERAL TAX I.D. NUMBER   SSN ☐ EIN [X]
11-123452

26. PATIENT'S ACCOUNT NO.
17-6

27. ACCEPT ASSIGNMENT? (For govt. claims, see back)
☐ YES ☐ NO

28. TOTAL CHARGE
$ 120 00

29. AMOUNT PAID
$

30. BALANCE DUE
$

31. SIGNATURE OF PHYSICIAN OR SUPPLIER INCLUDING DEGREES OR CREDENTIALS (I certify that the statements on the reverse apply to this bill and are made a part thereof.)
ERIN A HELPER MD
SIGNED _____   DATE MMDDYYYY

32. NAME AND ADDRESS OF FACILITY WHERE SERVICES WERE RENDERED (If other than home or office)

33. PHYSICIAN'S SUPPLIER'S BILLING NAME, ADDRESS, ZIP CODE & PHONE #
(101) 111 1234
ERIN A HELPER MD
101 MEDIC DRIVE
ANYWHERE US 12345
PIN# _____   GRP# _____

PHYSICIAN OR SUPPLIER INFORMATION

(SAMPLE ONLY - NOT APPROVED FOR USE)

PLEASE PRINT OR TYPE

SAMPLE FORM 1500
SAMPLE FORM 1500 SAMPLE FORM 1500

FIGURE 17-13 Completed CMS-1500 claim for Mary Sue Patient encounter form in Figure 17-6

- Temporary disability
- Permanent disability
- Vocational rehabilitation
- Death of the worker

● Providers are required to accept workers' compensation reimbursement as payment in full. Balance billing of patients is prohibited.

● Many workers' compensation programs incorporate managed care to improve quality of medical benefits and services provided as well as to control costs.

● The *First Report of Injury* form is completed when the patient first seeks treatment for a work-related illness or injury. The report is filed in quadruplicate with a copy distributed to the:

- State workers' compensation board/commission
- Employer-designated compensation carrier
- Ill or injured party's employer
- Patient's work-related injury chart

● When employers initially deny workers' compensation claims, the employee has the right to appeal the denial.

● Detailed narrative progress/supplemental reports document significant changes in the employee's medical or disability status.

● When completing workers' compensation CMS-1500 claims for case studies in this text and the Workbook, the following special instructions apply:

- Block 1a—Review the encounter form to determine whether the patient's SSN (first claim) or workers' compensation carrier assigned number (subsequent claims) is reported.
- Block 14—Review the encounter form to locate the date of the on-the-job illness or injury.
- Block 15—Review the encounter form to locate the date of any prior episode of same or similar illness or injury.
- Block 16—Review the encounter form to locate the dates the patient was unable to work.
- Block 20—Enter an X in the NO box
- Block 23—Leave blank
- Block 24E—Enter one diagnosis reference number(s) from Block 21.
- Blocks 24H through Block 24K—Leave blank
- Block 25—Enter the EIN with a hyphen
- Block 26—Enter the case study number (e.g., 17-4).
- Block 31—Enter provider's complete name with credentials (instead of a signature as indicated in the chapter instructions). This will allow you to completely generate claims using the UHI software (instead of having to print the claim and sign it)
- Block 32—If Block 18 contains dates, enter the name and address of the responsible provider (e.g., hospital)

STUDY CHECKLIST

☐ Read the textbook chapter, and prepare the Insurance Plan Comparison Chart.

☐ Install the UHI software from the disk (instructions are in Appendix V), and become familiar with the software.

☐ Review CMS-1500 claims for each chapter encounter form, and complete them again.

☐ Complete the chapter review.

☐ Complete the chapter CD-ROM activities.

☐ Complete Web Tutor assignments, and take online quizzes.

☐ Complete workers' compensation claims for cases located in Appendices I and II.

☐ Complete the Workbook chapter, verifying answers with your instructor.

☐ Form a study group with classmates to discuss chapter concepts in preparation for an exam.

REVIEW

TRUE/FALSE

Indicate whether the definition is true or false.

1. ☐ T   ☐ F   Workers' compensation: Provision by employers to compensate their employees for medical expenses incurred from work-related injuries or illnesses.

2. ☐ T   ☐ F   State Compensation Fund: Regulates the workers' compensation program within a state.

3. ☐ T   ☐ F   State Compensation Board/Commission: A state-administered insurance program for on-the-job injury cases.

4. ☐ T   ☐ F   Temporary disability: The worker will be able to fully recover from the disorder and return to his or her regularly assigned job.

5. ☐ T   ☐ F   Permanent disability: The inability to be gainfully employed.

SHORT ANSWER

Briefly respond to the following.

6. List four types of workers' compensation programs that were created by state governments to meet mandates of the federal law.

7. Name four groups of workers covered solely by the federal workers' compensation program.

8. List the five classifications of compensation cases as stipulated by federal law.

9. Four copies must be made of the physician's *First Report of Injury* form. Explain where each copy must be sent or filed.

10. Explain why it is necessary to keep a patient's treatment and financial data covering a work-related injury separate from the patient's medical record for treatment of all other medical problems.

11. State the deadline for filing the physician's *First Report of Injury*.

12. Explain where billing for treatment of a workers' compensation case should be sent.

13. State the name of the form used for filing a claim for treatment of a workers' compensation case.

Appendix I

Case Studies: Set One

CASE STUDIES 1-1 THROUGH 1-20

The case studies in Appendix I (Table 1) provide additional practice in completing CMS-1500 claims. (Check with your instructor to determine whether you have accurately completed the claims.) Be sure to make special note of the following prior to completing claims for each case study:

- All information needed to complete the CMS-1500 claim, including diagnosis and procedure/service codes, is contained on each encounter form.

- Note that some encounter forms indicate that the patient has both primary and secondary health insurance coverage. This means that you will need to carefully review each claim to determine whether one or more CMS-1500 claim(s) are to be generated.

- Make copies of the CMS-1500 claim in Appendix III or use the CD-ROM to either print blank claims or complete claims using the software.

- Refer to the Insurance Plan Comparison Charts you created. When completing CMS-1500 claims using case studies, substitute the special instructions for the Blocks as indicated in Table 2.

NOTE: Enter EOB ATTACHED in the top margin of the CMS-1500 claim if two or more claims are generated due to the patient having primary and secondary insurance. •

NOTE: If the patient has more than one health insurance plan, refer to the special instructions at the end of the relevant chapter to properly complete the CMS-1500 claim. •

TABLE 1 List of cases according to payer for Appendix I

CASE	PAYER	CASE	PAYER
1-1	Commercial Insurance	1-11	Medicaid
1-2	Commercial Insurance	1-12	TRICARE
1-3	BCBS	1-13	TRICARE Standard
1-4	BCBS	1-14	Workers' Compensation
1-5	BCBS	1-15	Workers' Compensation
1-6	Medicare and Medigap	1-16	Commercial Insurance
1-7	Medicare and Medigap	1-17	Medicare and Medigap
1-8	BCBS and Medicare	1-18	TRICARE
1-9	Medicare/Medicaid	1-19	Commercial Insurance and TRICARE
1-10	Medicare	1-20	Workers' Compensation

TABLE 2 Special instructions for completing CMS-1500 claims in Appendix I and II (**Note:** For blocks that contain no special intructions, refer to your Insurance Plan Comparison Chart.)

BLOCK	COMMERCIAL	BCBS	MEDICARE	MEDICAID	TRICARE	WORKERS' COMP
1a	Enter payer ID #	Enter BCBS ID #	Enter Medicare ID #	Enter Medicaid ID #	Enter sponsor SSN	Enter WC carrier #
10d	Leave blank			Enter MCD and #	Leave blank	
12	Enter SIGNATURE ON FILE			Leave blank	Enter SIGNATURE ON FILE	Leave blank
13	Enter SIGNATURE ON FILE	Leave blank	Enter SIGNATURE ON FILE	Leave blank		
14	Leave blank					Enter date of on-the-job illness or injury
15	Leave blank					Enter date of prior episode of same illness or injury
16	Leave blank					Enter dates patient was unable to work
17a	Enter payer assigned PIN	Enter Medicare UPIN	Enter Medicaid PIN	Enter EIN or SSN		Enter SSN
19	Leave blank					
20	Enter an X in the NO box					
22	Leave blank					
23	Leave blank					
24C	Leave blank					Enter TOS code
24E	Enter one diagnosis reference number on each line	Enter multiple diagnosis reference numbers, if applicable	Enter one diagnosis reference number on each line			
24G	Enter 1-digit days or units (e.g., 1)	Enter 3-digit days or units (e.g., 001)	Enter 1-digit days or units (e.g., 1)			
24H-K	Leave blank					
25	Enter the EIN with the hyphen (e.g., 12-3456789)					
26	Enter the case study number (e.g., 1-1). If the patient has both primary and secondary coverage, and more than one CMS-1500 claim is generated, enter a P (for Primary) and S (for secondary) next to the case study number (e.g., 1-1P, 1-1S).					
27	Enter an X in the YES box					Leave blank
31	Enter the provider's complete name with credentials (e.g., SALLY M. JONES MD)					
32	If Block 18 contains inpatient dates or Block 20 contains an X in the YES box, enter name and address of responsible provider					
33	Leave PIN and GRP# blank	Enter payer assigned PIN and GRP#	Enter Medicare PIN; enter GRP# if assigned	Enter Medicaid PIN; leave GRP# blank	Enter TRICARE PIN	Enter payer assigned PIN; enter GRP# if assigned

CASE STUDY 1-1

Mary Sue Hightower encounter form

IRMINA M. BRILLIANT, M.D.

25 Medical Drive ■ Injury US 12347 ■ (101) 201-3145

Encounter Form

EIN:	11-765431	TRICARE PIN:	IBM7791
UPIN:	IB9821	BCBS PIN:	99531

PATIENT INFORMATION:

Name:	Mary Sue Hightower
Address:	61 Water Tower Street
City:	Anywhere
State:	US
Zip Code:	12345
Telephone:	(101) 201-6987
Gender:	Female
Date of Birth:	08-07-1951
Occupation:	Homemaker
Employer:	
Spouse's Employer:	Anywhere Water Co.

INSURANCE INFORMATION:

Patient Number:	1-1
Place of Service:	Hospital Outpatient Dept.
Primary Insurance Plan:	Aetna
Primary Insurance Plan ID #:	272034109
Group #:	NPW
Primary Policyholder:	Walter W. Hightower
Policyholder Date of Birth:	04-09-1951
Relationship to Patient:	Spouse
Secondary Insurance Plan:	
Secondary Insurance Plan ID #:	
Secondary Policyholder:	

Patient Status   ☒ Married   ☐ Divorced   ☐ Single   ☐ Student   ☐ Other

DIAGNOSIS INFORMATION

Diagnosis	Code	Diagnosis	Code
1. Coronary artery disease, graft	404.02	5.	
2.		6.	
3.		7.	
4.		8.	

PROCEDURE INFORMATION

Description of Procedure or Service	Date	Code	Charge
1. Left heart catheterization	01-10-YYYY	93510	2000.00
2. Injection for catheterization	01-10-YYYY	93540	250.00
3. Angiography, venous bypass graft	01-10-YYYY	93556	750.00
4.			
5.			

SPECIAL NOTES:
    Patient diagnosed with CAD 5 years ago (06-15-YYYY). Referring provider: I. M. Gooddoc, M.D.
    (PIN 777707070). Care rendered at Goodmedicine Hospital, Provider Street, Anywhere US 12345.
    Revisit 5 days. Admission/Discharge Date: 01-10-YYYY.

CASE STUDY 1-2

I. M. Gayle encounter form

SEJAL RAJA, M.D.

1 Medical Drive ■ Injury US 12347 ■ (101) 202-2923

EIN: 11-139799   CONN GEN PIN: SR9919

MCD: SR2995   BCBS PIN: 994321

Encounter Form

PATIENT INFORMATION:

Name:	I. M. Gayle
Address:	101 Happy Drive
City:	Anywhere
State:	US
Zip Code:	12345
Telephone:	(101) 111-9876
Gender:	Female
Date of Birth:	09-30-1945
Occupation:	Clerk
Employer:	Mail Boxes, Inc.
Spouse's Employer:	

INSURANCE INFORMATION:

Patient Number:	1-2
Place of Service:	Office
Primary Insurance Plan:	Conn General
Primary Insurance Plan ID #:	210010121
Group #:	101
Primary Policyholder:	I. M. Gayle
Policyholder Date of Birth:	09-30-1945
Relationship to Patient:	Self
Secondary Insurance Plan:	
Secondary Insurance Plan ID #:	
Secondary Policyholder:	

Patient Status   ☐ Married   ☐ Divorced   ☒ Single   ☐ Student   ☐ Other

---

DIAGNOSIS INFORMATION

Diagnosis	Code	Diagnosis	Code
1. Numbness, left arm	782.0	5.	
2. Osteoarthritis, cervical	715.98	6.	
3.		7.	
4.		8.	

PROCEDURE INFORMATION

Description of Procedure or Service	Date	Code	Charge
1. Office visit, established patient, level III	03-01-YYYY	99213	60.00
2. Trigger point injection, trapezius, left upper & mid	03-01-YYYY	20552	75.00
3.			
4.			
5.			

SPECIAL NOTES:

Patient paid $50 of today's total.

CASE STUDY 1-3
Katlyn Tiger encounter form

ARNOLD J. YOUNGLOVE, M.D.
21 Provider St ■ Injury US 12347 ■ (101) 202-7754

EIN:	11-123463	MCD PIN:	236598
UPIN:	AY9999	BCBS PIN:	991123

Encounter Form

PATIENT INFORMATION:

Name:	Katlyn Tiger
Address:	2 Jungle Road
City:	Nowhere
State:	US
Zip Code:	12346
Telephone:	(101) 111-2222
Gender:	Female
Date of Birth:	01-03-1954
Occupation:	Accountant
Employer:	John Lion, C.P.A.
Spouse's Employer:	

INSURANCE INFORMATION:

Patient Number:	1-3
Place of Service:	Inpatient Hospital
Primary Insurance Plan:	BCBS
Primary Insurance Plan ID #:	ZJW334444
Group #:	W310
Primary Policyholder:	Katlyn Tiger
Policyholder Date of Birth:	01-03-1954
Relationship to Patient:	Self
Secondary Insurance Plan:	
Secondary Insurance Plan ID #:	
Secondary Policyholder:	

Patient Status ☐ Married   ☐ Divorced   ☒ Single   ☐ Student   ☐ Other

DIAGNOSIS INFORMATION

Diagnosis	Code	Diagnosis	Code
1. Bronchopneumonia	485	5.	
2.		6.	
3.		7.	
4.		8.	

PROCEDURE INFORMATION

Description of Procedure or Service	Date	Code	Charge
1. Initial observation, comprehensive	02-28-YYYY	99220	$175.00
2. Discharge home	03-01-YYYY	99217	65.00
3.			
4.			
5.			

SPECIAL NOTES:

Care rendered at Goodmedicine Hospital, Provider Street, Anywhere US 12345.

CASE STUDY 1-4
Jeffrey A. Green encounter form

SEJAL RAJA, M.D.

1 Medical Drive ■ Injury US 12347 ■ (101) 202-2923

EIN:	11-139799	CONN GEN:	SR9919
MCD:	SR2995	BCBS PIN:	994321

Encounter Form

PATIENT INFORMATION:

Name:	Jeffrey A. Green
Address:	103 Mountain View Road
City:	Nowhere
State:	US
Zip Code:	12367
Telephone:	(101) 117-8765
Gender:	Male
Date of Birth:	02-03-1987
Occupation:	
Employer:	
Father's Employer:	Self-employed
Mother's Employer:	Goodmedicine Clinic

INSURANCE INFORMATION:

Patient Number:	1-4
Place of Service:	Office
Primary Insurance Plan:	BCBS
Primary Insurance Plan ID #:	XWV7794483
Group #:	876
Primary Policyholder:	Jeffrey G. Green
Policyholder Date of Birth:	07-01-1955
Relationship to Patient:	Father
Secondary Insurance Plan:	BCBS
Secondary Insurance Plan ID #:	XWV21928
Secondary Policyholder:	Janine Green
Relationship to Parent:	Mother
Policyholder Date of Birth	12-24-1957

Patient Status ☐ Married ☐ Divorced ☒ Single ☐ Student ☐ Other

---

DIAGNOSIS INFORMATION

Diagnosis	Code	Diagnosis	Code
1. Acute bronchitis	466.0	5.	
2. Purulent rhinitis	472.0	6.	
3.		7.	
4.		8.	

PROCEDURE INFORMATION

Description of Procedure or Service	Date	Code	Charge
1. Office visit, established patient, level II	03-10-YYYY	99212	26.00
2.			
3.			
4.			
5.			

SPECIAL NOTES:

Patient's mother paid $15 of today's total. Return visit prn.

CASE STUDY 1-5

Christine Noel encounter form

ARNOLD J. YOUNGLOVE, M.D.

21 Provider St ■ Injury US 12347 ■ (101) 202-7754

EIN: 11-123463   MCD PIN: 236598

UPIN: AY9999   BCBS PIN: 991123

Encounter Form

PATIENT INFORMATION:

Name:	Christine Noel
Address:	100 Christmas Tree Ln
City:	Anywhere
State:	US
Zip Code:	12346
Telephone:	(101) 115-8123
Gender:	Female
Date of Birth:	09-03-1977
Occupation:	Student (full-time)
Employer:	
Spouse's Employer:	Nowhere University

INSURANCE INFORMATION:

Patient Number:	1-5
Place of Service:	Office
Primary Insurance Plan:	BCBS
Primary Insurance Plan ID #:	ZJW35834
Group #:	624
Primary Policyholder:	Henry Noel
Policyholder Date of Birth:	02-21-1975
Relationship to Patient:	Spouse
Secondary Insurance Plan:	BCBS
Secondary Insurance Plan ID #:	123W476
Group #:	X23
Secondary Policyholder:	Christine Noel
Relationship to Patient:	Self

Patient Status   ☒ Married   ☐ Divorced   ☐ Single   ☒ Student   ☐ Other

DIAGNOSIS INFORMATION

Diagnosis	Code	Diagnosis	Code
1. Acute pharyngitis	462	5.	
2. Urinary frequency	788.41	6.	
3.		7.	
4.		8.	

PROCEDURE INFORMATION

Description of Procedure or Service	Date	Code	Charge
1. Office visit, established patient, level II	03-10-YYYY	99212	45.00
2. Urinalysis, dipstick and microscopy	03-10-YYYY	81000	8.00
3. Strep test (CLIA-approved office lab)	03-10-YYYY	87880	12.00
4.			
5.			

SPECIAL NOTES:

Patient paid $20 toward today's bill.

CASE STUDY 1-6

Elaine Blueberry encounter form

IRMINA M. BRILLIANT, M.D.

25 Medical Drive ■ Injury US 12347 ■ (101) 201-3145

EIN: 11-765431 TRICARE PIN: IBM7791

UPIN: IB9821 BCBS PIN: 99531

Encounter Form

PATIENT INFORMATION:

Name:	Elaine Blueberry
Address:	101 Bust St
City:	Anywhere
State:	US
Zip Code:	12345
Telephone:	(101) 555-5689
Gender:	Female
Date of Birth:	10-02-1925
Occupation:	
Employer:	
Spouse's Employer:	

INSURANCE INFORMATION:

Patient Number:	1-6
Place of Service:	Inpatient Hospital
Primary Insurance Plan:	Medicare
Primary Insurance Plan ID #:	102 62 3434B
Group #:	
Primary Policyholder:	Elaine Blueberry
Policyholder Date of Birth:	10-02-1925
Relationship to Patient:	Self
Secondary Insurance Plan:	BCBS Medigap
Secondary Insurance Plan ID #:	XWY123456
Secondary Policyholder:	Elaine Blueberry

Patient Status ☐ Married ☐ Divorced ☒ Single ☐ Student ☐ Other

---

DIAGNOSIS INFORMATION

Diagnosis	Code	Diagnosis	Code
1. Gastrointestinal bleeding	578.9	5.	
2. Perianal rash	691.0	6.	
3.		7.	
4.		8.	

PROCEDURE INFORMATION

Description of Procedure or Service	Date	Code	Charge
1. Inpatient consultation, level III	03-01-YYYY	99253	125.00
2.			
3.			
4.			
5.			

SPECIAL NOTES:

Care rendered at Goodmedicine Hospital, Provider Street, Anywhere US 12345. Admission Date: 03-01-YYYY. Discharge Date: 03-05-YYYY. Referring provider: I. M. Gooddoc, M.D. (SSN: 777707070)

CASE STUDY 1-7

Emma Berry encounter form

ARNOLD J. YOUNGLOVE, M.D.

21 Provider St ■ Injury US 12347 ■ (101) 202-7754

EIN:	11-123463	MCD PIN:	236598
UPIN:	AY9999	BCBS PIN:	991123

Encounter Form

PATIENT INFORMATION:

Name:	Emma Berry
Address:	Good Life Retirement Community, Golden Age Road
City:	Anywhere
State:	US
Zip Code:	12345
Telephone:	(101) 111-7700
Gender:	Female
Date of Birth:	03-08-1905
Occupation:	Retired
Employer:	Nowhere School District
Spouse's Employer:	

INSURANCE INFORMATION:

Patient Number:	1-7
Place of Service:	Inpatient Skilled Nursing Facility
Primary Insurance Plan:	Medicare
Primary Insurance Plan ID #:	888 44 1234A
Group #:	
Primary Policyholder:	Emma Berry
Policyholder Date of Birth:	03-08-1905
Relationship to Patient:	Self
Secondary Insurance Plan:	Aetna Medigap
Secondary Insurance Plan ID #:	995432992
Secondary Policyholder:	Emma Berry

Patient Status ☐ Married ☐ Divorced ☒ Single ☐ Student ☐ Other

---

DIAGNOSIS INFORMATION

Diagnosis	Code	Diagnosis	Code
1. Stable uncomplicated senile dementia	290.0	5.	
2. Peripheral edema	782.3	6.	
3.		7.	
4.		8.	

PROCEDURE INFORMATION

Description of Procedure or Service	Date	Code	Charge
1. SNF care, subsequent, level II	03-02-YYYY	99312	45.00
2.			
3.			
4.			
5.			

SPECIAL NOTES:

Care rendered at Good Life SNF, Golden Age Road, Anywhere US 12345. Daughter is Emma J. Peach, 1234 Beneficiary St, Faraway US 99999.

CASE STUDY 1-8

Stella Cartwheel encounter form

ANGELA DILALIO, M.D.

99 Provider Dr ■ Injury US 12347 ■ (101) 201-4321

EIN: 11-198234   TRICARE PIN: ADL1982

UPIN: AD9101   BCBS PIN: 991234

Encounter Form

PATIENT INFORMATION:

Name:	Stella Cartwheel
Address:	Red Wagon Rd
City:	Nowhere
State:	US
Zip Code:	12346
Telephone:	(101) 113-5567
Gender:	Female
Date of Birth:	01-02-1927
Occupation:	Retired
Employer:	Nowhere University
Spouse's Employer:	

INSURANCE INFORMATION:

Patient Number:	1-8
Place of Service:	Hospital Inpatient
Primary Insurance Plan:	BCBS
Primary Insurance Plan ID #:	XYZ332999009
Group #:	201
Primary Policyholder:	Fred W. Cartwheel
Policyholder Date of Birth:	01-03-1930
Relationship to Patient:	Spouse
Secondary Insurance Plan:	Medicare
Secondary Insurance Plan ID #:	332999999A
Secondary Policyholder:	Stella Cartwheel

Patient Status   ☒ Married   ☐ Divorced   ☐ Single   ☐ Student   ☐ Other

DIAGNOSIS INFORMATION

Diagnosis	Code	Diagnosis	Code
1. Uncontrolled hypertensive crisis, malignant	401.0	5.	
2. Acute vertigo	780.4	6.	
3.		7.	
4.		8.	

PROCEDURE INFORMATION

Description of Procedure or Service	Date	Code	Charge
1. Initial hospital visit, level III	03-14-YYYY	99223	165.00
2. Subsequent hospital visit, level III	03-15-YYYY	99233	60.00
3. Subsequent hospital visit, level II	03-16-YYYY & 03-17-YYYY	99232	100.00
4. Subsequent hospital visit, level I	03-18-YYYY & 03-19-YYYY	99231	80.00
5. Discharge, 30 minutes	03-20-YYYY	99238	55.00

SPECIAL NOTES:

Onset of illness 03-12-YYYY. Discharge home. Care provided at Goodmedicine Hospital, 1 Provider St, Anywhere US 12345. Hospital PIN: 1234GH.

CASE STUDY 1-9

Geraldine T. Makebetter encounter form

ARNOLD J. YOUNGLOVE, M.D.

21 Provider St ■ Injury US 12347 ■ (101) 202-7754

EIN:　11-123463　　MCD PIN:　236598

UPIN:　AY9999　　BCBS PIN:　991123

Encounter Form

PATIENT INFORMATION:

Name:	Geraldine T. Makebetter
Address:	7866A Memory Lane
City:	Injury
State:	US
Zip Code:	12346
Telephone:	(101) 111-9855
Gender:	Female
Date of Birth:	06-20-1945
Occupation:	
Employer:	
Spouse's Employer:	

INSURANCE INFORMATION:

Patient Number:	1-9
Place of Service:	Office
Primary Insurance Plan:	Medicare
Primary Insurance Plan ID #:	101278769W
Group #:	
Primary Policyholder:	Geraldine T. Makebetter
Policyholder Date of Birth:	06-20-1945
Relationship to Patient:	Self
Secondary Insurance Plan:	Medicaid
Secondary Insurance Plan ID #:	1198555W
Secondary Policyholder:	Geraldine T. Makebetter

Patient Status　☐ Married　☒ Divorced　☐ Single　☐ Student　☐ Other

---

DIAGNOSIS INFORMATION

Diagnosis	Code	Diagnosis	Code
1. Annual physical exam	V70.0	5.	
2. Bladder infection	595.9	6.	
3.		7.	
4.		8.	

PROCEDURE INFORMATION

Description of Procedure or Service	Date	Code	Charge
1. Preventive medicine, established patient	03-03-YYYY	99396	75.00
2. Established office visit, level II	03-03-YYYY	99212-25	40.00
3. Urinalysis with microscopy	03-03-YYYY	81000	8.00
4. Hemoccult	03-03-YYYY	82270	8.00
5. CBC auto	03-03-YYYY	85024	40.00
6. Health risk assessment	03-03-YYYY	99420	25.00

SPECIAL NOTES:

Hospital Info: Goodmedicine Hospital, Provider Street, Anywhere US 12345.

CASE STUDY 1-10

Gladys Phish encounter form

ANGELA DILALIO, M.D.
99 Provider Dr ■ Injury US 12347 ■ (101) 201-4321

EIN: 11-198234 TRICARE PIN: ADL1982

UPIN: AD9101 BCBS PIN: 991234

Encounter Form

PATIENT INFORMATION:

Name:	Gladys Phish
Address:	21 Windwhisper Dr
City:	Injury
State:	US
Zip Code:	12347
Telephone:	(101) 111-2397
Gender:	Female
Date of Birth:	11-21-1930
Occupation:	
Employer:	
Spouse's Employer:	

INSURANCE INFORMATION:

Patient Number:	1-10
Place of Service:	Hospital Outpatient Dept.
Primary Insurance Plan:	Medicare
Primary Insurance Plan ID #:	101891701A
Group #:	
Primary Policyholder:	Gladys Phish
Policyholder Date of Birth:	11-21-1930
Relationship to Patient:	Self
Secondary Insurance Plan:	
Secondary Insurance Plan ID #:	
Secondary Policyholder:	

Patient Status ☒ Married ☐ Divorced ☐ Single ☐ Student ☐ Other

---

DIAGNOSIS INFORMATION

Diagnosis	Code	Diagnosis	Code
1. Cellulitis, right hand	682.4	5.	
2.		6.	
3.		7.	
4.		8.	

PROCEDURE INFORMATION

Description of Procedure or Service	Date	Code	Charge
1. Incision & drainage, abscess, subcu.	03-10-YYYY	10060	450.00
2.			
3.			
4.			
5.			

SPECIAL NOTES:

Hospital Info: Goodmedicine Hospital, 1 Provider St, Anywhere US 12345.

Referring provider: I. M. Gooddoc, M.D. UPIN: IG7771. Admission/Discharge Date: 03-10-YYYY.

CASE STUDY 1-11

Fiona J. Filbert encounter form

SEJAL RAJA, M.D.

1 Medical Drive ■ Injury US 12347 ■ (101) 202-2923

EIN: 11-139799   CONN GEN PIN: SR9919

MCD: SR2995   BCBS PIN: 994321

Encounter Form

PATIENT INFORMATION:

Name:	Fiona J. Filbert
Address:	1 Butternut Street
City:	Anywhere
State:	US
Zip Code:	12345
Telephone:	(101) 791-8645
Gender:	Female
Date of Birth:	03-08-1977
Occupation:	
Employer:	
Spouse's Employer:	

INSURANCE INFORMATION:

Patient Number:	1-11
Place of Service:	Hospital Outpatient Dept.
Primary Insurance Plan:	Medicaid
Primary Insurance Plan ID #:	119850B
Group #:	
Primary Policyholder:	Fiona J. Filbert
Policyholder Date of Birth:	03-08-1977
Relationship to Patient:	Self
Secondary Insurance Plan:	
Secondary Insurance Plan ID #:	
Secondary Policyholder:	

Patient Status   ☐ Married   ☒ Divorced   ☐ Single   ☐ Student   ☐ Other

---

DIAGNOSIS INFORMATION

Diagnosis	Code	Diagnosis	Code
1. Papilloma with cystic changes, benign, left breast (3.0 x 1.5 x 0.2 cm)	217	5.	
2.		6.	
3.		7.	
4.		8.	

PROCEDURE INFORMATION

Description of Procedure or Service	Date	Code	Charge
1. Excision, mass, left breast	03-10-YYYY	19120	75.00
2.			
3.			
4.			
5.			

SPECIAL NOTES:

Hospital Info: Goodmedicine Hospital, Anywhere Street, Anywhere US 12345.

Medicaid PIN: 9H019076. Referred by Arnold J. Younglove, M.D. Medicaid PIN: 00919919.

Patient paid $10 toward today's charges. Admission/Discharge Date: 03-10-YYYY.

CASE STUDY 1-12

Gregory Willowtree encounter form

ANGELA DILALIO, M.D.
99 Provider Dr ■ Injury US 12347 ■ (101) 201-4321

EIN: 11-198234   TRICARE PIN: ADL1982
UPIN: AD9101   BCBS PIN: 991234

Encounter Form

PATIENT INFORMATION:

Name:	Gregory Willowtree
Address:	150 Tree Lane
City:	Nowhere
State:	US
Zip Code:	12347
Telephone:	(101) 555-2356
Gender:	Male
Date of Birth:	12-12-1942
Occupation:	Retired Army Captain
Employer:	
Spouse's Employer:	

INSURANCE INFORMATION:

Patient Number:	1-12
Place of Service:	Hospital Outpatient Dept.
Primary Insurance Plan:	TRICARE
Primary Insurance Plan ID #:	071269845
Group #:	
Primary Policyholder:	Gregory Willowtree
Policyholder Date of Birth:	12-12-1942
Relationship to Patient:	Self
Secondary Insurance Plan:	
Secondary Insurance Plan ID #:	
Secondary Policyholder:	

Patient Status   ☐ Married   ☐ Divorced   ☒ Single   ☐ Student   ☐ Other

---

DIAGNOSIS INFORMATION

Diagnosis	Code	Diagnosis	Code
1. Medial meniscus tear, rt knee	836.0	5.	
2. Plica, right knee	717.9	6.	
3.		7.	
4.		8.	

PROCEDURE INFORMATION

Description of Procedure or Service	Date	Code	Charge
1. Arthroscopy with medial meniscectomy	03-19-YYYY	29881	2000.00
2.			
3.			
4.			
5.			

SPECIAL NOTES:

Hospital Info: Goodmedicine Hospital, 1 Provider St, Anywhere US 12345.

Date of injury: 03-17-YYYY. Return visit in 3 days. Admission/Discharge Date: 03-19-YYYY.

CASE STUDY 1-13

Agnes Patty encounter form

IRMINA M. BRILLIANT, M.D.

25 Medical Drive ■ Injury US 12347 ■ (101) 201-3145

EIN: 11-765431   TRICARE PIN: IBM7791

UPIN: IB9821   BCBS PIN: 99531

Encounter Form

PATIENT INFORMATION:

Name:	Agnes Patty
Address:	1 Patty Cake Drive
City:	Nowhere
State:	US
Zip Code:	12367
Telephone:	(101) 112-2701
Gender:	Female
Date of Birth:	09-03-1947
Occupation:	Domestic engineer
Employer:	
Spouse's Employer:	

INSURANCE INFORMATION:

Patient Number:	1-13
Place of Service:	Office
Primary Insurance Plan:	TRICARE Standard
Primary Insurance Plan ID #:	103236666
Group #:	
Primary Policyholder:	Gerry Patty
Policyholder Date of Birth:	03-09-1940
Relationship to Patient:	Spouse
Secondary Insurance Plan:	
Secondary Insurance Plan ID #:	
Secondary Policyholder:	

Patient Status   ☒ Married   ☐ Divorced   ☐ Single   ☐ Student   ☐ Other

---

DIAGNOSIS INFORMATION

Diagnosis	Code	Diagnosis	Code
1. Cardiac arrhythmia	427.9	5.	
2. Epistaxis	784.7	6.	
3.		7.	
4.		8.	

PROCEDURE INFORMATION

Description of Procedure or Service	Date	Code	Charge
1. Office visit, new patient, level III	03-01-YYYY	99203	100.00
2. Nasal cautery	03-01-YYYY	30901	65.00
3. EKG with interpretation	03-01-YYYY	93000	50.00
4.			
5.			

SPECIAL NOTES:

First symptoms: 02-10-YYYY. Patient paid $35.00 towards today's charges. Spouse's Duty Station: USS George Bush CVN-02. Mailing Address: FPO AE 00599-2871.

CASE STUDY 1-14

Iona J. Million encounter form

ANGELA DILALIO, M.D.

99 Provider Dr ■ Injury US 12347 ■ (101) 201-4321

EIN:	11-198234	TRICARE PIN:	ADL1982
UPIN:	AD9101	BCBS PIN:	991234

Encounter Form

PATIENT INFORMATION:

Name:	Iona J. Million
Address:	100A Follish Pleasures Ct
City:	Anywhere
State:	US
Zip Code:	12345
Telephone:	(101) 759-0839
Gender:	Female
Date of Birth:	01-01-1970
Occupation:	Supervisor of Grounds
Employer:	Anywhere Golf Course
Social Security #:	235-56-8956

INSURANCE INFORMATION:

Patient Number:	1-14
Place of Service:	Hospital Outpatient Dept.
Primary Insurance Plan:	High Risk Insurance
Primary Insurance Plan ID #:	10173
Group #:	
Primary Policyholder:	Anywhere Golf Course
Policyholder Date of Birth:	
Relationship to Patient:	Employer
Secondary Insurance Plan:	
Secondary Insurance Plan ID #:	
Secondary Policyholder:	

Patient Status ☐ Married ☐ Divorced ☒ Single ☐ Student ☐ Other

---

DIAGNOSIS INFORMATION

Diagnosis	Code	Diagnosis	Code
1. Retained hardware	V54.0	5.	
2. Status post fracture surgery	V45.89	6.	
3. Pain, healed fracture site	719.47	7.	
4.	905.4	8.	

PROCEDURE INFORMATION

Description of Procedure or Service	Date	Code	Charge
1. Removal, internal fixation device, left ankle, deep	03-10-YYYY	20680	650.00
2.			
3.			
4.			
5.			

SPECIAL NOTES:

Hospital Info: Goodmedicine Hospital, 1 Provider St, Anywhere US 12345.

Date of injury: 09-08-YYYY. Patient may return to work 03-31-YYYY.

Admission/Discharge Date: 03-10-YYYY.

CASE STUDY 1-15

Mike Roe Scope encounter form

ANGELA DILALIO, M.D.

99 Provider Dr ■ Injury US 12347 ■ (101) 201-4321

EIN: 11-198234   TRICARE PIN: ADL1982

UPIN: AD9101   BCBS PIN: 991234

Encounter Form

PATIENT INFORMATION:

Name:	Mike Roe Scope
Address:	10 Laboratory Ct
City:	Nowhere
State:	US
Zip Code:	12347
Telephone:	(101) 113-5567
Gender:	Male
Date of Birth:	06-20-1972
Occupation:	Technician
Employer:	Bio Labs
Social Security #:	356-89-8459

INSURANCE INFORMATION:

Patient Number:	1-15
Place of Service:	Office
Primary Insurance Plan:	High Risk Insurance
Primary Insurance Plan ID #:	10173
Group #:	
Primary Policyholder:	Bio Labs
Policyholder Date of Birth:	
Relationship to Patient:	Employer
Secondary Insurance Plan:	
Secondary Insurance Plan ID #:	
Secondary Policyholder:	

Patient Status   ☐ Married   ☐ Divorced   ☒ Single   ☐ Student   ☐ Other

DIAGNOSIS INFORMATION

Diagnosis	Code	Diagnosis	Code
1. Cervical strain	847.0	5.	
2. Low back strain	847.2	6.	
3.		7.	
4.		8.	

PROCEDURE INFORMATION

Description of Procedure or Service	Date	Code	Charge
1. Office visit, established patient, level II	03-20-YYYY	99212	26.00
2.			
3.			
4.			
5.			

SPECIAL NOTES:

WC assigned claim number: BL3636. Onset of illness 03-12-YYYY. Discharged home.

CASE STUDY 1-16

Sandy Spencer encounter form

IRMINA M. BRILLIANT, M.D.

25 Medical Drive ■ Injury US 12347 ■ (101) 201-3145

EIN: 11-765431   TRICARE PIN: IBM7791

UPIN: IB9821   AFLAC PIN: 562659

Encounter Form

PATIENT INFORMATION:

Name:	Sandy Spencer
Address:	101 High Streeet
City:	Anywhere
State:	US
Zip Code:	12345
Telephone:	(101) 555-5698
Gender:	Female
Date of Birth:	08-05-1985
Occupation:	Manager
Employer:	Goodmedicine Medical Center
Spouse's Employer:	

INSURANCE INFORMATION:

Patient Number:	1-16
Place of Service:	Office
Primary Insurance Plan:	Aflac
Primary Insurance Plan ID #:	5623569
Group #:	
Primary Policyholder:	Sandy Spencer
Policyholder Date of Birth:	08-05-1985
Relationship to Patient:	Self
Secondary Insurance Plan:	
Secondary Insurance Plan ID #:	
Secondary Policyholder:	

Patient Status   ☐ Married   ☐ Divorced   ☒ Single   ☐ Student   ☐ Other

DIAGNOSIS INFORMATION

Diagnosis	Code	Diagnosis	Code
1. Hypertension	401.9	5.	
2.		6.	
3.		7.	
4.		8.	

PROCEDURE INFORMATION

Description of Procedure or Service	Date	Code	Charge
1. Office visit, new patient, level IV	10-15-YYYY	99214	100.00
2.			
3.			
4.			
5.			

SPECIAL NOTES:

CASE STUDY 1-17

Peter Cartright encounter form

ANGELA DILALIO, M.D.
99 Provider Dr ■ Injury US 12347 ■ (101) 201-4321

EIN:	11-198234	TRICARE PIN:	ADL1982
UPIN:	AD9101	BCBS PIN:	991234

Encounter Form

PATIENT INFORMATION:

Name:	Peter Cartright
Address:	250 Hill Street
City:	Anywhere
State:	US
Zip Code:	12345
Telephone:	(101) 555-7843
Gender:	Male
Date of Birth:	12-24-1935
Occupation:	Retired
Employer:	Anywhere Pharmacy
Spouse's Employer:	

INSURANCE INFORMATION:

Patient Number:	1-17
Place of Service:	Office
Primary Insurance Plan:	Medicare
Primary Insurance Plan ID #:	235689569A
Group #:	
Primary Policyholder:	Peter Cartright
Policyholder Date of Birth:	12-24-1935
Relationship to Patient:	Self
Secondary Insurance Plan:	Medigap
Secondary Insurance Plan ID #:	5626598
Secondary Policyholder:	Peter Cartright

Patient Status ☐ Married ☐ Divorced ☒ Single ☐ Student ☐ Other

---

DIAGNOSIS INFORMATION

Diagnosis	Code	Diagnosis	Code
1. Diabetes mellitus	250.00	5.	
2.		6.	
3.		7.	
4.		8.	

PROCEDURE INFORMATION

Description of Procedure or Service	Date	Code	Charge
1. Office visit, established patient, level II	04-15-YYYY	99212	50.00
2.			
3.			
4.			
5.			

SPECIAL NOTES:

CASE STUDY 1-18

Terry Lewis encounter form

ANGELA DILALIO, M.D.
99 Provider Dr ■ Injury US 12347 ■ (101) 201-4321

EIN: 11-198234   TRICARE PIN: ADL1982
UPIN: AD9101   BCBS PIN: 991234

Encounter Form

PATIENT INFORMATION:

Name:	Terry Lewis
Address:	9 Randolph Road
City:	Anywhere
State:	US
Zip Code:	12345
Telephone:	(101) 555-5169
Gender:	Male
Date of Birth:	05-05-1945
Occupation:	Navy Seal
Employer:	
Spouse's Employer:	

INSURANCE INFORMATION:

Patient Number:	1-18
Place of Service:	Office
Primary Insurance Plan:	TRICARE
Primary Insurance Plan ID #:	562356989
Group #:	
Primary Policyholder:	Terry Lewis
Policyholder Date of Birth:	05-05-1945
Relationship to Patient:	Self
Secondary Insurance Plan:	
Secondary Insurance Plan ID #:	
Secondary Policyholder:	

Patient Status   ☐ Married   ☐ Divorced   ☒ Single   ☐ Student   ☐ Other

---

DIAGNOSIS INFORMATION

Diagnosis	Code		Diagnosis	Code
1. Anxiety	300.00	5.		
2.		6.		
3.		7.		
4.		8.		

PROCEDURE INFORMATION

Description of Procedure or Service	Date	Code	Charge
1. Office visit, established visit, level II	06-19-YYYY	99212	35.00
2.			
3.			
4.			
5.			

SPECIAL NOTES:

CASE STUDY 1-19

Mary Parker encounter form

ANGELA DILALIO, M.D.
99 Provider Dr ■ Injury US 12347 ■ (101) 201-4321

EIN:	11-198234	TRICARE PIN:	ADL1982
UPIN:	AD9101	BCBS PIN:	991234

Encounter Form

PATIENT INFORMATION:

Name:	Mary Parker
Address:	15 Main St
City:	Anywhere
State:	US
Zip Code:	12345
Telephone:	(101) 555-5658
Gender:	Female
Date of Birth:	06-06-1975
Occupation:	Provost
Employer:	Anywhere University
Spouse's Employer:	US Navy

INSURANCE INFORMATION:

Patient Number:	1-19
Place of Service:	Office
Primary Insurance Plan:	Aetna
Primary Insurance Plan ID #:	562156
Primary Policyholder:	Mary Parker
Policyholder Date of Birth:	06-06-1975
Relationship to Patient:	Self
Secondary Insurance Plan:	TRICARE Standard
Secondary Insurance Plan ID #:	23562598
Secondary Policyholder:	Mark Parker
Secondary Policyholder Date of Birth:	04-30-1970

Patient Status ☒ Married ☐ Divorced ☐ Single ☐ Student ☐ Other

DIAGNOSIS INFORMATION

Diagnosis	Code	Diagnosis	Code
1. Asthma	493.90	5.	
2.		6.	
3.		7.	
4.		8.	

PROCEDURE INFORMATION

Description of Procedure or Service	Date	Code	Charge
1. Office visit, established visit, level II	06-19-YYYY	99212	35.00
2.			
3.			
4.			
5.			

SPECIAL NOTES:

Mark Parker is stationed on the USS Eisenhower. FPO AE 11600-3982.

CASE STUDY 1-20

Jim Gallo encounter form

ANGELA DILALIO, M.D.

99 Provider Dr ■ Injury US 12347 ■ (101) 201-4321

EIN: 11-198234	TRICARE PIN: ADL1982
UPIN: AD9101	BCBS PIN: 991234

Encounter Form

PATIENT INFORMATION:

Name:	Jim Gallo
Address:	115 Glenn St
City:	Anywhere
State:	US
Zip Code:	12345
Telephone:	(101) 555-8457
Gender:	Male
Date of Birth:	05-02-1975
Occupation:	Public Relations Director
Employer:	Anywhere University
Social Security #:	467-90-9560

INSURANCE INFORMATION:

Patient Number:	1-20
Place of Service:	Office
Primary Insurance Plan:	High Risk Insurance
Primary Insurance Plan ID #:	10173
Group #:	
Primary Policyholder:	Anywhere University
Policyholder Date of Birth:	
Relationship to Patient:	Employer
Secondary Insurance Plan:	
Secondary Insurance Plan ID #:	
Secondary Policyholder:	

Patient Status	☐ Married	☐ Divorced	☒ Single	☐ Student	☐ Other

DIAGNOSIS INFORMATION

Diagnosis	Code	Diagnosis	Code
1. Muscle spasms, back	724.8	5.	
2.		6.	
3.		7.	
4.		8.	

PROCEDURE INFORMATION

Description of Procedure or Service	Date	Code	Charge
1. Office visit, established patient, level II	02-15-YYYY	99212	35.00
2.			
3.			
4.			
5.			

SPECIAL NOTES:

Onset of illness 02-15-YYYY. Return to work 02-20-YYYY.

Case Studies: Set Two

CASE STUDIES 2-1 THROUGH 2-21

The case studies in Appendix II provide additional practice in completing CMS-1500 claims. Be sure to make special note of the following information prior to completing claims for each encounter form:

- All EIN, PIN, and GRP# information needed to complete each CMS-1500 claim is documented on each encounter form.

- The Goodmedicine Hospital address is listed on the encounter form when that information is to be reported in Block 32. If applicable, be sure to report the Medicare/Medicaid PIN as GHA123.

- All providers participate in Medicare, Medicaid, and BCBS. Be sure to complete the CMS-1500 claims for these payers appropriately. *Carefully review encounter forms to determine provider participation status for other payers.*

- Table 1 (page 586) contains place of service (POS) codes reported in Block 24B of the CMS-1500 claim.

- Table 2 (page 587) contains type of service (TOS) codes reported in Block 24C of the CMS-1500 claim. *Be sure to review step-by-step instructions in the relevant chapter to determine whether these codes are to be reported (including the format).*

- Table 3 (page 588) contains CPT E/M codes with level of service.

- Table 4 (page 589) contains the list of case studies set two according to payer.

- Be sure to carefully review the patient record to properly assign ICD-9-CM diagnosis codes and CPT and HCPCS level II (national) procedure and service codes. The encounter form contains the name of procedure or service and charge, but you still need to review the patient record to accurately assign codes. Table 3 contains a partial listing of CPT E/M subsections (or categories), subcategories, code numbers, and corresponding level. *Be sure to refer to this table when levels are referenced on encounter forms so that you assign the proper E/M code.*

- None of the patients has paid on his or her account, which means 0 00 is reported in Block 29, when required by the payer.

- Some encounter forms document primary, secondary, and even tertiary payer information, which means more than one CMS-1500 claim is to be generated. *Be sure to refer to special instructions at the end of the relevant chapter to properly complete multiple CMS-1500 claims.*

- Make copies of the CMS-1500 claim in Appendix III (page 634), or print blank claims using the Student Practice software. You can also complete CMS-1500 claims using the Student Practice software.

- Use the Insurance Plan Comparison Charts you created to complete CMS-1500 claims for each case study. *Be sure to substitute the special instructions in Table 1 (Appendix I, page 564) when completing claims for case studies.*

- Enter TRANSMITTAL NOTICE ATTACHED in the top margin of the CMS-1500 claim if two or more claims are generated due to the patient having primary and secondary insurance.

TABLE 1 Place of service codes for CMS-1500 claim, Block 24B

CODE	DESCRIPTION	CODE	DESCRIPTION
00–02	Unassigned	35–40	Unassigned
03	School	41	Ambulance—Land
04	Homeless Shelter	42	Ambulance—Air or Water
05	Indian Health Service Free-Standing Facility	43–49	Unassigned
06	Indian Health Service Provider-Based Facility	50	Federally Qualified Health Center
07	Tribal 638 Free-Standing Facility	51	Inpatient Psychiatric Facility
08	Tribal 638 Provider-Based Facility	52	Psychiatric Facility Partial Hospitalization
11	Office	53	Community Mental Health Center
12	Home	54	Intermediate Care Facility/Mentally Retarded
13–14	Unassigned	55	Residential Substance Abuse Treatment Facility
15	Mobile Unit	56	Psychiatric Residential Treatment Facility
16–19	Unassigned	57–59	Unassigned
20	Urgent Care Facility	60	Mass Immunization Center
21	Inpatient Hospital	61	Comprehensive Inpatient Rehabilitation Facility
22	Outpatient Hospital	62	Comprehensive Outpatient Rehabilitation Facility
23	Emergency Room—Hospital	63–64	Unassigned
24	Ambulatory Surgical Center	65	End-Stage Renal Disease Treatment Facility
25	Birthing Center	66–70	Unassigned
26	Military Treatment Facility	71	State or Local Public Health Clinic
27–30	Unassigned	72	Rural Health Clinic
31	Skilled Nursing Facility	73–80	Unassigned
32	Nursing Facility	81	Independent Laboratory
33	Custodial Care Facility	82–98	Unassigned
34	Hospice	99	Other Unlisted Facility

TABLE 2 Type of service codes for CMS-1500 claim, Block 24C

CODE	DESCRIPTION	CODE	DESCRIPTION
1	Medical Care	F	Ambulatory Surgery Center (ASC) (facility usage for surgical services)
2	Surgery	G	Immunosuppresive Drugs
3	Consultation	H	Hospice
4	Diagnostic Radiology	I	Purchase of DME (installment basis)
5	Diagnostic Laboratory	J	Diabetic Shoes
6	Therapeutic Radiology	K	Hearing Items and Services
7	Anesthesia	L	ESRD Supplies
8	Assistant at Surgery	M	Monthly Capitation Payment for Dialysis
9	Other Medical Items or Services	N	Kidney Donor
0	Whole Blood	P	Lump Sum Purchase of DME, Prosthetics, Orthotics
10	Unassigned	Q	Vision Items or Services
Codes 11–18 are for use on Medicaid claims only		R	Rental of DME
11	Used DME	S	Surgical Dressings or Other Medical Supplies
12	DME Purchase	T	Outpatient Mental Health Limitation
18	DME Rental	U	Occupational Therapy
A	Used Durable Medical Equipment (DME)	V	Pneumococcal/Influenza Virus Vaccine
B	High-Risk Screening Mammography	W	Physical Therapy
C	Low-Risk Screening Mammography	Y	Second Opinion on Elective Surgery
D	Ambulance	Z	Third Opinion on Elective Surgery
E	Enteral/Parenteral Nutrients/Supplies		

TABLE 3 Partial listing of CPT Evaluation & Management (E/M) codes and levels

SUBSECTION (CATEGORY)	SUBCATEGORY	CODE	LEVEL
Office or Other Outpatient Services	New Patient	99201	I
		99202	II
		99203	III
		99204	IV
		99205	V
	Established Patient	99211	I
		99212	II
		99213	III
		99214	IV
		99215	V
Hospital Inpatient Services	Initial Hospital Care	99221	I
		99222	II
		99223	III
	Subsequent Hospital Care	99231	I
		99232	II
		99233	III
Consultations	Office or Other Outpatient Consultations	99241	I
		99242	II
		99243	III
		99244	IV
		99245	V
Preventive Medicine Services	New Patient	99381	I
		99382	II
		99383	III
		99384	IV
		99385	V
		99386	VI
		99387	VII
	Established Patient	99391	I
		99392	II
		99393	III
		99394	IV
		99395	V
		99396	VI
		99397	VII
Nursing Facility Services	Comprehensive Nursing Facility Assessments	99301	I
		99302	II
		99303	III
	Subsequent Nursing Facility Care	99311	I
		99312	II
		99313	III
Home Services	New Patient	99341	I
		99342	II
		99343	III
		99344	IV
		99345	V
	Established Patient	99347	I
		99348	II
		99349	III
		99350	IV

TABLE 4 List of cases according to payer for Appendix II

CASE	PAYER	CASE	PAYER
2-1	Commercial Insurance	2-12	Medicaid
2-2	Commercial Insurance	2-13	TRICARE
2-3	Commercial Insurance	2-14	TRICARE as Secondary
2-4	BCBS	2-15	Workers' Compensation
2-5	BCBS	2-16	Workers' Compensation
2-6	Medicare/Medicaid	2-17	Commercial Insurance with TRICARE as Secondary
2-7	Medicare as Primary		
2-8	Medicare/Medigap	2-18	TRICARE
2-9	Medicare as Secondary	2-19	Medicare/Medicaid
2-10	Medicare/Medigap	2-20	BCBS with Medicare as Secondary
2-11	Medicaid	2-21	Medicare

CASE STUDY 2-1

GOODMEDICINE CLINIC

1 Provider Street ■ Anywhere US 12345 ■ (101) 111-2222

EIN: 11-123456   MCARE GRP#: J1110   BCBS GRP#: GC12340

Encounter Form

PROVIDER: HENRY C. CARDIAC, M.D.

PATIENT INFORMATION:		INSURANCE INFORMATION:	
Name:	Jose X. Raul	Patient Number:	2-1
Address:	10 Mexico Street	Place of Service:	Office
City:	Anywhere	Primary Insurance Plan:	Bell Atlantic
State:	US	Primary Insurance Plan ID #:	222304040
Zip Code:	12345	Group #:	MD1
Telephone:	(101) 111-5454	Primary Policyholder:	Self
Gender:	Male	Policyholder Date of Birth:	12-24-1957
Date of Birth:	01-01-1968	Relationship to Patient:	
Occupation:	Lineman	Secondary Insurance Plan:	
Employer:	Anywhere Telephone Co.	Secondary Insurance Plan ID #:	
Spouse's Employer:		Secondary Policyholder:	

Patient Status ☐ Married ☐ Divorced ☒ Single ☐ Student ☐ Other

DIAGNOSIS INFORMATION

Diagnosis	Code	Diagnosis	Code
1.		5.	
2.		6.	
3.		7.	
4.		8.	

PROCEDURE INFORMATION

Description of Procedure or Service	Date	Code	Charge
1. Office consultation, level II	06-20-YYYY		$ 100.00
2.			
3.			
4.			
5.			

SPECIAL NOTES:

Referring Physician is I. M. Gooddoc, M.D. (SSN 777707070).

GOODMEDICINE CLINIC

1 Provider Street ■ Anywhere US 12345 ■ (101) 111-2222

Patient Record

PROVIDER: HENRY C. CARDIAC, M.D.

OFFICE CONSULTATION   06/20/YYYY

S: Patient is adult Mexican-American single male, referred by Dr. I. M. Gooddoc for consultation. He noted umbilical mass roughly five days ago, two days after the onset of pain in this region. There is no known etiology. He had been physically active, but within the past two months he has not engaged in normal physical activity. He has erratic bowel habits with defecation 2-3-4 days and has history of having some bright red blood in the stool and on the toilet tissue. He has had no melanotic stool or narrowing of the stool. He denies episodic diarrhea. He has had bronchitis and sinus difficulties, particularly in the fall. He is a nonsmoker. He has no GU symptoms of prostatism. Health history reveals chronic nonspecific dermatitis of eyes, ears, hands and groin, and in fact, felt that bleeding in perianal region was secondary to this. He was a full-term delivery. History reveals maternal uncle had hernia similar to this. Medications include use of halogenated steroid for skin condition. HE HAS ALLERGIES IN THE FALL TO POLLEN. HE HAS SENSITIVITY TO PERCODAN OR PERCOCET, CAUSING NAUSEA, although he has taken Tylenol #3 without difficulty. He takes penicillin without difficulty. The rest of the family and social history are noncontributory. Details can be found in patient's history questionnaire.

O: Supraclavicular fossae are free from adenopathy. Chest is clear to percussion and auscultation. No cutaneous icterus is present. Abdomen is soft and nontender, without masses or organomegaly. Penis is circumcised and normal. Testicles are scrotal and normal. No hernia is palpable in the groin. At the base of the umbilicus, there is suggestion of crepitus but no true hernia at this time. Rectal examination reveals normal tone. There is some induration of perianal tissues. The prostate is 3x4 cm and normal in architecture. Hemoccult testing of the formed stool is negative for blood.

A: 1. Umbilical mass. Possible umbilical cyst, possible umbilical hernia.
     2. Rectal bleeding.

P: 1. Schedule endoscopic evaluation of lower colon.
     2. Schedule follow-up visit to evaluate progression of umbilical change.
     3. Note dictated to Dr. Gooddoc.

Henry C. Cardiac, M.D.

Henry C. Cardiac, M.D.

CASE STUDY 2-2

GOODMEDICINE CLINIC

1 Provider Street ■ Anywhere US 12345 ■ (101) 111-2222

EIN: 11-123456   MCARE GRP#: J1110   BCBS GRP#: GC12340

Encounter Form

PROVIDER: HENRY C. CARDIAC, M.D.

PATIENT INFORMATION:

Name:	Kay Moutaine
Address:	634 Goodview Avenue
City:	Anywhere
State:	US
Zip Code:	12345
Telephone:	(101) 115-1234
Gender:	Female
Date of Birth:	06-01-1955
Occupation:	Pharmacist
Employer:	Goodmedicine Pharmacy
Spouse's Employer:	General Electric

INSURANCE INFORMATION:

Patient Number:	2-2
Place of Service:	Office
Primary Insurance Plan:	Connecticut General
Primary Insurance Plan ID #:	877345567
Group #:	V143
Primary Policyholder:	Charles W. Moutaine
Policyholder Date of Birth:	03-04-1952
Relationship to Patient:	Spouse
Secondary Insurance Plan:	
Secondary Insurance Plan ID #:	
Secondary Policyholder:	

Patient Status   ☒ Married   ☐ Divorced   ☐ Single   ☐ Student   ☐ Other

---

DIAGNOSIS INFORMATION

Diagnosis	Code	Diagnosis	Code
1.		5.	
2.		6.	
3.		7.	
4.		8.	

PROCEDURE INFORMATION

Description of Procedure or Service	Date	Code	Charge
1. Office visit, level III	06-20-YYYY		$ 75.00
2.			
3.			
4.			
5.			

SPECIAL NOTES:

Schedule return visit p.r.n. Patient paid $30 on account ($45 still due).

GOODMEDICINE CLINIC

1 Provider Street ■ Anywhere US 12345 ■ (101) 111-2222

Patient Record

PROVIDER: HENRY C. CARDIAC, M.D.

OFFICE VISIT - PREVENTIVE MEDICINE   06/20/YYYY

S: This white female, who appears her stated age, is seen for the first time and will undergo routine annual physical examination. She has history of sensory seizure disorder for which she takes Tegretol. This was diagnosed on EEG in California. Tegretol has been quite efficacious in controlling her symptoms. She has sensations of "slipping away," auditory hallucinations, and déjà vu with these attacks, which last for 45 seconds. She also has history of migraines for which she takes Inderal, with no exacerbation in several years. (I discussed with her the advantages and disadvantages of discontinuing prophylaxis in light of no recurrence of migraines.) She has history of allergies and asthma for which she takes Vanceril daily and Ventolin on a p.r.n. basis. She has history of fibrocystic breast disease for which she takes Vitamin E and follows a low-caffeine diet. Recently, she was found to have heme positive stools with negative colonoscopy, BE, and sigmoidoscopy. Currently on Colace and Fiberal for hemorrhoids. No complaints today. Had Pap smear and mammogram in October.

O: NAD. HEENT: PERRL, funduscopic benign. Sinuses nontender. NECK: Supple, no nodes or masses. CHEST: Clear. HEART: RRR, without murmur. ABDOMEN: Soft, nontender. NEURO: Cranial nerves II-XII, sensory, motor, cerebellar grossly intact. Gait coordinated. LAB: Peak expiratory flow equals 510 liters/second.

A: 1. Temporal lobe epilepsy, doing well on Tegretol.
    2. Migraines, doing well on prophylaxis.
    3. Bronchial asthma, doing well.
    4. Allergic rhinosinusitis, doing well on Vanceril.
    5. Fibrocystic breast disease, no breast exam done today as it was done in October.
    6. History of hemorrhoids.

P: Renew medications: Tegretol, 200 mg, 1 P.O., b.i.d. #100, 1 refill.

Henry C. Cardiac, M.D.
Henry C. Cardiac, M.D.

CASE STUDY 2-3

GOODMEDICINE CLINIC

1 Provider Street ■ Anywhere US 12345 ■ (101) 111-2222
EIN: 11-123456   MCARE GRP#: J1110   BCBS GRP#: GC12340

Encounter Form

PROVIDER: JANET B. SURGEON, M.D.

PATIENT INFORMATION:

Name:	Chang Li Ping
Address:	100 Dragon St
City:	Injury
State:	US
Zip Code:	12347
Telephone:	(101) 111-4545
Gender:	Male
Date of Birth:	01-06-1945
Occupation:	Clerk
Employer:	Good Growth, Inc.
Spouse's Employer:	Hunan Inc.

INSURANCE INFORMATION:

Patient Number:	2-3
Place of Service:	Office
Primary Insurance Plan:	Connecticut General
Primary Insurance Plan ID #:	333669999
Group #:	93939
Primary Policyholder:	Song Ling
Policyholder Date of Birth:	06-01-1942
Relationship to Patient:	Spouse
Secondary Insurance Plan:	
Secondary Insurance Plan ID #:	
Secondary Policyholder:	

Patient Status   ☒ Married   ☐ Divorced   ☐ Single   ☐ Student   ☐ Other

DIAGNOSIS INFORMATION

Diagnosis	Code	Diagnosis	Code
1.		5.	
2.		6.	
3.		7.	
4.		8.	

PROCEDURE INFORMATION

Description of Procedure or Service	Date	Code	Charge
1. Office visit, level III	06-14-YYYY		$ 75.00
2. Proctectomy with one-stage colostomy	06-16-YYYY		800.00
3.			
4.			
5.			

SPECIAL NOTES:

Admitted to Goodmedicine Hospital on 6/16/YYYY, discharged 6/20/YYYY.

GOODMEDICINE CLINIC

Patient Record

1 Provider Street ■ Anywhere US 12345 ■ (101) 111-2222

PROVIDER: JANET B. SURGEON, M.D.

OFFICE VISIT   06/14/YYYY

S: Mature adult Asian-American male patient, seen for the first time today, was off work due to hypertension when he noted a change in quality of bowel movements in that they became segmented. Two weeks ago occult blood was found in stool on Hemoccult testing x3. Bowel movements occur every 2-3 hours, and stool is flat and hemispheric. He has no weight loss except that following preparation for his barium enema. Appetite is good. In June, he had abdominal cramping. Health problems include hypertension, present for over 20 years, and a recent episode of parotitis. He admits to NO ALLERGIES.

O: No supraclavicular adenopathy. Chest clear to percussion and auscultation. Diminished breath sounds are present. Cardiac exam revealed regular rhythm without extra sound. Abdomen is soft, nontender. Groin is free from adenopathy. Rectal exam revealed normal tone. There is an external hemorrhoid anteriorly. Prostate is 4x4 cm, normal in architecture. Hemoccult testing of stool is positive. No masses palpable in rectum. Written report of BE is not yet available, but verbal report from pathology reveals 2 cm apple core type lesion in lower sigmoid colon, findings compatible with carcinoma.

A: Constricting lesion, lower sigmoid colon.

P: Admit to Goodmedicine Hospital for complete colonoscopy and evaluation to include CSR, CEA, and liver function. Surgery to follow, if tests prove positive.

Janet B. Surgeon, M.D.
Janet B. Surgeon, M.D.

INPATIENT HOSPITALIZATION   **Admission:** 06/16/YYYY   **Discharge:** 06/20/YYYY

Patient admitted for surgery due to constricting lesion, lower sigmoid colon. On 6/16/YYYY, complete prostatectomy with one-stage colostomy was performed. Pathology report revealed Duke's C carcinoma, colon. Patient was discharged 6/20/YYYY to be seen in the office in 1 week. Patient is to see Dr. Chemo, oncologist, in 3 weeks.

Janet B. Surgeon, M.D.
Janet B. Surgeon, M.D.

CASE STUDY 2-4

GOODMEDICINE CLINIC
1 Provider Street ■ Anywhere US 12345 ■ (101) 111-2222
EIN: 11-123456   MCARE GRP#: J1110   BCBS GRP#: GC12340

Encounter Form

PROVIDER: JANET B. SURGEON, M.D.

PATIENT INFORMATION:

Name:	John J. Recall
Address:	10 Memory Lane
City:	Anywhere
State:	US
Zip Code:	12345
Telephone:	(101) 111-4444
Gender:	Male
Date of Birth:	06-03-1942
Occupation:	Research Analyst
Employer:	Will Solve It, Inc.
Spouse's Employer:	

INSURANCE INFORMATION:

Patient Number:	2-4
Place of Service:	Inpatient Hospital
Primary Insurance Plan:	BCBS
Primary Insurance Plan ID #:	ZJW55544
Group #:	650
Primary Policyholder:	Self
Policyholder Date of Birth:	
Relationship to Patient:	
Secondary Insurance Plan:	
Secondary Insurance Plan ID #:	
Secondary Policyholder:	

Patient Status ☐ Married   ☒ Divorced   ☐ Single   ☐ Student   ☐ Other

---

DIAGNOSIS INFORMATION

Diagnosis	Code	Diagnosis	Code
1.		5.	
2.		6.	
3.		7.	
4.		8.	

PROCEDURE INFORMATION

Description of Procedure or Service	Date	Code	Charge
1. Office visit, level II	06-18-YYYY		75.00
2. Open cholecystectomy	06-19-YYYY		1360.00
3.			
4.			
5.			

SPECIAL NOTES:

New patient referred by Arnold Younglove, M.D. for surgery; UPIN AY9999.

GOODMEDICINE CLINIC

1 Provider Street ■ Anywhere US 12345 ■ (101) 111-2222

Patient Record

PROVIDER: JANET B. SURGEON, M.D.

OFFICE VISIT 06/18/YYYY

S: This new patient is a white adult, divorced male research analyst who was well until approximately early December when he noted nonradiatiang pain in the right upper quadrant with bloating. He had possible fever with chills several weeks ago, but has had no recurrence of this. He has chronically had increased gas, which was relieved with belching, and he has had some heartburn. He does have fatty food intolerance dating back several years. His pain has been intermittent since the initial episode. He has been slightly constipated. He has no alcoholic stools, jaundice, or liver disease. He drinks two highballs each night and smokes one pack of cigarettes per day. His weight has decreased 55 lbs in the past six months. As a child, he had jaundice. His family history is negative for gallbladder disease. He has NO KNOWN ALLERGIES. His other medical problems include diabetes, diagnosed 5 years ago; arteriosclerotic cardiovascular disease, without CVA or angina, congestive heart failure or arrhythmia. Studies reveal cholelithiasis and a normal upper gastrointestinal series.

O: Supraclavicular fossae are free from adenopathy. Chest is clear to percussion and auscultation. Cardiac examination reveals a regular rhythm, which is slow, without murmur or extra sound. The abdomen is soft and nontender, without masses or organomegaly. There is a suggestion of a left inguinal hernia. Groin is free of adenopathy. Rectal examination reveals normal tone without masses.

A: Cholelithiasis and chronic cholecystitis. Adult onset diabetes mellitus. Arteriosclerotic cardiovascular disease. Status post five-coronary artery bypass.

P: Admission for cholecystectomy. Obtain films for review.

Janet B. Surgeon, M.D.
Janet B. Surgeon, M.D.

INPATIENT HOSPITALIZATION   **Admission:** 06/19/YYYY   **Discharge:** 06/20/YYYY

Procedure: Cholecystectomy, open, performed yesterday.

Diagnosis: Chronic gallbladder with stones.

Discharge 10:00 AM today. To be seen in 5 days.

Janet B. Surgeon, M.D.
Janet B. Surgeon, M.D.

CASE STUDY 2-5

GOODMEDICINE CLINIC

Encounter Form

1 Provider Street ■ Anywhere US 12345 ■ (101) 111-2222

EIN: 11-123456   MCARE GRP#: J1110   BCBS GRP#: GC12340

PROVIDER: HENRY C. CARDIAC, M.D.

PATIENT INFORMATION:		**INSURANCE INFORMATION:**	
Name:	Philamena Islander	Patient Number:	2-5
Address:	129 Coconut Court	Place of Service:	Office
City:	Anywhere	Primary Insurance Plan:	BCBS
State:	US	Primary Insurance Plan ID #:	XWJ473655
Zip Code:	12345	Group #:	101
Telephone:	(101) 111-7218	Primary Policyholder:	Richard T. Islander
Gender:	Female	Policyholder Date of Birth:	02-11-1952
Date of Birth:	11-21-1953	Relationship to Patient:	Spouse
Occupation:	Secretary	Secondary Insurance Plan:	
Employer:	Nixon Modeling Agency	Secondary Insurance Plan ID #:	
Spouse's Employer:	Wonderful Photos	Secondary Policyholder:	

Patient Status	☒ Married	☐ Divorced	☐ Single	☐ Student	☐ Other

---

DIAGNOSIS INFORMATION

Diagnosis	Code	Diagnosis	Code
1.		5.	
2.		6.	
3.		7.	
4.		8.	

PROCEDURE INFORMATION

Description of Procedure or Service	Date	Code	Charge
1. Anoscopy with biopsy	06-20-YYYY		100.00
2.			
3.			
4.			
5.			

SPECIAL NOTES:

GOODMEDICINE CLINIC

Patient Record

1 Provider Street ■ Anywhere US 12345 ■ (101) 111-2222

PROVIDER: HENRY C. CARDIAC, M.D.

OFFICE VISIT   06/20/YYYY

S: This patient had no complaints since her last visit until 3 weeks ago when she noted some intermittent soft stool and decrease in the caliber of stools, with some bleeding that discontinued 4
days ago. She had no crampy abdominal pain.

O: External examination of the anus revealed some external skin tags present in the left anterior
position. Anal examination revealed an extremely tight anal sphincter. This was dilated manually
to allow instrumentation with the anoscope, which was accomplished in a 360-degree orientation.
There was some prominence of the crypts and some inflammation of the rectal mucosa, a portion
of which was sent for biopsy. This was friable. In the left anterior position there was a fistula that
was healing with some formation of a sentinel pile on the outside, which had been noticed on
external examination.

A: Anal fissure, unusual position, nontraumatic.

P: Rule out inflammatory bowel disease with air contrast barium enema examination and reflux into
terminal ileum. Patient to return for sigmoidoscopy after BE.

Henry C. Cardiac, M.D.
Henry C. Cardiac, M.D.

CASE STUDY 2-6

GOODMEDICINE CLINIC

1 Provider Street ■ Anywhere US 12345 ■ (101) 111-2222

EIN: 11-123456   MCARE GRP#: J1110   BCBS GRP#: GC12340

Encounter Form

PROVIDER: NANCY HEALER, M.D.   MCARE PIN: N3333   MCAID PIN: NJH3333

PATIENT INFORMATION:		INSURANCE INFORMATION:	
Name:	Imogene Sugar	Patient Number:	2-6
Address:	120 Young Street	Place of Service:	Home
City:	Injury	Primary Insurance Plan:	Medicare
State:	US	Primary Insurance Plan ID #:	777228888W
Zip Code:	12345	Group #:	
Telephone:	(101) 111-8675	Primary Policyholder:	Self
Gender:	Female	Policyholder Date of Birth:	
Date of Birth:	03-09-1924	Relationship to Patient:	
Occupation:	Retired	Secondary Insurance Plan:	Medicaid
Employer:		Secondary Insurance Plan ID #:	1155773388
Spouse's Employer:		Secondary Policyholder:	Self

Patient Status   ☐ Married   ☐ Divorced   ☒ Single   ☐ Student   ☐ Other

DIAGNOSIS INFORMATION

Diagnosis	Code	Diagnosis	Code
1.		5.	
2.		6.	
3.		7.	
4.		8.	

PROCEDURE INFORMATION

Description of Procedure or Service	Date	Code	Charge
1. Home visit, level II	06-20-YYYY		45.00
2.			
3.			
4.			
5.			

SPECIAL NOTES:

GOODMEDICINE CLINIC

1 Provider Street ■ Anywhere US 12345 ■ (101) 111-2222

Patient Record

PROVIDER: NANCY HEALER, M.D.

HOME VISIT 06/20/YYYY

S: Patient was visited at home in follow-up for her Type I uncontrolled diabetes with circulatory problems. On 05/10/YYYY, while visiting her daughter in Somewhere, MD, she saw an orthopedic surgeon who admitted her to the hospital and did a transmetatarsal amputation of her foot. She had not notified Dr. Bones or me that she had received a second opinion or that she had gone through with surgery.

O: Her blood pressure is 130/70; she looks well. Chest is clear and cardiac examination is unremarkable. Examination of the leg shows no edema, redness, or heat in the lower extremity. The patient had strict instructions not to allow me to unwrap the wound.

A: This patient underwent transmetatarsal amputation although neither Dr. Bones nor I felt a BKA was warranted. I encouraged the patient to be compliant with follow-up planned by her orthopedic surgeon. I will inform Dr. Bones she had gone ahead with surgery and if problems develop, she is to contact me.

P: Schedule office follow-up visit in 2 weeks.

Nancy Healer, M.D.

Nancy Healer, M.D.

CASE STUDY 2-7

GOODMEDICINE CLINIC

1 Provider Street ■ Anywhere US 12345 ■ (101) 111-2222
EIN: 11-123456   MCARE GRP#: J1110   BCBS GRP#: GC12340

Encounter Form

PROVIDER: HENRY C. CARDIAC, M.D.   MCARE PIN: H4444

PATIENT INFORMATION:

Name:	Esau Gonzales
Address:	14 Adobe St
City:	Nowhere
State:	US
Zip Code:	12347
Telephone:	(101) 115-7689
Gender:	Female
Date of Birth:	09-10-1933
Occupation:	Retired
Employer:	
Spouse's Employer:	

INSURANCE INFORMATION:

Patient Number:	2-7
Place of Service:	Office
Primary Insurance Plan:	Medicare
Primary Insurance Plan ID #:	101234591A
Group #:	
Primary Policyholder:	Self
Policyholder Date of Birth:	
Relationship to Patient:	
Secondary Insurance Plan:	
Secondary Insurance Plan ID #:	
Secondary Policyholder:	

Patient Status   ☐ Married   ☐ Divorced   ☒ Single   ☐ Student   ☐ Other

DIAGNOSIS INFORMATION

Diagnosis	Code	Diagnosis	Code
1.		5.	
2.		6.	
3.		7.	
4.		8.	

PROCEDURE INFORMATION

Description of Procedure or Service	Date	Code	Charge
1. Office visit, level II	06-20-YYYY		100.00
2. EKG, routine with interpretation	06-20-YYYY		65.00
3.			
4.			
5.			

SPECIAL NOTES:

GOODMEDICINE CLINIC

1 Provider Street ■ Anywhere US 12345 ■ (101) 111-2222

Patient Record

PROVIDER: HENRY C. CARDIAC, M.D.

OFFICE VISIT   06/20/YYYY

S: Elderly African-American male returns, after a two-year hiatus, for follow-up of coronary artery disease and associated problems. Since triple coronary bypass surgery four years ago, he has had no chest discomfort. It should be noted that he had no chest discomfort during a markedly abnormal stress test performed just two weeks before the bypass surgery. He now reports intermittent dyspnea that occurs at rest, and spontaneously abates. He does not notice any discomfort on exertion, but he does report that his lifestyle is sedentary. He denies orthopnea, paroxysmal nocturnal dyspnea or edema. He has continued to follow up with his internist, Dr. Gooddoc, for treatment of his dyslipidemia and hypertension. He is on Cholestin and Tenormin.

O: Patient is a mildly obese, African-American male appearing his stated age, in no acute distress. Weight is 210. Height is 5'8". Pulse 16. BP 162/82, 172/82, and then 188/82 in the office. HEENT grossly unremarkable. Neck reveals normal jugular venous pressure, without hepatojugular reflux. Normal carotid pulses; no bruits present. Lungs are clear to A&P. Heart reveals regular rhythm, S1 and S2 are normal. There is no murmur, rub, click, or gallop. Cardiac apex is not palpable. No heaves or thrills are detected. Abdomen is soft, nontender, with normal bowel sounds, and no bruits. No organomegaly, including abdominal aorta, or masses noted. Extremities reveal a surgical scar in the right leg, presumably from saphenous venectomy. Femoral pulses are normal, without bruits. Dorsalis pedis and posterior tibial pulses are also normal. There is no cyanosis, clubbing, or edema. Neurological is grossly within normal limits.

A: 1. Status post aortocoronary bypass surgery four years ago.
     2. Coronary artery disease. Today's abnormal EKG suggests, but does not prove, that an inferior myocardial infarction may have occurred sometime in the past. There is independent suggestion of this on stress-thallium test performed six months ago. Additionally, he still has symptoms of dyspnea.
     3. Hypertension.
     4. Hypercholesterolemia.

P: 1. Patient was instructed to follow up with Dr. Gooddoc for hypertension and dyslipidemia.
     2   Schedule treadmill stress test for next week.

Henry C. Cardiac, M.D.

Henry C. Cardiac, M.D.

CASE STUDY 2-8

GOODMEDICINE CLINIC

1 Provider Street ■ Anywhere US 12345 ■ (101) 111-2222
EIN: 11-123456   MCARE GRP#: J1110   BCBS GRP#: GC12340

Encounter Form

PROVIDER: NANCY J. HEALER, M.D.   MCARE PIN: N3333

PATIENT INFORMATION:		INSURANCE INFORMATION:	
Name:	Mary Blooming Bush	Patient Number:	2-8
Address:	9910 Reservation Rd	Place of Service:	Office
City:	Nowhere	Primary Insurance Plan:	Medicare
State:	US	Primary Insurance Plan ID #:	071269645B
Zip Code:	12347	Group #:	
Telephone:	(101) 111-9922	Primary Policyholder:	Self
Gender:	Female	Policyholder Date of Birth:	
Date of Birth:	04-01-1930	Relationship to Patient:	
Occupation:	Retired	Secondary Insurance Plan:	Cigna
Employer:		Secondary Insurance Plan ID #:	
Spouse's Employer:		Secondary Policyholder:	Self

Patient Status	☐ Married	☐ Divorced	☒ Single	☐ Student	☐ Other

DIAGNOSIS INFORMATION

Diagnosis	Code	Diagnosis	Code
1.		5.	
2.		6.	
3.		7.	
4.		8.	

PROCEDURE INFORMATION

Description of Procedure or Service	Date	Code	Charge
1. Office visit, level IV	06-20-YYYY		100.00
2.			
3.			
4.			
5.			

SPECIAL NOTES:

GOODMEDICINE CLINIC

1 Provider Street ■ Anywhere US 12345 ■ (101) 111-2222

Patient Record

PROVIDER: NANCY J. HEALER, M.D.

OFFICE VISIT 06/20/YYYY

S: This elderly, widowed Native American woman returns to the office today after having a possible seizure at dinner last night. She reports that she was sitting at the table and suddenly fell to the floor. She had urine incontinence at that time and awoke in a slightly confused state with a bad headache. She denies any recent trauma, blows to the head, chest pain, palpitation, paresthesias, aura, or other symptoms. Her history is remarkable for a well-differentiated nodular lymphoma on the upper right arm that was diagnosed and treated with radiation by Dr. Raes in Anywhere, US. She has had no clinical evidence of recurrence. There has been no prior hospitalization other than for childbirth. Para: 1001. She has had mild COPD for the past 10 years. Her husband died of an unexpected myocardial infarction 2 years ago. She now lives with her daughter. The review of systems is noncontributory. She has no current medications and the only known allergy is to penicillin.

O: Physical exam shows a well-nourished, well-developed female in no acute distress at this time. Her clothed weight is 155 lbs. Blood pressure: 120/72, both arms, with no orthostasis. Pulse: 70 and regular. Respirations: Unlabored at 18. HEENT: Head is nomocephalic and atraumatic. PEERLA with intact EOMs. Sclerae are white and the conjunctivae are pink. Funduscopic exam is benign. Ears are normal bilaterally. There is no evidence of Battle's sign. The mouth and throat are unremarkable. Tongue is midline without atrophy or fasciculation. Neck is supple without JVD, adenopathy, thyromegaly, or bruits. The lungs are clear to P&A. Breasts are pendulous with no masses, dimpling, or nipple retraction. Heart rate and rhythm is regular with a grade II/VI SEM along the LSB without gallop, rub, clicks, or other adventitious sounds. Abdomen is soft and nontender without organomegaly, masses, or bruits. Bowel sounds are normal. Rectum has good sphincter tone without masses. Stool is hemoccult negative. Extremities have no edema, cyanosis, jaundice, clubbing, or petechiae. The peripheral pulses are full and palpable. There is no significant cervical, supraclavicular, axillary, or inguinal adenopathy noted. The mental status is normal. Cranial nerves II-XII are intact. Motor, sensory and cerebellar function is normal. Romberg sign is normal. The Babinski is absent. Reflexes are 2+ and symmetrical in both upper and lower extremities.

A: New onset seizure disorder. Rule out tumor, metabolic and vascular etiologies.

P: The patient will be scheduled ASAP for MRI of the brain and an EEG at Goodmedicine Hospital. Obtain blood for electrolytes, calcium, albumin, LFTs, and CBC with platelet count and sed rate, and send to the lab. Patient was instructed to call immediately if she has any further difficulty or questions.

Nancy J. Healer, M.D.

Nancy J. Healer, M.D.

CASE STUDY 2-9

GOODMEDICINE CLINIC

Encounter Form

1 Provider Street ■ Anywhere US 12345 ■ (101) 111-2222

EIN: 11-123456   MCARE GRP#: J1110   BCBS GRP#: GC12340

PROVIDER: T. J. STITCHER, M.D.   BCBS PIN: 12342   MCARE PIN: T2222

PATIENT INFORMATION:		INSURANCE INFORMATION:	
Name:	Mary A. Cadillac	Patient Number:	2-9
Address:	500 Carr St	Place of Service:	Inpatient Hospital
City:	Anywhere	Primary Insurance Plan:	BCBS
State:	US	Primary Insurance Plan ID #:	XWY111111
Zip Code:	12345	Group #:	GM103
Telephone:	(101) 222-3333	Primary Policyholder:	James D. Cadillac
Gender:	Female	Policyholder Date of Birth:	06-06-1933
Date of Birth:	04-30-1929	Relationship to Patient:	Spouse
Occupation:		Secondary Insurance Plan:	Medicare
Employer:		Secondary Insurance Plan ID #:	001266811B
Spouse's Employer:	Anywhere Auto Dealer Association	Secondary Policyholder:	Self

---

Patient Status	☒ Married	☐ Divorced	☐ Single	☐ Student	☐ Other

---

DIAGNOSIS INFORMATION

Diagnosis	Code	Diagnosis	Code
1.		5.	
2.		6.	
3.		7.	
4.		8.	

PROCEDURE INFORMATION

Description of Procedure or Service	Date	Code	Charge
1. Laparoscopic cholecystectomy	06-20-YYYY		1350.00
2. Intraoperative cholangiogram	06-20-YYYY		0.00
3. Liver biopsy	06-20-YYYY		100.00
4. Lysis of adhesions	06-20-YYYY		0.00
5.			

SPECIAL NOTES:

Inpatient care provided by Goodmedicine Hospital, Anywhere St, Anywhere US 12345.

GOODMEDICINE CLINIC

1 Provider Street ■ Anywhere US 12345 ■ (101) 111-2222

Patient Record

PROVIDER: T. J. STITCHER, M.D.

INPATIENT HOSPITAL SURGERY   06/20/YYYY

PREOPERATIVE DIAGNOSIS: Chronic cholecystitis and cholelithiasis without obstruction.

POSTOPERATIVE DIAGNOSIS: Same.

SURGEON: T. J. Stitcher, M.D.

PROCEDURE: Laparoscopic cholecystectomy, intraoperative cholangiogram, lysis of adhesions, liver biopsy.

ANESTHESIA: General endotracheal.

OPERATIVE FINDINGS: Numerous adhesions around the gallbladder area. Gallbladder was distended. Cystic duct normal in caliber. Common bile duct normal. No residual stone on cholangiogram. Patient has two nodules on each side of inferior lobe, close to the gallbladder, proximally and distally.

OPERATIVE PROCEDURE: The patient was placed in the dorsal supine position after adequate anesthesia, and the abdomen was prepped and draped in the usual fashion. A right lateral infraumbilical incision was made and dissected to the fascia. The fascia was entered, and dissection of the pre-peritoneum was done to enter the peritoneal cavity. Adhesions were lysed with blunt dissection. Hasson trocar was inserted and anchored to the fascia after 1-0 Vicryl was preset on each side of the fascia. Insufflation was started with CO_2. After adequate insufflation, patient was placed in the Trendelenburg position, and antrocar was placed under direct visualization. Skin was infiltrated with 0.5% Marcaine. After adequate placement of trocars, grasping forceps were inserted. Gallbladder was grasped on the lateral port along the subcostal area, anterior axillary line to lift the gallbladder up for dissection and lysis of the adhesions around the gallbladder. After adequate lysis of adhesions, neck of gallbladder was grasped with the midclavicular subcostal grasping forceps to expose the triangle of Calot. Careful dissection of cystic branch going to the gallbladder was identified and skeletonized, small clip was placed distal to the cystic duct toward the gallbladder, and small opening was made. Cholangiocath was introduced, cholangiogram was performed using 50% dye and completed with no evidence of retained stone. Cholangiocath was removed. Cystic duct was clamped twice distally and proximally using endoclips and divided. Gallbladder was excised from liver bed using the spatula cautery. Copious irrigation of liver bed was clear with no evidence of bile leak or bleeding. Gallbladder was removed from liver bed and brought out toward subxyphoid opening under visualization. Bile content was removed and some stones had to be crushed prior to removal of the gallbladder through the 1-cm opening. Trocar was reinserted and biopsy of nodule noted on liver was made, using a true cut needle, cutting going through skin under direct visualization. Two specimens were removed (two nodules). Patient was placed in reverse Trendelenburg position and irrigation fluid was removed. All trocars and grasping forceps were removed under direct visualization. Gas was deflated. Hasson was removed under laparoscope. Fascia layer on umbilical area was closed using preset sutures and figure of eight. Fascia and subxyphoid were closed using 0 Vicryl, figure of eight. Subcuticular reapproximation using 4-0 Vicryl was completed and skin was Steri-stripped after application of Benzoin Tincture. Patient tolerated procedure well. Estimated blood loss was less than 25 cc. Foley catheter was removed, and nasogastric tube was removed prior to the patient being extubated. The patient left the operating room in satisfactory condition.

T.J. Stitcher, M.D.

T. J. Stitcher, M.D.

CASE STUDY 2-10

GOODMEDICINE CLINIC

1 Provider Street ■ Anywhere US 12345 ■ (101) 111-2222
EIN: 11-123456   MCARE GRP#: J1110   BCBS GRP#: GC12340

Encounter Form

PROVIDER: T. J. STITCHER, M.D.   MCARE PIN: T2222

PATIENT INFORMATION:

Name:	John W. Hammerclaw
Address:	111 Lumber St
City:	Anywhere
State:	US
Zip Code:	12345
Telephone:	(101) 111-9191
Gender:	Male
Date of Birth:	05-30-1930
Occupation:	Retired
Employer:	
Spouse's Employer:	

INSURANCE INFORMATION:

Patient Number:	2-10
Place of Service:	Office
Primary Insurance Plan:	Medicare
Primary Insurance Plan ID #:	101101010A
Group #:	
Primary Policyholder:	Self
Policyholder Date of Birth:	
Relationship to Patient:	
Secondary Insurance Plan:	BCBS Medigap
Secondary Insurance Plan ID #:	YXW10110
Secondary Policyholder:	Self

Patient Status   ☐ Married   ☐ Divorced   ☒ Single   ☐ Student   ☐ Other

DIAGNOSIS INFORMATION

Diagnosis	Code	Diagnosis	Code
1.		5.	
2.		6.	
3.		7.	
4.		8.	

PROCEDURE INFORMATION

Description of Procedure or Service	Date	Code	Charge
1. Excision, 4.1 cm cyst, back	06-20-YYYY		360.00
2. Excision, 2.5 cm cyst, neck	06-20-YYYY		300.00
3.			
4.			
5.			

SPECIAL NOTES:

Referring physician is Erin Helper, M.D. UPIN: EH8888.

GOODMEDICINE CLINIC

1 Provider Street ■ Anywhere US 12345 ■ (101) 111-2222

Patient Record

PROVIDER: T. J. STITCHER, M.D.

OFFICE SURGERY   06/20/YYYY

PREOPERATIVE DIAGNOSIS: 4.1-cm infected sebaceous cyst, back; 2.5-cm infected sebaceous cyst, posterior neck.

POSTOPERATIVE DIAGNOSIS: Same.

OPERATION: Excision, 4.1-cm benign cyst, back. Excision, 2.5-cm benign cyst, neck.

PROCEDURE: The patient was placed in the prone position and the back and posterior neck were prepared with Betadine scrub and solution. Sterile towels were applied in the usual fashion, and 0.25% Marcaine was injected subcutaneously in a linear fashion transversely over each of the cysts asynchronously. The lower cyst was excised and the cavity was irrigated with copious amounts of Marcaine solution. The skin edges were loosely reapproximated throughout with # 3-0 nylon suture. Following this, Marcaine was injected around the superior cyst, an incision was made transversely, and the cyst was completely excised. The wound was irrigated with Marcaine and packed with Iodoform, and sterile dressings were applied. The patient was discharged with verbal and written instructions, as well as Tylenol #3 for pain and a prescription for 30. Return visit in 3 days for packing removal.

T.J. Stitcher, M.D.

T. J. Stitcher, M.D.

CASE STUDY 2-11

GOODMEDICINE CLINIC

1 Provider Street ■ Anywhere US 12345 ■ (101) 111-2222

EIN: 11-123456   MCARE GRP#: J1110   BCBS GRP#: GC12340

Encounter Form

PROVIDER: HENRY C. CARDIAC, M.D.   MCAID PIN: HCC4444

PATIENT INFORMATION:

Name:	Germane Fontaine
Address:	132 Canal St
City:	Injury
State:	US
Zip Code:	12346
Telephone:	(101) 111-9685
Gender:	Female
Date of Birth	05-07-1965
Occupation:	Unemployed
Employer:	
Spouse's Employer:	

INSURANCE INFORMATION:

Patient Number:	2-11
Place of Service:	Office
Primary Insurance Plan:	Medicaid
Primary Insurance Plan ID #:	11347765
Group #:	
Primary Policyholder:	Self
Policyholder Date of Birth:	
Relationship to Patient:	
Secondary Insurance Plan:	
Secondary Insurance Plan ID #:	
Secondary Policyholder:	

Patient Status   ☐ Married   ☐ Divorced   ☒ Single   ☐ Student   ☐ Other

---

DIAGNOSIS INFORMATION

Diagnosis	Code	Diagnosis	Code
1.		5.	
2.		6.	
3.		7.	
4.		8.	

PROCEDURE INFORMATION

Description of Procedure or Service	Date	Code	Charge
1. Office visit, level II, established patient	06-20-YYYY		26.00
2. Strep test			12.00
3.			
4.			
5.			

SPECIAL NOTES:

GOODMEDICINE CLINIC

Patient Record

1 Provider Street ■ Anywhere US 12345 ■ (101) 111-2222

PROVIDER: HENRY C. CARDIAC, M.D.

OFFICE VISIT 06/20/YYYY

S: This patient has had a sore throat for the past several days, temperature to 101 degrees Fahrenheit with pleuritic cough. She has had abundant postnasal drip.

O: NAD. Sinuses are tender about the maxillary and frontal areas. TMs, gray bilaterally. Pharynx is injected and there is obvious purulent material in the left posterior pharynx. Neck: supple, no nodes. Chest: clear. COR: RRR without murmur. Lab: sinus films normal.

A: Clinical chronic sinusitis; her sore throat is probably from this, but will obtain a Strep test to rule out that possibility, at her request.

P: Beconase nasal spray, 1 whiff to each nostril q.i.d. for 1 week, then 1 whiff b.i.d. to each nostril. If she has not improved in 3 weeks, refer to ENT specialist.

Henry C. Cardiac, M.D.
Henry C. Cardiac, M.D.

CASE STUDY 2-12

GOODMEDICINE CLINIC

1 Provider Street ■ Anywhere US 12345 ■ (101) 111-2222
EIN: 11-123456   MCARE GRP#: J1110   BCBS GRP#: GC12340

Encounter Form

PROVIDERS:	HENRY C. CARDIAC, M.D.	MCAID PIN: HCC4444
	T. J. STITCHER, M.D.	MCAID PIN: TJS2222
	JANET B. SURGEON, M.D.	MCAID PIN: JBS1111

PATIENT INFORMATION:

Name:	James Apple
Address:	1 Appleblossom Court
City:	Hometown
State:	US
Zip Code:	1523
Telephone:	(201) 111-2011
Gender:	Male
Date of Birth:	11-12-1984
Occupation:	Unemployed
Employer:	
Spouse's Employer:	

INSURANCE INFORMATION:

Patient Number:	2-12
Place of Service:	Inpatient Hospital
Primary Insurance Plan:	Medicaid
Primary Insurance Plan ID #:	1234567
Group #:	
Primary Policyholder:	Self
Policyholder Date of Birth:	
Relationship to Patient:	
Secondary Insurance Plan:	
Secondary Insurance Plan ID #:	
Secondary Policyholder:	

Patient Status   ☐ Married   ☐ Divorced   ☐ Single   ☒ Student   ☐ Other

DIAGNOSIS INFORMATION

Diagnosis	Code	Diagnosis	Code
1.		5.	
2.		6.	
3.		7.	
4.		8.	

PROCEDURE INFORMATION

Description of Procedure or Service	Date	Code	Charge
1. Inpatient visit, level III (Cardiac)	06-19-YYYY		165.00
2. Laparoscopic appendectomy (Stitcher)	06-19-YYYY		1400.00
3. Laparoscopic appendectomy (Surgeon)	06-19-YYYY		280.00
4.			
5.			

SPECIAL NOTES:
Dr. Cardiac is the attending physician. Dr. Stitcher is the surgeon. Dr. Surgeon is assistant surgeon. Care was provided at Goodmedicine Hospital, Anywhere St, Anywhere US 12345.

GOODMEDICINE CLINIC

1 Provider Street ■ Anywhere US 12345 ■ (101) 111-2222

Patient Record

PROVIDER: HENRY C. CARDIAC, M.D.; T. J. STITCHER, M.D.; JANET B. SURGEON, M.D.

INPATIENT HOSPITALIZATION   Admitted: 06/19/YYYY   Discharged: 06/20/YYYY

06/19/YYYY   Patient admitted with acute appendicitis. Dr. Stitcher called in as surgeon.

Henry C. Cardiac, M.D.
Henry C. Cardiac, M.D.

06/19/YYYY   PREOPERATIVE DIAGNOSIS: Acute appendicitis.

POSTOPERATIVE DIAGNOSIS: Acute appendicitis.

OPERATION: Laparoscopic exploration with appendectomy.

SURGEON: T. J. Stitcher, M.D.

ASSISTANT SURGEON: Janet B. Surgeon, M.D.

PROCEDURE: Patient anesthetized with general anesthesia via endotracheal tube. Abdomen prepped and draped in sterile fashion. Because of patient's size (he is 9 years old and quite small) it was not possible to place a catheter in the bladder. Patient was placed in Trendelenburg position. Abdominal wall was palpated, no masses felt. Incision was made below the umbilicus and Verres needle inserted toward the pelvis. This was tested with normal saline; when it appeared to be in the peritoneal cavity, the abdomen was insufflated with 3 liters of $CO2$. A 1/2-cm camera was introduced through this opening. There was no evidence of injury from the needle or trocar, and the area of the appendix was visualized and some exudates and free fluid in the area noted. Under direct vision, a 1/2-cm trocar was passed through the right edge of the rectus sheath in the midabdomen. Using blunt and sharp dissection, the appendix and cecum were mobilized. The mesoappendix was serially ligated with hemoclips and then divided and the appendix freed to its base. The base was identified by the fact it was supple and it lay at the convergence of the tinea. A single 0 chromic suture was laced approximately 1 cm distally and then the appendix divided between and through the 11-mm trocar. The abdomen was irrigated with normal saline and the contents aspirated. Skin closed with 4-0 Vicryl, and Benzoin and steristrips applied. Estimated blood loss was 10 cc. Sponge and needle counts were correct. Patient tolerated the procedure well and returned to the recovery room awake and in stable condition.

T.J. Stitcher, M.D.
T. J. Stitcher, M.D.

06-20-YYYY   Patient was unremarkable postoperatively. Discharged 9 a.m. today. Mother was given standard, written pediatric appendectomy discharge sheet. Patient to be seen in the office of J. H. Cutdown, M.D. in 5 days for postop follow-up.

T.J. Stitcher, M.D.
T. J. Stitcher, M.D.

CASE STUDY 2-13

GOODMEDICINE CLINIC

1 Provider Street ■ Anywhere US 12345 ■ (101) 111-2222

EIN: 11-123456   MCARE GRP#: J1110   BCBS GRP#: GC12340

Encounter Form

PROVIDER: JANET B. SURGEON, M.D.

PATIENT INFORMATION:

Name:	Stanley N. Banana
Address:	1 Barrack St
City:	Anywhere
State:	US
Zip Code:	12345
Telephone:	(101) 111-7676
Gender:	Male
Date of Birth:	11-11-1956
Occupation:	US Army
Employer:	
Spouse's Employer:	

INSURANCE INFORMATION:

Patient Number:	2-13
Place of Service:	Outpatient
Primary Insurance Plan:	TRICARE
Primary Insurance Plan ID #:	123445555
Group #:	
Primary Policyholder:	Self
Policyholder Date of Birth:	
Relationship to Patient:	
Secondary Insurance Plan:	
Secondary Insurance Plan ID #:	
Secondary Policyholder:	

Patient Status   ☐ Married   ☒ Divorced   ☐ Single   ☐ Student   ☐ Other

---

DIAGNOSIS INFORMATION

Diagnosis	Code	Diagnosis	Code
1.		5.	
2.		6.	
3.		7.	
4.		8.	

PROCEDURE INFORMATION

Description of Procedure or Service	Date	Code	Charge
1. Flexible sigmoidoscopy	06-20-YYYY		600.00
2.			
3.			
4.			
5.			

SPECIAL NOTES:

Nancy Healer referred patient. UPIN: NH3333.

GOODMEDICINE CLINIC

1 Provider Street ■ Anywhere US 12345 ■ (101) 111-2222

Patient Record

PROVIDER: JANET B. SURGEON, M.D.

OFFICE VISIT 06/20/YYYY

PROCEDURE: Flexible left sigmoidoscopy was performed. The lining of the colon to this point was normal throughout. No signs of inflammation ulceration, or mass formation were noted. Anoscope was introduced into the anal canal and this was examined in 4 quadrants. To the left of the midline posteriorly a 4–5 mm, very small fissure was seen, apparently exposing an underlying vein that was slightly darker. There was no sign of heaped up margin or any true ulceration.

DIAGNOSIS: Fissure in ano.

PLAN: 1. Dietary modification to increase fluid and bulk in diet.

2. Avoid straining.

3. Use simple measures such as sitz baths and Tucks pads when the fissure is symptomatic.

4. Return visit on a prn basis should any additional bleeding be seen.

Janet B. Surgeon, M.D.

Janet B. Surgeon, M.D.

CASE STUDY 2-14

GOODMEDICINE CLINIC

Encounter Form

1 Provider Street ■ Anywhere US 12345 ■ (101) 111-2222

EIN: 11-123456   MCARE GRP#: J1110   BCBS GRP#: GC12340

PROVIDER: JANET B. SURGEON, M.D.

PATIENT INFORMATION:		INSURANCE INFORMATION:	
Name:	Reginald T. Karot	Patient Number:	2-14
Address:	15 Caring St	Place of Service:	Office
City:	Anywhere	Primary Insurance Plan:	Metropolitan
State:	US	Primary Insurance Plan ID #:	222 22 222A
Zip Code:	12345	Group #:	ASD1
Telephone:	(101) 222-2022	Primary Policyholder:	Louise Karot
Gender:	Male	Policyholder Date of Birth:	10-11-1936
Date of Birth:	10-01-1936	Relationship to Patient:	Spouse
Occupation:	Construction worker	Secondary Insurance Plan:	TRICARE Standard
Employer:	Is A Construction Co.	Secondary Insurance Plan ID #:	012346543
Spouse's Employer:	Anywhere School District	Secondary Policyholder:	Self

Patient Status   ☒ Married   ☐ Divorced   ☐ Single   ☐ Student   ☐ Other

DIAGNOSIS INFORMATION

Diagnosis	Code	Diagnosis	Code
1.		5.	
2.		6.	
3.		7.	
4.		8.	

PROCEDURE INFORMATION

Description of Procedure or Service	Date	Code	Charge
1. Office visit, level II, new patient	06-20-YYYY		75.00
2.			
3.			
4.			
5.			

SPECIAL NOTES:

Nancy J. Healer referred patient. UPIN: NH3333.

GOODMEDICINE CLINIC

1 Provider Street ■ Anywhere US 12345 ■ (101) 111-2222

Patient Record

PROVIDER: JANET B. SURGEON, M.D.

OFFICE VISIT 06/20/YYYY

S: Three years ago today, this patient was noted to have a bulge in his left side. He has had possible weakness on the right side, noted in Dr. Healer's evaluation today. He does not smoke; he runs frequently and does not do any heavy lifting or straining. He has had some minor changes in his urinary stream and has been noted to have an enlarged prostate in the past. He reports terminal dribbling, but has no difficulty with initiating a stream and has noticed no change in the force of the stream. He reports his bowel movements have been normal. There has been no blood or black stools. He has no other significant medical problems. See the attached Family and Social History Data Sheet elsewhere in this chart.

O: The supraclavicular fossae are free of adenopathy. The chest is clear to percussion and auscultation. The abdomen is soft and nontender, without masses or organomegaly. There is a right lower quadrant appendectomy incision that is well healed. The penis is circumcised without masses. The testicles are scrotal and normal. In the standing position, there is a left inguinal hernia that exits the external right and a right inguinal external right that is beginning to do this. Rectal examination revealed normal tone. The prostate is 4.0 x 4.0 cm and normal in architecture. The stool was hemoccult negative.

A: Bilateral inguinal hernias, left greater than right.

P: Schedule for bilateral inguinal herniorrhaphy in early July.

Janet B. Surgeon, M.D.

Janet B Surgeon, M.D.

CASE STUDY 2-15

GOODMEDICINE CLINIC

1 Provider Street ■ Anywhere US 12345 ■ (101) 111-2222

EIN: 11-123456   MCARE GRP#: J1110   BCBS GRP#: GC12340

Encounter Form

PROVIDER: T. J. STITCHER, M.D.

PATIENT INFORMATION:		INSURANCE INFORMATION:	
Name:	James Lawrence Butcher	Patient Number:	2-15
Address:	14 Pigsfeet Rd	Place of Service:	Emergency Department
City:	Anywhere	Primary Insurance Plan:	Workers' Comp Fund
State:	US	Primary Insurance Plan ID #:	321458765
Zip Code:	12345	Group #:	
Telephone:	(101) 333-4567	Primary Policyholder:	Piglet Meat Packers
Gender:	Male	Policyholder Date of Birth:	
Date of Birth:	02-29-1977	Relationship to Patient:	
Occupation:	Meat cutter	Secondary Insurance Plan:	
Employer:	Piglet Meat Packers	Secondary Insurance Plan ID #:	
Spouse's Employer:	Anywhere US 12345	Secondary Policyholder:	

Patient Status   ☐ Married   ☐ Divorced   ☐ Single   ☐ Student   ☐ Other

DIAGNOSIS INFORMATION

Diagnosis	Code	Diagnosis	Code
1.		5.	
2.		6.	
3.		7.	
4.		8.	

PROCEDURE INFORMATION

Description of Procedure or Service	Date	Code	Charge
1. Extensor tendon repair	06-19-YYYY		1400.00
2.			
3.			
4.			
5.			

SPECIAL NOTES:

Workers' Compensation Fund, 113 Insurance Ave, Anywhere US 12345.

GOODMEDICINE CLINIC

1 Provider Street ■ Anywhere US 12345 ■ (101) 111-2222

Patient Record

PROVIDER: T. J. STITCHER, M.D.

ED VISIT 06/19/YYYY

DIAGNOSIS: 2-cm laceration, dorsum of left thumb, with laceration of extensor tendon.

PROCEDURE: Repair of extensor tendon and laceration, dorsum of left thumb.

HISTORY: 22-year-old male seen with chief complaint of 2-cm laceration of the back of his left thumb. Patient said, "I was cutting the feet off of hogs when the knife slipped and cut the back of my thumb." He cannot extend his thumb since the accident, and he had some bleeding, which he stopped with pressure. Patient had tetanus toxoid administered last year when he sustained a wound to the forearm while at work. He has no past history of serious illnesses, operations, or allergies. Social and family history are noncontributory.

PHYSICAL FINDINGS: Examination reveals a well-developed, well-nourished white male appearing his stated age and in no acute distress. He has no abnormal findings other than the left thumb, which shows a laceration of the dorsum of the thumb proximal to the interphalangeal joint. The patient cannot extend the thumb; he can flex, adduct, and abduct the thumb. Sensation at this time appears to be normal.

PROCEDURE: With the patient in the supine position the area was prepped and draped. A digital nerve block using 1% of Carbocaine was carried out. When the block was totally effective, the wound was explored. The distal severed end of the tendon was located. The proximal end could not be found. A vertical incision was then made down the lateral aspect of the thumb starting at the corner of the original laceration, thus creating a flap. When the flap was retracted back, the proximal portion of the tendon was located. Both tendon ends had a very clean-cut surface; therefore, the tendon was not trimmed. Examination revealed the joint capsule had been lacerated. After thorough irrigation of the wound with normal saline the joint capsule was repaired with two sutures of 5-O Dexon. The tendon repair was then carried out using 4-O nylon. When the tendon repair was complete, the patient was allowed to flex the thumb gently and then fully extend it. The thumb was then held in full extension. The wound was again irrigated well and the skin was then closed with 4-O nylon. Dressings were applied and a splint was applied holding the interphalangeal joint in neutral position, in full extension but not hyperextension. The patient tolerated the procedure well and left the surgical area in good condition.

DISPOSITION OF CASE: Patient was instructed to elevate the hand, keep his fingers moving, keep the dressing clean and dry, and not to remove the splint or dressing at home. He is to take Percocet, one q4h as needed for pain. He will take Augmentin, 250 mg t.i.d. If he has any problems or difficulties he is to call or return to the emergency department; otherwise, he will be seen in the office for follow-up in three days.

T.J. Stitcher, M.D.

T. J. Stitcher, M.D.

CASE STUDY 2-16

GOODMEDICINE CLINIC

1 Provider Street ■ Anywhere US 12345 ■ (101) 111-2222
EIN: 11-123456   MCARE GRP#: J1110   BCBS GRP#: GC12340

Encounter Form

PROVIDER: GAIL R. BONES, M.D.

PATIENT INFORMATION:

Name:	David J. Hurts
Address:	4321 Nowhere St
City:	Anywhere
State:	US
Zip Code:	12345
Telephone:	(101) 314-1414
Gender:	Male
Date of Birth:	02-25-1955
Occupation:	Painter
Employer:	UC Painters, Anywhere US
Spouse's Employer:	

INSURANCE INFORMATION:

Patient Number:	2-16
Place of Service:	Office
Primary Insurance Plan:	Industrial Indemnity Co.
Primary Insurance Plan ID #:	112102121
Group #:	
Primary Policyholder:	UC Painters
Policyholder Date of Birth:	
Relationship to Patient:	
Secondary Insurance Plan:	
Secondary Insurance Plan ID #:	
Secondary Policyholder:	

Patient Status   ☐ Married   ☐ Divorced   ☒ Single   ☐ Student   ☐ Other

---

DIAGNOSIS INFORMATION

Diagnosis	Code	Diagnosis	Code
1.		5.	
2.		6.	
3.		7.	
4.		8.	

PROCEDURE INFORMATION

Description of Procedure or Service	Date	Code	Charge
1. X-ray, forearm, complete	06-20-YYYY		80.00
2. Closed fracture repair, left radius	06-20-YYYY		300.00
3. Wound repair, 2-cm	06-20-YYYY		80.00
4.			
5.			

SPECIAL NOTES:

Industrial Indemnity Co., 10 Policy St, Anywhere US 12345

GOODMEDICINE CLINIC

Patient Record

1 Provider Street ■ Anywhere US 12345 ■ (101) 111-2222

PROVIDER: GAIL R. BONES, M.D.

OFFICE VISIT 06/20/YYYY

S: At 10:30 this morning, Mr. Ima Boss presented himself at the front desk and announced that he was the supervisor at UC Painters, Inc., and he had an injured worker in the car. The patient is David J. Hurts, who was injured when he fell from a ladder while painting a 543 House St. in Anywhere. The injury occurred at 10:15 a.m. The patient says he fell when a step broke on the ladder.

S: X rays revealed a Colles' fracture of the left radius with only minor displacement.

S: Colles' fracture, left radius. Multiple abrasions and lacerations.

S: The fracture was reduced and a plaster cast applied. The patient was given a prescription for Tylenol #3, instructed in cast care, and told to return tomorrow for a cast check. A 2.0-cm medial mandible laceration was closed with 3 black silk sutures. The supervisor and patient were told the patient would not be able to return to his regular painting job for approximately 6 weeks. The doctor stated she does not anticipate any permanent disability.

Gail R. Bones, M.D.

Gail R. Bones, M.D.

CASE STUDY 2-17

GOODMEDICINE CLINIC

1 Provider Street ■ Anywhere US 12345 ■ (101) 111-2222
EIN: 11-123456   MCARE GRP#: J1110   BCBS GRP#: GC12340

Encounter Form

PROVIDER: JANET B. SURGEON, M.D.

PATIENT INFORMATION:

Name:	Peter M. Smith
Address:	1000 Main St, Apt B
City:	Anywhere
State:	US
Zip Code:	12345
Telephone:	(101) 562-9654
Gender:	Male
Date of Birth:	02-20-1965
Occupation:	Accountant
Employer:	Peebles & Clark
Spouse's Employer:	State University

INSURANCE INFORMATION:

Patient Number:	2-17
Place of Service:	Office
Primary Insurance Plan:	Aetna
Primary Insurance Plan ID #:	235 23 6594
Group #:	3002
Primary Policyholder:	Sandy Smith
Policyholder Date of Birth:	05-20-1967
Relationship to Patient:	Spouse
Secondary Insurance Plan:	TRICARE Standard
Secondary Insurance Plan ID #:	23562658
Secondary Policyholder:	Self

Patient Status   ☒ Married   ☐ Divorced   ☐ Single   ☐ Student   ☐ Other

---

DIAGNOSIS INFORMATION

Diagnosis	Code	Diagnosis	Code
1.		5.	
2.		6.	
3.		7.	
4.		8.	

PROCEDURE INFORMATION

Description of Procedure or Service	Date	Code	Charge
1. Office visit, level III	06-20-YYYY		100.00
2.			
3.			
4.			
5.			

SPECIAL NOTES:

GOODMEDICINE CLINIC

1 Provider Street ■ Anywhere US 12345 ■ (101) 111-2222

Patient Record

PROVIDER: JANET B. SURGEON, M.D.

OFFICE VISIT   06/20/YYYY

Mr. Smith came to the office today complaining of severe left hand pain. I performed tendon repair on his left hand in the emergency department two days ago.

The dressing and splint were removed, taking care to keep the finger in extension. It should be noted that when the dressing was removed, there was a slight flexion to the thumb as it was lying in the splint as the patient had replaced it. The wound was inflamed and hot.

The wound was cleaned with Aqueous Zephiran; Betadine ointment was then applied and it was redressed. A new splint was put on, holding the thumb in a fully extended position.

The patient was instructed to keep the dressing clean and dry and not remove the splint or the dressing. He is to continue his Augmentin. He will continue on Darvocet-N 100 as needed for pain. He was given a prescription for penicillin. If he has any problems or difficulties he is to call me or return to the emergency department; otherwise, he will be seen in the office in 2 days.

Diagnosis: Postoperative wound infection, left hand.

Janet B. Surgeon, M.D.

Janet B. Surgeon, M.D.

CASE STUDY 2-18

GOODMEDICINE CLINIC

1 Provider Street ■ Anywhere US 12345 ■ (101) 111-2222

EIN: 11-123456   MCARE GRP#: J1110   BCBS GRP#: GC12340

Encounter Form

PROVIDER: JANET B. SURGEON, M.D.

PATIENT INFORMATION:

Name:	Mary A. Martin
Address:	5005 South Ave
City:	Anywhere
State:	US
Zip Code:	12345
Telephone:	(101) 111-7676
Gender:	Female
Date of Birth:	10-05-1955
Occupation:	US Navy
Employer:	
Spouse's Employer:	

INSURANCE INFORMATION:

Patient Number:	2-18
Place of Service:	Outpatient
Primary Insurance Plan:	TRICARE
Primary Insurance Plan ID #:	23258957
Group #:	
Primary Policyholder:	Self
Policyholder Date of Birth:	
Relationship to Patient:	
Secondary Insurance Plan:	
Secondary Insurance Plan ID #:	
Secondary Policyholder:	

Patient Status   ☐ Married   ☐ Divorced   ☒ Single   ☐ Student   ☐ Other

DIAGNOSIS INFORMATION

Diagnosis	Code	Diagnosis	Code
1.		5.	
2.		6.	
3.		7.	
4.		8.	

PROCEDURE INFORMATION

Description of Procedure or Service	Date	Code	Charge
1. Hysteroscopic endometrial ablation	06-20-YYYY		950.00
2.			
3.			
4.			
5.			

SPECIAL NOTES:

Surgery performed at Goodmedicine Hospital, 1 Provider St, Anywhere US 12345.

GOODMEDICINE CLINIC

1 Provider Street ■ Anywhere US 12345 ■ (101) 111-2222

Patient Record

PROVIDER: JANET B. SURGEON, M.D.

OUTPATIENT SURGERY 06/20/YYYY

PREOPERATIVE DIAGNOSIS: Menorrhagia

POSTOPERATIVE DIAGNOSIS: Same

PROCEDURE PERFORMED: Endometrial ablation

Patient was anesthetized with general anesthesia via endotracheal tube, and prepped and draped in a sterile fashion. Operative hysteroscope was inserted through the vagina and the cervix into the uterus, and the uterus was filled with saline solution. Thermal ablation of the endometrium was successfully performed, and the hysteroscope and saline were removed. The patient was transferred to the recovery room where her output is to be carefully monitored.

Janet B. Surgeon, M.D.

Janet B. Surgeon, M.D.

CASE STUDY 2-19

GOODMEDICINE CLINIC

1 Provider Street ■ Anywhere US 12345 ■ (101) 111-2222
EIN: 11-123456   MCARE GRP#: J1110   BCBS GRP#: GC12340

Encounter Form

PROVIDER: NANCY HEALER, M.D.   MCARE PIN: N3333   MCAID PIN: NJH3333

PATIENT INFORMATION:

Name:	Cindy Santos
Address:	3902 Main St
City:	Anywhere
State:	US
Zip Code:	12345
Telephone:	(101) 111-5128
Gender:	Female
Date of Birth:	04-29-1935
Occupation:	Retired
Employer:	
Spouse's Employer:	

INSURANCE INFORMATION:

Patient Number:	2-19
Place of Service:	Office
Primary Insurance Plan:	Medicare
Primary Insurance Plan ID #:	53231589A
Group #:	
Primary Policyholder:	Self
Policyholder Date of Birth:	
Relationship to Patient:	
Secondary Insurance Plan:	Medicaid
Secondary Insurance Plan ID #:	231562584
Secondary Policyholder:	Self

Patient Status   ☐ Married   ☐ Divorced   ☒ Single   ☐ Student   ☐ Other

DIAGNOSIS INFORMATION

Diagnosis	Code	Diagnosis	Code
1.		5.	
2.		6.	
3.		7.	
4.		8.	

PROCEDURE INFORMATION

Description of Procedure or Service	Date	Code	Charge
1. Office visit, level II	06-20-YYYY		$ 50.00
2.			
3.			
4.			
5.			

SPECIAL NOTES:

GOODMEDICINE CLINIC

1 Provider Street ■ Anywhere US 12345 ■ (101) 111-2222

Patient Record

PROVIDER: NANCY HEALER, M.D.

HOME VISIT   06/20/YYYY

S: Patient was seen in the office today in follow-up for chronic hypertension. She has no complaints today.

O: Her blood pressure is 120/80. Chest is clear to auscultation and percussion. Heart is unremarkable. Extremities reveal no edema or redness.

A: Chronic hypertension, controlled with medication.

P: Renew hypertensive medication. Schedule office follow-up visit in 3 months.

Nancy Healer, M.D.

Nancy Healer, M.D.

CASE STUDY 2-20

GOODMEDICINE CLINIC

1 Provider Street ■ Anywhere US 12345 ■ (101) 111-2222

EIN: 11-123456   MCARE GRP#: J1110   BCBS GRP#: GC12340

Encounter Form

PROVIDER: T. J. STITCHER, M.D.   BCBS PIN: 12342   MCARE PIN: T2222

PATIENT INFORMATION:		INSURANCE INFORMATION:	
Name:	Lana Tobias	Patient Number:	2-20
Address:	3920 Hill St	Place of Service:	Inpatient Hospital
City:	Anywhere	Primary Insurance Plan:	BCBS
State:	US	Primary Insurance Plan ID #:	ABC123456
Zip Code:	12345	Group #:	AB103
Telephone:	(101) 555-1235	Primary Policyholder:	Carey Tobias
Gender:	Female	Policyholder Date of Birth:	05-05-1965
Date of Birth:	12-15-1967	Relationship to Patient:	Spouse
Occupation:		Secondary Insurance Plan:	Medicare
Employer:		Secondary Insurance Plan ID #:	23256258A
Spouse's Employer:	State University	Secondary Policyholder:	Self

---

Patient Status   ☒ Married   ☐ Divorced   ☐ Single   ☐ Student   ☐ Other

---

DIAGNOSIS INFORMATION

Diagnosis	Code	Diagnosis	Code
1.		5.	
2.		6.	
3.		7.	
4.		8.	

PROCEDURE INFORMATION

Description of Procedure or Service	Date	Code	Charge
1. Office visit, level II, established patient	06-20-YYYY		50.00
2.			
3.			
4.			
5.			

SPECIAL NOTES:

GOODMEDICINE CLINIC

1 Provider Street ■ Anywhere US 12345 ■ (101) 111-2222

Patient Record

PROVIDER: T. J. STITCHER, M.D.

INPATIENT   06/20/YYYY

S: Patient seen in the office today with complaint of left hip pain. She states that she fell down some stairs in her home two days ago while carrying laundry to her basement. She says when she awakes in the morning her hip "really hurts her."

O: Physical examination reveals good range of motion of her left hip, and she can walk without pain. Bruising is noted in the left hip area.

A: Left hip pain.

P: The patient was instructed to take over-the-counter acetaminophen for pain, as directed. If the pain worsens, she is to call the office.

T.J. Stitcher, M.D.

T. J. Stitcher, M.D.

CASE STUDY 2-21

GOODMEDICINE CLINIC

1 Provider Street ■ Anywhere US 12345 ■ (101) 111-2222
EIN: 11-123456   MCARE GRP#: J1110   BCBS GRP#: GC12340

Encounter Form

PROVIDER: HENRY C. CARDIAC, M.D.   MCARE PIN: H4444

PATIENT INFORMATION:		INSURANCE INFORMATION:	
Name:	Larry Kane	Patient Number:	2-21
Address:	2359 Green St	Place of Service:	Office
City:	Anywhere	Primary Insurance Plan:	Medicare
State:	US	Primary Insurance Plan ID #:	23259586B
Zip Code:	12345	Group #:	
Telephone:	(101) 555-8950	Primary Policyholder:	Self
Gender:	Male	Policyholder Date of Birth:	
Date of Birth:	09-10-1937	Relationship to Patient:	
Occupation:	Retired	Secondary Insurance Plan:	
Employer:		Secondary Insurance Plan ID #:	
Spouse's Employer:		Secondary Policyholder:	

Patient Status   ☐ Married   ☐ Divorced   ☒ Single   ☐ Student   ☐ Other

---

DIAGNOSIS INFORMATION

Diagnosis	Code	Diagnosis	Code
1.		5.	
2.		6.	
3.		7.	
4.		8.	

PROCEDURE INFORMATION

Description of Procedure or Service	Date	Code	Charge
1. Office visit, level III	06-20-YYYY		100.00
2.			
3.			
4.			
5.			

SPECIAL NOTES:

GOODMEDICINE CLINIC

1 Provider Street ■ Anywhere US 12345 ■ (101) 111-2222

Patient Record

PROVIDER: HENRY C. CARDIAC, M.D.

OFFICE VISIT 06/20/YYYY

S: Elderly caucasian male returns for follow-up of recently diagnosed hypercholesterolemia. He has no complaints other than some occasional indigestion. He is tolerating his Cholestin medication well.

O: Patient is somewhat obese, appears his stated age, and is in no acute distress. Weight is 200. Height is 5'10". Pulse 18. BP 120/80. HEENT grossly unremarkable. Neck reveals normal jugular venous pressure, without hepatojugular reflux. Normal carotid pulses; no bruits present. Lungs are clear to A&P. Heart reveals regular rhythm, S1 and S2 are normal. There is no murmur, rub, click, or gallop. Cardiac apex is not palpable. No heaves or thrills are detected. Abdomen is soft, nontender, with normal bowel sounds, and no bruits. No organomegaly, including abdominal aorta, or masses noted. Extremities reveal a surgical scar in the right leg, presumably from saphenous venectomy. Femoral pulses are normal, without bruits. Dorsalis pedis and posterior tibial pulses are also normal. There is no cyanosis, clubbing, or edema. Neurological is grossly within normal limits.

A: Hypercholesterolemia.

P: Patient was instructed to refill prescription for Cholestin, and schedule 3 month follow-up appointment.

Henry C. Cardiac, M.D.
Henry C. Cardiac, M.D.

Appendix III

Forms

You are welcome to copy the following forms for use when completing exercises in the text-book and workbook:

- CMS-1500 claim
- Coding Case Study Form (for Chapter 10 exercises)
- Insurance Plan Comparison Chart
- E/M CodeBuilder

NOTE: These forms can also be printed from the CD-ROM that accompanies this textbook. ●

PLEASE
DO NOT
STAPLE
IN THIS
AREA

(SAMPLE ONLY - NOT APPROVED FOR USE)

CARRIER

| | PICA | | | **HEALTH INSURANCE CLAIM FORM** | PICA | | |

| PICA | **HEALTH INSURANCE CLAIM FORM** | PICA |

1. MEDICARE MEDICAID CHAMPUS CHAMPVA GROUP HEALTH PLAN FECA BLK LUNG OTHER
☐ (Medicare #) ☐ (Medicaid #) ☐ (Sponsor's SSN) ☐ (VA File #) ☐ (SSN or ID) ☐ (SSN) ☐ (ID)

1a. INSURED'S I.D. NUMBER   (FOR PROGRAM IN ITEM 1)

2. PATIENT'S NAME (Last Name, First Name, Middle Initial)

3. PATIENT'S BIRTH DATE
MM   DD   YY   SEX
M ☐   F ☐

4. INSURED'S NAME (Last Name, First Name, Middle Initial)

5. PATIENT'S ADDRESS (No. Street)

6. PATIENT RELATIONSHIP TO INSURED
Self ☐   Spouse ☐   Child ☐   Other ☐

7. INSURED'S ADDRESS (No. Street)

CITY   STATE

8. PATIENT STATUS
Single ☐   Married ☐   Other ☐

CITY   STATE

ZIP CODE   TELEPHONE (Include Area Code)
(   )

Employed ☐   Full-Time Student ☐   Part-Time Student ☐

ZIP CODE   TELEPHONE (INCLUDE AREA CODE)
(   )

9. OTHER INSURED'S NAME (Last Name, First Name, Middle Initial)

10. IS PATIENT'S CONDITION RELATED TO:

11. INSURED'S POLICY GROUP OR FECA NUMBER

a. OTHER INSURED'S POLICY OR GROUP NUMBER

a. EMPLOYMENT? (CURRENT OR PREVIOUS)
☐ YES   ☐ NO

a. INSURED'S DATE OF BIRTH
MM   DD   YY   SEX
M ☐   F ☐

b. OTHER INSURED'S DATE OF BIRTH
MM   DD   YY   SEX
M ☐   F ☐

b. AUTO ACCIDENT?   PLACE (State)
☐ YES   ☐ NO

b. EMPLOYER'S NAME OR SCHOOL NAME

c. EMPLOYER'S NAME OR SCHOOL NAME

c. OTHER ACCIDENT?
☐ YES   ☐ NO

c. INSURANCE PLAN NAME OR PROGRAM NAME

d. INSURANCE PLAN NAME OR PROGRAM NAME

10d. RESERVED FOR LOCAL USE

d. IS THERE ANOTHER HEALTH BENEFIT PLAN?
☐ YES   ☐ NO   If yes, return to and complete item 9 a – d.

READ BACK OF FORM BEFORE COMPLETING & SIGNING THIS FORM.
12. PATIENT'S OR AUTHORIZED PERSON'S SIGNATURE I authorize the release of any medical or other information necessary to process this claim. I also request payment of government benefits either to myself or to the party who accepts assignment below.

SIGNED _____ DATE _____

13. INSURED'S OR AUTHORIZED PERSON'S SIGNATURE I authorize payment of medical benefits to the undersigned physician or supplier for services described below.

SIGNED _____

PATIENT AND INSURED INFORMATION

14. DATE OF CURRENT:
MM   DD   YY   ◀ ILLNESS (First symptom) OR INJURY (Accident) OR PREGNANCY (LMP)

15. IF PATIENT HAS HAD SAME OR SIMILAR ILLNESS, GIVE FIRST DATE   MM   DD   YY

16. DATES PATIENT UNABLE TO WORK IN CURRENT OCCUPATION
MM   DD   YY   MM   DD   YY
FROM   TO

17. NAME OF REFERRING PHYSICIAN OR OTHER SOURCE

17a. I.D. NUMBER OF REFERRING PHYSICIAN

18. HOSPITALIZATION DATES RELATED TO CURRENT SERVICES
MM   DD   YY   MM   DD   YY
FROM   TO

19. RESERVED FOR LOCAL USE

20. OUTSIDE LAB? $ CHARGES
☐ YES   ☐ NO

21. DIAGNOSIS OR NATURE OF ILLNESS OR INJURY. (RELATE ITEMS 1, 2, 3, OR 4 TO ITEM 24E BY LINE)
1. |___.___| 3. |___.___|
2. |___.___| 4. |___.___|

22. MEDICAID RESUBMISSION CODE   ORIGINAL REF. NO.

23. PRIOR AUTHORIZATION NUMBER

24. A DATE(S) OF SERVICE					B	C	D PROCEDURES, SERVICES, OR SUPPLIES (Explain Unusual Circumstances)		E	F	G	H	I	J	K
From			To			Place of Service	Type of Service	CPT/HCPCS	MODIFIER	DIAGNOSIS CODE	$ CHARGES	DAYS OR UNITS	EPSDT Family Plan	EMG	COB	RESERVED FOR LOCAL USE
MM	DD	YY	MM	DD	YY											
1																
2																
3																
4																
5																
6																

25. FEDERAL TAX I.D. NUMBER   SSN EIN
☐ ☐

26. PATIENT'S ACCOUNT NO.

27. ACCEPT ASSIGNMENT?
(For govt. claims, see back)
☐ YES   ☐ NO

28. TOTAL CHARGE
$

29. AMOUNT PAID
$

30. BALANCE DUE
$

31. SIGNATURE OF PHYSICIAN OR SUPPLIER INCLUDING DEGREES OR CREDENTIALS
(I certify that the statements on the reverse apply to this bill and are made a part thereof.)

SIGNED _____ DATE _____

32. NAME AND ADDRESS OF FACILITY WHERE SERVICES WERE RENDERED (if other than home or office)

33. PHYSICIAN'S SUPPLIER'S BILLING NAME, ADDRESS, ZIP CODE & PHONE #

PIN#   GRP#

PHYSICIAN OR SUPPLIER INFORMATION

(SAMPLE ONLY - NOT APPROVED FOR USE)   *PLEASE PRINT OR TYPE*   SAMPLE FORM 1500
SAMPLE FORM 1500 SAMPLE FORM 1500

Coding Case Study Form

Page _____

CASE STUDY NO.	DIAGNOSIS CODE #s	PROCEDURE CODE #s
Sample: 2-1	789.35, 569.3	99242

Insurance Plan Comparison Chart

Page _____

BLOCK										

E/M CODEBUILDER

(For use with 1995 and 1997 *CMS Documentation Guidelines for Evaluation & Management Coding*)

Introduction

The E/M code reported to a third-party payer must be supported by documentation in the patient's record (e.g., SOAP or clinic note, diagnostic test results, operative findings). While providers are responsible for selecting the E/M code at the time patient care is rendered, insurance specialists audit records to make sure that the appropriate level of E/M code was reported to the third-party payer.

This *E/M CodeBuilder* form can be used for that purpose, and it can also be used as a tool to teach appropriate assignment of E/M level codes. To assign a code, just review the documentation in the patient's record, record your findings below (based on the directions provided), and refer to the CPT coding manual to select the E/M code to be reported.

E/M code selection is based on three key components: *history, examination*, and *medical decision making*. This E/M CodeBuilder form emphasizes those components. It is important to be aware that contributory components (*counseling* and *coordination of care*) also play an important role in selecting the E/M code when documentation in the patient record indicates that counseling or coordination of care dominated the visit. In this situation, the contributory component of *time* can be considered a key or controlling factor in selecting a level of E/M service (code).

NOTE: *Time* and *nature of presenting problem* are listed in some E/M code descriptions to assist in determining which code number to report. ●

Selecting the Level of History

To select the level of history, review the following elements in the patient record. If an element is not documented, it cannot be considered when selecting the level of E/M service code.
● History of Present Illness (HPI)
● Review of Systems (ROS)
● Past, Family, and/or Social History (PFSH)

History of Present Illness (HPI)

Review the clinic or SOAP note in the patient's record, and for each documented HPI element (below), enter an X in the box located in front of the element on this form. Then, total the Xs and enter that number on the line located in front of the Total Score (below). Finally, select the level of HPI based on the total number of elements documented, and enter an X in the appropriate box.

☐ **Location:** of pain/discomfort (e.g., is pain diffused/localized or unilateral/bilateral; does it radiate or refer?).

☐ **Quality:** a description of the quality of the symptom (e.g., is pain described as sharp, dull, throbbing, stabbing, constant, intermittent, acute or chronic, stable, improving, or worsening?).

☐ **Severity:** use of self-assessment scale to measure subjective levels (e.g., on a scale of 1-10, how severe is the pain?), or comparison of pain quantitatively with previously experienced pain.

☐ **Timing:** establishing onset of pain and chronology of pain development (e.g., migraine in the a.m.).

☐ **Context:** where was the patient and what was he doing when pain began (e.g., was patient at rest or involved in an activity; was pain aggravated or relieved, or does it recur, with a specific activity; did situational stress or some other factor precede or accompany the pain)?

☐ **Modifying factors:** what has patient attempted to do to relieve pain (e.g., heat vs. cold; does it relieve or exacerbate pain; what makes the pain worse; have over-the-counter drugs been attempted—with what results)?

☐ **Associated signs/symptoms:** clinician's impressions formulated during the interview may lead to questioning about additional sensations or feelings (e.g., diaphoresis associated with indigestion or chest pain, blurred vision accompanying a headache, etc.).

_____ **Total Score:** Enter the score for number of Xs entered above (representing number of HPI elements), and enter an X in front of the HPI type below:

      ☐ Brief HPI (1–3 elements)

      ☐ Extended HPI (4 or more elements)

Review of Systems (ROS)

Review the clinic or SOAP note in the patient's record, and for each documented ROS element (below), enter an X in the box located in front of the element on this form. Then, total the Xs and enter that number on the line located in front of the Total Score (below). Finally, select the level of ROS based on the total number of elements documented, and enter an X in the appropriate box.

NOTE: To properly assess review of systems documentation, have *CMS Documentation Guidelines for Evaluation & Management Coding* available as you review the patient's record. ●

- [ ] Constitutional symptoms
- [ ] Eyes
- [ ] Musculoskeletal
- [ ] Ears, nose, mouth, throat
- [ ] Cardiovascular
- [ ] Respiratory
- [ ] Gastrointestinal
- [ ] Integumentary (including skin & breast)
- [ ] Genitourinary
- [ ] Allergic/Immunologic
- [ ] Hematologic/Lymphatic
- [ ] Neurologic
- [ ] Endocrine
- [ ] Psychiatric

____ **Total Score:** Enter the score for number of Xs entered above (representing number of ROS elements), and enter an X in front of the ROS type below:
- [ ] None
- [ ] Problem pertinent (1 body system documented)
- [ ] Extended (2–9 body systems documented)
- [ ] Complete (all body systems documented)

Past, Family, and/or Social History (PFSH)

Review the clinic or SOAP note in the patient's record, and for each documented PFSH element (below), enter an X in the box located in front of the element on this form. Then, total the Xs and enter that number on the line located in front of the Total Score (below). Finally, select the level of PFSH based on the total number of elements documented, and enter an X in the appropriate box.

- [ ] Past history (patient's past experience with illnesses, operations, injuries, and treatments)
- [ ] Family history (review of medical events in the patient's family, including diseases that may be hereditary or place the patient at risk)
- [ ] Social history (an age appropriate review of past and current activities)

____ **Total Score:** Enter the score for number of Xs entered above (representing number of PFSH elements), and enter an X in front of the PFSH type below:
- [ ] None
- [ ] Pertinent (1 history area documented)
- [ ] Complete (2 or 3 history areas documented)

Level of History

Circle the type of HPI, ROS, and PFSH determined above; then circle the appropriate Level of History below.

HPI	Brief	Brief	Extended	Extended
ROS	None	Problem Pertinent	Extended	Completd
PFSH	None	None	Pertinent	Complete
Level of History	Problem Focused	Expanded Problem Focused	Detailed	Comprehensive

Selecting the Level of Examination

To select the level of examination, first determine whether a *single organ examination* (specialist exam; e.g., ophthalmologist) or a *general multisystem examination* (e.g., family practitioner) was completed.

NOTE: To properly assess review of systems documentation, have *CMS Documentation Guidelines for Evaluation & Management Coding* available as you review the patient's record. ●

Single Organ System Examination

Refer to the single organ system examination requirements in the *CMS Documentation Guidelines for Evaluation & Management Services*, and enter an X in front of the appropriate exam type below.

☐ PROBLEM FOCUSED EXAMINATION (1–5 elements identified by a bullet)

☐ EXPANDED PROBLEM FOCUSED EXAMINATION (at least 6 elements identified by a bullet)

☐ DETAILED EXAMINATION (at least 12 elements identified by a bullet)

NOTE: For eye and psychiatric examinations, at least 9 elements in each box with a shaded border and at least one element in each box with a shaded or unshaded border is documented. ●

☐ COMPREHENSIVE EXAMINATION (all elements identified by a bullet; document every element in each box with a shaded border and at least 1 element in each box with an unshaded box)

General Multisystem Exam

Refer to the General Multisystem Examination Requirements in the *CMS Documentation Guidelines for Evaluation & Management Services*. Enter an X in front of the organ system or body area for up to the total number of allowed elements (e.g., up to 2 elements can be documented for the Neck exam).

☐ Constitutional (2)   ☐ Respiratory (4)   ☐ Genitourinary (male–3; female–6)

☐ Eyes (3)   ☐ Gastrointestinal (5)   ☐ Musculoskeletal (6)

☐ Ears, nose, mouth, throat (6) ☐ Chest (breasts) (2)   ☐ Neurologic (3)

☐ Neck (2)   ☐ Skin (2)   ☐ Psychiatric (4)

☐ Cardiovascular (7)

_____ **Total Score:**   Enter the score for number of Xs entered above (representing number of Exam elements), and enter an X in front of the Exam type below:

☐ PROBLEM FOCUSED EXAMINATION (1-5 elements identified by a bullet on *CMS Documentation Guidelines for Evaluation & Management Services*)

☐ EXPANDED PROBLEM FOCUSED EXAMINATION (at least 6 elements identified by a bullet on *CMS Documentation Guidelines for Evaluation & Management Services*)

☐ DETAILED EXAMINATION (at least 2 elements identified by a bullet from each of 6 organ systems or body areas, or at least 12 elements identified by a bullet in two or more systems or areas, on *CMS Documentation Guidelines for Evaluation & Management Services*)

☐ COMPREHENSIVE EXAMINATION (documentation of all elements identified by a bullet in at least 9 organ systems or body areas, and documentation of at least 2 elements identified by a bullet from each of 9 organ systems or body areas, on *CMS Documentation Guidelines for Evaluation & Management Services*)

Medical Decision Making

Select the appropriate level of medical decision making based upon the following criteria:

Number of diagnoses or management options	Amount/complexity of data to be reviewed	Risk of complications and/or morbidity/mortality	Medical Decision Making
Minimal	Minimal or None	Minimal	Straightforward
Limited	Limited	Low	Low Complexity
Multiple	Moderate	Moderate	Moderate Complexity
Extensive	Extensive	High	High Complexity

E/M Code Selection

Select the E/M code based on selection of level of history, examination, and medical decision making:

History	Problem focused	Expanded problem focused	Expanded problem focused	Detailed	Comprehensive
Examination	Problem focused	Expanded problem focused	Expanded problem focused	Detailed	Comprehensive
Medical Decision Making	Straightforward	Low complexity	Moderate complexity	Moderate complexity	High complexity

Go to the appropriate E/M category/subcategory, and select the code based upon the information above.

Appendix IV

Answers to Coding Exercises

Answers to ICD-9-CM Coding Exercises (Chapter 6)

NOTE: The underlined word is the condition found in the Index. ●

Exercise 6-1

1. Bronchiole <u>spasm</u>	519.1
2. <u>Congenital candidiasis</u>	112.9
3. <u>Irritable</u> bladder	596.8
4. Earthquake injury	E909.0
(No site mentioned. See Injury in Index to External Causes)	
5. <u>Exposure</u> to AIDS virus	V01.7
6. Ground <u>itch</u>	126.9
7. <u>Nun's</u> knees	727.2
8. <u>Mice</u>, right knee joint	717.6

Exercise 6-2

1. Acute purulent <u>sinusitis</u>	461.9 - (purulent) is a nonessential modifier
2. <u>Fracture</u>, mandible	802.20 - (closed) is a nonessential modifier
3. Actinomycotic <u>meningitis</u>	039.8, 320.7 - sequence bracketed code second
4. Psychomotor akinetic <u>epilepsy</u>	345.40 - requires fifth digit
5. 3 cm <u>laceration</u>, right forearm	881.00 - *See also* wound, open
6. <u>Contusion</u>, abdomen	868.00 - NEC
7. <u>Pneumonia due to</u> *H. influenzae*	482.2 - Subcategory
8. Delayed healing, open <u>wound</u>, abdomen	879.3 - Boxed Note describes "delayed healing" as "complicated"
9. Bile duct <u>cicatrix</u>	576.8 - "Trust the index."
10. Uncontrolled noninsulin dependent <u>diabetes</u> with osteomyelitis	250.82, 731.8 - Bracketed code

Exercise 6-3

1. 515	Postinflammatory pulmonary <u>fibrosis</u>	C
2. 250.1	Noninsulin-dependent <u>diabetes</u>	250.10
3. 727.67	Nontraumatic <u>rupture</u> of Achilles tendon	C
4. 422.0	Acute <u>myocarditis</u> due to Coxsackie virus	074.23, 422.0

5. 813.22   <u>Malunion</u>, closed, right radial fracture   733.81
6. 483.0   Mycoplasmic <u>pneumonia</u>   C
7. 795.71   Positive <u>HIV</u> test, asymptomatic   V08
8. 796.2   <u>Elevated</u> blood pressure   C
9. 718.06   Old <u>tear</u> of right knee meniscus   717.5

Exercise 6-4

1. <u>Pregnancy</u> complicated by gonorrhea   647.13, 098.3 - fifth digit
2. Benign <u>neoplasm</u>, ear cartilage   215.0 - ear cartilage is not excluded
3. <u>Cervicitis</u>, tuberculous   016.70 - Includes
4. Uncontrolled Type II <u>diabetes</u> with polyneuropathy   250.62, 357.2 - Use additional code
5. Congenital <u>hemangioma</u> on face   228.01 - Site is skin. Includes
6. <u>Hiss-Russell</u> shigellosis   004.1 - "Trust the Index."
7. Closed <u>fracture</u>, right leg   827.0 - NOS
8. Diabetic <u>cataract</u>   250.50, 366.41 - Use additional code
9. Muscular <u>atrophy</u>, left leg   728.2 - NEC
10. Chronic smoker's bronchitis with   466.0 (the acute disorder) and
    acute <u>bronchitis</u>   491.0 - Includes (the underlying chronic condition)

Exercise 6-5

1. Essential <u>hypertension</u> with cardiomegaly   402.90 - Includes
2. Transient <u>hypertension</u> due to pregnancy   642.30 (episode of care is not stated)
3. Malignant <u>hypertensive</u> crisis   401.0
4. Renal and heart disease due to <u>hypertension</u>   404.90 - Hypertension, Cardiorenal

Exercise 6-6

1. <u>Kaposi's</u> sarcoma   176.9
2. <u>Lipoma</u>, skin, upper back   214.1
3. <u>Carcinoma</u> *in situ*, skin, left cheek   232.3
4. Scrotum <u>mass</u>   608.89
5. <u>Neurofibroma</u>   215.9
6. <u>Cyst</u> on left ovary   620.2
7. <u>Ganglion</u>, right wrist   727.41
8. <u>Yaws</u>, frambeside   102.2
9. Breast, chronic <u>cystic</u> disease   610.1
10. Hurtle cell <u>tumor</u>   226
11. Bile duct <u>cystadenocarcinoma</u>   155.1
12. Mixed <u>glioma</u>   191.9

Exercise 6-7

1. Ca (carcinoma) of the lung   162.9
2. Metastasis from the lung   162.9 (lung is primary),
                                                      199.1 (unknown secondary site)

3. Abdominal mass   789.30
4. Carcinoma of the breast (female) with   174.9, 196.3
   metastasis to the axillary lymph nodes
5. Carcinoma of axillary lymph nodes and   174.9 (breast is primary)
   lungs, metastatic from the breast (female)   196.3, 197.0 (secondary sites)
6. Astrocytoma (Unspecified site)   191.0
7. Skin lesion, left cheek   709.9

Exercise 6-8

1. Adverse <u>reaction</u> to pertussis vaccine   995.2 (unspecified adverse effect),
   (<u>Table of Drugs and Chemicals, Therapeutic</u>)   E948.6
2. Cardiac <u>arrhythmia</u> caused by interaction   971.2 (poisoning, ephedrine),
   between prescribed ephedrine   980.0 (poisoning, alcohol),
   and alcohol, not prescribed (<u>Table of Drugs and</u>   427.9 (arrhythmia), E980.4,
   <u>Chemicals, Poisoning</u>)   E980.9 (undetermined external cause)

3. Stupor due to overdose of Nytol (suicide attempt) (Table of Drugs and Chemicals, Poisoning, Suicide)

963.0 (poisoning, Nytol), 780.09 (stupor), E950.4 (suicide attempt)

Exercise 6-9

1. Family history of epilepsy with no evidence of seizures — V17.2
2. Six-week postpartum checkup — V24.2
3. Premarital physical (examination, marriage) — V70.3
4. Consult with dietitian for patient with diabetes mellitus — V65.3, 250.00
5. Rubella screening — V73.3
6. Exposure to TB — V01.1

Exercise 6-10

1. Patient is HIV positive with no symptoms — V08
2. AIDS patient treated for Candida — 112.9, 042
3. Open fracture maxilla — 802.5
4. Greenstick fracture, third digit, right foot — 826.0
5. Multiple fractures, right femur, distal end — 821.29

Exercise 6-11

1. Malunion due to fracture, right ankle, 9 months ago — 733.81, 905.4 (Late Effect)
2. Brain damage due to subdural hematoma, 18 months previously — 348.9, 438.9 (nontraumatic) or 907.0 (traumatic) (depending on documentation)
3. Second-degree burn, anterior chest wall — 942.22, 948.00 (extent of body surface burned is 9%)
4. Scalding with erythema, right forearm and hand — 943.11, 944.10, 948.00
5. Third-degree burn, back, 18% body surface — 942.34, 948.11

Exercise 6-12

1. Automobile accident, highway, passenger — E819.1 (Accident, motor vehicle)
2. Worker injured by fall from ladder — E881.0
3. Accidental drowning, fell from power boat — E832.1
4. Soft tissue injury, right arm, due to snow-mobile accident in patient's yard — 884.0, E820.9 (Accident, snow vehicle) E849.0 (Accident, occurring at or in)

Answers to CPT Coding Exercises (Chapter 7)

NOTE: The underlined words are found in the Index. Words in parentheses are substitutions to help you locate the procedure/service in the index, or provide explanations of special coding situations. ●

Exercise 7-1

1. False   The asterisk indicates a variable minor surgical procedure only. Pre- and postop services are billed separately.
2. False   The Evaluation and Management and Anesthesia sections are excluded from the list. Nuclear medicine is a subsection of Radiology. Pathology should be listed as Pathology and Laboratory.
3. False   The triangle indicates a code description revision.
4. False   CPT requires a two-digit modifier to be attached to the five-digit CPT code.
5. True   While parenthetical notes apply to specific codes or refer the reader to additional codes, blocked notes provide instruction for codes listed below the heading.
6. True   Semicolons save space in CPT where a series of related codes are found.
7. False   Qualifiers may appear in main and subordinate clauses.
8. False   Parenthetical statements beginning with "E.g." provide examples of terms that might be in the health care provider's description of the service performed. They do not have to be included in the documentation.
9. True   Horizontal triangles ▶ ◀ are found in revised guidelines, notes, and procedure descriptions.
10. True   The bullet (●) located to the left of a CPT code indicates a new code has been added to CPT.
11. False Code 50620 would be reported for a *ureterolithotomy* performed on the middle one-third of the ureter.

Exercise 7-2

2. Marsupialization means creating a pouch.
3. 47350   management of liver hemorrhage; simple suture of liver wound or injury
   47360   complex suture of liver wound or injury, with or without hepatic artery ligation
   47361   exploration of hepatic wound, extensive debridement, coagulation, and/or suture with or without packing of liver
   47362   re-exploration of hepatic wound for removal of packing

Exercise 7-3

1. Assistant surgeon reporting patient's cesarean section, delivery only.	-80
2. Cholecystectomy reported during postoperative period for treatment of leg fracture.	-79
3. Treatment for chronic conditions at same time preventative medicine is provided.	-25
4. Inpatient visit performed by surgeon, with decision to perform surgery tomorrow.	-57
5. Office consultation as preoperative clearance for surgery.	No modifier is assigned.
6. Postoperative management of vaginal hysterectomy.	-55
7. Repeat gallbladder X-ray series, same physician.	-76
8. Arthroscopy of right elbow and closed fracture reduction of left wrist.	-51
9. Needle core biopsy of right and left breast.	-50
10. Consultation required by payer.	-32

Exercise 7-4

1. Closed treatment of wrist dislocation	25660, 25675, 25680
2. Dilation of cervix (See Dilation and Curettage)	57800-57820
3. Placement of upper GI feeding tube (Placement, nasogastric tube)	43752
4. Radiograph and fluoroscopy of chest, 4 views (See Radiology, Diagnostic; X-ray) X-ray, Chest, Complete (Four Views), with Fluoroscopy	71034
5. Magnetic resonance imaging (MRI), Spine, Lumbar	72148, 72158
6. Darrach procedure (See Excision, Ulna, Partial)	25150-25151, 25240
7. Manual CBC (See Blood Cell Count, Complete Blood Count [CBC])	85025-85027
8. Electrosurgical removal, skin tags	11200-11201

Exercise 7-5

1. Incision and drainage (I&D) finger abscess	26010
2. Percutaneous I&D, abscess, appendix	44901
3. Anesthetic agent injection, L-5 paravertebral nerve	64475
4. Laparoscopic cholecystectomy with cholangiography	47563
5. Flexible esophagoscopy with brushing and specimen collection and removal of foreign body and radiologic supervision and interpretation (S&I) (Esophagus, Endoscopy, Removal, Foreign Body **or** Endoscopy, Esophagus, Removal, Foreign Body. See parenthetical note below 43215 for second code.)	43215, 74235
6. Anterior interbody approach, arthrodesis with minimal diskectomy, L-1 through L-3 vertebrae (Arthrodesis, Vertebra, Lumbar, Anterior, Anterolateral Approach. There are two interspaces between L-1 & L-3. Use add-on code for the second interspace.)	22558, 22585

Exercise 7-6

1. Diagnostic arthroscopy, right wrist, with biopsy (BX)	29840
2. Simple vaginal mucosal biopsy	57100
3. Diagnostic nasal endoscopy, bilateral and	31231
Facial chemical peel	15788
4. Diagnostic thoracoscopy, pleural space and biopsy right lung	32602

Exercise 7-7

1. Excision, 2.5 cm malignant lesion, left cheek (Excision, Skin, Malignant)	11643

2. Excision 1-1/2 inch benign lesion, scalp   11424
   (Lesion is 3.81 cm. Excision, Lesion, Skin, benign)
3. Remove 10 <u>skin</u> tags upper back, 3 right   11200 (first 15 lesions)
   arm, 4 chest, 2 left thigh, 3 abdomen   11201 (remaining 7 lesions)
4. Suture, 1 inch simple laceration, left forearm, and 2-1/2 inch   12004
   simple laceration, right arm (<u>Repair</u>, Wound, Simple. Instructional
   note at Repair-Simple states "sum of lengths of repairs."
   Therefore, add 1 inch and 2-1/2 inch repairs together,
   convert to centimeters, and wound length is 8.89 cm.)
5. <u>Excision</u> 2.5 cm malignant <u>lesion</u> forehead   11643
   with intermediate closure   12051
   (See parenthetical note regarding closure at
   Excision-Malignant Lesions)

Exercise 7-8

1. <u>Exploration</u> of right wrist with removal of deep foreign body   25248
2. <u>Manipulation</u> of right thumb <u>dislocation</u>   26641
3. Reapplication of short leg walking <u>cast</u>   29425
4. Open reduction with screws, compound <u>fracture</u>,   27758
   shaft, left tibia and fibula, and application of a long
   leg cast (No code for cast. See casting notes at
   beginning of Application of Casts and Strapping.)
5. Diagnostic <u>arthroscopy</u> followed by removal   29870
   of the medial meniscus by <u>arthrotomy</u>   27332
   (Surgery was not performed through the arthroscope.)

Exercise 7-9

1. <u>Laparoscopy</u> cholecystectomy with cholangiography   47563
2. <u>Anoscopy</u> with removal of polyp by snare   46611
3. Diagnostic flexible bronchoscopy (Bronchi, Exploration)   31622
4. Fibroscopic full colonoscopy, with removal of polyps   45385
   by snare (Endoscopy, Colon, Removal)
5. Nasal endoscopy with partial ethmoidectomy   31254

Exercise 7-10

1. Cardiac catheterization, right side only   93501
   (<u>Catheter</u>, Cardiac, Right Heart) with conscious <u>sedation</u>, IV   99141
2. Routine <u>EKG</u>, tracing only   93005
3. <u>Spirometry</u>   94010
4. <u>CPR</u>, in office   92950
5. <u>Psychiatric diagnostic</u> examination   90801
6. Influenza <u>vaccine</u>   90657 or 90658 or 90659 or 90660
        and 90471
7. <u>Whirlpool</u> and   97022
   <u>paraffin bath</u> therapy   97018
8. WAIS-R and MMPI psychological tests and report,   96100
   1 hour (Psychiatric Diagnosis, Psychological Testing)
9. Office services on emergency basis (Office, Medical Service)   99058

Exercise 7-11

1. GI series <u>X-ray</u>, with small bowel and air studies, without KUB   74246
2. Chest <u>X-ray</u>, PA & Left Lateral   71020
3. Cervical spine, complete, with flexion and extension (xray, spine)   72052
4. <u>X-ray</u> pelvis, AP only   72170
5. Abdomen, flat plate, AP (X-ray)   74000
6. BE, colon, with air (X-ray colon)   74280
7. Postoperative radiological supervision and   74305
   interpretation of <u>cholangiography</u> by radiologist
8. <u>SPECT</u> exam of the liver   78205
9. Retrograde pyelography with KUB   74420

Exercise 7-12

1.	Hepatic function <u>panel</u>	80076
2.	Hepatitis <u>panel</u>	80074
3.	<u>TB</u> skin test, PPD	86580
4.	<u>Urinalysis</u> with microscopy, automated	81001
5.	<u>CBC</u> w/Diff, manual	85032
6.	Stool for <u>occult blood</u>	82270
7.	Wet mount, vaginal <u>smear</u>	87210
8.	<u>Glucose</u>/blood sugar, <u>quantitative</u>	82948
9.	<u>Sedimentation</u> rate (Need method for definitive code)	85651 or 85652
10.	Throat <u>culture</u>, bacterial	87070 or 87081
11.	Urine <u>sensitivity, disk</u>	87184
12.	Hematocrit, spun	85013
13.	<u>Monospot</u>	86403
14.	Strep test, rapid (<u>Streptococcus, Group A</u>, Direct Optical Observation)	87880

Exercise 7-13

1.	Home visit, problem focused, est pt	99347
2.	Emer dept service, new pt, low complexity DX: Low-grade chest pain	99282
3.	Hosp visit, new pt, initial, high complexity	99223
4.	Hospital care, subsequent, detailed	99233
5.	Emergency care, hospital, est pt, problem focused, counseling 15 min. DX: Bladder infection.	99281
6.	Pt requested consult, new pt, moderate complexity, no 3rd party confirmation requested	99274
7.	Office consult, high complexity, est pt, surgery scheduled tomorrow	99245
8.	Follow-up consult, office, problem focused, counseling 15 min. full encounter 25 min. (There is no follow-up outpatient consult; use Est. Office Visit. Counseling becomes the key factor, selection is based on time.)	99214
9.	Follow-up consult, inpatient, detailed, 35 min.	99263

Exercise 7-14

1.	New pt, routine preventative medicine, age 11 Risk factor discussion, 20 min.	99383
2.	Critical care, 1.5 hr	99291, 99292
3.	NFS visit, subsequent visit, expanded problem focused H&PE	99312
4.	Medical team conference, 50 min.	99362
5.	Follow-up visit, ICU pt, stable, expanded problem focused (Patient is stable, use subsequent inpatient category)	99232
6.	Resuscitation, newborn, initial	99440
7.	Telephone call with social worker, brief	99371
8.	Custodial care, est pt, detailed H&PE, high complexity	99333
9.	Pediatrician on standby, high-risk birth, 65 min.	99360 x 2
10.	Heart risk factor education, group counseling, nonsymptomatic attendees, 65 min.	99412
11.	Prolonged care of subsequent inpatient level III with CPR, 1 hr 45 min. (Neither the inpatient visit nor CPR is bundled with prolonged care; code separately.)	99233, 99356, 99357 x 2, 92950

Answers to Chapter 8 Exercises
Exercise 8-1

1.	J3490	Key word(s): unclassified drug
2.	Q0114	Key word(s): fern test

3. L3214   Key word(s): Benesch boot
4. K0031   Key word(s): belt, safety
5. A4913   Key word(s): dialysis, supplies
6. G0105   Key word(s): screening examination, colorectal cancer

Exercise 8-2

Local Medicare Carrier:	G0105
DMERC:	L3214, K0031
Local Medicare Carrier or DMERC:	J3490, Q0114, A4913

Answers to Chapter 10 Exercises

Exercise 10-1

1. Acute pharyngitis
2. Musculoligamentous sprain, left ankle
3. Benign prostatic hypertrophy (BPH) with urinary retention
4. Bacterial endocarditis
5. Partial drop foot gait, right
6. Cervical osteoarthritis

Exercise 10-2

CASE 1	Ref #	Procedure/Service
	2	Hemoccult lab test
	2	Proctoscopy with biopsy
	3	Proctectomy

NOTE: The hemoccult lab test and proctoscopy with biopsy are done because the patient presents with the symptom blood in the stool. Occult blood is present in such minute amounts in stool that it is not visible to the naked eye. Patients who present with blood in their stools undergo the hemoccult lab test to determine the cause of the bleeding (e.g., colorectal cancer versus hemorrhaging hemorrhoids). A positive hemoccult test would indicate a need for proctoscopy with biopsy, which, in this case, was done to determine the cause of the bleeding. While pathological diagnosis upon biopsy indicates Duke's C Carcinoma of the colon, at the time the CMS-1500 claim is submitted, this diagnosis was unknown; therefore, link the proctoscopy with biopsy to the blood in the stool.

CASE 2	Ref #	Procedure/Service
	1, 2, 4	Office visit
	1	Urinalysis
	4	Rapid strep test

NOTE: Do not link sore throat with the office visit or the rapid strep test because it is a symptom of strep throat, which was diagnosed during the visit.

NOTE: Urinary frequency with dysuria, sore throat with cough, and headaches are signs and symptoms; therefore, link all with the office visit. The urinalysis was specifically done because of the urinary frequency with dysuria. The rapid strep test was performed because of the sore throat with cough, but it came back positive; therefore, link "strep throat" with the test.

CASE 3	Ref #	Procedure/Service
	1	Office visit
	1	Chest X-ray

NOTE: Do not report wheezing, congestion, and labored respirations because these are symptoms of pneumonia, which was diagnosed during the office visit.

NOTE: Unlike pathological diagnoses, which can require several days prior to the establishment of a definitive diagnosis, a chest X-ray can be evaluated immediately upon completion and a diagnosis rendered. Because wheezing, congestion, and labored respirations are signs detected on physical examination, and pneumonia is a definitive diagnosis, report the pneumonia only on the CMS-1500 claim.

CASE 4	Ref #	Procedure/Service
	1, 3, 4, 5	Nursing facility visit

NOTE: Malaise and fatigue are assigned the same ICD code number, so report the Ref # just once.

NOTE: The CMS-1500 claim allows only four ICD-9-CM codes to be reported; therefore, report diagnosis reference numbers 1, 3, 4, and 5 only.

CASE 5	Ref #	Procedure/Service
	3	Emergency department visit

NOTE: Do not report chills and fever because they are a symptom and sign, respectively, of the acute diverticulitis.

NOTE: Do not link signs/symptoms (chills and fever) with the service reported because a definitive diagnosis of acute diverticulitis is documented.

Exercise 10-3

1. Procedures	Codes	Diagnoses	Codes
Prevent Med, est, age 66	99397	Annual exam	V70.0
Outpatient visit, est, level III	99213-25	Elevated BP	796.2

CBC, auto	85025	Screening, blood	V78.9
UA, dipstick, auto, micro	81001	Screening, GU	V81.6
Chest X-ray, 2 views	71020	Exam, Radio, NEC	V72.5
Vaccination, influenza	90659, 90471	Vaccination	V04.8

NOTE: The only disorder reported is the elevated BP. V codes are used to justify the screening tests.

2. **Procedures**

Procedures	Codes	Diagnoses	Codes
Arthroscopy, shoulder	29805	Pain, shoulder NOS	719.41
Outpatient, est pt	99214	Tired and weak	780.71
		Depression	311

3. **Procedure**

Procedure	Code	Diagnosis	Code
Inpatient, initial, level II	99222	Appendicitis with abscess	540.1

4. **Procedure**

Procedure	Code	Diagnosis	Code
Inpatient, initial, level III	99223	Cholecystitis NOS	575.10

5. **Procedure**

Procedure	Code	Diagnosis	Code
Appendectomy, open	44900-55	Aftercare, surgery	V58.3

NOTE: Do not code the office visit because modifier -49 is required to receive reimbursement for the postoperative care. Do not code appendicitis; the appendix is not longer present.

Exercise 10-4

Diagnoses	ICD Code No.
1. Atrophic gastritis	535.10
2. Cholecystitis with cholelithiasis;	574.10
metastatic Adenocarcinoma (liver).	197.7
3. Rheumatoid arthritis, NOS	714.0
4. Unstable angina	411.1
5. Exudative tonsillitis	463
6. Seizure disorder, onset	780.39

Exercise 10-5

CASE 1	Diagnoses:	Granulation, tissue, skin	701.5
		History, personal, malignant, skin	V10.83
	Procedure:	Excision, lesion, benign, (0.3 cm, scalp)	11420
CASE 2	Diagnosis:	Atypical neoplasm, skin (uncertain behavior)	238.2
		(Pathology ordered the reexcision because of atypical cells)	
	Procedures:	Excision, lesion, benign, return to OR (skin of back)	11406-78
		Closure, intermediate	12032
CASE 3	Diagnoses:	Neoplasm, benign, intestine, sigmoid	211.3
		Melanosis coli	569.89
	Procedure:	Colonoscopy, with biopsy of polyp	45380
		and fulguration of polyp	45384
CASE 4	Diagnosis:	Serous otitis media, acute	381.01
	Procedure:	Myringotomy (Tympanostomy) with insertion of ventilating tubes (Procedure performed bilaterally)	69433-50
CASE 5	Diagnosis:	Lesion, buccal, mucosa	528.9
		NOTE: If working in a physician's office, do not code diagnosis until biopsy results are received—results could indicate a malignant lesion.	
	Procedure:	Biopsy, buccal mucosa	40812
CASE 6	Diagnosis:	Pilonidal cyst—no mention of abscess	685.1
	Procedure:	Excision pilonidal cyst (No mention of extensive or complicated excision.)	11770
CASE 7	Diagnosis:	Femoral hernia, incarcerated (Incarcerated equals strangulated)	552.00
	Procedure:	Herniorrhaphy, femoral (Not stated as recurrent)	49553

Appendix V

Using the Student Practice CD-ROM

USING THE STUDENT PRACTICE CD-ROM

The Student Practice CD-ROM, found inside the back cover of this textbook, is designed to help you practice completing CMS-1500 claims. The CD-ROM Procedure Manual along with tutorials for using the Blank Form, Study, and Self Test modes are located on the disk. They can be viewed on your computer screen or printed. Brief instructions to get you started using the software follow.

System Requirements

- 386 Processor or higher, with hard drive, 3.5 floppy disk drive, and CD-ROM drive
- Microsoft® Windows
- 4 MB RAM
- 2.5 MB free hard drive space
- Mouse
- Printer with 4 MB memory

Installing and Uninstalling the Student Practice Software Program

1. Insert the Student Practice disk into the CD-ROM drive.

2. Click **Start** and then click **Run**.

3. Type **D:\SETUP** and click **OK**.

4. In a few moments, you will see an installation screen; click **Next** to start the installation.

5. A dialog box will appear, and you will be asked to identify the drive and directory to install the software. Click **Next** so that the default directory (**C:\DELMAR\UHI**) is selected. If you want to change the directory location, click Browse and enter the drive and directory name into which the program should be installed.

6. The installation will begin at this time; you can stop the installation at any time by clicking **Cancel**.

7. A Delmar UHI icon will be added to the Program Manager on your computer, and a Start menu item will be created.

8. When you see the **Installation is complete** message, click **OK**.

   To remove the program from your computer, you can uninstall it by selecting **Delmar Applications** from the **Programs** menu and then selecting **Uninstall UHI 7**.

General Hints

- Proofread each entry before moving to the next block of the CMS-1500 claim.
- Press the **Caps Lock** key on your keyboard to activate it.
- Follow Optical Scanning Guidelines when completing the CMS-1500 claim.
- Enter reference numbers (not ICD code numbers) in Block 21.
- Enter the provider's full name and credentials in Block 31.
- Press the **Num Lock** key on your keyboard to activate it, before using the numeric keypad to enter long strings of numbers.
- Use the Study mode for Case Studies 1-1 through 1-15 (Appendix I of this textbook) when working in diagnosis and procedure **Skill Builders.**

Optical Scanning Guidelines

- Do not interchange a zero (0) with the alpha character O.
- When manually preparing the CMS-1500 claim, use pica type (10 characters per inch) and type all alphabetic characters in upper case (capital letters).
- Do not enter the dollar sign ($) for charges, payments, or balances due.
- Enter a space instead of any of the following:
  - Decimal point in charges, payments, or balances
  - Decimal point in a diagnostic code number
  - Dash in front of a procedure code number or a telephone number
- Do not type the parentheses when entering the area code of the telephone number (they are printed automatically on the form).
- Leave one blank space between the patient's/policyholder's last name, first name, and middle initial.
- Do not use any punctuation in a patient's/policyholder's name, except for a hyphen in a compound name.
- Do not use a patient's or policyholder's title or other designations such as Sr., Jr., II, or III on a claim unless they appear on the patient's insurance ID card.

EXAMPLE:

The name on the ID card reads:
  Wm. F. Goodpatient, IV

This name on the claim is written:
  GOODPATIENT IV WILLIAM F ●

Exceptions:

- TRICARE/CHAMPUS active duty sponsor required rank or grade after the name.
- Use two zeros (00) in the cents column when a fee or monetary total is expressed in whole dollars.

EXAMPLES:

Six dollars is written 6 00

Six thousand dollars is written 6 000 00

- Dates should be entered as eight digits with spaces between the digits representing the month, day, and year. Care should be taken to ensure that none of the digits fall on the vertical separations within the block.

Two-digit code numbers for the months are:

Jan	01	Apr	04
July	07	Oct	10
Feb	02	May	05
Aug	08	Nov	11
Mar	03	June	06
Sept	09	Dec	12

EXAMPLES:

03 04 1897 for March 4, 1897

03 04 1997 for March 4, 1997

Exceptions:

- Blocks 24A, 24B, and 31 do not allow for spacing between month/day and day/year.
- Enter the hyphen in all Employer Identification Numbers (EIN).
- Enter social security numbers as a continuous number, without the hyphens or spaces.
- In Block 31, enter the provider's full name and credentials.
- Review the claim to be sure all blocks that require an X to be placed within the block are so marked.

Completing Case Study Claims

When starting the program, you are asked to designate whether you want to store your data on a floppy disk or on the computer's hard drive. It is simpler to use a floppy disk, using the same disk every time you work, so that you have access to your previous work. Just insert the floppy disk before you start the program, and select **Use Floppy.**

1. YOU CAN USE THE CD-ROM TO:
   - Print blank CMS-1500 claims to manually complete a claim (e.g., handwritten or type-written).
   - Complete Case Studies 1-1 through 1-20 (Appendix I of this textbook) in the Blank Form mode, where no feedback is provided and completed claims can be printed.
   - Complete Case Studies 2-1 through 2-21 (Appendix II of this textbook) using the Study mode, where feedback is provided as you enter information in each Block of the CMS-1500 claim, and reports can be printed.
   - Complete Case Studies 2-1 through 2-21 (Appendix II of this textbook) using the Self Test mode, where *no* feedback is provided, the completed claim is graded, and reports can be printed.
   - Use Skill Builders, in either the Study or Self Test mode, to practice coding diagnoses and procedures/services based on Case Studies 2-1 through 2-21 (Appendix II of this text-book). As you enter data, the software checks your entries against expected answers and either provides feedback immediately or upon completion of the case, depending on which feedback procedure you selected.

     EXAMPLE: To print just your current work on a claim, click off (deselect) the Print Summary Report options.

2. KEYSTROKES TO HELP MANEUVER AROUND THE CLAIM:

Go To A Specific Block the block number	Ctrl-G and key in
Go To Next Block	Ctrl-N
Go To Previous Block	Ctrl-P
Go To Top Of Claim	Ctrl-T

   To help you use these shortcuts, click on **View** in the toolbar and select the action you desire.

3. Using **Enter** or **Tab** keys when working on the claim in Study mode provides immediate feedback.

4. TO SAVE A CLAIM: All case study claims must be saved manually to your floppy disk or hard disk after you have completed work with a claim.

On the top menu bar, choose **File > Save As...**

In the **Save As...** dialog box, choose the desired disk drive and folder, and specify a file-name. (Please review the File Naming Conventions discussion that follows.)

In the **Save file as type:** area on the dialog box, be sure that **Health Insurance (*.UHI)** is selected as the file type, and then click **OK**.

File Naming Conventions

- You should name each file to correspond with the case study it represents.
- If the case study you are working on requires two or more claims, be sure to indicate Primary (P) or Secondary (S) in your file-name.
- Your filename can include hyphen (-) and underscore (_) characters, but it cannot include most other symbols.
- To maintain compatibility across operating systems, it is best to limit your filename to no more than eight (8) characters, plus the three-character .UHI file type extension.

Printing Blank and Completed CMS-1500 Claims

1. TO PRINT A BLANK CMS-1500 CLAIM:
   - At the UHI main menu, click on **Blank CMS-1500** in the Blank Form box.
   - Click **OK** (you are not required to enter the form's destination).
   - When the blank CMS-1500 claim appears on your computer screen, click **Print** and then click **OK**.

2. TO PRINT A COMPLETED CMS-1500 CLAIM:
   - Once you have completed a CMS-1500 claim using either the Study or Self Test mode, click **Print**.
   - A **Printing Options** dialogue box will appear, and you can click on any checked box to deselect a particular option.
   - Note that the check mark disappears when you click on a box. To select that printing option again, click in the box and the check mark reappears.

LICENSE AGREEMENT FOR DELMAR LEARNING, A DIVISION OF THOMSON LEARNING, INC.

Educational Software/Data

You the customer, and Delmar Learning, a division of Thomson Learning, Inc. incur certain benefits, rights, and obligations to each other when you open this package and use the software/data it contains. BE SURE YOU READ THE LICENSE AGREEMENT CAREFULLY, SINCE BY USING THE SOFTWARE/DATA YOU INDICATE YOU HAVE READ, UNDERSTOOD, AND ACCEPTED THE TERMS OF THIS AGREEMENT.

Your rights:

1. You enjoy a non-exclusive license to use the software/data on a single microcomputer in consideration for payment of the required license fee, (which may be included in the purchase price of an accompanying print component), or receipt of this software/data, and your acceptance of the terms and conditions of this agreement.
2. You acknowledge that you do not own the aforesaid software/data. You also acknowledge that the software/data is furnished "as is," and contains copyrighted and/or proprietary and confidential infor-mation of Delmar Learning, a division of Thomson Learning, Inc. or its licensors.

There are limitations on your rights:

1. You may not copy or print the software/data for any reason whatsoever, except to install it on a hard drive on a single microcomputer and to make one archival copy, unless copying or printing is expressly permitted in writing or statements recorded on the diskette(s).
2. You may not revise, translate, convert, disassemble or otherwise reverse engineer the software/data except that you may add to or rearrange any data recorded on the media as part of the normal use of the software/data.
3. You may not sell, license, lease, rent, loan or other-wise distribute or network the software/data except that you may give the software/data to a student or and instructor for use at school or, temporarily at home.

Should you fail to abide by the Copyright Law of the United States as it applies to this software/data your license to use it will become invalid. You agree to erase or otherwise destroy the software/data immediately after receiving note of termination of this agreement for violation of its provisions from Delmar Learning.

Delmar Learning, a division of Thomson Learning, Inc gives you a LIMITED WARRANTY covering the enclosed software/data. The LIMITED WARRANTY follows this License.

This license is the entire agreement between you and Delmar Learning, a division of Thomson Learning, Inc. interpreted and enforced under New York law.

LIMITED WARRANTY

Delmar Learning, a division of Thomson Learning, Inc. warrants to the original licensee/purchaser of this copy of microcomputer software/data and the media on which it is recorded that the media will be free from defects in material and workmanship for ninety (90) days from the date of original purchase. All implied warranties are limited in duration to this ninety (90) day period. THEREAFTER, ANY IMPLIED WARRANTIES, INCLUDING IMPLIED WARRANTIES OF MERCHANTABILITY AND FITNESS FOR A PARTICULAR PURPOSE, ARE EXCLUDED. THIS WARRANTY IS IN LIEU OF ALL OTHER WARRANTIES, WHETHER ORAL OR WRITTEN, EXPRESS OR IMPLIED.

If you believe the media is defective please return it during the ninety day period to the address shown below. Defective media will be replaced without charge provided that it has not been subjected to misuse or damage.

This warranty does not extend to the software or information recorded on the media. The software and information are provided "AS IS." Any statements made about the utility of the software or information are not to be considered as express or implied warranties.

Limitation of liability: Our liability to you for any losses shall be limited to direct damages, and shall not exceed the amount you paid for the software. In no event will we be liable to you for any indirect, special, incidental, or consequential damages (including loss of profits) even if we have been advised of the possibility of such damages.

Some states do not allow the exclusion or limitation of incidental or consequential damages, or limitations on the duration of implied warranties, so the above limitation or exclusion may not apply to you. This warranty gives you specific legal rights, and you may also have other rights which vary from state to state. Address all correspondence to: Delmar Learning, a division of Thomson Learning, Inc., 5 Maxwell Drive, P.O. Box 8007, Clifton Park, NY 12065-8007. Attention: Technology Department

Appendix VI

UB-92

INTRODUCTION

This appendix provides an introduction to the use of the UB-92 (Uniform Bill, implemented in 1992) claim for institutional services (e.g., hospitals and skilled nursing facilities).

UB-92

The UB-92 claim contains data entry blocks called *form locators* (FLs) that are similar to the CMS-1500 claim blocks used to input information about procedures or services provided to a patient. While some institutions actually complete the UB-92 claim (Figure VI-1) and submit it to third-party payers for reimbursement, most perform data entry of UB-92 information using commercial software (Figure VI-2). What this means is most institutions do *not* actually complete a UB-92 claim for submission to a payer (unlike providers who usually complete the CMS-1500 claim either manually or on-screen using a software package). Instead, personnel who render services to institutional patients (e.g., nursing, laboratory or radiology) enter UB-92 data into the commercial software product. The data resides in the patient's computerized account, and upon discharge of the patient from the institution, the data is verified by billing office personnel and transmitted electronically either directly to the third-party payer or (more likely) to a clearinghouse that processes electronic claims by editing and validating them to ensure that they are error-free, reformatting them to the specifications of the payer, and submitting them electronically to the appropriate payer.

EXAMPLE: During an inpatient admission, the attending physician writes an order in the patient's record for a blood glucose level to be performed by the laboratory. The patient's nurse processes the order by contacting the laboratory (e.g., telephone or computer message), which sends a technician to the patient's room to perform a venipuncture (blood draw, or withdrawing blood from the patient's arm using a syringe). The blood specimen is transported to the laboratory by the technician where the blood glucose test is completed. The technician enters the results into the patient record information technology (IT) system using a computer terminal. At the same time, the UB-92 data elements are input into the patient account IT system using a computer terminal. This data resides in the patient's

APPROVED OMB NO. 0938-0279

ST11843 1PLY UB-92

1

2

3 PATIENT CONTROL NO.

4 TYPE OF BILL

5 FED. TAX NO.

6 STATEMENT COVERS PERIOD FROM THROUGH

7 COV D. | 8 N-C D. | 9 C-I D. | 10 L-R D. | 11

12 PATIENT NAME

13 PATIENT ADDRESS

14 BIRTHDATE | 15 SEX | 16 MS | ADMISSION 17 DATE | 18 HR | 19 TYPE | 20 SRC | 21 D HR | 22 STAT | 23 MEDICAL RECORD NO. | CONDITION CODES 24 | 25 | 26 | 27 | 28 | 29 | 30 | 31

32 OCCURRENCE CODE DATE | 33 OCCURRENCE CODE DATE | 34 OCCURRENCE CODE DATE | 35 OCCURRENCE CODE DATE | 36 OCCURRENCE SPAN CODE FROM THROUGH | 37 A B C

a
b

38

39 VALUE CODES CODE AMOUNT | 40 VALUE CODES CODE AMOUNT | 41 VALUE CODES CODE AMOUNT

a
b
c
d

	42 REV. CD.	43 DESCRIPTION	44 HCPCS / RATES	45 SERV. DATE	46 SERV. UNITS	47 TOTAL CHARGES	48 NON-COVERED CHARGES	49	
1									1
2									2
3									3
4									4
5									5
6									6
7									7
8									8
9									9
10									10
11									11
12									12
13									13
14									14
15									15
16									16
17									17
18									18
19									19
20									20
21									21
22									22
23									23

50 PAYER | 51 PROVIDER NO. | 52 REL INFO | 53 ASG BEN | 54 PRIOR PAYMENTS | 55 EST. AMOUNT DUE | 56

A
B
C

57 DUE FROM PATIENT ▶

58 INSURED'S NAME | 59 P. REL | 60 CERT. - SSN - HIC. - ID NO. | 61 GROUP NAME | 62 INSURANCE GROUP NO.

A
B
C

63 TREATMENT AUTHORIZATION CODES | 64 ESC | 65 EMPLOYER NAME | 66 EMPLOYER LOCATION

A
B
C

67 PRIN. DIAG. CD. | OTHER DIAG. CODES 68 CODE | 69 CODE | 70 CODE | 71 CODE | 72 CODE | 73 CODE | 74 CODE | 75 CODE | 76 ADM. DIAG. CD. | 77 E-CODE | 78

79 P.C. | 80 PRINCIPAL PROCEDURE CODE DATE | 81 OTHER PROCEDURE CODE DATE A | OTHER PROCEDURE CODE DATE B | 82 ATTENDING PHYS. ID

OTHER PROCEDURE CODE DATE C | OTHER PROCEDURE CODE DATE D | OTHER PROCEDURE CODE DATE E

83 OTHER PHYS. ID A (a, b)

OTHER PHYS. ID B (a, b)

84 REMARKS
a
b
c
d

85 PROVIDER REPRESENTATIVE X | 86 DATE

UB-92 HCFA-1450 | OCR/ORIGINAL | I CERTIFY THE CERTIFICATIONS ON THE REVERSE APPLY TO THIS BILL AND ARE MADE A PART HEREOF.

FIGURE VI-1 Sample UB-92 claim (Reprinted according to CMS's reuse policy at http://cms.hhs.gov)

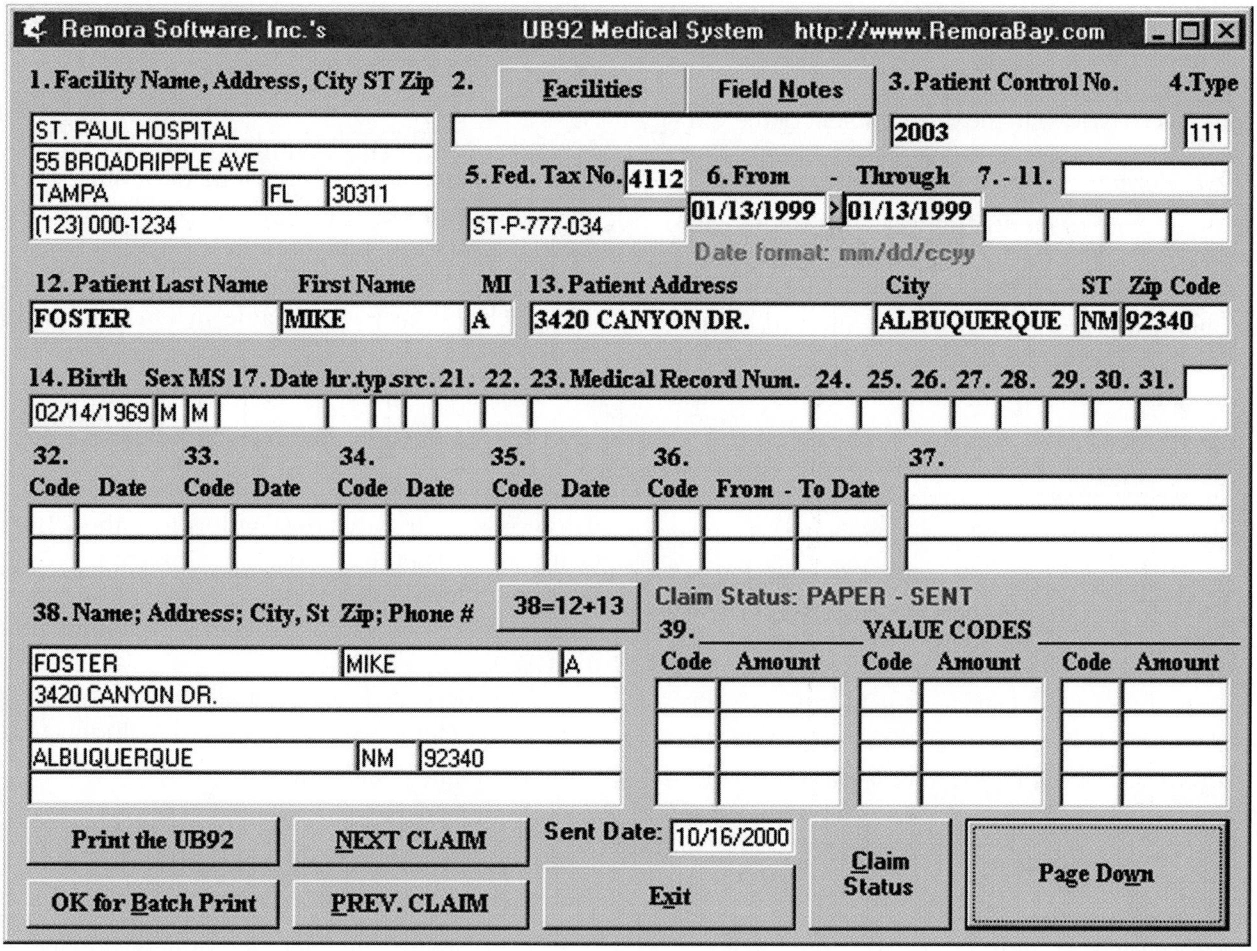

FIGURE VI-2 Sample data entry screen using UB-92 electronic data interchange software (Permission to reprint granted by Remora Software, Inc.)

computerized account until it is verified by the billing office (at patient discharge) and is then transmitted to a clearinghouse that processes the claim and submits it to the third-party payer. The clearinghouse also uses the network to send an acknowledgment to the institution upon receipt of the submitted claim. ●

UB-92 Claim Development and Implementation

Institutional and other selected providers submit UB-92 (CMS-1450) claim data (Figure VI-2) to payers for reimbursement of patient services. The National Uniform Billing Committee (NUBC) is responsible for developing data elements reported on the UB-92 in cooperation with State Uniform Billing Committees (SUBCs).

NOTE: UB-92 claim data for Medicare Part A reimbursement is submitted to *fiscal intermediaries (FIs),* which are private insurance companies contracted by CMS to serve as the financial agent between providers and the federal government for the purpose of handling Medicare Part A reimbursement. The FI processes payments for hospitals, skilled nursing facilities, home health and hospice agencies, dialysis facilities, rehabilitation facilities, and rural health clinics. ●

HINT: The role of the FI is similar to that of the Medicare carrier associated with Medicare Part B claims processing. ●

National Uniform Billing Committee (NUBC)

Like the role of the National Uniform Claims Committee (NUCC) in the development of the CMS-1500 claim, the *National Uniform Billing Committee (NUBC)* is responsible for identifying and revising *data elements* (information entered into UB-92 form locators or submitted by institutions using electronic data interchange), and it originally designed the first uniform bill (called the UB-82 because of its 1982 implementation date). The current claim is called the UB-92 because it was implemented in 1992.

The NUBC was created by the American Hospital Association (AHA) in 1975 and is represented by major national provider (e.g., AHA State Hospital Association Representatives) and payer (e.g., Blue Cross and Blue Shield Association) organizations. The intent was to develop a single billing form and standard data set that could be used by all institutional providers and payers for health care claims processing. In 1982, the NUBC voted to accept the UB-82 and its *data set* (a compilation of data elements that are reported on the uniform bill) for implementation as a national uniform bill. Once the UB-82 was adopted, the focus of the NUBC shifted to the state level, and a *State Uniform Billing Committee (SUBC)* was created in each state to handle implementation and distribution of state-specific UB-82 manuals (that contained national guidelines along with unique state billing requirements).

When the NUBC established the UB-82 data set design and specifications, it also implemented an evaluation process through 1990 to determine whether the UB-82 data set was appropriate for third-party payer claims processing. The NUBC surveyed SUBCs to obtain suggestions for improving the design of the UB-82, and the UB-92 was implemented in 1992 to incorporate the best of the UB-82 with data set design improvements (e.g., providers no longer need to include as many attachments to UB-92 claims submitted).

Data Specifications for the UB-92

When reviewing data specifications for the UB-92, the NUBC balances the payers' need to collect information against the burden of providers to report that information. In addition, the administrative simplification principles required of the Health Insurance Portability and Accountability Act of 1996 (HIPAA) are applied when developing data elements. Each data element required for reporting purposes is assigned to a unique UB-92 *form locator (FL)*, which is the designated space on the claim identified by a unique number and title, such as the patient name in FL12 (Refer to Figure VI-1).

UB-92 Claim Submission

Whether completed manually (Figure VI-1) or using on-screen software (Figure VI-2), the UB-92 claim contains 86 form locators (Table VI-1). The data is entered according to third-party payer guidelines that contain instructions for completing the UB-92.

Providers that submit the UB-92 claim (or UB-92 data elements in EDI format) include:

- ambulance companies.
- ambulatory surgery centers (ASC).
- home health care agencies (HHA).
- hospice organizations.
- hospitals (emergency department, inpatient, and outpatient services).
- psychiatric drug/alcohol treatment facilities (inpatient and outpatient services).
- skilled nursing facilities (SNFs).
- subacute facilities.
- stand-alone clinical/laboratory facilities.
- walk-in clinics.

The UB-92 (CMS-1450) and its data elements serve the needs of many third-party payers, and while some payers do not collect certain data elements, it is important to capture all NUBC-approved data elements for audit trail purposes. In addition, NUBC-approved data elements are reported by facilities that have established coordination of benefits agreements with the payers.

NOTE: All Medicare claims are currently submitted either manually on the UB-92 paper claim, or processed according to electronic data interchange (EDI) guidelines. Form locator definitions are

TABLE VI-1 UB-92 form locators and brief description of information to be entered

FORM LOCATOR	BRIEF DESCRIPTION OF INFORMATION TO BE ENTERED ON THE UB-92	FORM LOCATOR	BRIEF DESCRIPTION OF INFORMATION TO BE ENTERED ON THE UB-92
1	Provider Name, Address & Telephone #	46	Units of Service
2	Unlabeled Field - State Use	47	Total Charges (by Revenue Code Category)
3	Patient Control Number (Account Number)	48	Non-Covered Charges
4	Type of Bill	49	Unlabeled Field - National Use
5	Federal Tax Number	50A-C	Payer Identification
6	Statement Covers Period	51A-C	Provider Number
7	Covered Days	52A-C	Release of Information Certification Indicator
8	Non-Covered Days	53A-C	Assignment of Benefits Certification Indicator
9	Coinsurance Days	54A-C, P	Prior Payments - Payers and Patient
10	Lifetime Reserve Days	55A-C, P	Estimated Amount Due
11	Unlabeled Field - State Use	56	DRG Number and Grouper ID
12	Patient Name	57	Unlabeled Field - National Use
13	Patient Address	58A-C	Insured's Name
14	Patient Birthdate	59A-C	Patient's Relationship to Insured
15	Patient Sex	60A-C	Health Insurance Claim Identification Number
16	Patient Marital Status	61A-C	Insured Group Name
17	Admission Date	62A-C	Insurance Group Number
18	Admission Hour	63A-C	Treatment Authorization Code
19	Type of Admission	64A-C	Employment Status Code
20	Source of Admission	65A-C	Employer Name
21	Discharge Hour	66A-C	Employer Location
22	Patient Status	67	Principal Diagnosis Code
23	Medical/Health Record Number	68-75	Other Diagnosis Codes
24-30	Condition Codes	76	Admitting Diagnosis
31	Unlabeled Field - National Use	77	External Cause of Injury Code (E-Code)
32-35a,b	Occurrence Codes and Dates	78	Principal Diagnosis Code
36a,b	Occurrence Span Codes and Dates	79	Procedure Coding Method Used
37	Internal Control Number (ICN)	80	Principal Procedure Code and Date
38	Responsible Party Name and Address	81A-E	Other Procedure Codes and Dates
39-41a-d	Value Codes and Amounts	82a-b	Attending Physician ID
42	Revenue Code	83a-b	Other Physician ID
43	Revenue Description	84	Remarks
44	HCPCS/Rates	85	Provider Representative Signature
45	Service Date	86	Date Bill Submitted

(Reprinted according to content reuse policy at http://cms.hhs.gov)

identical and in some situations, the electronic claim contains more characters than the corresponding item on the paper form. ●

UB-02

The National Uniform Billing Committee (NUBC) is working on the proposed UB-02, which is scheduled to replace the UB-92. (The implementation date has not yet been announced.) Revisions will emphasize clarification of definitions for data elements and codes to eliminate amibiguity and to create consistency. The UB-02 will also address emergency department (ED) coding and data collection issues to respond to state public health reporting systems. The NUBC continues to emphasize the need to stay involved so that data sources can continue to support public health data reporting needs.

Bibliography

BOOKS AND MANUALS

American Medical Association. (2002). *CPT 2003*. Chicago, IL: Author.

Austin, M. S. (2000). *Managed health care simplified: A glossary of terms*. Clifton Park, NY: Delmar Learning.

Blue Cross Association. (1972). *The Blue Cross story*. Chicago, IL: Author.

Blue Cross and Blue Shield Association. (1987). *The history of Blue Cross and Blue Shield plans*. Chicago, IL: Author.

Davis, J. B. (2000). *Reimbursement manual for the medical office: A comprehensive guide to coding, billing & fee management*. Los Angeles, CA: Practice Management Information Corporation.

Davison, J., & Lewis, M. (2000). *Working with insurance and managed care plans: A guide for getting paid*. Los Angeles, CA: Practice Management Information Corporation.

Garrett, T. M., Baillie, H. W., & Garrett, R. M. (2001). *Health care ethics: Principles and problems*. Upper Saddle River, NJ: Prentice Hall.

Ingenix Publishing. (2002). *2003 HCPCS*. Salt Lake City, UT: Author.

Ingenix Publishing. (2002). *2003 hospital & payer ICD-9-CM*. Salt Lake City, UT: Author.

Johnson, S. L. (2002). *Understanding medical coding: A comprehensive guide*. Clifton Park, NY: Delmar Learning.

Medicode. (2002). *2003 coder's desk reference*. Salt Lake City, UT: Ingenix Publishing.

Medicode. (2002). *2003 Medicode's encoder pro,* Salt Lake City, UT: Medicode.

Medicode. (2002). *Code It Right 2003*. Salt Lake City, UT: Ingenix Publishing.

Medicode. (2002). *Coders' desk reference 2003*. Salt Lake City, UT: Ingenix Publishing.

Medicode. (2002). *Encoder pro 2003*. Salt Lake City, UT: Ingenix Publishing.

Medicode. (2002). *ICD-10 made easy*. Salt Lake City, UT: Ingenix Publishing.

Medicode. (2002). *Medicare billing guide 2003*. Salt Lake City, UT: Ingenix Publishing.

Medicode. (2002). *Modifiers made easy 2003*. Salt Lake City, UT: Ingenix Publishing.

National Association of Blue Shield Plans. *The Blue Shield story: All of us helping each of us*. Chicago, IL: Blue Cross and Blue Shield Association.

Rizzo, C. D. (2000). *Uniform billing: A guide to claims processing*. Clifton Park, NY: Delmar Learning.

St. Anthony's. (2002). *St. Anthony's complete guide to coverage issues: A reference to covered and non-covered services*. Salt Lake City, UT: Ingenix Publishing.

BROCHURES AND BULLETINS

2002 guide to health insurance for people with Medicare. Washington, D.C: Health Care Financing Administration.

CMS-1500 claim filing instructions. Albuquerque, NM: BlueCross BlueShield of New Mexico.

Coverage policy bulletins. Hartford, CT: Aetna US Healthcare, Aetna Life Insurance Company.

Federal Employees Program (FEP) claim form Completion Instructions. Chicago, IL: Blue Cross and Blue Shield Federal Employees Program.

FEP service benefit plan brochure. Chicago, IL: Blue Cross and Blue Shield Federal Employees Program.

Health Insurance Portability and Accountability Act of 1996—Administrative simplification care fact sheet. Washington, D.C.: Health Care Financing Administration.

Health insurance, the history. Seattle, WA: Health Insurance Association of America.

Medicare & you 2003. Washington, D.C.: Health Care Financing Administration.

Medicare and other health benefits: Your guide to who pays first. Washington, D.C.: Centers for Medicare and Medicaid Services.

Medicare fraud and abuse. Washington, D.C.: Centers for Medicare and Medicaid Services.

Medicare savings for qualified beneficiaries. Washington, D.C.: Centers for Medicare and Medicaid Services.

Medigap policies and protections. Washington, D.C.: Centers for Medicare and Medicaid Services.

TRICARE grand rounds. Falls Church, VA: TRICARE Management Activity.

Understanding your Medicare choices. Washington, D.C.: Centers for Medicare and Medicaid Services.

Your Medicare benefits. Washington, D.C.: Centers for Medicare and Medicaid Services.

INSURANCE MANUALS

Blue Cross and Blue Shield of Maryland guide to programs & benefits. (2003). Owings Mills, MD: Blue Cross and Blue Shield of Maryland, Inc.

CHAMPVA handbook. (2003). Denver, CO: VA Health Administration Center.

CMS's state Medicaid manual. (2003). Washington, D.C.: Centers for Medicare and Medicaid Services.

Medicare & Medicaid program manuals. (2003). Washington, D.C.: Centers for Medicare and Medicaid Services.

TRICARE/CHAMPUS policy manuals. (2003). Falls Church, VA: TRICARE Management Activity.

TRICARE Standard provider handbook. (2003). Falls Church, VA: TRICARE Management Activity.

JOURNALS, NEWS-MAGAZINES AND NEWSLETTERS FOR ADDITIONAL READING

Advance for health information professionals. King of Prussia, PA: Merion Publications.

American medical news. Chicago, IL: American Medical Association.

BlueReview for BlueCross and BlueShield of Illinois institutional & professional providers. Chicago, IL: Blue Cross and Blue Shield of Illinois.

Claims for compensation under the Federal Employees' Compensation Act, Final Rule, 11/25/1998. Federal Register. Washington, D.C: National Archives and Records Administration.

CodeCorrect news. Yakima, WA: CodeCorrect.com.

Coding edge. San Clemente, CA: Laguna Medical Systems.

CPT assistant. Chicago, IL: American Medical Association.

Family practice management. Leawood, KS: American Academy of Family Physicians.

For the record. Valley Forge, PA: Great Valley Publishing.

HealthInk. Owings Mills, MD: CareFirst Blue Cross and Blue Shield.

Journal of the American health information management association. Chicago, IL: American Health Information Management Association.

Medical office management. Pensacola, FL: Professional Association of Health Care Office Managers.

Medicare part B news. Denison, TX: Trailblazer Health Enterprises, LLC., a CMS Contracted Intermediary/Carrier.

Medicare part B special bulletins. Denison, TX: Trailblazer Health Enterprises, LLC., a CMS Contracted Intermediary/Carrier.

Part B news, Rockville, MD: United Communications Group.

Professional medical assistant. Chicago, IL: American Association of Medical Assistants.

Provider news brief. Albuquerque, NM: BlueCross BlueShield of New Mexico.

Solutions for health care providers. Camp Hill, PA: Healthcare Management Solutions, Inc.

INTERNET-BASED REFERENCES

http://www.codecorrect.com – CPT, ICD-9, CCI, Coding Crosswalk and APC data, and searchable Medicare newsletters and *Federal Register.*

http://www.firstgov.gov – resource for locating government information on the Internet

http://cms.hhs.gov/medlearn – self-paced Medicare training by downloading free interactive courses and attending free satellite programs designed to teach Medicare billing guidelines.

http://mxcity.com – a gateway to up-to-date reimbursement, coding, and compliance information.

http://www.trailblazerhealth.com – Medicare Part A and Part B Newsletter and Special Bulletins.

Glossary

abuse (5) - actions inconsistent with accepted, sound, medical, business, or fiscal practices.

accept assignment (4) - provider accepts as payment in full whatever is paid on the claim by the payer (except for any copayment and/or coinsurance amounts).

accounts receivable aging report (4) - shows the status (by date) of outstanding claims from each payer, as well as payments due from patients.

accreditation (3) - voluntary process that a health care facility or organization (e.g., hospital or managed care plan) undergoes to demonstrate that it has met standards beyond those required by law.

adjudication (17) - judicial dispute resolution process in which an appeals board makes a final determination.

adjusted claim (15) - payment correction resulting in additional payment(s) to the provider.

Advance Beneficiary Notice (ABN) (6) – document that acknowledges patient responsibility for payment if Medicare denies the claim.

adverse effect (6) - also called *adverse reaction*; the appearance of a pathologic condition due to ingestion or exposure to a chemical substance properly administered or taken.

adverse reaction (6) - *see* adverse effect.

adverse selection (3) - covering members who are sicker than the general population.

Alliance of Claims Assistance Professionals (ACAP) (1) – professional association that represents professionals dedicated to the effective management of health insurance claims; its membership includes professional electronic billers who work for providers as well as professional claims assistance professionals who work for patients.

allogeneic bone marrow transplant (14) - healthy donor stem cell or bone marrow is obtained and prepared for intravenous infusion.

allowed charge (4) - the maximum amount the payer will reimburse for each procedure or service, according to the patient's policy.

ambulance fee schedule (9) - payment system for ambulance services provided to Medicare beneficiaries.

Ambulatory Payment Classification (APC) (2) – prospective payment system used to calculate reimbursement for outpatient care according to similar clinical characteristics and in terms of resources required.

ambulatory surgical center (ASC) (9) - state-licensed, Medicare-certified supplier (not provider) of surgical health care services that must *accept assignment* on Medicare claims.

Amendment to the HMO Act of 1973 (3) – legislation that allowed federally qualified HMOs to permit members to occasionally use non-HMO physicians and be partially reimbursed.

American Academy of Professional Coders (AAPC) (1) – professional association established to provide a national certification and credentialing process, to support the national and local membership by providing educational products and opportunities to network, and to increase and promote national recognition and awareness of professional coding.

American Health Information Management Association (AHIMA) (1) – professional association that represents more than 40,000 health information management professionals who work throughout the health care industry.

American Hospital Association (AHA) (13) - national organization that represents and serves all types of hospitals, health care networks, and their patients and communities; the AHA began as the accreditation agency for new prepaid hospitalization plans in 1939.

ANSI ASC X12N 837 (5) - variable-length file format used to bill institutional, professional, dental, and drug claims.

aplastic anemia (14) - decreased formation of red blood cells and hemoglobin.

appeal (4) - documented as a letter, signed by the provider, explaining why a claim should be reconsidered for payment.

arbitration (17) - dispute resolution process in which a final determination is made by an impartial person who may not have judicial powers.

assessment (10) – contains the diagnostic statement and may include the physician's rationale for the diagnosis.

assignment of benefits (4) - the provider receives reimbursement directly from the payer.

Association of Medical Care Plans (2) - a national coordinating agency for physician sponsored health insurance plans.

authorization (5) – a document that provides official instruction, such as the customized document that gives covered entities permission to use specified protected health information (PHI) for specified purposes or to disclose PHI to a third party specified by the individual.

autologous bone marrow transplant (14) - uses the patient's own (previously stored) cells to treat acute leukemia in remission, resistant non-Hodgkin lymphomas, recurrent or refractory neuroblastomas, or advanced Hodgkin disease.

Away From Home Care® (13) - provides continuous BCBS health care coverage for subscribers who will be out of their service area for more than 90 consecutive days.

axis of classification (6) - organizes entities, diseases, and other conditions according to etiology, anatomy, or severity.

balance billing (9) – billing beneficiaries for amounts not reimbursed by payers (not including copayments and coinsurance amounts); this practice is prohibited by Medicare regulations.

Balanced Budget Act of 1997 (BBA) (2) - addresses health care fraud and abuse issues, and provides for Department of Health & Human Services (DHHS) Office of the Inspector General (OIG) investigative and audit services in health care fraud cases.

base period (2) - period of time that usually covers 12 months and is divided into four consecutive quarters.

batched EOB (4) - payer reports multiple payments on one explanation of benefits document.

BCBS basic coverage (13) - Blue Cross and Blue Shield (BCBS) coverage for the following services: hospitalization, diagnostic laboratory services, X-rays, surgical fees, assistant surgeon fees, obstetric care, intensive care, newborn care, and chemotherapy for cancer.

BCBS major medical (MM) coverage (13) – BCBS coverage for the following services, in addition to basic coverage: office visits, outpatient nonsurgical treatment, physical and occupational therapy, purchase of durable medical equipment (DME), mental health visits, allergy testing and injections, prescription drugs, private duty nursing (when medically necessary), and dental care required as a result of a covered accidental injury.

beneficiary (4) - the person eligible to receive health care benefits.

beneficiary services representative (BSR) (16) - employed at a TRICARE Service Center, provides information about using TRICARE and assists with other matters affecting access to health care (e.g., appointment scheduling).

benefit period (Medicare) (14) - begins with the first day of hospitalization and ends when the patient has been out of the hospital for 60 consecutive days.

benign (6) - not cancerous.

billing entity (11) - the legal business name of the provider's practice.

birthday rule (4) - determines coverage by primary and secondary policies when each parent subscribes to a different health insurance plan.

black box edits (5) - nonpublished code edits, which were discontinued in 2000.

BlueCard® Preferred Provider Organization (PPO) (13) - program that allows BCBS subscribers access to a large national health care network of participating hospitals and physicians, specialists, and other health care practitioners.

BlueCard® Program (13) - program that allows BCBS subscribers to receive local Blue Plan health care benefits while traveling or living outside of their plan's area.

BlueCard® Worldwide (13) - program that allows BCBS subscribers who travel or live abroad to receive covered inpatient hospital care and physician services from a network of hospitals and doctors around the world.

Blue Cross (13) - insurance plan created in 1929 when Baylor University Hospital, in Dallas, TX, approached teachers in the Dallas school district with a plan that guaranteed up to 21 days of hospitalization per year for subscribers and each dependent for a $6 annual premium.

Blue Cross Association (BCA) (2) - replaced the American Hospital Association (AHA) in 1972 as the approval agency for new Blue Cross health plans.

Blue Cross/Blue Shield (BCBS) (13) - joint venture between Blue Cross and Blue Shield where the corporations shared one building and computer services but maintained separate corporate identities.

Blue Shield (BS) (13) - began as a resolution passed by the House of Delegates at an American Medical Association meeting in 1938; incorporates a concept of voluntary health insurance that encourages physicians to cooperate with prepaid health plans.

BlueCross BlueShield Association (BCBSA) (2) - an association of independent Blue Cross and Blue Shield plans.

BluesCONNECT® (13) - program that allows subscribers to access a national network of physicians and hospitals and provides: urgent care for sudden illnesses or injuries that require immediate attention while traveling, guest membership for subscribers living in another city for at least 90 days, and follow-up care while traveling.

breach of confidentially (5) - unauthorized release of patient information to a third party.

business associate (5) - person or entity that provides certain functions, activities, or services for, or to, a covered entity, involving the use and/or disclosure of protected health information (PHI).

cafeteria plan (3) - also called *triple option plan*; provides different health benefit plans and extra coverage options through an insurer or third-party administrator.

capitation (3) - provider accepts pre-established payments for providing health care services to enrollees over a period of time (usually one year).

carcinoma (Ca) *in situ* (6) - a malignant tumor that is localized, circumscribed, encapsulated, and noninvasive (has not spread to deeper or adjacent tissues or organs).

care plan oversight services (7) - cover the physician's time supervising a complex and multidisciplinary care treatment program for a specific patient who is under the care of a home health agency, hospice, or nursing facility.

carrier (5) - organization (e.g., insurance company) that contracts with the Centers for Medicare and Medicaid Services (CMS) to process Medicare Part B claims.

case law (5) - also called *common law*; based on a court decision that establishes a precedent.

case management (3) - development of patient care plans to coordinate and provide care for complicated cases in a cost-effective manner.

case management services (7) - process by which an attending physician coordinates and supervises care provided to a patient by other providers.

case manager (3) - submits written confirmation, authorizing treatment, to the provider.

catastrophic cap benefit (16) - protects TRICARE beneficiaries from devastating financial loss due to serious illness or long-term treatment by establishing limits over which payment is not required.

catchment area (16) - the region defined by code boundaries within a 40-mile radius of a military treatment facility.

Category I codes (7) - procedures/services identified by a five-digit CPT code and descriptor nomenclature; these are codes traditionally associated with CPT and organized within six sections.

Category II codes (7) - optional performance measurement tracking codes that are assigned an alphanumeric identifier with a letter in the last field (e.g., 1234A); these codes will be located after the Medicine section; *their use is optional.*

Category III codes (7) - temporary codes assigned for data collection purposes that are assigned an alphanumeric identifier with a letter in the last field (e.g., 0001T); these codes are located after the Medicine section, and they will be archived after five years unless accepted for placement within Category I sections of CPT.

Centers for Medicare and Medicaid Services (CMS) (1) - formerly known as the Health Care Financing Administration (HCFA), it is an administrative agency within the federal Department of Health and Human Services (DHHS).

CHAMPUS Reform Initiative (CRI) (2, 16) - conducted in 1988 and resulted in a new health program called TRICARE, which includes three options: TRICARE Prime, TRICARE Extra, and TRICARE Standard.

chargemaster (4) - term hospitals use to describe a patient encounter form.

check digit (5) - one-digit character, alphabetic or numeric, used to verify the validity of a unique identifier.

civil law (5) - area of law not classified as criminal.

Civilian Health and Medical Program of the Department of Veterans Affairs (CHAMPVA) (2) - program that provides health benefits for dependents of veterans rated as 100% permanently and totally disabled as a result of service-connected conditions, veterans who died as a result of service-connected conditions, and veterans who died on duty with less than 30 days of active service.

Civilian Health and Medical Program—Uniformed Services (CHAMPUS) (2) – originally designed as a benefit for dependents of personnel serving in the armed forces and uniformed branches of the Public Health Service and the National Oceanic and Atmospheric Administration; now called TRICARE.

claim attachment (11) - medical report substantiating a medical condition.

Classification of Drugs by AHFS List (6) - Appendix C of ICD-9-CM that contains the American Hospital Formulary Services list number and its ICD-9-CM equivalent code number; organized in numerical order according to AHFS list number.

Classification of Industrial Accidents According to Agency (6) - Appendix D of ICD-9-CM and is based on employment injury statistics adopted by the Tenth International Conference of Labor Statisticians.

clean claim (4) - a correctly completed standardized claim (e.g., CMS-1500 claim).

clearinghouse (5) - performs centralized claims processing for providers and health plans.

Clinical Data Abstraction Center (CDAC) (5) - requests and screens medical records for the Payment Error Prevention Program (PEPP) to survey samples for medical review, DRG validation, and medical necessity.

clinical laboratory fee schedule (9) - data set based on local fee schedules (for outpatient clinical diagnostic laboratory services).

Clinical Laboratory Improvement Act (CLIA) (2) - established quality standards for all laboratory testing to ensure the accuracy, reliability, and timeliness of patient test results regardless of where the test was performed.

Clinical Laboratory Improvement Act (CLIA) certification number (14) - 10-digit number assigned by CMS for clinical laboratory services performed by a practice.

clinical trials (16) - research studies that help find ways to prevent, diagnose, or treat illnesses and improve health care.

closed assigned claims (4) - claims for which all processing, including appeals, has been completed.

closed fracture treatment (7) - fracture site was not surgically opened when treated.

closed-panel Health Maintenance Organization (HMO) (3) - health care is provided in an HMO-owned center or satellite clinic or by physicians who belong to a specially formed medical group that serves the HMO.

CMS Office of Managed Care (3) - facilitates innovation and competition among Medicare HMOs.

CMS-1500 (2) - form used to submit Medicare claims; previously called the HCFA-1500.

code pairs (5) - edit pairs included in the Correct Coding Initiative (CCI) that cannot be reported on the same claim.

coding (1) - process of reporting diagnoses, procedures, and services as numeric and alphanumeric characters on the insurance claim.

coding conventions (6) - rules that apply to the assignment of ICD-9-CM codes.

coinsurance (4) - also called *coinsurance payment;* the percentage the patient pays for covered services after the deductible has been met and the copayment has been paid.

coinsurance payment (4) - *see* coinsurance.

common data file (4) - abstract of all recent claims filed on each patient.

common law (5) - also called *case law;* is based on a court decision that establishes a precedent.

comorbidity (6) - secondary diagnosis or concurrent condition that coexists with the primary condition, has the potential to affect treatment of the primary condition, and is an active condition for which the patient is treated or monitored.

competitive medical plan (CMP) (3) - an HMO that meets federal eligibility requirements for a Medicare risk contract, but is not licensed as a federally qualified plan.

complication (6) - condition that develops subsequent to inpatient admission.

comprehensive assessment (7) - must include an assessment of the patient's functional capacity, identification of potential problems, and a nursing plan to enhance, or at least maintain, the patient's physical and psychosocial functions.

concurrent review (3) - review for medical necessity of tests and procedures ordered during an inpatient hospitalization.

conditional primary payer status (14) - Medicare claim process that includes the following circumstances: a plan that is normally considered to be primary to Medicare issues a denial of payment that is under appeal; a patient who is physically or mentally impaired failed to file a claim to the primary carrier; a workers' compensation claim has been denied and the case is slowly moving through the appeal process; or there is no response from a liability carrier within 120 days of filing the claim.

confidentiality (5) - restricting patient information access to those with proper authorization and maintaining the security of patient information.

confirmatory consultation (7) - evaluation and management (E/M) service requested by the patient, the patient's family, or a third party for the purpose of rendering a second or third opinion about the necessity or appropriate nature of a previously recommended diagnosis, or surgical or medical procedure.

congenital anomaly (6) - disorder diagnosed in infants at birth.

consent (5) - document that gives health care providers, who have a direct treatment relationship with a patient, permission to use and disclose all personal health information (PHI) for purposes of treatment, payment, or health care operations (TPO).

Consolidated Omnibus Budget Reconciliation Act of 1985 (COBRA) (2) - allows employees to continue health care coverage beyond the benefit termination date.

consultation (7) - examination of a patient by a health care provider, usually a specialist, for the purpose of advising the referring or attending physician in the evaluation and/or management of a specific problem with a known diagnosis.

consumer-driven health plans (2) - encourage individuals to locate the best health care at the lowest possible price with the goal of holding down health care costs.

contiguous site (6) - also called *overlapping sites;* occurs when the origin of the tumor (primary site) involves two adjacent sites.

contract (5) - agreement between two or more parties to perform specific services or duties.

contributory components (7) - include counseling, coordination of care, nature of presenting problem, and time.

conversion factor (9) - dollar multiplier that converts relative value units (RVUs) into payments.

coordinated care plan (CCP) (14) - also called *managed care plans;* includes health maintenance organizations (HMOs), preferred provider organizations (PPOs), and provider sponsored organization (PSO), through which a Medicare beneficiary may choose to receive health care coverage and services. CCPs often provide a greater array of services and smaller copayment than conventional Medicare.

coordinated home health and hospice care (13) - allows patients with this option to elect an alternative to the acute care setting.

coordination of care (7) - physician makes arrangements with other providers or agencies for services to be provided to a patient.

copayment (copay) (2) - provision in an insurance policy that requires the policyholder or patient to pay a specified dollar amount to a health care provider for each visit or medical service received.

Correct Coding Initiative (CCI) (2) - developed by HCFA (now called CMS) to promote national correct coding methodologies and to eliminate improper coding.

cost-based HMO (14) - type of Medicare HMO that allows beneficiaries to receive care through an HMO without the loss of traditional Medicare benefits.

counseling (7) - discussion with a patient and/or family concerning one or more of the following areas: diagnostic results, impressions, and/or recommended diagnostic studies; prognosis; risks and benefits of management (treatment) options; instructions for management (treatment) and/or follow-up; importance of compliance with chosen management (treatment) options; risk factor reduction; and patient and family education.

Coverage Issues Manual (CIM) (8) - advises the local Medicare carrier (LMC) whether a service is covered or excluded under Medicare regulations.

covered lives (3) - employees and dependents who join a managed care plan; known as beneficiaries in private insurance plans.

CPT-5 (7) - fifth edition of CPT, developed by the American Medical Association in response to the electronic data interchange requirements of the Health Insurance Portability and Accountability Act of 1996 (HIPAA).

CPT-5 Project (7) - improvements to CPT that address the needs of hospitals, managed care organizations, and long-term care facilities.

CPT Coding Conventions (7)

  boldface type - highlight main terms in the CPT index and categories, subcategories, headings, and code numbers in the CPT manual.

  bundled codes - CPT codes that are included with certain codes and may not be reported separately in addition to certain codes.

  cross reference term (See) - directs coders to a different CPT index entry because no codes are found under the original entry.

  descriptive qualifiers - terms that clarify assignment of a CPT code.

  guidelines - define terms and explain the assignment of codes for procedures and services located in a particular section.

  inferred words - used to save space in the CPT Index when referencing subterms.

  instructional notes - appear throughout CPT sections to clarify the assignment of codes.

  italicized type - used for the cross reference term, *See,* in the CPT Index.

separate procedure - follows a code description that identifies procedures that are an integral part of another procedure or service.

surgical package - includes the procedure, local infiltration, metacarpal/digital block or topical anesthesia when used, and normal, uncomplicated follow-up care.

CPT Extent of Examination (7)

problem focused - limited examination of the affected body area or organ system.

expanded problem focused - limited examination of the affected body area or organ system and other symptomatic or related organ system(s).

detailed - extended examination of the affected body area(s) and other symptomatic or related organ system(s).

comprehensive - general multisystem examination or a complete examination of a single organ system.

CPT Extent of History (7)

problem focused - chief complaint, brief history of present illness or problem.

expanded problem focused - chief complaint, brief history of present illness, problem-pertinent system review.

detailed - chief complaint, extended history of present illness, problem-pertinent system review extended to include a limited number of additional systems, pertinent past/family/social history directly related to patient's problem.

comprehensive - chief complaint, extended history of present illness, review of systems directly related to the problem(s) identified in the history of the present illness, plus a review of all additional body systems and complete past/ family/social history.

CPT Symbols (7)

● bullet located to the left of a code number identifies new CPT procedures and services.

▲ triangle located to the left of a code number identifies a revised code description.

►◄ horizontal triangles surround revised guidelines and notes. *This symbol is not used for revised code descriptions.*

; semi-colon saves space in CPT so that some code descriptions are not printed in their entirety next to a code number; the entry is indented and the coder refers back to the common portion of the code description located before the semicolon.

* asterisk (or star) located next to minor procedure code number indicates variable preoperative and postoperative services.

+ plus symbol identifies add-on codes for procedures that are commonly, but not always, performed at the same time and by the same surgeon as the primary procedure.

Ⓞ symbol identifies codes that are not to be appended with modifier -51.

criminal law (5) - public law governed by statute or ordinance that deals with crimes and their prosecution.

critical care services (7) - reported when a physician directly delivers medical care for a critically ill or critically injured patient.

critical pathway (16) - sequence of activities that can normally be expected to result in the most cost-effective clinical course of treatment.

***Current Dental Terminology* (CDT) (5)** - medical code set maintained and copyrighted by the American Dental Association.

***Current Procedural Terminology* (CPT) (1)** - published by the American Medical Association and includes five-digit numeric codes and descriptors for procedures and services performed by providers (e.g., 99203 identifies a detailed office visit for a new patient).

cystourethroscopy (7) - passage of an endoscope through the urethra to visualize the urinary bladder.

day sheet (4) - also called *manual daily accounts receivable journal;* chronological summary of all transactions posted to individual patient ledgers/ accounts on a specific day.

deductible (2) - amount for which the patient is financially responsible before an insurance policy provides coverage.

Defense Enrollment Eligibility Reporting System (DEERS) (16) - computer system that contains up-to-date Defense Department Workforce personnel information.

delinquent claim (4) - claim usually more than 120 days past due; some practices establish time frames that are less than and more than 120 days past due.

delinquent claim cycle (4) - advances through various aging periods (30 days, 60 days, 90 days, and so on), with practices typically focusing internal recovery efforts on older delinquent accounts (e.g., 120 days or more).

demonstration project (16) - tests and establishes the feasibility of implementing a new program during a trial period, after which the program is evaluated, modified, and/or abandoned.

Department of Defense (DoD) Cancer Treatment Clinical Trials (16) - offers TRICARE beneficiaries the latest in cancer preventive care and treatment.

Dependents Medical Care Act of 1956 (2) - provides health care to dependents of active military personnel.

deposition (5) - legal proceeding during which a party answers questions under oath (but not in open court).

diagnosis reference numbers (11) - item numbers 1 through 4 preprinted in Block 21 of the CMS-1500 claim.

diagnosis related groups (DRGs) (2) - prospective payment system that reimburses hospitals for inpatient stays.

***Diagnostic & Statistical Manual* (DSM) (16)** - published by the American Psychiatric Association, classifies mental health disorders, and is based on ICD.

Diagnostic Coding and Reporting Guidelines for Outpatient Services: Hospital-Based and Physician Office (6) - developed by the federal government for use in reporting diagnoses for claims submission.

dialysis (14) - process by which waste products are removed from the body.

direct contract model HMO (3) - contracted health care services delivered to subscribers by individual physicians in the community.

direct laryngoscopy (7) - performed by passing a rigid or fiberoptic endoscope into the larynx.

direct patient contact (7) - refers to face-to-face patient contact (outpatient or inpatient).

direct treatment provider (5) - one who treats a patient directly, rather than based on the orders of another provider, and/or provides health care services or test results directly to patients.

disability (14) - an individual's inability to work.

disability insurance (2) - reimbursement for income lost as a result of a temporary or permanent illness or injury.

discharge planning (3) - involves arranging appropriate health care services for the discharged patient (e.g., home health care).

disease oriented panel (7) - also called *laboratory panel* or *organ panel;* the panel consists of a series of blood chemistry studies routinely ordered by providers at the same time for the purpose of investigating a specific organ or disorder.

domiciliary care (7) - covers evaluation and management services provided to patients who live in custodial care or boarding home facilities that do not provide 24-hour nursing care.

downcoding (4) - assigning lower level codes than documented in the record.

dual eligibles (15) - individuals entitled to Medicare and eligible for some type of Medicaid benefit.

durable medical equipment (DME) (8) - canes, crutches, walkers, commode chairs, blood glucose monitors, and so on.

durable medical equipment, prosthetics, orthotics, and supplies (DMEPOS) dealers (8) - supply patients with durable medical equipment.

durable medical equipment, prosthetics, orthotics, and supplies (DMEPOS) fee schedule (9) - Medicare reimburses DMEPOS dealers according to either the actual charge or the amount calculated according to formulas that use average reasonable charges for items during a base period from 1986 to 1987, whichever is lower.

durable medical equipment regional carriers (DMERC) (8) - covers a specific geographic region of the country and is responsible for processing DMEPOS claims for their specific region.

E codes (6) - located in the ICD-9-CM Tabular List, describe external causes of injury, poisoning, or other adverse reactions affecting a patient's health.

Early and Periodic Screening, Diagnostic, and Treatment (EPSDT) services (15) - legislation that mandates states to provide routine pediatric checkups to all children enrolled in Medicaid.

electronic claims processing (1) - sending data in a standardized machine-readable format to an insurance company via disk, telephone, or cable.

electronic data interchange (EDI) (1) - mutual exchange of data between provider and payer.

electronic transaction standards (5) – also called *transactions rule;* a uniform language for electronic data interchange.

emergency care (16) - sudden and unexpected onset of a medical or mental health condition that is threatening to life, limb, or sight.

emergency department services (7) - services provided in an organized, hospital-based facility, which is open on a 24-

hour basis, for the purpose of "providing unscheduled episodic services to patients requiring immediate medical attention."

employer group health plan (EGHP) (9) - contributed to by an employer or employee pay-all plan; provides coverage to employees and dependents without regard to the enrollee's employment status (i.e., full-time, part-time, or retired).

employer-sponsored retirement plan (14) - conversion plan offered to employees by certain companies at the time of retirement.

Employment Retirement Income Security Act of 1974 (ERISA) (2) - mandated reporting and disclosure requirements for group life and health plans (including managed care plans), permitted large employers to self-insure employee health care benefits, and exempted large employers from taxes on health insurance premiums.

encounter form (4) - financial record source document used by providers and other personnel to record treated diagnoses and services rendered to the patient during the current encounter.

encrypted (5) - information converted to a secure language format for transmission.

endoscopic guide-wire dilation (7) - passage of a guide-wire through an endoscope into the stomach.

end-stage renal disease (ESRD) (2, 14) - chronic kidney disorder that requires long-term hemodialysis or kidney transplantation because the patient's filtration system in the kidneys has been destroyed.

Energy Employees Occupational Illness Compensation Program (17) - provides benefits to eligible employees and former employees of the Department of Energy, its contractors and subcontractors, certain survivors of such individuals, and certain beneficiaries of the Radiation Exposure Compensation Act.

enrollees (3) - also called *covered lives;* employees and dependents who join a managed care plan; known as beneficiaries in private insurance plans.

established patient (4) - person seen within the last 36 months by the health care provider or another provider of the same specialty in the same group practice.

ethics (1) - principle of right or good conduct; rules that govern the conduct of members of a profession.

Evaluation and Management (E/M) (2) - services that describe patient encounters with health care professionals for evaluation and management of general health status.

Evaluation and Management Documentation Guidelines (7) - federal (CMS) guidelines that explain how E/M codes are assigned according to elements associated with comprehensive multisystem and single system examinations.

exclusive provider organization (EPO) (3) - managed care plan that provides benefits to subscribers if they receive services from network providers.

explanation of benefits (EOB) (1) - report that details the results of processing a claim (e.g., payer reimburses provider $80 on a submitted charge of $100).

external quality review organization (EQRO) (3) - responsible for reviewing health care provided by managed care organizations.

extra coverage plan (14) - specialized insurance plan that covers specific diagnoses or falls into the special hospital indemnity class.

face-to-face time (7) - amount of time the office or outpatient care provider spends with the patient and/or family.

Fair Debt Collection Practices Act (FDCPA) (4) - specifies what a collection source may or may not do when pursuing payment of past due accounts.

Federal Black Lung Program (17) - enacted in 1969 as party of the *Black Lung Benefits Act;* provides medical treatment and other benefits for respiratory conditions related to former employment in the nation's coal mines.

Federal Claims Collection Act of 1966 (5) - requires carriers and fiscal intermediaries (as agents of the federal government) to attempt the collection of overpayments.

Federal Employee Health Benefits Program (FEHBP) (13) - also called the *Federal Employee Program (FEP);* an employer-sponsored health benefits program established by an Act of Congress in 1959, which now provides benefits to over nine million federal enrollees and dependents through contracts with about 300 insurance carriers.

Federal Employee Program (FEP) (13) – *see* Federal Employee Health Benefits Program (FEHBP).

Federal Employees' Compensation Act (FECA) (2) - replaced the 1908 workers' compensation legislation; civilian employees of the federal government are provided medical care, survivors' benefits, and compensation for lost wages.

Federal Employment Liability Act (FELA) (17) - not a workers' compensation statute, but it provides railroad employees with protection from employer negligence, making railroads engaged in interstate commerce liable for injuries to employees if the railroad was negligent.

Federal False Claims Act (5) - passed by the federal government during the Civil War to regulate fraud associated with military contractors selling supplies and equipment to the Union Army.

Federal Medical Assistance Percentage (FMAP) (15) - portion of the Medicaid program paid by the federal government.

federal poverty level (FPL) (15) - income guidelines established annually by the federal government.

Federal Register (5) - legal newspaper published every business day by the National Archives and Records Administration (NARA).

federally qualified HMO (3) - certified to provide health care services to Medicare and Medicaid enrollees.

fee-for-service (3) - reimbursement methodology that increases payment if the health care service fees increase, if multiple units of service are provided, or if more expensive services are provided instead of less expensive services (e.g., brand-name vs. generic prescription medication).

fee schedule (2) - list of predetermined payments for health care services provided to patients (e.g., a fee is assigned to each CPT code).

first party (5) - person designated in the contract to receive a contracted service.

First Report of Injury (17) - workers' compensation form completed when the patient first seeks treatment for a work-related illness or injury.

fiscal intermediary (FI) (5) - organization that contracts with CMS to process Medicare Part A claims.

fiscal year (16) - for the federal government, October 1 of one year to September 30 of the next.

flat file (5) - series of fixed-length records (e.g., 25 spaces for patient's name) submitted to third-party payers to bill for health care services.

for-profit corporation (13) - pays taxes on profits generated by the corporation's for-profit enterprises and pays dividends to shareholders on after-tax profits.

fraud (5) - intentional deception or misrepresentation that someone makes that could result in an unauthorized payment.

gag clause (3) - prevents providers from discussing all treatment options with patients, whether or not the plan would provide reimbursement for services.

gatekeeper (3) - primary care provider for essential health care services at the lowest possible cost, avoiding nonessential care, and referring patients to specialists.

general enrollment period (GEP) (14) - enrollment period for Medicare Part B held January 1 through March 31 of each year.

global period (9) - includes all services related to a procedure during a period of time (e.g., 10 days, 30 days, 90 days, depending on payer guidelines).

global surgery (7) - also called *package concept* or *surgical package;* includes the procedure, local infiltration, metacarpal/digital block or topical anesthesia when used, and normal, uncomplicated follow-up care.

Glossary of Mental Disorders (6) - Appendix B of ICD-9-CM, corresponds to the psychiatric terms that appear in Chapter 5, Mental Disorders; consists of an alphabetic listing of terms and definitions based on those contained in ICD-9-CM and input from the *American Psychiatric Association's Task Force on Nomenclature and Statistics.*

Government-Wide Service Benefit Plan (13) - phrase printed below the BCBS trademark on federal employee plan (FEP) insurance cards, which indicates that the enrollee has federal employer-sponsored health benefits.

group health insurance (2) - health care coverage available through employers and other organizations (e.g., labor unions, rural and consumer health cooperatives); employers usually pay part, or all, of premium costs.

group medical practice (2) - three or more health care providers who share equipment, supplies, and personnel, and divide income by a prearranged formula.

group model HMO (3) - contracted health care services delivered to subscribers by participating physicians who are members of an independent multi-specialty group practice.

group practice without walls (GPWW) (3) - contract that allows physicians to maintain their own offices and share services (e.g., appointment scheduling and billing).

grouper software (9) - determines appropriate group (e.g., diagnosis related group, home health resource group, and so on) to classify a patient after data about the patient is input.

guarantor (4) - person responsible for paying health care fees.

guardian (5) - person legally designated to be in charge of the patient's affairs.

HCFA-1500 (2) - now called CMS-1500 claim.

HCPCS level II code types (8)

dental codes - contained in *Current Dental Terminology* (CDT).

miscellaneous codes - reported when a DMEPOS dealer submits a claim for a product or service for which there is no existing HCPCS level II code.

modifiers - provide additional information about a procedure or service (e.g., left-sided procedure).

permanent codes - maintained by HCPCS National Panel, comprised of representatives from the Blue Cross/Blue Shield Association (BCBSA), the Health Insurance Association of America (HIAA), and CMS.

temporary codes - maintained by the CMS and other members of the HCPCS National Panel; independent of permanent level II codes.

Health Affairs (HA) (16) - refers to the Office of the Assistant Secretary of Defense for Health Affairs, which is responsible for both military readiness and peacetime health care.

health care (2) - expands the definition of medical care to include preventive services.

Healthcare Common Procedure Coding System (HCPCS) (1) - coding system that consists of CPT, national codes (level II), and local codes (level III); local codes were discontinued in 2003; previously known as HCFA Common Procedure Coding System.

health care finder (HCF) (16) - registered nurse or physician assistant who assists primary care providers with preauthorizations and referrals to health care services in a military treatment facility or civilian provider network.

health care provider (1) - physician or other health care practitioner (e.g., physician's assistant).

health insurance (2) - contract between a policyholder and a third-party payer or government program to reimburse the policyholder for all or a portion of the cost of medically necessary treatment or preventive care by health care professionals.

health insurance claim (1) - documentation submitted to an insurance plan requesting reimbursement for health care services provided; e.g. CMS-1500 and UB-92 claims.

Health Insurance Portability and Accountability Act of 1996 (HIPAA) (2) - mandates regulations that govern privacy, security, and electronic transactions standards for health care information.

health maintenance organization (HMO) (2) - responsible for providing health care services to subscribers in a given geographical area for a fixed fee.

Health Maintenance Organization Assistance Act of 1973 (2) - authorized grants and loans to develop HMOs under private sponsorship; defined a federally qualified HMO as one that has applied for, and met, federal standards established in the HMO Act of 1973; required most employers with more than 25 employees to offer HMO coverage if local plans were available.

Health Plan Employer Data and Information Set (HEDIS) (2) - created standards to assess managed care systems using data elements that are collected, evaluated, and published to compare the performance of managed health care plans.

hemodialysis (14) - passing patient's blood through an artificial kidney machine to remove waste products; cleansed blood is subsequently returned to the patient's body.

Hill-Burton Act (2) - provided federal grants for modernizing hospitals that had become obsolete because of a lack of capital investment during the Great Depression and WWII (1929-1945). In return for federal funds, facilities were required to provide services free, or at reduced rates, to patients unable to pay for care.

history (7) - interview of the patient that includes the following components: history of the present illness (HPI) (including the patient's chief complaint), a review of systems (ROS), and a past/family/social history (PFSH).

hold harmless clause (1) - patient is not responsible for paying what the insurance plan denies.

Home Assessment Validation and Entry (HAVEN) (9) - data entry software used to collect OASIS assessment data for transmission to state databases.

Home Health Prospective Payment System (HH PPS) (2) – reimbursement methodology for home health agencies that uses a classification system called home health resource groups (HHRGs), which establishes a predetermined rate for health care services provided to patients for each 60-day episode of home health care.

home health resource group (HHRG) (9) - classifies patients into one of 80 groups, which range in severity level according to three domains: clinical, functional, and service utilization.

home services (7) - health care services provided in a private residence.

hospice (14) - autonomous, centrally administered program of coordinated inpatient and outpatient palliative (relief of symptoms) services for terminally ill patients and their families.

hospital discharge service (7) - includes the final examination of the patient, discussion of the hospital stay with the patient and/or caregiver; instructions for continuing care provided to the patient and/or caregiver; and preparation of discharge records, prescriptions, and referral forms.

host plan (13) - plan in which the subscriber originally enrolled.

iatrogenic illness (6) - illness that results from medical intervention (e.g., adverse reaction to contrast material injected prior to a scan).

ICD-9-CM Index to Diseases Coding Conventions (6)

code in slanted bracket - always reported as secondary codes because they are manifestations (results) of other conditions.

eponym - disease (or procedure) named for an individual (e.g., physician who originally discovered the disease, first patient diagnosed with the disease).

essential modifier - subterms that are indented below the main term in alphabetical order (except for "with" and "without"); clarifies the main term and must be contained in the diagnostic statement for the code to be assigned.

main term - condition printed in boldface type and followed by the code number.

NEC (not elsewhere classified) - identifies codes to be assigned when information needed to assign a more specific code cannot be located in the ICD-9-CM coding book.

nonessential modifiers - subterms enclosed in parentheses following the main term that clarify code selection, but do not have to be present in the provider's diagnostic statement.

notes - contained in boxes to define terms, clarify index entries, and list choices for additional digits (e.g., fourth- and fifth-digits).

See - directs the coder to a more specific term under which the code can be found.

See also - refers the coder to an index entry that may provide additional information to assign the code.

See Category - refers the coder directly to the Tabular List category (three-digit code) for code assignment.

subterm - essential modifiers that qualify the main term by listing alternate sites, etiology, or clinical status.

incident to (9) - Medicare regulation which permitted billing Medicare under the physician's billing number for ancillary personnel services when those services were "incident to" a service performed by a physician.

indemnity coverage (13) - offers choice and flexibility to subscribers who want to receive a full range of benefits along with the freedom to use any licensed health care provider.

independent practice association (IPA) HMO (3) - also called *individual practice association (IPA);* type of HMO where contracted health services are delivered to subscribers by physicians who remain in their independent office settings.

Index to Diseases (Volume 2) (6) - contains Alphabetical Index of Diseases and Injuries, Table of Drugs and Chemicals, and Index to External Causes of Injury and Poisoning.

ICD-9-CM Index to Procedures and Tabular List Coding Conventions (6)

omit code - term that identifies procedures or services that may be components of other procedures; this instruction means that the procedure or service is not coded.

code also any synchronous procedures - refers to operative procedures that are to be coded to completely classify a procedure.

ICD-9-CM Tabular List Coding Conventions (6)

and - when two disorders are separated by the word "and," it is interpreted as "and/or" and indicates that either of the two disorders is associated with the code number.

bold type - all category and subcategory codes and descriptions are printed in bold type.

braces - enclose a series of terms, each of which modifies the statement located to the right of the brace.

brackets - enclose synonyms, alternate wording, or explanatory phrases.

category - printed in bold upper- and lowercase type and are preceded by a three-digit code.

chapter heading - printed in uppercase letters and is preceded by the chapter number.

code first underlying disease - appears when the code referenced is to be sequenced as a secondary code; the code, title, and instructions are italicized.

colon - used after an incomplete term and is followed by one or more modifiers (additional terms).

excludes - an excludes note directs the coder to another location in the codebook for proper assignment of the code.

format - all subterms are indented below the term to which they are linked; if a definition or disease requires more than one line, that text is printed on the next line and further indented.

includes - includes notes appear below a three-digit category code description to further define, clarify, or provide an example.

major topic heading - printed in bold uppercase letters and followed by a range of codes enclosed in parentheses.

not otherwise specified (NOS) - indicates that the code is unspecified; coders should ask the provider for a more specific diagnosis before assigning the code.

parentheses - enclose supplementary words that may be present or absent in the diagnostic statement, without affecting assignment of the code number.

subcategory - indented and printed in the same fashion as the major category headings.

subclassification - requires the assignment of a fifth digit.

use additional code - indicates a second code is to be reported to provide more information about the diagnosis.

with - when codes combine one disorder with another (e.g., code that combines primary condition with a complication), the provider's diagnostic statement must clearly indicate that both conditions are present and that a relationship exists between the conditions.

indexing (6) - cataloging diseases and procedures by code number.

indirect laryngoscopy (7) - larynx is visualized using a warm laryngeal mirror.

individual practice association (IPA) HMO (3) – *see* independent practice association (IPA).

initial enrollment period (IEP) (14) - seven-month period that provides an opportunity for the individual to enroll in Medicare Part A and/or Part B.

initial hospital care (7) - covers the first inpatient encounter the *admitting/attending physician* has with the patient for each admission.

injury (6) - traumatic wound or damage to an organ.

inpatient (2) - admitted to the hospital for treatment with the expectation that the patient will remain in the hospital for a period of 24 hours or more.

inpatient prospective payment system (IPPS) (9) - system in which Medicare reimburses hospitals for inpatient hospital services according to a predetermined rate for each discharge.

Inpatient Rehabilitation Facilities Prospective Payment System (IRF PPS) (2) - implemented as a result of the BBA of

1997; utilizes information from a patient assessment instrument to classify patients into distinct groups based on clinical characteristics and expected resource needs.

insurance (2) - contract that protects the insured from loss.

integrated delivery system (IDS) (3) - organization of affiliated provider sites (e.g., hospitals, ambulatory surgical centers, or physician groups) that offer joint health care services to subscribers.

integrated provider organization (IPO) (3) - manages the delivery of health care services offered by hospitals, physicians employed by the IPO, and other health care organizations (e.g., an ambulatory surgery clinic and a nursing facility).

International Classification of Diseases (ICD) (2) - classification system used to collect data for statistical purpose.

***International Classification of Diseases, 9th Revision, Clinical Modification* (ICD-9-CM) (1)** - coding system used to report diagnoses (e.g., diseases, signs, and symptoms) and reasons for encounters (e.g., annual physical examination and surgical follow-up care) on physician office claims.

interrogatory (5) - document containing a list of questions that must be answered in writing.

Joint Commission on Accreditation of Healthcare Organizations (JCAHO) (3) - provides voluntary accreditation of a variety of health care organizations (e.g., hospitals, long-term care and ambulatory care facilities).

key components (7) - extent of history, extent of examination, and complexity of medical decision making.

kidney transplant (14) - involves surgically inserting a healthy kidney from another person (a kidney donor) into the patient who has ESRD; the new kidney does the work that the patient's kidneys cannot.

laboratory panel (7) – *see* disease oriented panel.

large group health plan (LGHP) (9) - provided by an employer who has 100 or more employees *or* a multi-employer plan in which at least one employer has 100 or more full- or part-time employees.

late effect (6) - residual effect or sequela of a previous acute illness, injury, or surgery.

Lead Agent (LA) (16) - serves as a federal health care team created to work with regional military treatment facility commanders, uniformed service headquarters' staffs, and Health Affairs (HA) to support the mission of the Military Health Services System (MHSS).

legislation (3) - laws.

lesion (6) - any discontinuity of tissue (e.g., skin or organ) that may or may not be malignant.

leukemia (14) - progressive proliferation of abnormal white blood cells.

level of service (7) - reflects the amount of work involved in providing health care to patients.

liability insurance (2) - policy that covers losses to a third party caused by the insured, by an object owned by the insured, or on the premises owned by the insured.

lifetime maximum amount (2) - maximum benefit payable to a health plan participant.

lifetime reserve days (14) - may be used only once during a patient's lifetime and are usually reserved for use during the patient's final, terminal hospital stay.

limited license practitioners (LLPs) (14) - psychologists, clinical psychologists, and clinical social workers.

limiting charge (9) - maximum fee a physician may charge.

List of Three-Digit Categories (ICD-9-CM) (6) - found in Appendix E of ICD-9-CM, contains a breakdown of three-digit category codes organized beneath section headings.

listserv (5) - subscriber-based question-and-answer forum that is available through email.

litigation (4) - uses legal action to recover a debt, it is usually a last resort for a medical practice.

local codes (level III codes) (1) - developed by local insurance companies and include five-digit alphanumeric codes for procedures, services, and supplies that are also not classified in CPT.

local Medicare carrier (LMC) (8) - responsible for processing Medicare claims in the local area.

lock-in provision (14) - neither the HMO nor Medicare will pay for nonemergency services provided by health care providers who are not part of the HMO's community-based network unless referred outside the network by the primary care physician.

Longshore and Harbor Workers' Compensation Program (17) - administered by the U.S. Department of Labor, provides medical benefits, compensation for lost wages, and rehabilitation services to longshoremen, harbor workers, and other maritime workers who are injured during the course of employment or suffer from diseases caused or worsened by conditions of employment.

major medical insurance (2) - provided coverage for catastrophic or prolonged illnesses and injuries.

major surgical procedure (7) - one with no asterisk (*) after the code number, is considered by CPT to be a surgical package and includes the operation, any local anesthesia administered, and normal, uncomplicated follow-up care.

malignant (6) - cancerous.

managed care (2) - allows patients to receive care from a group of participating providers to whom a copayment is paid for each service.

managed care organization (MCO) (3) - responsible for the health of a group of enrollees; can be a health plan, hospital, physician group, or health system.

managed health care (managed care) (3) - combines health care delivery with the financing of services provided.

management service organization (MSO) (3) - usually owned by physicians or a hospital and provides practice management (administrative and support) services to individual physician practices.

mandates (3) - laws

manipulation of a fracture (7) - also called *reduction of a fracture;* the application of manually applied forces to restore normal anatomical alignment.

manual daily accounts receivable journal (4) - also called the *day sheet;* is a chronological summary of all transactions posted to individual patient ledgers/ accounts on a specific day.

Material Safety Data Sheet (MSDS) (17) - contains information about chemical and hazardous substances used on-site.

Medicaid (Title XIX of the SSA of 1965) (2) - cost-sharing program between the federal and state governments to provide health care services to low-income Americans; originally administered by the Social and Rehabilitation Service (SRS).

Medicaid eligibility verification system (MEVS) (15) - sometimes called *recipient eligibility verification system* or *REVS;* allows providers to electronically access the state's eligibility file through point of sale device, computer software, and automated voice response.

Medicaid remittance advice (15) - sent to the provider; serves as an explanation of benefits from Medicaid and contains the current status of all claims (including adjusted and voided claims).

medical assistance program (15) - program for individuals with incomes below the federal poverty level.

medical care (2) - includes the identification of disease and the provision of care and treatment as provided by members of the health care team to persons who are sick, injured, or concerned about their health status.

medical decision making (7) - refers to the complexity of establishing a diagnosis and/or selecting a management option as measured by the number of diagnoses or management options, amount and/or complexity of data to be reviewed, and risk of complications and/or morbidity or mortality.

medical emergency care rider (13) - covers immediate treatment sought and received for sudden, severe, and unexpected conditions that, if not treated, would place the patient's health in permanent jeopardy or cause permanent impairment or dysfunction of an organ or body part.

medical foundation (3) - nonprofit organization that contracts with and acquires the clinical and business assets of physician practices; the foundation is assigned a provider number and manages the practice's business.

medical necessity (1) - involves linking every procedure or service reported to the insurance company to a condition that justifies the necessity for performing that procedure or service.

medical necessity denial (14) - denial of otherwise covered services that were found to be not "reasonable and necessary."

medical savings account (MSA) (3) - tax-exempt trust or custodial account established for the purpose of paying medical expenses in conjunction with a high-deductible health plan; allows individuals to withdraw tax-free funds for health care expenses, which are not covered by a qualifying high-deductible health plan.

medical treatment (17) - illness or injuries for which the patient receives treatment and/or services.

medically managed (10) - a particular diagnosis (e.g., hypertension) may not receive direct treatment during an office visit, but the provider had to consider that diagnosis when considering treatment for other conditions.

medically unnecessary (4) - procedure or service does not match up with an appropriate diagnosis.

Medicare (Title XVIII of the SSA of 1965) (2) - reimburses health care services to Americans over the age of 65.

Medicare Bulletin **(5)** - published by CMS as a legal notice to providers (e.g., physicians and suppliers) about requirements imposed by Medicare laws, regulations, and guidelines.

Medicare Carrier Manual (MCM) (8) - provides direction to local Medicare carriers (LMC) to the process for paying and denying claims for services/procedures.

Medicare Part A (14) - reimburses institutional providers for inpatient, hospice, and some home health services.

Medicare Part B (14) - reimburses noninstitutional health care providers for outpatient services.

Medicare private contract (14) - agreement between Medicare beneficiary and physician or other practitioner who has "opted out" of Medicare for two years for *all* covered items and services furnished to Medicare beneficiaries; physician/practitioner will not bill for any service or supplies provided to any Medicare beneficiary for at least two years.

Medicare Risk Program (3) - federally qualified HMOs and competitive medical plans (CMPs) that meet specified Medicare requirements provide Medicare covered services under a risk contract.

Medicare Secondary Payer (MSP) (9) - situations in which the Medicare program does not have primary responsibility for paying a beneficiary's medical expenses.

Medicare SELECT (14) - type of Medigap policy available in some states where beneficiaries choose from one of 10 standardized Medigap plans, A through J.

Medicare Summary Notice (MSN) (9) - previously called an *Explanation of Medicare Benefits* or *EOMB;* notifies Medicare beneficiaries of actions taken on claims.

Medicare supplemental plans (13) - augment the Medicare program by paying for Medicare deductibles and copayments.

Medicare+Choice (M+C or Medicare Part C) (3) - program which expands Medicare coverage options by creating managed care plans, to include HMOs, PPOs, and MSAs.

Medicare-Medicaid crossover (14) - combination of Medicare and Medicaid programs; available to Medicare-eligible persons with incomes below the federal poverty level.

Medigap (11) - supplemental plans designed by the federal government but sold by private commercial insurance companies to cover the costs of Medicare deductibles, copayments, and coinsurance, which are considered "gaps" in Medicare coverage.

member (13) - subscriber.

member hospital (13) - hospital that has signed a contract to provide services for special rates.

Merchant Marine Act (Jones Act) (17) - not a workers' compensation statute, but provides seamen with the same protection from employer negligence as FELA provides railroad workers.

metastasize (6) - the spread of cancer from primary to secondary sites.

metastatic (6) - descriptive term that indicates a primary cancer has spread to another part of the body.

Military Health Services System (MHSS) (16) - entire health care system of the U.S. uniformed services and includes military treatment facilities (MTFs) as well as various programs in the civilian health care market, such as TRICARE.

Mine Safety and Health Administration (MSHA) (17) - helps reduce deaths, injuries, and illnesses in U.S. mines through a variety of activities and programs.

minimum data (5) - enough information to schedule the appointment (e.g., reason for the referral and office visit); minimum data is defined by each state.

Minimum Data Set (MDS) (2) - data elements collected by long-term care facilities.

minor surgical procedure (7) - an asterisk (*) following the CPT code number indicates a "relatively small surgical service, too variable to be billed as an all-inclusive package."

modifier (5) - 2-digit code attached to the main code that indicates a procedure/service has been altered in some manner (e.g., bilateral procedure).

morphology (6) - indicates the tissue type of a neoplasm, and while M codes are *not reported on provider office claims,* they are reported to state cancer registries.

Morphology of Neoplasms (M codes) (6) - Appendix A of ICD-9-CM, contains a reference to the World Health Organization publication entitled *International Classification of Diseases for Oncology* (ICD-O).

mother/baby claim (15) - submitted for services provided to a baby under the mother's Medicaid identification number.

multiple myeloma (14) - form of bone marrow cancer.

multiple surgical procedure (7) - two or more surgeries performed during the same operative session.

narrative clinic note (10) - using paragraph format to document health care.

National Association of Blue Shield Plans (2) - name of the former Associated Medical Care Plans.

National Center for Health Statistics (NCHS) (6) - one of the U.S. Department of Health and Human Services agencies responsible for overseeing all changes and modifications to the ICD-9-CM.

national codes (level II codes) (1) - commonly referred to as HCPCS codes, which include five-digit alphanumeric codes for procedures, services, and supplies that are not classified in CPT (e.g., J-codes are used to assign drugs administered).

National Committee for Quality Assurance (NCQA) (3) - a private, not-for-profit organization that assesses the quality of managed care plans in the United States and releases the data to the public for its consideration when selecting a managed care plan.

National Drug Code **(NDC) (5)** - maintained by the Food & Drug Administration (FDA); identifies prescription drugs and some over-the-counter products.

National Health PlanID (PlanID) (5) - unique identifier, previously called PAYERID, that will be assigned to third-party payers and is expected to have 10 numeric positions, including a check digit in the tenth position.

National Individual Identifier (5) – unique identifier to be assigned to patients.

National Provider Identifier (NPI) (5) - unique identifier to be assigned to health care providers as an 8- or possibly 10-character alphanumeric identifier, including a check digit in the last position.

National Standard Employer Identifier Number (EIN) (5) - unique identifier assigned to employers who, as sponsors of health insurance for their employees, need to be identified in health care transactions.

National Standard Format (NSF) (5) - flat file format used to bill physician and non-institutional services, such as services reported by a general practitioner on a CMS-1500 claim.

nature of the presenting problem (7) - defined by CPT as a disease, condition, illness, injury, symptom, sign, finding, complaint, or other reason for the encounter, with or without a diagnosis being established at the time of the encounter.

neonatal intensive care (7) - care provided by a physician who directs the care of a critically ill newborn (or the very low birth weight infant).

neoplasm (6) - new growths, or tumors, in which cell reproduction is out of control.

network model HMO (3) - contracted health care services provided to subscribers by two or more physician multi-specialty group practices.

network provider (3) - physician or health care facility under contract to the managed care plan.

new patient (4) - person who has not received any professional services from the health care provider or another provider of the same specialty in the same group practice within the last 36 months.

newborn care (7) - covers examinations of normal or high-risk neonates in the hospital or other locations, subsequent newborn care in a hospital, and resuscitation of high-risk babies.

nonavailability statement (NAS) (16) - certificate issued by a military treatment facility that cannot provide needed care to TRICARE Standard beneficiaries.

noncovered procedure (4) - also called *uncovered benefit* or *uncovered procedure;* any service determined to be a non-covered benefit.

nonparticipating provider (nonPAR) (4) - does not contract with the insurance plan; patients who elect to receive care from nonPARs will incur higher out-of-pocket expenses.

nonphysician provider (14) - physician assistants, nurse practitioners, nurse midwives, clinical nurse specialists, clinical psychologists, clinical social workers, and Certified Registered Nurse Anesthetists.

nonprofit corporations (13) - charitable, educational, civic, or humanitarian organizations whose profits are returned to the program of the corporation rather than distributed to shareholders and officers of the corporation.

nurse advisor (16) - available 24/7 for advice and assistance with treatment alternatives and to discuss whether a TRICARE sponsor should see a provider based on a discussion of symptoms.

nurse practitioner (NP) (9) - has two or more years of advanced training, has passed a special exam, and often works as a primary care provider along with a physician.

nursing facility services (7) - performed at the following sites: skilled nursing facilities (SNFs), intermediate care facilities (ICFs), and long-term care facilities (LTCFs).

objective (10) - documentation of measurable or objective observations made during physical examination and diagnostic testing.

observation services (7) - E/M category includes subcategories for observation care discharge services and initial observation care, and no differentiation is made as to patient status (new vs. established).

Occupational Safety and Health Administration (OSHA) (17) - agency created to protect employees against injuries from occupational hazards in the workplace.

Occupational Safety and Health Administration Act of 1970 (OSHA) (2) - legislation designed to protect all employees against injuries from occupational hazards in the workplace.

Office of Workers' Compensation Programs (OWCP) (17) - administers programs that provide wage replacement benefits, medical treatment, vocational rehabilitation, and other benefits to federal workers (or eligible dependents) who are injured at work or acquire an occupational disease.

Omnibus Budget Reconciliation Act (OBRA) (2) - federal law that requires physicians to keep copies of any government insurance claims and copies of all attachments filed by the provider for a period of five years; also expanded Medicare and Medicaid programs.

on-the-job-injury (17) - occurrence when the employee is either injured while working within the scope of the job description, injured while performing a service required by the employer, or succumbs to a disorder that can be directly linked to employment, such as asbestosis or mercury poisoning.

open assigned claims (4) - submitted to the carrier, but processing is not complete.

open fracture treatment (7) - fracture site was surgically opened, the bone ends visualized, aligned, and internal fixation may have been applied.

open-panel HMO (3) - health care provided by individuals who are not employees of the HMO or who do not belong to a specially formed medical group that serves the HMO.

operative reports (10) - vary from a short narrative description of a minor procedure that is performed in the physician's office to more formal reports dictated by the surgeon in a format required by the hospitals and ambulatory surgical centers (ASCs).

optical character reader (OCR) (11) - device used for optical character recognition.

optical scanning (11) - uses a device (e.g., scanner) to convert printed or handwritten characters into text that can be viewed by an optical character reader.

organ panel (7) - *see* disease oriented panel.

Original Medicare Plan (14) - fee-for-service or traditional pay-per-visit plans for which beneficiaries are usually charged a fee for each health care service or supply received.

other health insurance (OHI) (16) - insurance policy considered primary to TRICARE (e.g., civilian insurance plan, workers' compensation, liability insurance plan).

Outcomes and Assessment Information Set (OASIS) (2) - group of data elements that represent core items of a comprehensive assessment for an adult home care patient and form the basis for measuring patient outcomes for purposes of outcome-based quality improvement.

outpatient (6) - person treated in one of three settings: health care provider's office; hospital clinic, emergency department, hospital same-day surgery unit, or ambulatory surgical center (ASC) where the patient is released within 23 hours; or hospital admission solely for observation where the patient is released after a short stay.

outpatient pretreatment authorization plan (OPAP) (13) - also called *prospective authorization or precertification;* requires preauthorization of outpatient physical, occupational, and speech therapy services.

Outpatient Prospective Payment System (OPPS) (2) - uses Ambulatory Payment Classification (APCs) to calculate reimbursement; was implemented for billing of hospital-based Medicare outpatient claims.

outsource (4) - contract out.

overlapping site (6) - *see* contiguous site.

overpayment (5) - funds a provider or beneficiary has received in excess of amounts due and payable under Medicare and Medicaid statutes and regulations.

package concept (7) - *see* global surgery.

participating provider (PAR) (4) - contracts with a health insurance plan and accepts whatever the plan pays for procedures or services performed.

pass-through payments (8) - temporary additional payments (above the OPPS payment) made for certain innovative medical devices, drugs, and biologicals provided to Medicare beneficiaries.

patient account record (4) - also called *patient ledger;* a computerized permanent record of all financial transactions between the patient and the practice.

patient ledger (4) - *see* patient account record.

Payment Error Prevention Program (PEPP) (5) - requires facilities to identify and reduce improper Medicare payments and, specifically, the Medicare payment error rate.

payment error rate (5) - number of dollars paid in error out of total dollars paid for inpatient prospective payment system services.

payment system (9) - reimbursement method the federal government uses to compensate providers for patient care.

Peer Review Organization (PRO) (2) – replaced Professional Standards Review Organizations (PSROs) as part of the Tax Equity and Fiscal Responsibility Act of 1983.

per diem (2) - Latin term meaning "for each day," which is how retrospective cost-based rates were determined; payments were issued based on daily rates.

percutaneous skeletal fixation (7) - neither an open or closed treatment, bone fragments are never directly visualized but fixation (pins) is placed across the fracture site, usually under radiologic guidance.

perinatal condition (6) - occurs before birth, during birth, or within the perinatal period.

perinatal period (6) - first 28 days of life.

peritoneal dialysis (14) - involves passage of waste products from the patient's body through the peritoneal membrane into the peritoneal (abdominal) cavity where a solution is introduced and periodically removed.

permanent disability (17) - refers to an ill or injured employee's diminished capacity to return to work.

physical examination (7) - assessment of the patient's organ (e.g., extremities) and body systems (e.g., cardiovascular).

physician assistant (PA) (9) - has two or more years of advanced training, has passed a special exam, works with a physician, can do some of the same tasks as the doctor.

physician fee schedule (PFS) (9) - formerly called Resource-Based Relative Value Scale (RBRVS), the PFS payment system reimburses providers for services and procedures by dividing all services into relative value units (RVUs).

physician incentive plan (3) - requires managed care plans that contract with Medicare or Medicaid to disclose information about physician incentive plans to CMS or State Medicaid agencies before a new or renewed contract receives final approval.

physician incentives (3) - includes payments made directly or indirectly to health care providers to serve as encouragement to reduce or limit services (e.g., discharge an inpatient from the hospital more quickly) to save money for the managed care plan.

physician standby service (7) - involves a physician spending a prolonged period of time without patient contact, waiting for an event to occur that will require the physician's services.

physician-hospital organization (PHO) (3) - owned by hospital(s) and physician groups that obtain managed care plan contracts; physicians maintain their own practices and provide health care services to plan members.

place of service (POS) (7, 9) - the physical location where health care is provided to patients (e.g., office or other outpatient settings, hospitals, nursing facilities, home health care, or emergency departments); the two-digit location code is required by Medicare.

plan (10) - statement of the physician's future plans for the work-up and medical management of the case.

plan identification number (PlanID) (14) – *see* National Health PlanID.

point-of-service plan (3) - delivers health care services using both an HMO network as well as traditional indemnity coverage so patients can seek care outside the HMO network.

poisoning (6) - occurs as the result of an overdose, wrong substance administered or taken, or intoxication (e.g., combining prescribed drugs with nonprescribed drugs or alcohol).

policyholder (or subscriber) (4) - person in whose name the insurance policy is issued.

PPN provider (13) - provider who has signed a PPN contract and agrees to accept the PPN allowed rate, which is generally 10% lower than the PAR allowed rate.

practice guidelines (16) - decision making tools used by providers to determine appropriate health care for specific clinical circumstances.

preadmission certification (PAC) (3) - review for medical necessity of inpatient care prior to the patient's admission.

preadmission review (3) - review for medical necessity of inpatient care prior to the patient's admission.

preadmission testing (PAT) (6) - completed prior to an inpatient admission or outpatient surgery to facilitate the patient's treatment and reduce the length of stay.

preauthorization (1) - prior approval.

precedent (5) - standard.

precertification (13) - *see* outpatient pretreatment authorization plan (OPAP).

pre-existing condition (4) - any medical condition that was diagnosed and/or treated within a specified period of time immediately preceding the enrollee's effective date of coverage.

Preferred Provider Health Care Act of 1985 (3) - eased restrictions on preferred provider organizations (PPOs) and allowed subscribers to seek health care from providers outside of the PPO.

preferred provider network (PPN) (13) - program that requires providers to adhere to managed care provision.

preferred provider organization (PPO) (3) - network of physicians and hospitals that has joined together to contract with insurance companies, employers, or other organizations to provide health care to subscribers for a discounted fee.

preoperative clearance (7) - occurs when a surgeon requests that a specialist or other physician (e.g., general practice) examine a patient and certify whether or not that patient can withstand the expected risks of a specific surgery.

prepaid health plan (2) - contract between employer and health care facility (or physician) where specified medical services were performed for a predetermined fee that was paid on either a monthly or yearly basis.

preventive medicine services (7) - routine examinations or risk management counseling for children and adults exhibiting no overt signs or symptoms of a disorder while presenting to the medical office for a preventive medical physical, that is, "wellness visits."

preventive services (2) - designed to help individuals avoid health and injury problems.

primary care manager (PCM) (16) - provider (e.g., physician) assigned to a sponsor and is part of the TRICARE provider network.

primary care provider (PCP) (3) - responsible for supervising and coordinating health care services for enrollees and preauthorizing referrals to specialists and inpatient hospital admissions (except in emergencies).

primary diagnosis (6) - the most significant condition for which services and/or procedures were provided; it is entered first in Block 21 of the CMS-1500 claim.

primary insurance (4) - associated with how an insurance plan is billed—the insurance plan responsible for paying health care insurance claims first is considered primary.

primary malignancy (6) - original cancer site.

primary policyholder (4) - person to whom the policy is issued.

principal diagnosis (6) - condition determined *after study* that resulted in the patient's admission to the hospital.

principal procedure (6) - procedure performed for definitive treatment rather than diagnostic purposes; one performed to treat a complication; or that which is most closely related to the principal diagnosis.

privacy (5) - right of individuals to keep their information from being disclosed to others.

Privacy Act of 1974 (5, 14) - forbids the Medicare regional carrier from disclosing the status of any unassigned claim beyond the following: date the claim was received by the carrier; date the claim was paid, denied, or suspended; general reason the claim was suspended.

Privacy Rule (5) - creates national standards to protect individuals' medical records and other personal health information.

private fee-for-service (PFFS) (14) - health care plan offered by private insurance companies; not available in all areas of the country.

professional component (7) - supervision of procedure, interpretation, and writing of the report.

Professional Standards Review Organizations (PSROs) (2) - physician-controlled nonprofit organizations that contracted with HCFA (now called CMS) to provide review of hospital inpatient resource utilization, quality of care, and medical necessity; PSROs were replaced by Peer Review Organizations, or PROs, as a result of the Tax Equity and Fiscal Responsibility Act of 1982, or TEFRA; PROs were replaced by Quality Improvement Organizations (QIOs).

Program Integrity (PI) Office (16) - responsible for the worldwide surveillance of fraud and abuse activities involving purchased care for beneficiaries in the Military Healthcare System.

prolonged services (7) - assigned in addition to other E/M services when treatment exceeds by 30 minutes or more the time included in the CPT description of the service.

prospective authorization (13) - *see* outpatient pretreatment authorization plan (OPAP).

prospective cost-based rates (9) - rates established in advance, but based on reported health care costs (charges) from which a prospective per diem rate is determined.

prospective payment system (PPS) (2) - issues predetermined payment for services.

prospective price-based rates (9) - rates associated with a particular category of patient (e.g., inpatients) and are established by the payer (e.g., Medicare) prior to the provision of health care services.

provider identifying number (PIN) (14) - unique number issued by regional carriers and reported in Block 33 of the CMS-1500 claim to identify the provider who rendered services.

provider-sponsored organizations (14) - managed care organizations owned and operated by a network of physicians and hospitals rather than by an insurance company.

qualified diagnosis (6) - working diagnosis that is not yet proven or established.

qualified Medicare beneficiary (QMB) (14) - program in which the federal government requires state Medicaid programs to pay Medicare premiums, patient deductibles, and coinsurance for individuals who have Medicare Part A, a low monthly income, limited resources, and who are not otherwise eligible for Medicaid.

quality assessment and performance improvement (QAPI) (3) - program implemented so that quality assurance activities are performed to improve the functioning of M+C organizations.

quality assurance program (3) - activities that assess the quality of care provided in a health care setting.

quality improvement organization (QIO) (2) - previously called a peer review organization (PRO); performs utilization and quality control review of health care furnished, or to be furnished, to Medicare beneficiaries.

Quality Improvement System for Managed Care (QISMC) (3) - established by Medicare to assure the accountability of managed care plans in terms of objective, measurable standards.

***qui tam* (5)** - abbreviation for the Latin phrase *qui tam pro domino rege quam pro sic ipso in hoc parte sequitur,* which means "who as well for the king as for himself sues I this matter." It is a provision of the Federal Civil False Claims Act that allows a private citizen to file a lawsuit in the name of the U.S. Government, charging fraud by government contractors and other entities.

radiologic views (7) - studies taken from different angles.

recipient eligibility verification system (REVS) (15) - also called *Medicaid eligibility verification system (MEVS);* allows providers to electronically access the state's eligibility file through point of sale device, computer software, and automated voice response.

reduction of a fracture (7) - also called *manipulation of a fracture;* the application of manually applied forces to restore normal anatomical alignment.

re-excision (6) - occurs when the pathology report recommends that the surgeon perform a second excision to widen the margins of the original tumor site.

referral (7) - a patient who reports that another provider referred him.

regulations (5) - guidelines written by administrative agencies (e.g., CMS).

relative value units (RVUs) (9) - payment components consisting of physician work, practice expense, and malpractice expense.

religious fraternal benefit society plan (14) - may restrict enrollment to members of the church, convention, or group with which the society is affiliated.

remission (14) - symptoms lessen in severity.

report card (3) - contains data regarding a managed care plan's quality, utilization, customer satisfaction, administrative effectiveness, financial stability, and cost control.

Resident Assessment Validation and Entry (RAVEN) (9) - data entry system used to enter MDS data about SNF patients and transmit those assessments in CMS-standard format to individual state databases.

Resource Utilization Groups (RUGs) (2) - based on data collected from resident assessments (using data elements called the Minimum Data Set, or MDS) and relative weights developed from staff time data.

Resource-Based Relative Value Scale system (RBRVS) (2) - payment system that reimburses physicians' practice expenses based on relative values for three components of each physician's services: physician work, practice expense, and malpractice insurance expense.

respite care (14) - the temporary hospitalization of a hospice patient for the purpose of providing relief from duty for the nonpaid person who has the major day-to-day responsibility for the care of the terminally ill, dependent patient.

retrospective reasonable cost system (9) - reimbursement system in which hospitals report actual charges for inpatient care to payers after discharge of the patient from the hospital.

retrospectively (3) - relating to after care has been administered.

rider (13) - special contract clauses stipulating additional coverage above the standard contract.

risk contract (3) - an arrangement among providers to provide capitated (fixed, prepaid basis) health care services to Medicare beneficiaries.

risk pool (3) - created when a number of people are grouped for insurance purposes (e.g., employees of an organization); the cost of health care coverage is determined by employees' health status, age, sex, and occupation.

risk-based HMO (14) - type of Medicare HMO that requires the HMO to provide all Medicare benefits but may offer additional benefits not available to regular Medicare patients.

roster billing (14) - enables Medicare beneficiaries to participate in mass PPV (pneumococcal pneumonia virus) and influenza virus vaccination programs offered by Public Health Clinics (PHCs) and other entities that bill Medicare carriers.

scope of practice (9) - health care services, determined by the state, that a NP and PA can perform.

second party (5) - the person or organization providing the service.

second surgical opinion (SSO) (3, 13) - second physician is asked to evaluate the necessity of surgery and recommend the most economical, appropriate facility in which to perform the surgery (e.g., outpatient clinic or doctor's office versus inpatient hospitalization).

secondary diagnosis (6) - also called *concurrent condition* or *comorbidity;* coexists with the primary condition, has the potential to affect treatment of the primary condition, and is an active condition for which the patient is treated or monitored.

secondary malignancy (6) - tumor has metastasized to a secondary site, either adjacent to the primary site or to a remote region of the body.

secondary procedure (6) - additional procedure performed during the same encounter as the principal procedure.

security (5) - involves the safekeeping of patient information by controlling access to hard copy and computerized records; protecting patient information from alteration, destruction, tampering, or loss; providing employee training in confidentiality of patient information; and requiring employees to sign a confidentiality statement that details the consequences of not maintaining patient confidentiality.

self-referral (3) - enrollee who sees a non-HMO panel specialist without a referral from the primary care physician.

sequelae (6) - late effects of injury or illness.

service location (13) - location where the patient was seen.

severe combined immunodeficiency disease (SCID) (14) - defective immune system due to a defect in the immune mechanism or another disease process.

site of service differential (9) - reduction of payment when office-based services are performed in a facility, such as a hospital or outpatient setting, because the doctor did not provide supplies, utilities, or the costs of running the facility.

Skilled Nursing Facility Prospective Payment System (SNF PPS) (2) - implemented (as a result of the BBA of 1997) to cover all costs (routine, ancillary, and capital) related to services furnished to Medicare Part A beneficiaries.

skin lesion (7) - any discontinuity of the skin.

SOAP notes (10) - using outline format to document health care; "SOAP" is an acronym derived from the first letter of the headings used in the note: Subjective, Objective, Assessment, and Plan.

Social Security Administration (SSA) (14) - an agency of the federal government.

source document (4) the routing slip, charge slip, encounter form, or superbill from which the insurance claim was generated.

special accidental injury rider (13) - covers 100% of nonsurgical care sought and rendered within 24 to 72 hours (varies according to policy) of the accidental injury.

special enrollment period (SEP) (14) - a set time when individuals can sign up for Medicare Part B if they did not enroll in Part B during the initial enrollment period.

special report (7) - must accompany the claim when an unlisted procedure or service code is reported to describe the nature, extent, and need for the procedure or service.

specified low-income Medicare beneficiary (SLMB) (14) - federally mandated program that required states to cover just the Medicare Part B premium for persons whose income is slightly above the poverty level.

spell of illness (14) - formerly called *spell of sickness;* is sometimes used in place of *benefit period.*

staff model HMO (3) - health care services are provided to subscribers by physicians employed by the HMO.

standards (3) - requirements.

Stark II regulations (5) - released in 1998 to regulate physician referral to monitor physician profits for Medicare services.

State Children's Health Insurance Program (SCHIP) (15) - also abbreviated as CHIP; provides health insurance coverage to uninsured children whose family income is up to 200% of the federal poverty level (monthly income limits for a family of four also apply).

State Insurance Fund (or State Compensation Fund) (17) - a quasi-public agency that provides workers' compensation insurance coverage to private and public employers and acts as an agent in workers' compensation cases involving state employees.

statistical analysis durable medical equipment regional carrier (SADMERC) (8) - responsible for providing suppliers and manufacturers with assistance in determining HCPCS codes to be used.

statutes (5) - also called *statutory law;* laws passed by legislative bodies (e.g., federal congress and state legislatures).

statutory law (5) - *see* statutes.

subjective (10) - part of the note that contains the chief complaint and the patient's description of the presenting problem.

subpoena (5) - an order of the court that requires a witness to appear at a particular time and place to testify.

subpoena duces tecum (5) - requires documents (e.g., patient record) be produced.

subrogation (2) - process of the third-party payer recovering health care expenses from the liable party.

subscriber (or policyholder) (4) - person in whose name the insurance policy is issued.

subsequent hospital care (7) - includes the review of the patient's chart for changes in the patient's condition, the results of diagnostic studies, and/or the reassessment of the patient's condition since the last assessment performed by the physician.

subsequent nursing facility care (7) - reported when the evaluation of the patient's assessment plan is not required and/or when the patient has not had a major or permanent change of health status.

superbill (4) - term used for an encounter form in the physician's office.

supplemental plan (11) - covers the deductible and copay or coinsurance of a primary health insurance policy.

surgical package (7) - *see* global surgery.

surveillance and utilization review system (SURS) (15) - safeguards against unnecessary or inappropriate use of Medicaid services or excess payments and assesses the quality of those services.

survey (3) - conducted by accreditation organizations (e.g., JCAHO) and/or regulatory agencies (e.g., CMS) to evaluate a facility's compliance with standards and/or regulations.

survivor benefits (17) - claim that provides death benefits to eligible dependents, which are calculated according to the employee's earning capacity at the time of illness or injury.

suspense (4) - pending.

Tabular List (Volume 1) (ICD-9-CM) (6) - contains 17 chapters that classify diseases and injuries, two supplemental classifications, and five appendices.

Tabular List and Index to Procedures (Volume 3) (ICD-9-CM) (6) - included only in the hospital version of the commercial ICD-9-CM; is a combined alphabetical index and numerical listing of inpatient procedures.

Tax Equity and Fiscal Responsibility Act of 1982 (TEFRA) (2) - created Medicare risk programs, which allowed federally qualified HMOs and competitive medical plans that met specified Medicare requirements to provide Medicare-covered services under a risk contract.

technical component (7) - use of equipment and supplies for services performed.

Temporary Assistance to Needy Families (TANF) (15) - makes cash assistance available on a time-limited basis for children deprived of support because of a parent's death, incapacity, absence, or unemployment.

temporary disability (17) - claim which covers health care treatment for illness and injuries, as well as payment for lost wages.

third party (5) - one who is not involved in the patient/provider relationship.

third-party administrator (TPA) (2, 13) - company that provides health benefits claims administration and other outsourcing services for self-insured companies, provides administrative services to health care plans; specializes in mental health case management; and processes claims, serving as a system of "checks and balances" for labor-management.

transmittal notice (4) - report of payments from payer to provider; or a memo distributed by CMS informing providers of government program (e.g., Medicare) changes.

TRICARE (16) - health care program for active duty members of the military and their qualified family members, CHAMPUS-eligible retirees and their qualified family members, and eligible survivors of members of the uniformed services.

TRICARE beneficiary (16) - includes sponsors and dependents of sponsors.

TRICARE Dental Program (TDP) (16) - voluntary, comprehensive dental program offered worldwide by the Department of Defense to family members of all active duty uniformed service members and to Selected Reserve and Individual Ready Reserve (IRR) members and/or their family members.

TRICARE Extra (16) - allows TRICARE Standard users to save 5% of their TRICARE Standard cost-shares by using health care providers in the TRICARE network.

TRICARE For Life (14) - permanent health care benefit that provides expanded medical coverage for uniformed service beneficiaries who are age 65 or older, are Medicare-eligible, and have purchased Medicare Part B.

TRICARE Management Activity (TMA) (16) - formerly OCHAMPUS; the office that coordinates and administers the TRICARE program and is accountable for quality health care provided to members of the uniformed services and their families.

TRICARE Pharmacy Plan (16) - allows active duty military members to fill prescriptions for reduced costs.

TRICARE Prime (16) - managed care option similar to a civilian health maintenance organization (HMO).

TRICARE Program Management Organization (PMO) (16) - manages TRICARE programs and demonstration projects.

TRICARE Retiree Dental Program (TRDP) (16) - provides comprehensive dental benefits program to uniformed services retirees and their family members.

TRICARE Senior Pharmacy Program (14) - authorizes uniformed services beneficiaries 65 years of age and over to obtain low-cost prescription medications from the National Mail Order Pharmacy (NMOP) and TRICARE network and non-network civilian pharmacies.

TRICARE Service Center (TSC) (16) - business offices staffed by one or more beneficiary services representatives and health care finders who assist TRICARE sponsors with health care needs and answer questions about the program.

TRICARE sponsor (16) - uniformed service personnel who are either active duty, retired, or deceased.

TRICARE Standard (16) - new name for traditional CHAMPUS.

triple option plan (3) - usually offered by either a single insurance plan or as a joint venture among two or more insurance carriers, and provides subscribers or employees with a choice of HMO, PPO, or traditional health insurance plans.

two-party check (4) - check made out to both patient and provider.

type of service (TOS) (7) - refers to the kind of health care services provided to patients, a code required by Medicare to denote anesthesia services.

UB-92 (5) - flat file used to bill institutional services, such as services performed in hospitals.

unassigned claim (4) - generated for providers who do not accept assignment; organized by year.

unauthorized procedures and services (4) - procedures and services that are provided to a patient without proper authorization or that are not covered by a current authorization.

unbundling (4) - submitting multiple CPT codes when one code should be submitted.

uncertain behavior (6) - it is not possible to predict subsequent morphology or behavior from the submitted specimen.

uncovered benefit (4) - *see* noncovered procedure.

uncovered procedure (4) - *see* noncovered procedure.

uniformed services (16) - U.S. military branches that include the Army, Navy, Air Force, Marines, Coast Guard, Public Health Service, and the North Atlantic Treaty Organization (NATO).

unique provider identification number (UPIN) (14) - number issued by Medicare during processing of a provider's application; the UPIN is reported in Block 17A by providers who order services *or* refer patients.

unit/floor time (7) - amount of time the provider spends at the patient's bedside and managing the patient's care on the unit or floor (e.g., writing orders for diagnostic tests or reviewing test results).

unlisted procedure (7) - also called *unlisted service;* assigned when the provider performs a procedure of service for which there is no CPT code.

unlisted service (7) - *see* unlisted procedure.

unspecified nature (6) - neoplasm is identified, but there is no further indication of the histology or nature of the tumor reflected in the documented diagnosis.

upcoding (5) - assignment of an ICD-9-CM diagnosis code that does not match patient record documentation for the purpose of illegally increasing reimbursement (e.g., assigning the ICD-9-CM code for heart attack when angina was actually documented in the record).

usual and reasonable payments (2) - based on fees typically charged by providers in a particular region of the country.

usual, customary, and reasonable (UCR) (13) - amount commonly charged for a particular medical service by providers within a particular geographic region for establishing their allowable rates.

utilization management (utilization review) (3) - method of controlling health care costs and quality of care by reviewing the appropriateness and necessity of care provided to patients prior to the administration of care.

utilization review organization (URO) (3) - entity that establishes a utilization management program and performs external utilization review services.

V codes (6) - located in the Tabular List and assigned for patient encounters when a circumstance other than a disease or injury is present.

verbal contract (5) - established between the patient and the health care provider when the patient asks a provider to perform medical services.

vocational rehabilitation (17) - claim that covers expenses for vocational retraining for both temporary and permanent disability cases.

voided claim (15) - claim Medicaid should not have originally paid, resulting in a deduction from the lump sum payment made to the provider.

Wiskott-Aldrich syndrome (14) - cross-linked immunodeficiency disorder that occurs in male children.

without direct patient contact (7) - includes non-face-to-face time spent by the physician on an outpatient or inpatient basis and occurring before and/or after direct patient care.

workers' compensation (2) - insurance program, mandated by federal and state governments, that requires employers to cover medical expenses and loss of wages for workers who are injured on the job or who have developed job-related disorders.

Workers' Compensation Board or Commission (17) - state agency responsible for administering workers' compensation laws and handling appeals for denied claims or cases in which a worker feels compensation was too low.

World Health Organization (WHO) (2) - developed the International Classification of Diseases (ICD).

Index

FOR LICENSE AGREEMENT PERTAINING TO THE STUDENT PRACTICE CD-ROM, SEE PAGE 650.